Dedicated
to my beautiful daughter
Violet Ann Harris

Contents

Acknowledgements

I am deeply indebted to a number of people who have supported me throughout the development of this book. Firstly to Kathryn Jenkins, Heidi Anderson and Umber Ahmed who provided the initial impetus to consider youth services from a wider perspective, which became the foundation of this book. Plus, for the enduring faith they have placed in me in the development and design of adult and youth services across Torfaen and Monmouthshire. Whilst the future is uncertain, I am so proud of what we have achieved together over the years in terms of innovation of services, and feel privileged to have worked with you. Special thanks must also go to Kevin Fisher for such wise and softly spoken counsel, along with the Dyfed commissioning teams for welcoming me into the continued development of services.

My unstinting admiration goes out to the Choices, Prism and Contact Ceredigion Youth Services for piloting the ideas described in this book, as well as to the Cornish and Somerset youth substance misuse teams for running with the torch. All the debates I have had with the teams have shaped my thinking enormously in the development of these ideas. Special thanks must go to Rob Tuttle and Mick Soper for trialling the Complexity Index and all the counties mentioned above who provided such clear data. And to Rowan Miller and Jo Bush at the Training Exchange for everything, but especially the Needs Analysis that provided such fantastic data sets. One day Rowan you will learn to love statistics.

Recognition must go to the Russell House Publishing team – Geoffrey, Rupert and Martin – for their Herculean editing, re-editing and de-editing. This was an enormously complex book, and their incredible eye for detail never ceased to amaze me. From within a maze of inter-related concepts they have brought clarity, consistency and a pragmatism I could not have scaled myself. I am indebted to them as ever. Also to Molloy May McNeil, who proved to be such a diligent research assistant during her work placement with me. Even though I still wait on my half of the award that she won it was great to work with her.

At home, special thanks to my wife, Dr Jessica Gwyther, for her love, encouragement and tolerance of my messy office space. To my daughter Violet for not crayoning too often on my draft copies. And to my many friends who care so little about what I do, but so much for who I am. To Chris Flook, Simon Hall, Ian Hand, Neil Cross, Wayne Roberts and Edmund Scammell. We shared the years described in this book and more. Thinking of adolescent development so deeply, and connecting it to my own youth only makes me value you all the more. Thanks for watching my back, carrying me home, never breaking a secret, forgiving my folly and sharing my joys. It was a hell of ride and I could not have done it without you all.

Introduction

Whilst the substance misuse field universally accepts that young people are not adults, it has been difficult to articulate what the differences actually are. This is an important question to address, if the best efforts to successfully divert or support young people with substance misuse disorders are to be effective. This book hopes to address the question by examining the burgeoning research base that has illuminated not simply young people's drug and alcohol use but also the wider social and developmental context that frames it.

Numerous books about adolescent substance misuse have examined issues such as prevalence patterns, adolescent development, substance misuse problems, prevention and treatment. However, no book has attempted to understand the connection between these multiple domains. This book attempts to integrate these disciplines into a cohesive vision of young people's substance misuse. As such, its structure tries to follow a linear sequence through these topics as well as cross-reference their inter-connectedness. To address a multi-disciplinary area it has relied upon an immense research base, whose multifacetedness I hope does not prove too distracting, as the attempt is made to improve understanding by casting light from different directions.

The structure of this book

Chapter 1 examines the patterns of consumption in young people across and within cultures. Mapping these consumption patterns and identifying cross-cultural comparisons reveals critical patterns. It demonstrates that consumption and problems are shaped by forces greater than the relationship between the substance and the individual. Young people's consumption occurs within a wider context of dynamic historical and cultural forces. These forces not only establish the patterns of consumption, but also exert huge influence over the type, range and frequency of problems that young people experience. Placing young people's drug and alcohol consumption in this context opens up new terrain in understanding the process of intoxication and subsequent behaviors. It also offers critical insight into approaches that hope to ameliorate these problems.

Chapter 2 then demonstrates how these cultural forces do not simply shape drug and alcohol use, but also define the structure of adolescent development itself. Adolescence cannot be understood outside of the social context in which it occurs, as it is the key life stage that prepares young people for the adult roles they must occupy within a pre-established social order. This chapter will tease out the distinct elements of adolescent development, including biological and psychological maturation, life task achievement, identity formation and the shifting patterns of relationships. It then examines how drug and alcohol use impacts on these developmental processes and results in profound levels of developmental delay. Consideration will also be given to the impact of adolescent mental health problems which can also influence these developmental processes.

Chapter 3 then charts the evolution of drug and alcohol problems in young people. Combining research on adolescent development, risk and protection factors and longitudinal studies reveals how drug and alcohol problems are rooted in these developmental processes. Substance misuse does not simply occur at random points in a young person's life but operates at key moments within the life course. This research demonstrates that problematic drug and alcohol using youth are not a homogenous group. Instead they are locked into highly predictable pathways that create distinct sub-populations with remarkably similar clinical profiles. Understanding the patterns, needs and responses of these sub-groups is imperative in the evolution of effective interventions for young people. It offers a radically different perspective on problematic using youth, one that requires a profound revision in prevention and treatment approaches.

Chapter 4 investigates the exact nature of substance misuse problems, and identifies specific differences between young people's and adults' problematic use. It begins with a thorough exploration of the diagnostic criteria that are currently used. The majority of diagnostic criteria have been developed to identify the needs of those adults who have gravitated to the severest level of problematic consumption. As young people's use has not progressed to such an extreme at this stage in their life course, this chapter will demonstrate why adult criteria represent a poor fit for young people who are often under- or over-diagnosed in terms of problematic use. Instead, it will offer a deeper analysis of how young people's use evolves through clearly identifiable phases. This can provide a framework for improved assessment and care planning, matching young people's needs. Alternative assessment processes are suggested which are not only designed to provide a more accurate understanding of young people's use, but can also make a significant contribution to enhancing their treatment outcomes.

Based on this deeper understanding of the development of problematic use in young people, *Chapter 5* examines the effectiveness of prevention and education programmes. It takes a historical perspective that charts the development of prevention models since the 19th Century. This historical angle is important as it identifies many of the deep assumptions of prevention models, that have primarily reflected adult concerns as opposed to connecting to the reality of young people's lives. It will help dispel many established myths in the field of prevention and education, and explain what is effective and why. Based on an increasingly optimistic evidence base, which demonstrates that prevention and education can be effective, this chapter will also establish why the benefits of these approaches have eluded the field, leading to an unwarranted degree of pessimism regarding their value. Instead, it will describe how the benefits of prevention and education reside up-stream from the point of delivery. It will demonstrate that even modest gains from these approaches can lead to disproportionately large outcomes over time.

Finally, *Chapter 6* will examine the impact of treatment on young people. Summarising the previous research outlined in this book, it will examine the outcomes that have been achieved with young people, and why their treatment responses vary considerably. The variations offer insight into a reorientation of treatment services to account for the multiple pathways that lead young people into problematic consumption. Such a reorientation involves understanding several elements of treatment. First, this chapter will demonstrate how the working alliance between the practitioner and the young person is the central driver of positive outcomes. Furthermore, it will demonstrate how these outcomes are highly predictable. Based on these key findings it will explain how factors can be optimised to double young people's successful outcomes from treatment. This chapter will then highlight the critical elements that are necessary within a comprehensive treatment framework to truly assist all young people. It will also review the evidence which supports those specific modalities that have been found to be effective. This will entail identifying interventions that are aimed at reducing substance use as well as specific interventions that are necessary to support young people with more complex needs. Additional consideration is given to how families may be involved in the treatment process in different ways. Finally, the much neglected area of aftercare is explored. Longer term aftercare is essential if the most vulnerable youth are to sustain treatment gains, given that they are also the least likely to complete treatment. This section will then review the optimal length and intensity of aftercare, as well offer innovative new strategies to dramatically increase take-up of this service.

The aspirations of this book

I must confess to having many sincere hopes for this book. In the extensive research base which it presents, I have tried to capture the natural history of young people's drug and alcohol use as it actually evolves, establishes itself and recedes in their lives. Based on this, I assume that interventions can be enhanced when they directly address the reality of young people's lives. In this I have deliberately ignored policy as a factor to be taken into account. This is because, all too often, treatment systems are developed that are based on political agendas rather than the clinical needs of those they try to help; and because evolving treatment systems that do not account for the specific needs of the people within them will always end in failure. All too often I see that political imperatives lead to unrealistic targets, restrictive treatment interventions or cumbersome outcome processes that are all unhelpful. Misdirected policy leads to poorer outcomes for the most vulnerable young people, demoralisation in the staff teams trying to assist them and wasted resources. Policy must account for young people's needs rather than expect young people to comply with requirements of policy. Therefore, even though this book does not specifically address policy, I hope that it assists policy makers to orientate their approaches towards what is possible with young people, in what time frames, and to how best to assess the effectiveness of the services that they procure.

My second hope is for practitioners. On the whole I find youth workers to be energetic, passionate, imaginative and highly skilled in translating the complexities of adult life into the emergent understanding of young people. However, there is a tendency to operate from broader perspectives. Youth work, generic counseling approaches and empowerment models are all important frameworks in which to understand young people's needs. However, they do not always provide sufficient attention to the specific elements of developmental processes or clinical outcomes. Research can be perceived as restrictive or an impediment to the real work. I hope for the opposite. We still lack truly developmentally informed approaches to young people. Considerable progress has been made but further development is essential. I hope the research presented in this book inspires new directions and possibilities by offering clear directions for the immense imagination of youth workers.

Finally, I sincerely hope that the translation of the ideas in this book leads to better outcomes for young people themselves. It is impossible to write a book on adolescent development without considerable reflection on one's own youth. It can be easy to forget that the numbers, analysis and statistics described in this book measure powerful forces that shape real people's lives in powerful ways. The experience of social deprivation, disadvantage and family discord shaped my early life as much as it does many of the young people described in this book. I am aware that, even amidst relentless poverty, hardship and marginalisation, there is also love and joy and most importantly hope. It is the most grievous injury to rob young people of this. I hope that the ideas described within this book provide a framework where young people's hopes can be articulated, valued and expressed in their fullness. After all, many young people from highly disadvantaged backgrounds go on to achieve great things. We do not know which young people will do this, so we should treat all as capable. So, whilst this book spends a great deal of time describing the pathways into profound difficulties, I hope it also contributes as much to shaping pathways to profound recoveries.

Who is this book for?

Substance Misuse Youth Workers: Youth workers face the most significant challenges in supporting the most vulnerable young people with complex substance misuse needs. This often occurs in a setting that stresses the importance of helping relationships, but which can lack deeper guidance on substance abuse problems, mental health issues and an understanding of effective treatment processes. Uncertainty can be compounded, as substance misuse youth workers are confronted with a diverse population of young people with multiple needs, which can range from young people who require brief interventions to those with the highest support needs. They are often called upon by professionals with wider responsibilities for further guidance and support. This book will provide a state-of-the-art understanding of young people's substance misuse problems. Furthermore, it gives guidance on effective prevention strategies, and practical recommendations of how to assess young people's needs, as well as clear indication regarding optimal treatment approaches. It also details specific tools that provide validated outcome measures with young people which improve their treatment gains. This radically new model will also inform the development of treatment pathways for young people and clarify roles amongst multi-disciplinary teams. Further guidance is also included that demonstrates how the wider family can be incorporated into the treatment process.

Lecturers, Students and Researchers: The study of adolescent development is a multidisciplinary field including biology, genetics, psychology, family, peer and cultural influences. *Youthoria* draws together this wide range of subjects in one text, evaluating their individual contributions as well as integrating them into a unified framework. Furthermore, few books on adolescent development make specific reference to how these processes shape the lives of young people in terms of social exclusion, substance abuse and mental health. This book offers a unique understanding of the connection between theoretical research and everyday practice. Furthermore, the state of the art research offers an up-to-date picture of central issues in understanding adolescence and substance use as well as clear structural guidance on effective practice in areas such as prevention and treatment.

Youth Workers: Increasingly, youth workers are being tasked to effect change in young people, especially amongst the most socially excluded who are also most likely to be involved in drug and alcohol use. Whilst empowerment models are important in this process they often lack sufficient attention to developmental or substance misuse issues. This book will explain the major issues in young people's drug and alcohol use, the evolution of problems and the treatment outcomes. This will assist youth workers to recognise not just when to intervene but which young people will require higher levels of support. The section on prevention provides important guidance on the provision of effective prevention and education programmes, which can be a core activity in general youth work settings. Not only does the book describe the most important elements of programmes, it also demonstrates the value of aspects of these programmes which are often unrecognised.

Criminal Justice Workers: Young offenders often have the most complex substance misuse problems and mental health needs, as well as experiencing the most profound levels of development delay. This book illuminates the trans-generational nature of these problems, and why substance misuse occurs within a cluster of problem behaviours. Young offenders represent the most under-served and vulnerable population of young people. This book will provider deeper insight into the development of their behavioural and substance misuse difficulties and outline clear strategies that will effect enduring change in this most marginalised of groups.

Teachers: Drug education and prevention are now part of the national curriculum and teachers are tasked with providing advice, guidance and wider input on a range of substance related issues. The substance misuse field can be dominated by a number of myths and assumptions regarding the development of substance related problems. This book provides in-depth and clear descriptions of the nature of young people's drug and alcohol use. Whilst teachers can feel confident discussing substances, this book also explains the key processes of substance misuse problems. It not only provides an extensive examination of what works in terms of education and prevention, but also offers practical guidance in the delivery of these programmes. It also demonstrates that prevention and education has a major impact on drug and alcohol use, but why this is not recognised at the point of delivery. As teachers are also liable to encounter substance misuse in their daily practice, it offers further guidance on how to recognise and respond to problems.

Social Workers: Social workers are often the last line of defence for families experiencing problematic use. This can included trans-generational substance abuse issues, profound mental health problems or families at a loss as to how to support their offspring. This book charts the vying needs of young people with substance misuse issues as well key treatment recommendations. Not only does it provide clear direction in how to support young people and their families, it also describes critical markers of progression and describes the key time frames in which change is likely to occur. This can help inform care planning processes as well as offer vital insight into the level and rate of progression.

Housing Workers and Officers: Young people with complex needs are liable to end up in supported accommodation. The developmental delay generated by substance use can curtail young people's ability to achieve independent living. This book offers deeper insight into the process and offers guidance on these wider support needs. Offering a clear understanding of these complex issues can create greater rapport with young people at the frontline of social exclusion and provide direction to best support them.

Family Workers: This book will increase the range of family workers' skills base to help address the more specialist and often most intractable area of substance misuse. It offers a deep, empirically based understanding of parent-youth interactions and how they are influenced by substance use. It not only recognises that young people who use drugs and alcohol problematically are not a homogenous group, it also describes how this is mirrored in different sub-types of family. Family therapy has often failed to account for these differences. Besides reviewing the evidence base of family therapy, this book also offers new ways of understanding, involving and supporting families as they address substance misuse.

Counsellors: Generic counselling models can find it difficult to account for young people with complex needs. As a client population they often present with diverse and opposing needs. This book explains the evolution of substance misuse problems in young people, and details the specific needs within different sub-groups of youth. Mapping the risk factors for consumption does challenge the deeply held assumptions of many models, but at the same time offers greater focus to address the prevailing forces that govern problem use. This book also provides in-depth analysis of what counts in treatment, as well as describing how outcomes follow predictive pathways. Drawing on this research, this book offers practical suggestions that can double the occurrence of successful clinical outcomes with young people who otherwise show a poor response to treatment.

Families: Although written with a professional audience in mind this book will also be useful to families concerned about their offspring's use. Families can often experience high levels of guilt and self-blame when their offspring have problems. This book presents a clear, research-based explanation of how young people actually develop substance misuse problems. It challenges many assumptions regarding problematic use and the influence of parenting. It also provides a clear framework to assess problem use and explains treatment processes clearly. Research shows that families can mobilise their own resources and become involved in supporting their loved one to enter treatment. This book explains these processes, as well as how families might be involved in the treatment process itself.

Adult Drug and Alcohol Workers: Whilst the focus of this book is on young drug and alcohol users, the key ideas in this book have major implications for adult problem users as well. Examining the evolution of drug and alcohol problems across adolescence offers considerable insight into the diverse needs of presenting adult populations. This will demonstrate why adult problem users' needs differ. Critically, it will offer insight into those clients who are most liable to naturally remit or respond to treatment, in contrast to those whose use will become more protracted without additional levels of support. Dispelling many established myths in the field, it will illuminate critical issues in diagnosis and provide vital background material to develop psycho-educational approaches to adult substance misuse.

Commissioners: Commissioners are tasked with purchasing services for young people with complex substance misuse needs. It is imperative that the services which are purchased have specific relevance to young people rather than reflect adult treatment services. Furthermore, it is also important that the targets which are set for the services are realistic. This book not only identifies the key differences in treating young people but also describes an optimal integrated treatment pathway for them. It provides extensive guidance on the most effective prevention and treatment programmes for universal as well as targeted services. By detailing the outcomes for young people, it offers clear benchmarking to assess the performance of agencies against normative standards; it also describes the treatment frequency and length that maximises treatment outcomes. This can ensure that treatment systems can account for the full spectrum of young people's needs in the most realistic timeframes, thus providing guidance on the most efficient use of precious resources.

CHAPTER 1

How Common is Substance Use in Young People?

Introduction

Oscar Wilde was a controversial figure in his day. Even before his reputation was rocked by the scandal of his sexuality he would cause a storm of reaction whenever he would appear on stage. These cameos were a frequent occurrence after the performance of his plays, and young men would rush the stage to be closer to their pre-scandalised idol. However, there was one facet of Wilde's public behavior that caused utter outrage at the time. It is difficult from our current historical perspective to understand any reaction, let alone an overreaction, to this one particular facet of Wilde's appearance. It would seem wholly innocuous by today's standards. The public furor centred on the fact that Wilde would always appear on stage smoking a cigarette.

For the Victorians, Wilde was breaking an important unspoken law. The smoking of cigarettes had evolved over a century before amongst the nimble-fingered women who worked long hours in Spanish cigar factories. After work they would sweep up the loose tobacco that had been destined for cigars and roll this windfall in paper and smoke it. Smoking cigarettes was established and enshrined as a strictly female pastime in comparison to the masculine cigar and pipe. Wilde publically and unashamedly broke this cultural code. It was an enormously powerful symbolic gesture, and one that was adopted by his legion of admirers and reported widely throughout the national press. As such, Wilde would become a trigger for a cultural shift in consumption. The cigarette would cross the gender divide and become a drug for men.

This case example illustrates many of the key features of the shifting prevalence patterns of alcohol and drug consumption that are reviewed in this chapter. First, it is important to recognise that the consumption rate of drugs and alcohol is not constant, but is locked into powerful over-arching historical forces, and changes as they change. As young people are particularly sensitive to induction into new patterns of consumption, they are highly sensitive markers of

such trends in a culture's consumption. Moreover, whilst it is important to acknowledge changes in levels of consumption, it is equally important to recognise that the range and incidence of substance-related problems also vary. It is often assumed that there is a strong relationship between these factors, but cross-cultural studies reveal a more complex picture. In the example of Oscar Wilde's cultural context, the shift from smoking cigars to cigarettes did not necessarily mean people smoked more. But the inhalation of cigarette smoke causes greater health problems, such as lung cancer, than are experienced by pipe and cigar smokers, who only draw smoke into the mouth. This illustrates that substance-related problems are not proportionate to consumption. This chapter will explore the complex underlying cultural and social factors that determine substance-related problems beyond the act of consumption itself.

The case of Oscar Wilde also indicates that consumption of any substance is never culturally neutral. Substances are imbued with social meanings and functions. These codes are imprinted in the customs and social relationships of tribes, sub-cultures and societies. Whilst they are mutable, it is these social influences that regulate and contain consumption. Young people are inducted into the cultural mores of their time, enact them and transmit them to the next generation. These expectancies and norms are disseminated through contact with other users, as well as vicariously through the wider mass media.

Finally, this chapter will examine the everyday reality of young people's use, including how they procure drugs and alcohol and where they use them. This will demonstrate how consumption is more than intoxication. Consumption is a set of commitments and experiences that young people share with each other in their social networks. As such, this chapter, together with the more general look at adolescent development in Chapter 2, will provide the broad overview that will be examined in more detail in subsequent chapters.

Historical trends

Consumption rates of drugs and alcohol are not static. Even in the case of culturally permissible substances, such as alcohol and cigarettes, consumption rates rise and fall over time. There is limited research on these wider historical trends as most studies on prevalence only examine current substance use. This illuminates the current generation's use as if they exist outside of a historical continuum. In contrast Johnson & Gerstein (1999) studied the age of initiation of eleven substances in 69,490 people born between the years 1919–75. This large representative sample was grouped by birth dates and adjusted for mortality figures in the older age sample groups.

Their historical review demonstrates dramatic variations. For example, people born in the years 1930–40 only made use of three substances prior to the age of 35 (as defined by more than 1 per cent of the sample using a substance). The three substances consumed at this time were alcohol (used by 84 per cent), cigarettes (used by 78 per cent) and cannabis (used by 6 per cent). The range of substances consumed expanded dramatically in those born in the years 1951–55.

In this generation, 10 substances were used by at least 5 per cent of the population by the age of 35. The only substance which was used by a smaller percentage was heroin, which had still increased from 0.2 per cent to 3 per cent of the population. Whilst cigarette use remained fairly stable in both age groups, there was a 700 per cent increase in illicit drugs between these two periods. The use of cannabis and cocaine peaked at its highest in those born in the years 1961–65, when they entered adulthood in the 1970s. This represents a 250 per cent increase in cannabis use (from 6 to 21 per cent) and 200 per cent increase in cocaine use (from 2 to 6 per cent) from the lowest levels of use. Although this rate of consumption began to decline with later cohorts, subsequent generations are yet to eradicate these significant increases in use compared to those amongst people who were born in 1951–55 (See Graph 1.1).

This research also demonstrated that the age of initiation into drug and alcohol use has also been decreasing historically. The number of young people using alcohol prior to the age of 15 has doubled from 14 per cent in those born in 1951–55 to 33 per cent in those born in 1970–75. Rates of consumption have also equalised between genders. Amongst those born in 1919–29, the

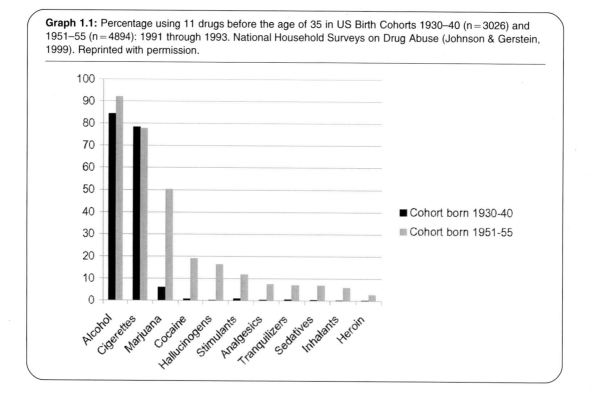

Graph 1.1: Percentage using 11 drugs before the age of 35 in US Birth Cohorts 1930–40 (n = 3026) and 1951–55 (n = 4894): 1991 through 1993. National Household Surveys on Drug Abuse (Johnson & Gerstein, 1999). Reprinted with permission.

■ Cohort born 1930-40
■ Cohort born 1951-55

Alcohol, Cigerettes, Marjuana, Cocaine, Hallucinogens, Stimulants, Analgesics, Tranquilizers, Sedatives, Inhalants, Heroin

study found that 79 per cent of men and 49 per cent of women had used alcohol prior to the age of 21. In the 1966–70 cohort, 90 per cent of men and 83 per cent of women had initiated alcohol use prior to 21. The difference between male and female consumption has continued to narrow for all substances in subsequent generations. Alcohol and cigarette use was already narrowing as World War Two approached, but differences have closed so dramatically that women's consumption of alcohol now exceeds men's in many Western countries.

Social changes

Through these shifting demographics of consumption we can see how consumption is locked into wider social and historical forces. Johnson & Gerstein (1999) suggested that changes in consumption were determined by social changes occurring in the US at this time. For example, women gained increasingly equal status in the workplace but also increasing career strain, too. This occurred without reallocation of domestic responsibility, placing even greater pressures on women. Furthermore, social taboos regarding women's use, whilst still prevalent, became eroded through the increase of gender equalities.

Social changes also affected young people. The 1960s saw a dramatic increase in the relative size of the youth population after World War Two. This began to dilute social contact between the young and older generations, as a financially self-sufficient youth began to emerge after the post-austerity years. Older and more conservative attitudes towards alcohol and drug use did not percolate an increasingly independent youth culture that was experiencing greater social freedoms, and a war in Vietnam, that forced them to question social norms. The relative cost of alcohol and drugs also decreased as global trade increased, bringing a wider range of intoxicants to Western populations. This not only increased the availability of drugs through reduced cost, but also reduced the efforts needed to procure the drugs by an anti-establishment youth who applied new symbolic meanings to drug use. Consumption of drugs became an expression of personal freedom, a personal value that this generation cherished. Numerous historical studies on prevalence have identified similar forces in operation in cultures other than the US. For example, Neve et al. (1993) suggested

that the 300 per cent increase in alcohol use in Holland from 1961 to 1985 was driven by a combination of social factors, such as increased prosperity and fashion, that offered new symbolic meanings for alcohol that were disseminated through the mass media.

Whilst the overall historical trend shows an increase in the prevalence of substance use, it must be recognised that the consumption of certain substances has also decreased. Dramatic declines in cannabis use throughout Scandinavia, Germany and Holland in the 1970s had little to do with changes in social policy or the law. It was the decline of the hippy movement in Western Europe, which had gone out of fashion and taken associated behaviours such as cannabis use with it (Cohen, 1981). This change in fashion meant the social value in cannabis use changed amongst young people. What had been de rigueur was now passé. The pace of these changes can be rapid. Vaillant's (1995) long-term research has followed the drinking patterns of inner city and college-educated males born in 1935 across their entire life course. The study found significant variations in drinking patterns between their sample and a comparison group born only a year later.

This suggests that social and historical forces exert a more powerful influence on consumption rates amongst young people than legal or biological factors. Historically, the lowering age of initiation is particularly important as it serves as a powerful indicator of trends within any culture. Adolescence is the window of opportunity for new substances to enter a culture. Young people are more open to explore novel or alternative behaviours, including experimenting with new substances. This can be seen in the case of alcohol beverage preference. The take-up of new drinking technologies such as alco-pops is negligible in older adults. Conversely, new forms of alcohol such as shots, alco-pops or flaming Sambucas are rapidly assimilated by young people. The same processes occur with other drugs, where we see the rapid adoption of new illicit drugs but also novel substances such as oxycotton, methadrone, GHB or DMT. Research demonstrates that people are highly unlikely to initiate a new drug use after the age of 20 (Johnston et al., 1998). As such, each new generation represents an entry point into a culture for new substances and new patterns of consumption.

This also explains why patterns of drug use are often cyclical. Young people are receptive to the emergence of new substances. Once fashionable youth or their heroes initiate use of a novel substance they become powerful attractors to initiate others into use. These early adopters are 'vectors' that promote, glamorise and disseminate the new substance to wider peer groups. As new converts, they are unlikely to have experienced any adverse effects from the substance themselves at this time in their using career (Behrens et al., 1999; 2000; 2002). However, as they progress into heavier use they become more susceptible to health or social problems.

This reverses the recruitment process. The problematic user becomes the personification of the negative associations with the consumption of that drug. Haggard, sick or excluded, they now repel new initiates as the substance becomes increasingly stigmatised. Consumption of the once novel drug begins to decline as this generation ages and shrinks. Musto (1987) suggested that an 'upswing' back into use occurs as the generation gap widens. As the old cohort pass over the generational horizon, a new generation of young people discover the outmoded drug anew, without the cultural memory of its previous impact. And so the cycle begins again. Research has found a strong cohort effect in that each generation sets its own benchmark of consumption which they then carry with them throughout the life course. So even though consumption decreases with age, each generation preserves its rank order in relation to other cohorts, as consumption rates pulse across history.

Prevalence rates of tobacco, alcohol and drug use

Initiation into use varies according to the availability of the substance. This places legal drugs such as nicotine and alcohol at the vanguard of youth consumption due to their low cost and the ease of attainment. The substance that young people are most likely to experiment with first is tobacco. Overall, smoking rates in young people appear to be in slow decline at present in affluent social groups, but not in poorer sections of the community. In the UK, the Harris et al. (2009) study of smoking patterns in young people found that 9 per cent of boys and 6 per cent of girls had tried smoking by the age of 11. The numbers of regular smokers in this age-range is much smaller at 0.5 per cent. This figure increases with age whereby 14 per cent of young people were regular smokers by the age of 15. Girls were more likely than boys to be regular smokers at age 15. This study found that 17 per cent of girls smoked regularly at this age whilst only 11 per cent of boys did. Smoking rates escalate across adolescence, with a peak in the twenties and thirties before declining across the life course (see Graph 1.2).

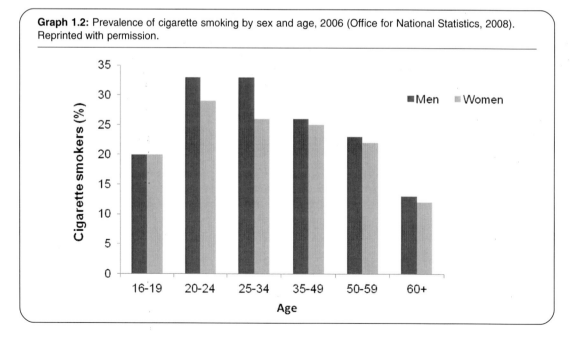

Graph 1.2: Prevalence of cigarette smoking by sex and age, 2006 (Office for National Statistics, 2008). Reprinted with permission.

The Office for National Statistics (2008) found that patterns of nicotine consumption closely align with other patterns of substance use, suggesting tobacco involvement is a strong indicator of other drug involvement. There is a particularly strong relationship between tobacco use and the other legal drug, alcohol. In the UK the Schools and Students Health Education Unit (SHEU, 2001) studied 42,073 young people aged 12–15 and fount that half the young people questioned drank at home, half of whom did so without their parents' knowledge. Other UK studies have found that 1.5 million children aged 11–17 drank alcohol in the last week, of which 704,000 were aged 11–15. More recently, the Chief Medical Officer's Report (2009) suggested that approximately 360,000 children are estimated to have been drunk 'within the last week'. Furthermore it found that 20 per cent of children will have consumed an alcoholic drink by the age of 11. Alcohol consumption follows a similar pattern as tobacco. The prevalence of alcohol consumption increases with age, with 54 per cent of 13-year-olds and 81 per cent of 15-year-olds having consumed alcohol. The volume of alcohol consumed also appears to increase with age from 8 units per week for 11–13 year olds to 15 units a week for 15-year-olds. There does appear to be a decline in alcohol consumption amongst young people in the UK in general; however, there is an upward trend in the amount of alcohol units consumed by young people who do drink.

International studies of alcohol use

International studies of alcohol consumption show a similar pattern. A consistent finding in research is that alcohol shows a trend across the life course that mirrors tobacco use. For example, the Health Behaviour in School Aged Children Project (Gabhainn & Francois, 2000) surveyed alcohol use amongst 11-, 13-, and 15-year-olds in 22 countries. It included prevalence of lifetime consumption of alcohol, weekly consumption of alcohol and whether the young person had ever been drunk as a result of consuming alcohol. This research demonstrated that all three measures of consumption increased with age. All research on alcohol prevalence demonstrates that alcohol consumption rises across the adolescent years, peaks in the 20s, then begins to decline across the life course. Young people between the ages of 18 and 24 are most at risk from alcohol problems as they are the highest consumers at this time.

This pattern of alcohol consumption is influenced by several factors. Some societies with strongly religious cultures have strict prohibitions against alcohol, whilst in the Developing World alcohol is a luxury that most people cannot afford. However, amongst societies where alcohol consumption is permitted and available, it is evident from the research that there is huge variety in accepted drinking patterns, even within fraternal regions such as Europe and the different states of the US. These variations in the acceptability of consumption are reflected in the laws of each country or state, which set very different age limits on when that society deems a young person responsible enough to consume or purchase alcohol. This can range from 16 in Belgium to 21 in the US. There can also be considerable divergence between minimum drinking ages and minimum purchasing age. The UK has one of the lowest minimum drinking ages, set at 5 years old, but the purchasing age is set at 18. Countries may also place specific restrictions on the type of alcohol that can be bought by young people. Beer and wine may be purchased in Austria at the age of 16, but not spirits (see Table 1.1).

It is important to note that the legal status of alcohol and the actual rates of alcohol consumption in young people have very little relationship to each other. For example, in Spain it is possible to buy alcohol at the age of 16 or even younger if accompanied by a parent, whilst Sweden has far greater restrictions on the purchase of alcohol for young people: at 18 in a bar, 20 to purchase from an off-licence. Despite these variations, the two countries have very similar prevalence of consumption in 15- and 16-year-olds (see Table 1.2). It compares favourably to the Czech Republic, which has a high legal drinking and purchasing age at 18, but where only 5 per cent of 15–16-year-olds are still abstinent from alcohol. Similarly, Denmark sets the age limit for consumption and purchasing of alcohol at 18, but only 4 per cent of males and 5 per cent of females will be abstinent from alcohol by the age of 15–16. Other societies demonstrate higher levels of abstinence in this age range, but this occurs within the context of particular cultural patterns of consumption. For example, there are polarised drinking cultures in Northern Ireland, the Republic of Ireland, the Faroe Islands, Iceland and the US Bible Belt States. These countries show high rates of abstinence in young people aged 15–16, but also

Table 1.1:   Selected comparison of national drinking age limits and alcohol purchasing.

Country	Min. age drink alcohol	Min. age purchase alcohol	Notes
Argentina	18		
Austria	16 (15 in some areas)	18 in some areas for spirits	
Belgium	15	16	Under 16 years are not allowed to enter dance hall where alcohol is available
Canada	18* or 19	18* or 19	*Depending upon province. Consumption with adults is permissible in certain provinces
Czech Republic	18	18	
Denmark	18	18	No restrictions on sale from off licences
France	16	16	
Germany	16, 18	16, 18	Beer and wine can be consumed by under 16s if accompanied by parents. Spirits can only be consumed and purchased by 18 year olds or over
Greece		18	
Ireland	18	18	Under 18s allowed in bars – under 15s need to be accompanied by parents
Latvia		18	
Netherlands		16, 18	Beer and wine can be purchased at 16, spirits at 18
Slovenia		18	Only applies to buying or drinking in public places
Spain	16	16	Under 16s may purchase beer or wine if accompanied by parents
Sweden		18, 20	Class 1 (non-alcoholic beer) has no age restriction. Minimum age to buy from food store is 18. Minimum age to buy from off licence is 20
UK	18	18	Minimum age to purchase beer and cider is 16 if accompanied by a meal. Over 5s can consume alcohol in the home with parental consent
US	21*	21**	*In some States, alcohol consumption by under 21s is not illegal **Some exceptions exist for religious purposes, if with a parent, for medicinal purposes, in private members clubs or as part of employment

very much higher than average drinking levels in those that do drink.

International studies of drug use

It is also important to recognise important differences between the prevalence of alcohol use and drug use. Alcohol has earned a special role in Westernised societies due to its long-standing history. In Western Europe, water supplies were often so contaminated from the 8th Century onwards that beer became the staple diet. The high calorie value of beer also provided an important source of nutrition. As such, it acquired a normative status as the staple diet of the West, akin to rice or potatoes in other societies. This means that alcohol has wide cultural acceptability and societies have evolved norms of consumption over centuries.

However, societies have less cultural and historical experience of assimilating wider substance use into their ways of living. Drugs'

Table 1.2: Percentage abstinence rates amongst European and American 15- and 16-year olds during the last 12 months

Country	% All students	% Males	% Females
Austria	7	8	6
Belgium	14	13	15
Bulgaria	14	13	14
Croatia	18	15	21
Cyprus	21	16	26
Czech Republic	5	5	5
Denmark	5	4	5
Estonia	13	14	11
Faroe Islands	24	24	24
Finland	20	22	19
France	20	18	22
Germany	7	7	7
Greece	9	7	10
Greenland	27	32	23
Hungary	16	16	16
Iceland	36	38	35
Ireland	12	14	10
Isle of Man	6	8	4
Italy	18	15	20
Latvia	13	14	12
Lithuania	6	6	6
Malta	10	9	11
Netherland	15	14	15
Norway	24	26	21
Poland	15	12	17
Portugal	26	24	28
Romania	20	16	23
Russia (Moscow)	14	18	11
Slovak Republic	10	10	9
Slovenia	17	15	19
Spain	25	26	24
Sweden	23	23	23
Switzerland	12	12	13
Turkey	65	60	72
Ukraine	16	17	15
UK	9	10	8
US	41	43	39

2003 ESPAD Report (Hibell et al., 2004). Reprinted with permission.

illicit status also means that availability may be more varied than that of alcohol, and that consumption may be less socially acceptable. As a result, variations in drug consumption are likely to be accounted for by wider factors such as cultural acceptability, geographic proximity to sources of supply, leakage from established supply routes across borders and the efforts of enforcement to limit availability. However, despite these differences in availability between different societies, data suggest that the distribution of most illicit drugs within each society is stable, though with regional variation near international borders.

In the UK, data from the British Crime Survey estimates that approximately 1.1 million young people aged 16–24 have ever used a Class A drug such as heroin or cocaine, and half a million have used a class A drug in the last year, whilst a much smaller number of 294,000 have used a class A in the last month. Attaining accurate figures is difficult though, as school-based surveys are liable to miss high risk youth who are vulnerable to social exclusion from mainstream

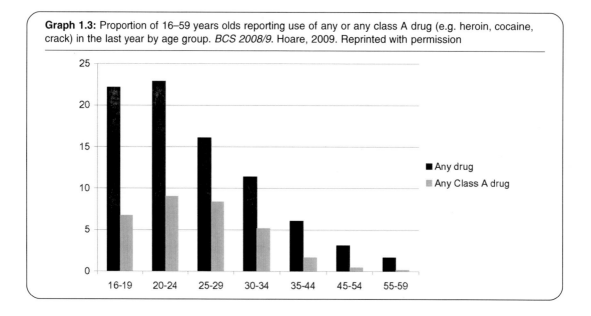

Graph 1.3: Proportion of 16–59 years olds reporting use of any or any class A drug (e.g. heroin, cocaine, crack) in the last year by age group. *BCS 2008/9*. Hoare, 2009. Reprinted with permission

school settings. Surveys which include excluded young people tend to report higher usage amongst young people as a whole (Goulden & Sondhi, 2001). The research from the British Crime Survey 2008/9 demonstrates that young people are by far the highest consumers of drugs of all age groups, but consumption declines significantly across the life course. As with nicotine and alcohol use, drug use increases across adolescence, peaking in the 20–24 age range, before again declining (see Graph 1.3).

Within this general distribution it appears that young people's use of drugs is principally, but not exclusively, limited to cannabis. Cannabis accounts for 84 per cent of 'Last Year Use'. The British Crime Survey (Hoare, 2009) also detected more subtle changes in patterns of use over time in recent years. Cannabis, hallucinogens and ecstasy all remain in decline, but tranquilisers, anabolic steroids and solvent use has remained stable in the UK. The biggest percentage increase has been in ketamine use which has more than doubled from 0.9 per cent in 2007/8 to 1.9 per cent in 2008/9. The UK data is showing a society whose drug use is in transition. Whilst opiate use had dominated the British drug scene throughout the 1980s and 1990s, research shows that young people are no longer initiating into heroin use. Moreover, the National Treatment Agency (NTA, 2010) figures reveal that the total number of drug users entering treatment for heroin or crack cocaine has fallen by 10,000 over the past two

years. The fall in heroin use is particularly profound among people under the age of 30. The number of 18- to 24-year-olds in treatment has halved, with the 25–29 age group almost matching this fall. Estimates from the University of Glasgow's Drug Misuse Research Centre put the number of heroin and crack users in England in 2009/10 at 306,000, down from 332,000 in 2008/09 (Hay et al., 2011). This shift in demographics suggests that opiate use has peaked in the UK and that fewer young people are initiating opiate use. Heroin, once perceived as an ultimate rock and roll drug, is now perceived by young people as a street homeless person drug. The drug has become less attractive to young people as it has acquired a negative public image. Instead, it is being replaced by a new generation of substances that are yet to acquire stigma in the eyes of young people, such as ketamine, M-CAT and legal highs.

The frequency of use in young people is often very different to the patterns of consumption seen in adults. The numbers of young people that have 'Ever Used' a drug tends to be an over-reported headline figure, but the actual regularity with which young people take drugs is far lower. This is especially true of Class A drug usage such as heroin, cocaine or crack. Whilst over 40 per cent of young people report having 'ever used' a drug, only 17 per cent report having used a Class A drug. The number of frequent users is even smaller: under 15 per cent of young people report that they used any drug in the 'last month', and less than 5 per cent report having used a Class A drug within the same time period. This suggests that drug use is opportunistic for many young people as opposed to a routine element of their life. So whilst 'harder' drugs are available to young people, very few use them with the regularity associated with problematic adult use, even at the high end of consumption.

Research into the prevalence of drug use in young people across Europe and the US demonstrates that a wide range of substances are available to young people, but prevalence rates again differ significantly from country to county. Table 1.3 presents data on 15–16 year-old students obtained from a large international survey. The method for data collection was anonymous classroom-based self-completion questionnaires, which were written in test conditions (www.emcdda.europa.eu). This large international sample demonstrates that the most common drug used by young people is cannabis. The prevalence of cannabis varies from 45 per cent lifetime use in the Czech Republic to only 4 per cent in Turkey and Romania. Inhalants are the next most commonly used substance by young people with the highest rate of use reported in the UK, where 17 per cent of young people in the survey reported lifetime use. Spain and Lithuania report the lowest use at 3 per cent. Drugs which are more expensive and harder to acquire, such as heroin, have uniformly low reported frequency of use across nearly all countries, with a slightly higher use of 3 per cent reported in France and Italy.

Natural remission

The prevalence studies in this chapter reveal an important trend. Just as with tobacco and alcohol, drug use increases across adolescence, peaks in the early 20s and then enters decline. Whilst large numbers of young people will initiate the use of drugs during adolescence, and experience a wide range of problems, the majority will not sustain this level of consumption in adulthood. The vast majority of young people who experiment with drugs, alcohol and nicotine will stop using as they exit their late twenties without the need to enter treatment. This process of change without treatment is referred to as 'natural remission'. Natural remission describes a maturing out effect, whereby young people change problematic behaviour themselves, without recourse to any

form of formal treatment. The Antony et al. (1994) review of drug prevalence studies found high rates of natural remission in young people as they aged. This may vary across different substances, with opiate users being the least likely to desist. However, even in terms of heroin use, just over 75 per cent of users will remit from use. Interestingly, this research found that tobacco users were least likely to desist across the life course. The studies suggest that natural remission from drug use is the primary exit route for the vast majority of young people (see Table 1.4).

Similar findings have been found with alcohol. For example, Filmore (1975) contacted 206 respondents who were followed up from a previous study of drinking patterns amongst 17,000 American college students. Whilst 42 per cent of the sample were identified as problem drinkers during their college years, only 17 per cent met this criterion in middle age. Interesting gender differences emerged between men, and women. Women had shown a lower incidence of problem drinking in the college years compared to men but had a much higher incidence of problems in later life. Natural remission was mostly seen in male populations. Further studies by Filmore and colleagues (Filmore & Midanik, 1984; Temple & Filmore, 1985; Filmore, 1987) re-iterated these findings with regard to the natural remission of heavy male drinking. Filmore et al.'s (1988: 29) findings, based on a review of multiple studies, summarised alcohol problems across the life course as 'a higher prevalence of problems in youth, but erratic and non-chronic with a 50–60 per cent chance of remission both in the long and short term among men and more than 70 per cent chance of remission among women in middle age, a much lower prevalence, but chronic with a 30–40 percent chance of remission among men and about a 30 percent chance among women: in older age, a great deal lower prevalence of problems, which were more likely to be chronic, with a 60–80 per cent change of remission among men and a 50–60 per cent chance of remission among women'.

Numerous studies have identified a similar pattern of decreasing consumption across the life course. However, in the case of alcohol this many not be as uniform as many studies have suggested. It is certain that heavy drug and alcohol using teens tend to preserve their rank order of consumption into adulthood. So, whilst their consumption declines, it remains relatively

Table 1.3:   Percentage lifetime prevalence of psychoactive substance use among students aged 15–16 years old from recent school surveys (2005–07)

Country	Notes	Year	Reference	Project	Sample size	Cannabis	Inhalants/ volatile substances	Ampheta- mines	Ecstasy	LDS and hallucino- gens	Cocaine	Heroin
Belgian	(2)	2007		ESPAD	1889	24	8	5	5	3	4	1
Bulgaria		2007		ESPAD	2353	22	3	6	6	3	3	2
Czech Republic		2007		ESPAD	3901	45	7	3	5	5	1	1
Denmark		2007		ESPAD	877	25	6	5	5	1	3	2
Germany	(2)	2007		ESPAD	5011	20	11	5	3	2	3	1
Estonia		2007		ESPAD	2372	26	9	4	6	3	3	1
Ireland		2007		ESPAD	2221	20	15	3	4	3	4	1
Greece		2007		ESPAD	3060	6	9	3	2	2	1	1
Spain	(1)	2007		PNSD	–	37	3	3	3	4	4	3
France		2007		ESPAD	2916	31	12	4	4	2	5	3
Italy		2007		ESPAD	9981	23	5	4	3	4	5	3
Cyprus		2007		ESPAD	6340	5	16	3	3	2	3	2
Latvia		2007		ESPAD	2275	18	13	6	7	4	2	1
Lithuania		2007		ESPAD	2411	18	3	3	3	2	2	1
Luxemburg		2005/6		HBSC/WHO	1507	23	–	–	–	–	–	–
Hungary		2007		ESPAD	2817	13	8	4	5	3	2	1
Malta		2007		ESPAD	3668	13	16	5	4	2	4	1
Netherlands		2007		ESPAD	2091	28	6	2	4	3	3	1
Austria		2007		ESPAD	2571	17	14	8	3	2	3	1
Poland		2007		ESPAD	2120	16	6	4	4	2	2	2
Portugal		2007		ESPAD	3141	13	4	2	2	1	2	2
Romania		2007		ESPAD	2289	4	4	1	1	1	2	0
Slovenia		2007		ESPAD	3085	22	16	2	3	2	3	2
Slovakia		2007		ESPAD	2468	32	13	2	6	4	3	1
Finland		2007		ESPAD	4988	8	10	1	2	1	1	1
Sweden		2007		ESPAD	3179	7	9	2	2	2	2	1
UK		2007		ESPAD	2179	29	9	2	4	3	5	1
England	(3, 4)	2007	1	NATCen/ NFER	1829	27	17	3	4	5	6	1
Scotland	(3, 4)	2006	1	Scot Gov	11980	25	5	3	5	4	5	2
N Ireland	(3, 4)	2007	1	Nat Age	–	17	11	3	5	4	5	1
Croatia		2007		ESPAD	3008	18	11	2	2	2	2	1
Turkey	(2)	2003		ESPAD	4177	4	4	2	2	2	2	2
Norway		2007		ESPAD	3482	6	7	1	1	1	1	1
US	(5, 6)	2005	1	NIDA	16200	34	13	4	4	6	5	2

Notes
The surveys for Belgium cover the Flemish region only, and those for Germany and Turkey are limited to the regions specified in the following notes. The European School Survey Project on Alcohol and other Drugs (ESPAD) is coordinated by the Swedish Council for Information on Alcohol and Other Drugs (CAN) and the Council of Europe (Pompidou Group). ESPAD research prevalence figures are taken from published ESPAD reports and may differ sometimes from those reported by member states. Sample sizes given refer to the number of participating 15-16-year-old students who filled in the questionnaire.

(1) ESPAD methods adopted to varying degrees.
(2) ESPAD 2007 Germany figures are based in seven regions only. ESPAD 2007. Belgium figures are based on Flanders only. ESPAD 2003 Turkey figures are based on one major city in each of six different regions (Adana, Ankara, Diyarbakir, Istanbul, Izmir and Samsun).
(3) The sample size given for these surveys is for a wider age range than 15-16 years.
(4) Only 15-year-old students are included in the United Kingdom ONS and Scottish Executive school surveys.
(5) Inhalants are adjusted for under-reporting of butyl nitrites.
(6) Amphetamines includes only drug use and not under a doctor's prescription.
Adapted from www.emcdda.europa.eu. Reprinted with permission.

high compared to their peers. However, reviewing the low consumers in adolescence, Pape & Hammer (1996) found that low-to-moderate users in adolescence increased their consumption across the life course. This suggests that as the population ages, both high and low consumers of alcohol both gravitate towards their national average of consumption.

Prevalence of alcohol and drug related problems

Prevalence studies such as these raise important issues. First, it appears that national differences in age of purchase have a fairly weak relationship to prevalence of use and consumption rates. Instead, historical and cultural trends tend to exert a more powerful influence over consumption. Within this, substance use does not remain static but accelerates through adolescence and peaks and declines in early adulthood. During this period the majority of young people are liable to experience a wide range of non-chronic problems, with a small minority experiencing more profound and entrenched problems. However, the types of problems young people experience also vary enormously across cultures. This is both in terms of dependency and in terms of negative social consequences of use.

It is often assumed that the prevalence of substance use within a society is indicative of the extent of problem use. But just as legal availability of alcohol has little relationship with consumption, so too the prevalence of drug and alcohol use has little association with the frequency of problematic use. For example, global drug and alcohol dependence rates show dramatic variation across different countries without any direct relationship to prevalence of consumption. Spain is one of the highest consumers of alcohol in the world, with 12.25 litres of pure alcohol being consumed per capita and has one of the lowest legal ages to purchase alcohol. Despite this, Spanish youth show exceptionally low rates of alcohol problems.

A study of Spanish 18-year-olds yielded a prevalence of any substance abuse disorder in only 0.3 per cent of the population sampled. In comparison the US consume less alcohol at 8.51 litres per capita, but exhibit higher rates of dependency amongst its youth. In the US the prevalence of alcohol dependence in young people ranges from between 4.6 per cent

Table 1.4:   Rates of uptake and subsequent dependence

Substance	Life time use	Life time dependence	Capture rate*
Tobacco	75.6%	24.1%	31.9%
Heroin	1.5%	0.4%	23.9%
Cocaine	16.2%	2.7%	16.7%
Alcohol	91.5%	14.1%	15.4%
Cannabis	48.3%	4.2%	9.1%

*Capture rate is the proportion of those who have ever used who have gone on to become dependent.
Antony et al., 1994. Reprinted with permission.

(Lewinsohn et al., 1993) to 32.4 per cent (Reinherz et al., 1993). These studies found that drug dependence occurred in 2.6 to 9.8 per cent of the youth population. Cohen et al. (1993) found in the US a rate of alcohol dependence in 20 per cent of 17–20-year-old males, but only in 8.9 per cent of females of the same age. Dependence to cannabis was rarer in the US, with only 4.8 per cent of males and 1.8 per cent of females meeting the Dependency criteria. Western European nations exhibit lower rates of Dependence than the US. For example, Verhulst et al. (1997) found that only 3.3 per cent of young people aged 13–18 met the criteria for physical dependence on any substance in the Netherlands. Whilst their neighbour Germany demonstrated that 12.3 per cent of young people aged 12–17 met the diagnosis for Dependence (Essua, 2000), where alcohol was the most common substance of dependence in 9.3 per cent of young people, and drug dependence occurred in 6.9 per cent of cases.

Types of substance misuse

Not only does the incidence of dependence vary across cultures but so do the types of substance misuse problems that youth experience. The ESPAD study (Anderson et al., 2007) compared the negative substance-related consequences experienced by young people born in 1985 across seven European countries. The study included a diverse range of cultures including Mediterranean countries (France, Greece, and Italy) as well as northern European countries (Sweden, Latvia, Poland, Slovak Republic). This research examined consumption and prevalence of problems that resulted from alcohol use. In general, northern European countries reported far higher individual problems with substance use. For example, 8 per cent of Slovak youth reported that alcohol had affected their 'schooling' compared to 1 per cent in France and Greece. 'Damage to objects or clothing' also figured more highly in northern European samples, with 36 per cent of young Swedish students reporting this consequence compared to only 3 per cent in Greece. The Swedish were also more likely to experience 'loss of money' (25 per cent) than students in Italy, France or Greece (5 per cent or lower). Accidents were also more common in northern European samples, with the highest incidence in Sweden which scored 14 per cent and, again, with less than 4 per cent of Mediterranean students experiencing similar problems.

In the relationship domain, 'quarrelling' figured highest in 27 per cent of the Swedish sample and 20 per cent of the Polish sample, yet only 4 per cent of the Greek sample. 'Arguments with teachers' were low in all groups at approximately 2 per cent. The highest incidences of 'quarrelling with friends or parents' were in Latvia and Poland, which reported 9 per cent and 14 per cent respectively. In terms of sexual problems, Swedish students were more likely to report having engaged in sex 'they regretted the next day' (17 per cent) compared to Mediterranean countries that cited this in less than 5 per cent of students. Likewise, 'unprotected sex' was also more likely to occur in the Swedish sample, where 15 per cent reported that they had engaged in this behaviour compared to 3 per cent in France, Italy or Greece. Incidents of delinquency related to alcohol were also dominated by northern European countries. Swedish (18 per cent), Latvian (15 per cent) and Polish (13 per cent) samples reported 'getting into a scuffle or fight' compared to Greece where only 2 per cent of students reported this, whilst the Latvia and Poland samples both reported having 'got into trouble with the police' because of alcohol in approximately 8 per cent of the sample. Greece scored very low in this category.

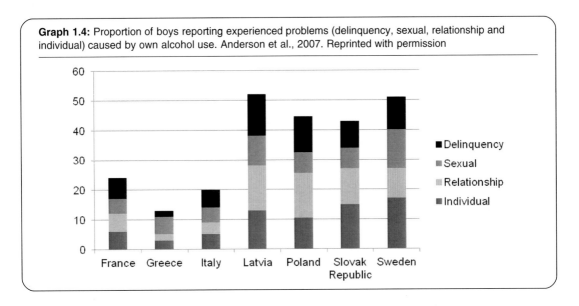

Graph 1.4: Proportion of boys reporting experienced problems (delinquency, sexual, relationship and individual) caused by own alcohol use. Anderson et al., 2007. Reprinted with permission

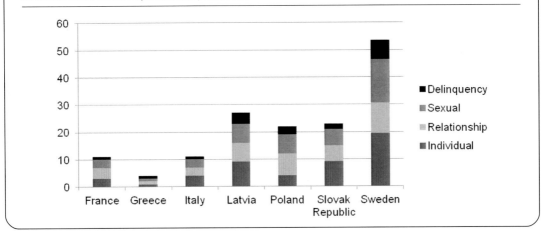

Graph 1.5: Proportion of girls reporting experienced problems (delinquency, sexual, relationship and individual) caused by own alcohol use. Swedish Council for Information on Alcohol and Other Drugs & The Pompidou Group. Alcohol and Drug Use among European 17–18 Year olds: Data from the ESPAD Project. Anderson et al., 2007. Reprinted with permission

Gender differences did emerge in the samples, with young males tending to report higher incidences of problems in all domains, with a few exceptions. For example, Swedish females were more likely to experience 'loss of money' and 'accidents' than Swedish males. Significant differences occurred in terms of 'quarrelling', which was much more likely to occur in male samples. Sexual problems remain relatively equal with males scoring slightly higher on 'sex that they regretted' and 'unprotected sex', except in Sweden (see Graphs 1.4 and 1.5).

This data is even more intriguing when compared to the actual consumption patterns of these seven populations. When this sample reviewed frequency of drinking in the last month, Greek students who had shown the lowest range of alcohol-related problems reported the highest frequency of drinking. This study identified that 23 per cent of Greek students reported that they had drunk alcohol 10 or more times in the last 30 days. Conversely, only 4 per cent of the Swedish sample and 9 per cent of Latvian young people reported consuming alcohol with this level of

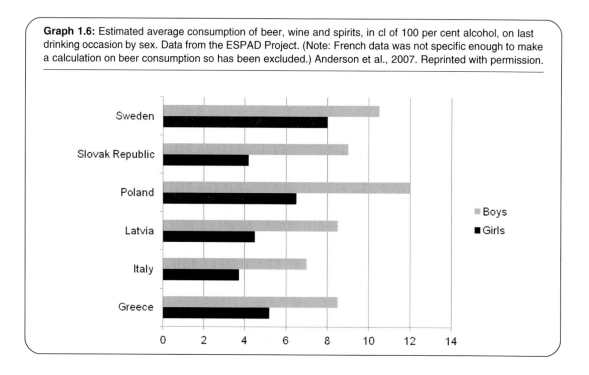

Graph 1.6: Estimated average consumption of beer, wine and spirits, in cl of 100 per cent alcohol, on last drinking occasion by sex. Data from the ESPAD Project. (Note: French data was not specific enough to make a calculation on beer consumption so has been excluded.) Anderson et al., 2007. Reprinted with permission.

frequency, even though their drinking patterns appear far more problematic. Again, gender differences emerged in drinking patterns, with males demonstrating more regular use. Greek males (30 per cent) were the highest consumers in this category, compared to Swedish males who were the lowest (5 per cent).

Based on reported levels of the last episode of consumption, this research calculated an estimation of the volume of alcohol consumed by these six samples (see Graph 1.6). It had to account for differences in types of drinks consumed (wine was preferred in the Mediterranean, for example) as well as the limitations of recall by the young people themselves. However, as the same calculations were used in all samples, it can be assumed that the bias in findings is consistent across cultures and that the figures offer an indication of overall consumption. In terms of drunkenness, the Swedish sample reported the highest rates of having been drunk in their lifetime (86 per cent) as well as of frequency of drunkenness. Around 49 per cent reported having been drunk more than 20 times. This compared to lower rates in southern Europe, with France showing the lowest prevalence rate for lifetime drunkenness at 61 per cent. France, Greece and Italy also reported the lowest levels of frequency of drunkenness (8–12 per cent).

Divergent responses

What is striking in this research is that overall consumption rates did not correlate with the range of problems that young people reported as a result of drinking. These differences are also apparent with drug use, where young people report divergent negative consequences from using the same substance. For example, the Plomp et al. (1996) study explored patterns of consumption of alcohol and cannabis in the border regions of Germany and Holland. Commonalities did exist between the two groups but so did important differences. Whilst the German sample of 567 school children showed lower than average consumption of alcohol and cannabis, they reported far higher levels of alcohol consumption when drinking and more frequent episodes of drunkenness. Amongst the 364 Dutch youth, cannabis consumption was similar to the national average though they showed higher than average levels of alcohol use. The German cannabis use was associated with far higher levels of social deviance such as 'truancy', whereas the Dutch consumption was associated with personal 'dissatisfaction'. Furthermore, alcohol use in Germany was also greatly associated with leisure, peer group bonding and social deviancy, but not in the Dutch sample. The researchers concluded that the social policy of each country had a weak influence over these consumption patterns, which appeared to be determined by the sub-cultural lifestyles of the peer groups in which young people found themselves.

These comparisons are intriguing. It is often anticipated that the extent of substance use and subsequent problems would be related, because substance related issues are widely assumed to be determined by the action of the substance on the human brain, which leads to predictable effects on behaviour. However, this research challenges this assumption. It appears that the experience of substance-related problems is influenced by factors other than simple consumption. These prevalence studies demonstrate that consumption is influenced by the cultural contexts in which it occurs. These cultural differences lead to divergent behaviours in young people, even when they take the same substance. To understand young people's consumption and problems it is essential to understand how this context influences intoxication and offers deeper insight into those young people most at risk of developing the most severe problems.

Variation in substance use across cultures

The fact that nearly every culture has used intoxicating substances has become a tired platitude. The statement misses the wide spectrum of consumption that cultures demonstrate and the diversity of responses from taking the same substances. Young people's use of drugs or alcohol does not occur in a void but is entwined in cultural norms. These norms and assumptions are difficult to detect within a culture, as societies tend to view their own behaviours as typical. Therefore, these cultural forces are most effectively exposed by cross-cultural comparison. If these behaviours are responses to drugs and alcohol that are purely the product of the pharmacological actions of the substance on the human brain, it would be reasonable to assume that they would be common in all societies. However, if responses to drug and alcohol use consistently vary from culture to culture, it suggests that intoxication is influenced by the cultural mores of those who use the substance. Alcohol is an ideal candidate for this kind of study as it is used by a wide range of

cultures in the Under-Developed, Developing and Developed Worlds. Alcohol use is often well established and integrated into a wide array of isolated cultural traditions. The cross-cultural study of alcohol use presents what Marshall (1979) described as a 'classic natural experiment' in understanding intoxication. This section will therefore focus primarily on alcohol studies and then extrapolate these findings to the use of a wider range of drugs.

Alcohol

Alcohol consumption produces clear physiological effects. Pharmacologically, alcohol is *bi-phasic* meaning that initial low doses have a stimulant like effect but as dosage increases it exerts an increasingly profound depressant effect on the human metabolism. This includes slowing central nervous system responses and delaying reaction time, slurring speech and even creating double vision. Alcohol consumption will also trigger the release of enzymes such as acetaldehyde dehydrogenase in order to metabolise alcohol in the liver, and may contribute a bilious hangover the next day. Alcohol affects the circulation system through vascular dilation, which is experienced as flushing, as fine blood capillaries in the skin expand and give off greater body heat. Alcohol influences the brain in a variety of ways, such as acting on opiate receptors, giving it a pain killing quality. Alcohol can narrow the individual's perception of time resulting in a disregard for the past or future. In higher doses it can cause nausea, blackouts and memory impairment. It is also a diuretic, causing increases in urination and dehydration. Alcohol increases libido but diminishes sexual arousal in both men and women. All these physical reactions, and others besides, are triggered by alcohol in the human body. They are a universal experience of consumption.

In contrast, advertisements for alcohol in Western societies portray alcohol as having a powerful influence on positive mood states. Alcohol is depicted being consumed in social settings, either in gender groups or couples. People are often attractive and sexually alluring. They may be witty or urbane. Advertisements are highly segmented in order to appeal to distinct social demographic groups. Different forms of alcohol are targeted at different groups because they are synonymous with lifestyles. This simple comparison reveals an important but often overlooked component of intoxication. When the pharmacological effects of alcohol are compared to the social representation of consumption we see that they contradict each other. Alcohol is a depressant but is associated with positive mood states. Alcohol decreases sexual arousal but is associated with sexual allure. Alcohol slurs speech but is associated with wit and revelry. Most people are drawn to alcohol use due to its social representation, even though no part of this representation is a pharmacological property of alcohol.

The social representations of alcohol use have a powerful influence on intoxication. Intoxication is governed by two key forces: the *objective* effect of a drug that will express its pharmacological action on the brain; and the *subjective* effects of intoxication that the user expects to occur. These *subjective* effects are sourced in the individual's wider cultural beliefs regarding the drug's action, because when a drug operates on the human brain these interactions do not reveal themselves to the user. For example, individuals are not aware of the action of alcohol on ion channels in the brain. Instead, the individual feels an internal sensation of intoxication. But how they value this experience, what emotional states they associate with this sensation, and how they conduct themselves under its influence are shaped by their cultural expectations. As different cultures have different expectancies of alcohol, individuals behave very differently under its influence, despite the neurological actions being the same.

Expectancies influence consumption in several ways. First, overtly positive expectations of use are strongly associated with the willingness of young people to initiate use in the first instance. Second, young people who do engage in drug or alcohol use will experience a wide range of internal and external consequences. As the expression of a drug on neurological processes does not reveal itself to the user, the individuals must interpret these internal responses. Young people interpret these experiences through the lens of their preceding expectations. For example, laughter and frivolity with friends when drinking alcohol tends to be associated with the alcohol being consumed, even though it is not a pharmacological action of the substance. If these individuals had received terrible news, alcohol would not make them laugh in the same way. Positive expectancies therefore bias the internal

appreciation of intoxication, where the user tends to attribute positive experiences to consumption. Conversely, negative consequences from consumption tend to be associated with other factors. For example, young people drinking heavily who get into conflict with others will associate this fracas with the other person's behaviour, not with their use. Third, research shows that we all have a strong memory bias in our recall of intoxication. We tend to recall the positive aspects of consumption and not the negative. This may be because memories are stored in the same area of the brain as expectancies, or be because we do not psychologically attend to difficulties in the same way. Whilst it is often believed that young people must recognise the consequences of their behaviour, it is rarely considered why young people do not see the consequences of their use in the first instance.

Mandelbaum (1965) suggested that this occurs as the cultural norms of a society create pre-existent expectations of the effects of drugs and alcohol and define how one should conduct oneself. Where a society expects disinhibited behaviour after consuming alcohol, it offers those who commit anti-social behaviour an excuse after the event. In Western societies, pleading clemency for one's anti-social behaviour because of being 'under the influence' is common, but is rare in Mediterranean cultures. Heath's (1998) review of double-blind or placebo experimental studies showed that people's response to alcohol is dependent on what they 'think' that they have drunk rather than what they have drunk. In these conditions, aggressive drinkers who are given a placebo that they think is alcohol will act aggressively. Alternatively, if they are given alcohol without being aware of it they do not become aggressive. Whilst the physiological influence of alcohol is common across cultures, the psychological, emotional and behavioural responses of those under the influence remain too inconsistent across cultures to be accounted for in terms of the action of the drug itself.

Anthropological research has consistently found that different culture groups display an extraordinarily diverse and contradictory response to alcohol (See Douglas, 1987; Pittman & White, 1991; Heath, 1998). Even in pre-literate societies, huge variations are found in consumption patterns. For example, Lemert (1964) compared drinking norms in three distinct Polynesian societies. In Tahiti alcohol was strongly associated with a pattern of benign festive drinking on weekends that were accompanied by singing, dancing and high levels of sociability. In Atiu, the population engaged in ritualised drinking, but it produced more belligerent behaviours, so the drinking ceremonies were overseen by a sober 'master of ceremony' who policed behaviour. In neighbouring Samoa, drinking was frequently associated with aggression, domestic violence and even rape. These three cultures' alcohol-behaviour varied enormously as a result of taking the very same substance.

Differences in intoxication patterns are even more vivid when examining the kissing cousin countries of Europe, who exhibit a wide range of alcohol-related behaviour. This occurs across a cultural fault line. Southern European countries such as Italy, Spain, France and Greece tend to be high consumers of alcohol without social complications. Northern European countries have lower rates of alcohol consumption but experience far higher rates of social problems. With the exception of liver cirrhosis, most problems associated with alcohol are *inversely* proportional to actual consumption levels (Heath, 1998). Furthermore, northern European countries also exhibit far higher rates of alcohol dependence than southern Europe, even though use is lower per capita.

One reason for this difference is the role of disinhibition with alcohol. MacAndrew & Edgerton's (1969) systematic study of global alcohol consumption demonstrated how some cultural groups show no signs of disinhibition, others have become increasingly disinhibited, whilst other societies display disinhibition within strict social limits. For example, when the British binge drinkers travel to a wine drinking region such as France, they drink wine in the same way that they drink beer and exhibit their domestic disinhibited behaviour patterns (MacDonald, 1994). This exportation of behaviour is contagious. Increasingly, Spanish youth are adopting the British binge drinking pattern of consumption, which had not been known before, particularly in holiday resorts frequented by the British (Gamela, 1995). To a lesser degree Italian youth are also adopting British binge drinking patterns, but they remain culturally more ambivalent. Wine continues to be consumed in the traditional context of meals at home, whereas novel drinks and heavier consumption occurs in the context of peer groups (Cottino, 1995).

Culture shapes these expectations in its members at a young age. In the UK, Jahoda & Cramond (1972) explored children's attitudes to alcohol between the ages of 5 and 10. Using games to evoke their opinions, even very young children had a very clear concept of alcohol and its effects. All the children in this study, including the girls, also displayed particular disapproval of alcohol consumption by women. Interestingly, these experiments were repeated 20 years later by Fossey (1994). This repeat study found exactly the same results, even though alcohol consumption had increased considerably in the UK during this period of time. Children from different cultures demonstrated different expectations of alcohol use, and this was reflected in their lower incidence of problematic use. For example, Greek, Jewish and Italian children are gradually exposed to alcohol at a young age. They do not associate consumption with special events or ceremonies, and consumption is regulated by strict family values that disapprove of anti-social behaviour under the influence (Blum & Blum, 1969; Glassner & Berg, 1980; Lolli et al., 1958).

In these cultures, alcohol consumption is seen as an ordinary daily event, and this can shape future expectancies in adolescence. Hibell et al. (2001) reviewed the expectations of alcohol use amongst 15-year-old adolescents throughout Europe, including six positive consequences and six negative consequences. Italian and French young people were far less likely to expect any positive consequences from use in comparison to young people from the UK, Sweden, Norway and Denmark. French and Italian students were far less likely to report that alcohol would make them 'happy' or that drinking was related to having 'a lot of fun'. However the negative expectations of alcohol use amongst all these groups were similar.

This also suggests that positive expectancies exert a greater influence over consumption than an awareness of the negative consequences of use. Numerous studies have demonstrated that positive expectations of alcohol use are strong predictors of future consumption in young people. Goldman et al. (1987a; 1987b) devised an Alcohol Expectancy Questionnaire – Adolescent (AEQ-A) form – to examine this issue. The questionnaire asked young people to rate different possible consequences of alcohol use as either true or false. From this data they identified seven key expectations of use in young people:

1. Global positive changes
2. Change in social behaviour
3. Improved cognitive and motor abilities
4. Sexual enhancement
5. Cognitive and motor impairment
6. Increased arousal
7. Relaxation and tension reduction

Positive expectancies of use tend to predict early and heavy alcohol involvement. This appears to be the case for alcohol (Leigh & Stacy, 1993). Christiansen et al. (1989) studied the development of alcohol expectancies over a year in young people aged 12–19. The youngest adolescents in this study had already developed clear expectations of alcohol prior to drinking. The study found that the more positive these expectations of drinking were then the more likely young people were to engage in early drinking behaviour. Specifically, item 2 (changes in social behaviour) and item 3 (improved cognitive and motor abilities), described above, were the biggest predictors of future use. These expectancies indicate that social acceptance and social competence were key drivers of consumption and reflected young people's concerns regarding fitting in with others. As such, alcohol was understood primarily as a social bonding agent amongst young people, even though this is not a pharmacological property of the substance.

Young et al. (2006) found a similarly complex relationship between expectancies and alcohol consumption in their study of university drinkers. Positive expectancies of alcohol use, such as 'alleviating stress', 'coping with worries' or 'sexual enhancement', were better predictors of dependent drinking than was the quantity of drinking. Young people were not without awareness of the negative consequences of use; however, in this study, negative expectancies of consumption exerted a very weak influence over young people's patterns of use. Other studies have found similar patterns. It appears that the negative consequences of actual consumption do not deter young people from use as much as positive expectancies promote it. This is not to say that the wider views of the young person do not have a role. Amonini & Donovan's (2006) study of 611 young people aged 14–17 found that use was directly related to the young person's moral view of the substance. Young people who believed that the use of alcohol, tobacco and cannabis was morally wrong under any

circumstances were least likely to use them; those who believed that the use of these substances was morally wrong under some circumstances were more likely to use them; whilst those who felt use was morally right under certain conditions were most likely to be users.

Other drugs

These same principles apply to a wider range of drugs than alcohol (Linkovich-Kyle & Dunn, 2001). Sub-cultures of youth evolve shared cultural beliefs and expectancies regarding illicit drug use. For example, smoking cannabis is often associated with 'giggles'. However, this only occurs at the initiation of use. Continued use of cannabis does not induce this response. The giggles may have nothing to do with cannabis but the may be driven by excited apprehension of first use. However, overtly positive expectations in youth will mean that they attribute this to the drug. Part of the induction process into drug consumption involves teaching the mode of use (rolling joint, loading pipes, preparing drugs for injection, etc.), what to notice in the experience, as well as how to act under the influence.

Expectations may also exert an even greater influence over consumption when the young person has positive expectancies for multiple substances. Smucker-Barnwell & Earlywine's (2006) online research on a sample of 2,600 users found that young people with simultaneous positive expectancies for alcohol and cannabis had a higher degree of involvement in both substances compared to those with positive expectations of one or the other substance alone. Strong correlations between positive expectations of substance use and alcohol use have also been found to predict other outcomes. Barnow et al. (2004) found that a strong correlation between positive expectations of drug and alcohol use predicted not only future consumption but also antisocial behaviour when under the influence of use.

There can be some differences between alcohol use and drug use. Expectancies regarding drug use may be shaped by sub-cultural influences as opposed to the broad cultural ones which shaped alcohol use. Youth sub-cultures ascribe different meanings to drug use which echo their own current concerns. LSD use in the sixties was a statement of dropping out, heroin use in the punk scene of the seventies was a statement of nihilism, ecstasy use in the eighties was a statement of freedom to party. None of these associations are pharmacological actions of the drugs. The symbolic meanings applied to specific drugs fuse them with fashion, music and attitudes to create clearly defined sub-cultures. Consumption of certain drugs at certain times is a badge of identity that indicates a young person's affiliation to a specific set of sub-cultural values. The preference young people have for a specific drug is not driven by the pharmacological effect, but by its symbolic affiliation to a set of values in their sub-culture.

The influence of having positive expectations is based on more than just individuals' anticipated effects of substances. Studies reveal that young people's expectations of how prevalent they believe consumption is amongst their peers also influence their own consumption. For example, a large English study (National Centre of Social Research, 2007) found that 15-year-olds who had consumed less than one unit of alcohol in the last week believed that only 9 per cent of other young people their age drank alcohol. In comparison, 15-year-olds who consumed more than 14 units of alcohol in the last week believed that 37 per cent of young people drank. This much stronger belief amongst heavier users that use was normal also occurred in relation to tobacco use. The study found that, 9 per cent of pupils smoked tobacco regularly, 5 per cent were occasional smokers, and 86 per cent didn't smoke. 63 per cent of non-smokers, 83 per cent of occasional smokers and 93 per cent of regular smokers believed that half their age group smoked.

Findings about drug use being normal were even more marked. Whilst very few young people took drugs at the age of 15 in this study, 20 per cent of those that had done so by this time believed that nearly *all* young people took drugs. In comparison, only 4 per cent of non-users thought that this was true.

As young people operate in peer groups with like-minded others, they tend to assume that their peer group behaviour is typical. This makes it easy for heavy-consuming youth to normalise their consumption, and strengthen the expectations that their behaviour is typical rather than problematic, regardless of the actual level of consumption.

Informal cultural control of use

Cultural forces also regulate consumption through establishing cultural norms. Room's

(2003) extensive studies into cultural variation in intoxication identified three critical rules that govern usage: the *mode*, *pattern* and *context* of use.

The *mode of use* describes how a society defines acceptable ways of taking the substance. This might include the form a substance takes and whether it is drank, snorted, smoked or injected. The *mode of use* can cause very specific problems in itself. For example, injecting drugs can increase risk of transmitting blood-borne viruses. Snorting drugs can damage the nasal passage. Much of the harm caused by nicotine is due to it being smoked in the form of cigarettes and thereby being inhaled into the lung.

The *pattern of use* relates to the amount, frequency and level of intoxication that is socially permissible. Northern European nations dominate the league table of those who drink '5 drinks or more' at least three times in a month. Malta is the only Mediterranean country where 20 per cent of youth reported drinking in this way. In comparison, young people in the UK, Sweden, Norway, the Netherlands, Ireland, Germany, Denmark and Belgium all scored above this rate (Hibell et al., 2004). Binge drinking is culturally acceptable in northern Europe but is not acceptable in southern Europe. This can have dramatic consequences. Norström's (2002) analysis of post-war drinking in 15 European countries found that every litre increase in per-capita alcohol consumption in northern European countries led to an almost three fold increase in the number of alcohol-related deaths compared to the same increase in Southern European countries.

The *context of use* states when it is permissible to use alcohol. Northern European countries make a strong association with alcohol consumption and 'carnival'. Drinking during festivities creates a strong cultural association between drinking and positive mood states. It promotes a 'time out' norm of alcohol use, where the normal rules of life are suspended during the festivity. This promotes greater disinhibition when consuming alcohol. Alcohol consumption in southern Europe is a daily occurrence and is not associated with special occasions. Its consumption is not associated with mood states and is more closely linked to the consumption of food. The *context of use* may also extend to what behaviours are permissible when intoxicated, for example whether it is permissible to drive under the influence of alcohol or perform other risk-sensitive tasks whilst taking prescription drugs.

Context also applies to the places where people prepare and consume a substance, both of which may also have a direct effect on their safety. Every culture designates sacred space for the consumption of alcohol. This can range from clearings in a forest, religious rituals or even bars and taverns. In Mediterranean cultures, where street drinking is common, drinking spaces are open and communal. Even in inclement weather, patrons eat and drink in 'glass houses' that facilitate all year round drinking on streets and in piazzas. These cultures display highly visible drinking in public spaces, where alcohol is imbibed by families. Consumption occurs within the context of everyday social relations.

Westernised nations consume alcohol in a 'hidden' world, in public houses and bars with frosted glass and heavy curtains. This drinking space is disconnected from people's everyday life, and thereby decreases any social consequences that might emerge as a result from heavy drinking. For example, if an individual gets inebriated and embarrasses themselves within their community they will experience social pressure from others. However, young people may now drink in anonymous bars where no-one knows them, removing this social consequence. These hidden drinking spaces offer far greater scope to create alcohol-induced 'fantasy worlds' where alternative 'ideal identities' are enacted. For example, McClelland et al.'s (1972) studies of western drinking found that males who felt powerless in their everyday life developed greater fantasies of power whilst intoxicated. Brown et al. (1980) found that Western male drinkers associated alcohol consumption with sexual power and aggression, whilst women expected more positive social experiences. Western societies experience far greater gender exaggeration, where males act more macho and women more feminine under the influence. Hence acts of 'quarrelling with friends' or regretful 'sexual encounters' are far more likely to occur in Western than Southern European youth (Anderson et al., 2007).

Symbolic meaning

Within these cultural rules governing use, each society attributes symbolic meaning to alcohol. These symbolic meanings shape the functions that alcohol has in each society. They can include alcohol's role in defining social situations. For example, whilst champagne is a 'situation definer' indicating celebration in the West, other beverages take on the meaning of 'situation definers' in different cultures, such as Brandy being drunk before foraging in East European Gypsy cultures. Alcohol offers an indication of social status. Beer drinking regions of Western Europe place great social prestige on expensive and high quality wine to indicate social status. However, in wine drinking regions, social status is indicated by imported beers.

There is an almost global experience of alcohol being used as a symbol of 'affiliation'. Sharing alcohol is a form of social bonding that can, for example, seal alliances, initiate people into friendship groups, endorse commitments or signify forgiveness amongst other kinds of pacts. Alcohol also serves as a marker of social 'transition'. This can occur on the micro-scale such as drinking on a Friday evening to mark the transition from labour to play. Or it can occur on a macro-scale to mark major life transitions. All major life transitions have their intrinsic alcohol-related ceremonies such as 'coming of age', 'wetting the baby's head', 'house warming' or 'wakes'. Alcohol provides an antidote to the stresses of these life transitions. Alcohol also has an important role in social cohesion. It plays a central role in festivals and public carnivals where the normal societal rules, social roles and distinctions are suspended, increasing social connection within a tribe or society. In the developed world this is nowadays often less connected with historical festivities, like Saints days, but more with major sports events. In this way alcohol is embellished with special meaning beyond its pharmacological action on the brain (see Table 1.5).

Taboos

Cultures also evolve restrictions on which people can consume, and how much, through the use of taboos. These taboos are policed by each member of society. Breaches in these unwritten laws are met with powerful verbal, emotional or group reactions which can range from shaming comments, group ridicule or even social exclusion. Research has identified that four critical taboos exist in nearly all cultures regarding the social regulation of consumption.

Although variations in these taboos exist, there are significant cross-cultural constants. For example, every culture operates a taboo regarding drinking in isolation. Drinking is a

Table 1.5:   Summary of the symbolic functions of alcohol

Area	Descriptors
Situation definer	• Beverage preference may denote specific occasions, such as champagne in Western culture. • Beverage preference may indicate social contexts as being formal or informal such as wine with a meal versus beer at informal social gatherings.
Status indicator	• Consumption of imported alcohol beverages holds higher social status than domestically produced alcohol. • Preference for high-status alcoholic beverages is indicative of social aspirations as opposed to social status. • Alcohol consumption and beverage preference differentiates gender behaviour. • Alcohol consumption signifies acceptance into an adult world.
Affiliation rituals	• Every culture has developed alcohol salutations, ceremonies of sharing alcohol and of reciprocity of alcohol. • Alcohol is the medium by which the links between groups, families and communities are initiated, sustained and affirmed. • Beverage preference can symbolise belonging to a group, social-class, nation or sub-culture. • Beverage preference can be a display of identifying with specific values and beliefs of sub-cultures. • The 'national drink' can symbolise the ideals, values and beliefs of the national character. • Refusal of a 'national drink' is construed as a rejection of national values.
Sacred spaces	• Alcohol provides designated physical space that is a separate social world. • Prescribed drinking spaces offer 'time out' from the normal demands of life (particularly in Western drinking patterns). • Separation of drinking space allows for the creation of 'ideal worlds' or an alternative reality where social roles and aspirations are transformed and played out. • Drinking spaces tend to be socially integrative and egalitarian. • Drinking space facilitate social bonding.
Transitional rituals	• Western cultures use alcohol to demarcate the transition from 'work' to 'play.' • Alcohol can serve as a ceremonial marker of life transitions (coming of age, graduation, marriage, parenthood, house warming etc.)
Festive rituals	• Alcohol is associated with festivity in nearly all cultures. • Ambivalent cultures use festivals as a reason to drink. • In moderate cultures, celebration is not invoked as a reason to drink.
Psychological function	• Transitions in life events induce anxiety that is antidote by alcohol. • Alcohol allows for the construction of ideal worlds under the influence as an escape from pressures of life.

rule-governed behaviour occurring within culturally prescribed rules. These have evolved to protect the consumer. The isolated drinker consumes alcohol outside of this protective framework and is not subject to the consequences of breaking social norms. Whilst some societies will countenance isolated drinking, isolated 'drunkenness' is not acceptable. Cultures also place prohibitions on female and underage drinking. Alcohol exerts a more profound pharmacological action on women due to their having more body fat and smaller livers, so their consumption is often judged by different standards to male drinking. Likewise children are protected from exposure to alcohol, with consumption being associated with coming of age or 'manliness' in many cultures (see Table 1.6). These findings create a contradiction in terms of the messages we give young people about the dangers of drugs. As Room (1983) suggested, overstating the disinhibiting aspect of alcohol and drug use may serve to reinforce these social norms in young people rather than warn young people away from use. Gusfield (1987) likewise warned that these messages may serve as justification and rationalisation in young people once they have acted in anti-social ways. As a result, the greater the power a society attributes to a drug then the greater the range of problems that they tend to experience.

Table 1.6:   Four constant cultural taboos regarding alcohol consumption

Constant	Description
Taboos against solitary drinking	• Nearly all cultures share taboos regarding solitary drinking. • Societies vary in their responses to solitary drinking but all are primarily negative from shaming to exclusion. • Societies do make exceptions from solitary drinking but not drunkenness. • In Western Europe, solitary drinking in a bar is more acceptable than solitary drinking at home.
Promotion of sociability	• Social drinking signifies social cohesion. • All cultures enforce etiquettes relating to sharing of alcohol. • Sharing of alcohol is conducted in an atmosphere of good will. • Alcohol is associated with reciprocation – alcohol is always exchanged for more alcohol, a gift, a favour etc.
Taboos regarding female and under-age drinking	• Most cultures reserve alcohol consumption for adult males and display at least degrees of prohibition regarding female drinking. • Multiple social theories have attempted to explain gender differences (feminism, male gender roles outside the home, women as source of values and probity, etc.) but have found little supporting evidence. • Differences may be due to the lower tolerance levels of females and the impact of consumption on pregnancy. • Restrictions are placed on underage drinking or even drinking in front of children. • Cultures vary in their prohibition of alcohol consumption by or with children, but all offer a degree of taboo. • Cultures which permit young children to taste alcohol at young age make provision for diluting alcohol with water or sugar cubes. • Western European drinking cultures have more inflexible restrictions on childhood drinking than Mediterranean cultures which are more permissive.
Social control	• Taboos and sociability promote control over consumption that minimises potential risks from consumption. • Informal social control has a greater influence on consumption behaviour than social policy. • Drinking rate is controlled by the group or designated individual. • Signs of drunkenness are disapproved of, whilst handling one's drink is met with prestige.

Young people's use and the media

Cultural norms are not simply learned by direct observation but are also acquired indirectly through the mass media such as television, film and music. The media is locked into a bi-directional relationship with its society where it both reflects and shapes public opinion. Young people are particularly susceptible to media influence due to their limited experience of adult life. The media is a powerful force for disseminating messages to a culture due to its mass and indiscriminate coverage. It can promote drug and alcohol use in many ways. This can be through consciously contrived messages about use such as news stories, documentaries or dramas that moralise on use, or through depiction of incidental alcohol and drug use in dramas that can augment social norms and normalise new ones. The media also has the power to lionise or demonise drug and alcohol users through positive or negative portrayals. In this way, the media can associate consumption with status figures and cultural icons that young people admire. Wakefield et al. (2003) summarised the media influence on cigarette smoking based on a deep analysis of the available research of media portrayals and young people's consumption. This showed how the media influences behaviours on a number of levels:

• The media influences and mirrors societal values regarding consumption.
• The media disseminates new information regarding substances to new audiences.
• The media is a source of observed learning for young people where they witness consumption and its consequences.

- Depictions of consumption can be positive or negative, influencing consumption or resistance.
- The media cannot directly influence what people think but it can influence the agenda of what people think about.
- The media can be effective in promoting interventions that increase the likelihood of avoiding substance use involvement.

It is difficult to assess the impact that the media has on young people's consumption. In general, research has found a stronger impact from the depiction of smoking (Wakefield et al., 2003) and alcohol (Austin et al., 2006) on young people's use than from the depiction of drug use. This is because media representation of illegal substances is governed by greater regulatory control. For example, the film industry has been subjected to strictures regarding the depiction of drug use since the 1920s. This code stated that drug use could not be glamourised for fear of influencing the young. This not only influenced the media presentation of drug use but spread to the lives of celebrities themselves. In the early days of Hollywood, the major studios went to great lengths to cover up drug scandals that rocked its major stars in order to preserve box office returns (Shapiro, 2003). In recent years this trend has reversed. Celebrity drug stories have become commonplace, along with public confessions and penance through the obligatory rehab stay. This modern strategy capitalises on substance use as a way of garnering increased publicity. Not only does this redeem the fallen idol, it also qualifies them as experts on substance misuse and offers opportunity for further career development through lecture tours and high profile media campaigns.

Visual media

In general, visual media like film and television have been the primary focus of research. Strong correlations have been found between the presentation of legal substances and their subsequent consumption amongst young people. These images are drawn from advertising, prevention campaigns and product placement as well as news coverage. Advertising has received the most research attention. Advertising's role is to increase routes into consuming substances. This includes encouraging initiation and experimentation, increasing consumption in present users, enticing users to switch brands and

stimulating ex-users to resume consumption. This may be particularly important in tobacco use because of the high mortality rates of those who do smoke. Advertising budgets for tobacco are huge with the industry spending over $9 billion dollars a year on advertising and a further $0.7 billion on free merchandise promoting their products prior to the ban on billboard advertising in 1999 (Federal Trade Commission, 1997). However, the television ban on advertising cigarettes has led to redirecting marketing funds into adverts in other areas, such as magazines often read by young people. As a result research has shown that partial bans on advertising have very little effect on consumption as these industries simply shift advertising dollars into new media (Pollay et al., 1996).

Research does show that young people who are exposed to cigarette advertising are more likely to smoke, even when other factors are taken into account (Difranza et al., 1991). Redmond (1999) was able to demonstrate a clear relationship between how increases in advertising budgets coincide with increases in prevalence of young people initiating into smoking. However, the promotion of tobacco or alcohol may not be restricted to the promotion of particular brands. Successful promotion can also be achieved by creating more attractive images of use, as well as by depicting social environments where drinking or smoking are portrayed as normal everyday activities. Through these characterisations, the media can promote consumption as a social norm. The use of free give-aways which are branded with cigarette or alcohol logos is also a very effective promotion strategy. Branded goods such as T-shirts increase the individual's personal identification with the product, cementing their attachment.

The depiction of teen idols smoking on and off screen is believed to enhance the prestige of substance use amongst their followers. Most research, however, has focussed on the frequency of substance use in the media rather than the meaning of substance use. For example, Furnham et al. (1997) studied media representation of alcohol in a sample of six UK soap operas. They identified that references were made to alcoholic beverages every 3.5 minutes and the cast were predominantly seen drinking alcohol twice as often as soft drinks. However, how the audience responded to the representation is not examined. Substance use can resonate with many powerful positive and negative associations and therefore simple frequency measures do not inform how these images influence young people. In one experimental study by Pechmann & Shih (1999), a film was shown to two groups of adolescents. One group watched an unedited version depicting smoking and the other watched a film that was edited to exclude images of smoking. Those exposed to the smoking depiction attributed greater prestige to smoking after the viewing and demonstrated greater intent to smoke than those who did not witness smoking on screen.

Product placement in films has become a new avenue to subsidise the cost of film production and offer tobacco and alcohol companies new media to reach predominantly young audiences. Product placement reached new heights in the 1980s where as much as 30–40 minutes of individual movies demonstrated product placement, accounting for a third of all film time (Hadju, 1988). Despite tobacco company claims that specific product placement fees had ceased since 1990, the reference to smoking has increased since this time. Furthermore, smokers within films are presented more positively than non-smokers, with little reference to any negative connotations from smoking. This finding is in accordance with experimental research on the powerful effects that exposure has on attitudes. Zajonc (1968) invited research participants to engage in a study that they thought was an investigation into how people learn foreign languages. During the first phase of the experiment, research candidates were shown ten Chinese-like words. Some were exposed to these symbols just once, some saw the images10 times and others 25 times. In phase two of the experiment, students were told that the Chinese symbols were adjectives with positive or negative meaning. The participants had to suggest which ones they thought were positive and which were negative. The more the research participant was exposed to the symbol, the greater the positive association became. Mere exposure creates a positive attitude towards neutral objects, and these findings have been replicated in numerous other studies (See Mita et al., 1977). Hence product placements in film and television need not promote specific brands but need to continually expose an audience to the idea of the product.

Music and magazines

One source of media influence that has been neglected is music. This is a particularly important media due to the strong association between youth lifestyle, sub-culture and drugs. Music has played a central role in identity formation of young people since the 1950s. Despite music's primacy and frequent moral panics associated with various youth movements, music has not been widely researched. One novel study was conducted by Primack et al. (2008) who analysed the content of 279 songs that were popular in 2005. Songs were grouped according to genre and were analysed for reference to substance use, context of use, motivation and consequences of use. In this sample, 2.9 per cent of songs referred to tobacco, 23.7 per cent referred to alcohol and 13.6 per cent referred to cannabis. Pop and rock songs had the least substance references whilst country and hip-hop had the highest frequency of references. Most references to use were positive. The consequences of use most referred to were social, sexual, financial or emotional benefits, usually with peers in party atmospheres. Whether music influences behaviour or whether the music depicts the priorities of youth sub-groups is difficult to discern. What this research did identify is that young people are exposed to 84 explicit references to substance misuse daily through the medium of music.

Magazines targeting youth have also become the focus of study in terms of how these publications depict substance use. This occurs in two distinct domains. Fashion magazines produce highly idealised images of youth and beauty that often incorporate smoking or substance use to enhance atmosphere in photography. Second, a new generation of gender specific magazine aimed at the youth market reflects and shapes young people's attitudes towards consumption. In terms of the fashion magazine, Gray et al. (1997) reviewed young people's interpretation and response to smoking in these magazines drawing on wider sociological theory. They suggest that a sociological change has occurred whereby people no longer construct a sense of identity from their class, gender or ethnicity. Instead, self-identity is now achieved through the 'lifestyle' people choose for themselves. Lifestyle has less do with the person's socio-economic history and more to do with their consumerist aspirations, expressed through the products, brands and logos that people purchase.

The explosion in fashion magazines for young people in the 1980s reflected this shift and disseminated the concept of the 'brand' to young people. Magazines like *The Face* did not simply inform young people about fashion choices, they began to depict fashion choices in new and symbolic ways. They brought top fashion photographers into their spreads who created highly stylised images that young people could relate to, and which embodied the readership's aspirations. Smoking in particular became an iconic symbol in these pages, representing the more exciting youthful world. This was a world that was free, cool and moody. Whilst the images in these fashion shoots were not direct advertising, but incidental, there is a strong suggestion that such constant exposure was a primer for cigarette smoking and for reduced guilt in adopting smoking behaviour amongst the young readership. Working with focus groups of young people, Gray et al. (1997) were able to establish a complex set of contradictory and complex meanings that young people associated with these images which largely support this sociological interpretation.

Whilst the 1980s saw an increase in the style magazine, the 1990s saw the emergence of the 'lad mag'. The proliferation of these gender specific youth magazines has received scant attention despite the highly bellicose style of reporting on young people's issues. This may be important as the development of these titles coincided with dramatic increases in binge drinking in the UK. Lyon et al. (2006) reviewed the representation of drinking in these youth-orientated magazines. They reviewed three magazines targeted at young men and three magazines targeted at young women over a three month period. They identified that 11.9 per cent of the articles in these magazines related to alcohol. There was a slightly higher prevalence in men's magazine but the overall the column inches were similar in both gender groups.

This study identified three recurrent narratives with regard to alcohol consumption in the magazines. First was 'alcohol-as-a-drug' story, which eulogised new alcoholic drinks in the images of illicit substances. This appeared to invest new power in alcoholic beverages beyond that of simply alcohol. For example, a new beverage might be like 'champagne and cocaine'. The second narrative was a powerful 'gender bias' in beverage preference. Beers were emphasised as a male drink whilst wine and newer beverages were 'disgraced' as being for women. Whilst women's magazines rarely commented on male beverage preference, men's magazines persistently referenced women's beverage preference in highly negative terms, usually describing it as 'piss'. Finally, high consumption of alcohol was depicted as 'normal' and always couched in highly masculine terms. Women's magazines connected alcohol with drinks after work, associating consumption with career strain. So women dined with friends after work, ate a meal and danced the night away 'fuelled' on 'champagne'. In contrast, male drinking was always pitched in hyper-masculine terms, largely calling upon warfare as a metaphor for drinking. They got 'hammered', drew up a 'line of attack' and took up an 'ambush-like' approach to shots. These youth magazines re-asserted the gender exaggeration associated with Western drinking cultures to a new generation.

The product as drug

Whilst this has not been studied in any great depth, there has also been a shift in mainstream advertising regarding drug use. This is not in the explicit selling of drugs but in the adoption of a 'product-as-a-drug' sales pitch. Advertisements now routinely display a monochrome and dull world where the protagonist is bored or engaged in some mundane activity. Then suddenly, on using the product such as confectionary, cleaning products or new electronic devices, they are transformed into a joyously altered state of consciousness. Colours are vivid, and added special effects create a sense of hyper-reality. The advertisements replicate exactly the rapid highs induced by drugs. They personify and stereotype the positive mood states associated with substances and attach them to new products and commodities. The fact that they do this, and that this advertising has gone largely unnoticed, also exemplifies the way in which drug use has become so mainstream in recent years.

Variation within cultures

Societies are not homogenous. Within their cultural boundaries and geographic borders there are a multiplicity of social classes, ethnic groups and sub-cultures which all have their own ways of living. Immigrant groups bring with them their own rituals and symbolic meanings which host cultures may meet with suspicion. Under-classes may cultivate values in opposition to the ruling classes who try to impose their norms on those beneath them. The young can reject the ways of the old and the old can vilify the young. These strata of society are locked in a dynamic interplay with each other producing ever more diverse mutations. Power, economic resources and media access are not evenly spread throughout the slipstreams. Likewise the prevalence of consumption is not evenly distributed amongst them either. Of all these forces, social deprivation exerts the greatest influence on variance of use within a culture.

Deprivation

Research has found a high correlation between substance use and social deprivation; this connection requires careful consideration. First, whilst the prevalence rates of consumption do appear higher in socially disadvantaged groups they do not have a monopoly on consumption, which can occur across any social group. Second, whilst substance misuse and poverty co-occur it is more difficult to suggest that poverty causes substance misuse. It could be the reverse, with heavy substance users experiencing greater poverty. Without a clear understanding of how the diffuse impact of poverty may initiate, sustain or escalate use, it can be difficult to establish that poverty causes increased use. Finally it is important to define what is meant by poverty, as different research studies may use different indicators.

Poverty is difficult to define and there is a debate in the research field whether it should be measured in *absolute* or *relative* terms. Absolute poverty is based upon a fixed scale whereas relative poverty indexes an individual's status in comparison to their national average. Most research has concluded that greater health and social problems are found amongst groups who experience relative poverty rather than absolute. Within this, deprivation is measured in wider terms than simple income, although lower income is an important measure. For example, substance use appears higher in those with no income but also amongst young people with low-paid or semi-skilled employment (Chau et al., 2008). Deprivation may also be found in housing conditions, educational disadvantage and length of unemployment, as well as in income poverty. It is also a subjective experience in which people feel disadvantaged in comparison to other social groups. This subjective experience of deprivation can be expressed through a feeling of worthlessness, loss of role, futility, loss of hope for a better life for oneself or one's children, as well as apathy.

Substance misuse has a strong relationship with deprivation whether the substances are legal or illegal. In the case of legal drugs, nicotine use shows a very high correlation with social deprivation. This has been a consistent finding as demonstrated by studies in the United States (Giovino et al., 1995; Barbeau et al., 2004) in the UK (Townsend et al., 1994) and other developed countries (Fernandez et al., 2001; Huismen et al., 2005). Every study has demonstrated that smoking increases as the socio-economic status decreases. In an Australian study for example, White et al. (2008) found that students in the most affluent areas were 35 per cent less likely to smoke cigarettes than students from poorer areas at all ages.

Similar patterns have been found with alcohol, albeit with some important differences. Numerous studies have found that poverty and family norms are associated with heavier drinking. Montgomery et al. (1998) found that unemployment of three years or more was strongly associated with smoking and heavier drinking in 2,887 males aged between 16–33 years old. Thundal et al. (1999) found similar results for women where alcohol consumption was closely related to less social support, lower socio-economic status and unemployment in the 414 women interviewed.

Alcohol does show some differences in spread of consumption due to its widespread cultural acceptability. The Health Study for England (1998) found that the percentage of men consuming more than the recommended 21 units of alcohol a week was similar for the wealthiest and the lowest socio-economic groups at 28 and 29 per cent of these populations respectively. However, the middle income groups showed the highest consumption with 35 per cent in the second most economically advantaged group and 31 per cent in the second most disadvantaged. The rich-poor drank more than the poor-poor. In contrast, women's alcohol consumption was more likely to exceed the recommended 14 units a week in the top three socio-economic groups

(20–22 per cent). Weekly unit consumption was significantly lower in the three most disadvantaged socio-economic groups where only 12 to 15 per cent exceeded the recommended daily limit on alcohol. So whilst tobacco is becoming increasingly the preserve of the poorest in society, high alcohol consumption tends to straddle the middle income earners rather than those at either end of the extremes of wealth.

Causality

Similar findings were reported by Coulthard et al.'s (2002) study of co-morbidity in 8,580 people aged 16–74 years old. Co-morbidity refers to groups of people who experience concurrently both substance abuse disorders and mental illnesses. Reviewing drinking patterns in these populations, they identified that young people aged 16–24 were the most likely group to engage in hazardous drinking. These young people were also more likely to be single or cohabiting rather than married (which showed a far lower rate of alcohol consumption). However, the highest consumers were not the most disadvantaged young adults. This study identified that 30 per cent of those that had a gross weekly income of £400 were hazardous drinkers. This compared to 19 per cent of those with a gross income of £200 per week. Heavy drinking is expensive and requires adequate financial resources. These higher alcohol consumers tended to be white, employed in manual occupations and experiencing greater financial difficulties than their counterparts. In contrast, the study found that heavy drug users were more likely to be single, unemployed and experiencing greater levels of financial pressure and stress. This was even the case of heavy cannabis use. Again, this raises the same issue of causality. Does heavy drug use lead to poverty or are poorer social groups more liable to use illicit drugs?

Numerous research studies have found a strong relationship between illicit drug use and social deprivation. One study conducted by Parker et al. (1988) in the Wirral area of North West England examined this relationship in detail. The study is interesting because the geographic area of Wirral contains a patchwork of areas with diverse income levels. The study identified 1,305 opioid users aged 16–24 who were contacted through local treatment agencies. The incidence of heroin use in the age range for the whole area was 18.2 per 1,000 people. However, research demonstrated that incidence of heroin use varied enormously in different neighbourhoods, from zero in some areas to 162 per 1,000 people in others. The research found a direct relationship between increasing social deprivation and the prevalence of consumption. The study went further by cross-referencing specific elements of poverty that related to consumption, using a co-efficient approach. A co-efficient describes how closely two variables move together. A score of 1.0 indicates that the two variables are absolutely related whilst a score of −1.0 describes a perfect negative relationship. A score of 0 means that the two variables are not related. This study found a significant relationship with all indicators of social deprivation and drug use. Some of the most powerful indicators included unemployment (0.72), council tenancy (0.67), overcrowding (0.62), large families (0.49), unskilled employment (0.39), single parent family (0.69) and lack of access to a car (0.58).

In the UK, the Advisory Council on the Misuse of Drugs report (ACMD, 1998) summarised how deprivation impacts on consumption, based on suggestive evidence. This occurs in two domains. The first domain describes how poverty influences an individual's choices whilst the second domain describes how poverty impacts on an individual's environment (See Table 1.7). Individual effects can include social disenfranchisement where the poor become excluded from access to wider social and economic opportunities. This can result in a rejection of the pro-social values of lifestyles that are beyond their reach. It may also promote greater involvement in anti-social behaviour as the only means of purpose available to them. Criminal or drug using 'careers' describe the structural involvement in these behaviours as an alternative means of achieving personal satisfaction in life. Scoring, using and dealing may offer the poor a purpose that they cannot access in mainstream social networks. At an environmental level, poverty increases the number of stressors that impact on an individual. For example, individuals in poverty do not have the economic resources to shield them from economic pressures. Poverty may weaken an individual's social supports through breaking family and wider community attachments, further undermining their resilience to stressors. This can promote mental health problems or

Table 1.7: Summary of the impacts of poverty. Adapted from the ACMD report, 1998

Personal impact	Environmental impacts
Individuals who grow up in disadvantaged areas may ignore or become detached from wider pro-social values.	Deprivation weakens family and community attachments.
Individuals may self-medicate as a coping strategy to deal with higher social pressures.	Deprivation can increase social stressors on the individual including anxiety and depression.
Drug use and dealing can provide alternative purposeful activity and structure to life without work.	Unemployment prevents young people from growing into developing social roles.
Drug dealing may be the only way of earning a living.	Low incomes may force individuals to secure money from the shadow economy of the community.
Hopelessness and apathy may pervade a community, tolerating a wider range of anti-social behaviour as it 'will never change.'	Deprived areas may not have the economic or social capitol to respond to the establishment of drug markets in their communities.

drive individuals to seek a livelihood in the shadow economy.

Rival theories have suggested that poverty acts on the individual in two different ways. One theory suggests that poverty exposes individuals to greater life stressors that produce dysfunctional coping styles. Other theorists have suggested that poverty creates a deficit in coping resources that makes those living in deprivation more susceptible to the adoption of unhealthy behaviours. For example, people in higher socio-economic groups may have more personal, social and material resources that buffer them from environmental stresses. The poor have no protection from these environmental stressors which impact directly on them.

The studies of Kooiker & Christiansen (1995) found that adults living in poverty do experience higher frequency of environmental problems and stresses, but personal coping was not such a significant factor. This situation may be different for young people whose emotional and social resourcefulness is not fully matured. Geckova et al. (2003) examined both theories amongst 2,616 Slovak adolescents with an average age of 14.9 years old. Their study found that both hypotheses were true for young people. Adolescents in the lowest socio-economic group were prone to higher rates of environmental stress, but it was their more limited ability to manage these social stresses that appeared more significant. They also found that that the type of social pressures that poor young people experienced tended to be much more profound, and that the incidence of problematic use increased in lower socio-economic groups compared to wealthy

social groups. This suggested that drug and alcohol use was an important coping strategy in an increasingly hostile environment.

The most insidious effect of poverty on people may be its influence on attitudes. Poverty can instil a sense of hopelessness and futility regarding an individual's potential achievement in a society. This lowering of expectation may be augmented by their everyday experiences. The children of affluent families grow up in households where the benefits of educational achievement are manifest in the material advantage of their parents. Poor children do not experience the benefits of education so directly and may not make such a strong connection to the value of education. Instead, poor children and young people are surrounded by those who remain trapped by their circumstances, have experienced no social mobility and feel unlikely to ever achieve anything in their society. This can lower or destroy any hope of wider social achievement. The result is that many young people may not only develop overtly positive expectations of drug and alcohol use but also inherit exceptionally negative expectations of other life achievements.

This may account for not only increased use of drugs and alcohol in the poorer social groups, but also for the increased rate of problematic usage that they also experience. As we have seen, the amount of substances an individual uses is not related to the problems that they can experience. For example, higher rates of mortality are found in smokers from lower socio-economic groups than in higher socio-economic groups. Whilst 7 per cent of males from the highest socio-economic standing will die before the age of 70 as a result of smoking tobacco, 22 per cent of males from the lowest socioeconomic status will die prematurely (Wanless, 2003). This is also true for other substances. Gruer et al. (1997) analysed postcodes of 3,715 admissions to hospital for a drug-related emergency in Glasgow. The admission rate for the poorest districts was 30 times that of the wealthiest. Admissions were over double for males to females, and the highest risk period was from age 25 to 29. This study concluded that the strongest relationship between drug related emergencies and hospital admission was deprivation. Research by Farrell et al. (1997) also identified that the prevalence of physical dependence on nicotine, alcohol or drugs was higher in disadvantaged socio-economic groups than in more affluent groups. The incidence of drug dependence increases with the severity of deprivation. Individuals scoring at the highest end of the deprivation scale were 10 times more likely to report dependence than those with no indicators of deprivation (see Graph 1.7).

Mental health and deprivation

In light of these findings, it is unsurprising that poverty also increases young people's susceptibility to significant mental illness. The Muntaner et al. (2004) review of research studies found a significant relationship between the rates of schizophrenia, bipolar disorder, depression and anxiety in general populations in lower socio-economic positions. Whilst not every study has found the same relationship, the vast majority of research has supported these findings. Again, the direction of causality remains an issue in these studies. For example, does lower socio-economic status increase mental illness or does mental illness lower people's socio-economic status? Comparing the socio-economic histories of the parents of those with mental illness, such as schizophrenia, does suggest that social disadvantage increases risk of the disorder.

However, the situation may be more complex than this research suggests. It requires deeper consideration of the nature of mental illness. Every mental health diagnosis, whether it be for mental illness, personality disorder or behavioural disorders, shares one common feature. For the diagnosis to be made, the disorder must affect the individual's social functioning. Social functioning is therefore critical in any diagnosis and yet it remains the most neglected symptom in psychiatry. Using the interruption of social function as the clinical cut-off point for serious mental illness introduces a random variable into diagnosis. This is because levels of social functioning can vary enormously. As we have seen, poverty can have a catastrophic

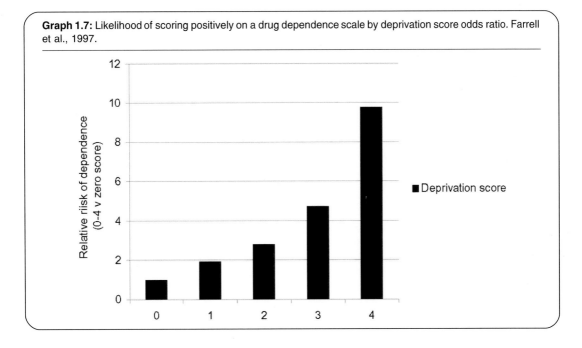

Graph 1.7: Likelihood of scoring positively on a drug dependence scale by deprivation score odds ratio. Farrell et al., 1997.

effect on social functioning whereas affluence can improve social functioning. Individuals from affluent backgrounds may have more personal resources (education, wealth, optimism) than those from poor backgrounds.

Furthermore, affluent individuals may have greater environmental supports (social support, job opportunities, qualifications and personal networks). The poor are managing more profound social stressors with fewer resources, curtailing their social functioning. This means that even lower levels of mental illness may have a more profound effect on their ability to manage disproportionately hostile environments. This suggests that the poor may not experience a higher rate of mental illness than other groups. However, as a greater range of difficulties is already implicit in their life, any mental health problems will compound this further. So, mental illness can have a far more dramatic impact on an individual who is already experiencing high levels of environmental pressure. This means that even milder forms of mental illness are more likely to impede their social functioning and so cross this diagnostic threshold.

Ethnicity

A great deal of research has focussed on ethnic differences in consumption within societies. As we have seen, every culture will develop its own patterns of consumption which have their specific internal symbolic meanings and rituals. However, there are considerable dangers in taking an absolute position on variance in consumption in ethnic groups. First, in a climate of racial discrimination it can be difficult to separate ethnic variance with other social factors such as poverty. The fact that poverty is also related to higher rates of mental illness clouds these issues further. Second, consideration of consumption within ethnic groups is susceptible to reinforcing racial stereotypes. For example, reports of drug use and dealing in different ethnic cultures are often caricatured by wider social prejudices. As Murji (1999) points out, drug dealing and consumption amongst British Afro-Caribbean populations tends to be represented in the media as a 'social problem' amongst 'gangs'. Whereas drug dealing and consumption amongst British Asian culture tends to be reported in terms of 'culture' and 'family'. Third, what constitutes problematic use may be dependent on cultural context. Diagnostic

frameworks used to assess problematic use are not understood by other cultures whose experience of use may be very different from Western populations (Room, 2007). Patterns and modes of consumption may integrate into one culture's social structure seamlessly but may not be transplanted into another without conflict. Finally, the concept of ethnic diversity can mask the issue of ethnic similarity. Within these discussions it is easy to omit the impact of Western imperialism which not only subjugated a diverse range of peoples but also systematically destroyed their indigenous culture. In its wake they imposed a Westernised morality on people which still resonates today. It is striking that individuals who live outside of Western economies and who aspire to Western values tend to have higher rates of alcohol and drug consumption than their peers.

Research into prevalence rates of consumption in ethnic minority groups has been contradictory. For example, three studies into the risk factors affecting ethnic groups report significant differences. Vega et al. (1993) reported that Black populations experienced significantly higher risks than Whites. Maddahian et al. (1988b) suggested Whites and Asians experienced the highest risk and Black populations the lowest. Whilst Newcomb et al. (1987) identified that Native American Indian populations had the highest risk and Black and Asian populations the lowest risk. The fact that these studies used very similar methodological approaches suggests that geographic location of these populations may have been a significant mediating factor on use. So, whilst many of the predictive factors of drug and alcohol use are similar across ethnic groups, this research suggests that fine-tuning approaches to specific populations and geographic areas may be valuable in the delivery of programmes.

These differences shown in these research findings may be due to the different degree that ethnic minority groups achieve cultural assimilation within different geographical areas. The rate of assimilation may show wide variance depending on the ethnic composition of each region, the predominant political climate and the levels of social disadvantage experienced by different sub-cultures who may be competing for the same limited resources. Cultural assimilation does have a major influence on consumption. So for example, Asian populations from the Pacific Rim experience a genetic condition called 'Oriental Flush'. They lack the ability to produce an enzyme to metabolise alcohol resulting in a high sensitivity to alcohol's effects and they suffer violent hangovers. The Native American Indian and the Inuit both have this condition and suffer the highest rates of alcoholism in the US. Simultaneously, Chinese and Japanese populations also have this genetic condition but show the lowest rates of alcoholism in the US. The cultural compatibility of their work ethics integrates the Chinese and Japanese into US culture, whereas the values of the Native American and Inuit are discordant with it.

Kandel (1995) suggested an alternative explanation. Whilst some ethnic groups' risk factors appear lower amongst young people, particularly in studies of Afro-Americans, their risk factors as adults are much higher. This 'paradox' might be accounted for by the fact that young Afro-American males are often excluded from school at a younger age than their white counterparts. Therefore they do not appear in these studies, which tend to be based on school populations, but do appear in later adult treatment samples. So this paradox may be indicative of structural racism rather than ethnicity. From this perspective, it remains difficult to separate multiple social forces such as ethnicity, poverty, cultural and political imperialism and the impact of structural racism on consumption rates.

How young people acquire drugs and alcohol

The issue of prevalence of drug and alcohol use in young people raises the issue of how young people acquire these substances. This may differ depending on the laws of society, with different routes of access for legal and illegal drugs. Even when legal substances are available there are limits to young people's access to them. As we have seen, the sale of alcohol is restricted to young people in nearly every culture. Whilst there is variance in the age ranges of consumption and purchase, young people still have to find ways around these restrictions. This means that underage drinkers must find other 'unofficial' avenues in which to purchase alcohol. These pathways are diverse. In the UK, research from the *Offending, Crime and Justice Survey* (Mathews et al., 2006) found that 48 per cent of 10- to 17-year-olds obtained alcohol from parents. A further 29 per cent acquired alcohol from

friends and 22 per cent purchased alcohol from bars and pubs. The heaviest drinkers were more likely to acquire alcohol from friends (50 per cent), bars & nightclubs (47 per cent) and shops (40 per cent). Amongst these more regular drinkers, just under a quarter of them obtained alcohol from parents.

The *Young Person's Behaviours and Attitudes Survey* (NISRA, 2007) in Northern Ireland identified that 27 per cent of young people who had consumed alcohol had actually bought it themselves. The majority (19 per cent) bought alcohol from a public house, a smaller group had purchased alcohol from an off-licence (14 per cent) and a small group from a shop (5 per cent). This research also identified the high rate of sociability attached with alcohol. Very few young people reported drinking alone. When asked about their last drinking episode, 39 per cent of young people said they drank with friends or a friend. Drinking with family figured highly as 15 per cent consumed alcohol with parents and 14 per cent with relatives. In a Scottish survey (BMRB, 2007), 61 per cent of 13-year-olds who drank reported that they never bought alcohol. Of those that had purchased alcohol, 22 per cent had obtained from friends or relatives, 11 per cent had purchased alcohol from shops, whilst 7 per cent had reported buying alcohol from an off-licence. As young people aged they were increasingly more likely to acquire alcohol from licensed premises but for many young people alcohol consumption is embedded in the family context.

Drug markets operate very differently to alcohol markets due to the illicit nature of the commodities being sold. In terms of distribution, drugs can be sold in either 'open' or 'closed' markets. An open market is a place where opportunistic purchases can be made. It may be a particular neighbourhood, public house, night club or street which is known to be frequented by dealers of a variety of substances. Operating in these markets carries more risk as the relationship between the buyer and seller is brief and the drugs can be of varying quality. The young person is also exposing themselves to a high degree of personal risk in being exploited, swindled or made the victim of a crime which they may be unable to report.

Closed markets (also referred to as social markets) are a network of associations. Buyers are introduced to sellers through a network of friends or family members. Buyers often complete transactions in the closed market dealer's home,

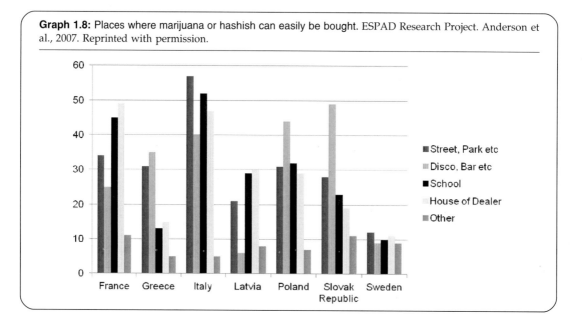

Graph 1.8: Places where marijuana or hashish can easily be bought. ESPAD Research Project. Anderson et al., 2007. Reprinted with permission.

and these closer social ties mean that buyers are less likely to be duped, swindled or extorted. The network of potential buyers is also informally vetted by individuals who already have a long-standing relationship with the closed market dealer. The introduction of a new buyer is often carefully managed in closed markets, through an established relationship with an existing buyer who will 'vouch' for the new person and seek clearance from the dealer prior to any formal transactions. This creates a circle of trust around the supplier that offers some protection through filtering out those whose behaviour would breach secrecy of the network. This informal system produces remarkably stable pricing and quality of drugs. Access to these vetted networks also offers a high degree of prestige to young people, who must be deemed sufficiently credible to be worthy of entry into them.

Research shows that the sources of drugs vary in different cultures, with a considerable difference between open and closed market access for young people. The ESPAD research project (Anderson et al., 2007) explored young people's perceptions of where they felt it would be easy for them to purchase cannabis. Young people had clear ideas as to where the drug could be purchased, even amongst those that did not use cannabis. Each country showed significant variations of where young people could acquire the drug. In general, it appeared that young people tended to purchase drugs

opportunistically in riskier open markets such as 'discos and bars' along with 'streets,' and 'park etc'. To a lesser extent, young people were also able to procure drugs from closed markets in 'school' and 'dealer's house'. The Swedish sample did not recognise any particular sources as more probable than any other (see Graph 1.8).

In-depth studies into young people's access to drugs such as cannabis are rare. An exception was research commissioned by the Joseph Rowntree Trust and conducted by Plymouth University. This study examined the supply of cannabis to young people in the UK (Duffy et al., 2008). They interviewed 182 young people aged 11–19 who had either used cannabis in the last six months or supplied cannabis in the preceding six months. Whilst this research is not directly comparable to the ESPAD studies (due to its different selection criteria for young people and methodology) it did suggest interesting similarities and differences amongst young people in the UK. Like the European cohort, young people in the UK study saw cannabis as 'very easy' or 'easy' to obtain. Furthermore, these young people saw their consumption as a shared activity with a purchasing pattern that was opportunistic. They would all 'chip in' to purchase cannabis in advance of an imminent social event. Nearly half the sample purchased the drug with money from parents or family whilst 29 per cent funded the cost of the drug through their wages. Almost a quarter of the young people in the UK sample did not buy the drug themselves but were given it by friends, whilst 16 per cent relied upon friends to buy the drug on their behalf.

Only 6 per cent of the cohort purchased cannabis from open markets. The majority of purchasers operated in tightly controlled closed markets. When they did buy from unknown sources, young people often went in groups for safety. Transactions were most likely to take place in public places like alleyways (28 per cent) or dealer's homes (22 per cent). Dealers were on average three years older than purchasers, typically aged 19. Whilst just under half the sample of young people had been involved in selling cannabis at some point, they did not perceive themselves as dealers in any formal sense. They were simply helping out friends. This study concluded that the supply of cannabis amongst young people was not driven by financial profit in the first instance. 'Young people's patterns of cannabis acquisition had little or nothing to do with "drug markets" as they have been conventionally described, and were primarily based around friendship and social networks. Young people were introduced to cannabis by friends, accessed and maintained supplies via friends, as well as passed on and sold cannabis to friends.' (Duffy et al., 2008 p.viii). Furthermore, the self-contained nature of these largely youth dealing networks protected young people from entering, or being influenced by, more adult dealing networks. Strikingly, the pattern of young people's cannabis use appeared similar to the patterns of alcohol consumption. Its use is a form of social currency in sorting out and sharing with friends. This included reciprocation, where young people would purchase and share the drug in lieu of being given the drug by friends on previous occasions.

Summary

Drug and alcohol use is not a static process but is locked into a dynamic relationship with historical and cultural forces. Within these overarching trends in consumption we see that drug and alcohol use, and incumbent problems, vary according to the cultural context of their use. International studies reveal that levels of consumption and problems do not correlate in young people. Instead, we see that the cultural context sets the mode, frequency and types of consumption. These patterns of consumption imbue drugs and alcohol with symbolic social meanings, rituals and customs. They do not simply demarcate the pattern of use but also shape the internal experience of intoxication itself. Expectancies influence the anticipated effects of substances, their influence on mood as well as what behaviours are culturally permissible under the influence. Furthermore, these expectancies also shape a young person's sense of normalcy of use, where they see their own consumption as typical.

Expectancies are derived from direct and indirect learning. This direct experience may emanate from family and the immediate social group. Indirect sources include the broader media who shape expectancies through positive representations of smoking or alcohol. The media also normalises patterns of behaviour in its representation of what constitutes everyday life. Patterns of consumption can vary within a culture depending on a wide range of factors. Consumption patterns show a particularly strong correlation with different socio-economic positions. Heroin, and increasingly tobacco, use occurs within the poorer social groups. The wide availability and acceptability of alcohol has wider socio-economic reach across social groups. Poverty not only increases consumption but can also increase the range, and severity, of substance misuse problems that people experience. As such, young people's use is governed by the social context in which it occurs. Whilst this cultural context has often been ignored, we shall see how it governs not only young people's consumption but also the entirety of their lives.

CHAPTER 2

What is Adolescent Development?

Introduction

A new born human baby is a particularly feeble specimen in comparison to its primate cousins such as the chimpanzee, gorilla and monkeys. Not only is the human baby physically much smaller than its counterparts but it is also completely immobile. Whilst our primate cousins are quick to explore the world around them, we remain at the mercy of our care giver. By the time other primates are problem solving and playing with their siblings we have not mastered walking. Biologists calculate that in comparison with other primates the human infant is born too soon. The gestation period for a primate of our size should be twenty-one months and not the nine-month term in which we are typically carried. This means that humans are born a year premature; hence our particularly helpless state. The reason for this early ejection is the size of the human brain. It is simply too large for the birth canal of a primate that walks on two feet. Premature birth is a biological necessity.

The human baby maybe an evolutionary ugly duckling but it will become a cultural swan. From these humble beginnings the infant will grow and develop the skills, ability and understanding to operate in the most sophisticated animal habitat in the world: human society. The transition from helpless infant to autonomous adult is the central focus of adolescent development and is the central focus in this chapter. Adolescent development is a multi-disciplinary science, drawing on biology, genetics, sociology, psychology and history. Needless to say it is not a discipline characterised by agreement. Many theorists and researchers in the field might offer rival definitions of the words 'adolescence' and 'development'. It is impossible to review the full range of issues, research and disagreements in a chapter of this size. Therefore, it will examine just the critical elements of adolescent development that relate to substance misuse. This will serve as a benchmark for considering risk factors, problematic use, prevention and treatment in subsequent chapters.

In reviewing adolescence it is easy to fall into the trap of believing that our current cultural and historical situation represents a universal norm. But it is important to acknowledge that adolescence and the study of it have a history. Examining the development of both these elements can be helpful in illuminating the assumptions that are so prevalent in current thinking, which can then be scrutinised from a deeper research perspective. Once this context has been established, this chapter will examine critical developmental processes. It begins by examining the building blocks of development: personality and genetics. Whilst conclusive findings are scant in these domains, they are often alluded to in adolescent drug and alcohol research. So it is essential to have a basic working knowledge of these core concepts. This chapter will then partition adolescent developmental processes into four strands. The strands are inter-related, but for clarity they will be examined in isolation. They are: the life tasks to be accomplished across adolescence, the physical and cognitive changes that occur as part of puberty, how young people formulate a new emergent 'adult' identity for themselves and the shifts in their relationships that will transform their future lives irrevocably.

Finally, this chapter will consider disruptions to the natural developmental process. Before considering how drug and alcohol use interrupt this process it is important to acknowledge that other issues can deflect young people from the normal developmental course. Primary amongst them are adolescent mental health issues that can have an equally catastrophic effect on development. So, whilst the themes presented in this chapter may appear disparate at first, understanding the developmental context of young people's lives becomes critical in later chapters. This is because the emergence of drug and alcohol problems is deeply entwined in these developmental processes.

The evolution of the modern family

No social institution is as vulnerable to shifting historical, economic and cultural tides as the family unit. In considering adolescence, the family unit is of particular interest, largely due to widespread assumptions regarding the influence of parenting on the establishment of personality, and its perceived influence on child and adolescent behaviour. In any tragedy regarding young people, it is impossible to escape the immediate riposte that any form of anti-social behaviour is essentially the fault of the parents. These prevalent assumptions are located in the development of increased theorising (and moralising) of the family from the perspectives of psychology and psychotherapy in the 20th Century. These theories have led to the idealisation of both childhood and parenting into rarefied forms that few can actually achieve. But it is important to examine family and parenting style in this context to address the monopoly that many recent psychological theories of family currently exert over the notion of family influence.

It is important to recognise that family structures vary enormously across cultures. As Mead (1928) noted, many societies outside of Western cultures pay little attention to the role of parenting in the life course. Mead identified that in Samoa, infants were given over to the next older sibling to raise at the age of two to three. Malinowski's (1922) anthropological study found that Trobriand children were given enormous freedom compared to Western peers with little parental involvement. In this society, discipline was not a father's responsibility, this task befell the mother's brother. Similarly, Harris' (1999) extensive study of parenting styles across cultures describes a multiplicity of family structures. Harris also identified that, in the majority of cultures, siblings have a direct parenting role.

Even within Western societies, family structures have changed enormously over the course of history. DeMause's (1976) historical analysis of the family unit described these changes in detail. In the 4th Century, children were seen as largely expendable members of the family. Even though child mortality rates were high, infanticide was a common practice, particularly of baby girls who were seen as an economic liability in those austere times. Children had fewer rights than livestock who contributed significantly more to the survival of families. By the 13th Century children had become perceived as 'non-entities' who could soon be abandoned to others to raise them without sentimentality. Children were dispatched into apprenticeships or servitude as early as six to seven years old. Whilst these children did have some 'play time' outside of work, they were largely perceived in economic terms. In return they could learn a trade to sustain them in their adult life.

As life expectancy increased, children became more involved in the emotional life of parents. The 18th Century saw a marked shift in parental responsibility. For the first time parenting took on the role of 'shaping the future adult'. As children in the West were still marked by Original Sin, this responsibility entailed breaking the will of a child and civilising it in the name of God. However, during this period children were not seen as a distinct social group. Rather they were perceived as little adults and there was little legal or cultural separation of childhood as a distinct life phase. The recognition of childhood really emerged in the 19th Century. During this period the parental role shifted towards taking responsibility for socialising children. For the very first time it established a clear role for fathers in parenting. The father's role changed from disinterested other into one that fused education and corporal punishment into the family authoritarian.

Contemporary ideals of family

Contemporary ideals of family really began to take root in the Edwardian period early in the 20th Century. The emergent disciplines of psychotherapy believed it could provide scientific guidance to create ideal forms of parenting. This occurred when social and economic changes had liberated the middle classes from the necessity of constant toil, allowing middle classes the time and emotional energy to invest in family life in a manner that had not possible in any previous age. It was in the writings of this new middle class that began to ferment modern conceptions of family structures. These writers idealised family in their own image. The assumption was that after a period of non-sexual courtship based on romantic love, marriage would be the stable institution necessary in which to have children, and that both parents were essential to their emotional well-being and future social adjustment. The family structure itself reflected that of the middle classes. This consisted of a breadwinning father, a home-based nurturing mother and one to four children under the age of 18. This became understood as an ideal unit of social organisation and any departure from this structure would invariably lead to developmental and behavioural problem in children. Furthermore, the Edwardians extended the Victorian concept of parents as educators. They emphasised that the future life of a child was determined wholly by parenting style. This created new pressures and responsibilities for parents who were now believed to be accountable for their offspring's future actions. For the first time, the failure of a child was understood as a failure in parenting.

Even during the Edwardian period, when theorists such as Freud began exploring parenting style and personality development, high infant mortality rates, short life expectancies and lack of contraception meant that women endured a reproductive cycle that could span forty years. Outside of the middle classes, in the economic pressures of working life, this ideal family structure was simply not possible. Men worked long hours in physically demanding labour. Emotional availability, creativity and the hope for 'quality time' are difficult attributes to maintain in the physically demanding and monotonous labour of mines and factories. Male unavailability led working class women to forge relationships with other women during this period. Today we grieve the loss of 'community'. However, these communities were largely of women who were forced together through economic hardships and adversity rarely seen in the West today. During this time, children were raised through a network of neighbourly matriarchs. For example, the extended relationship between mothers and their mothers became increasingly important for the first time. This occurred as working class women had to enter the workplace due to economic necessity, and 'grandparenting' as a form cheap child care became vital to families' survival.

By the 20th Century, Western society experienced an explosion of interest in the impact of the family unit on development. This brought a wealth of new modes of parenting into the popular imagination. Increasingly it advocated both parents being emotionally and physically involved in a child's life as nurturing helpers. This led to the development of increasingly permissive forms of parenting and has reversed power relationships within the family unit compared to the Victorian period. Dr Spock's popular humanistic model of parenting presented in his seminal book *Baby and Child Care* (which at one stage was said to be the second best-selling book after the Bible), suggested that a child has a greater understanding of their own developmental needs than their parents. Parental responsibility requires them to now understand the needs of the child and translate this into their daily care. Thus power relationships are reversed, and the child is seen as the educator of the parents. Increasingly now, parents report that they are their child's 'friend' rather than parent. This has equalised child-parent relationships. Although this represents an advance in children's rights it has also had consequences. In many ways, modern parenting has reverted back to an 18th Century notion of children as 'little adults' rather than a unique sub-category of human development. Clear demarcation between child and adult life has become increasingly blurred in the contemporary world.

The 20th Century pre-occupation with parenting has produced widely contradictory results. A proliferation of parenting books has now been published claiming to be scientific and instructional. However, their wholly contradictory guidance has created deeper uncertainty and anxiety in parents who are more concerned than ever that they are doing it in the 'right way'. For example, Watson (1928) and the behavioural tradition emphasise the necessity for discipline, consistency and emotional detachment from children. In contradiction, Dr Spock (2011) suggested that mothers indulge their children, feed them on demand and shower them with affection. Bowlby (1961), following in a Freudian tradition, presented a theory of maternal deprivation that placed guilt specifically at the feet of mothers. He suggested that children could only form one meaningful attachment and that was with the mother. Prolonged separation induced a profound grieving process in a child which would have life-long consequences. This occurred at a time when changes in the labour market were giving women increasing economic freedom and independence, and has generated a deeper conflict in mothers between providing immediate physical availability to their infants versus providing material benefit. Ironically, the increased interest in parenting has left 20th Century parents feeling less confident in their abilities than at any other time.

Whilst the assumptions regarding the ideal family unit advocated by Edwardian theorists persist to this very day, research has questioned the validity of their claims. Modern day family structures fail to meet their ideal. High divorce rates, multi-culturalism, cohabitation, women's increasing role as economic breadwinners, the erosion of male social roles, same sex civil partnerships, second families and step families and have created a multiplicity of family structures. For example, Stacey (1996) identified that less than 7 per cent of households in the US conformed to the ideal Edwardian family structure. Furthermore, whilst parents are continually held responsible for their children's actions, research has questioned this core assumption. The long-term impact of parenting appears considerably weaker than the Edwardians imagined, with young people's lives also being shaped by wider cultural forces.

Perspectives on adolescent development

Like the family structure itself, adolescence has changed considerably over time (see Cunningham, 2006). It was not until Western society achieved a substantial level of material comfort in the Victorian period that the concept of adolescence began to emerge. The intense pace of social progress at this time gave rise to new forms of labour, which placed new demands on the workforce. Prior to this, labour markets open to lower socio-economic groups were based on the artisan, agriculture or industry, and workers had primarily toiled with their hands rather than their heads. Education had been the preserve of the ruling classes. New professions in an increasingly sophisticated social epoch required a more skilled workforce. For example, a cabal of social reformers and industrialists in 1869 in the UK increasingly pressured Government to establish compulsory state education for all. The 1870 Education Act allowed for the provision of schools in areas without educational opportunities, but it had no compulsory element. Various Royal Commissions up to the 1878 Factory Act recommended that compulsory education was necessary to end child labour. This led to the 1880 Education Act, which made education compulsory between the ages of five and ten.

Though the actual take up of children in education remained low, these parliamentary acts were indicative of a shift in social structure. Apprenticeship to a skilled labourer had been an adequate to bridge from childhood to adulthood in simpler times. However, the increasing complexity of industrialised societies required children to be better prepared for adult life. A latency period began to emerge between childhood and adulthood where more complex skills could be mastered prior to entry into the labour force. The adolescence phase of the life course was born (Eisenstadt, 1956). Outside of the developed and developing world there is no equivalent to this life stage.

The systematic study of adolescent development began early in the 20th Century, shortly after its evolution. The early pioneer of these studies was G. Stanley Hall (1916). Hall was deeply influenced by the popular ideas of the time, particularly the evolutionary concepts suggested by the 18th Century biologist Lamarck, whose evolutionary theory pre-dated Darwin's theory of natural selection, which had not yet gained acceptance. Lamarck supposed that higher order mammals had to mature through every previous evolutionary zone as part of their development. Hence the fertilised human embryo was an amoeba, and subsequent development continued through each genus such as fish, amphibian, bird, etc. until birth as a human. Even after birth, this process continued. Once born, the human infant passed through every stage of human history from primeval hunter-gatherer to modern man. Hall believed that adolescence marked the exact historical transition from primitive caveman to civilised modern man. As such, it was inevitably a time of 'storm and stress' where brutal desires were transformed into civilised manners.

Other theorists soon entered the debate proffering alternative explanations but ones which still emphasised the tumultuous nature of adolescence. For example, Freud (1958) suggested that the onset of puberty initiated the genital phase of psychosocial development, where increasing sexual desire and isolation from parents led to inner psychological conflicts. Whilst contemporary research has questioned whether adolescence is necessarily a difficult transition phase (Arnett, 1999; Schlegal & Barry, 1991), the idea that this developmental phase is intrinsically difficult has remained active in the popular imagination ever since.

Life stages

The re-examination of adolescent development led to the increased use of stage models of development. This extended the concept of development beyond childhood and considered how development continues across the life course. Primary amongst these are the life stages as described by Erick Erickson (1995). Erickson suggested that each life stage was characterised by key dilemmas that needed to be resolved before the individual could progress to the next stage of the life course. Should the individual fail to resolve these dilemmas, then they were somewhat doomed to a kind of psychological purgatory. These life stages were largely determined by the age of the individual. For example, the first dilemma entailed an infant forging a bond of trust with their care-giver. The second stage involved a child developing self-control. During adolescence the dilemma was to forge a sense of individual and social identity. Each stage was broad in its definition in order to make it relevant to a wide range of cultures (see Table 2.1).

Erickson's ideas remain highly influential but are essentially untestable. Some of his core assumptions have been challenged. Subsequent research has questioned whether Erickson's stages are universally applicable to all societies. Pre-literate societies appear to have fewer stages. In these cultures a *rites of passage* ceremony can transform the social roles of individuals in one sweep. Erickson's stages appear more reflective of a traditional 'modern' society. They describe an individual's life course that resided within an industrial world that was fixed and inflexible. As Hunt (2005) observed, many of Erickson's later

stages such as marriage, retirement and old age would be hard to apply in the mid-18th Century when 60 per cent of males died between the ages of 25 and 65.

It is important to recognise that the life stages have their own history. As we have seen in terms of the emergence of adolescence itself, life stages shift and change in the wider social context in which they occur. Each generation of youth is subject to unique social, cultural and economic forces. They can vary from the dramatic, such as World War Two, to the insidious, such as global recessions. The nature of our lives is highly dependent upon the historical, economic, social, geographical and class situation that we are born into. These wider social forces change the nature of the adult life that befalls each generation of young people and groups them into 'cohorts' who share the historical circumstances of their birth.

These historical and social changes relate to a second criticism of Erickson's stage model: that it describes a 'traditional' life. The 20th Century saw the establishment and dissemination of widely held social norms that cast men, women, children and adolescents in clearly demarcated social roles. Linked to these roles there was a broad agreement on age-related behaviour. For example Neugerten (1965) found a wide consensus of agreement in terms of age-related definitions, such as 'young man', and when to marry, when to become a grandparent, etc. In our post-modern age, these certainties have become

Table 2.1:   Erickson's stages of psychosocial development.

Approx. age	Stage	Crises	New virtue	Social manifestation
0–1	Infancy	Basic trust versus basic mistrust	Hope	Religion and faith
1–6	Earl childhood	Autonomy versus shame and doubt	Will	Law and Order
6–10	Play age	Initiative versus guilt	Purpose	Economics
10–14	School age	Industry versus inferiority	Competence	Technology
14–20	Adolescence	Identity versus role confusion	Fidelity	Ideology
20–35	Young adulthood	Intimacy versus isolation	Love	Ethics
30–39	Career consolidation*			
35–65	Maturity	Generativity versus stagnation	Care	Education, art and science
50–59	Keeping the meaning versus despair*			
65 +	Old age	Ego integrity versus despair and disgust	Wisdom	All major cultural institutions

*Additional stages suggested by Vaillant, 1977

increasing blurred. Multiculturalism brings within it variation on themes in terms of development. The decline of Western industry has brought different forms of labour where women's roles have changed considerably. Redundancy, retraining, early retirement have not only changed people's life stages but even reversed them. The rise of meritocracy and a bias towards youth have changed power relationships in the workplace between the old and the young. The old certainties of a bygone 'modern' age are gone. Adolescence is not just a preparation stage for adult life. During adolescence young people must develop the preparedness to enter into a shifting concept of what adult life is.

By the 1950s, theorists not only questioned the assumption of adolescence as a time of difficult transition but re-orientated the study of adolescence considerably as well. Where early theorists such as Hall and Freud took an explicitly biological view of an individual's development, recent theorists have stressed the importance of the context of a young person's development. For example, Havinghurst (1952) identified a series of culturally defined life tasks that a young person must accomplish within certain age ranges to achieve maturity. Other theorists have taken an even greater context-person view (Bronfenbrenner, 1979; Lerner et al., 1997). Here the young person's development is not simply the product of their biological development. Instead development is highly reliant on the environmental context in which they develop. Development is not a simple growth pattern, but is multi-dimensional and the product of a dynamic interplay between an individual young person and the world that they inhabit. Periods of stability and change in a young person are the product of this interplay with their environment. In this modern view, adolescence is not an intrinsically difficult phase of life. It is only difficult where the environmental conditions contrive to make it so (Petersen & Leffert, 1995). For example, whilst biology remains important in this equation, an individual remains locked in a highly influential cultural context which can even influence the rate of biological maturation itself (Silbereisen & Kracke, 1997). Recent research developments have all stressed that young people's development must always be understood in the social context in which it occurs.

Parent and adolescent interactions

The transitions to adulthood occur on many levels. However, the most immediate context of young people's development is the family. Young people must make the transition from being embedded in a family unit towards increasingly autonomous adult life. This renegotiation of relationships requires a difficult balancing act, for teenagers and for parents. An adolescent must demonstrate greater personal autonomy whilst preserving their relationships with parents. At the same time, parents must offer increasing degrees of freedom that are within a young person's competence to manage effectively. As Kegan (1982) suggests, parenting requires holding on to a child and letting them go, in a timely manner. Whilst the consistency of parenting style appears important during childhood, this status quo is increasingly challenged during adolescence and new parenting styles need to be adopted.

Parenting style

Two researchers have been highly influential in understanding these shifts. Baumrind (1971) suggested that there were two critical dimensions of parenting which have been continually supported in subsequent research studies. 'Parental responsiveness' describes the degree that the parent responds to a child's needs and offers support and encouragement. 'Parental demandingness' is the extent to which the parent expects more mature, self-directed and responsible behaviour from a child. These are two independent variables that occur on a spectrum from high to low. They may not be absolute measures in that parents may show some variance along the two continuums. Maccoby & Martin (1983) further developed a scheme that demonstrated how parents varied in their application of these two elements. Cross-referencing these two variables gave a simple classification system of parenting style, comprising four sub-groups of parenting style (adding to Baumrind's original three) demarcated by whether parents score high or low on responsiveness or demandingness (See Table 2.2).

In practice, most parenting styles fall somewhere in between the sub-groups of this structure. Authoritarian parents place a high value on obedience and conformity, and tend to discourage autonomy. Authoritative parents tend

Table 2.2:   Classifying parenting types

		Demandingness	
		High	**Low**
Responsiveness	**High**	**Authoritative** High expectations of maturity. Teach children to regulate emotion. Find appropriate outlets to solve problems. Extensive verbal give-and-take is allowed. Warm and nurturing toward the child. When punishing a child, the parent will explain his or her motive for their punishment.	**Indulgent** Few behavioral expectations for the child. Parents are nurturing and very responsive to the child's needs and wishes. Not required to behave appropriately. Children tend to be more impulsive.
	Low	**Authoritarian** High expectations of conformity and compliance to parental rules. Little open dialogue between parent and child. Do not explain the reasoning for the rules or boundaries. More likely to use corporal punishment.	**Indifferent** Parents are low in warmth and control. Not involved in their child's life. Dismiss the children's emotions and opinions. Other aspects of the parents' lives are more important than children.

Based on Maccoby & Martin, 1983

to be warm, but set clear boundaries. They are also more likely to explain their decisions and reason with their children. Indulgent parents have low expectations of their children and tend to be passive in parenting style. Highly accepting of their children's behaviour they are unlikely to use any form of punishment. They are likely to be over-protective of their children; whilst indifferent parents are neglectful, offer little parental supervision and spend little time with their children as they focus on other priorities. Research demonstrates that children who are from authoritative parents tend to out-perform children from other parenting styles in terms of self-esteem and perspective taking, and engage in less substance use and under-age sexual activity (Steinberg et al., 1991). Adolescents in indulgent households tend to be more immature and demonstrate higher group conformity. Whilst those who hail from neglectful families tend to be highly impulsive and engage in high risk activities from a young age (Kurdek & Fine, 1994). However, it is important to recognise that not all studies have been conclusive.

Studies of parenting style across ethnic cultures are limited but do appear to suggest that the authoritative parenting style tends to be more common in White ethnic groups, though other ethnic youth appear to benefit from this parenting style as much as their white peers (Steinberg et

al., 1992). Authoritarian parenting is more common in non-white ethnic groups, though this parenting style tends to have a more aversive impact on White youth rather than other ethnic youth. This more restrictive parenting style may be useful in constraining youth who live in hostile and impoverished communities which are more likely to be experienced by non-white ethnic groups. Shucksmith et al.'s (1995) study of adolescents in Scotland found that authoritative and authoritarian styles were common in parents of young adolescents but there was a tendency towards increasingly permissive parenting with older adolescents. However, the study found that parenting style had little influence on adolescents in comparison to the wider social and economic factors.

Personality

Parenting style is often cited in studies of young people's problems. Whilst blaming parents for their offspring's behaviour has become a cultural standard in Western societies, most studies of parenting omit a critical factor. Young people are not 'blank slates' whose personalities are waiting to be written by the family environment that engulfs them. Young people are born with temperaments of their own that will influence how they respond to their environments, including parents. In turn, the temperament of a child will influence parenting style. Understanding the nature of temperament is difficult as there is no unified grand theory of personality. Instead there are rival schools of thought on the nature and formation of personality, from environmental to genetic theories. This remains a contentious area of study. So this section will limit itself to those themes which are recurrent in the addiction research on young people, and which therefore have relevance for subsequent chapters.

Key to an understanding of temperament is the study of genetics. Before reviewing these ideas though, it is important to clarify some key misunderstandings. It is important to stress that the idea of inheritability does not equate to determinism. Geneticists use a shorthand for the expression of genes which lacks an important caveat. The expression of a gene occurs in 'a standard environment'. If the environment changes then the trait can also change. For example, you can clone a seed so that it has a genetically identical twin. If one is planted in a nurturing environment and the other is planted in a hostile environment, you will not end up with two identical plants.

This applies to human traits too. For example, whilst intelligence has been linked to genetic inheritance, it does not rule out the possibility that enriching the environment improves intelligence. As a result, studies demonstrate that the inheritability of intelligence varies across social environments. Inheritability accounts for 10 per cent of variance in intelligence amongst poor families and 72 per cent amongst wealthy families (Turkheimer et al., 2003), whilst environment accounts for the rest. Again, there can be a misunderstanding regarding what these percentages of 'inheritance' refer to. If a trait such as intelligence was 0 per cent inheritable, intelligence as a trait would be solely influenced by the environment. If it were 100 per cent inheritable it would mean that the trait of intelligence would be wholly genetic and would not be influenced by the environment at all. These studies of inheritability of intelligence across social classes suggest that poorer children's intelligence is highly influenced by their environments in a way that wealthier children's intelligence is less susceptible to environmental influence. This may reveal more about their environments than their genes. The potential expression of a gene may be thwarted by environmental factors in the poor groups in a way that highly supportive environments allow the genes to be expressed fully.

A further misunderstanding is that inheritance statistics do not describe variation in an individual. Inheritance percentages do not suggest that 10–70 per cent of a person's intelligence is caused by their genes. It is simply describing the variance *amongst a population*, not in a person. The nature versus nurture debate does not apply to individuals, only to populations as a whole. Finally, it is important to recognise that the expression of genes is not static, but changes across the life course. As we age we experience greater influence of genes and are less prone to influence by our environments. Inheritability of genes is low when our environments are controlled by our parents, but increases with age as we begin to select our own environments as adults. This is because our life choices are influenced by our genes; we select environments suited to our temperaments (Plomin & Spinath, 2004).

Defining personality is difficult and, historically, not only have different definitions been applied, but also different words have been used. The terms 'temperament', 'character' and 'disposition' have been applied to denote what is referred to here as 'personality'. Definitions struggle to capture the range of internal thoughts, social effects, qualities, inner goals and motivations of the individual. Larsen & Buss define personality thus: '**Personality** *is the set of psychological traits and mechanisms within the individual that are organized and relatively enduring and that influence his or her interactions with, and adaptions to, the intrapsychic, physical, and social environments.*' (2005: 4, original bold and italics). This definition includes as characteristics of a person both traits, such as whether they are shy or outgoing, and mechanisms, such as how someone evaluates, makes decisions and acts. The traits are enduring in that they are governed by rules and demonstrate a consistent pattern of response to the world. Interactions refer to the way in which we select environments, react to situations and try to influence the situations we find ourselves in. This also entails how we adapt and cope with pressures and opportunities in our environments.

If we are asked to describe someone we know, we tend to call upon adjectives such as friendly, outgoing, warm, funny, etc. In a similar way, trait psychologists believe that personality is constructed from a small group of traits in each person. These traits may be latent, in that they are not always expressed, but they are still present. For example, a dominant person does not always take charge of every situation they are in, but will show that tendency in a variety of environments over time. There is disagreement over the number of basic traits human beings exhibit. Cattell (1947) suggested that there were 16 personality traits, Eysenck (1952) suggested that there were three core traits, and more recently McCrae & Costa (1990) have suggested a five factor model. However all trait theorists share the idea that personality can be adequately described by these basic units of character.

The Five Factor trait model has been very influential in recent years. Within this model McCrae and Costa define a trait as 'dimensions of individual differences in tendencies to show consistent patterns of thoughts, feelings and actions.' (McCrae & Costa 1990: 23). The Five Factor model is a lexicographical approach, with origins in Allport & Odbert's (1936) analysis of all the words in a dictionary that could describe human beings. They identified 17,953 words that described human traits and then began to categorise them. They found that 4,500 words described stable traits. Cattell (1943) was able to reduce this number of words further to a smaller set of 171 clusters. With the advent of computers, more sophisticated analysis became possible. It was through this more detailed factor analysis that Fiske (1949) identified that the clusters could be reduced to five key traits. These findings were replicated by a number of researchers (Norman, 1963; Botwin & Buss, 1989; McCrae & Costa, 1990). The final five traits have been termed as the Five Factor Model or the High Five (see Table 2.3). Individuals are assumed to reside between two poles for each attribute. For example, an individual will reside somewhere on a spectrum between very extroverted to highly introverted. These traits are supposed to be mutually exclusive in that a person cannot be both highly extroverted and highly introverted at the same time.

The personality of each individual is a combination of these five traits, which gives rise to a wide variety of possible combinations. For example, a child with high extroversion and low neuroticism may be highly impulsive and less concerned about risk. A child who scores highly on introversion and neuroticism may be insular and fretful. The traits identified by the Five Factor

Table 2.3:   Five Factor Model

Trait	Description
Extroversion	Talkative-Silent Sociable-Reclusive Adventurous-Cautious Openness-Secretive Impulsive-Reserved
Agreeableness	Good Natured-Irritable Cooperative-Negativistic Gentle-Headstrong Not Jealous-Jealous
Conscientiousness	Responsible-Undependable Scrupulous-Unscrupulous Persevering-Quitting Fussy-Careless
Emotional Stability	Calm-Anxious Composed-Excitable Non-hypochondria-Hypochondria Poised-Nervous
Culture	Intellectual-Unreflective Artistic-Uncreative Imaginative- Direct Polished-Crude

Adapted from Norman, 1963.

model have demonstrated remarkable stability across people's life course. Whilst they do change over time they preserve rank order. So an extroverted 16-year-old is less extroverted at 90-years-old but will remain very extroverted in comparison to their peers. The Five Factors also show remarkable stability across cultures, though some debate remains regarding the exact definition of the fifth factor, Culture, which has been defined differently by different researchers.

The traits described in the Five Factor model have been studied extensively by geneticists who have tried to evaluate how inheritable they are in general and clinical populations. This has produced mixed results. Henderson's (1982) review of 25,000 twin studies found a strong relationship in the inheritability of traits such as extroversion and neuroticism (60 per cent). Pederson's (1993) adoption studies also found that these two traits were the most inheritable, but to a lesser degree, with extroversion at 40 per cent and neuroticism at 30 per cent inheritability. Observational studies by Borkenau et al. (2001) found that there was approximately 40 per cent inheritability of all the Five Factor traits. Whilst Boucharde & McGue's (1990) studies, of 45 sets of identical twins reared apart and 26 sets of fraternal twins raised apart found evidence that a range of traits appeared to be genetically influenced, such as traditionalism, imagination, alienation and inhibition control, the most inheritable was neuroticism. This study concluded that there was 20–40 per cent inheritability for the Five Factor traits. It is also important to state that the trait models have critics and that the area remains hotly debated beyond the scope of this book. (For a comprehensive review of the research see Larsen & Buss, 2005).

Family interaction

The lower ranges of variance of genetically inherited personality traits in Boucharde and McGue's studies of twins emphasises the inter-relationship of genes and environment operating together. For example, a highly extrovert child with low neuroticism may be more prone to acting out and less sensitive to verbal criticism. Conversely, the introverted and neurotic child may be highly sensitive to critical environments. In this way, temperament and parenting style collide. It is very easy to parent a compliant child in the ideal authoritative manner. However, parenting a child with temperament difficulties can disrupt this idealised parenting approach.

Parenting is easier when the child is young because the child is so dependent on the parents who can exert considerable influence over their environment. However, parental confidence can become increasingly eroded across childhood as offspring become less reliant on parents and press for greater autonomy. When parents feel that they are losing control they opt for one of two strategies. One is to become increasingly authoritarian in style, employing corporal punishments. This tends to worsen the family situation and a child's behaviour. The alternative is to become increasingly depressed and feel that the situation cannot be controlled. Emotionally exhausted parents can revert to the indifferent style of parenting as they give up. Again, this has a negative effect on a child's behaviour that can become more extreme as it remains unchecked. Alternatively, if a child is introverted and fretful, the parental style may shift towards becoming increasingly indulgent as parents lower expectations of the child and increase support, which may protect the child from overcoming

their anxieties, sustaining their anxiety in the longer term. In this way, parenting and temperament interact to forge the nature of family relationships. Adjusting parenting to account for temperament differences is important. However, this may not simply be a question of skills. Goodnow & Collins (1990) developed the idea of *perceived control* as an important coping strategy for parents. This feeling of control strengthens parenting skills as they become more confident in their ability.

Many do not like the ideas of genetic inheritability of personality traits due to the determinism that it implies. However, the alternative is to fall into the same trap by supposing that parenting style determines personality. This assumption entered popular thinking through early theorists such as Freud, who believed that parenting style exerted a powerful influence on the development of the child that endured into their future life. Research into the developmental process does not support this theory. Furedi's (2001) extensive research into the impact of parenting demonstrated that the notion of *infant determinism* driven by parental style is significantly weaker than is commonly believed. Parental influence is high during infancy because parents control a child's environment. But as the child moves into other social structures and becomes increasingly autonomous, parental influence declines dramatically across childhood. Furedi demonstrates that children are highly adaptive and can develop a high level of social functioning in all but the most abusive environments. As a result, the influence of parental style recedes to almost zero by early adulthood. It is important to stress this is not suggesting that something as powerful as abuse does not have long term implications. It is suggesting that, in normative development, parenting style is simply not as enduring as is often assumed.

A preoccupation with parental style in early childhood neglects this shift in the balance of power that occurs across adolescence. Adolescents make increasingly autonomous life choices, select their own interests, evolve their own values and chose their own peer groups. These choices may be informed by a young person's temperament rather than their family norms. It was long assumed that this invariably generated conflicts between adults and their parents as the generation gap between the two widened. Recent research has challenged this assumption and demonstrates that relationships between parents and adolescents remain remarkably positive at this time (Douvan & Adelson, 1966). Adolescence is a critical time when parent-adolescent relationships undergo renegotiation rather than separation.

Young people and their parents must manage a careful balance of achieving greater individuation whilst at the same time maintaining emotional connection. For example, Grotevant & Cooper (1986) found that individuality is expressed through the development of separateness and self-assertion in a young person, whilst connectedness is expressed through greater mutualism and permeability with parents. They noted that young people who maintained both cohesion with and separation from parents had greater scope for identity exploration and perspective taking. Steinberg & Silverberg (1986) tried to measure this transition through the development of the Emotional Autonomy Scale. It measured four key areas: 'de-idealisation of parents,' seeing parents 'as people', 'non-dependency' in terms of greater self-reliance, and the degree that youth felt 'individuation' from their parents. The study found that all measures increased between the ages of 10 and 14 with the exception of seeing parents as people in their own right. After 14 there was little change in any of the scores, suggesting that the renegotiation in parent-adolescent relationship occurred at that point.

Kracke & Noacke (1998) found that it was during middle adolescence that the most intensive period of renegotiation of the parental relationship occurred. They identified that as young people enter into their mid-teens (age 14–16) they demand more personal autonomy, whilst parents are less likely to surrender to these demands and try to maintain high levels of control. They observed a shift in family communication at this time characterised by an increase in verbal negotiation rather than conflict, which was surprisingly low. Fogelman's (1976) study of 11,000 young people and parents in the UK found that the vast majority of youth and parents also reported very positive relationships. Not only did young people respect their parents' opinion, they also sought their advice. Where conflict does exist at this time, they found that it tended to be symptomatic of conflicted families and that this pattern emerged in childhood and persisted into adolescence, rather than took root there (see Haggerty et al. 1994).

The generation gap effect appears weak. Gecas & Seff (1990) found wide agreement between parents and teenagers regarding work, religious beliefs and personal qualities that were important to them. In fact, greater variation in world views existed between groups of young people than it did between young people and their own parents, although adolescents often assumed that their parents were far more conservative than the parents believed themselves to be. Smetana (1988; 1989) suggested that disagreements between parents and adolescents occurred because the different generations interpreted the problem from different perspectives. For example, parents may view dress as a matter of social convention, whereas young people will interpret the choice of dress as an expression of personal autonomy. Hence young people and parents do not necessarily clash over different world views but over who has the right to express authority in the given situation. Similarly, Drury et al. (1998) found that conflict was most likely to occur where parents and adolescents fail to see the other person's point of view.

The shift in power across adolescence appears to be facilitated by a change in parenting style. Parents must concede power gradually and thereby tend to move into an increasingly democratic style of parenting. Parents begin to explain their decisions rather than impose them on young people simply because 'they said so'. Communication also appears to be key to understanding parental monitoring during adolescence (Stattin & Kerr, 2003). For example, unmonitored youth are more likely to be engaged in high risk behaviours such as sex and substance use. However monitoring behaviour relies upon the young person's willingness to disclose their behaviour to their parents. Parental monitoring is determined by the communication flow from a young person to a parent rather than by an expression of control emanating from a parent to an adolescent.

Developmental processes of adolescence

Temperament, parenting style and family interaction are the building blocks of development across childhood, but the transition into adulthood introduces new developmental forces during adolescence. Whilst there are rival schools of thought on the nature of these

Table 2.4: Summary of the four key development processes of adolescence

Processes	Description
Life task achievement	Young people must master increasingly complex psychological, relational and social demands. The mastery of these tasks promotes autonomy and independence.
Puberty	Puberty triggers a wide range of physical and cognitive changes in adolescents. The onset of puberty has specific cultural meanings as well give rises to distinct and novel patterns of thinking.
Identity formation	Increased processing power in the brain and the movement towards entry into adult life generates re-evaluation of identity and greater consideration of the future self.
Transformation of relationships	Peer relationships are of primary importance in the lives of young people. However, across adolescence power relationships with adults equalise until the adolescent becomes an adult themselves.

developments, research has centred on four key processes (Schulenberg et al., 1997). These four processes encompass the richness of human life occurring at the biological, neurological, psychological, familial, social and cultural level. Each of these processes will be reviewed separately for clarity but they are deeply interrelated. The four key process of adolescent development are summarised in Table 2.4.

Puberty: physical changes

Adolescence is a period of rapid physiological change. Whilst the onset of puberty signals sexual maturation, it has a far wider effect on young people, encompassing physiological and cognitive changes. This chapter will review these two components separately even though they co-occur. Physiologically, puberty triggers a growth spurt in adolescence (see Graph 2.1). This can be so rapid that it can outpace a young person's neurological spatial awareness, often leaving an adolescent clumsy and awkward. However, these physiological changes also extend to wider processes, triggering changes at this time to the heart, lungs, respiration and muscle density. In general, young women advance into puberty before young men, but there can be wide variance in each gender.

The actual age of onset of puberty can have a very contradictory impact on females and males. Early onset of puberty in young women tends to have a detrimental effect. It sets them apart not only from the pre-pubescent male peers, but also from their female peers. This may promote an increased self-consciousness and the development of a poor self-body image, as well

single them out for bullying (Silbereisen & Kracke, 1997). The opposite occurs in young males. As puberty increases muscle density, early onset males tend to be much physically stronger than their pre-pubescent peers and diminishes bullying or teasing. Instead early puberty singles them out as leaders. Late developing females and males tend to be less popular and less confident than those who mature 'on-time' (Simmons & Blythe, 1987). Late onset males in particular may be prone to excessive worry about their smaller physique and height. Shorter young males who have not entered puberty are likely to increase in height when puberty does occur.

Puberty in general can lead young people, and particularly young women, to become pre-occupied with ideals of physical beauty. It also brings the challenges of negotiating the development of a sexual identity. This is particularly powerful, as the onset of puberty coincides with a shift in gender relationships. Between the ages of 5 and 7 gender differences emerge between boys and girls. Girls start to swap instructions whilst boys stop taking orders. This means that during this period, boys find girls bossy and girls find boys uncooperative. Furthermore, gender differences in play at this time mean that boys and girls split into distinct gender groups. Girls play unstructured games which are intended to restore harmony from conflict. Boys play highly structured games, and conflicts are only resolved in order to reinitiate the game. These gender differences are carried into adolescence where young woman have deeper and more intimate relationships with each other, whilst young men will seek out a female rather than a male peer to share deeper thoughts with (Shucksmith & Hendry, 1998).

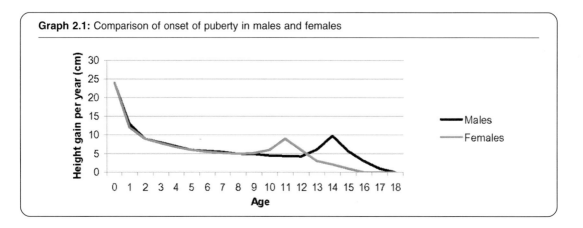

Graph 2.1: Comparison of onset of puberty in males and females

Gender differences become more apparent during the onset of puberty, when the initiation of sexual exploration begins and sexual identity is formed. Brooks-Gunn & Paikoff (1997) identify four key challenges to the development of a sexual identity during adolescence. They include becoming comfortable with one's own body and the changes it is undergoing, and extend to becoming comfortable with sexual feelings and the experience of arousal. Next is the understanding that sexual relationships should be mutual and consensual. Finally, a young person must attain the sexual confidence to practice safer sex and feel able to protect themselves from the consequences of sexual encounters.

This presents a more complex challenge for young people who are gay. These young people must not only accomplish the same process of sexual identity formation, but must do so within a social context that can stigmatise, ridicule and reject them because of their sexual orientation. Shame, guilt or fear of exclusion, that is imagined or real, can stifle this process and generate powerful internal pressures. 'Coming out' is often considered to be the final realisation of homosexual identity. However, it is not an event but a process. Young gay people must continue to 'come out' for the rest of their lives, as they enter into new relationships, work and social groups.

Certainly, the desire for romantic partners is especially strong in the adolescent years and is the result of changes in the brain. Oxytocin is a hormone that surges in mothers around birth. It was believed that this hormone was just responsible for uterine contractions and milk production, but it appears to be responsible for a wider range of functions as well. The release of oxytocin during childbirth is the primary mechanism by which a mother and child bond. We see this in a wide variety of mammals. For example, species which live solitary lives produce low levels of oxytocin, whilst mammals who live in large social groups produce high rates of this hormone (Instel, 1992). Oxytocin production begins in adolescence, where levels rise dramatically across puberty for the first time. It is this bonding hormone that gives rise to puppy love, teen-crushes and infatuations that can appear and disappear so inexplicably, and explains why young people may be utterly inconsolable when even the shortest term relationships break up.

Across adolescence romantic encounters intensify and create greater freedom for sexual intimacy. This intimacy becomes increasingly dominant by late adolescence and these partnering relationships will eventually become so powerful that they will usurp the previously dominant influence of the peer group. Whilst it is normal that adolescents develop sexual awareness, this desire can lead to participation in unplanned and even non-consensual sexual activity. Young women who enter romantic relationships with partners more than two years older than themselves are particularly vulnerable to sexual coercion (Gowen et al., 2004). Research suggests that young people are not only becoming sexually active at a younger age but they are also engaging in different kinds of sexual activity. The wide availability of internet pornography, discussions of sexuality in youth magazines and young people being treated as little adults have re-shaped young people's expectations of sex. They have become exposed to idealised visions of sexual behaviour.

Adolescents are more likely to engage in less conventional forms of sexual behaviour from a younger age. For example young people report more frequent engagement in anal sex than they did 20 years ago (Breakwell & Fife-Shaw, 1992).

Sexual maturation tends to raise other dilemmas for young women as well. Whilst the desire to form romantic partnerships is as central to young women as to young men, their sexual behaviour can easily lead them to be stigmatised. Young women must therefore resolve a conflict between being available enough to secure a romantic partner and not being so available as to acquire a negative reputation amongst their peers. Udry & Billy (1987) studied the release and levels of hormones associated with sexual maturation such as androgen in males and females. High levels of androgen predicted sexual involvement in young males in a way it did not predict sexual involvement in young women. So whilst puberty is essentially a biological process it is still shaped by cultural contexts such as these.

Puberty: cognitive changes

Puberty is not limited to physiological maturation but extends to brain functioning, including neurological and psychological adaptions. Brain development continues across adolescence into early adulthood and even beyond. During adolescence structural changes to the brain occur in the cerebral white matter; increased density and refinement of neural pathways and synaptic pruning allow for more complex reasoning, and distinct thinking styles emerge at this time (Paus et al., 1999). *Synaptic pruning* occurs as the adolescent brain re-boots itself. The human brain is unique as an organ in its ability to send signals from one cell to another. This ability is part of the learning process. When we learn new information, the human brain forges inter-connections between brain cells forming large neural networks. The more profound our learning, the greater the neural associations. However, a child is exposed to a wide variety of experiences, not all of which are strengthened through repetition. During adolescence, these weaker associations are *pruned* out to improve the efficiency of brain function (Giedd et al., 1999).

Pruning memory means that weaker prior experiences are cleared from the memory banks. For example, a French child can say 'this' and

'that'. But as the French language does not use the sound '*th*', a French child's brain does not build a strong neural web on the phoneme 'th'. Therefore in adolescence it may be pruned out, leaving the French teenager to say 'zis' and 'zat' only. Hence our accents are shaped through pruning. This pruning process strips back our neurological associations to their core templates of understanding. This increases the efficiency of the brain on the one hand, but may lay down a set of inflexible templates from which we view the world on the other. For example, if a child experiences relationships as loving and giving, this can become a core template of what relationships are. Alternatively, children who experience hostile interactions in relationships may develop this as a core template. In this way, deep assumptions, that we are not always consciously aware of, may be written into the fabric of the brain at this time. These templates can change over time, but doing so in adult life is effortful.

There are also gender differences in brain development. Young women develop verbal processing skills far more quickly than males (Levin et al., 1991). This may allow them to articulate internal mood states and develop a level of emotional literacy that males only achieve much later in adolescence. As males may not be able to express emotions verbally, they are prone to acting out their feelings as a behavioural response to intolerable mood states that cannot be expressed by any other means. Substance use or aggression may relieve internal tension generated by emotional mood states that are beyond their capacity to verbalise. This may be particularly salient to the experience of contradictory feelings. The increase in brain processing during adolescence means that young people may experience contradictory emotions simultaneously for the first time, but they may find it difficult to understand or process competing emotions. It is a striking feature of books, music and films aimed at the teenage market that so many of them feature heroes or heroines torn by contradictory emotions or dilemmas.

Changing patterns of thought

These changes in brain functioning have a profound effect on how a young person views the world. Children demonstrate a very concrete egocentric thinking style which tends to be inflexible. Children for the most part place themselves at the centre of the universe and life orbits around their own perspective. This is a locked down view of the world which is immediate, direct and narrow. For example, in one of Piaget's (2001) many fascinating experiments testing children's cognition, an array of toys were arranged on a table separated by screens of various heights. Children were asked to identify which toys could 'see' each other. For example, could the teddy bear see the doll? If a child could see the doll they always assumed that the teddy could as well, regardless of the height of the screen that separated them. But if the child could not see the doll themselves, they would assume that the teddy could not see the doll either, again regardless of the height of the screen. Hence, Piaget concluded that a child's world view is always 'egocentric', in that events are solely understood from their own perspective.

As a child moves into puberty, increases in the brain's processing power give rise to a major transition in thinking. They move from this direct concrete thinking style to 'meta-cognition'. Meta-cognition allows an adolescent to think about how they think. It offers a more flexible and adaptable way of understanding the world by allowing young people to dislocate their perception from their own immediate point of view. For the first time they can see the world from other people's perspectives as they become capable of empathy. There are many benefits to empathy. It gives young people the ability to think about events in alternative ways, shift perspective, offer rival explanations and to infer deeper psychological explanations that hide beneath other people's behaviour. However, this new ability also comes at a psychological cost.

Changes in behaviour

Elkind (1967) demonstrated that this shift in thinking is a double bind. Whilst the emergence of meta-cognition frees an adolescent from the restrictions of child-like concrete thinking, it embroils them into to new thinking traps. Although young people become capable of empathy, adolescents still find it difficult to differentiate their thoughts from the thoughts of others. As a result they tend to invert their empathy. Adults use their empathy to see the world through the eyes of others. Adolescents use their empathy to see themselves through the eyes of others. This gives rise to a new kind of

egocentric worldview where a young person considers themselves in the centre of everyone else's attention. Furthermore, the attention of others is a direct reflection of their own concerns. For example, if a young person is preoccupied with an aspect of their own appearance, they assume everyone else must also be preoccupied with their appearance in exactly the same way.

This leads to an 'invisible audience' effect whereby the young person operates in real or imagined social settings where they are continually anticipating the thoughts and reactions of others. When a young person preens before a mirror they are not performing these actions for themselves. They are staring beyond the mirror into the audience of admirers who appreciate their charms in exactly the same manner that they do. Equally, a teenager who has some anxiety regarding their appearance or behaviour carries with them an invisible audience who also see this fault as vividly as they do, leading to deep anxiety. This means that during puberty, the confident outgoing child shifts towards the self-conscious and withdrawn teenager who wants to be alone. The 'coolness' of youth can be understood as a form a self-protection. An adolescent's external display of disregard and aloofness can mask an intensive self-scrutiny that pores over inadequacy before an equally judgemental audience. Coolness hides these insecurities, which, if exposed, would represent a terrifying form of humiliation for a young person.

The invisible audience creates a feeling of specialness, whereby by a young person is cast as the central hero or heroine amongst the life events that engulf them. This specialness means that young people believe themselves to be different from others. This 'personal fable' distorts their perception of risk. Adolescents can recognise that bad things can happen in the world but do not recognise that bad things will happen to people like them. This disconnects young people from the magnitude of risk, believing that only others will fall prey to problems. So health messages, including those about the negative consequences or long term problems resulting from substance use, are difficult for young people to comprehend, as they cannot connect these risks with themselves.

This can create problems for young people in other ways. An attractive, popular young person can experience the 'halo effect', where others assume that because the popular young person has a pleasing personality, they are more competent and self-reliant than they actually are. This can flatter a young person on the one hand, but it can also lead them to conforming to this image. As a result of this halo effect, young people can be offered less support and be placed under higher demands than others. They may try to maintain this identity and therefore find it more difficult to ask for help. This can lead to a deep sense of isolation and depression even in a crowd (Munsch & Kinchen, 1995), which is why it is not uncommon for popular, high achieving youth to be found to have been secretly self-harming, or suffering from depression or anorexia for long periods of time. The most popular young people can be the loneliest.

Elkind suggested that addressing these personal fables, invisible audience or even halo effects in young people would be important in helping them adjust their anti-social behaviours. A range of studies have supported Elkind's findings (see Enright et al., 1980), though some critics have argued that adolescent egocentrism is more closely related to young people's understanding of interpersonal relationships than to cognitive development (Jahnke & Blanchard-Fields, 1993). For example, young people's perception of risk can be highly situational. When asked in isolation, a young person's assessment of risk is similar to that of adults, but within the peer group the assessment of risk appears to diminish (Gardner and Steinberg, 2005).

Another key shift between adolescent and child thought patterns are the development of expectancies. Expectancies are particularly powerful for young people as their novice life situation means that they have no personal experience to draw upon in assessing situations. Therefore young people tend to operate on what they assume will occur as a result of their actions. These assumptions may or may not be realistic. As a result, young people may be more likely to engage in risk taking behaviours that are beyond their competence. Only with experience do they gain the opportunity to begin to reflect on their actual ability. With regards to drug and alcohol use, Dunn & Goldman (1998) found that children's largely negative expectations of consumption moved across the teenage years towards positive expectancies of arousal and enhanced social interaction. As we saw in Chapter 1, positive expectancies have been found to be very strong predictors of future substance

consumption in children (Goldman et al., 1999). Young people with the most positive expectancies of consumption initiated use earlier and were heavier consumers. Similar findings have been identified in other studies (Roehrich & Goldman, 1995; Stein et al., 2000).

Another significant change in adolescence, and a perennial point of conflict with adults, is the shifting sleep pattern. Whilst children's sleep requirements fluctuate, neurological and developmental changes in adolescence increase a young person's sleep requirement. In general terms, adolescents require 8.5 – 9.25 hours of sleep a night (Wolfson and Carskadon, 1998). However, adolescent sleep patterns are interrupted, particularly during the intrinsic sleep phase. This means that adolescents do not experience sleep cues. They do not feel tired until late at night and then have a greater inclination to sleep late in the day. This means that adolescents sleep for much shorter periods than they need, on average 7–7.75 hours per night. Whilst longer sleep periods at weekends address this deficit to a small degree, cumulative sleep deprivation means that adolescents are the most at-risk population to suffer from pathological sleepiness. This can affect their academic performance, increase risk of accidents and have profound effects on negative moods.

Adolescent brain regions do not mature at the same rate. This is especially true of the pre-frontal cortex which is the last brain region to become fully operational. The pre-frontal cortex is located behind the forehead and is responsible for higher cognitive functions such as forethought, emotional regulation and behavioural self-regulation. So whilst emotional impulses develop in childhood, regulation does not emerge in young women until 16 years old and up to 18 years old in young men. This means that the adolescent brain can be considered as having an accelerator but no brake. Besides increasing the impulsivity of young people, this makes them prone to acting without regard to the immediate consequences of their behaviour.

Young people read the world in a very different way to either children or adults. Whilst a child's view is limited by parenting style, these restrictions wane across adolescence, removing the amount of external control. Young people are not only moving into a new world, but also have a new way of understanding it. This can be difficult for adults to understand as they are more cognitively sophisticated than adolescents. It is easy for them to forget their own transition experience when caught up in the pressures of adult life. Young people can even understand their problems in a very different ways to adults. Young people may place a high prestige on their problems because these difficulties are symbolic of their maturation. Sophisticated problems become emblems of their more 'grown up' life (see Table 2.5 for summary).

Life tasks

Brain development does not occur in a vacuum. A unique feature of the human brain is its plasticity which is reflected in human beings' ability to learn and adapt to their environments. The environments in which we operate make constant mental demands of us, which shape the brain in terms of developing neural pathways and networks of association. The mental demands comprise mastering ourselves, our relationships and our environments. These demands are the life tasks that we must attain to integrate effectively in our social world. As we share a similar biology and growth rate, and inhabit the same social structures, the life tasks are similar for everyone embedded in a given society.

Havinghurst was an early researcher in this area and defined a life task as 'a task which arises at or about a certain period in the life of the individual, successful completion of which leads to . . . happiness and to success with later tasks, while failure leads to unhappiness in the individual, disapproval by the society, and difficulty with later tasks' (1952: 2). He suggested that life tasks are the bridge between an individual's developmental need and a societal demand. As humans are born into a pre-fabricated social world with its own established rules, each person must acquire the necessary skills to enter and operate effectively in this environment. Life tasks are the critical skills that allow young people to enter into this social environment and to maintain responsibilities within it.

Life tasks are sourced in biological maturation, cultural pressures and individuals' own personal desires. For example, learning to walk relies upon both physical maturation and the cultural expectancy of parents. Havinghurst believed that early life tasks were driven primarily through the interaction between an individual and their environment. This shifts in adulthood, where life tasks are driven by motivations and personal goals of the individual, such as choosing jobs or partners. Newman & Newman (1995) identified a broad range of life tasks that shape people's development in predominantly Western industrial societies. Kegan (1982) added a new dimension to this by recognising that life tasks are embedded in the social structures which we inhabit across the life course (see Table 2.6).

The life tasks of early infancy require the mastery of physical movement, spatial awareness and the formation of special bonds with primary carers. Learning at this age is primarily through perception and mimicry. A toddler begins to engage in wider family relationships, masters greater use of language and begins to exert greater control over emotions, for example by developing the ability to self-soothe. This gives rise to the ability to operate in social groups such as nursery and school, which require greater emotional regulation as well as the ability to adapt to social roles. Fantasy role-play and the development of moral awareness are essential in this early level of social engagement. Parents tell their children up to 15 stories an hour at this phase of the life course. Every story is a moral parable, allowing the development of ethics to occur through the medium of stories.

It would be a harsh society that did not prepare its children for adult life. Education reflects the demands of adult life. In Western societies, children must prepare for entry into the marketplace of adult life. In this marketplace they will buy and sell specialist knowledge, and the more specialist knowledge they acquire through education then the better the price they will get for it. But in a market place they also have to have the social skills to broker these deals. Education most therefore account for both processes: educational attainment and socialisation. As Lasch (1979) observed, Western children must learn to be ruthlessly competitive with a smile. Likewise, as children get older the nature of play begins to change. Agricultural societies give their children agricultural toys and warrior societies give their children warrior toys. In the cyber age, societies give their children Grand Theft Auto and high speed internet access. Whilst older generations may bemoan children's preoccupation with video games instead of tree climbing, they fail to recognise this important cultural shift. In the past the labour market was often about physical endurance and strong

Table 2.5: Summary of key changes in hormone, brain function and psychology in adolescence

Process	Description	Example
Hormonal changes		
Oxytocin production	Hormonal release governing bonding. Can lead to crushes and puppy love during adolescence and an increased desire for romantic involvement.	Karen is heartbroken. She will not stop crying about the break-up of her relationship to Kyle. She is depressed and inconsolable. She texts him constantly looking to get back together. Her mother says she is young and not to worry about it but she has started to hate herself and blame herself for Kyle finishing with her. Karen says her parents don't understand, they have never loved anyone, that it was 'real' between her and Kyle. She cannot believe that after all they shared in the last two weeks it is over.
Androgen production	Sexual drive hormone that predicts sexual involvement in males but not females due to social strictures.	At 15 Alfie has become fiercely protective of his bedroom. When cleaning his mother found a collection of men's magazines, stashed under his bed.
Brain function changes		
Pruning	Weak neural webs and associations are eliminated to increase efficiency in brain function but this sets templates of experience.	Kasim has dropped out of services, but at 15 he is back. The worker raises the issues that they had discussed 18 months previously. Kasim looks blank and uncomfortable, as if the worker is trying to put words in his mouth.
Pre-frontal cortex underdevelopment	Higher brain functions of anticipation, fore thought and emotional regulation are not fully developed until late adolescence giving rise to impulsive or emotionally driven behaviour.	Saffi is in trouble. She has set fire to her bedroom. She and her friend Alisha were having a sleep over. They started heating up a tin of beans on her electric face steamer. It was taking ages so they started to play on the Play Station whilst waiting when they forgot about the beans. The label burst into flames setting fire to the curtains it was leaning against.
Sleep patterns	Sleep cues are not triggered in the brain leading the adolescents to stay up later. Increased requirement for sleep may lead them to sleep for longer in the day.	Charlie does nothing around the house. He is moody, staying up late, playing online games and talking to his friends over the head mic. Sleeping all day he is driving his parents to distraction.
Psychological changes		
Meta-cognition	The ability to see the world from other perspectives than one's own. Gives rise to empathy, psychological explanation of other behaviours and reflection on one's own thoughts.	Roman used to belong to a lot of school clubs and showed promise in athletics, particularly gymnastics. But he has dropped out of all this now. He won't say why. Insular and quiet he spends most of his time in his bedroom, rarely speaks and seems painfully shy in front of others. Always with his hood up and sleeves pulled over his hands he makes no effort to communicate.
Invisible audience	Product of meta-cognition, young people may be able to view the world as others do but tend to confuse their thoughts with others. Gives rise to a sensation of being watched at all times by an audience that mirrors their own thoughts, fears or hopes.	Allie spends hours in front of the mirror. She is perpetually playing with her hair and pouting deeply into the mirror. She is obsessed with her clothes and appearance. Venturing out she has decided to bleach her hair really blonde-white. After having it done she is heart-broken -she says it is orange, cries and refuses to go to school.

Table 2.5:   *Continued*

Process	Description	Example
Personal fable	Product of meta-cognition, the invisible audience effect gives rise to a sense of prominence in the eyes of others. The young person may see themselves as special. They can recognise that risk taking behaviour has consequences, but not for people like them.	Sam is into dance music and ketamine. He reads everything that is available on the drug and has a file of cuttings and information downloaded from the internet. He can tell people anything about ketamine – even all the health complications such as Bristol bladder and kidney failure. Every weekend he canes as much as he can.
Expectancies	Young people's lack of life experience means that they operate on their expectations of what will happen rather than experience.	Leigh is now based in a Pupil Referral Unit due to repeat truancy and poor behaviour at school. He does not take any of his studies seriously. He says there is no point and that he does not have to. When asked what he is going to do after he leaves school he says that he will be a professional footballer or rapper. He is not sure which. He is currently involved in neither of these activities.
Halo effect	Young people who appear attractive and smart tend to be attributed with greater responsibility and less support. This can render the apparently capable, popular adolescent lonely and isolated.	Cherry is a bright young woman. She has lots of friends and hangs out with different groups. She always has boys chasing after her and she is engaging and funny. As she is doing well at school, her parents were shocked to find that she has been self-harming for the last six months and is deeply depressed.

hands. Now the market place is now dominated by IT. This requires rapid data processing skills and nimble fingers honed by different types of play.

Critical in life task achievement is the age of 16. As Kegan (1982) observed, at this point young people make the biggest transition since their birth. They separate from the external world provided for them in the form of primary carer, parents, family and school, and they create an adult world of their own. Western society is unique in making such a dramatic transition to autonomy. In other cultures, adult life is pre-planned for its youth through remaining in the family home, having life partners chosen in advance and having careers determined by parents. Young people in these cultures do not make such life-shaping decisions at such a young age. In Western society this transition period is compensated for by a *moratorium*. This is a period of time where young people are given the freedom to explore roles, relationships, identities and careers well into early adulthood. The longer education that an individual has, the later they will enter into the fullness of adult

responsibilities. But once young adults enter into adult life their responsibilities begin to change dramatically in selecting a career, a life partner and raising families. Divorce, second careers, second families may add increasing levels of complexity. Increased life expectancy also requires contemporary adults not only to raise their own children but also to take care of their own ageing parents. This has added new strains and pressures on the 'sandwich generation'. It is telling to think that 300 hundred years ago we would have been dead at the age of thirty. Now we are only just beginning to enter into adult life.

Reviewing the life course demonstrates how the nature of life tasks becomes increasingly complex as we age. The life tasks of a 5-year-old are very different to the life tasks of a 45-year-old. It is essential that we are able to cultivate the skills and abilities to master these increasingly complex demands. Kegan (1982) suggested that life tasks are 'staged' in increasing levels of complexity that enable young people to master them in a timely progression. In this way, each stage of life is preparing us with the skills for the next more complex one. During infancy, play

Table 2.6: Life stages and developmental tasks

Life stages	Developmental tasks	Social environment
Infancy Early infancy (0–2 years)	Social attachment Maturation of sensory, perceptual and motor functions Sensorimotor intelligence and primitive causality Understanding the nature of objects and the creation of categories Emotional development	Primary Carers
Toddlerhood (2–4 years)	Elaboration of locomotion Fantasy play Language development Self-control	Family
Childhood Early school age (4–6 years)	Sex-role identification Early moral development Self-theory Group-play	Children of a similar age regardless of gender
Middle childhood (6–12 years)	Friendship Concrete operations Skills learning Self-evaluation Team play	School
Adolescence (12–18 years)	Physical maturation Formal operations Emotional development Membership in the peer group Sexual relationships	Peers
Adulthood Youth (18–22 years)	Autonomy from parents Gender identity Internalised morality Career choice	Moratorium
Young adulthood (22–40)	Explore intimate relationships Child-bearing Work Lifestyle	Adult institutions
Middle adulthood (40–60 years)	Management of career Nurturing the couple relationships Expanding caring relationships Management of household	2nd Adult institutions
Early-late adulthood (60–75 years)	Promotion of intellectual vigour Redirection of energy toward new role and activities Acceptance of one's life Development of a point a view regarding death	Retirement
Late-late-adulthood (75 years onward)	Coping with physical changes of ageing Development of a psycho-historical perspective Travel through uncharted terrain.	

Adapted from Newman & Newman, 1995; Kegan, 1982.

revolving around motor skills, like building blocks and the attachment to 'teddy bear' or 'blankie', is actually key learning for the next stage of development. It fosters basic mastery of physical co-ordination as well as the ability to form relationships with others. This assists us to shift into toddlerhood.

In toddlerhood, fantasy role play allows children to rehearse social roles, whilst story telling is a form of moral instruction through metaphors. This prepares them to enter into wider family and school life. Schooling prepares children for adult life through the development of specialised knowledge and socialisation. Other developmental processes parallel this. Pocket money, Saturday jobs and holiday jobs, prepare young people for the marketplace of work. The ephemeral friendships of childhood give way to the deep friendships of the adolescent peer group. These become a rehearsal for romantic partnerships and then life partnerships of sacrifice and commitment. The increasing complexity of young people's social, academic and relational life tasks make higher intellectual demands upon each human brain to process increasingly sophisticated data. In turn, the brain's adaptions allow for a more sophisticated level of understanding, which results in greater analysis of these environmental demands.

Intensification in adolescence

Adolescence is characterised by a rapid acceleration in the accumulation of life tasks as a young person approaches adulthood. For example, the life tasks of a 35-year-old are very similar to those of a 55-year-old. But the life tasks of a 13-year-old are not the same as those of a 17-year-old. Adolescence is the most intensive period of life task achievement. Young people are expected to undertake increasing levels of responsibility for their own life choices, relationships, behavioural regulation, identity formation and sense of future as they emerge from childhood. This places new social, cultural and legal expectations on them, and occurs on a micro and macro scale. At the micro level young people become increasingly responsible for basic life skills such as choosing and preparing their own food, managing study and leisure time, deciding when to sleep, what to wear, etc. On the macro scale they must renegotiate their relationship with their family of origin, select educational options, prepare for occupational life,

become accountable by law and ultimately leave home (see Table 2.7).

The attainment of these life tasks is central to the development of the young person. The well prepared young person will move through these developmental processes smoothly without even noticing the transition that is unfolding. However, when young people are not prepared for the next stage of their development they will struggle. Small delays in life task accomplishment can make subsequent transitions ever more difficult. Within normative development, life task achievement can be disrupted in two different

Table 2.7: Summary of key life tasks across adolescence

Life tasks	Contexts
Life skills	Choice of clothes
	Personal grooming
	Budgeting
	Cooking
	Cleaning
	Sleeping
	With parents
	With friends
	With romantic partner
	On campus
	Army
	Alone
Education	Selecting educational options
	Secondary school
	VI Form/college
	University
	Apprenticeship
	Saturday jobs
	Summer jobs
	Part time vs fulltime employment
	Career development
	Unemployment
	Romantic partners
	Cohabitation
Relationships	Dating and sexual behaviour
	Socialisation and peer groups
	Starting a family
	Marriage/cohabitation
Occupational development	Completion of education
	Vocational
	Entering higher education
	Start career
Legal	Driving
	Criminal liability
	Financial responsibility
	Voting

ways. This can be through the impact of random life events or through the impact of the structural effects of social policy.

The impact of life events

The study of life events has increased in recent years, particularly the study of how people deal with loss or crises (Moos, 1986; Parkes, 1991). Non-events are included in this, as failure to achieve a desired life task, such as failing entry into university or inability to conceive children, can have the same effect as hostile events (Baltes et al., 1980). In contrast to life tasks that are carefully sequenced, life events are haphazard accidents that impact and shape young people's lives when any event or non-event 'results in changed relationships, routines, assumptions and roles' (Schlossberg et al., 1995: 27). The frequency of occurrence of life events is increasing for contemporary youth. Social changes such as technological developments, greater geographic movement, changes in the labour market and higher rates of divorce means that the younger generation face a higher incidence of life events than their grandparents did. The likelihood of a life event occurring tends to increase with age, but they can occur at any time.

The impact of a life event may depend upon several key variables (Reese & Smyer, 1983), including the objective dimensions of the event, the individual's subjective perception of the event, and the subsequent consequences of the event. The objective element of an event for a young person may include whether or not the young person felt it was their fault, whether it is a typical occurrence at this stage in the life course, where it occurs, such as home or school, and how long the event takes to happen. For example, the impact of a divorce may affect young people differently. Its impact will be influenced by the age at which it happens, whether they feel responsible for it and how protracted the process becomes. Subjective perception includes an assessment of whether events were chosen or not, how expected the outcome was, the perceived severity of consequences and possible negative social judgements. The consequence element includes the assessment of whether the impact is positive or negative, whether it involves changing social roles, what areas of life are affected and how much an individual must change in light of the event. As in the divorce example, a young male might see that they must become 'the man

of the house' if a father leaves, whereas a young woman might step in to the mother's vacant role if she leaves.

Not only does the impact of life events differ, so does the individual's ability to cope with them. Schlossberg et al. (1995) identified four key domains that influence an individual's ability to adjust to life events. Besides the 'situation' identified by Reese & Smyer (1983), Schlossberg et al. identified 'coping strategies in the self', 'support', and 'coping styles of the individual'. 'Coping strategies in the self' refers to 'who' experiences the event, and refers to things such as their economic status, gender, ethnicity and age, all of which influence their ability to cope with the event. For example, an assured, economically advantaged 18-year-old may deal with a parental separation more readily than a fretful 13-year-old who already lives in an unpredictable and unstable environment. The sum total of these internal resources can be considered as an inherent resilience or vulnerability within the person simply by the virtue of who they are and their current life position.

'Support' describes the "interpersonal transactions that include one or more of the following key elements: affect, affirmation, and aid" (Kahn & Antonucci, 1980: 267). It can include finances, time, advice and guidance as well as confidence in these supportive alliances. By providing these, social networks can form 'stability zones'. Belonging to a number of supportive social networks offers stability when other networks are threatened. For example, strong peer networks may offer a stability that provides respite from the conflict of a divorce. Difficulties at school like bullying may be assuaged by a stable home network. But social networks can be destabilising. For example, it is easy on occasions for the families, which can be over-intimate, claustrophobic and fallible, and for peers to misdirect or compound problems. A family network, a peer network or a school network can all be sources of tensions as well as of support. When all stability zones come under threat young people especially can become overwhelmed.

'Coping styles of the individual' refers to what someone does to deal with pressures and stresses. Whilst some people are expressive and share their emotions, others may deploy different key behavioural coping strategies such as distraction or avoidance of taking action in difficult circumstances. Others may have a more cognitive coping style involving problem solving, reframing experiences or reflecting on experiences and troubles.

The impact of the structural effects of social policy

Life task achievement can also be arrested by the structural effects of social policy. As many of the elements of young people's lives are touched by statutory services, young people are particularly prone to the reach of policy in health, education, welfare, child protection and housing and how that policy shapes society.

Educational achievement is a key marker of young people's development in a Western society due to its significance in social mobility and employment. So how it is impacted by social structures is particularly important. Hendry et al. (1993) researched young people's attitudes to social structures such as school, peers, parents and adult authority. The study identified clear sub-populations of young people. One group was peer- and school-orientated; a second group was peer-orientated and a third group was disaffected from pro-social structures. These groups related directly to their parents' socio-economic status. For example, the most disaffected youth belonged to 'manual labour' households, and were the most likely to leave school with few qualifications and more likely to experience unemployment. Success at school and work also appears to be influenced by the social structure defined as 'race'. White Europeans and Asians performed similarly, with the Afro-Caribbean young people performing half as well as their counter-parts (Drew et al., 1992).

Structural social inequalities are also to be found amongst populations who become long term unemployed and dependent on welfare. Hendry et al. (1993) also found that young people whose head of the house was unemployed were twice as likely to become long term unemployed themselves, whilst young people growing up in non-manual labour families were least likely to experience unemployment. Vocational qualifications have diversified the opportunities for young people, but the courses by which these qualifications are attained are perceived by young people as having low prestige.

In general, educational standards in young people have risen, but this has not improved the social status of those young people who experience structural inequalities. For example,

whilst university is no longer the preserve of the social elite, a number of factors still restrain young people from the poorest sections of society from progressing into professional roles. Despite increases in the number of young people entering into university, the future prospects of students remain stratified. Students from the newer universities still face the most difficulties in the labour market as opposed to Oxbridge or Ivy League candidates (Brown & Scase, 1994). Higher student fees and resulting increases in student debt may deter the poorest from entry to the best universities. So, even though educational attainment has risen in young people, inequality in attainment throughout the social classes has widened. Educational achievement remains largely predicated by parents' employment status, rather than by a young person's ability (Bourdieu, 1977; Ball et al., 1996).

A second major critical life task for achieving independence during adolescence and the transition to adulthood is leaving home. With marriage declining, the capacity for young people to leave home has changed. As Jones & Wallace (1992) noted, the ability for young people to leave home is highly reliant on many social factors including employment income, family support and access to affordable housing, all of which are in turn impacted by social policy. As many of these factors are curtailed for young people in particular socio-economic groups, the shift into adulthood which is marked by leaving home can be forestalled by these social forces. Hendry et al. (1993) found that only 6 per cent of 17- to 18-year-olds had left home. Young women were more likely to leave home sooner than young men with 50 per cent of males still residing at home at the age of 23–24.

Identity formation

Increases in brain functioning, increasing complexity of life tasks and the imminent transition into adulthood give rise to a central challenge in adolescence, the formation of an adult identity. This is double-ended. Young adolescents are able to think about themselves more deeply post-puberty and therfore they become preoccupied with self. This gives rise to new evaluations and assessments of who they are. At the other end of the adolescent spectrum they must formulate a future sense of identity. Identity formation becomes particularly salient as the critical age of 16 looms. This is when young people will leave a world provided for them through primary carers, family and school and must instead build an adult life for themselves. It becomes imperative that young people cultivate an idea of who they will be in this adult world. These future life orientations are bounded by social, historical, culture, gender and economic factors as well as by individual preferences linked to temperament.

Understanding self and identity formation is difficult as it centres on highly subjective internal states that are difficult to measure. Researchers have used divergent definitions of self and identity. A simple but concise definition of self was offered by Harter (1988) who suggested that it was the theory that one constructs about oneself. Self can be understood primarily as an internal vision that organises multiple elements of the persona into a cohesive framework. Identity encompasses this and more. Identity includes all the things that make us what we are, including our history, aspirations, social status, occupations, tastes, ethnicity, sexual orientation, class and social roles. So whilst self is an internal concept, identity conveys this and external elements as well. An important quality of self and identity is cohesion. As Festinger (1957) observed, human beings have a deep internal drive towards a cohesive sense of self akin to those for food or sex. For example, it would be difficult to be both a probation officer and a shop lifter at the same time. This is because the values espoused by this individual would be too divergent from their actual behaviour. Whenever human beings realise that there is a discrepancy between their values and their behaviour they experience psychological discomfort. Festinger described this as 'cognitive dissonance'. This is a unique form of stress characterised by anxiety, restlessness, appetite suppression, increased heart rate and perspiration. Cognitive dissonance drives us towards internal consistency in order to restore psychological harmony.

Children tend to universalise their own behaviour. For example, a child might describe themselves as lazy at school. The increase in their brain processing power means that adolescents begin to see elements of themselves in context – 'I am lazy in English but work hard in PE'. This ability to recognise various elements of their self fosters deeper introspection. Adolescents become increasingly aware of contradictions within themselves and attempt to organise their sense of

self in more harmonious and continuous ways (Harter, 1990). The struggle to resolve internal contradictions makes young people hypersensitive to hypocrisy in others, particularly adults. Concepts such as 'authenticity', 'realness' and 'genuineness' become important in their wider relationships, as they reflect their own struggles to resolve confounding elements of themselves. It is the resolution of these contradictions that leads to the creation of a more organised sense of identity. Offer et al. (1992) identified several distinct elements of self that had to be reconciled, including a person's psychological view of self, sexual identity, social relationships and styles of coping (Figure 2.1).

The development of identity in adolescents is not simply a preoccupation with their current sense of self. Children are locked into and share their family's world view. As young people emerge from the constraints of childhood they enter into new social niches, face new opportunities and can make more independent choices. The expression of these choices becomes the fabric of their identity. However, this is difficult because a young adolescent will know that they are no longer identified by their family but will not yet have a strong sense of who they are as an individual. They must also be increasingly mindful of the future transition into adulthood and orientate themselves towards who they will be in this world too. Young people must not simply formulate any identity, but one that can carry them across the threshold into an adult life.

Figure 2.1: Components of self concept

Psychological self
Impulse control
Emotional health
Body image
Social self
Social functioning
Vocational attitudes
Familial self
Family functioning
Sexual self
Sexuality
Coping self
Self reliance
Self-confidence
Mental health

Offer et al., 1992

The Dream

Levinson (1978) described the development of a future sense of self as a critical life task that emerges in early adulthood, from the age of 17 onward. He referred to the future sense of self as the 'Dream'. 'In its primordial form, the Dream is a vague sense of self-in-an-adult-world. It has the quality of a vision, an imagined possibility that generates excitement and vitality.' (Levinson, 1978: 91).

This Dream may range from concrete images, like winning the World Cup, to dramatic forms in which they may take the form of a heroic persona – such as a successful businessman, artist or musician. The Dream can be mundane or extravagant but must be incorporated into a young person's life structure to some degree. If this does not occur, the Dream dies and takes the individual's vitality or sense of purpose with it. Levinson's research identified that individuals were often conflicted between making life choices that could encompass the Dream and making life choices that did not. So, whilst the Dream formation is influenced by family, class, gender and culture, its attainment is likewise influenced by social realities. Parental pressure, economic and social class, deprivation and temperament all increase or decrease the likelihood of the Dream being realised. Failure to realise the Dream can have significant consequences in later life.

Levinson's study of Dream formation focussed on white males entering adult life. Their dreams hinged on occupational roles, and their attainment of them shaped their life direction. This encompassed the young person forming a mentoring relationship that would assist them to achieve their Dream. In males, marriage was seen as a vehicle for achieving their Dream, where it was assumed that the wife would share in the vitality of the husband's Dream and support their husband's pursuit of his Dream. The nature of the Dream has since been examined more widely in terms of gender, sexuality and ethnicity in ways that highlight important differences. Roberts & Newton (1987) reviewed unpublished research into women's life course development that utilised a similar methodology to Levinson's male sample group. They found that women's Dreams tended to be more complex and multi-faceted than males'. Their Dreams placed them in particular environments rather than occupational roles. Within this they were often divided by contrary loyalties between their own personal

aspirations, and accounting for others in their lives. In other ethnic groups, studies have highlighted an additional component of racial identity in the Dream development. For example, a middle class Afro-American's Dream tended to include the concept of progressing in a White world to achieve occupational security (Ruffin, 1989). The Dream is also influenced by class. Afro-Americans from poor backgrounds did not share this occupation-based Dream (Gooden, 1989).

Identity formation

The process of identity formation was first explored by Erickson (1968). As we have seen, Erickson suggested that individuals had to successfully resolve internal dilemmas before they were able to move to the next phase of their life. In adolescence, this dilemma is characterised by a young person establishing an identity versus being in identity confusion. This is driven by the rapid changes a young person experiences, combined with the life-defining decisions that must be made during this period of their life (school options, exams, college/university, etc). However, Erickson's work remained largely theoretical and untested until Marcia (1966; 1993) was able to develop his ideas into a testable theory. Based on Erickson's work, Marcia noted that there were four key identity statuses that dominated adolescence:

1. **Identity diffusion**: The individual has not yet experienced a crisis in identity or made any commitment to future vocations. There is no sign of any activity towards establishing future commitment.
2. **Identity foreclosure**: The individual has not had a crisis of identity but has commitment to a future vocation, usually under the direction of another.
3. **Moratorium**: The individual has yet to resolve a struggle over current identity. They are actively exploring their choices to locate an identity.
4. **Identity achievement**: The individual has experienced the crises and resolved them on their own terms. They are now committed to a vocation, belief and social role.

Marcia believed that these statuses occurred in sequence, but unlike Erickson, did not believe that all stages must be resolved in order to progress towards identity formation. Only the moratorium phase appears essential to the formulation of an adult identity.

For Marcia, the young adolescent is in a state of *personality diffusion*, where they are embedded in an external world that provides for them. They still exist on the natural gradient of childhood. This established balance is disrupted when the external world retreats and they become expected to make larger life decisions. Young people then enter a *moratorium* period where they evaluate options, explore roles and sample experiences as they feel their way to finding a new sense of identity. This struggle can only be resolved in one of two ways. *Identity achievement* is when the young person finds an identity that is reflective of their inner self concept. This motivates them to strive towards its realisation. The alternative is *identity foreclosure* where the young person is pressured into a social role that does not fit with their own aspirations. This may occur even without a moratorium, where parents or others drive them along a specific path which is not of their own choosing. Research has supported Marcia's general thesis. Identity achievers appear far more psychologically balanced than young people in the other stages. Individuals in the moratorium status score highly on anxiety and show the greatest conflict with authority. Those who experience identity foreclosure score highly on the need for social approval, low on autonomy and are most authoritarian in style. These difficulties are derived from a conflict between the aspirations of the self being discordant with the identity that is established, whilst those who remain in identity diffusion have high levels of psychological and interpersonal problems (see Kroger, 1993; 1996; Phinney & Goosens, 1996).

Changing relationships

Identity formation is closely linked with shifts in relationships across adolescence. As we have seen, young people emotionally separate from their parents by approximately 14 years old. Whilst a young person has come to realise that they are not indelibly defined by their family of origin, they lack the developmental maturation to assert who they are as an independent person in their own right. As young people cannot derive identity from their own internal processes at this stage, they draw upon identity through external means. The peer group becomes a transitional structure that provides these external trappings of identity. Peer influence tends to peak between the ages of 14 and 16, between the point of parental separation and engagement into early adulthood. Young people make clear choices with regards to which peer groups they join. They gravitate towards like-minded others who share common interests, values and tastes. Dunphy (1972) found that peer groups took on a cell-like structure. The peer group itself took the form of a close-knit friendship group. These peer groups then aggregated together to form a larger 'scene'. This was a cluster of like-minded peer groups where less intimate relationships are managed between members of various individual peer groups.

Identification of belonging to a peer group takes on common symbolic forms, drawing on music, fashion and even drug and alcohol use as symbols of belonging. So, whilst adults become concerned about the music that young people listen to, this is not simply on the grounds of taste. Different genres of music espouse different values, lifestyles and ambitions that are attractive to distinct sub-groups of young people. Likewise, fashion is a uniform of belonging and not simply about appearance. Whilst young people over-emphasise the need for personal expression, fashion is a statement of compliance with a particular sub-culture. These are all external props to identity formation at this fledgling stage.

Popularity and acceptance are central drivers of young people's behaviour as they offer them access to peer groups. Peer group membership can also improve social standing in other social cliques. Popular individuals tend to be attractive, have a sense of humour, are sensitive to others and have a friendly disposition. Other young people may gain popularity from specialising, such as being smart, sporty or fashionable. Young people who do not belong to a peer group face isolation and lack of social support. As identity is externally driven, this also deprives them of a wider sense of self. Finally, the lack of a peer group may make young people vulnerable in more immediate ways. A peer group may be the only form of physical protection available to young people in hostile neighbourhoods.

The extent of peer groups' centrality to adolescence is also determined by other factors. Dunphy (1972) suggested that the formation of peer groups is only necessary in a society where family, kinship groups and social forums cannot provide young people with the skills and opportunities they need for their development.

These extra-curricular activities are more commonly described as taking risks, particularly in enacting adult behaviours that they are forbidden from doing in other, more supervised areas of life. In this sense, the peer group is the platform where young people can explore and experiment with new behaviours more freely under the watchful gaze of like-minded others. Risk taking is an important maturational process in that it offers an opportunity to master key social competences in readiness for the autonomy adult life. A peer group is a pivotal opportunity for learning that cannot be obtained from the protective structures of family, school or other supervised activities. In this way, young people leave home in degrees as the peer group, not the family, becomes the central forum of young people's development. This divide increases across adolescence. Parents will have increasingly less knowledge of the peers that the young person associates with, let alone what they do together.

Peer-based learning is not limited to new or risky activities and behaviours, but includes socialisation as well. Harris (1999) identified that children and young people make a very clear separation between their private home life and their public life. Young people police the divide between home and public life vehemently. They may allow information regarding their public life to enter the home but will not let home life go public. This makes young people's behaviour highly situational as they may act very differently in the home, the classroom and the playground. This is because, even at a young age, a child soon learns that what is permissible at home is not permissible in the playground. Harris' research suggests that children socialise each other through activities in the peer group.

This process is driven by the consequences of their behaviour. Young people who do not conform to peer norms can soon be met with powerful forms of social coercion such as rejection and humiliation. Peers will criticise, tease, barrack or praise a completely different set of behaviours than parents do. Children and young people will soon learn to adapt in light of these social pressures. For example, if a child's peer group judge a behaviour as babyish, such as liking a particular TV show, the child will soon abandon it. Likewise in adolescence, if a young woman hints that she finds an unpopular young man attractive, the teasing of her peers means she will soon abandon the object of her affection.

Whilst these forces are often perceived negatively by adults, they can be powerful in shaping pro-social behaviour and group cohesion. For example, aggressive males who project violence into their peer group will soon be rejected. This rejection will temper the behaviour. Equally, whilst the peer group may endorse the use of certain substances, it may legislate against others through the denigration of those who use a stigmatised drug. Likewise, prestige behaviour can be enhanced through envy, recognition or mimicry. A classic example of peer socialisation is amongst immigrant children who do not speak the host country's language. Whilst they continue to speak their native tongue at home, through socialisation with new peers they acquire a second language rapidly (Genesee, 1989).

Peer pressure is often perceived by adults as a very negative experience. It is often assumed that peer pressure emanates from a ringleader who coerces the others into risk-taking or anti-social behaviour. However, it tends to be the overall values of the group that are most influential in shaping young people's responses rather than the behaviour of individuals within the group. Peer pressure can be understood as a willingness to participate in group activities and not an external pressure to do so. In this way peer influence can exert positive and negative influences. Statistically, a child is better off growing up in a dysfunctional family in a good neighbourhood, as the peer influence may assuage difficulties in socialisation and promote pro-social aspirations. In contrast, a child growing up in a well-functioning family in a bad neighbourhood is more likely to be drawn into anti-social behaviour, regardless of parental style. Again, this is not to say that abusive parenting does not affect children and adolescents. It does suggest, though, that supportive structures later in the life course can mediate problems located in early ones.

Further to this, the peer group is a barometer of the personal power of young people. In general, whilst young people have far less personal power compared to adults, as long as they have the same freedoms enjoyed by their peer group they feel in control. Any request that they make to parents that is denied will result in the immediate riposte 'But Sam's parents let him go . . .' The peer group can also amplify young people's power. While young people cluster into like-minded groups, their behaviour within these groups is remarkably similar. However, when they encounter a rival peer group, they amplify their norms in contradiction to the other group. For example, young women can be very competitive in sports. However, if a peer group of males crosses their path they will suddenly act less competitively. In contrast, this male peer group will act 'more masculine' in their presence. Likewise when demographically identical groups of young people encounter each other, it automatically amplifies in-group norms and fosters antagonism regarding the out-group norms (Sherif et al., 1961). This can lead to aggression and violence between groups of young people who otherwise share remarkably similar lives.

The monopoly of the peer group over a young person becomes compromised under different conditions. In later adolescence, young people establish a more autonomous sense of identity that becomes increasingly incompatible with the group. In this way, young people can 'knife off' from peer groups whose collective values become increasingly discordant with these future hopes. This phrase was first coined in relation to the US military during World War Two. Reception centres for new recruits had to sever the new recruit from their old social ties to re-mould them as a soldier. Knifing off is thus breaking free of one's old social networks in order to re-invent oneself and embed into new social contexts (Maruna & Roy, 2007). The same process can also occur when a young person forms an important romantic attachment in later adolescence. The young person starts to invest more time in this relationship than in the group. This can generate conflict between peers and the romantic partner who can appear to compete for the young person's attention. The conflict can result in the torn young person exiting the peer group in favour of the new relationship.

Whilst the peer group dominates mid-adolescence, it will also become superseded by other relationships. In childhood and early adolescence young people hold vertical relationships with adults who have power and control over them. Meanwhile, they hold horizontal relationships with their peers which are collusive. The nature of these relationships changes dramatically across adolescence. As the peer group begins to dissolve, other relationships come to the fore. Whilst young adolescents perceive adults as a restraining force, in later adolescence they come to see adults as people in their own right. The desire for greater levels of

autonomy means that adults must gradually rescind power over young people at this stage in their lives. As the peer groups splinter, power relationships with adults begin to equalise. This is hastened as young people leave school from the age of 16. Life choices that lead to university, employment or the creation of family bring young people into contact and broader relationships with peers of a wider age range. By the end of adolescence, young people need to have achieved a new relational life task: having a relationship with adults as equals. Ultimately it is their capacity to make this key transition that will determine the adult life that follows and which represents the full fruition of adolescent development.

Developmental delay and substance use

Adolescence is a period of rapid transition in terms of life task achievement, puberty, identity and relationship shifts. The pace of transition across multiple domains makes young people particularly susceptible to drug and alcohol problems at this time. Drug and alcohol use has significant ramifications across all four of these developmental strands.

Cognitive processes

In the realm of puberty, accelerated changes in the adolescent brain make it highly susceptible to the toxicity of various substances, and there is growing evidence that the neurological impact of drugs and alcohol is more profound in young people than in adults (Monti et al., 2005; Smith, 2003).

More research has been conducted on the effects of alcohol than other substances. This research has demonstrated that alcohol consumption in adolescence has a profound influence on learning and cognitive processes that can endure into adult life (Spear, 2000; Tomlinson et al., 2004). Alcohol affects the adolescent brain in a different way from adults' (Slotkin, 2002; White & Swartzwelder, 2004). For example, adolescents who experience alcohol use disorders demonstrate poorer memory retrieval and visual-spatial awareness (Brown et al., 2000a). High doses of alcohol appear to inhibit memory function, especially in binge drinking episodes (Blitzer et al., 1990). Animal behavioural studies also highlight that an area of the brain called the hippocampus is particularly sensitive to the effects of alcohol. Damage to this area of the brain appears to de-sensitise adolescents to the sedative effects of alcohol. This means that they do not feel drowsy when drinking, which can prolong drinking episodes. This can increase risk of further problems. In this situation, young people also appear unable to self-assess their own levels of intoxication or the negative consequences of their use, which are key factors in moderating consumption (Graham & Diaz-Granados, 2006). This has been supported by wider research. De Belis et al. (2005) found that hippocampus volumes were much smaller for adolescents with alcohol use disorders compared to their peers.

Young people who use cannabis prior to the age of 17 appear more vulnerable to cognitive impairment (Pope et al., 2003). Ashtari et al. (2009) conducted a small study of brain functioning in 14 adolescents who were heavy users of cannabis in comparison to 14 non-users. They found that heavy users displayed abnormal water diffusion in the brain which suggested arrested development of myelin sheaths. These sheaths insulate brain cells and assist in the signalling of messages from one brain cell to another, a core function of the brain. As such, cannabis appeared to have a direct impact on halting brain development. It can be difficult to identify clean samples where the young people being studied only use one drug, however, so this research must be considered tentative due to the fact that it might be reflecting poly-drug use.

The problem of finding clean samples may mask problems associated with other drugs. For example, the abnormal water diffusion could be amplified by the fact cannabis is often taken with tobacco. The effects of nicotine in the adolescent brain differ from that of adults and even pre-natal exposure. Nicotine can have long term effects on the reward pathways, memory and mood leading to increased probability of continued high use (Slotkin, 2002). Studies in this area are limited as they tend to be conducted on small research samples, or results are inferred from animal behavioural studies. It is not clear whether the changes in brain functioning occur as a result of consumption or whether they pre-date initiation in substance use. Also, when differences are found, there is not a complete research base to establish how reversible these effects may be. What is clear in the emergent research is that young people present a distinct sub-group who

are at risk of heightened impacts of consumption of nicotine that may be enduring into their adult lives.

In terms of sexual maturation, the early onset of puberty in young women also places them at heightened risk of becoming involved in problematic drug or alcohol use. Early onset puberty in young women can lead to teasing and alienation from the peer group. This leaves them vulnerable to entering into romantic relationships with older males who are more developmentally advanced in their drug and alcohol consumption. Deardorff et al. (2005) studied the link between early puberty in young women, alcohol consumption and the initiation of sexual behaviour. They questioned 666 females aged 18–22 from 4 different ethnic groups who had been pregnant in their teens or early twenties. They identified that the age of young women's first menstrual period was the greatest predictor of subsequent early involvement in sexual activity and alcohol initiation, regardless of ethnic group. The earlier the onset of puberty also predicted a greater risk of sexual activity involving alcohol.

Other studies have shown that early sexual initiation also predicts: multiple sexual partners prior to adulthood, teen pregnancy, terminations, sexually transmitted diseases, increased emotional disturbance and pregnancy complications in young women (Moore et al., 1995; Zabin et al., 1979; Zabin, 1990). Furthermore, pregnancy at a young age has long term consequences for young women that shape their future life course, including long-term unemployment, educational disadvantage and depression in later life (Berry et al., 2001). Early puberty and involvement with older males can thus have profound consequences on the life course of these young women who are at increased risk. Other studies support these findings. Wider factors have been implicated in increasing such risks, with a particular focus on divorce, and where a parent has multiple partners (Crockett et al., 1996; Miller & Bingham, 1989).

Social impact of consumption

The social impact of consumption on a user's life can be profound. Melrose et al.'s (2007) extensive interviews with young cannabis users were able to identify a range of difficulties connected to their use such as poor educational achievement, conflict with parents, being thrown out of home or criminal involvement. Many of the young people interviewed had been excluded from school due to cannabis involvement or had truanted from school in order to smoke cannabis. This is a common finding. Studies of alcohol use also found that drop-out and truancy were more likely to occur amongst young people who drank frequently (O'Malley et al., 1998). Wichstrom (1998) found that young people were more likely to skip school in order to drink rather than miss school as a result of heavy drinking. These findings are not necessarily uniform for every young person. Lyskey & Hall (2000) found that only youth from the most disadvantaged backgrounds tended to report this experience. However, it is illustrative of the impact that cannabis has on life task achievement. For example, failure in education can compound the cycle of deprivation for youth living in poverty by curtailing subsequent career opportunities later in the life course.

Consumption can also affect other areas of a young person's life. The formation of a romantic partnerships and marriage decreases consumption, whilst being single increases consumption (Sadava & Pak, 1994; Bachman et al., 1997). Early alcohol involvement predicts early entry into the work force and higher early wages (Bachman & Schulenberg, 1993) though continued use predicts lower work status and frequent employment changes over time (Jones, 2002). Whilst this is not solely influenced by the level of consumption, Neale (2006) found that the heaviest users of cannabis were immersed in cannabis using networks, compared to moderate users who were more likely to be engaged in wider non-using social networks. Baumrind & Moselle (1985) highlighted the high cost of early initiation in terms of its impact on the development of coping skills and healthy relationships. Furthermore, Newcomb & Bentler (1987) suggested that early drug and alcohol use was liable to shorten adolescence, moving young people into an adult world early. This lowered their educational achievements and chances of establishing successful occupational careers.

Consumption and achievement of life tasks

The social complications arising from consumption can halt the achievement of life tasks. When a young person is over-invested in

their use they become embedded in using groups and increasingly excluded from the pro-social structures of the normal life course. This social exclusion denies young people the opportunity to prepare for the increasingly complex demands of life. When life task achievement is interrupted in this way, developmental delay is rapid and consuming, because of the pace of transition during this period. Even short periods of social exclusion can have profound consequences. It is important to note that there is complex relationship between life task achievement and consumption. For example, in Melrose et al.'s study, 'the high-heavy users tended, on the whole, to be experiencing the greatest number of pre-existing social or personal problems, for example homelessness/hostel dwelling, low educational achievement, unemployment, criminality and, for a small number, former Class A drug use' (Melrose et al., 2007: 42.). This begs the question whether interruptions in the life course increase drug and alcohol use, or whether drug and alcohol use interferes with the life-course. Gotham et al. (2003) explored this issue. They hypothesised that pre-existing factors, substance use and the achievement of life tasks could interact in four different ways. They attempted to identify which of these theories best accounted for substance use amongst 489 young people over a seven year period (see Table 2.8).

Gotham et al.'s (2003) results found little evidence for the widely accepted Causation Theory. This is to say that alcohol use did not appear to cause specific problems in young people who proceed to self-medicate with continued consumption. There was strong evidence that the Selection Theory did account for a great deal of consumption. Their data showed that pre-existing variables had a significant impact on young people's accomplishment of life tasks. These pre-existing variables appear to influence the choices young people make regarding substance use and life tasks. For example, young people that achieved a baccalaureate degree were more likely to be religiously involved and to have demonstrated higher educational achievement seven years previously. Those with alcohol-related disorders were less likely to achieve a degree but their failure to do so was predicted by pre-existent difficulties rather than their alcohol use. This suggests that underlying problems can influence life task achievement and substance use. Young people whose lives are already compromised

Table 2.8:   Four theories of substance misuse and life tasks

Theory	Explanation
Selection theory	This theory assumes pre-existing factors influence a young person's life choices before they make transitions. For example, poor educational attainment means that they might not chose to go into further education, or impulsive behaviour may make them prone to use drugs and alcohol.
Causation theory	Suggests that drug and alcohol use causes cognitive or emotional damage that result in youth distress. This distress in turn promotes continued use as a means of self-medicating. This fosters increasing reliance on external coping like substance use, diminishing their own internal ability to self-sooth negative moods.
Socialisation theory	Drug and alcohol involvement is part of the process of maturation. Young people become involved in drug and alcohol use at key moments within their own development. Intoxication management and bonding with others is a life task in itself.
Reciprocal effects	This theory assumes that selection, causation and socialisation processes are all at work in prompting young people's involvement with drug and alcohol. Furthermore, involvement in drugs and alcohol will affect the selection, causation and social roles young people adopt. For example, young people might choose peers, partners or a job that allows them to use substances.

Based on Gotham et al., 2003.

with other life stresses appear to struggle in educational settings and then make life choices that lead to increased drug and alcohol involvement. These young people may drop out of school early, take up employment and even marry early in order to facilitate their consumption. However the gains of this *pseudo-maturity* are unlikely to be sustained over time (Schulenberg et al., 2004).

This supports the findings of Melrose et al. (2007) who found that the heaviest cannabis users in their study already had more complex life situations prior to the onset of cannabis use. These heavy users were likely to abandon the pursuit of life tasks, such as applying for a job, and reported that they did not feel that they were reaching their potential. Light cannabis users were more likely to procrastinate on life tasks rather than neglect them. This suggests that life task accomplishment is not necessarily catastrophically halted by *any* consumption, but rather that delay occurs on a spectrum.

Bachman et al. (2008) produced the most definitive analysis of drug and alcohol impact on educational achievement in their studies of over 50,000 young people aged 14–22 as part of the Monitoring The Future project in the US. They especially examined the impact of tobacco, marijuana, alcohol and cocaine use and found a strong correlation between early delinquency and substance use, particularly with tobacco. They

also found a strong correlation between drug involvement and poor educational achievement. Within these broad statements, though, there were interesting differences between substances and age ranges. The Monitoring The Future survey also found that the most predictive variables in young people's educational attainment existed prior to the onset of their drug or alcohol consumption. Ethnic status, poor parental educational background, low parental support, being held back a year and suspension/expulsion prior to eighth grade all predicted delinquency, substance involvement and poor educational achievement. These factors are reflective of the increased life stresses and limited coping resources in the poorest social groups. They also explain why environments express a greater influence than genetics on intelligence in poorer social groups than amongst the more affluent.

Early school exclusion was the most significant predictor of early involvement of substance use. The substance that was most revealing was tobacco use, where the early onset of smoking predicted overall educational achievement. Cannabis use was also strongly related to poor educational achievement but did not 'cause' poor performance. Again, pre-existing social variables in the young people were better predictors of their educational failure. Initiation into cocaine use occurred much later in adolescence and therefore patterns of educational achievement were already established by this time.

In this study, alcohol had a more complex relationship with educational attainment. Initiated in early adolescence (age 14–16), it appeared similar to smoking tobacco in terms of predicting poor educational attainment amongst already disadvantaged youth. However, academic achievers' (students aged 18 or above) levels of alcohol consumption surpassed that of their educationally disadvantaged peers once they initiated use. This research strongly suggests that the early initiation of substance use and delinquency can be understood together as part of an 'anti-social behavioural syndrome' in youth, located in the pre-existing social structures of young people's lives that hinder academic achievement, and by proxy, influence their long-term socio-economic status. Later onset drinking in student populations appears linked with leaving home for university and experiencing lower social responsibilities at such times. So the study demonstrated a U-shaped curve of alcohol problems across the educational spectrum. Alcohol use tended to compound pre-existing problems for the educationally disadvantaged, but diminished the potential of the most educationally advantaged.

College and university represent a high risk period for substance involvement as attendance coincides with the peak period of consumption in the life course. Whilst students may engage in drinking prior to attendance, going to college and university tends to increase their consumption rapidly (Moos, 1977). Johnston et al. (1991) found that 40 per cent of students engaged in bouts of heavy drinking compared to only 34 per cent of their non-university peers, with 4 per cent of students drinking every day. Approximately 23 per cent of female students engage in heavy drinking compared to only 8 per cent of non-university counterparts. These elevated consumption rates are driven by a number of variables. The convergence and high concentration of young men and women who are free from wider social responsibilities at this point in their life course increases their use dramatically. This in turn contributes to a high normative drinking culture. Marketing of alcohol is also aggressive in and around the student campus (Ryan & Mosher, 1991). The fact that many students experience their first taste of independent living, experience insecurity in a new environment and a need to create new social

relationships all increase the risk factors, which amplify the cultural importance of alcohol as a social bonding agent.

Besides having a wider social impact on crime and health, drug and alcohol use diminishes academic achievement dramatically. Several studies have shown a strong and direct correlation between drinking rates and grades (Hill & Bugen, 1979). Studies have demonstrated that alcohol plays a role in 40 per cent of problems on campus and that 28.3 per cent of college drop-out is attributable to alcohol alone (Anderson & Gadaleto, 1991). So, even in these high achieving young adults, the social consequences of drug and alcohol use can be very high in impeding life task achievement.

Consumption and social identity

Young people in school and in higher education select peer groups of like-minded others. This like-mindedness is highly influenced by their sense of identity, values and aspirations. Young people select life choices that are harmonious with this sense of self. In this way, they may select peer groups or make life choices which facilitate consumption. This idea is supported by research into substance abuse and identity formation. Anderson (1993; 1994) has suggested that young people are motivated to seek out a drug using identity when they experience marginalisation in pro-social networks. This marginalisation can take several forms such as stigmatisation, unpalatable personality traits or negative social status.

As we saw in Chapter 1, trauma and abuse can also increase young people's sense of marginalisation. This is especially the case when negative life events have happened only to them and not others, and these life events may invoke negative social judgements about them in those who are not affected. These young people can feel singled out and fear exposure or shame. The invisible audience effect can amplify this alienation. A young person will find it hard to separate their thoughts from others', and so may believe that others can 'see' the difference in them which they feel. This can make integration into pro-social groups psychologically difficult for them. Alternatively, the impact of their trauma may influence their behaviour, leading them to act in different ways than their peers. This can lead to an increase in teasing and rejection by peers. This social judgement, or anticipation of it, generates an ego discomfort in the young person who becomes increasingly uncomfortable in social networks that devalue them.

Kaplan et al. (1986) refer to this as *self-derogation*, where the young person makes increasingly negative statements about themselves. These statements are symptomatic of a deeper struggle in a young person who is developing a negative self-image. They avoid social situations where they feel uncomfortable and seek out alternative social contexts that enhance their sense of self. The ego discomfort which they have been experiencing blocks them from formulating a positive identity within the pro-social structures they had been inhabiting. In contrast, heavy drug and alcohol sub-cultures are highly accepting and offer young people ceremonies, structures, belonging and shared norms that are more compatible with a dislocated sense of self.

Anderson & Mott (1998) tested this idea among 228 drug-using adults who initiated drug use at an average age of 15. This sample reported a wide range of marginalisation prior to initiating use such as frequent moves, sexual abuse, parental death or divorce. These individuals sought out alternative social networks where they felt more psychologically comfortable. The intensity of their ego discomfort was not as significant in their selection of using peer groups as was the inability to formulate a positive identity elsewhere or their strong identification with drug-using sub-cultures. Most importantly though, once a drug use was initiated, all individuals reported reductions in ego discomfort.

Drugs and alcohol offered a form of identity achievement that was most compelling to those who could not find adequate self–expression within the confines of pro-social structures. Drug and alcohol use for this population is not merely a behaviour but an assertion of identity. Hence, as Gotham et al. (2003) found, young people choose to enter into peer groups where they do not feel marked out as different. This cements consumption into the fabric of an individual's self-concept, which can sustain consumption well into the life course.

A substance user's identity formation also relates to their peer relationships as the peer group constitutes their social environment. As Baumeister stated 'When all of one's social relationships remain constant, personality change is considerably more difficult, because people tend to assume that others' personalities will remain stable and consistent' (Baumeister, 1994: 283). Induction into drug and alcohol using peer groups isolates the individual from wider social relationships. This subjects them to bonding, social norms and obligations in this peer group. In this social niche, adolescence and anti-social norms, values and attitudes are preserved into adulthood. As Erickson (1968) noted, the peer group promotes an 'adolescent existentialism' where individual choice, freedom from responsibility and distrust of adults are sustained well into an adult life course. The using peer group is a time capsule that sustains these behaviours and normalises heavy consumption within the context of its own rules. The problem-using youth will therefore not make the transition into a wider range of relationships that breaks the monopoly of the peer group. Instead, they remain locked into the narrow norms of the group well into early adulthood.

Consumption and developmental delay

Drug and alcohol involvement can therefore interrupt each of the key developmental processes in critical ways. The result of these interruptions is that the problem user becomes increasingly developmentally delayed across every domain of their life. As young people are excluded from the social structures of the life course, they lack exposure to the critical life tasks that are embedded in those structures. Educational, social, relational and recreational skills are not developed. As the life course becomes increasingly complex, these excluded youth become increasingly adrift and lacking in their skills repertoire, making reintegration more difficult with each passing month. The impact of substance misuse in these four domains is summarised in Table 2.9.

Adolescent mental health

Developmental processes can be interrupted by other factors. In particular, mental health problems can have dramatic impact on adolescence. The impact of mental illness is similar to that of substance use. Whilst there are a wide range of mental illnesses that can affect young people, all diagnostic criteria share one key symptom. The mental illness must affect the individual's social functioning to be deemed a

Table 2.9:   Summary of disruptions in the maturational process

Developmental process	Impact of substance use
Life task achievement	Over investment in drug and alcohol use leads to neglect of life task achievements. The social consequences of use may also lead to social break down. The resulting social exclusions deprive young people of the rehearsals and preparedness for an increasingly complex life course.
Physical and cognitive development	• Early onset puberty can increase young women's risk of involvement with older male peers whose drug and alcohol use is developmentally ahead of their own. This increases the risk of sexually transmitted disease, multiple partners and teen pregnancy which has an impact on their life course. • The transitional nature of brain development makes young people especially susceptible to the toxicity of alcohol and drug use. This can lead to impairment of key cognitive skills, de-sensitise the young person to intoxication as well interrupting normal brain maturation. • Young problem users may operate in a less demanding environment, reducing the intellectual demands that shape brain functioning and learning.
Identity	Young people may respond to trauma or deprivation by formulating a negative identity. This can be exacerbated in pro-social peer groups where young people feel singled out or different. This generates an ego discomfort and identification with alternative peer groups. Entry into peer relationships with other disenfranchised youth may alleviate this discomfort but contribute to the formation of a negative identity.
Peers	Embedding into an alienated peer group may prevent the natural separation from relationships with peers to creating relationships with adults as equals. Alienated peer groups may normalise and sustain adolescent behaviours into the life course.

clinical issue (Tyrer & Casey, 1998). Yet this is also the least understood and least researched symptom. The diagnostic difference between sadness and depression is that the depressed individual cannot sustain their relationships and commitments. In other words, mental illness will affect developmental processes in exactly the same way that substance misuse does in terms of interfering with life task completion, eroding relationships and having a stigmatising influence on identity formation. Reviewing the impact of mental health problems on young people reveals that they not only experience high levels of social exclusion, but also that these disadvantages can be carried into adult life (Grant et al., 2005). This suggests that the developmental delay can be as profound and enduring as that linked to substance misuse.

Diagnostic criteria have been classified to describe over 150 mental health disorders that apply to young people. Most of the diagnostic criteria are based on studies of adults or are rare in adolescence. Some, such as Bipolar disorder in particular, remain highly controversial diagnoses in children (Birmaher et al., 2006). Two broad classifications are used to describe adolescent mental health problems: externalised and internalised. Externalised disorders are those

disorders that are characterised by a cluster of problem *behaviours* that are acted out. They include ADHD/ADD, Conduct Disorder and Oppositional Defiance Disorder. They are more common in boys and have a higher prevalence rate in children growing up in poverty (West, 1982). Early temperament difficulties in children, such as reactive and intense responses to stress and frustration, tend to be highly predictive of conduct disorders (Nigg and Huang-Pollock, 2003). Their early onset in infancy suggests a genetic origin. Externalised children tend to have personality traits such as high impulsivity and low inhibition. In contrast, an introverted temperament appears to protect children from externalised disorders (Burke et al., 2002).

Internalised disorders are *psychological* problems and are inferred from withdrawn behaviour. Internalised disorders include anxiety, depression, self-harm and eating disorders. They tend to occur in early adolescence at around the same time as meta-cognition is developed, whereby young people can see themselves through the eyes of others. Internalised disorders tend to be more common in girls who appear to be more sensitive to fear. Anxiety is the most common adolescent mental health problem and can emerge earlier than other internalised disorders. Again, this suggests that there may be a genetic influence. Temperament factors such as anxiety sensitivity, temperamental sensitivity and behavioural inhibition in childhood are predictive of anxiety disorders (Donovan & Spence, 2000). A summary of the principle disorders is described in Table 2.10.

It is important to stress that both externalised and internalised disorders are not solely governed by genetic factors but are profoundly influenced by social environments. Externalised disorders evolve in contexts of clear environmental pressures. Whilst the early age of onset of an externalised disorder is a predictor of poorer treatment prognosis and suggests a strong genetic-temperament link, Rutter et al. (2006) found that environmental stresses tend to predict the form and the severity of the disorders in ways that reflect on the parenting–temperament dynamic reviewed earlier in this chapter. Highly impulsive children may have this trait dampened in a family that consistently manages its boundaries, whereas high impulsivity may be exacerbated in a permissive family structure. Maternal warmth may limit the severity of ADHD and halt the development of Conduct Disorder. Family difficulties that result in inconsistent, coercive or low parental management also increase problematic Conduct or Oppositional Defiance Disorder (Weiss & Trokenberg-Hechtman, 1993).

Externalised disorders are locked into a dynamic relationship with parenting and their impact can be profound. Parents of ADHD children are far more likely to divorce (Wymbs et al., 2008). Parents of Conduct Disorder children tend to experience a wealth of social problems themselves. Loeber et al. (1998) found high levels of parental conflict, violence and stress, whilst Steinberg (2001) identified high rates of depression, drug and alcohol problems, criminal behaviour and anti-social personality disorder in these parents. There are also high rates of sexual or physical abuse reported within these families. Needless to say, these complexities in the parents' lives lead to increased family poverty, unemployment and educational disadvantage (Dadds, 1996).

Internalised disorders are also influenced by the environment. Within the realm of anxiety disorders, high parental anxiety, parental over-control, over-protection and hypercriticism are strongly linked to the disorders' development (Warren et al., 1997; Donovan & Spence, 2000).

Some research suggests that parental influences have been overstated though, with genetic research suggesting that parental style only accounts for 4 per cent of variance. These studies suggest that over-control is the most significant single factor within the context of parent influence (McLeod et al., 2007). Velting et al. (2004) suggested that parental anxiety is most likely to shape the disorder when a child is young. This is the time when parents are most likely to accommodate the child's anxiety through permissive parenting styles, particularly when the parents themselves also have an anxiety or related disorder. Social and cultural change is nowadays placing increasingly sophisticated demands on youth. With regards to anxiety, Twenge (2000: 1017) observed that 'The birth cohort change in anxiety is so large that by the 1980s normal child samples were scoring higher than child psychiatric patients from the 1950s'. Such increases in rates of anxiety disorders are driven by increasing social pressures on young people.

Parental depression is a risk factor for subsequent depression in young people (Kane & Garber, 2004). Family influences are less well established in populations with eating disorders or self-harming behaviours, but both tend to have concurrent internalised disorders and report high rates of sexual abuse (Yager et al., 2002). Socio-economic position also has an influence, which may be due to the increased probability of poorer young people experiencing traumatic life events, or to the sense of helplessness that people in deprivation are more likely to experience.

Summary

Adolescent development is a dynamic process that is driven both by maturational processes and by the environments that young people are embedded in. Social, cultural and historical forces play powerful roles in shaping the landscape in which young people develop and which they must account for. Young people's lives simply cannot be understood without this context – the social structures that we inhabit, which shift as we age into adult life.

As we progress through these culturally prescribed networks, the balance of external influence begins to wane. Children operate in highly controlled environments with little personal power. At this time, environmental

Table 2.10: Summary of the major mental health disorders in adolescence

Disorder	Description
Externalised Disorders	
Hyperkinetic Disorder (ADHD/ADD)	Children are restless, fidgety and overactive. They are easily distracted and do not finish tasks. Highly impulsive they have difficulty waiting their turn in play, conversation or queues. Signs will have been obvious since a toddler. For a diagnosis, a child must display symptoms in more than one situation, such as at home and school. Diet can impact on the behavior of some children. Estimate of prevalence vary widely for ADHD / ADD, occurring in 2–18 per cent of young people.
Conduct Disorders	Children with this disorder may get involved in physical fights, temper tantrums and may steal, without any sign of remorse or guilt. Cruelty to others or animals, running away from home and criminal behavior is common. They may stay out all night and truant from school. Teenagers with this disorder may also take risks with little regard for their own safety. Boys are more likely to experience this disorder (69 per cent). The condition affects 4 per cent of the population with an onset at the age of 5.
Oppositional Defiance Disorder	This disorder is more common in boys and starts by age 8 but may start as early as preschool. They do not follow requests, are angry, resentful and blame others for their own mistakes. Often they have no, or have lost, friends. Constantly in trouble at school, they are spiteful or seek revenge. To fit this diagnosis, the pattern must last for at least 6 months and must be more than normal childhood misbehaviour. The condition occurs in 6–10 per cent of the population.
Internalised Disorders	
Self-Harm	Young people report feeling desperate about a problem and don't know where to turn for help. They feel the self-harming behaviour helps them to feel more in control. It can be linked to trauma or abuse. Young people report feelings of 'numbness' or 'deadness' and self-harm makes them feel more connected and alive. In a proportion of young people it may be accompanied by suicidal thinking. Research suggests it affects 6.9 per cent of young people and is more common in girls (11.2 per cent) than boys (3.2 per cent). The average age of onset is 12 years. Suicide rates are very low in children, but start to increase from the age of 11.
Anxiety including PTSD	This disorder can be generalised, be the result of trauma or be specific to a situation or object; for example school or separation from a parent. It can cause panic, fear, hyper-vigilance, nightmares, psycho-somatic illness and obsessive thinking. For very young children it can emerge as *selective mutism*. Here, the child may not speak, appear to be deaf and freeze like a statue at times. It often occurs with depression, eating disorders or substance abuse. Behavior needs to present as an exaggeration of normal developmental trends for a diagnosis. It is the most common mental health disorder and occurs in 13 per cent of children and adolescents.
Depression	Symptoms include sadness, irritability and loss of interest in activities. Associated features include changes in appetite, sleep disturbance and tiredness, difficulty concentrating, feelings of guilt, worthlessness and suicidal thoughts. The typical age of onset is 11. It is estimated that 1 per cent of children and 3 per cent of adolescents suffer from this condition in any one year.
Anorexia/Bulimia	Key signs are weight loss or unusual weight changes, irregular periods or stopping. They miss meals, avoiding 'fatty' foods or engage in secret eating. They may over-exercise. It can lead to medical conditions including osteoporosis and cardiovascular problems. This condition occurs in 1 in 60 young people and has the highest mortality rate of all mental illnesses with 5–10 per cent of patients dying within 5–10 years. The death rate is 12 times higher than all other causes of death for young women between the ages of 12–14. Typical onset is between the ages of 12–25.
Obsessive Compulsive Disorder	Typical onset is at the age of 10 and is characterised by a thought, image or urge that keeps coming to mind that is distressing. These can include: worry about illness; fears about disease; worry about harm happening to them or someone else; or worrying about things being tidy. It causes anxiety and the person then feels an irresistible urge to 'put it right.' This disorder affects 1–3 per cent of young people.

influence is high. As adolescence shifts towards autonomy, young people self-select life choices within the confines of their socio-economic strata. Temperament and personality factors increasingly shape such choices.

Parenting style and the child's temperament have received a great deal of individual attention in isolation. It is clear that family cohesion is the product of an interplay between these two domains. However, parental influence diminishes across adolescence as the young person strives towards greater personal independence. The achievement of this independence encompasses four key processes: puberty, life task achievement, identity formation and a shift in relationships. These four processes are integral to each other rather than separate.

Substance misuse and other factors such as mental illness can disrupt these processes, leading to profound levels of social exclusion and developmental delay. This curtails young people's preparation for adult life, which is the central function of this period of the life course. The following chapter will review the relationship between substance misuse and adolescent development further, establishing how young people develop substance misuse problems. Within the patterns of development that have been described in this chapter, we will see that the evolution of substance misuse problems is not a random occurrence. Drug and alcohol problems are inextricably entwined in the developmental processes. This reality creates starkly delineated pathways into substance involvement that have profound consequences for not just prevention and treatment, but also for how we understand young people in their entirety.

CHAPTER 3

How do Substance Misuse Problems Develop?

Introduction

There is some debate amongst historians regarding which is the oldest trick in the book. The weight of evidence supports the Cup and Balls routine. This trick involves the appearance and disappearance of small balls that takes place beneath three cups. In the grand finale, a ball is transformed into an object such as orange or even a bird. Evidence to support the Cup and Balls trick is found in Beni Hassan, a small village outside Cairo. There is a mural depicting what appears to be a magician conducting the Cup and Balls trick on the wall of a tomb dating to 2,000 BC. Early writers such as Seneca the Younger (born in 3 BC) also describe witnessing the trick. Alichron of Athens wrote a detailed account of the trick in AD 200 where the performer's grand finale ended with him plucking missing balls from his ears and mouth. However, the Egyptian mural is a bas-relief depiction of two people sat by up-turned cups. It cannot be established with certainty that it is a Cup and Balls routine and not just a popular game.

An ancient Egyptian Papyrus dating to 2,600 BC describes another contender for the oldest trick. Pharaoh Cheops, builder of the Great Pyramid at Giza, asked his sons to bring the great conjuror Dedi to his court. At the venerable age of 70 Dedi performed a series of miracles that included the decapitation of a goose, a duck and then an ox. Shortly after, these slaughtered beasts were restored to life with no apparent injury. Cheops asked Dedi to repeat the spectacle with a human but Dedi declined. Either he did not have the correct apparatus or the original decapitated animals were not as intact as their subsequent replacements suggested.

The third contender for the oldest trick in the book is in the writings of Hero of Alexander in 62 BC who amazed Greeks and Egyptians alike with his array of magic conducted in his temple. This included doors opening mysteriously, stone idols that spoke and libations of wine poured freely from empty vessels. Some of Hero's magic has been discredited, with some researchers suggesting that these tricks were accomplished through changes in air pressure in the Temple caused by fires. Whilst this does not appear to account for all eyewitnesses' accounts, it is a possibility.

So the oldest trick in the book remains lost in the murk of history. The weight of evidence supports the Cup and Balls routine as the most likely candidate. Ironically, it was this routine that began to spark neurological interest in acts of magic, which began in 1975 with two avant-garde stage magicians who would come to call themselves Penn and Teller. After one gig Teller practiced his adaption of the Cups and Balls trick, but had no props. So he used crumpled napkins and everyday transparent glasses. Although it was now possible to follow the crumpled napkins as Teller variously palmed them, squished them and moved them from cup to cup, the illusion persisted. It became a part of their stage show and, despite the transparency, audiences remained baffled. This was because Teller's hands moved faster than the audience's brains could process. Such blatant trickery attracted the interest of neurologists who studied such tricks to understand brain function better.

Neurological research has demonstrated that many magical illusions simply exploit blind spots in the human brain. For example, a stage pickpocket, Apollo Robbins, worked with a team of neuroscientists who wanted to understand how he could pick the pocket of someone whom he had just told that he would. The pickpocket explained that the feat could only be achieved if he moved a free hand in an arc and not in a straight line. They realised the feat was achieved because of 'saccades'. Saccades are the rapid movement of the eye that precedes the conscious decision of where to look and is one of the fastest movements that humans can make. When the hand moves in a straight line, the eyes automatically gaze on the end point of the movement. However, the arcing motions prevent this from happening, leaving the victim watching the moving hand for a fraction longer than they would otherwise, allowing the pick pocket enough time to lift the wallet with his other hand.

Stage magicians do not rely only upon the flaws of human neurology in order to astonish their audiences. Psychology and engineering also have their part. The good magician knows what to over-emphasise and what to underplay. They have to control the human eye with their patter and body language in a way that the audience does not realise what is happening. This is coupled with good engineering. For example some tricks such as the Pepper Ghost Apparition that was popular in the Victorian period demanded purpose built theatres to house the illusion. But again, even where mechanical devices are used, the magician understands human psychology. The magician knows that audiences tend to look for one simple explanation of how the trick might be achieved. Therefore multiple mechanisms are used and the audience is confused, not because the trick is inexplicable, but because of the habits of the audience's thinking.

These imponderable acts of magic reveal something interesting. Human beings are not very good at understanding cause and effect. When we see a dramatic effect that has no apparent cause we fall into traps of thinking. We may think of the dramatic gesture that the magician made, we may think it was all done with mirrors, we may wonder whether the cards were marked in some way. In other words we look for obvious causes and ignore the little details. When we come to consider the evolution of drug and alcohol problems, we fall prey to the very same errors. We look for simple and singular dramatic causes such as genetics, a troubling life event or social breakdown. What is fascinating is that whilst research has categorically established that no one single explanation can account for the development of drug and alcohol problems, 'single cause' illusions persist in the thinking of people involved in addictions work. This is because of our own personal biases, allegiances or sympathies, which mean that we look for the evidence that supports our pre-existing views and discount the rest.

This chapter will begin with an overview of various more complex causal relationships that have been identified by research, and illustrate how substance misuse and substance-related problems are easily misconstrued. Based on this overview, this chapter will then examine the evolution of drug and alcohol problems from the perspective of a constellation of risks that are located in both the individual and their environments, and which shift as a young person moves through adolescence. The research will reveal how substances and their use do not occur randomly in young people's lives, but are enmeshed in the core development processes that were reviewed in Chapter 2. This phenomenon not only gives rise to predictable pathways of involvement with substances, but also influences young people's use in more profound ways, as risk factors cluster together to form distinct substance misuse careers that arc into adult life. The chapter will describe why the age of initiation of use refracts young people into distinct sub-trajectories of use thereafter, and will examine the common clinical features of groups of young people on each of these trajectories. This will unify the key processes of adolescent development with the evolution of substance misuse problems, and offer a radically new perspective on understanding young people and their needs. This is critically important in understanding how young people can be supported more effectively in terms of prevention and treatment.

Models of cause and effect

Understanding the development of drug and alcohol problems demands a much deeper understanding of cause and effect than is usually brought to bear on it. We are in the habit of assuming that when two things happen close together, which in research is called correlation, one event causes the other. For example, if someone drank alcohol and then got in to a fight, we might assume that drinking alcohol caused the aggression. However, just because two events correlate does not mean that one causes the other. For example, in New York in the early 1980s there was a strong correlation between being HIV positive and owning a Liza Minnelli album. But this does not suggest that owning a Liza Minnelli album caused the HIV infection. To establish the relationship between two events requires establishing the nature and the direction of causality.

Research has advanced considerably in understanding causal relationships, and this has underpinned studies of the development of drug and alcohol problems. These studies have revealed four different types of causal pathways. Let's consider an example of a young man who becomes violent after drinking alcohol. One explanation is that he has engaged in this behaviour *because* alcohol disinhibited him. This assumes that alcohol caused the violence. Alternatively, a second explanation is that the young man may have intended to be aggressive prior to the event and alcohol gave him the courage to follow through on this intent. In this way, the direction of causality is reversed. Aggression caused him to drink alcohol. Alternatively, a third explanation is that both drinking and violence could both have been caused by a third factor, such as temperament. He could have a strong disregard for his own and others' welfare. In both cases alcohol and violence are caused by a third factor – not alcohol in itself. Finally, a fourth explanation is that peer pressure, temperament, expectancies, social norms, environmental pressure and alcohol may have *all* contributed to the resulting behaviour. In this way, alcohol was just one factor amongst a constellation of influences that led to violence. It is this more complex model of causal pathway which best accounts for the majority of human behaviours.

It is rare for human behaviour to be driven solely by a single cause. In reviewing the evolution of complex behaviours, such as those linked to mental health, criminal activity or even personality formation itself, we see it is multifactorial. In this model, behaviours are governed by a host of factors that, when combined, increase the probability of the behaviour occurring. Within this, it is important to assess how much influence each factor contributes to the outcome. For example, how much does alcohol contribute as opposed to environmental stress? And how much alcohol would need to be consumed in order to makes its contribution significant? There is no clarity regarding whether one drop or a large dose of alcohol is needed for it to influence subsequent behaviour. The analysis of causal relationships and addressing the particular issues briefly highlighted here have illuminated the dynamics of drug and alcohol problems, and what it is that drives them.

Risk and protection factors

Whilst many young people become involved in drug and alcohol use, some develop problems and others do not (Hingson et al., 2003). In light of these findings, increased interest developed in what factors accounted for these differences. It

has been driven by a public health approach which assumes that, to prevent a problem from happening, it is essential to address that factors that create it. Whilst the development of disorders such as drug and alcohol abuse do not present until adolescence, many of the factors are often present in childhood. Identification of these factors across childhood and adolescence can inform education and prevention programme developers about which of them to target and about when to divert young people from use. It can also guide the selection of optimum treatment approaches for those who experience difficulties.

To identify these factors researchers have called upon longitudinal research studies that profile large populations of young people and follow them up over long periods of time. These studies allow them to identify which particular factors at the start of the studies (intake) predict subsequent drug and alcohol involvement later (at follow-up). They are referred to as risk and protection factors. Clayton defines a risk factor as 'an individual attribute, individual characteristic, situational condition, or environmental context that increases the probability of drug use or abuse or a transition in level of involvement with drugs' (Clayton, 1992: 15). In contrast, protection factors are defined as 'an individual attribute, individual characteristic, situational condition or environmental context that inhibits, reduces, or buffers the probability of drug use or abuse or a transition in the level of involvement' (Clayton, 1992: 16). Both risk and protection factors can be present or absent, and they can occur in an individual or in the environment that they inhabit.

Whilst the concept of risk and protection factors has been widely adopted in the field, there are competing views of how they operate. One way of understanding their interaction is that risk and protection reside at either end of the same pole. The protection factor may represent the high end of one condition and the risk factor is at the lower end of the same condition. For example high parental support decreases probability of drug and alcohol use, in contrast to low family support which may increase it. Liability to use drugs and alcohol may be the result of the balance of these opposing forces. Alternatively, protection factors can be seen as buffers that limit the expression of risk factors. For example, high parental support may prevent a young person from entering a high drug-using peer group, thus reducing risk. Finally, the influence of protection factors may only be important when there is heightened risk. A young person with no risk factors in their life situation would not benefit from added protection factors. On the other hand, young people with multiple risk factors and no protection factors suffer poor outcomes. It is also important to recognise that not all young people in high-risk groups succumb to use. This introduces the concept of resilience. Resilience is the capability by which a young person is free to choose to use or refrain *regardless of the protection factors*.

In line with ecological models of adolescent development, risk and protection factors are located in both an individual young person (genetics, temperament, attitudes, social expectations, class and gender) and in their environment (family, socio-economic status, neighbourhood and peer groups). Hawkins et al.'s (1992) extensive review of studies of risk factors identified that they occur across four domains: biogenetic factors that relate to the inherited susceptibility; socio-behavioural factors including personality, activities and attitudes; the interpersonal domain which includes relationships such as with family and peers; and the cultural and social domain that contributes broader environmental influences. Their initial extensive review was criticised for failing to include coping styles, depression, anti-social personality disorder and the effect of life events like trauma or sexual abuse. Frisher et al. (2007) repeated the literature review and included a broader range of risk factors. Dillon et al. (2006) expanded this further by identifying which risk factors were amenable to change and which were not (see Table 3.1).

Research has also suggested that there are specific risk and protection factors that influence use in minority ethnic groups and which differ from use in the majority population. Background variables appear poor to be predictors of use in minority ethnic groups whereas lifestyle variables were stronger predictors. Lifestyle variables include intent to use drugs and alcohol (Maddahian et al., 1988a); family histories of alcoholism (Russell et al., 1990); perceptions of drug and alcohol using peers and role models (Newcomb & Bentler, 1986); individual and social disapproval of use (Wallace & Bachman, 1993); and experience of disruptive life events (Castro et al., 1987). Attempts to predict use in ethnic minority groups have demonstrated a greater

split. Some studies found that fixed background variables such as parents' education have the greatest influence. Other studies have suggested that lifestyle variables such as truancy, job involvement or religious involvement exert greater influence.

So, whether in mainstream or minority groups, research has consistently identified that the cause of differing probabilities of drug and alcohol involvement is multi-factorial, and that it is a combination of risk and protection factors that defines a young person's potential to experience drug or alcohol problems. Despite the identification of specific risk factors, there is no one determinant of either initiation or escalation of use. Rather, multiple risk factors combine to increase a person's risk of developing problematic behaviours. An individual's multiple risk profile is referred to as their Risk Factor Index, which shows very high reliability in predicting drug and alcohol use. For example, Bry et al. (1982) identified six risk factors for the use of ten different substances in young people. Results revealed a direct relationship between the number of risk factors and the probability of consumption and problem use. Young people in the sample with one risk factor were 1.4 times more likely to experience problem drug or alcohol use than those with no risk factors, whilst those with four risk factors were 4.5 times more likely.

These results have been replicated in other independent studies, and increasing the number of risk factors being researched has increased the predictive validity. For example, Newcomb et al.'s (1987) study included twelve risk factors in a cross section of adolescent students in seventh, ninth and eleventh grade in the US. In populations with no risk factors, only 1 per cent went on to experiment with nicotine. For those young people with seven or more risk factors, 56 per cent smoked nicotine, 18 per cent abused alcohol, 40 per cent abused cannabis, 7 per cent used cocaine and 18 per cent used other illicit drugs.

Becker & Roe (2005) identified that young people with complex life situations (such as homeless young people, truants, offenders, cared for children, young people in the sex industry and the children of drug using parents) had the highest incidence of use of Class A drugs such as heroin and cocaine. The incidence of use of Class A drugs varied within these sub-populations with truants showing the highest rates of use (16

Table 3.1: Risk factors by domain

Hawkins et al. (1992)	Frisher et al. (2007)
Culture and society: mostly outside of individuals' control (expanded by Dillon et al., 2006)	
Laws favourable to drug use	Socio-economic status
Social norms favourable to use	Education & school management
Group norms	Availability
Cost	Effective intervention
Availability	
Extreme deprivation	
Neighbourhood disorganisation	
Interpersonal: relations with family and peers can be amended or changed	
Parent and family use	Family structure (young or divorced parents)
Positive family attitudes towards drug use	Low parental discipline and monitoring
Lack of maternal warmth	Older sibling use
Poor or inconsistent family management practices	Family substance use and disorders
Permissive parenting	Parental mental health issues
Hostile father relationship	Peer use
Family conflict and disruption	
Peer rejection	
Association with drug using peers	
Psycho-behavioural: easier to address these factors through social policy or lifestyle choice	
Early/persistent problem behaviour	Early onset use
Academic failure	Other substance use
Low commitment to school	Perception of use
Alienation	Non-religious involvement
Rebelliousness	Sport
Favourable attitude to drug use	Treatment
Poor adjustments	Aggressive or violent
Early aggression	Early sexual involvement
Externalised disorders	
Positive attitude to use	
Early onset and intensity of use	
Truancy	
Social inhibition	
Biogentics: difficult or impossible to change	
Inherited genetic susceptibility to use	Gender
Psycho-physiological vulnerability to drug effects	Age
Sensation seeking and low harm avoidance	Ethnicity
Poor impulse control	Life events
	Self esteem
	Hedonism
	Depression/anxiety
	Mental illness
	ADHD
	Genetics

Based on Hawkins et al., 1992; Frisher et al., 2007; Dillion et al., 2006.

per cent) and cared for children showing the lowest (5 per cent), compared to 4 per cent of young people in the general population. However, children that belonged to more than one vulnerability group showed higher rates of use than those with any single vulnerability. Amongst young people who fell into two classifications, 39 per cent of them had used a Class A drug such as heroin or cocaine in the previous twelve months.

Newcomb & Felix-Ortiz (1992) took a slightly different approach. Rather than looking simply at risk factors, they evaluated the relationship between risk and protection factors. They assessed 14 psycho-social variables that were coded on a continuum from risk level (lower 20 per cent) to protection level (upper 20 per cent). Seven of these variables were based on typical risk factors and seven on typical protection factors. Their cross-sectional and longitudinal study of 117 teenagers found that the number of risk factors was highly predictive of use of cigarettes, alcohol, cannabis, cocaine and other hard drugs, as well as predictive of the quantity of use for cigarettes, alcohol and cannabis. A high number of protection factors demonstrated a negative association with all drug and alcohol use, with the exception of cigarette use in men. A strong relationship within each variable was not identified, suggesting that protection factors are independent of risk factors. They also identified that individuals with lower risk were less likely to use drugs regardless of the number of protection factors in their lives. In contrast, those with high risk profiles were more likely to have their use moderated by protection factors. This suggests that protection factors exert a greater influence on high risk than low risk youths, which may be why risk factors are a stronger predictor of use than protection factors. For example, Newcomb's (1995) study of Latino youths' drug and alcohol use found that young

people with a low number of risk factors were unlikely to use substances regardless of the number of protection factors in their life, whereas consumption rates in high risk groups were significantly reduced by having a high number of protection factors. This finding has been replicated in numerous studies (Sullivan & Farrell, 1999; DeWit et al., 1995; Scheier et al., 1994).

Key issues in risk and protection theory

It is important to recognise that the contribution of risk factors is not even. Some risks may account for a considerably higher degree of involvement than others. In this respect, it is important to understand the 'weight' of each risk factor in contributing to the likelihood of drug and alcohol involvement. This can be established through statistical analysis, which can identify variance amongst different risk factors, or by odds ratios. Odds ratios describe how the chances of drug and alcohol involvement are increased in young people who have a specific risk factor compared to those who do not. Dillon et al. (2006) and Sutherland (2004) used odds ratios to identify a hierarchy of risk factors in a large sample of young people (see Table 3.2).

Research regarding the weighting of risk shows a consistent pattern. The highest risk groups are strongly associated with high substance abuse

Table 3.2:   Comparison of risk factors by rank order

Analysis of 10–16-year-olds' risk factors in rank order (Dillon et al., 2006)	Analysis of 17–24-year-olds' risk factors in rank order (Dillon et al., 2006)	Odds ratios in rank order (Sutherland, 2004)*
Serious anti-social behaviour	Anti-social behaviour	High use families (Drugs)
Weak parental attitude towards bad behaviour	Early smoking	High use families (Alcohol)
Truancy & exclusion	Truancy and exclusion	Family with a substance abuser
Friends in trouble with the law	Being impulsive in temperament	Peer influence
Unhelpful temperament	Being un-sensitive in temperament	Self-esteem
Early initiation into smoking	Belonging to few or no groups	Lack of self-concern
Not receiving school meals		Delinquency
Minor anti-social behaviour		Depression
		Genetic (Drugs)
		Low academic achievement
		Sensation seeking
		Genetic (Alcohol)
		Anxiety

*Based on higher ranges shown in Sutherland (2004).
Adapted from Dillon, 2006 & Sutherland, 2004.

within families, alongside impulsive traits in young people. This research also challenges many deeply held assumptions in the field regarding perceived risks for youth, notably those concerning genetics and self-esteem. But as these two particular risk factors are given so much prominence in the field they demand further investigation.

Whilst genetic inheritance does appear to contribute to increased risk in males with alcohol (there is no evidence for a female link), this contribution is often much smaller than imagined. Sutherland's research suggested that genetic ancestry of substance problems only increased the odds ratio of having problems to 2:1 for alcohol and 2.5:1 for drug use. In other words, a genetic ancestry of this kind may double the risk in a young person compared to a peer without this family tree. In contrast, heavy peer use increases a young person's odds ratio to 7:1. Research has tried to separate those who are genetically susceptible to problematic use versus those whose consumption is environmentally driven. This has produced very mixed results. Vaillant's (1995) longitudinal study of alcoholism across the entire life span found that 27 per cent of those born to an alcoholic parent developed alcohol problems, as opposed to 5 per cent of those with difficult childhoods but no alcoholic parent. However, it also demonstrated that 73 per cent of those with alcoholic relatives did not develop problems, and that those without a family history of alcoholism were also prone. Furthermore, individuals without an alcoholic ancestry experienced earlier onset of problem drinking (29.2 years) and had poorer treatment outcomes; whilst the high genetically correlated group drank problematically much later in life (onset at 40.1) and had the best treatment outcomes. So whilst genetics make a contribution to the evolution of drug and alcohol problems, they are by no means the definitive factor.

Self-esteem is an idea that dominates youth work. Sometimes definitions of the word are confused. Self-esteem describes how much an individual values themselves, as opposed to self-efficacy which is an individual's belief in their ability to perform a task at a given level. There is often an implicit assumption that young people do bad things because they feel bad about themselves. This position misses the truism that many anti-social young people derive a huge amount of self-esteem from their anti-social behaviour. Being able to score drugs, take heroic amounts of substances, or undertake successful expeditions in shoplifting to fund substance use can be very gratifying to them. Young risk takers may be liable to have very high self-esteem that may discount the level of risk they are exposed too. Either way, poor self-esteem features as a low risk factor for youth in the vast majority of studies.

Frisher et al.'s (2007) literature review did identify four studies where there was an association between low self-esteem and use, but the correlations tended to be very low. Baumeister et al. (2003) reviewed over 15,000 studies on self-esteem and found little correlation between self-esteem and behaviour. They identified that self-esteem was only minimally related to personal success. Furthermore, self-esteem levels had no relationship to smoking, alcohol abuse or drug abuse. Low self-esteem even had a very low relationship with depression. The Monitoring the Future study (Bachman et al., 2008) of over 50,000 young people's substance use and educational attainment found that self-esteem levels had a minimal relationship with alcohol, cannabis, or cocaine use, educational achievement and delinquency. So, whilst there was a small relationship between self-esteem and these variables, self-esteem levels did not predict involvement. This suggested that self-esteem was a non-related, general variable that happens to coincide with these other factors rather than drives them.

There is even strong evidence to suggest that high self-esteem could be unhelpful. In research undertaken by Donnellan et al. (2005), individuals with high self-esteem tended to regard themselves as smarter, more attractive or more popular than they actually were. In some youth this equated with a perceived sense of specialness that they were entitled to different treatment or that rules everyone else had to follow did not apply to them. These individuals were more liable to become increasingly aggressive when this was challenged in them, making them more prone to violent outbursts. Raising self-esteem levels in young offenders, who already have a low disregard for others, can actually increase their anti-social behaviour.

The currently common overstatement of the role of self-esteem may be the result of a misunderstanding regarding the relationship between self-esteem and self-confidence. If we increase a young person's confidence that they can perform a task to a given standard and they subsequently achieve their desired goals they will experience an increase in self-esteem as a by-product of their achievement. However, it is not a balanced equation. Raising self-esteem does not increase their ability or their confidence in achieving goals. It may just leave young people feeling good about themselves in their current situation, and leave them vulnerable to increased frustration that the rest of the world does not respond to their specialness by offering them privileged entitlements. Encouraging young people to value themselves more, simply will not increase their ability to achieve any level of behavioural change.

It is also important to recognise that risk factors are not static. Some risk factors can be short-lived, such as mood, whilst others can be enduring such as genes. Risk and protection factors may occur in different levels at different ages in the life course. Protection factors may reverse their influence. For example, high parental monitoring may be a protection factor in early adolescence, but may become a risk factor if it continues into late adolescence. Frisher et al. (2007) conceptualised this shifting pattern of risk and protection factors from pre-natal lifestyles to early adulthood (see Table 3.3)

1. Maternal smoking; maternal drug use.
2. Parental discipline, family cohesion, parental substance use, parental monitoring, sibling drug use, early life trauma.
3. Truancy, educational attainment, problems at school, school rules.
4. Friends' drug use, friends' anti-social behaviour.
5. Low self-esteem, hedonism, attention deficit hyperactivity disorder, phobias, depression, anxiety, aggressive behaviour to solve problems.
6. Getting intoxicated, escape from negative moods.
7. Low household income, lack of neighbourhood amenities.
8. Early onset of smoking (age 11) and drinking (age 12).
9. As well as the inverse, there may be a range of additional protective factors such as negative consequences of drug taking, not considering drugs as part of lifestyle, not being exposed to drugs, adherence to conventional values, involvement in religious or sporting activities, strategies for resisting peer pressure to use drugs, positive future plans.

If we transpose the key ideas developed in Chapter 2, we see the same background factors of genetics, family structure and parenting style accord with many of the key risk factors identified. 'Prenatal Environment' and 'Family Experience' present the earliest range of risk as the child's environment exerts such as powerful influence at this stage. Early risk also emerges in the temperament domain due to its strong link with 'Genetic' inheritability. As a young person begins the transition from childhood into adolescence, these forces wane. Key developmental processes such as cognitive and physical development, relational shifts into peer groups, identity formation, life task achievements and positive expectancies of use become increasingly prominent in early adolescence. Hence 'School', 'Friends' and 'Socio-economic' position exert the greatest influence at this time. An adolescent is increasingly capable of expressing greater autonomy in making life choices, influenced by their 'Psychological Traits'. Young people select peer environments that match their temperaments (Gotham et al., 2003). 'Psychological Traits' and 'Reason for Use' drive personal motivation to use and may set them on a path to 'Early Life Use' of drugs and alcohol. Reviewing risk factors by age demonstrates that they do not occur at random but are embedded in the fabric of the life course.

The order of risk factors reveals an interesting pattern. Risk factors are accumulative as opposed to additive. This is to say that young people are not born with a fixed number of risk factors that they must evade in order to avoid drug or alcohol involvement. Instead risk factors accumulate across the life course in a stratified process. Young people may be born with a genetic heritage or in impoverished social environments. These account for background vulnerability factors, which make use more probable rather than definite. Genes do not 'know' that drugs and alcohol are out there. There needs to be an inclination in the individual towards initiation of use. These initiation risk factors include up-bringing, family use and positive expectancies as well as opportunity, availability, cost and social permissiveness (Boys et al., 1999).

This demonstrates why positive expectancies are so critical in the evolution of drug and alcohol problems. A young person may have a bank of vulnerability factors in their life prior to use. But these risk factors are not activated until a young person initiates consumption. When young

Table 3.3: Potential development framework for risk factors for drug use among young people. Frisher et al., 2007)

Risk and protective factors

Age	Prenatal environment (1)	Genetic	Family experience (2)	School (3)	Friends (4)	Psychological traits (5)	Reason for drug use (6)	Socio-economic (7)	Early life use (8)	Protective factors (9)
– 9 mths	●	●								
Birth	●	●								
Infancy (0–2)		●	■							
Early childhood (3–8)		●	●	■						
Middle childhood (9–11)		●	●	●		●		■	●	■
Adolescence (12–18)		●	■	●	●	●	●	■	●	●

● indicates a relatively strong factor; ■ indicates a relatively weak factor.

people have positive expectations of use they tend to use more drugs and alcohol and do so at a younger age (Boys et al., 2001; Boys & Marsden, 2003). Positive expectancies become the bridge that connects existing risk factors in a young person's life to possible future risk derived from continued use. As positive expectancies bias young people's perception and recall of intoxication, they also negate young people's awareness of this new tier of risks. This provides a latency period that allows consumption to become established whilst these overtly positive expectancies reduce young people's ability to recognise or adjust to problems.

This new tier of risk factors operates to maintain consumption once initiated. It includes identity, belonging, euphoria and excitement, and it may satisfy an impatience for adulthood. Use may also be sustained to avoid negative mood states such as boredom, alienation, coping or relieving ego discomfort in marginalised youth. Continued involvement can interrupt normal social functioning through increased aggression, the formation of an anti-social identity or truancy. This increased involvement then elicits a wider range of risk factors. Involvement with a heavy using peer group may bring a young person into new social networks where a more diverse array of substances becomes available. They may begin to experience social problems as a result of their use, such as family conflict, exclusion from school or involvement with the law. These stresses can escalate use as a means of coping. Immersion in a drug using sub-culture will bring with it a range of difficulties such as violence, victimisation, bereavements and stigmatisation. At this stage drug and alcohol use devours itself by generating the crises that continued consumption hopes to avail.

So, just because a young person is susceptible to early vulnerability factors does not mean that they will inevitably progress. It does mean that if they do move forward in their use they will encounter a new tier of risk factors. And should they trigger this new tier, they will encounter additional levels of risk. In this way, risk factors snowball across the life course in a cascading effect. Drug and alcohol problems in later adolescence are the expression of risk factors established at an earlier age (Silva & Stanton, 1996). Alternatively, Oetting & Beauvais (1986) argued that risk factors should be understood only in so far as they lead a young person to enter into a high consuming peer group. This is

because the peer group will hold so much influence over a young person in between their emergence from their family and their establishment of an autonomous self.

Age of initiation

As risk factors for drug and alcohol problems are embedded in the life course, the age at which young people initiate use is particularly important. In the vast majority of studies, age of initiation is the single biggest predictor of future drug and alcohol problems during adolescence and early adulthood (Robins & Przybeck, 1985; Humphrey & Friedman, 1986; Grant et al., 2006). Vega et al.'s (2002) studies of alcohol initiation in young people across seven Western countries all demonstrated a strong relationship between the age of initiation and subsequent increased risk of problematic use. In US studies, despite considerable variation in drinking laws from state to state, the link between age of initiation and subsequent problems remains remarkably similar, and the pattern appears to hold true in all Western countries (Ferri et al., 2003). Research differs in opinion regarding the critical age for initiation that leads to problem use. The cut-off point for early initiation varies between 'the age of 13' (Gruber et al., 1996), 'before the age of 14' (Muthen & Muthen, 2000), or 'at the age of 15' (Chou & Pickering, 1992). Initiation of use prior to the age of 14 substantially increases risk in later adolescence (Grant et al., 2001) with risk at its greatest when consumption starts very early at age 11 (Dawson, 2000).

But while the precise critical age is moot, it is certain that the greatest risk that an individual will develop problematic alcohol use occurs in those individuals who initiate consumption prior to the age of 15 (Dryfoos, 1990; Hawkins, E. et al., 1987; Higgins, 1988). These individuals are six-to-ten times more likely to experience problematic use in later life than their peers (Robins & Przybeck, 1985). Hingson et al.'s (2006) survey of 43,093 adults found that young people who began drinking prior to the age of 14 were far more likely to experience alcohol dependence within 10 years of initiation compared to the later onset group who commenced drinking at age 21. Amongst the early onset drinking population, 47 per cent met the criteria for dependence by the age of 21 and 66 per cent met the criteria by the age of 25. They also experienced a far higher rate of dependence symptoms 'within the last year' and experienced multiple dependence episodes. Similar results were found by Grant & Dawson (1997) in their analysis of 42,862 adults as part of the National Longitudinal Alcohol Epidemiologic Study. They found that 45 per cent of adults who had begun drinking prior to the age of 14 developed symptoms of alcohol dependence compared to only 10 per cent of those who began after the age of 21.The risk of developing alcohol problems decreased by 14 per cent for every year of delayed initiation. This finding has been substantiated across ethnic groups within the US (Gil et al., 2004) as well as within European (Pitkanen et al., 2005) and South American populations (Viera et al., 2007) but with smaller samples. In contrast, initiating alcohol use 'on time' fosters social bonding, cohesion and harmony with peers.

Similar findings have been identified in drug initiation. King & Chassin (2007) explored drug and alcohol initiation in a sample of 454 adolescents with an average age of 13.22. Of this population, 246 had at least one biological or custodial parent with alcohol dependency whilst 208 had no alcoholic parents. These young people were followed up periodically until the average age of 25. Interestingly, they did not find that early initiation of alcohol use predicted future alcohol dependence but found that social and economic factors did. The early onset of alcohol use was strongly related to the later drug dependence. This suggests that early alcohol involvement can serve as a primer for other substances. In this regard, early age of onset of alcohol use serves as a 'marker' of future risk. It may also be important to distinguish the level of consumption with future problem use. Early light experimentation and early heavy consumption are not always separated in these studies but may lead to different outcomes (Weber et al., 1989).

There are two rival theories regarding the significance of the age of initiation. The General Vulnerability Hypothesis (Prescott & Kendler, 1999) suggests that early initiation and later onset of problems are generated by the same underlying susceptibility in the individual. This could be genetic, parental, linked to a personality trait or psychopathological in origin (Zucker, 1994). The second theory is the Causation Hypothesis (Gotham et al., 2003). This suggests that earlier use places the young person on a trajectory towards heavier and more frequent use that has its own direct and indirect consequences.

This is akin to the snowballing effect of risk factors, where the triggering of one risk factor opens up new levels of risk, which might include negative labelling, segregation into older and more deviant peer groups or even legal sanctions. These can all interfere with the mastery of normal developmental tasks or healthy coping strategies, which leaves a young person developmentally delayed in their life course. This delay is carried into the subsequent phases of the individual's life, curtailing educational-occupational development and relationship formation. As such, the Causation Hypothesis supposes that, if the age of initiation into substance use is delayed for as long as possible, it would have significant impact on curtailing future problem use, and young people would be better equipped for future transitions. At present there is not sufficient evidence to support either position definitively, although research does side with the Causation Hypothesis, and this has important implications for prevention and education programmes.

Gateway Theory

The age of initiation also predicts the typical sequence of progression through use of different types of substances. Gateway Theory is the name given to the exploration of these drug using sequences. The idea is often confused with the discredited 'Stepping Stone Theory'. Stepping Stone Theory was developed in the 1930s and posited that a young person using soft drugs would *inevitably* progress into harder substances. This conclusion was derived from a misreading of clinical evidence. Heroin users incarcerated in prison or seeking treatment often reported that they had used cannabis first. Researchers at this time assumed that cannabis use led to heroin use. Their research failed to account for the huge population of cannabis users that did not progress into other drugs, and end up in prison or require treatment.

Gateway Theory was developed by Kandel (1975) and explored the sequence of use more deeply. The theory was based on research findings which demonstrated that patterns of drug and alcohol consumption tended to be progressive and hierarchical. Kandel identified that involvement began with initiation into tobacco, then beer and wine, and then moving through cannabis. This was followed by initiation into cocaine, solvents, hallucinogens and heroin for some. The Gateway Theory suggested that the movement through this sequence was probabilistic, rather than deterministic as Stepping Stone theory had posited. It suggests that involvement in one substance increased the risk of involvement in other substances, but this progression is not inevitable. 'The notion of development stages in drug behaviour does not imply, however, that these stages are either obligatory or universal, nor that all persons must progress through each in turn.' (Kandel, 2002: 3). Engaging in drug or alcohol consumption at one stage does not equate with progressing to the next. The sequence may be interrupted by other factors. For example, protective factors such as good academic achievement and good parental communication appear able to impede movement from lower orders of drug and alcohol use to progressively higher levels (Stronski et al., 2000).

Certainly, studies of the sequence of substance initiation support a probabilistic gateway sequence. Young adolescents tend to use the substances that are cheap and widely available to them such as tobacco and then alcohol. Research suggests that the use of these substances by the age of 11 increases the probability that young people will go on to cannabis. This then increases their risk of using other substances such as stimulants, hallucinogens and opiates. Furthermore, young people who initiate use at a young age tend use higher amounts, and are most liable to progress through the full sequence of use than those with a later onset of initiation. For example, in one study (Kandel & Yamaguchi, 1993) over 71 per cent of young people who smoked cannabis more than 300 times went on to use cocaine. In comparison, only 38.7 per cent of those who smoked cannabis 12–100 times, and only 12.8 per cent of those who had only smoked cannabis once or twice moved into cocaine use. Kandel & Yamaguchi (2002) also found that heroin users in their sample had all initiated tobacco use at the earliest age, 12.6 years old on average. Cocaine but non-heroin users started smoking tobacco at an average age of 14. Individuals who went on to use cannabis but no other drug started smoking tobacco at 14.6 years old. Whilst individuals that went on to only drink alcohol commenced smoking at age 15.8 years old on average. The age of initiation of tobacco use is the strongest predictor of the subsequent sequence of drug involvement across the rest of adolescence.

It is also important to note that the sequence of use is not always fixed, with some users reporting that cocaine and heroin were their entry point into substance misuse (Sanju & Hamday, 2005). This appears to be the case with heavy inner-city users. These young people appear to enter into higher levels of drug use at initiation. For example Mackesey-Amiti et al. (1997) found 33 per cent of drug users in an inner-city New York sample moved through the predicted alcohol-cannabis-hard drug sequence. Others entered into the post-alcohol sequence with harder substances first. In this study, 60 per cent of young people started the post-alcohol sequence with cannabis compared to 90 per cent in other general samples. This leap-frogging might occur for a number of reasons. Practically, young people may initiate into harder substances first due to their wider availability in certain inner-city locations. Second, inner-city areas may cultivate different norms regarding drug use which do not stigmatise harder drugs, making their use more socially acceptable. Third, it may also be the result of a gender divide. Young women may be at risk of leap-frogging into initiation of harder drug use before cannabis, if they engage in relationships with older males. These older males will have already progressed through a typical sequence and have established use of harder substances. Young women who experience early onset puberty can accelerate their consumption if they form attachments to these older males.

The existence of a sequence of consumption, and the fact that some young people can subvert its order, invites an examination of why these sequences occur. Hawkins et al. (2002) examined this question in a study that followed 808 students from the age of 11 until they were 22. These young people were interviewed nine times during this period, with particular regard to their favourable attitudes to nicotine, alcohol and cannabis. In general, young people consistently showed higher degrees of favourability to alcohol throughout this period, with nicotine next and then cannabis last. Based on these findings, they then examined the ages of initiation of these substances in order to test the Gateway Theory. They hypothesised that young people would follow an initiation sequence that matched their social norms (alcohol-nicotine-cannabis). Furthermore, with its high favourability, they also expected that young people would be more likely to use alcohol as a sole substance or alcohol and tobacco in combination. Conversely, they hypothesised that cannabis use should be more likely to occur after they had tried alcohol and tobacco.

Hawkins et al.'s (2002) subsequent findings supported these assumptions. At the time of the first interview, 26 per cent of young people used alcohol solely, 5 per cent had initiated tobacco solely and none had initiated cannabis. Whilst the rate of initiation into use increased over the research period, these figures preserved rank order over subsequent interviews. Initiation into one substance did increase the likelihood that the individual would progress into other substances' use, but this did not mean that all young people progressed though all levels. Alcohol and tobacco were more likely to be used in combination across the study, whilst cannabis use tended to follow the initiation of these legal substances. Combinations of tobacco and cannabis only or tobacco and hard drugs only were non-existent (see Graph 3.1).

This research identified key differences in social norms regarding alcohol and other substances. As young people's attitudes become increasingly favourable to tobacco and cannabis use they were more likely to initiate the use of these substances. This was not the case with alcohol. Parental norms regarding alcohol use were a stronger restraining factor on initiation of

alcohol than parental supervision and monitoring. This may be the product of alcohol's wider social acceptability. Parents may enforce boundaries on young people whilst at the same time be more permissive about their offspring's use of alcohol. Parental supervision and monitoring style was a bigger influence on delaying initiation of cannabis use, but parents were also more likely to have a negative view of cannabis at the same time. Interestingly, the strength of maternal attachment had little impact on either drug or alcohol consumption. This may be the result of the re-negotiation of the parent-child relationship in early adolescence, where the young person detaches from parents by the age of 14. This was also the point in the life course where their expectancies of use became increasingly positive.

The progression through the gateway may also be driven by other factors. Young people must also have the opportunity to physically access these substances. This is difficult for them to do in light of legal restrictions regarding illicit drugs and the complexity of finding social networks willing to supply them. As we have seen, the majority of young people remain embedded in narrow and protected environments that are removed from adult dealing networks. Golub & Johnson (2002) suggested that the sequence of substance involvement is simply a reflection of

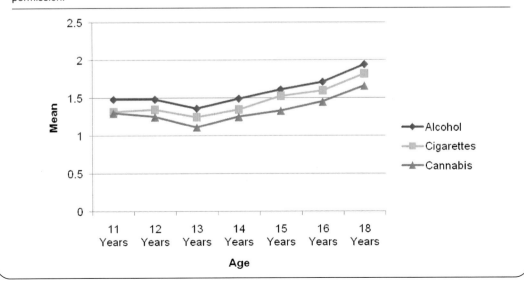

Graph 3.1: Mean level of norms favouring cigarette, alcohol, and marijuana use across time (n = 764). All mean norm levels were significantly different at 0.5 level or better. Hawkins et al., 2002. Reprinted with permission.

the ordering of opportunities to access different drugs across the life course. Early initiation is most likely to occur with low-cost and highly accessible substances such as tobacco and alcohol. Peer supply of cannabis offers a second tier of accessibility. In early adolescence the opportunity to obtain harder drugs is significantly limited as these drugs are expensive and remote from their sphere of relationships. They have to find, and be permitted to enter into, wider drug dealing networks to access them. This caps their access and restricts consumption. But as the young people's social world expands through increasing levels of autonomy and financial independence, access to a wider range of substances expands with it.

Informal social restrictions on availability have changed. Use of the internet to access mail order legal highs is circumventing both the formal legal barriers and informal social barriers to consumption. The internet offers anonymous and unfettered access to a myriad of substances. This has accelerated shifts in consumption as the suppliers of these substances adapt rapidly to changes in the law. As these 'under-the-net' substances become outlawed, new substances soon take their place. The short and long term effects of these substances is unknown. This makes even the most pragmatic approach, such as harm minimisation, difficult to apply. No research to date has been conducted on the sequence of over the net legal highs. But the use of new technology is likely to have circumvented the previous ordering of drug involvement. Legal substances such as tobacco and alcohol are still liable to remain the gateway substances, but they will become a portal to a much wider exotic range of intoxicants. The fact that young people have rapidly adopted both this new route of access and a broader range of unknown substances accords with Morral et al.'s (2002) findings. They suggested that drug and alcohol involvement and the willingness to seek them out are predicted by a strong desire in a young person to want to take substances. And once they master intoxication of one substance it may increase their confidence that they can then manage other substances that are perceived as harder.

Substance abuse trajectories

Research on the evolution of young people's drug and alcohol problems reveals that several strands of influence converge to increase the probability of involvement. They include the stratified risk factors that occur across the life course, the age at which use is initiated and the sequence of substance involvement that is followed from licit to illicit drugs. Advances in research have illuminated how these three areas combine. Longitudinal studies that follow up young people over the course of adolescence can track young people's risk profiles, the age in which they initiate use and their subsequent level of consumption over time. These studies have revealed how risk factors cluster together at certain points in the life course and create distinct pathways into problem use. These pathways are referred to as trajectories or sub-trajectories. 'A trajectory is a pathway or line of development during the life span, such as work life, parenthood, or criminal behaviour. Trajectories refer to long term patterns of behaviour and are marked by a sequence of transitions.' (Hser et al., 2007b: 518). The current research base has consistently revealed four primary sub-trajectories of drug and alcohol involvement which account for over 90 per cent of young people's usage, though it needs to be understood that some linguistic confusion does arise as various researchers use different terms to name the populations of young people in these sub-trajectories. Based on data from the large scale Alcohol Misuse Prevention Study, Chassin et al. (2002) identified distinct sub-trajectories of binge alcohol use in young people. This revealed a very typical pattern of consumption, with Early Heavy users demonstrating the highest frequency of binge use. Later Onset youth showed more moderate patterns, whilst non-bingers in adolescence carried this low incidence into adulthood (see Graph 3.2).

All trajectory research shows this pattern, regardless of the substance. *Normative* substance consumption has a late adolescent onset and tends to be limited to tobacco and alcohol use with some light cannabis use. This is the most common trajectory amongst those whose consumption remains low across adolescence and into adulthood. These youth tend show the highest level of social functioning and psychological adjustment as they have almost completed adolescence by the time they have initiated use. These young people account for 20–66 per cent of research populations according to different studies (White et al., 2000; Hill et al., 2000). *Stable-moderate* drinkers engage in some heavy drinking across adolescence and early

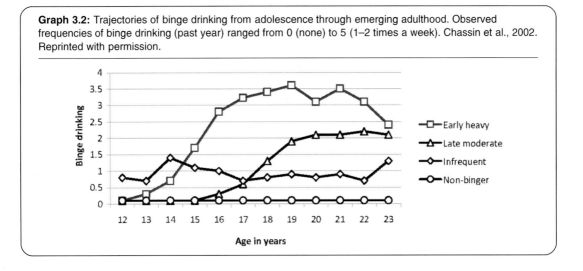

Graph 3.2: Trajectories of binge drinking from adolescence through emerging adulthood. Observed frequencies of binge drinking (past year) ranged from 0 (none) to 5 (1–2 times a week). Chassin et al., 2002. Reprinted with permission.

adulthood but do not increase or decrease use dramatically. They account for approximately 33 per cent of young people (Chassin et al., 2002; Tucker et al., 2003). *Fling* drinkers experience a period of limited heavy drinking that peaks and then declines in late adolescence, often corresponding with the university years (Chassin et al. 2002; Tucker et al., 2003).

The high risk groups include *chronic heavy* drinkers and *late onset heavy* drinkers who do not decrease their drinking in their twenties (Bates & Labouvie, 1997; Schulenberg et al., 1996a; White et al., 2000). The *chronic heavy* group always display the earliest onset of initiation and is predictive of the highest subsequent level of involvement. Whilst they are the smallest group, these young people are the most at risk from developing severe substance related problems by early adulthood. Early drinking is also associated with a greater risk of a wide array of health problems including obesity, hypertension and physical illness (Oesterle et al., 2004). In nearly all cases, the *early chronic* group hailed from problematic backgrounds, had the poorest social functioning and were the least likely to make the transition into full adult life. *Late-onset* drinkers start drinking in their late teens but with a rapid escalation (Casswell et al., 2002; Flory et al., 2004).

Some *early heavy* users did decrease consumption across adolescence, and we can see some adjustment in these early onset populations. For example Colder et al. (2002) found that *decreasers* begin drinking heavily in early adolescence but reduce consumption across the later teen years. Schulenberg et al. (2005) found

the same process could occur in *early onset heavy* cannabis users. *Decreasers* in this study were remarkably similar to the *long-term chronic* users at the start of the research. However, they were able to turn their life around profoundly across adolescence and came to more closely resemble *abstainers*. Likewise, the *late onset fling* users in the same study were akin to *increased* users but their ability to find a pathway into pro-social life also brought them closer to abstainers. This demonstrates that these sub-trajectories are not inflexible, which is important in understanding both the potential and the focus of treatment programmes for young people (see Table 3.4 which simplifies the various categories of alcohol and substance users described in the research just reviewed).

The picture of drugs' and alcohol's capacity to interrupt the developmental process is most vivid when seen from this vantage point of the patterns of trajectories and sub-trajectories. Early initiators all demonstrate profound developmental delay and high levels of social exclusion. In comparison, every study shows that the late onset group demonstrate higher social functioning and a greater capacity to integrate into a pro-social adult life. Furthermore, the earlier that young people become involved in drug and alcohol use then the longer their subsequent using trajectory becomes. This is borne out in Hser et al.'s (2007a) research which was a 33-year follow-up of heroin users. Their study found that some opiate users used across the entire reporting period, some stopped using in their thirties and others stopped use in their twenties. They differed little in terms

Table 3.4:   Comparisons of sub-trajectory populations in longitudinal research

Research Substance Sample size	Chassin et al. (2002) Alcohol (binge drinking) 446	Schulenberg et al. (2005) Cannabis 19,952	Flory et al. (2004) Alcohol and cannabis 481	Hser et al. (2007a) Heroin 471
	Heavy early onset (13–14) users were more likely to have parents with alcohol problems, show anti-social behaviour, and have peers involved in heavy drinking. Boys showed high externalised symptoms but low on depression. They were also more likely to be involved in drug use. Showed the highest risk for adult substance misuse disorders.	**Chronic** users were more likely to be unemployed, living away from an active social life with other users. Showed binge drinking, crime, aggression and high levels of risk taking. Smoked cannabis as a coping mechanism. Poor academic achievement and truancy.	**Early onset** (10–12) alcohol users were less school/religiously involved, and showed conduct disorder, low peer resistance high sensation seeking and had positive expectations of use.	**Stable high users had** problem behaviours at school, family difficulties, mental health issues and were drug involved before age 15. Earlier onset of use than early quitters and left home earlier. Reported higher levels of childhood poverty and family mental health problems. Also had a high rate of alcohol problems.
	Infrequent early onset (13–14) users showed a low frequency of alcohol consumption. They had a high incidence of parental alcoholism and, for girls, showed signs of internalised disorders, particularly depression.	**Increased** users were more likely to be unemployed, living away from parents, with an active social life, and started smoking as a coping strategy. Greater difficulty in establishing an adult role for themselves than fling users.	**Early onset** cannabis users were more likely to be involved with alcohol, have lower self-esteem, low school involvement, higher conduct disorder symptoms, poor family relationship and positive expectancies of use.	**Late decelerator** users had problem behaviours at school, family difficulties, mental health issues and were drug involved before age 15. Earlier onset of use than early quitters. More likely to have been involved in treatment.
	Late moderate (16–17) users had a later onset of consumption and scored higher on all measures of psychological adjustment compared to early onset groups. Parents were less likely to have problems. Peers were less likely to be heavy alcohol or drug using. Lowest incidence of substance misuse problem in later life.	**Fling** users were similar to the increased group at intake. With an active social life, they reduced their binge drinking pattern into adulthood. Appeared to find a life path for themselves that reduced their consumption.	**Later onset** (15–16) alcohol users were more likely to be school or religiously involved and low on conduct disorder and impulsive behaviour.	**Early quitters** had problem behaviours at school, family difficulties, and mental health issues and were drug involved before age 15, with later onset in heroin initiation. More likely to still be employed at follow up, had better scores in mental health and had been involved in treatment.

Non-bingers had the best range of psycho-social variables and were the least at risk for developing alcohol or drug problems. They were more likely to be involved in higher education.

Decreased users were similar to the chronic users at intake but use subsided dramatically. More likely to be married and be parents in early adulthood. Became less inclined to smoke as a coping strategy. Reduced binge drinking pattern. Reported the highest increase in wellbeing.

Abstainers were more likely to be married and be parents in early adulthood. More likely to be college graduates and employed, religiously involved, socialised less. Had less cannabis using friends and were not involved in crime. Reduced binge drinking pattern

Rare users were more likely to be college graduates, living away from parents.

Later onset (14–16) cannabis users had better family relationships and higher self-esteem.

Non-alcohol involved users were similar to the later alcohol scores.

Non-cannabis users had better positive relationships, were school involved and had negative using expectancies.

of their background profiles other than the age of onset of use. Heroin users who continued to use the drug across their life course initiated opiate use at the age of 14. The sub-population of heroin users that remitted in their twenties initiated heroin use at an average age of 14.6 years old. The difference in age of onset between these two groups was small but it had a dramatic effect on their outcomes. The rate of development is so great during adolescence that even short disruptions in developmental progression can have catastrophic impacts. For example, an adult who takes a year out on sabbatical will not find it too difficult to re-adjust to everyday life on its completion because of the relative stability of adult life course. In comparison, a 13-year-old who loses a year will experience profound delays in development. Not only will they be under greater pressure to catch up with their peers, they will also be confronting additional life tasks for which they are unrehearsed.

Understanding these sub-trajectories becomes vital in the development of effective prevention and treatment approaches. Historically, young people have been treated as a homogenous group. They tend to assessed on the amounts that they use, first and foremost. Where greater recognition of their needs has occurred this has largely been organised by *where* (or what) young people are, rather than *who* the young people are. For example, policy has often recognised higher support needs in offenders, truants, care leavers etc. But these policies have not been clear on the nature of their needs. The reason that this separation of specific sub-populations has not occurred is largely due to the problems posed by *equifinity* and *mulitifinity*. *Equifinity* describes the fact that multiple pathways can lead to the same outcome, whilst *mutlitfinity* describes how pathways can diverge from a common point. If a large population of young people are taking the same amount of drugs it is easy to assume they are similar. However, the pathways that led them to this point, and the pathways that will lead them out can be completely different. Failure to recognise this has led to young people having received the same intervention, regardless of the complexity of their need.

Trajectories and mental health

The age of initiation and length of using careers in young drug and alcohol users in these sub-trajectories is, on its own, quite revealing. But the ability of trajectory research to examine the psychological and social risk profiles of young people within these sub-trajectories demonstrates further complexity in the pattern of drug and alcohol involvement. This research has also been found able to predict a wide range of multi-problem trajectories in young people, such as changes in offending behaviour across the life course (D'Unger et al., 1998; Moffit, 1997; Nagin et al., 1995). There is a significant crossover in these studies between crime, mental health and drug and alcohol problems (Bui et al., 2000; Ellickson & Morton, 1999). For example, Ferdinand et al. (2001) found that risk factors developed in a chain that led to engagement with deviant peers, followed by delinquent behaviour and ended in substance abuse. Their studies have identified that each trajectory shares common features. A Youth Lifestyles Study (Goulden & Sondhi, 2001) showed that rates of exclusion from school, truancy, offending, homelessness and running away predicted the use of Class A drugs such as heroin. From this perspective it is clear that young people cannot be filtered into neat categories of substance misuse *or* mental health *or* offending. There are not disparate groups, but rather individuals with disparate needs. These needs transcend the artificial boundaries that exist in the traditional organisation of service provision.

Pre-eminent in this overlap is the relationship between significant mental health problems and substance misuse. Every study has demonstrated a higher prevalence of substance use in groups with significant mental health problems (Poulin et al., 2005; Brook et al., 1998; Weinberg et al., 1998; Kandel et al., 1999). Grant et al. (2004) conducted a large-scale survey of 43,093 people in the general population that included consideration of every diagnosis for all mood disorders. This sample was then weighted to be representative of the US population as a whole. The incidence of diagnosed mental illness was small at less than 1 per cent of the population. However, all mood disorders were strongly related to substance misuse problems within the last 12 months – even when drug induced disorders were accounted for. The exception was with alcohol when it occurred with a single mental health disorder where the relationship was less strong. In general, the more severe cases of dependence on drugs and alcohol showed the highest correlation with mental health disorders.

Based on these figures, 40.7 per cent of problem alcohol users seeking treatment would have at least one concurrent mood disorder. Amongst problem drug users seeking help, 60 per cent had a concurrent mood disorder and 43 per cent had an anxiety disorder.

In the UK, considerable covariance has been identified between mental illness and substance use amongst adolescents. Boys et al.'s (2003) study of 2,624 young people aged 13–15 identified that heavy involvement in one drug predicted involvement in other substances, particularly tobacco, alcohol and cannabis. Within this sample, 171 young people had an emotional disorder, whilst 136 had other problems such as behavioural, disruptive or eating disorders. Depressed young people were five times more likely to smoke tobacco, had double the risk of regular drinking and of lifetime cannabis use. Regular cannabis users were seven times more likely to have a mental health problem than non-users in the sample. Regular smokers were five times more likely to report an 'other' mental health diagnosis. These risks increased with poly-use, where smokers and drinkers were 6.92 times more likely to have a disorder. Young people that used tobacco, alcohol and cannabis were 8.77 times more likely to have an 'other' mental health diagnosis. These findings are in accordance with other studies on the relationship between cannabis and psychotic illness. Green et al. (2005) reviewed 53 studies of young cannabis users and psychosis. A higher prevalence of psychotic illness was found in nearly all studies. It is important to stress that this study did not examine whether cannabis caused these problems, but the focussed on prevalence of both disorders.

Externalised and internalised disorders

Kuperman et al. (2001) studied the relationship between externalised mental health disorders (ADD/ADHD, Oppositional Defiance Disorder and Conduct Disorder) and the development of alcohol dependence in 13–17 year olds. This research concluded that the externalised disorders occurred first and was followed by misuse of all classes of drugs. Giancola & Parker (2001) examined the relationship between increased drug use in young people aged 10–16 and psychiatric disorders, aggression, and relationships with delinquent peers. Aggressive behaviour and peer involvement figured highly

in the development of substance misuse problems, whilst psychiatric features such as poor cognitive functioning and poor attention levels also predicted higher levels of use. When social exclusion and psychiatric disorders are combined it produced an even higher range of risk. Lee et al. (2010) followed 310 children into adulthood, gathering data regarding their use of alcohol and cannabis at ages 18, 20 and 22. They identified two clear trajectories for young people who go on to develop dependence on both these substances. Risk factors included being male, dropping out of school, early age of initiation and being involved with other drugs. They were also more likely to have received a diagnosis of an externalised disorder such as Conduct Disorder or Oppositional Defiance Disorder in childhood. Attention Deficit Disorder was not such a high predictor of late life dependence.

Similarly, young people with internalised mental health disorders also appear to be at higher risk of the development of substance related problems. Crum et al. (2008) followed two cohorts of children (sample sizes of 1,196 and 1,115 respectively) into adolescence. This research found that there was a strong relationship between high levels of depression in childhood and subsequent alcohol involvement. Those with severe depression in childhood were twice as likely as those without depression to develop alcohol dependence, and to do so at a much faster rate. Wu et al.'s (2006) study of 1,119 Puerto Rican 10 to 13-year-olds identified a similar pattern. Subsequent alcohol problems were predicted by the severity of pre-adolescent depression. However, they found that protection factors of parental involvement and support could diminish the risk. Conversely, exposure to parental mental health problems or violence could increase it. Woodward & Fergusson (2001) followed 1,265 children over a 21-year period. They found a strong association with the number of anxiety disorders in childhood and increased risk of anxiety disorder in later life. They also found higher rates of tobacco, alcohol and drug use in this population, and that they were more likely to experience alcohol or drug dependence in later life. Similarly Rey et al. (2002) found that in a population of 1,261 young people, 14 per cent of depressed youth used cannabis compared to 6 per cent of non-depressed youth. A summary of prevalence studies is described in Table 3.5.

Brown et al.'s (2005b) analysis of these various research studies suggested that these problems

Table 3.5: Summary of co-occurring mental health and substance abuse prevalence studies.

Disorder	Prevalence with substance abuse
Hyperkinetic disorder (ADHD/ADD)	• Chan et al. (2008) found, in under 15s, that 63.3 per cent of alcohol use disordered youth also had ADHD. • Molina et al. (2002) identified 30 per cent of youth in a treatment population had severe ADHD symptoms.
Conduct disorders	• Chan et al. (2008) found, in under 15s, 74.2 per cent of substance use disordered youth also had conduct disorder. • Molina et al. (2002) identified 73 per cent of youth in an alcohol treatment population who had conduct disorder symptoms.
Oppositional defiance disorder	• Clark et al. (1997) found ODD youth were twice as likely to experience substance use disorders. • Armstrong & Costello (2002) identified ODD as the most common disorder associated with substance misuse problems in youth.
Self-harm	• Bell et al. (2010) found 63.3 per cent of A&E presentation for self-harm involved alcohol use. • Greydanus & Shek (2009) found a high correlation between self-harm and substance abuse. • Klonsky (2011) found 15.4 per cent of self-harmers were also in substance abuse treatment programmes.
Anxiety including PTSD	• Clark et al. (1994) found anxiety to be the most common disorder in substance treatment populations. • Kessler et al. (1995) found 5 per cent of young substance misusers had PTSD. • Abram et al. (2004) found 11 per cent of young offenders exhibited symptoms of PTSD.
Depression	• Chan et al. (2008) found 52.7 per cent of substance use disordered youth also had depression. • Kaminer & Bukstein (2008) found 24–50 per cent of adolescents with substance problems had depression.
Anorexia/Bulimia	• Krug et al. (2008) found 35 per cent of women with an eating disorder had a substance misuse disorder. • Root et al. (2010) found a higher incidence of substance misuse issues in anorexic and bulimic women. • Wiederman & Pryor (1996) found higher incidence of substance abuse in bulimic rather than anorexic adolescent girls.
Obsessive compulsive disorder	• Understudied area, but Rasmussen & Tsuang (1986) reported that 12 per cent of OCD clients in a clinical population had a lifetime history of alcoholism.

converge in young people producing three critical trajectories for adolescent alcohol problems, and that they are likely to also be relevant to substance misuse.

Three critical trajectories

In the early onset trajectory, 'personality/ temperament' risk begins prior to exposure to drug and alcohol use and originates in high sensation seeking, behaviour disinhibition, low impulse control and hyperactive traits. Initiating smoking in late childhood and early adolescence, their use is liable to cluster with a wide range of problem behaviours. This includes early offending, early truancy and poor educational achievement. These young people can be characterised as being an *externalised* group. They are more likely to experience trans-generational issues, growing up in problem-using households that experience high rates of deprivation, poverty, unemployment; and they are exposed to a greater risk of abuse. These risk factors are the most heavily weighted, leading them into consumption at an early age. At this younger age range they are also under greater environmental influence as they have not developed personal autonomy nor made the emotional separation from parents. High parental use also gives them immediate access to a wider range of substances in unsupervised environments at an early age.

The mid-onset trajectory initiates consumption around the onset of puberty (and can be defined as a 'psychopathological risk' group. Psychopathological risk refers to the type of mental health problems that also occur at this time). As we saw in Chapter 2, during puberty the adolescent brain increases its processing power giving rise to more complex thinking styles. The development of meta-cognition allows young people to scrutinise themselves through the eyes of others. This inures self-consciousness in young people in a way that is associated with an increase in the rates of depression, anxiety, self-harm and eating disorders that occurs at this same time of life. These *internalised* disorders may be influenced by life events such as trauma or abuse, but can also be driven by temperament. Highly neurotic and introverted young people may be particularly sensitive to overcritical environments or to the wider cultural pressures of contemporary life. These risk factors occur later in the schema of development, hence the later onset of consumption in comparison to externalised youth. Internalised disorders appear to influence not only the age of initiation but the rate at which alcohol problems are acquired. This may be due to substance use alleviating the negative mood states that drive higher consumption.

The late onset trajectory is referred to as the *normative* risk group. These young people have far less psychological, familial and social risk factors prior to initiation. Their use is initiated between the ages of 14 and 16 when peer groups have the greatest influence over their lives. Normative use is embedded in peer experimental and recreational use that can become pathological and chronic. As this occurs far later in the adolescent phase of the life course, these individuals are more likely to have mastered critical life tasks, and thus have more ability to facilitate remission from use than earlier onset groups. By this time young people have emotionally separated from parents and so this source of influence has receded dramatically.

Increased levels of autonomy mean that young people are free to select their own peer groups at this stage and are particularly reliant on this surrogate structure to provide the external trappings of identity. As we have seen, fashion, music and drugs triangulate as markers of identity within particular sub-groups. Young

people do not select drugs for their specific pharmacological effects but because of their symbolism, such as LSD and hashish use in the hippy movement of the 1960s, ecstasy use in the dance scene of the 1980s, opiates in the grunge scene of the 1990s, etc. It is interesting to consider how the underlying trajectories of adolescent mental health influence the composition of these sub-cultures in attitude. For example, youth movements associated with the poor working classes such as Skinheads, Hip-Hop/Rap and Punk are all very externalised in their attitudes. They are often aggressive, militant and have been associated with violence. Conversely, middle class youth fashions such as Goths and Emos are more pre-occupied with personal identity, the expression of personal creativity and insular self-reflection. These youth movements are more internalised in their attitudes. As such, different youth movements appeal to different sensibilities and may account for the high degree of friction between them.

Outside of Brown's three categories are fling users. Fling use tends to occur in early adulthood in the college years, when their consumption rate at this time can exceed that of the early groups. These young adults have high levels of academic achievement and social functioning. However, leaving the strictures of home, the need to establish new peer groups and the pressures of study lead to higher rates of consumption. As the onset of problems tends to occur after the age of 18, they often reside outside the remit of most youth services. But problems at this stage may not warrant referral to an adult service either, so this population can fall through the gaps in services. All these major trajectories are described in Figure 3.1.

Aligning substance misuse, age of onset, life course and the social structures we inhabit explains why some individuals appear resilient to use whilst others succumb to more severe problems that persist deep into adulthood (Jessor et al., 1991). The timing of onset of use can be matched to the interruption in social functioning, where the achievement of key tasks is stalled. Furthermore, the environmental influence on consumption shifts as young people pass though different social structures. Early onset use is more strongly influenced by family whereas peers have greater influence in later adolescence.

Evidence for the first three sub-trajectories was examined in a large, international review of trajectory research conducted by Zucker (2008).

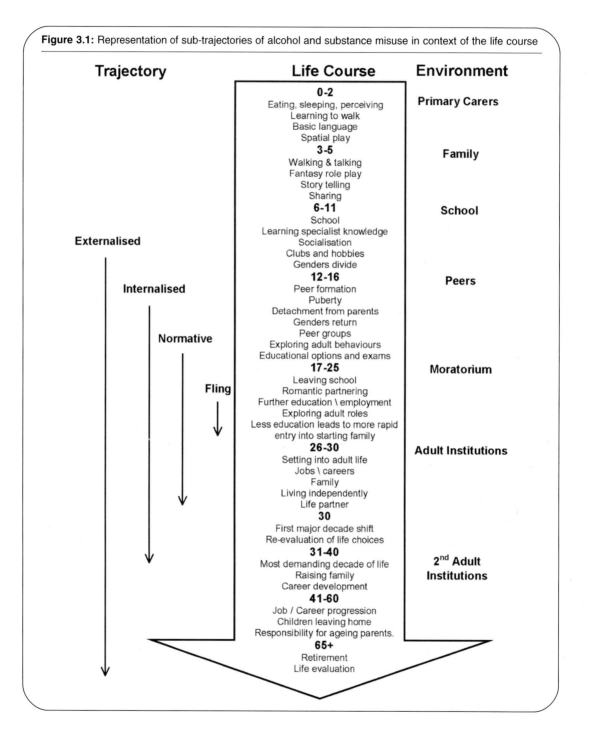

Figure 3.1: Representation of sub-trajectories of alcohol and substance misuse in context of the life course

Trajectory

Life Course

Environment

0-2
Eating, sleeping, perceiving
Learning to walk
Basic language
Spatial play

Primary Carers

3-5
Walking & talking
Fantasy role play
Story telling
Sharing

Family

6-11
School
Learning specialist knowledge
Socialisation
Clubs and hobbies
Genders divide

School

Externalised

12-16
Peer formation
Puberty
Detachment from parents
Genders return
Peer groups
Exploring adult behaviours
Educational options and exams

Peers

Internalised

Normative

17-25
Leaving school
Romantic partnering
Further education \ employment
Exploring adult roles
Less education leads to more rapid
entry into starting family

Moratorium

Fling

26-30
Setting into adult life
Jobs \ careers
Family
Living independently
Life partner

Adult Institutions

30
First major decade shift
Re-evaluation of life choices

31-40
Most demanding decade of life
Raising family
Career development

**2ⁿᵈ Adult
Institutions**

41-60
Job / Career progression
Children leaving home
Responsibility for ageing parents.

65+
Retirement
Life evaluation

This examined data from six independent studies based in the US, Great Britain and Finland but was limited to patterns of alcohol use. The studies tracked young people from pre-teen years into adulthood, except for one study which began at age 18. This broad range of cultural and geographic locations displayed a wide range of social drinking patterns, from the highest consumers in Great Britain to the lowest consumers in New York.

With regard to the existence of an externalised pathway, there was very strong agreement that poor impulse control, thrill seeking and early truancy were very strong predictors of heavy alcohol involvement across all countries. There was also strong evidence that this heavy drinking that continued into adulthood was a strong pathway itself.

In terms of an internalised pathway, evidence was inconsistent. The presence of internalised disorders at 11 was sometimes predictive of high consumption and sometimes predictive of very low consumption. This suggests that anxiety and depressive disorders can be protective for some young people and a risk factor for others. This may occur for a number of reasons. First, young people with internalised disorders are more likely to become socially isolated from peers restricting access to substances. Second, an anxious disposition may make these young people more fearful of alcohol consumption. However, for those internalised young people that do overcome the initial fear barrier, they can experience immediate relief of symptoms. This drives higher rates of consumption, once initiated. The later onset of internalised disorders may suggest a more complex interaction between the mental health issues and substance use. Substance use may amplify symptoms of internalised disorders which in turn may increase consumption.

In terms of a normative pathway through social relationships, there was again a more complex relationship. Popularity, social competence and educational attainment could increase or decrease the risk of involvement. Risk increased for those young people who were under the greatest stress, experienced greater social disadvantage and had poorer social competence. Risk also increased for those with the greatest social mobility. Normative users could be characterised as trying to 'serve two masters'. Alcohol served as an important form of social bonding for this group, bringing them closer to others. At the same time it also increased interpersonal difficulty, decreased social capability and could lead to abuse and dependence.

This section's survey shows that research currently supports the theory that risk factors cluster and accumulate into distinct pathways of substance involvement. Whilst ongoing research continues to unify this broad range of studies, it is also clear that substance misuse does not simply happen in adolescents but is deeply entwined in the developmental forces of this phase in the life course. The highly predictive nature of these trajectories offers considerable insight into optimising prevention and treatment approaches by identifying and targeting specific risk factors in each sub-population of young people. Programmes of interventions for young people should not simply focus on their consumption but also on the specific risk profiles that will trigger or sustain their use. These risk factors are located in the environments and temperament of early onset youth, in the mental health status of the mid-onset youth and in the peer relationships of late onset youth. At the onset of any such programmes of interventions, greater screening would be required to establish whether it is possible to identify these sub-trajectories in a population of young people presenting for help.

Diagnosis, labelling and stigmatisation

It is important to recognise that there is often a profound distaste in the field to applying diagnostic language to young people. This approach can be deemed as 'labelling'. This supposes that the description of a young person's problems leads to stigmatisation. Whilst it is important to always be mindful that people are not the diagnostic labels, it must also be stressed that there is no evidence to suggest that the use of diagnostic categories leads to stigmatisation. The reality is quite the contrary. People who experienced profound mental health problems experienced greater stigmatisation prior to the development of a diagnostic understanding of mental illness. Furthermore, the impact of behavioural problems or mental illness in young people is liable to lead to greater exclusion and stigma than its professional recognition and treatment. In this way, the use of terms such as externalised, internalised and normative is simply shorthand to describe categories of *problem* that young people experience. It does not assume that this describes young people in their fullness.

Identifying sub-trajectories

The issue of whether these sub-trajectories could be identified in young people who are seeking support from treatment services in the community was addressed through the development of a Complexity Index (Revised)

(Harris, 2011d). This risk-profiling tool rates the complexity of young people's needs from 0–15 points. The Complexity Index (Revised) was derived from identifying the key risk factors that could differentiate each sub-trajectory. As early onset consumption increased the risk of problem consumption, 'use prior to the age of 14' was selected as a key factor to differentiate externalised and internalised from normative users. The key risk factors unique to externalised disorders included early onset and a range of behavioural difficulties such as diagnosis of a behavioural disorder, as well as a wider range of indicators, including: offending prior to 11, persistent truancy prior to the age of 11 and social work involvement prior to the initiation of use. Internalised disorders were defined by the presence by mental health problems such as depression, self-harm and suicidal thinking.

The most difficult sub-group to isolate was the normative group. Externalised and internalised users were likely to pass through normative consumption patterns as their use escalated. However, externalised and internalised users were much more likely to use in isolation, and therefore identifying whether a young person only used in a peer setting was likely to be a clear indication of a normative pattern of use. A second loaded question was used asking whether the young person had only recently abandoned pro-social activities in favour of use. This question was based on the diagnostic criteria for abuse rather than dependence (see Chapter 4). It is a loaded question in that it assumes that the young person has been involved in pro-social activity until recently, something which may be less likely to occur in externalised or internalised populations.

Based on these research findings the Complexity Index (Revised) was then arranged into sub-scales and weighted. As externalised problems are the least treatment-responsive and carry the highest level of complexity, four questions were asked regarding this population to reflect their higher needs. This was followed by three questions regarding internalised use and only two questions for the later onset normative group, who have the highest level of treatment responsiveness. In this way, it was hoped that the Complexity Index (Revised) would score externalised and internalised sub-groups respectively higher to reflect the higher needs of these groups. A dummy question, that is not scored, was also included asking whether the

young person in question did not experience any of these listed symptoms. An answer that they did not would trigger further investigation to assess if any key variables were missing in the profile.

In terms of substance use, all drugs were weighted the same. Young people's problematic consumption, even of harder drugs, is sporadic and opportunistic as opposed to adult's problematic use that tends to be continuous. Therefore the Complexity Index (Revised) assumes that poly-use would be indicative of higher levels of need in young people. Furthermore, young people who used harder substances would also score highly on the psychosocial variables as well. This would separate them by the overall risk score rather than by consumption. All types of substance are weighted the same, with each young person scoring one point for each type of substance that they used. The total score for the substances sub-scales would therefore render the overall complexity of their needs, as opposed to stacking one substance as potentially more problematic than another. The classification of substances was based on the UK classifications: Alcohol, Class C, Class B, Class A and Other (including solvents, legal highs etc.). This meant that the young person could score a maximum of five points if they were poly-users of all types. The final Complexity Index (Revised) is described in Table 3.6.

The Complexity Index (Revised) was then piloted in two counties of Wales by youth workers in a variety of services as part of a Needs Analysis study. The response rate was high, with each major treatment agency providing information on their current client group with a final sample size of 81. Feedback on the use of the tool was positive with workers reporting that the tool was easy and straightforward to use. The one dummy variable in the Complexity Index (Revised), 'the client does not fit any of these criteria,' only identified one false positive. The client who had received a positive score on this item also had a positive score in the normative sub-scale rendering it redundant. This suggests that the range of risk factors in the Complexity Index (Revised) were relevant to the treatment population of young people sampled. The average results for the total sample by variable are illustrated in Graph 3.3.

The overall picture of this treatment-involved sample revealed an interesting picture. In general

Table 3.6: The Complexity Index (Revised) with sub-scales and scoring

Item	Sub-Scale	Points
1. Did they initiate regular drug or alcohol use before the age of 14?	Early onset	1
2. Did they have a history of offending under the age of 11?	Externalised	1
3. Have they been diagnosed with ADHD, Defiance or Conduct Disorder, or were they statemented for special educational needs?	Externalised	1
4. Have they had social work involvement prior to treatment entry?	Externalised	1
5. Do they have, or report, low commitment to school through persistent truancy before the age of 11?	Externalised	1
6. Do they have, or report, a history of depression or anxiety?	Internalised	1
7. Do they have, or report, a history of self-harm prior to treatment?	Internalised	1
8. Do they have, or report, a history of feeling suicidal?	Internalised	1
9. Do they report that previous pro-social activities they once enjoyed are no longer interesting?	Normative	1
10. Do they report only using drugs or alcohol with peers or partners?	Normative	1
11. This young person does not fit any of these criteria.	Screening	Not scored
12. Do they use Alcohol?	Substance	1
13. Do they use Class C Drugs? (Benzos, GHB, Ketamine, etc.)	Substance	1
14. Do they use Class B Drugs? (Cannabis, Ecstasy, Amphetamine, etc.)	Substance	1
15. Do they use Class A Drugs? (Heroin, Cocaine, Crack, etc.)	Substance	1
16. Do they use steroids, solvents, other non-classified drugs (Legal Highs, OTC, prescriptions drugs, etc.)	Substance	1

Harris, 2011d.

this population showed a high rate of early initiation as might be expected in a treatment-involved youth population who were more likely to be experiencing problematic use. Incidences of externalised diagnosis were low compared to higher ranges of associated problems such as truancy, family history involving social work or offending, which suggested there may be under-diagnosis in this population. The rates of internalised diagnosis such as anxiety and depression scored most highly of the mental health disorders, and this reflects the fact that these are the most common disorders in adolescence. Normative scores were also high demonstrating the powerful influence of peer settings on youth consumptions and the early onset of problems in terms of the abandoning of pro-social activity. Finally, in terms of consumption, alcohol and Class B drugs (predominately cannabis) were the most heavily used substances. Again, this would fit the expected profile of youth consumption seen in all prevalence studies. The patterns of use identified in the Complexity Index (Revised) appeared to reflect the anticipated pattern of consumption in young people.

The average level of complexity score across the entire sample was 7.6. However, the range and type of complexity varied across the different support services in the sample. Community based drug and alcohol services demonstrated remarkably similar outcomes as well as some key differences. The highest overall complexity scores were found in the agency that was dedicated to supporting young people Not in Education, Employment or Training (NEETS) who scored 9.83. These young people often hail from the most disadvantaged backgrounds, are liable to experience trans-generational unemployment and have very poor educational achievement. The lowest score was in the Youth Offending Service (YOS) who scored 6.75. The Youth Offending Service is a dedicated young people's community sentence probation service. The Youth Offending Service scores may have been reduced by those of the young people who were on their deterrence programme and who had not yet entered into more chaotic lifestyles, or they may have been lowered by reduced consumption as a result of treatment that they were receiving. Had the sample been taken on treatment entry these complexity scores may have been higher.

In terms of the sub-scales, the community based Street Agency treatment provider demonstrated notably high externalised scores (2.375) as did the young people's Housing Provider (2.46) and Community Groupwork Programme (2.4); and all reported significantly lower rates of internalised disorders. In contrast

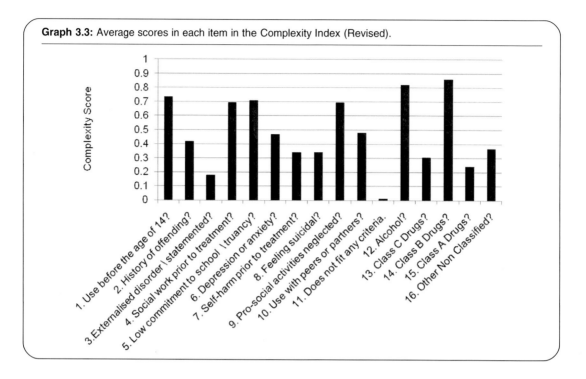

Graph 3.3: Average scores in each item in the Complexity Index (Revised).

the Child and Adolescent Mental Health Service (CAMHS) demonstrated higher scores for mental illness at 1.09. Again, this was to be expected due to their close working relationship with National Health Service mental health services. The NEETS service was unusual in reporting high levels of externalised and internalised youth. This reflects the older age range of the young people they work with, who present in crises with multiple needs. Data taken from a second research site (Miller, 2012) found that, as externalised youth aged, they were also increasingly vulnerable to experiencing internalised disorders. This may be due to the fact that, as their externalised behaviour had led to increasing social exclusion and stigma, their mental health also deteriorated. The rate of normative use was consistently lower in all agencies, scoring in the range of 1–1.2 points. This data suggests that the divergent needs of young people were being addressed within different agencies. However, the high rate of undiagnosed externalised youth suggests they are more likely to present in community based programmes than receive the specialist interventions that the internalised peers received. A comparison of outcomes is described in Table 3.7.

Reviewing the data based on the sub-scales and consumption revealed interesting patterns. The Complexity Index (Revised) found high levels of externalised problems in the young people presenting for help. In total, 40 per cent of the young people sampled demonstrated externalised behaviours though only 17.2 per cent had been formally diagnosed. The rate of internalised disorders was also high, accounting for 46.9 per cent of the young people with 33 per cent reporting suicidal thoughts. Whilst there was little difference in the percentage of young people presenting with externalised or internalised disorders, the weighting of the Complexity Index (Revised) did elevate the needs of the externalised disorders as higher than the internalised problems by approximately one third. Externalised disorders were rated as a complexity index of 1.58 versus 1.1 for pathological problems. Normative users scored slightly higher than internalised youth. This higher percentage may be reflective of a higher range of non-chronic problems, or the variables used for normative use were not distinct enough to isolate this population.

In terms of substance use, 23.4 per cent of the sample used Class A drugs and this was strongly associated with mental health problems. Amongst young people reporting Class A use, 31 per cent had been diagnosed with an externalised disorder diagnosis. Furthermore, 63 per cent of

Table 3.7: Average Complexity Index (Revised) scores by agency.

	Street agency	CAMHS	Group work	NEETS	YOS	Housing provider
Alcohol	0.875	0.96	0.80	0.83	0.68	0.60
Class C	0.50	0.419	0.20	0.33	0.0625	0.26
Class B	1.00	0.955	0.80	1.00	0.625	0.86
Class A	0.375	0.354	0.20	0.16	0.0625	0.13
Legal highs/solvents	0.50	0.387	0.40	0.66	0.1875	0.33
Total substance score	**3.25**	**3.075**	**2.40**	**2.98**	**1.6175**	**2.18**
Total substance score	3.25	3.075	2.40	2.98	1.6175	2.18
Under 14	1.00	0.77	1.00	0.30	0.68	0.66
Externalised	2.375	1.58	2.40	2.50	1.93	2.46
Internalised	0.75	1.09	0.60	2.50	1.37	0.80
Normative	1.00	1.16	1.20	1.50	1.125	1.20
Total complexity	**8.375**	**7.675**	**7.60**	**9.78**	**6.7225**	**7.30**

Class A users recorded problems with depression and anxiety. Class A use was also associated with earlier onset, in 73 per cent of cases. High rates of poly-drug use were also found in this sample with 16 per cent of the young people being recorded as having tried every classification of substance. These populations were again correlated with high rates of internalised disorders, depression in particular. Amongst the 13 poly-drug users, 10 also scored on the depression and anxiety item (76.9 per cent) and 11 initiated use under the age of 14 (84 per cent). Poly-users are more likely to have more complex behavioural, emotional or mental health needs than those that use only one substance. In contrast, individuals who used only one substance demonstrated less complex needs. A sample of 17 per cent of young people reported only using one substance. Amongst the single substance users, 85 per cent had initiated use after the age of 14. Furthermore, none of the group had a diagnosis of externalised disorders, whilst 42 per cent demonstrated signs of depression or anxiety.

The Complexity Index (Revised) has been adjusted as a result of on-going research and larger samples. It has demonstrated utility in identifying sub-populations of adolescent substance misuse in everyday treatment settings. The development of this tool could be extremely useful in a number of ways. First, the tool can be used to assess not simply the number of young people in treatment but also to indicate the range of complexity within a treatment service as well. Furthermore it may also help multiple agencies in a treatment system to identify whether young people are receiving treatment from the most appropriate service. Tracking the sub-populations through outcome monitoring may also indicate whether all young people are responding to the treatment being provided. As we shall see, late onset users are often the most treatment responsive. Their higher response rate may cause failure to differentiate poor treatment response rates in the most vulnerable groups. Tracking and measuring the treatment response rates for each sub-trajectory is vital in the development of more effective services. This is because outcomes based on all young people in a treatment service can mask differences between groups. High rates of treatment success with normative youth will detract from poorer rates of treatment outcomes of externalised youth. This means that the most disenfranchised young people, who are liable to experience personal and social harm from their use, may not receive the help they need the most. Their issues are liable to be carried on deep into adulthood and beyond. Where this occurs, the trans-generational issues that have shaped their lives will then be bestowed upon their own children.

Summary

Singular explanations of the development of drug and alcohol problems dominate the popular imagination, but no one single explanation can account for the diversity of substance misuse problems in young people. Advances in research methodologies have demonstrated unequivocally that substance misuse problems arise from multiple influences that occur across the biological, psychological, relational and environmental realms. The probability of experiencing substance misuse problems is directly related to the number of risk factors present in the young person's life. Whilst risk and protection factors have increasingly been utilised in treatment programmes for young people, the interaction of these opposing forces is complex and not well understood. It is important to recognise that not all risk factors are amenable to change. Furthermore, the research strongly suggests that treatment should not simply reduce risk factors, but should also increase the protection factors in the lives of the most vulnerable.

Risk factors are not static but peak in influence at different ages. This is because, while some risk factors are located in young people themselves, other risk factors are also located in the social environments that they occupy. Risk factors are accumulative in a stratified sequence with vulnerability factors leading to greater probability of initiation; initiation open up the possibility of increased risk of maintaining consumption; this opens greater risks of diversification and escalation of consumption. Central to the full expression of these risk factors are positive expectations of use that lead to initiation. Expectations trigger the potential of established risk factors as well open up the young person to the possibility of increased future risk. So whilst expectancies do not give a complete account of substance misuse problems, they

represent a pivotal moment of transition. In this way, risk factors cascade across young people's lives with increased momentum. Furthermore, risk factors cluster in their life to create distinctive trajectories of consumption. These sub-trajectories share remarkably similar clinical features from person to person, which demonstrates that young people's pathways in and out of problem use are not homogenous. Instead they represent distinct sub-populations with distinct needs.

The early initiation of substance use not only predicts the length of their subsequent using careers. It also heightens the probability that young people will progress through increasingly harder categories of intoxicants as well as experience the most profound range of problems. These robust and consistent research findings have generally not been integrated into prevention or treatment programmes, in the UK or elsewhere, where young people have tended to be treated as a homogenous group. The research brought together in this chapter offers considerable scope for innovation in interventions that can intercept use through prevention or optimise outcomes within treatment. This not only requires deeper understanding of the evolution of substance misuse problems but also greater clarity on the nature of adolescent substance misuse itself, steps towards which are offered in this book. This is because the kinds of problem that young people experience differ radically from adult problem use.

CHAPTER 4

What is Problematic Use in Young People?

Introduction

In 1970 Elvis Presley met President Nixon to offer his services in the fight against drugs. A gun fixated Elvis asked to be appointed as a 'special agent at large' in order to secretly fight the drug menace that he believed was deeply un-American. His offer was declined but they awarded him a special badge. A year later Nixon launched his 'War on Drugs' that has shaped global drug policy ever since. In 1977 Elvis was found dead in his Graceland bathroom with a cocktail of ten different drugs in his system including codeine, ethinamate, methaqualone, unidentifiable barbiturates, Placidyl, Valium, Demerol, Meperidine, morphine and chloropheniramine. His private physician, Dr George 'Nick' Nichopoulos, had prescribed him 10,000 doses of sedative, amphetamines and other narcotics in the first eight months of 1977 alone. He had been using prescribed drugs since the 1960s.

Successive US presidents have continued the War on Drugs with some duplicity. President Bill Clinton admitted smoking cannabis but not inhaling. He justified his consumption by stating 'Well, I did smoke pot, but I didn't inhale. And I was in England, so it really doesn't count. Plus, no one saw me. So what's the big fuss? The half million people arrested for pot last year are just sore losers.' President Barack Obama admitted smoking cannabis and when asked if he had inhaled he replied 'That was the point.' Republican George W. Bush avoided drug involvement but was arrested for Driving Under the Influence in 1976.

In 1997, eight-time Grand Slam winner Andre Agassi failed a drug test. He had tested positive for methamphetamine that he had been using heavily that year following a wrist injury. One of the world's greatest tennis players of all time had slumped to a 141 in the world rankings. He received no ban from tennis as many believed him to be too important to the sport. In 2009 Olympic swimmer Michael Phelps, who won eight medals for the U.S. at the Beijing Olympics, was pictured smoking marijuana at a party at the University of South Carolina. Observers said that

the he drank beer and smoked the drug in a glass bong. In 2005 Steve Jobs, the visionary founder of Apple, told a reporter that his youthful experiments with LSD were one of two or three most important things he had ever done in his life. He credited the drug with enabling him to create visionary products that continue to shape the 21st century, long after his premature death. He even suggested that Bill Gates, his rival at Microsoft, would be a "broader guy" if he too had taken hallucinogenic drugs. Little did he know that Bill Gates had already admitted to taking LSD in an interview in 1994.

In November 1995 a media crusade was initiated in the UK, following the death of a girl called Leah Betts. She had taken ecstasy on her 18th birthday and died a few days later when her life support machine was switched off. Whilst her father called for the person who supplied with the drug to be charged with murder and hanged, she had taken the drug on at least four other occasions and was supplied the drug by her best friend. An autopsy revealed that Leah had died of water intoxication. In May 2000 the body of a young woman, Rachel Whitear, was found crouched on her hands and knees having died from a heroin overdose. The photograph of the 21-year-old's dead body was used to spearhead another anti-drug campaign in UK. The idea was that Rachel was an ordinary girl and that drugs could affect anyone. In August 2005, Mark Shields was found dead in bed at his home in Northumberland by his father Graeme on the morning of his 18th birthday. Celebrating the night before, he had drunk at least three pints of lager, five double whiskies and up to three double shots of the liqueur Aftershock. A toxicology report showed that Mark had 491mg of alcohol in 100ml of blood, five times the drink drive limit. His death only made the local paper.

Addressing the confusion of diagnosis

Media representations of substance abuse problems are confused, fragmented and disproportionate regarding the nature of drug and alcohol problems. This distorted image occurs as reporting tends to fixate on the dramatic deaths which attract media interest by their novelty. Alternatively, stories focus on the famous to feed popular interest in celebrity. This may be a form of atonement for discredited public figures or be used as a sales pitch to publicise a biography of the 'My Drug Hell' ilk. It also qualifies public figures to comment on drug and alcohol policy, prevention and treatment with regard to nothing other than their own experience. The media angle on these stories presents a confused and distorted message to young people regarding drug use and alcohol use. It is difficult to discern whether drugs and alcohol will:

- Result in an anonymous death.
- Result in a high profile death.
- Enhance your fame and notoriety.
- Turn you into a visionary genius.
- Make you president of the most powerful country in the world.

This is a fairly wide spectrum of possible outcomes. It is little wonder that there remains a great deal of uncertainty regarding the exact nature of drug and alcohol problems, even within the field. This chapter will review the nature of substance misuse problems in young people. Their pattern of problematic use differs from that experienced by problematic adult users. To understand these differences it is essential to have a clear understanding of the diagnostic criteria that have evolved in recent decades. This chapter will chart these developments and identify how different diagnostic systems serve different functions within clinical settings. Describing the key features of drug and alcohol problems, we will then review the relevance of these diagnostic criteria to young people's drug and alcohol use. This comparison will reveal young people's issues and how they diverge from adults' experiences. Furthermore, we will then review how problematic use unfolds, by identifying the sequence of symptoms that occurs within both abuse and dependence. It will then be shown how this can inform effective screening and assessment processes with young people. Effective assessment processes not only increase young people's awareness of the need for change but, if done well, can also make a substantial contribution to the young person's outcomes, even before treatment begins.

Origins of diagnosis

Accurate and consistent diagnostic criteria are essential for a number of reasons. First, having clear diagnostic criteria helps us identify the severity of problem use and assess whether it requires treatment. Second, they allow researchers to look at the key symptoms of a disorder in an organised way, so they can help to identify underlying core processes. Third, clear criteria offer practitioners and researchers a common conceptual language in which to debate, research and treat young people. They also ensure that research is undertaken on a specified range of problems when they are evaluating who responds to treatment across different treatment samples. Historically, defining substance misuse problems has been prone to confused and contradictory descriptions because it is both multi-faceted and divergent in appearance. Whilst they may be supposed to represent one identifiable condition, the symptoms of substance misuse problems retain a plasticity that is difficult to discern. This led early theorists to segment substance misuse problems into separate types or sub-species. An early pioneer of this model was Jellinek (1960) whose five-part typology attempted to define distinct drinking patterns in problem users. Whilst it was not exhaustive in its definitions, this model became quickly established (see Table 4.1).

Jellinek's typology has been both influential and misunderstood. His classification system has been commonly interpreted as defining 'fixed' drinking patterns when they in fact represent shifts in drinking styles. For example, even highly socially excluded Gamma 'street' drinkers, who would be supposed to maintain high levels of continuous drinking in this model, often experience protracted periods of abstinence (Schuckit et al., 1997). This occurs during prison stays or when in dry hostels. Likewise, heavy bout Epsilon drinkers often report case histories of continuous drinking.

In light of the limitations of Jellinek's classification system, the World Health Organisation approached two researchers to develop specific diagnostic criteria that could identify physically dependent drinkers *who required medical attention*. These researchers, Edwards & Gross (1976), suggested that alcoholism could be understood as occurring on a spectrum of severity rather than as an absolute condition, which is to say that individuals were

Table 4.1: Jellinek's drinking typology

Sub-type	Description
Alpha alcoholism	Drinking for psychological reasons without tolerance.
Beta alcoholism	Excessive drinking which has led to tissue damage but no dependence on alcohol.
Gamma alcoholism	Excessive drinking with tolerance and withdrawal, variable alcohol intake and characterised by a loss of control over consumption.
Delta alcoholism	Excessive drinking where there is evidence of tolerance and withdrawal accompanied by steady alcohol use. These clients may find more difficulty in abstaining rather than exercising control of what they drink.
Epsilon alcoholism	Bout or binge drinking.

Jellinek, 1960.

not simply alcoholic or not, but could experience degrees of alcohol-related problems. They also found that alcohol dependence could be separated from alcohol-related problems based on their clinical observations of the symptoms that physically dependent drinkers tended to exhibit. Examination of physically dependent drinkers revealed a cluster of seven common symptoms which they formulated into the Alcohol Dependence Syndrome. A 'syndrome' is a medical term that describes a disorder which is defined by a set of symptoms that appear sufficiently regularly to make a diagnosis, but where not all symptoms need to be present. The symptoms of the Alcohol Dependence Syndrome are described in Table 4.2.

Edwards & Gross (1976) assumed that symptoms of the dependence syndrome should be proportional to each other due to the central role of *tolerance* and *physical withdrawal*. Tolerance and withdrawal are interrelated physiological processes. At its simplest, tolerance can be understood as the body's response to the presence of a drug. For example, alcohol has a depressant effect on biological processes. Therefore the body compensates for this

Table 4.2: The Alcohol Dependence Syndrome

Key symptoms	Descriptors
Narrowing of repertoire	The problem individual begins to drink the same regardless of social context. With advanced drinking, consumption follows a strict daily timetable.
Salience of drinking	Priority is given to maintaining alcohol intake over time, relationships and finances.
Increased tolerance	The drinker can tolerate and still operate under the influence of large doses of alcohol that would incapacitate an ordinary drinker. Will also develop cross-tolerance to other depressant drugs.
Withdrawal	The client will experience severe and multiple symptoms, usually on waking, that include tremor, nausea, sweating and mood disturbance.
Relief or avoidance of withdrawal by further drinking	Drinking occurs earlier in the day as dependence progresses to alleviate the onset of withdrawal. Usually the periods of abstinence are limited to 3–4 hours. Drinking is triggered by mild withdrawal in anticipation of worsening symptoms. Often early drinking becomes ritualised with the client knowing the exact amount to consume to avoid rather than alleviate withdrawal.
Subjective awareness of compulsion to drink	May be ruminating on alcohol during a period of withdrawal as well as loss of control over drinking once it has been initiated.
Reinstatement after abstinence	A rapid return to pre-treatment drinking levels after relapse.

Edwards & Gross, 1976.

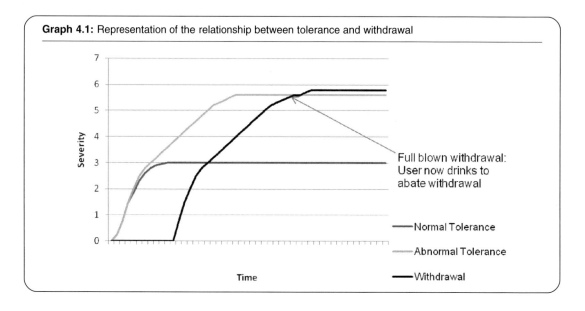

Graph 4.1: Representation of the relationship between tolerance and withdrawal

Full blown withdrawal: User now drinks to abate withdrawal

———Normal Tolerance

———Abnormal Tolerance

———Withdrawal

depressant effect by working harder in order to sustain biological functioning. The body does this in two ways. The first is through metabolic tolerance, where the liver produces more enzymes to metabolise the substances. The more routinely a substance is used then the higher the rate of enzyme production. The second route is cellular tolerance where neurological functions adapt to the presence of a drug. The mechanism of cellular tolerance may vary depending upon the action of the drug. The net result of both processes is that as tolerance increases, the individual can withstand higher doses of the substance, or needs to consume more to get a desired effect. Tolerance will not continue to rise forever but will plateau at a saturation level, which is why Edwards and Gross' classification of symptoms refers to *increased* tolerance rather than *increasing* tolerance.

Tolerance is therefore an adjustment the body makes to compensate for the action of a drug. When the substance subsequently wears off, the metabolic rate of the tolerant individual will be left over-compensating for a period of time. This is experienced as withdrawal. The withdrawal of a drug is therefore the exact opposite to its effects. This is called the *law of rebound*. For example, cocaine stimulates the metabolism, increasing energy levels, and this forces the body to compensate by slowing down. When the drug wears off, the body is functioning too slowly for a short period and the user experiences lethargy. Conversely the depressant effect of heroin leaves

the user sedated, and this forces their body to overcompensate in the presence of the drug by working harder. When the substance wears off, the body is operating too fast, leading to agitation and restlessness. The relationship between tolerance and withdrawal is represented in Graph 4.1.

There can be a considerable delay between increased tolerance and the onset of withdrawal. Tolerance is rapidly achieved through continued exposure, whilst withdrawal can take years to develop. This means that the heavy drinker can consume large doses of alcohol with apparent impunity for extended periods of time, until the experience of physical withdrawal sweeps upon them. Once withdrawal is initiated though, the problem drinker begins to consume alcohol to *alleviate* its physical symptoms. Drinkers tend to do this on the onset of physical *withdrawal* rather than when its symptoms become full blown. If alcohol is not available to them during this period, they will fixate and experience *subjective awareness of compulsion* to drink, knowing the discomfort that looms. As a result, they begin to plan their daily routine around alcohol consumption in order to ensure alcohol is available to them at the critical times, giving rise to *narrowing of repertoire*. This schedule of drinking becomes more important to them than other responsibilities and so it becomes increasingly *salient* to them. *Reinstatement* refers to repeated failed attempts to cut down on alcohol or stop drinking. Individuals return to drinking despite knowing it has serious consequences for them, such as peptic ulcers, for example, or that their spouse will leave them. Repeated failed attempts to end or control use signal loss of control over an individual's capacity to manage their consumption.

Reviewing this classification of symptoms it is important to make a distinction. Symptoms such as tolerance and withdrawal are physical, whereas *subjective awareness of compulsion, reinstatement, salience* and *narrowing of repertoire* are all behavioural. As such, these behavioural symptoms are more liable to change. Probably the most vivid feature of *narrowing of repertoire* are the habits of 'secret drinkers'. These individuals hide alcohol around the house or in the office desk. Their day will be punctuated by the necessity to have rapid access to alcohol, not to get inebriated, but to keep the sickness of physical withdrawal at bay. On the other hand, an example of not needing to narrow the repertoire would be a landlord of a bar who will not need to take special steps to plan their life around alcohol, as it is already a central component of their daily life. *Reinstatement* may depend on how long the person has experienced these symptoms before attempting to quit. In contrast, physical tolerance and withdrawal cannot be changed easily. An individual may be able to focus their attention on something other than alcohol or plan their daily activities in a way that they cannot choose to drink in response to withdrawal or not. But, as Edwards et al. state 'for clinical purposes it is probably best to restrict the diagnosis of alcohol dependence to patients who have experienced withdrawal symptoms to at least some degree' (Edwards et al., 2003: 59).

As such, the presence of *tolerance* and *withdrawal* are taken to be the defining symptoms of the diagnostic criteria of physical dependence. There is a particularly strong relationship between tolerance and withdrawal with depressant drugs such as alcohol, heroin and benzodiazepines. Abrupt withdrawal from alcohol and benzodiazepines can cause fitting and death. Whilst this is not the case with opiates, the experience of withdrawal from this drug can be protracted and physically difficult, making clinical management a helpful way of easing profound discomfort. Stimulants, cannabis and hallucinogenic substances will all produce a law of rebound effect, due to the body's adjustment to the presence of the drug. But the withdrawal process is not of significant magnitude to warrant

medical interventions. So, as a general rule, it is only possible to become physically dependent on depressant substances such as alcohol, opiates and benzodiazepines. All these depressant drugs demonstrate a pattern of use that is consistent with the classification of symptoms described in the Alcohol Dependence Syndrome. A mass of subsequent research has supported the idea that the Alcohol Dependence Syndrome is indeed a clinical reality (See Stockwell et al., 1979; 1983; Chick, 1980; Meehan et al., 1985; Feingold & Rounsaville, 1995; Heather et al., 1983; Rankin et al., 1982; Grant et al., 1992; Cottler, 1993). However, not all symptoms are such strong predictors as others. *Narrowing of repertoire, subjective awareness of compulsion* and *reinstatement* have proved more difficult to validate. This led Cottler et al. (1995) to suggest that physical withdrawal should be the key symptom for diagnostic purposes.

Substance abuse

The Alcohol Dependence Syndrome has been hugely influential in the development of more recent diagnostic criteria. Two key diagnostic assessments are currently used. The first is the *Diagnostic and Statistical Manual of Mental Health Disorders (Edition IV – Text Revised)* (APA, 2000) abbreviated to *DSM (IV-TR)*. The *DSM (IV-TR)* was developed by the American Psychiatric Association who have based their model upon a wide range of clinical research, field studies and consultation with expert panels to derive its diagnostic criteria. They also undertook structured interviews with people with all the major mental health disorders for adults and children. The other commonly used model of diagnostic criteria is the *World Health Authority's International Classification of Disease (Edition 10)*, which is abbreviated to *ICD (10)*. However, the *ICD (10)* tends to be used for research purposes and not everyday clinical practice. Therefore, this section will focus on the American *DSM (IV-TR)* as it utilises the criteria most used in everyday practice.

The *DSM (IV-TR)* makes a clear distinction between two different types of substance use problem: Abuse and Dependence. It assumes that Abuse is a milder condition that precedes the onset of the more profound Dependence syndrome. Therefore, individuals cannot experience Abuse *and* Dependence in connection

Table 4.3: *DSM (IV-TR)* Criteria for alcohol and substance abuse

Item	Alcohol abuse symptoms	Drug abuse symptoms
1	Role impairment: Frequent intoxication leading to failure to fulfil major role obligations at work, school, or home (such as repeated absences or poor work performance related to alcohol use; alcohol-related absences, suspensions, or expulsions from school; or neglect of children or household).	Role impairment: Recurrent substance use resulting in a failure to fulfil major role obligations at work, school, or home (such as repeated absences or poor work performance related to substance use; substance-related absences, suspensions, or expulsions from school; or neglect of children or household).
2	Hazardous use: Recurrent use in situations in which it is physically hazardous (such as driving an automobile or operating a machine when impaired by alcohol use).	Hazardous use: Recurrent substance use in situations in which it is physically hazardous (such as driving an automobile or operating a machine when impaired by substance use).
3	Legal problems: Recurrent alcohol-related legal problems (such as arrests for alcohol related disorderly conduct).	Legal problems: Recurrent substance-related legal problems (such as arrests for substance related disorderly conduct).
4	Social problems: Continued alcohol use despite having persistent or recurrent social or interpersonal problems caused or exacerbated by the effects of the alcohol (for example, arguments with spouse about consequences of intoxication and physical fights).	Social problems: Continued substance use despite having persistent or recurrent social or interpersonal problems caused or exacerbated by the effects of the substance (for example, arguments with spouse about consequences of intoxication and physical fights).

with a particular substance simultaneously. The *DSM (IV-TR)* defines alcohol or substance Abuse as 'a maladaptive pattern of substance use manifested by recurrent and significant adverse consequences related to the repeated use of substances.' (APA 2000: 198). This distress can be caused by health and/or psychological problems. Abuse is manifested by one or more of the following symptoms, occurring within a 12-month period, as described in Table 4.3.

The diagnostic concept of Abuse has tended to be used to denote the negative social consequences rather than any physical harm resulting from use such as liver damage. However, many of the diagnostic criteria of Abuse in *DSM (IV-TR)* actually measure risk-taking behaviour rather than negative consequences. Items 1 (role impairment), 3 (legal problems) and 4 (social problems) all describe *conflicts within relationships* as a result of behaviour. Only Item 2 (hazardous use) actually relates to physical health consequences. This includes engaging in risk-taking behaviour under the influence, such as driving under the influence. The hazardous use criteria appears to be the opposite of the other three. Whilst the other criteria of Abuse in *DSM (IV-TR)* describe interference with pro-social attachments, the hazardous use criteria is describing the

engagement in anti-social activities, indicating the degree of involvement in anti-social behaviours that are associated with use.

All the other criteria of Abuse in the *DSM (IV-TR)* refer to changes in relationships or commitments such as failure to manage social responsibilities, conflict with relationship or rule violation. This is unusual in classifications of diagnostic criteria. Every other diagnosis of mental health disorders in the *DSM (IV-TR)* assumes that they are the result of impaired neurological or psychological mechanisms. However, the Abuse criteria focus on the continuation of behaviour despite negative personal, social and legal consequences means the diagnosis is based on 'poor decisions'. For example, when using *DSM (IV-TR)* we can diagnose Abuse based solely on whether an individual makes choices (to use drugs or alcohol) that are disapproved of, such as by their family. This is not describing a psychological impairment, but something based on the judgments of others. It would be hard for any other mental illness diagnosis to be determined by the same benchmark of what essentially may be nothing more than social or legal disapproval. The Abuse criteria are organised in a completely different way to all other diagnoses. As a result, Abuse as defined in *DSM (IV-TR)* has been heavily criticised as a 'category without content' (Langebucher and Martin, 1996: 270A). However, understanding the impact that drugs and alcohol have on social functioning is vitally important in understanding young people's use. This is because they are far more likely to be afflicted by social consequences of use than any other clinical issues.

The social consequences of abuse

The problem of clearly identifying Abuse may lie in the lack of research that is conducted on understanding the social consequences of use. Whilst research on the medical consequences of alcohol and drug use has been extensive, very little research has been conducted on understanding the social aspect of consumption. An exception to this is a series of papers edited into a book format by Klingemann & Gmel (2001). This extensive review of studies of the social consequences of alcohol recognised the limited research in this area, referring to the social consequences of the 'forgotten dimension' (Klingemann & Gmel 2001: 1). Whilst this collection of studies is limited to alcohol, these findings may also be relevant to drug using populations.

One paper by Rehm (2001) attempted to classify different types of social consequence from alcohol use, beyond the physical health problems such as liver damage. These domains include three areas: psychological consequences, social-environmental consequences and the wider social consequences. Psychological consequences may be influenced to some degree by biological process, for example, drinking alcohol regularly can cause neurological damage. But alcohol may also influence the young person's psychology by changes in consciousness, loss of control, hangovers and depression that may result from use. Heavy drinking may in itself produce these changes in mood but so can behaviours enacted under the influence. People may experience shame or remorse after disinhibited behaviour such as unplanned sexual encounters, aggression or overly sentimental behaviour. In addition, consumption of alcohol as a mood control agent may inhibit the development of psychological processes such as the ability to internally manage emotional mood states. If young people increasingly rely upon alcohol as an external mode of mood control they become less rehearsed at managing their own mood states

internally. As such, the young person may be unable to achieve landmarks in their own personal development in terms of emotional coping.

The social-environmental consequences may include disruptions in social responsibilities and commitments to others. These might include conflict with family, interruptions of school and disengagement from other pro-social activities or networks. The heavy-consuming young person may experience alienation from friends as a result of behaviour when drunk. Young people may fail to cultivate relationships without alcohol as a social lubricant. In this way, alcohol use may interfere with the broader social functioning of the young person. For example, studies have found that social competence is often inversely proportional to alcohol consumption. Young abstainers appear to have higher social competence than moderate drinkers, whilst heavy alcohol consumers appear to the most socially inept (Hover & Gaffney, 1991).

As a result of continued use, the impact of the social consequences for young people on their social-environment can be profound, leading to the complete breakdown in pro-social attachments. They may become excluded from social networks such as school, alienated from family or incarcerated for criminal behaviour. Once they are disconnected from the pro-social networks their exposure to the life tasks embedded in the life course becomes curtailed. They become disconnected from exams, employment opportunities, building healthy relationships, recreational life, life skills, financial management, etc. Without exposure to these activities young people's social development is curtailed, leaving them increasingly developmentally delayed in their ability to manage the responsibilities and opportunities of life as we saw in Chapter 2. Furthermore, they may be even less prepared for the increasingly complex demands of life that follow adolescence.

The complications of alcohol use can also extend into the wider environment of the young person, beyond their own immediate social world. The wider environmental consequence can involve breaking the law, stigmatisation or intimidation of strangers, as locations where drug and alcohol use is consumed become 'no-go' areas to the wider public. The social costs also include public expenditure on health to treat those with health-related problems or accidents under the influence. Ironically, when viewed in this way, the consequences of alcohol appear to

Table 4.4: Comparison of positive expectancies and social consequences of alcohol use

Domain	Positive expectancies	Social consequences
Psychological	• Enhanced mood • Increased confidence • Stress release	• Depression/over-sentimentally • Shame and regret • Moribund thinking
Social environment	• Group cohesion • Intimacy • Appearing grown up • Belonging	• Violence • Unwanted sexual contact • Reduced ability to manage developmental life tasks • Conflict in pro-social networks of family, school, peer group
Wider society	• Coming of age • Cultural identification • Participation in social/cultural norms • Generate tax revenues	• Signal of immaturity • Stigmatisation • Legal and social rule violation • Increased economic expenditure on health and treatment services

Adapted from Rehm, 2001.

be the exact polar opposite of many of the perceived benefits of use (see Table 4.4).

Whilst the concept of abuse appears to be very poorly defined, the social consequences of use can be profound and enduring. The magnitude of the impact may be influenced not necessarily by the pharmacology of the drug itself, but by the social attitudes towards to the substance in question. The social response to the use of drugs such as heroin and crack cocaine is often more profound than that of alcohol due to the highly negative social norms regarding these substances. Alcohol use in young people is more likely to be tolerated as 'part of growing up'. However, all substances can lead to breakdowns in psychological well-being and social attachments, and to social rule violations. As the social consequences affect the functioning of the individual, they are not necessarily substance specific. Any substance, be it alcohol, cannabis, legal highs, cocaine or ketamine, has the potential to generate social consequences.

These ruptures in social functioning and incumbent developmental delay should become the central focus of psycho-social treatment. Young people who meet the criteria for a diagnosis of abuse, such as in *DSM (IV-TR)* or another model, are liable to social exclusion and therefore must reconnect to their life course and increase their competence in managing the demands of everyday life. As a result, we do not see benefits in *substance specific* psycho-social treatment interventions. Programmes that focus on cannabis or ketamine or alcohol may provide

additional information about these particular substances but, regardless of the substance, the challenge remains to address the social functioning of the young person. So whilst 'abuse' can be considered at best a rudimentary measure, the behaviour linked to abuse is the common denominator in the psycho-social impact of, and treatment for, all substances.

Dependence

The *DSM (IV-TR)* assumes that people will pass through an initial stage of Abuse before progressing on to the more profound diagnosis of Dependence. Based on the Alcohol Dependence Syndrome, the *DSM (IV-TR)* defines Dependence as 'a cluster of cognitive, behavioural, and physiological symptoms indicating that the individual continues use of the substance despite significant substance-related problems.' (APA, 2000: 192). The substance Dependence criteria include 10 categories of drugs, plus an 'other' section as well as poly-drug use. For a diagnosis of Dependence to be made the client must meet at least 3 of the 7 criteria in the last 12 months. Alcohol and substances also share similarities, as described in Table 4.5.

The *DSM (IV-TR)* retains many of the core features of Edward and Gross' original Alcohol Dependence Syndrome (ADS) though it couches them in a different language. *DSM (IV-TR)* diagnostic symptoms such as 'important activities are given up', 'long time spent obtaining the

Table 4.5: Comparison of diagnostic criteria for dependence

DSM (IV-TR) substance dependence	*DSM (IV-TR)* alcohol dependence
(1) Tolerance, as defined by either of the following: (a) A need for markedly increased amounts of the substance to achieve intoxication or the desired effect, or (b) Markedly diminished effect with continued use of the same amount of the substance.	(1) Tolerance, as defined by either of the following: (a) A need for markedly increasing amounts of alcohol to achieve the desired effect or (b) Markedly diminished effect with continued use of the same amount of alcohol.
(2) Withdrawal, as manifested by either of the following: (a) The characteristic withdrawal syndrome for the substance, or (b) The same (or closely related) substance is taken to relieve or avoid withdrawal symptoms.	(2) Withdrawal, as manifested by either of the following: (a) The characteristic withdrawal syndrome for alcohol, or (b) Alcohol (or a closely related drug such as Valium) is used to relieve or avoid withdrawal symptoms.
(3) The substance is often taken in larger amounts or over a longer period than intended.	(3) Alcohol is used in larger amounts or over a longer period than was intended.
(4) There is a persistent desire or unsuccessful efforts to cut down or control substance use.	(4) There is a persistent desire or unsuccessful efforts to cut down or control use.
(5) A great deal of time is spent in activities necessary to obtain the substance, use the substance, or recover from its effects.	(5) A great deal of time is spent in activities necessary to obtain alcohol, use alcohol, or recover from its effects.
(6) Important social, occupational, or recreational activities are given up or reduced because of substance use.	(6) Important social, occupational, or recreational activities are given up or reduced because of alcohol use.
(7) The substance use is continued despite knowledge of having a persistent physical or psychological problem that is likely to have been caused or exacerbated by the substance (for example, current cocaine use despite recognition of cocaine-induced depression).	(7) Alcohol use is continued despite knowledge of having a persistent or recurrent physical or psychological problem that is likely to have been caused or exacerbated by alcohol (e.g. continued drinking despite recognition that an ulcer was made worse by alcohol consumption).

APA, 2000.

substance' and 'persistent desire to quit' are reminiscent of ADS's *'salience'*, *'subjective awareness of compulsion'* and *'reinstatement'* respectively. Separate *withdrawal* syndromes for each substance are also described in sub-tables in *DSM (IV-TR)*, each combined with the fact that withdrawal must cause distress and impair social functioning (though withdrawal is not presented as a diagnostic criteria for cannabis, hallucinogens, phencyclidine or inhalant dependence.) The biggest difference in the *DSM (IV-TR)* is that, unlike the ADS, *increased tolerance* and *withdrawal* are not mandatory elements of diagnosis of physical Dependence. Previous editions of the *DSM* did require the presence of both increased tolerance and physical withdrawal in order for a diagnosis to meet the criteria for Dependence. Instead, the *DSM (IV-TR)* demarcates two sub-groups of Dependence: *physiologic dependence* (with physical withdrawal

and tolerance) and *non-physiologic dependence* (without physical withdrawal and tolerance). But this change has not worked well in follow-up studies. Research shows that the *DSM (IV-TR)* does not discriminate well between heavy substance users and physically dependent users (Schuckit et al., 1998; Hasin et al., 2000).

Indeed, the demarcation of two sub-groups is a controversial idea, as physical withdrawal is such a clear marker of severe physical dependence. As we have already seen, Edwards & Gross (1976) identified that physical withdrawal could only occur after the establishment of tolerance and both were necessary for a diagnosis. This has led some researchers to suggest that the criteria of dependence should be restricted to the presence of withdrawal alone. This is because populations of problem users with withdrawal symptoms perform far worse in follow-up studies than those who do not have these particular symptoms. For example, Hasin et al. (2000) found that problem alcohol users who had withdrawal symptoms were almost three times more likely to still be meeting the *DSM (IV-TR)* criteria for Dependence 12 months later, compared to those drinkers without withdrawal symptoms. When the alcohol symptoms of tremens are included in the withdrawal criteria (which they currently are not in the *DSM (IV-TR)*), drinkers were also six times more likely to relapse. Withdrawal, at the least, should be taken to serve as an indicator that the severest levels of physical dependence have been reached, and also be indicative of who requires medical attention to assist in the detoxification process.

When assessing the *DSM (IV-TR)*, it must be remembered that it has been developed for use in the American health care system. This private insurance based health care approach requires that the individual seeking treatment must have a formal diagnosis in order to qualify for financial assistance. Therefore, the *DSM (IV-TR)* and its various editions often formulate broad diagnostic criteria in order to capture the largest possible treatment population. However, in the UK this financial eligibility assessment is not relevant, as everyone is entitled to access to services. But resources are not infinite, and it is essential that those seeking professional support receive appropriate treatment. It is a poor use of resources to undertake detoxification with young people who do not need it, and it is dangerous to fail to medically intervene with young people who may experience potentially harmful consequences of unassisted withdrawal. Balancing this requires a greater recognition of the presenting symptoms of dependence.

Any treatment programme will have to account for two distinct problems. Interventions for abuse are primarily psychosocial. They must assist young people to re-construct the ruptured attachments to the social networks that shape normative development. Treatment for dependence is primarily medical. The identification and assessment of withdrawal is essential to manage it effectively, especially when the young person is using depressants. Tolerance levels govern whether substitute prescribing or detoxification is required and indicate the dosage. Therefore, for a complete package of care, both the social relationships of the young person requiring restoration, and their physical need for the substance, need to be managed. When treatment interventions confuse these two issues, treatment inevitably fails.

Young people and diagnostic criteria

Whilst there remains some debate about diagnostic criteria for adults (for a review see Martin and Chung, 2008) these issues are more critical of young people. For example, research has been conducted on the *DSM (IV-TR)* criteria in comparison to other diagnostic critera in order to assess their consistency. The alternative diagnostic criteria is the World Health Organisation's International Classification of Diseases *ICD-(10)*. This diagnostic framework is largley used for research purposes and has a dependence criteria as well as a lower order Hazardous Use criteria which is the equivalent of abuse. Comparisons of these two diagnostic systems show strong agreement with each other in terms of Dependence but far weaker agreement on lower order problems such as Abuse/Hazardous use. For example, a large scale international study was conducted on young people in 11 different countries in order to establish cultural sensitivity in the criteria for diagnosing drug and alcohol related problems (See Cottler et al., 1997; Hasin et al., 1997; Pull et al., 1997; Ustun et al., 1997). These studies were conducted in Developed, Developing and Third World countries. The incidences of the various diagnostic criteria for Dependence as described by the *DSM (IV-TR)* and *ICD-(10)* showed a very high level of agreement with each other in the various countries. However, the comparisons of the *DSM (IV-TR)* diagnosis of Abuse and the equivalent *ICD-(10)* diagnosis of Harmful Use showed very little agreement. The reason why both diagnostic frameworks agree at the extreme end of Dependence is because they are both derived from the Alcohon Dependence Syndrome. As we have seen, this is a diagnostic framework developed for adults at the chronic end of problem use. Neither the *DSM (IV-TR)* or the *ICD-(10)* appear sensitive to the early onset of substance misuse problems which are the one's most likely to be experienced by young people in the emergent using careers.

Furthermore, Chung et al. (2002) found little concordance in the incidence of symptoms of Abuse, as defined by *DSM (IV-TR)*, within a specific country. This study compared young people's symptoms in community settings compared to those of young people in clinical treatment settings. Whilst it would be anticipated that young people in clinical settings would have more severe problems than those in the community, this was not the case. Furthermore, when reviewing four community samples, Chung et al. (2002) found that the incidence of alcohol Abuse ranged from 0.4 per cent in one population to 9.6 per cent in another population of young people. The rates of Dependence, again as defined by *DSM (IV-TR)*, varied from 0.6 per cent to 4.3 per cent. Regional differences are to be expected in any sample study, but the differences identified by Chung when using the same diagnostic criteria represent a huge discrepancy in scores, questioning its validity for young people.

Indeed, in terms of Dependence, the *DSM (IV-TR)* appears to be a poor fit for young people. Research shows that the Dependence diagnosis tends to produce a high proportion of 'diagnostic orphans' amongst young people. Diagnostic orphans are individuals that demonstrate one or two symptoms of Dependence over a twelve month period, but not the three symptoms required to establish a full diagnosis. Yet adolescents who are diagnostic orphans do not differ from those who do meet the full diagnosis on a number of external measures and outcomes (Pollock & Martin, 1999). In contrast to this, using the *DSM (IV-TR)* Dependence criteria reveals a high incidence of adolescent 'diagnostic imposters' (Martin, 1999). These young people meet the *DSM (IV-TR)* criteria for Dependence but do not have significant problems.

This poor fit of criteria can lead to a significant level of misdiagnosis of adolescent substance misuse problems. For example, Pollock & Martin (1999) studied 199 male and 173 female drinkers aged between 13 and 19. Using the *DSM (IV-TR)* criteria, they assessed these young people at the start of the study and then reassessed them all one year later. Of the total sample, 135 received a current diagnosis of alcohol Dependence and 110 met the criteria for Abuse. However, 127 young drinkers were diagnostic orphans. They had no abuse symptoms, and only met two of the dependence criteria but not the three necessary for a formal diagnosis. This population accounted for 31 per cent of the sample. The symptoms that these orphans did exhibit included tolerance (41 per cent), drinking longer than intended (33 per cent), unsuccessful efforts to quit or cut down (26 per cent) and much time spent using (21 per cent). However, the orphans' consumption and likely progression into more problematic use were identical to those who met the full Dependence criteria.

DSM (IV-TR)'s key symptoms of dependence are highly distorted in young people (Martin & Winters, 1998). This problem is located in the structure of its diagnostic approach. The original impetus of the diagnostic criteria was developed in order to identify problem drinkers from those who required medical attention. This focuses the diagnostics at the highest threshold of problem use, after years of consumption. Conversely, young people are still in the early stages of drug or alcohol involvement and so would not have reached this high cut-off point. As a result, the criteria for a diagnosis of dependence amongst adult users do not fit the drug and alcohol using patterns of young people, or can be distorted by a range of age-related issues creating false positive and false negative scores. Reviewing specific key symptoms reveals where these disjunctures occur.

The manifestation of key symptoms

In terms of abuse, a review shows that the *DSM (IV-TR)* diagnostic approach is highly generalised. The social consequences of use are very different for young people than for adults by virtue of their position in the life course. Interruptions in social functioning may be highly age- or status-specific in young people. The difficulty with the *DSM (IV-TR)* Abuse diagnosis is that most of the criteria are based on social responses to the user, which can be highly varied. For example, alcohol use in a 13-year-old may be met with social problems, such as conflict with parents, in a way that it is not in a 16-year-old. Social acceptability of drug use in the family or neighbourhood may mean that there is no family response at all to drug use in young people. School policies on drug and alcohol use may vary greatly, creating divergent levels of role impairment. A young person may be excluded from one school as a result of use, but a young person at a different school may not be excluded, even when they are using the same amount.

Different problems emerge in attempting to apply *DSM (IV-TR)* Dependence criteria to young people. Tolerance is defined there as the need for increasing consumption to achieve a similar effect. A 50 per cent increase to attain a similar effect within 12 months is the benchmark of the increased tolerance criteria. However, young people can experience this increased tolerance as part of the normal developmental process. Young people who have never imbibed alcohol will have an initially low tolerance but this will increase quickly as they continue to consume. For example, Chung & Martin (2001) found that young people who initiate alcohol use and are initially intoxicated on low doses often increase tolerance very quickly to large doses (from 2 to 8 drinks). Those with a higher starting tolerance increase it more slowly (from 6 to 8 drinks). This means that the use of the *DSM (IV-TR)* would positively identify novice drinkers as problematic drinkers simply through this natural process of tolerance development creating a false score. Furthermore, problems in diagnosis relate to withdrawal following increased tolerance. Long term exposure is required to develop a high range of tolerance before the withdrawal process begins. Because of this extensive time period, physical withdrawal is rarely observed in young people in medical settings. But, this may be because that withdrawal develops over a relatively long time span, or it could be that withdrawal manifests itself differently in adolescent populations.

Other non-physiological symptoms also manifest themselves differently for young people than for adults. For example, *DSM (IV-TR)* dependence symptom 3 – 'The substance is often taken in larger amounts or over a longer period than intended' – refers in adults to a loss of control over their ability to regulate their consumption. For example a binge drinker might find that, once they have begun drinking, they cannot stop or control their intake. However, young people may consume larger amounts or for longer than intended because of peer influence rather than lack of personal control. Likewise, symptom 5 – 'A great deal of time is spent in activities necessary to obtain the substance, use the substance, or recover from its effects' – describes in adult populations a subjective compulsion to acquire a substance at all costs to alleviate physical or psychological need. Young people may spend a great deal of time trying to acquire substances because of its high social prestige combined with its limited availability within their social network.

Longitudinal studies show that symptoms of abuse can occur faster in young people than in adult populations (Deas et al., 2000). However, there does not appear to be a linear progression in the *DSM (IV-TR)* model from Abuse through to dependence as suggested in its diagnostic criteria. If an alternative method of diagnosis is used, such as Latent Class Analysis, it suggests that young people's substance-related problems exist on a continuum rather than move through distinct categories of abuse, then dependence. Whilst abuse is considered to be the least problematic condition, symptoms of the more clinically severe dependence tend to precede abuse (Martin et al., 1995; Wagner et al., 2002). Harrison et al. (1998) assessed 74,008 students as part of a state-wide survey in Minnesota of young people's drug and alcohol use in the US. They found that students who reported three or more of the *DSM (IV-TR)* symptoms of Abuse or dependence used more than one substance. However, 'the major finding with respect to the DSM-IV (sic) criteria for adolescents was that the abuse/dependence diagnostic framework was not supported in this epidemiological study.' (Harrison et al., 1998: 491) This research demonstrated that making a distinction between abuse and dependence was simply not found in young people's use.

Research into the evolution of young people's substance-related problems suggests that the symptoms emerge in stages. A number of researchers (Chung et al., 2002; Martin et al., 1995) found that the development of tolerance was the first symptom to evolve in youth for most substances. This would be expected due to the low initial tolerance levels most young people experience at the outset of their use. Martin et al. (1996) and Wagner et al. (2002) found that the first two years of regular drinking tended to display the onset of 'drinking more and for longer than intended', followed by increases in interpersonal problems related to drinking. From the third to fourth years, symptoms such as 'increased time spent using' appear. The third stage is characterised by the experience of 'physical withdrawal', but it does not emerge for most young people. Wagner et al. (2002) found that alcohol-related social problems tended to occur within the first two years of consumption. Rosenberg & Anthony (2001) found that cannabis users experienced 'using for longer than intended' in the first year of use. This was followed by cannabis-related health or psychological problems in the second year. Nearly all studies identified that the emergence of withdrawal was rare in young people, even in the case of alcohol, heroin or cocaine (Chung & Martin, 2005).

This research suggests that young people's problematic use tends to move through a sequence. The first phase of consumption is characterised by increased tolerance, using for

Table 4.6: The evolution of substance abuse problems over time

Symptom

Phase 1
- Tolerance *(d)*
- Drinking larger amounts or for longer than intended *(d)*
- Much time spent using *(d)*
- Role impairment *(a)*
- Social problems *(a)*

Phase 2
- Unsuccessful attempt or persistent desire to quit or cut down *(d)*
- Reduce activities *(d)*
- Hazardous use *(a)*
- Legal problems *(a)*

Phase 3
- Withdrawal *(d)*

Based on Martin & Winters, 1998

longer than intended, social problems and role impairment. These symptoms describe an increasing involvement with substance use during this time. The second phase is characterised by attempts to stop or reduce use, reductions in other social activities, hazardous use and legal problems. At this stage, the nature of the problems shifts from failure to manage social roles and responsibilities into experiencing direct negative consequences of use. These problems appear to be of sufficient magnitude to trigger motivation to try and cut down or to quit use. Finally, the crowning symptom of dependence is experienced in the form of physical withdrawal. This is liable to be far more profound in depressant drugs such as alcohol, heroin and benzodiazepines. Table 4.6 sets out this sequence and identifies the onset of either dependence *(d)* or abuse *(a)* symptoms, as originally defined by *DSM (IV-TR)*.

The rate of acquisition of substance-related problems

In general, studies into alcohol have found an earlier onset of alcohol-related problems in young women (14.6 years old) than young men (16.1 years old). Males then appear to acquire problems at a faster rate than females once consumption is initiated (Lewinsohn et al., 1996). However, it is difficult to place fixed schedules on the development of substance use disorders as

some social groups are prone to 'telescoping'. Telescoping was a term was first used in the 1950s to describe the more rapid acceleration in drinking-related problems that appeared to occur in women in comparison to men. Alcohol-related problems could emerge within two years of onset in women compared to seven years in men. These studies were limited to adult drinking populations and were confounded by the fact that women often presented for treatment more rapidly than men did. Thus telescoping could be an illusion created by a propensity for women to seek professional help more quickly than men.

Research into telescoping has broadened to other populations, specifically children of alcoholics. These young people have been demonstrated to show a high vulnerability to the rapid onset of alcohol-related problems in comparison to other young people (Chassin et al., 1996). A number of mechanisms have been suggested for this rapid onset. Some research has suggested a biological/genetic sensitivity. Newlin & Thomson (1999) found that children of alcoholic parents had a greater sensitivity to alcohol's effects in comparison to the quantities tolerated by their peers. This greater sensitivity could decrease their opportunity to learn controlled drinking skills as they were catapulted into problematic consumption at a faster rate. At the same time, fraternising with heavy drinkers in and around their families creates little social resistance to increasing use. This population is prone to the externalised behavioural disorders and associated risk factors that we reviewed in Chapter 3. They tended to exhibit disinhibited temperament, deviant behaviours and externalised symptoms that make them more prone to engage in consumption without considering social or interpersonal consequences (Zucker, 2006; Wong et al., 2006).

Hussong et al. (2008) tested which of these biological, social and temperament factors had the greatest impact on the rate of development of alcohol problems. Their research was based on interviews with 454 families over a three-year period who were followed up 5 and 10 years later. They found that the children of alcoholics were 2.7 times more likely to experience alcohol problems than their peers. Furthermore, the children of alcoholics experienced the onset of alcohol disorder within 4 years of initiation into drinking compared to 7 years for the non-alcoholic parent group. Gender, age and ethnicity were not significant in this finding. This research concluded that the main drivers of the telescoping effect appeared to be the severity of *externalised symptoms prior to use*. Telescoping effects were similar whether parents were in active or inactive alcoholism. Hence historically impaired parenting through intoxication, poor role modelling, or provision of greater access to alcohol did not have any less impact on the rate of onset of problems than currently impaired parenting. But concurrent alcohol and mental health problems in parents, such as depression or anti-social personality disorder, did have a major effect on telescoping. This may suggest a genetic link. Or, alternatively, the co-morbidity of parents may have even greater impact on their ability to parent effectively than alcohol problems on their own. Interestingly, early onset of drug use was strongly associated with telescoping effects for drug-related problems, but not in the case of alcohol. Children of alcoholics who initiated consumption later in adolescence had the highest risk of telescoping.

Screening

Many of the risk factors described in Chapter 3 appear to influence the rate at which substance-related problems are acquired. When considering the risk factors that have already been identified, it appears that the lives of many young people who are most at risk of developing problems are characterised by weak social relationships to begin with. This means that a high level of consumption may not initially be necessary to compromise these strained attachments. The social impairment described in the *DSM (IV-TR)* Abuse criteria may already be in place for many of these young people prior to use. So, as screening for drug and alcohol problems has become increasingly standard practice in recent years, it can play a critical role in the early detection of these social problems, if they are to be addressed before they become entrenched, once exacerbated by the drug and alcohol problems.

Screening tools are designed to identify the possible presence of substance-related problems in young people. To be effective, they need to be conducted, when it is practical, in universal services for young people such as schools, youth centres or medical settings, as young people are unlikely to voluntarily present to services specifically based on substance misuse. As screening is conducted by non-specialists, its

function should simply be to identify positive and negative cases for intervention. This requires that screening tools are brief, accurate and cost effective. A positive test on screening indicates (what some might call the negative circumstances) that further assessment and/or referral is required. Most screening tools tend to use scoring systems with a clinical cut-off point which is taken to indicate the presence of a drug- or alcohol-related problem.

Issues concerning how substance misuse disorders differ in adolescents compared to adults mean that many screening tools are not configured to identify young people's substance-related problems effectively. For example, a screening tool that detects the late-onset withdrawal symptoms is liable to be wholly insensitive to young people's use as withdrawal is such a rare phenomenon in this population. Attention to earlier-onset symptoms of drug- and alcohol-related problems may be more sensitive to detecting the emergence of drug- and alcohol-related problems in young people. Furthermore, no score on any screening tool, no matter how high, should automatically be considered indicative of substance misuse problems; a deeper assessment is necessary. Likewise, a low score may not suggest that the young person does not have any problems. Considering the age of the young person, it may be that they are on a wider trajectory towards problem use than the particular screening can pick up. Research and evaluation has suggested that two screening tools demonstrate the greatest sensitivity in identifying adolescent substance abuse problems. These are the *Alcohol Use Disorder Identification Test (AUDIT)* (Barbor et al., 1989) and the *CRAFFT* (Knight, 1999).

The *AUDIT* is a ten-item questionnaire which explores alcohol consumption and alcohol-related problems. Each question can be scored from 0–4, offering a total score of 40. However, this raw total is not the whole picture. The ten questions are ordered into sub-scales to give a deeper reading of the type of problems that are being experienced. Questions 1–3 relate to Hazardous Use; questions 4–6 relate to the presence of Dependence; whilst questions 7–10 identify symptoms of Harmful Use. Hence, high scores within these sub-scales give a more accurate picture of the types of alcohol problems that young people are experiencing (see Table 4.7) than the overall score.

In adults, a total score of 8 or more tends to

Table 4.7: *AUDIT* sub-scales

Domains	Question	Item content
Hazardous use	1	Frequency of drinking
	2	Typical quantity
	3	Frequency of heavy drinking
Dependence	4	Impaired control over
	5	drinking
	6	Increased salience of
		drinking
		Morning drinking
Harmful use	7	Guilt after drinking
	8	Blackouts
	9	Alcohol related injuries
	10	Others concerned about
		drinking

Barbor et al., 1989.

indicate problem use with a score 20 indicating severe problems. Amongst young medical patients, *AUDIT* worked best with a clinical cut-off score of 3 (Knight et al., 2003) or 4 (Chung et al., 2000). *AUDIT* has proved a reliable measurement of dependence and problem drinking across gender and age (Saunders et al., 1993) and culture (Allen et al., 1997). The limitation of *AUDIT* is that it is restricted to alcohol. A drug equivalent is available, *DUDIT*, though this has received far less evaluation of its effectiveness.

A second screening tool that is effective for drug and alcohol use in young people is *CRAFFT* (Knight et al., 2002). This is an acronym for a 6-item questionnaire which, when evaluated, did not differ to *AUDIT* in its sensitivity in identifying Abuse in problem drinkers, and had a similar sensitivity with drug users as well. *CRAFFT* indicates a substance misuse problem with a cut off of 2 and has demonstrated superiority to other screening tools in comparative trials (Knight et al., 2003). It is also endorsed by the American Academy of Pediatrics (2002). *CRAFFT* is available in self-administration and interview formats and includes such questions as:

- Have you ridden in a **Car** driven by some (including yourself) who had been drinking or using drugs?
- Do you use drugs or alcohol to **Relax**, feel better about yourself or fit in?
- Do you use drugs or alcohol when you are by yourself or **Alone**?

- Do you **Forget** things you did while using alcohol or drugs?
- Do your family or **Friends** tell you that you should cut down on your drinking or your drug use?
- Have you gotten into **Trouble** while using drugs or alcohol?

The *CRAFFT* score predominantly focuses on abuse symptoms. Whilst these are more apposite than dependence symptoms to young people's use, it does not give such a comprehensive overview of their consumption as *AUDIT* does, as it assumes that the young person's consumption level is explored separately. However, it does benefit from being easy to use in a wide variety of settings without recourse to paper by the screener, as long as the key questions can be recalled. This may give it a more informal feel that young people value.

A wide array of alternative screening tools is available. These tools have become increasingly complex and sophisticated. It is important to remember, though, that the function of a screening tool is simply to identify positive and negative cases, usually by non-specialists in substance misuse. Long screening tools may actually drift into formal assessment rather than screening. Not only is this cumbersome but it also requires a greater depth of knowledge, which can make any subsequent assessment repetitious. This may be particularly hard for young people who have a low boredom threshold. Therefore, in selecting a screening tool, it is important to ensure limited cross-over with any follow-up assessment. Table 4.8 describes a wide range of screening tools that are currently available, and their validation.

In the use of screening tools, it is important that there is a planned response to both positive and negative results. A negative result, suggesting no current problem, does not necessarily preclude the possibility of a future positive result, especially for young people who are at risk of early involvement in drug and alcohol use. For this population, even a delay in the onset of use can have significant consequences in reducing the impact of their overall substance-using trajectory. In this context, it is important to note that there is emergent research that positive verbal reinforcement in light of a negative screen can have a significant impact on delaying subsequent initiation (Hancock, 2002; Henderlong & Lepper, 2002). Positive praise, genuine respect from a

Table 4.8:   Review of screening tools for adolescent substance abuse

Screening tool	Description
Client Substance Index (Thomas, 1990)	15 item yes/no questionnaire used for identification of drug and alcohol abuse in youth justice environments. Shows good reliability and matches consumption to offending behaviour.
Drug and Alcohol Problem (DAP) Quick Screen (Schwartz & Wirtz, 1990)	30 item questionnaire that assesses overall drug and alcohol problem severity. Not validated.
Drug Use Screening Inventory – Revised (DUSI-R) (Tarter et al., 1992)	159 true/false questions yield scores on 10 adolescent problems such as drug and alcohol use, health, mental health, family, peers, education, vocational status, social skills, leisure and recreation as well as delinquency. Also includes a lie scale, and is available in lifetime, past-year and past month versions. It has shown very high validity.
Perceived benefit of drinking and drug use (Petchers & Singer, 1990)	10 item questionnaire assessing the young person's perceived benefits of alcohol and other drug use. Developed as a non-threatening screen, it operates on the assumptions that the positive expectancy of use tends to be associated with actual use. Has been validated.
Personal Experience Screening Questionnaire (PESQ) (Winters, 1992)	40 item questionnaire that provides measures of overall problem severity, using history, psychosocial problems and accounts for distortion of presenting information. Validated tool.
Problem Orientated Screening Instrument for Teenagers (POSIT) (Rahdert, 1991)	139 item yes/no questionnaire developed by the National Institute on Drug Abuse. It addresses 10 problem areas in the same areas as the DUSI-R described above.
Substance Abuse Subtle Screening Inventory (SASSI) (Miller, 1985)	81 item questionnaire that assesses the severity of alcohol and drug problems. Includes additional measures on denial. Validated tool.
Adolescent Alcohol Involvement Scale (AAIS) (Mayer & Filstead, 1979)	14 item questionnaire establishes past and current alcohol use and perceptions of consumptions. Score demonstrated alcohol involvement. Validated tool.
Adolescent Drinking index (ADI) (Harrell & Wirtz, 1989)	24 item questionnaire addressing alcohol related problems in psychological, physical and social functioning. It has two sub-scales to identify self-medicating drinking and rebellious drinking. A validated tool.
Rutgers Alcohol Problem Index (RAPI) (White & Labouvie, 1989)	23 item questionnaire assessing the consequences of alcohol use on family life, social life, psychological functioning, delinquency physical problem and neurological disorders. Validated tool.

professional for a young person's decisions and rewards can all be powerful reinforcers to remain drug or alcohol free. This can be coupled with feedback on the health or social risks that the young person is avoiding as a result of their decision not to use drugs or alcohol.

Screening may also identify young people who are using drugs or alcohol but whose scores are not high enough to warrant referral to treatment. In this situation the professional should utilise brief advice in order to encourage the young person to quit or reduce at this stage. Objective feedback on the impact of drugs and alcohol on their development can be very helpful along with exploring options for change. Motivational

Interviewing is one such brief approach that has demonstrated a high degree of success in helping young people reduce or quit, and is reviewed extensively in Chapter 6.

Young people who test positive at screening should be interviewed more deeply regarding their consumption pattern and consequences. Establishing the history of their use may be important in assessing whether use is escalating or not. Assessing frequency and amounts consumed in more detail may also indicate how likely it is that the young person is experiencing profound difficulties in controlling their use.

Table 4.9:   Summary of the stages of change

Stages	Description
Pre-contemplation	Not considering change
	May not recognise problems
	Recognise positives in use
	Rationalise or justify use
	Attribute problems to others, such as parents' over-reaction
Contemplation	Increasing awareness of substance-related issues
	Use may create and alleviate internal stress
	Experience mixed feelings regarding change
	A 'near miss' accident can tip change
	Resolved by committing to change
Preparation	Future orientated
	Planning
	Considering options
	Resolved by turning intentions into action
Action	Stop using drugs/alcohol
	Managing to cope without use
	Separate from using peer groups
	Keeping occupied
	Resolved if sustained for six months
Maintenance	Reintegrating into new pro-social networks
	Wider life goals
	Resolution of a new personal and social identity
Relapse	Failure to sustain change
	Slips
	Lapses
	Relapse

Change in response to screening

Young people's recognition and willingness to discuss these issues may be indicative of their motivation for change. It is important to recognise that motivation for change occurs on a spectrum. Prochaska & DiClemente's (1992) influential Stages of Change model demonstrated that change occurs in a sequence. This begins with *pre-contemplation*, where the individual does not recognise any need for change and only perceives the benefits of use. However, as the consequences of use increase, they become increasingly aware of the impact of their use. This can elicit *contemplation* of change. Contemplation is difficult to resolve as young people recognise the problems that stem from their use whilst at the very same time experience benefits in use. Contradictory feelings towards the same object are described as ambivalence. Resolving these mixed feelings requires self-evaluation before any commitment to change can be made. This moves the young person into *preparation* for change where they are open to reviewing options and making plans. These plans must be enacted upon and put into *action*. In these early stages their confidence in change is low, and therefore avoidance of, and separating from, using peers becomes essential. If they sustain this for six months they enter the *maintenance* of change stage, where they create new peer groups and engage in alternative sources of satisfaction. In *relapse* they may revert back to their old using behaviour. As they progress through these stages they may require very different levels of support to assist them in the process (see Table 4.9).

Young people are more likely than adults to be in the pre-contemplative stage of change for a number of reasons. The under-developed pre-frontal cortex means that young people lack consequential thinking. Furthermore, overtly positive expectations of use, normalisation of high consumption amongst peers and a lack of immediate health-threatening consequences may militate against the young person considering change. Even where they recognise that they are experiencing difficulties they do not automatically attribute problems to their consumption, or can believe that they are capable of managing these difficulties without assistance (Botvin & Tortu, 1998).

This may be amplified by the 'personal fable' where young people find it hard to contemplate that bad things can happen to them. For many young people, being willing to take on the risks of use can serve as a badge of identity as an 'outsider'. Furthermore, externalised and internalised youth may have experienced extensive professional support which was not necessarily helpful. This can deepen their pessimism about the value of yet more treatment which may appear futile to them. As a result, research suggests that 50 per cent of young people are in pre-contemplation regarding changing their substance use (Connors et al., 2001). They are often far more likely to enter into treatment through legal coercion, while at reachable moments such as entering an A & E department, or through family pressure, rather than to self-present for help.

If a young person has recognised the need to make change, the referral process is straight forward. It is important that the professional who conducts the screening process has a good knowledge of the treatment services and options available. This can help allay fears and address any negative expectations of entering treatment that the young person may have. Encouraging parental/guardian involvement can increase attendance and improve subsequent treatment outcomes. Routine follow-up after brief advice or referral is essential to monitor the changes or levels of engagement the young person managed to attain. Where a young person does not acknowledge the need for change, Motivational Interviewing can assist in this process. Alternatively, for a highly unmotivated young person, interventions can be provided through parents or guardians who can have a huge influence on their motivation to change. These processes are reviewed in more detail in Chapter 6.

Comprehensive assessment: overview

Comprehensive assessment of young people's needs presents unique challenges for the practitioner. The assessment process needs to be thorough but not monotonous, due to the boredom factor that young people can experience in relatively short periods of time. The assessment must identify the presence and severity of dependence as well as the impact of use on a young person's wider social functioning. This entails assessing the breakdown of, or threats to, a young person's attachments in each social domain, including housing, family, education/training, crime, mental health and physical health. Whilst adult social functioning tends to remain fairly static across the life course, adolescence is a period of rapid developmental change. The life tasks of an 11-year-old differ greatly from those of a 16-year-old. Greater attention is needed to the 'age-appropriateness' of a young person's development. For example, a 15-year-old young person with a romantic partner might be considered developmentally on track in a way that a similar relationship at 9 years old would not be. In addition, the assessor should be mindful of the additional complications that young people can bring to treatment, such as adolescent mental health problems. A good understanding of externalised and internalised disorders may be necessary, especially in terms of referral to specialist mental health services. Broader issues such as Safeguarding, Child Protection and other legal requirements also require sensitive handling.

The purpose of an assessment is to establish a mutual understanding of a young person's current situation. At the same time as the assessor is assessing the young person, the young person is assessing the assessor. Through an evolving rapport, the former will be assessing the latter's authenticity, and this will influence their willingness to co-operate. These two processes can be at cross-purposes, where the information-gathering element can create a barrier to establishing rapport. For example, a cold and impassionate interviewer style will have a negative effect on assessment regardless of its structure. Literature reviews have continued to highlight the importance of effective assessment of young people's needs and its relationship to increased engagement rates (Baker, 2008; Hutchings & Levesley, 2008; Lipsey & Wilson, 1998). This first encounter can affect young people's subsequent responses to treatment in profound ways. A comprehensive assessment may also be the first opportunity that a young person has been offered to tell their story and consider their use in a systematic way. It affords them the opportunity to establish the connection between their drug and alcohol use and the wide range of difficulties that they are experiencing. Supporting young people to make these connections can be intrinsically important to the change process. For the first time, a young person will elucidate the negative consequences of use, which can challenge their overtly positive expectations of consumption.

The possibility of the comprehensive assessment itself providing impetus for change has been established by clinical research. Research demonstrates that many young people are susceptible to experiencing *Baseline Assessment Reactivity* (Epstein et al., 2005; Kypri et al., 2006), which refers to the phenomena whereby significant changes are made to drug or alcohol consumption that occur *in between* the completion of the assessment and the beginning of the first treatment session. As such, it offers early gains even before the 'active' treatment phase commences. These effects have been found both in adults (Clifford et al., 2000; 2007) and in young people (McCambridge & Strang, 2005).

Kaminer et al. (2008) examined whether Baseline Assessment Reactivity occurred in adolescents and whether it was possible to identify what made young people sensitive to this effect. To test the theory, assessments were conducted on 177 adolescents with alcohol problems on a nine-week therapy programme. These young people were screened for alcohol and drug use in the 30 days prior to the formal full clinical assessment and again just prior to the first treatment session. In terms of alcohol, 51.4 per cent of the young people who subsequently tested positive at the assessment were negative prior to the first session. Whilst for drugs, 29 per cent who had tested positive at assessment were negative at the first session. These are substantial gains considering that active treatment had not commenced between these two points in time. Waiting time, gender, age and criminal involvement were not related to Baseline Assessment Reactivity.

Baseline Assessment Reactivity was strongly associated with two key predictors. There was a strong relationship to the young person's readiness to change. Those with high motivation at the assessment made significant immediate gains. Reactivity was also predicted by the self-efficacy of the young person. Young people with high confidence in their capacity to change made significant pre-treatment gains. It is important to state that the adolescents who made gains between assessment and treatment in this

study continued to make additional gains during the treatment process. However, this early baseline improvement contributed substantially to the overall outcome.

The more beneficial that clients perceive the early engagement with professional support to be, the better they will do in any subsequent treatment, and this begins with the assessment process itself. The fact that Baseline Assessment Reactivity can have such a considerable impact on treatment gains should not be overlooked in the design and implementation of comprehensive assessment. These two key predictors should be woven into the assessment process itself in order to maximise treatment gains. Designing assessment tools to explicitly increase the motivation of young people as well as increase their belief in their capacity to change is vital to enhance the long term outcome of their treatment. However, this has generally not yet been fully developed or integrated into daily practice, in the UK or elsewhere.

Comprehensive assessment: dependence

A striking feature of most comprehensive assessments of young people is the limited attention given to the assessment of the severity of dependence. This may be as a result of a lack of understanding of the diagnostic criteria of dependence in everyday practice. The fact that young people may present with significant risk of severe health problems resulting from their consumption demands that a deep understanding of dependence be obtained through a thorough assessment of young people's health needs. But, instead of assessing dependence, both youth and adult substance misuse services assess consumption. Nearly all comprehensive assessment tools contain a drug and alcohol use consumption table which charts primary and secondary substance use, the amounts used, route of administration and prescription status (see Figure 4.1).

Establishing consumption offers a clear mutual understanding of current usage. It gives an indication of the severity of use and, importantly, whether medically assisted detoxification is necessary. This data also offers a baseline measure of use at intake that may be a useful marker of any subsequent treatment's effectiveness if repeated at treatment completion.

Figure 4.1: Example of a consumption table

Substance	Amount	Frequency/week	Route	Prescribed?
Alcohol	20 units	2	Drank	No
Grass	¼ oz	7	Smoked	No

However, there are limitations to consumption tables. They tend to rank substances in order of severity of use. Hence, the 'primary' substance of abuse is entered first, followed by 'secondary' substance, etc. This could be adapted to offer greater insight into a young person's progression in substance use. As we saw in Chapter 3, young people's use is often sequenced in a gateway order of initiation. This begins with nicotine, followed by alcohol and then cannabis. The more frequently they use these substances, the more probable it becomes that they will progress to other substances.

The consumption table could be adapted to map the young person's involvement in substances if they are recorded in order of *initiation* rather than *problem severity*. This should always include nicotine, as it appears to be highly predictive of future substance use. Age of initiation of each substance also reveals important information. First, it will give an indication of the sub-trajectory that the young person is on. Second, it may highlight the length of social exclusion that may have occurred, offering insight into possible treatment. Third, it will offer insight into the current progression of the young person's use and the likelihood of their advancing into heavy substance use. In this way, a sequenced consumption table may not simply establish current consumption but may also establish the case history of substance involvement and predict future involvement. This might trigger education or prevention approaches to interrupt the possible sequence (see Figure 4.2).

It is important to reiterate that consumption and dependence are not the same thing. For example, one young person might report drinking 50 units of alcohol a week. If they are drinking at this rate and have not developed withdrawal, they are a heavy drinker. However another young person might report drinking 50 units a week and have developed withdrawal-like symptoms when they stop. They are a physically dependent drinker and would require a medically supervised detoxification. So whilst the consumption rate is exactly the same, the treatment they require is very different. A further limitation is that young people perceive their own consumption as typical. Assessing consumption rates in isolation of any other

Figure 4.2: Example of a sequence consumption table

Substance	Age of first use	Amount	Freq/ week	Route	Prescribed	Are you still using this substance? If no, when did you stop?
Tobacco	11	9/day	7 days	Smoked	No	
Alcohol	11	15 units	3 days	Drunk	No	
Grass	12	1/16	7 days	Smoked	No	
Ecstasy	13	½ tablet	1 only once	Oral	No	

comparative information will not foster an opportunity to increase the young person's insight into the severity of their use.

Assessing the severity of dependence is difficult as many young people can present as diagnostic orphans or imposters. The Centre for Substance Abuse Treatment (CSAT, 1999) offered a different set of criteria for calibrating a young person's use on a spectrum of severity. This ranged from abstinence at the low end of consumption to dependence at the extreme end. This system may offer an opportunity to establish current status of use in young people. The status should be monitored frequently due to the rapid rate at which young people may develop drug or alcohol abuse symptoms. For example, Martin et al. (1995) found that young people could develop dependence in under 12 months, as compared to adults where this process tends to take years to establish. As a result, the following criteria might not only be best used as an indication of current status for assessment purposes, but may also be indicative of the most appropriate intensity of treatment. Whilst the CSAT scales offer greater insight into the process of dependence, they too remain limited. The criteria are subjective and assume that abuse precedes dependence. As such, it does not offer deeper insight into the severity of the problem in a young person:

1. Abstinence: no reported use.
2. Experimental use: minimal use, often associated with recreational activities and usually limited to alcohol.
3. Early abuse: more established pattern of use, usually involving more than one substance, greater frequency of use and the emergence of some social complications or problems.
4. Abuse: regular and frequent use over an extended period, several adverse consequences occur.
5. Dependence: continued use despite repeated severe negative consequences, signs of tolerance, adjustment in activities to account for usage, and failed attempts to reduce or stop using.

CSAT, 1999

A more effective assessment process for dependence can be derived from the data that has consistently shown how the sequence of abuse and dependence symptoms emerge over time in a sequence. This can be converted into a checklist of symptoms within the assessment process in order to assess a young person's progression into problematic use. The sequence of symptoms can be ordered in the phases in which they are likely to occur. In the first two years of use, Phase 1 symptoms are characterised by increasing involvement in use. In the third to fourth years of use, Phase 2 tends to show increasing negative social consequences of use and failed attempts to quit. Phase 3 is characterised by the emergence of physical withdrawal symptoms (see Figure 4.3). This deeper assessment of dependence should be completed on the primary drug of abuse and not on all substances. This is because the primary drug will impact on the young person's social functioning more profoundly than the other substances. For example, if the young person uses ketamine heavily, and cannabis and alcohol occasionally, ketamine will have the greater social impact first and foremost. The primary drug of choice can be considered as the pacesetter for subsequent problems.

There are many benefits to assessing severity of problems in this sequence. First, the typical sequence of symptoms allows the practitioner to assess severity of problematic use as it develops in young people. In piloting this approach with family members, adults and young people, the author has found the relevance of these questions to be a powerful engagement process. The questions are poignant. Their authenticity appears prescient in articulating experiences that may have previously only occurred in a young person's private thoughts. When treatment interventions speak so directly of a young person's experience, it increases their confidence in the assessor. Whilst discussions of consumption can be normalised by young people, the experience of these problems cannot be so casually dismissed, especially when they are indicative of escalating problems. This raises the opportunity to give feedback regarding the current severity of their problems. This psycho-education role can have beneficial effects on prompting change.

Furthermore, the likely consequences of continued use can also be explored. These future consequences are highly predictable. Those experiencing several Phase 1 symptoms are liable to progress to Phase 2 symptoms. Those experiencing Phase 2 symptoms are vulnerable to progressing to Phase 3 symptoms of physical withdrawal, but only in the case of depressants such as alcohol, heroin or benzodiazepines. Feedback on this may be useful in countering overtly positive expectations of continued use

Figure 4.3: Symptom severity checklist

Symptom	Indication	What have you noticed?
Phase 1 **Tolerance:** Have you noticed that you have to use more of the substance to get the same effect?	Yes/No	
Larger amounts: Have you found yourself using more or for longer than intended?	Yes/No	
Time spent: Do you spend a great deal of time trying to find or buy the substance?	Yes/No	
Role impairment: Have you noticed that you are not doing things like school or homework anymore?	Yes/No	
Social problems: Have you noticed that your use is leading to arguments with people close to you (family, partners, peers etc.)?	Yes/No	
Phase 2 **Persistent desire to cut down or quit:** Have you made any attempts to cut down or stop using by yourself?	Yes/No	
Reduced activity: Have you noticed that you would rather use than do anything else?	Yes/No	
Hazardous use: Has use led you to taking risks such as travelling with a drink driver?	Yes/No	
Legal problems: Have you got into trouble with the police or been to court as a result of your use?	Yes/No	
Phase 3 **Withdrawal:** Do you experience any physical problems when the substance has worn off?	Yes/No	

with objective feedback about the negative realities of use. As we have seen, expectancies play a significant role in the initiation and maintenance of substance misuse. Social acceptance, mood enhancement, recreation and stress reductions were identified by Petraitis et al. (1995) as prime drivers for consumption in young people. This can be challenged through encouraging young people to reflect on their own experiences. Such feedback should not be delivered as a dire warning of the future consequences. Instead, it should be offered as part of an educative role where the practitioner invites the young person's own views on these eventualities. Even if this does not increase motivation for behavioural change at this stage, it can heighten future sensitivity when these predicted symptoms do emerge.

Comprehensive assessment: social functioning

As we have seen, the diagnostic criteria used to define Abuse largely describe the impact of drug and alcohol use on the social functioning of the young person. Whilst physical dependence is limited to depressant type substances, any substance can interfere with the social attachments and responsibilities of young people. A comprehensive assessment should measure this impact in each domain of the young person's life. Whilst there is not universal agreement on the social domains that ought to be assessed, they should include family, school, recreation, promiscuity, physical & mental health and future aspirations. These domains may need to be broken down further. For example, family might encompass more than family of origin but step families and foster families, too. Social recreation might need to accommodate more than one peer group and make distinction between partnering relationships and peer relationships.

Whilst assessments have often increased in length, the quality of assessment has not always improved. To show improvement, an assessment should identify what factors are sustaining consumption at present rather than just take detailed case history. In this way, a comprehensive assessment must identify the relevant factors in a young person's life, and identify the potential risks from use for them. The impact that consumption has on these social domains may vary. Later onset youth may show signs of deterioration such as dropping grades at school, greater conflict with parents, arrests etc. Whereas early onset youth are liable to have experienced catastrophic damage in their social ties or have neglected responsibilities for

extended periods of time. The severity and duration of social exclusion may give a strong indication for treatment prognosis. High functioning youth may benefit from brief interventions where highly excluded youth with complex needs will require extensive and extended support due to profound developmental delay.

The comprehensive assessment offers the opportunity to support young people in making a connection between their drug and alcohol use and any wider social problems that they are experiencing. Assessment of each social domain may not in itself foster insight into the impact substance misuse may have on a young person. But assessing each social domain in direct relationship to substance use can 'split' an assessment of life domains into two separate areas: the young person's functioning in each domain 'before' they used, and how they are functioning 'after' use. This provides a stronger point of comparison for the young person where they are able to see the impact that their substance use is having across their life. Conducting these split assessments over multiple domains is important because it easy for a young person to discount problems in one area, such as

Figure 4.4: Example of a split assessment of life domains

	Before	**After**
Family		
School		
Peers		
Partners		
Interests		
Physical health		
Mental health		
Future self		

school. The split assessment can reveal multiple difficulties that all pertain to drug or alcohol use making it harder for them to dismiss the pattern of social consequences (see Figure 4.4).

Split assessments reveal different patterns across various sub-trajectories of young people's development and consumption. Externalised youth will have experienced a wide range of problems prior to the initiation of use. As a consequence, pre-existing problems may simply drown out any post-initiation problems. Where entrenched underlying problems persist, they are likely to undermine any future treatment gains if they are not addressed. In these cases, special attention should be given to key areas of the assessment that may have greater relevance in the lives of young people than adults. Family history may impact on a young person's use in several ways. Genetic ancestry of substance abuse may increase a young person's potential risk, particularly in young male drinkers. However, high consuming or problematic using families will increase the risk of problems for young people in other ways as well, due to the normalisation of use, increased availability of substances, poor modelling of intoxication management or failure to set unacceptable thresholds of consumption (McGue, 1999).

McGue's further research identified that the children of problematic drug users were more likely to suffer from a wider range of undiagnosed health problems or the effects of malnutrition. Therefore profound pre-existent family dysfunction should trigger further investigations into the health of a young person, whether with their GP or with another doctor they have been seeing, if they have been suffering any long term health problems. For example, exposure to drugs and alcohol may have a significant impact on an adolescent's brain function. Deeper exploration of the young person's cognitive and neurological functioning where there appears to be significant impairment to their recall, or insensitivity to intoxication, is important. Establishing any diagnosis of co-existing mental health problems is also vital in the assessment process. As reviewed earlier, young people who experience the most severe drug and alcohol problems tend to have co-existing behavioural problems. These young people are also prone to a wider range of abuse including neglect and physical, sexual or emotional abuse.

Comprehensive assessment with internalised youth may raise other issues. They may exhibit good social functioning prior to the onset of mental health and substance misuse issues. Careful attention needs to be paid to the experience of any specific trauma event that may have contributed to the emergence of the disorder and in what life domain it occurred. This may raise specific issues of emotional, sexual or physical abuse that may require a more in-depth assessment. Identification of problem areas can also highlight 'stability zones' in the young person's life. These are the social networks that offer support, such as peers, partners or family, and that can be invaluable havens for young people at such times. Alternatively, if the disorders do not appear to be related to trauma experiences, particular attention should be given to any hypercritical environments or hypersensitivity that may make a more generalised contribution.

Later onset normative youth consumption is more liable to be bound up in their social relationships. The comparison between social functioning prior to use and currently is liable to be the most stark for this group who often experience fairly stable family and school lives prior to the onset of use. Further attention should be given to the young person's peer group or partner. Adolescents are more likely to experience severe alcohol- and drug-related problems if they are attached to a high consuming peer group (Farrell & Danish, 1993). For example, Chilcoat & Breslau (1999) found that young people involved with drug using peer peers had a six-fold increased risk of drug problems compared to those who were not involved with drug using peers. As we saw in Chapter 2, young women in a relationship with a male two or more years older are at high risk of heavy consumption, as well as sexual exploitation, teen pregnancy and sexually transmitted diseases.

Sense of self

Drug and alcohol use interferes with young people's ability to make the ultimate transition from childhood to adulthood. A key issue in developing the resilience of a young person is the development of their future sense of self as an adult. The development of a Dream can assist young people in offering them clear long term goals, as well as help them orientate their current life course towards that aim. Therefore the current identity status of the young person should be an integral part of the assessment process, based on Marcia's four stages. If this future sense of self is clear to, desired by, and obtainable for the young person, any subsequent plan that facilitates this end will be innately more appealing and engaging to them. Young people without a future sense of self will be in what is called identity diffusion. Those struggling with dilemmas regarding future options are in the moratorium stage, whilst young people who hold an anti-social identity may experience the ego-discomfort that drives them from pro-social networks. Consideration should be given to how treatment interventions may help the young person resolve identity issues, cultivate a future sense of self and assist them to work towards a pro-social Dream.

An important component of increasing Baseline Assessment Reactivity, discussed earlier in this chapter, lies in the development of the self-efficacy of the young person that they can change. Self-efficacy refers to a specific kind of confidence. It describes our belief in our ability to perform a task *to a given standard*. As such, the 'given standard' can be positive if our belief is high, or negative if our belief is low. Research shows that our belief in our ability to perform a task is more important than our actual ability. This is because, if we have low self-belief in undertaking a task, we invest less in its completion and are liable to give up in light of any early setbacks. If our belief is high, we are more likely to persevere. Fostering a young person's belief in their ability to change is vital if they are to maintain it over a long period of time. The comprehensive assessment should include a review of the young person's strengths and resources to assist in the change process.

Self-confidence can be identified and increased by using scaling approaches. In scaling, a young person is asked to rate their confidence in achieving a specific goal on a scale of 1 to 10, with ten being at their most confident. Their score can then be explored in terms of 'what makes it a 6?' for them. What might raise their confidence to a 7? It is important to remember that the score young people give themselves is not as important in these scaling processes as the meaning that young people imbue in their score. In this way it depends on what resources, coping strategies, ideas or solutions that the scale elicits, rather than the number itself. Scaling can be used to help young people articulate their thoughts in important areas of change such as motivation, changing drug or alcohol use or addressing wider

problems in their lives. It is also a key finding in research that those young people most at risk of problematic drug and alcohol use benefit from increasing the number of protective factors in their life. This means that the assessment of strengths should extend beyond the young person and consider environmental supports in their life (see Figure 4.5).

Some young people may not have ever attempted to change their drug or alcohol use and therefore may not have a clear conception of their confidence in making change. This can be addressed simply by asking the young person to identify any previous success that they have had in their life such as a sport, being a good friend, etc. The same scaling question can be asked in terms of exploring how confident they were in achieving this aim instead. This will reveal their coping strategies and resources. The young person is then invited to consider whether these skills might help them achieve goals around their drug or alcohol use. This approach can be very effective because any achievement in any life domain demands the same set of skills. Persistence, teamwork, focus, learning, problem solving, different strategies, etc. are all important factors in the achievement of any goal. However, young people are unlikely to generalise these skills to new areas automatically.

Comprehensive assessment: treatment planning

Effective treatment planning should not be considered as a separate process from the comprehensive assessment but should be regarded as a direct continuation. Whilst a comprehensive assessment identifies the breakdowns in social functioning that contribute to use, a care plan should identify a treatment plan that addresses the specific ruptures that have been mapped. If the assessment plan and care plan are not linked directly, it renders assessment a redundant exercise. There is a danger that the treatment plan does not address the risk factors that are driving consumption. This will misdirect subsequent treatment, rendering it partially effective at best and irrelevant at worst. Therefore, care plans must tie-in directly with comprehensive assessments. Whilst there is no universal agreement on the social domains that should be assessed, it is imperative that the social domains in the

---

Figure 4.5: Strengths assessment

---

1. How important is it to you to change your drug or alcohol use right now?

1   2   3   4   5   6   7   8   9   10

What makes this your score?

What would need to happen for your score to be higher?

2. How confident are you that you could change your drug or alcohol use?

1   2   3   4   5   6   7   8   9   10

What makes this your score?

What would need to happen for your score to be higher?

3. How confident are you that you could address other problems in your life?

1   2   3   4   5   6   7   8   9   10

What makes this your score?

What would need to happen for your score to be higher?

4. How much support do you get from other people such as family, friends or school?

1   2   3   4   5   6   7   8   9   10

What makes this your score?

What would need to happen for your score to be higher?

---

comprehensive assessment tally with the social domains of the care plan.

Treatment options for young people with complex needs should also extend this continuum. They should offer interventions that assist young people to achieve the goals of their care plans. If there is a disconnection between the young person's stated goals and the subsequent support that they receive, they are unlikely to recognise the relevance of their treatment. Again, targeting treatment outside of the care plan may be interesting, but unhelpful to the young person's overall progress. It may also add additional pressure on the care co-ordinator who will need to provide additional support to assist the young person to achieve their core care plan goals at the same time as they are receiving more diverse support. This disparity between the young person's stated goals and the actual treatment they receive can cause confusion and is an inefficient use of treatment resources.

Historically, the addictions field has generally relied upon generic counselling models to support young people. However, studies with adult populations have suggested that generic models have limited value. Miller et al. (2003) have engaged in periodic reviews of research on the outcomes demonstrated by different treatment approaches to addressing alcohol problems. These findings are compiled in a large table where the treatment outcomes of 48 different modalities are evaluated and ranked in order of effectiveness. These evaluations are based on the clinical outcomes as well as on the quality of the research methodology. They suggest that the stand-alone generic counselling models were one of the least effective approaches to addressing addictions. This may be due to the fact that generic counselling approaches are too narrow in their focus and do not generalise to other domains. For example, a cognitive therapy approach might assist a young person to manage their depression but these gains do not appear to automatically improve functioning in other domains. It will not assist them to build new peer groups, manage family relationships or improve academic performance. Treatment outcomes with highly excluded youth appear to be enhanced by targeted interventions at each domain of their life. This is not to suggest that counselling interventions are not helpful. Rather, counselling services need to be orientated to specific goals within a care plan as part of an overall package of care. These findings were supported by Moos'

Figure 4.6: Rationalising assessment, care planning and interventions

Social functioning assessment domains . . .

Substance use	Mental health	Physical health	Family	School	Peers	Housing	Crime
⇩	⇩	⇩	⇩	⇩	⇩	⇩	⇩

Goals setting in care plan . . .

Substance use	Mental health	Physical health	Family	School	Peers	Housing	Crime
⇩	⇩	⇩	⇩	⇩	⇩	⇩	⇩

Range of interventions . . .

Substance use	Mental health	Physical health	Family	School	Peers	Housing	Crime

(2008) thematic review of treatment outcomes, where interventions that allowed problem users to reshape their whole environments were far more effective than discrete interventions.

It is important to reiterate that the social domains being assessed are not definitive. Rather, whichever social domains are assessed should be carried through the care planning and treatment stages. Neither early onset nor late onset users might experience compromises in every area of functioning. But the care plan should highlight those domains that require intervention. Furthermore, young people are liable to receive support from a number of possible sources, so their care needs to be managed through one commonly agreed treatment plan rather than through multiple ones. A schema of rationalised services is outlined in Figure 4.6.

Developing a meaningful care plan with young people is relatively straightforward when they have a strong sense of future self. When young people have clear life ambitions, the support they receive can be tailored to achieve this end. Care planning is much more difficult with young people who do not have such a strong sense of future self. Young people in an identity moratorium may have contradictory feelings regarding their aspirations or none at all. The golden rule of creating effective treatment plans is that, when exploring goals, the practitioner should never record the first thing that the young person says. This is because when asked what might improve their life they will always respond

by offering a general answer first. For example, in reviewing employment a young person is likely to state that they want to 'Get a job'. These general replies are simply not specific enough to generate motivation to pursue this stated ambition. Therefore it is vital to ask deeper questions to explore this more fully. The benchmark for working towards a well-formed goal is that the questions are specific. The treatment planner should consider whether the young person can see this goal in their mind's eye. Exploring where the young person would be working, what they would be doing, and who they would be doing this with can tease out the detail and create a deeper visualisation of the intended goal. Equally, it is important for the care planner to see the value that the young person sees in the goal. This can increase empathy, foster confidence and allay fears of judgement.

Whilst care planning offers a systematic approach to organising the care of young people with complex needs, it is often the weakest area of clinical functioning. Well-established models of care planning do exist but are often not deployed within everyday practice. The most effective care-planning model developed at present is Adolescent-Community Reinforcement Approach (A-CRA). It was developed in the US to support substance misusing runaway youth with complex needs. It has shown very positive outcomes with young people with complex needs and offers a gold standard care planning model that can be adapted to a range of service settings. This model is reviewed in more detail in Chapter 6.

Future developments in diagnostic criteria

Diagnostic criteria continue to evolve as a result of on-going clinical and research studies. These studies highlight weaknesses in the diagnosis, identify future developments and adjust ways of operating according to policy requirements. At the time of writing, the *Diagnostic Statistical Manual of Mental Disorders Edition V (DSM V)* (APA, in press) is under development. The new *DSM V* will make significant changes to the diagnostic structures of Abuse and Dependence. The biggest single change will be the abolishing of the Abuse and Dependence distinction identified in *DSM (IV-TR)*. As these did not appear to be distinct types of problems, they will be merged into one unified Substance Use Disorder that occurs on a spectrum of severity. Young people who experience 2–3 symptoms will receive the equivalent of an Abuse diagnosis whilst young people that meet 4 + symptoms will be deemed Dependent. These changes may shift the diagnostic focus towards the higher end of consumption. Early symptoms of problematic use in young people may be less likely to be detected by the new framework, leaving a 'diagnostic gap' in the identification of the early onset of substance use disorders.

The *DSM-V* will retain its distinction between non-physiological and physiological Dependence. However, the description of Dependence will not be applied to those patients being prescribed medications as part of planned treatment so as to distinguish them from 'addicts'. This is a rather judgemental view of non-clinical problem users, plus it may raise issues for people who develop problems as a result of prescribed medications. Whilst the actual symptoms of Dependence will remain the same, the *DSM-V* will broaden out its current distinction of alcohol and substance. Instead, each major drug of Abuse will have specific dependence criteria based on the same symptoms as *DSM (IV-TR)*. Furthermore, each substance will also have its own description of intoxication symptoms and withdrawal symptoms. Gambling has also been included in the same section as substance misuse disorders for the first time.

As the existing research on substance misuse has been conducted on the *DSM (IV-TR)* criteria, this chapter has focussed on these findings. Whilst *DSM-V* offers some alteration in the diagnostic framework, these amendments do not substantially revise the symptoms of Dependence. The new edition of the *DSM-V* will provide a new benchmark for future research. However, it will take a considerable period of time to develop a research base that can effectively evaluate the utility of the new criteria. As such the effectiveness of this new diagnostic model remains open to future examination, both in adults and in young people.

Summary

Considerable progress has been made in the identification of substance misuse problems. The development of the Alcohol Dependence Syndrome represented a major advance in clinical diagnosis. Its framework has shaped all subsequent diagnostic criteria since its inception. However, its explicit focus on identification of problem users who required *medical attention* has meant that its use is of limited value with young people who are unlikely to have progressed to this extreme level of use.

The *DSM (IV-TR)* criteria of Abuse and Dependence offered an opportunity to expand the diagnostic framework to account for both lower and higher ranges of severity. The Abuse criteria in particular, with their focus on interruption in social functioning, could have been far more relevant to the problems experienced by young people. But, the symptoms of Abuse did not appear to be sufficiently specific or sensitive to the problems young people are likely to experience; and the lack of clear separation between the onset of Abuse and the appearance of the more profound Dependence symptoms betrayed the validity of the approach. The criteria for physical Dependence were devised to assess the severity of symptoms in long term adult users. Furthermore, many of the key symptoms of Dependence have been misconstrued in the diagnosis of young people, which has led to a high rate of diagnostic orphans and imposters. Moreover, research has established that the symptoms of Abuse and Dependence occur in a typical sequence.

The development and structure of abuse and dependence has tended to be ignored in comprehensive assessment processes. However, the processes can be designed to encompass these critical issues and thereby offer greater insight into the progression and severity of young people's substance misuse problems. Doing this is especially important, as the comprehensive assessment can account for a significant proportion of treatment gains. They can be enhanced by the use of objective feedback, enhancing motivation and increasing a young person's confidence in their capacity to change.

Within this overall structure, comprehensive assessment, treatment planning and treatment interventions should not be seen as distinct activities but rather as a continuum of care. Harmonising these processes increases the relevance of treatment for young people, and improves the efficiency of resources. Treatment structures that help young people to identify goals in each domain of their life, and that provide support to attain them, tend to produce better outcomes than generalised approaches. Such goals need to account for young people's own future aspirations, which will increase their motivation to achieve them.

Future developments to the classification of diagnostic criteria may or may not enhance our understating of young people's substance-related problems. Not only does there need to be greater research attention given to the experience of problem use amongst young people, these findings need to be incorporated into daily practice.

CHAPTER 5

Can Substance Use Be Prevented in Young People?

Introduction

'I am told that you are neglecting your studies, and that you are giving yourself up to enjoyment. It is said that you wander about through the streets of an evening smelling of wine.' So begins a letter to a young man. The tone of the letter suggests that the issue has been brought to the writer's attention for serious scrutiny. Perhaps others had attempted to intervene to no effect and saw him as a last resort. Certainly, it reads stylistically as if written from a position of established authority. The fact that others had noticed the problems before the writer did also suggests he may well have been involved in duties beyond those of teaching. He may well have been the Dean of the university or held some other high-ranking position. Certainly, the brief, irksome tone suggests that there were things that he would rather be doing that day than writing to the errant student.

One can picture the young student at large in the city, enjoying his newfound freedom since leaving the strictures of home. He has obviously disregarded the pleas of others to curb the excessive elements of his lifestyle. One imagines him akin to the lazy and indulgent type of student who eulogises their indifference as a kind of superior wisdom. Perhaps it was this that made the tutor inflate the consequences of drinking alcohol, as a way of getting through to his indolent young ward. If the student actually understood the terrible risks he was taking he would surely stop. The majority of the letter is a list of evils associated with drinking. 'The smell of wine will make men avoid you. Wine will destroy your soul; you will become like a broken oar which cannot steer on either side.' And so he continues at considerable length. If that was not emphasis enough, he ends his letter with: 'Wine is an abomination.'

There is little in this story that might single it out as exceptional. The interaction between frustrated tutors and wayward students is hardly a unique phenomenon. What is striking about this letter is not who wrote it or why they wrote it but *when* it was written. This letter was found on a scroll dating from the Middle Kingdom of

Egypt, between the 11th and 14th Dynasties, which means it was written between 2080 and 1640 BC. Whilst the personalities within it feel very familiar to us today, they lived and died up to 4,000 years ago. It could be argued that this is the first recorded example of drug prevention work in history. It could also be argued that drug prevention work has not progressed a great deal in the intervening years.

Whilst prevention and education approaches have become a core activity in schools in the present day, attitudes towards these approaches are deeply ambivalent. On the one hand, alerting young people to the dangers of using drugs and alcohol represents a moral responsibility to their development. Nearly everyone would agree that this is inherently important. On the other hand, there is a deeper cynicism about the value of such approaches. This ambivalence is reflected in the multiple diverse formats that education and prevention programmes have adopted. A plethora of interventions are described under this banner from classroom-based teaching, diversionary activities, sports, legal restrictions, enforcement approaches or supply reductions, police information, the involvement of community groups, mentors and charities, mass media and family programmes. The programmes are delivered by an equally diverse range of providers including teachers, parents, police, ex-criminals, religious leaders, celebrities and glove puppets. The approaches can target young people who may not have taken drugs or alcohol, may be at risk of problems or may be already deeply involved. The range of substances also varies considerably in these approaches. Some programmes focus on all drugs whilst others focus on specific drugs. Alcohol and nicotine are sometimes included, and sometimes not. Likewise some of the programmes have been heavily influenced by research findings whilst others have been formulated at a grass roots level and operate on intuitive assumptions.

This chapter will focus on the evidence for education and prevention approaches. It will begin with a general review of key issues in the prevention and education research base, and then build on that to review the historical development of education and prevention approaches. This is important, as there is a lack of clarity regarding the aims, assumptions and strategies within many programmes. Divergent approaches can bleed into one another, resulting in confused programmes, making it difficult to evaluate what is or is not helpful in the various models on which they are based.

As part of this historical survey, the chapter will review a wide range of programmes that have demonstrated effectiveness in a range of settings. They include universal programmes delivered in schools, universities, families, mass media and community settings. They have been selected on the basis of their effectiveness or common usage. Specific programmes targeting high risk youth will then be examined in greater detail in light of the complex needs of those young people who are most vulnerable to experiencing profound problems.

The outcomes of prevention and education will then be evaluated in detail, specifically regarding the relationship between the modest gains that are achieved at the point of delivery and the longer term impact that prevention and education can achieve. As prevention models have been delivered in such a diverse range of formats, this chapter will then examine the core elements that influence outcomes. From this perspective we shall see how prevention and education can contribute significant gains for young people, but also why the true value of these approaches is often wholly unnoticed.

Prevention and education controversies

Advances in medicine over the last 100 years have extended life expectancies and eliminated many common and once fatal illnesses. This success has shifted the focus of health policy to address the rise in preventable diseases that are caused by lifestyle. Substance-related disorders have been considered one of the most critical lifestyle issues that affect the health of populations in both developed and developing countries. Whilst the prevention of both health and social problems caused by drug and alcohol use has broad support in principle, the reality is that the value of prevention and education programmes is questioned. Indeed, there is a general consensus that prevention programmes

are wholly ineffective. This conclusion has been drawn from a number of sources. The first is the self-evident fact that drug and alcohol problems persist in our society. Despite concerted efforts to convince them otherwise, young people remain involved in drug and alcohol use, which suggests substance use is inevitable. Second, the development of programmes has not generally been informed by research findings, and where evaluations have been conducted, programmes have shown poor outcomes and some have even appeared to increase consumption (Tobler, 1986). Third, prevention programmes have been driven by adult concerns regarding drug and alcohol use rather than young people's experiences. They have reflected the often highly uninformed assumptions, myths and fears that adults hold which are invariably wholly out of touch with the everyday experience of young people. For example, the myth of the evil dealer at the school gate who ensnares young people into addiction with the offer of free drugs has no truth whatsoever. This myth first appeared in a vapid drug prevention tome *The Black Candle* (Murphy, 1922) which extolled all the most horrifying visions of use. A bestseller in its day, it is striking that many of the fanciful myths purported by this book still remain unquestioned by many adults today.

A fourth major issue is that those evaluations of prevention programmes which have been undertaken have tended to be conducted over very short time frames. If attempts are made to prevent or limit use in a cohort of young people, those receiving such interventions need to be tracked for considerable periods of time as they move into adulthood. With time-limited research funding, the evaluation of these longer-term outcomes has been beyond reach. Longer-term longitudinal studies offer greater opportunity to identify both the risk factors that predict problematic use and the effectiveness of interventions which interrupt its development. However, these periods of time are often considered glacial in terms of availability of research grants. Moreover, even where long-term follow-up is conducted, the periods between sampling the study population can also mean that researchers miss the causal mechanisms of the changes they observe, unless the sampling is repeated regularly. This is a major obstacle to the development of an informed science of prevention.

A final problem is that drug and alcohol

prevention and education lacks a central co-ordinating body. Therefore the systematic assessment of the quality of interventions, evaluation of outcomes and dissemination of good practice simply does not occur. This has led to a fragmented field without any quality assurance. Prevention can be dominated by community champions who improvise interventions without monitoring or evaluation. Good practice does not become a norm and poor practice is not eliminated. The field of prevention has been populated by a colourful array of well-intended strategies with little evaluation.

All of this has led to a problem of circularity. Poor investment in prevention has led to the implementation of poor programmes. Poor outcomes have then justified further disinvestment. This lack of confidence in prevention strategies has resulted in its re-branding as 'education'. Education suggests a broader approach. Rather than eliminating use, educational approaches aim to raise awareness, help young people make more informed decisions regarding use and attempt to reduce rather than eliminate consumption.

The cynicism that has arisen as a result regarding the value of drug and alcohol prevention can be seen within the current research base in the UK. Whilst drug and alcohol education has become a core feature of the national curriculum in state schools, there have been very few research studies into the effectiveness of these programmes. For example, the National Institute of Clinical Excellence literature review (McGrath et al., 2006) on effective strategies to address drug education identified that none of the 29 research studies currently available regarding programme effectiveness were of gold standard. Seven papers were viewed as partly of a high standard. A further fourteen papers were deemed to contain some useful background and contextual material. And the remaining papers were classified as either relevant but not up-to-date, or were not relevant and discarded. The current research base is largely reliant upon conclusions from US studies which have made significant advances in organising both the discipline and the research base. However, most of these studies are conducted in schools, and miss the highest risk youth who are liable to be excluded. This means that no conclusive statements can be asserted regarding the effectiveness of drug and education

programmes. Current findings must be met with caution and considered indicative at best. However, these studies do provide direction to the development of new and innovative approaches that are demonstrating considerable potential in addressing young people's drug and alcohol use.

Defining drug and alcohol prevention and education

The furtherance of effective education and prevention approaches must begin with clear definition of the functions of prevention and education, their range and the criteria by which they should be assessed. Further to this, any programmes developed must be rooted in the epidemiology of drug and alcohol abuse if they are to intercept the drivers of use. This assertion is based on a 'public health' model that supposes that to prevent a problem prior to it occurring one must minimise the risk factors that trigger it (Catalano et al., 1998). As we have seen in Chapter 3, considerable progress has been made in the identification of the specific risk factors and long term trajectories of young people's involvement in drug and alcohol use. Without accounting for these specific drivers of consumption, prevention programmes are unlikely to be successful. Education programmes that have aligned themselves to addressing these causal factors of use demonstrate superior outcomes across a diverse range of populations and settings. Within this it is important to recognise that all risk is not equal. Some young people may experience not only higher ranges of risk than others but very different risk profiles. Education and prevention needs to account for this variance in order to span the needs of these wider sub-populations. Therefore prevention and education must be expansive in its aims. Three types of intervention have been identified as critical:

1. **Primary education:** Targeted at those who have not yet taken drugs or alcohol and designed to prevent the development of substance abuse problems. Besides providing universal coverage it may also target specific groups at highest risk of developing problems.
2. **Secondary education:** Aimed at those who are currently engaging in risky behaviour, to intercept them as early as possible in order to

reduce the severity of the disorder. Also known as early intervention.

3. **Tertiary education:** Designed to reduce the impairments and damage caused by a disorder and thus lead to treatment interventions.

Defining education is important in setting clear goals for any activity and in determining the most appropriate strategies. It also provides a benchmark to assess the effectiveness of approach. For example, the effectiveness of primary education could be assessed on the numbers of new cases that present for treatment who have received the intervention. A reduction in the incidence of new cases would determine whether it is effective. Secondary interventions should reduce the number of young people presenting for low threshold services; whilst tertiary interventions are closer to treatment and their effectiveness might be established by the numbers of young people that do not re-present in youth or subsequent adult services.

Whilst these definitions are common to the health promotion field, Kumpfer & Baxley (1997) suggested a more refined taxonomy for drug and alcohol education, based on the intended audience. This was based on distinctions first proposed by Gordon (1987). The strengths and weakness of this classification system are:

- **Universal prevention:** Targets a whole population or group, with the assumption that each member will experience some benefit from this broad application. Aims to prevent or delay the onset of drug and alcohol use. These large-scale programmes can be expensive to deliver.
- **Selective prevention:** Targets sub-groups who are exposed to greater risk of developing drug or alcohol problems than the average population. These groups are identified by the presence of biological, psychological or environmental risk factors. But these programmes can stigmatise young people in the specific target groups and, because risk factors are probability models, they do not necessarily determine who will experience problems.
- **Indicated prevention:** Targets individuals who are using drugs and alcohol and experiencing drug and alcohol problems but who do not meet medical criteria for dependence. This might include experimental use or binge patterns of use, or it might target young people

who show other problems such as depression or behavioural problems that may make them susceptible to escalations in use. These targeted individuals are usually identified for interventions through screening, but confidentiality may militate against recruitment of these target groups.

At the more targeted levels, these definitions can blur the divide between prevention and treatment of young people's drug and alcohol problems. Prevention and treatment occur on a continuum. Prevention is an attempt to intercept risk factors before they express their influence, whilst treatment attempts to address risk factors that are being expressed in a young person's life. In general, the risk and protection research can inform prevention in a number of ways. First, as the age of onset of use is so important, education and prevention should focus on delaying the initiation of use. Second, the sub-populations of young people most at risk of use should be identified as having specific needs regarding drug and alcohol consumption which are unlikely to be met through universal drug and alcohol education. In these high risk groups, use tends to be curtailed by the addition of protective factors, as opposed to low risk groups where such buffering is of less significance. Furthermore, as the risk factors for problem use span a wide range of individual, social and environmental domains, drug and alcohol education needs to target risk across these multiple domains too. It may need to reach beyond the individual young person and address these wider context influences. To be effective, this may require a much more systematic approach across the multiple agencies that are involved with young people and their families. For example, a young person growing up in an environment of high parental use is unlikely to benefit from a classroom-based approach.

School based approaches to prevention and education

In order to assess the value of drug and alcohol prevention, it is important to recognise its historical development and tease out the many diverse theoretical orientations that have shaped the discipline, particularly in the US. Drug and alcohol prevention has its roots in the

Temperance Movement that campaigned for prevention work to be delivered in schools as early as the 1840s. The Temperance Movement was an extraordinarily powerful religious movement in its day, in both the US and Western Europe. Its passionate advocacy of drug and alcohol prevention was rooted in the Protestant faith. As God had given mankind free will, and substance abuse removed this God-given choice, problematic consumption was perceived as a particular kind of sin. The eradication of all use was therefore more a matter of a proselytising moral duty than a public health concern. It was driven more by salvation than cirrhosis. In the US, the Temperance Movement campaigned vociferously to ensure that all States were required to teach the "evils of alcohol" in schools, and universal coverage was achieved by 1880. This religious message regarding the evils of alcohol did not change in the US until the repeal of alcohol prohibition in the 1930s.

The rational model

By the 1940s two opposing approaches emerged in prevention work. Whilst the 'evils of alcohol' approach was still popular in many States, the rise of public medicine and increasing secularisation gave rise to a more knowledge-based approach referred to as the 'rational model'. The rational model respected the fact that the fear of God might not scare young people into abstinence. Instead it suggested that young people could make informed life choices of their own based on the evidence. It assumed that young people involved themselves in risk taking behaviour because they were not aware of the problems associated with use. Therefore, if they were given information regarding the harmful effects of drugs and alcohol, young people would inevitably make the rational decision not to use them. By the 1950s, thinking based on the objective information derived from science became the dominant philosophy, and for the first time alcohol education became part of a broader health education curriculum. But, despite the movement towards a more scientific understanding of the effects and harm of alcohol, rational programmes were often of poor quality and factually incorrect. These programmes' over-emphasis on the long term negative consequences of heavy use was a new kind of

scare tactic. This fear-mongering also meant that these programmes had very little credibility amongst young people who disregarded their message. Despite this, rational programmes continued to dominate prevention work in the 1960s and, to a large degree, still inform many education strategies today.

Evaluation into the effectiveness of rational approaches has generally proved that they are either ineffective or less effective than other approaches. Bruvold (1993) extensive review of the effectiveness of education and prevention approaches found that the rational approach had very little if any impact on behaviour. Rundall & Bruvold (1988) found that rational programmes tended to be delivered in a less interactive and more didactic style resulting in poor outcomes for the young people. Other researchers found that knowledge was an important element of the effectiveness of prevention programmes, but not when delivered in a didactic way (White & Pitts, 1998; Lister-Sharp et al., 1999). Some research also found that this approach could increase use. This occurred in young people who were already drinking alcohol and who became increasingly anxious of the dire consequences that they were exposing themselves to (Stuart, 1974; Blum, 1976). The principal reason why rational approaches appear to be so ineffective is that they assume that young people take drugs and alcohol because they are not aware of the harmful consequences. However, lack of knowledge regarding use is simply not a risk factor that triggers consumption in young people. In fact, they often know more about drugs than those delivering the programme.

It is important to note that rational based prevention programmes are very diverse and often difficult to categorise. Tobler's (1986) first large scale review of prevention outcomes merged information, didactic teaching and fear arousal into a single category. Tobler & Stratton (1997) and Tobler et al. (2000) adopted a broader definition of rational programmes which makes a distinction between 'knowledge of media and social influences', and 'knowledge of actual drug use by peers (normative education)'. Knowledge of cultural influences appears to be closer to a social influence approach than a purely rational approach. This makes it difficult assess what element may or may not be helpful in this broad approach.

The affective and value clarification models

The limitations of the rational model stimulated interest in a wider set of variables that might influence involvement in drug and alcohol use. The 1970s saw prevention programmes shifting focus from the substance to the personality of the individual who was taking them. This 'affective model' assumed that young people took drugs in response to personal inadequacies. In particular, the affective model assumed that poor self-esteem was the critical mediating variable in substance use. This approach began to develop a wide range of strategies which focussed on building self-esteem, developing decision-making skills, clarifying values and other elements such as self-awareness and goal setting that were believed to relate to use (Carney, 1971; 1972).

An offshoot of the affective model (and sometimes included within it) was the 'value clarification' approach. Value clarification programmes aimed to highlight a discrepancy between the individual's values and the consequences of their behaviour to strengthen the idea 'that personal values are incompatible with substance use' (Hansen, 1992: 409). The simplistic assumption in this approach is that young people's deeper values are automatically incompatible with drug and alcohol use. As such the approaches incorporate decision-making on the assumption that enhanced decision-making skills will help young people resist temptation in a variety of problematic life situations, not just those around substance use.

Unfortunately, the connection between decision-making and substance use was not always explicit in these programmes. Many affective or value clarification programmes made no reference to substance use at all (Hansen, 1992). Whilst some studies showed that affective and value clarification could be effective in reducing use, most independent studies found that they had no impact whatsoever (Hansen, 1992; Tobler et al., 2000). Not only did they fail to reduce drug and alcohol use they also failed to raise esteem levels (Schaps et al., 1986). Some reviews did find that they could reduce drug and alcohol use in young people to some degree but were not as effective as other models (Bruvold, 1993; Tobler, 1986; Tobler & Stratton, 1997; Tobler et al., 1999).

There are several reasons why this model failed. First, as we have seen in Chapter 3, self-esteem has a weak relationship with drug and alcohol use at best (Shedler & Block, 1990; Schroeder et al., 1993). As a result, even if these programmes were successful in raising self-esteem, it would not necessarily lead to decreases in drug or alcohol involvement. Second, the relationship between personal values and behaviour is complex and not well understood. The overtly positive expectations of use in young people mean that their values may not be incompatible with consumption, but harmonious with it. Values are not always absolute and therefore cannot be relied upon to provide a cast iron principle which governs every action we take. This is particularly true for young people whose behaviour is highly situational. For example, whilst young people may believe it would be wrong to be drunk in front of their parents, they may apply a very different principle when with their peers. Third, these programmes often failed to link generalised interpersonal skills with specific drug- or alcohol-using situations. This created a knowledge gap where young people may have acquired a particular skills set but did not recognise its relevance in high risk situations. Again, affective models failed because they did not address the specific risk factors in the lives of young people. However, the approach was not entirely without merit. It appeared that creating a more positive attitude towards abstinence was an important element in these programmes.

The responsible use and harm reduction models

The failure to find robust outcomes for prevention gave rise to a deeper debate about the function of prevention and education in the 1980s. This re-evaluated the aims of prevention and considered why gains proved so limited. Weisheit (1983) suggested that abstinence-oriented programs failed because most adolescents drank by virtue of their life situation. This gave rise to a new direction in education, which shifted towards a 'responsible use' approach. The responsible use model took a harm reduction view to drug education for the first time, and adapted the rational model by assuming that informing young people about safe use would decrease their problems rather than eliminate consumption. These programmes focussed on safe and unsafe use, raising awareness of consequences of use as well on exploring the long-term negative consequences on adult life, such as risks to anticipated careers, insurance or foreign travel.

The difficulty in evaluating responsible use models highlights an important problem in the evaluation of prevention and education programmes. The vast majority of programmes are assessed on how successful approaches are at eliminating use. Alternative outcomes measures that might detect other changes from these programmes receive scant attention, such as reductions in use or in the negative consequences that they may initiate. These wider gains may be substantial. For example, McBride (2003) conducted a review of five alcohol studies that explored both use and misuse rates. This study found that programmes focusing on harm reduction outcomes for alcohol could significantly reduce problematic alcohol use. Likewise, McBride et al. (2000) reviewed Project SHAHRP (School Health and Alcohol Harm Reduction Project), a school programme based on harm reduction, and identified very positive results in reducing alcohol problems rather than alcohol use in itself. Whilst this responsible use model makes intuitive sense, Weisheit (1983) recognised that harm reduction was a difficult goal to define and even harder to evaluate. As any chance of successfully eliminating all use was remote, he suggested that the field should adopt alternative markers of success. A programme might be deemed successful if it satisfied parents, appeased taxpayers or if the school felt it useful.

Theory of Reasoned Action

It was not until the 1980s that prevention work began to draw upon wider psychological theories in order to shape the approach more effectively. The main source of inspiration was the Theory of Reasoned Action developed by Fishbein & Ajzen (1975). They suggested that behaviour is determined by the individual *intention* to perform the behaviour. Intention is the cognitive representation of a person's readiness to perform the behaviour and is determined by three factors: the attitude toward the specific behaviour, the subjective norms and the perceived behavioural control. As such, it supposes that there is a sequence that governs human behaviour. Increasing knowledge regarding the risks of use will alter attitudes towards substances leading to behavioural change (i.e. not using substances).

This promising new model was highly influential in the development of drug and alcohol prevention but the outcomes for young people remained poor. Studies revealed that the only impact these programmes had was to increase knowledge with little impact on attitudes or behaviour (Tobler, 1986). Staulcup et al (1979) reviewed 21 primary alcohol prevention programmes and found no link between knowledge or attitude change and behaviour change. Kinder et al (1980) reviewed 25 studies and found knowledge gains but no attitude or behaviour changes. The methodology and data collection was poor in both studies though. Schaps et al.'s (1981) review of 127 of these programmes found them to be ineffective in general. However, amongst the top 10 performing programmes they did find significant positive results. Goodstadt (1986) suggested that the evaluation methodology in these prevention programmes was often inadequate leading to inconsistent or negative findings. Programmes may appear to fail because evaluations fail to assess different effects on sub-groups. He also recognised that whilst knowledge is relatively easy to influence, deeper seated attitudes and behaviour are very difficult to modify.

Social influence models

A second generation of drug and alcohol programmes began to emerge in the 1980s, inspired by increasing interest in a 'social influence' approach. This gave rise to a cluster of new interventions derived from McGuire's (1964) social inoculation theory that argued prior exposure to persuasion inoculated people to its future influence. The original version of this model focussed on the external forces that pressurised young people into taking drugs and alcohol. These may be subtle and not necessarily conscious, such as an implicit desire to be accepted or look cool. The model acknowledged that young people are especially sensitive to these external pressures. As they make the transition from childhood to adulthood, they are prone to 'act' grown up by mimicking what they perceive as adult behaviours such as drug or alcohol use. The theory also combined elements of Bandura's (1977a) social learning theory which examined how the media modelled behaviour and created norms that people conformed to.

One version of the social influence model was the emergence of a resistance skills approach that focussed on the skills needed to address peer pressure, particularly the skills to refuse drug offers. These programmes are highly interactive and make extensive use of skills practice, discussion, drama and role playing strategies. They also make use of 'normative education' which has been defined as challenging 'erroneous perceptions of the prevalence and acceptability of drug and alcohol use and establish[ing] conservative group norms . . . Norm setting programs also utilise natural peer opinion leaders to establish or define standards of group behaviour . . . [they] are postulated to operate through lowering expectations about prevalence and acceptability of use and the reduced availability of substances in peer-oriented social settings' (Hansen, 1992: 411).

Normative programmes include the provision of factual information regarding the extent of young people's actual drug use (which is far lower than most young people think) as well as increasing resistance to use by building conservative group norms. As such, it examines the contribution of the media and of social influence in the young person's life. It also reversed the rational 'scaremonger' approach by examining the effect of drug and alcohol use on young people's lives in the immediate present rather than in the longer term health consequences (Ellickson & Robyn, 1987). These programmes are often peer led, using older teens to 'model' appropriate behaviour and provide credible non-using role models. These programmes promoted resistance skills in young people. 'Just Say No' was probably the most famous resistance skills approach. However this particular approach was a crass over-simplification and at odds with an informed decision approach to drug and alcohol education. It placed too much emphasis on direct peer pressure. Again, it centred on an adult interpretation of peer pressure as an explicit pressure placed on the young person to use drugs and alcohol. But, as we have seen, peer pressure amongst young people is experienced as willingness to comply with group norms. It has also been suggested that resistance approaches are unpopular outside the USA because of a general distain for their very blunt behavioural approach (Dorn & Murji, 1992) and the lack of credibility that is often associated with abstinence based models (Midford et al., 2002).

The Life Skills approach has been a particularly important programme in this context (Botvin et

al., 1990; 1997; 2001). It focuses on the development of generic social skills in young people but also includes elements of the social influences approach. Generic skills include decision-making and problem-solving skills, as in the affective approach, but with much greater focus on drug-and alcohol-using situations identified by young people. Botvin suggests that broad-based 'competence enhancement' approaches to drugs prevention are not effective unless some specific drugs resistance skills training is provided. The effectiveness of the social influence model also gave rise to greater involvement of research-led approaches that took far more account of the dominant risk factors that young people actually experienced. As we have seen, peer influence is a major contributory factor in the initiation of substances, and these programmes tacitly address this high-ranking risk factor with a clearly defined skills set. Life skills, social influences, resistance skills and normative approaches all share a common framework of social learning and social cognitive theory (Bandura, 1977b; 1986). These theories all assume that drug misuse arises from a skills deficit in the young person or from poor protection from the barrage of social pressures to use drugs (Coggans et al., 2003).

Research into the effectiveness of the social influence approach has shown promising results. Flay (1985) reviewed 27 studies of social influence prevention approaches and found evidence that the social influence approach was effective in preventing *increases* in smoking by 50 per cent for up to three years. However, there were flaws in the research base. Some studies assigned whole school populations to either randomised or non-randomised conditions. As some schools had much higher rates of smoking at baseline this made it difficult to compare the impact of the programmes at follow-up. Flay et al. (1985) also examined a social influence programme that addressed tobacco use alone. The Waterloo Smoking Study was delivered across 22 matched schools in experimental and control conditions. The core programme had three components: Socratic debate with students; development of skills to resist the social influence of family, peers and media to smoke; and decision-making skills not to smoke. Flay et al. (1985) found significant reduction in smoking, particularly amongst those most at risk. The Life Skills Model developed by Botvin et al. (1980) has also consistently shown reductions in smoking in young people. These reductions are between 5 and 8 per cent in targeted populations and can persist from 1 to 2 years after programme completion (Clearly et al., 1988). Booster sessions can increase this time period (Best et al., 1988). The social influence model has also demonstrated effectiveness in a wide range of different cultural groups (Botvin et al., 1989a; 1989b).

In regards to applying the model to other drugs, results have been equally promising. Project SMART (Self-Management and Resistance Training) compared the impact of a social influence model with an affective model of drug prevention. The affective model showed no gains. In contrast, the social influence model delayed initiation into tobacco and cannabis use by a year (Hansen et al., 1988). Project ALERT (Adolescent Learning Experiences in Resistance Training) was a large scale experiment conducted in 30 schools using a social influence model. This comprised 8 sessions with 3 booster sessions and covered beliefs about drugs and personal vulnerability to their risks, challenged expectations of use and built confidence in resisting offers of drug and alcohol. Trials were conducted with extensive consideration to robust evaluation in order to eliminate any outside factors that might influence outcomes. The results at 3-, 12- and 15-month follow-up showed that ALERT reduced tobacco and cannabis use. It delayed cannabis initiation in non-users and limited cannabis use in established users. It was also effective for both low and high risk youth. It was not effective for alcohol use though (Ellickson & Bell, 1990a; 1990b).

Reviews of education and prevention outcomes support the central finding that social influence models are effective in reducing drug and alcohol use. Bruvold's (1993) large scale review of studies found that programmes that were based on Social Reinforcement skills, and which were designed to resist pressures to use drugs, were generally the most effective of four different theoretical approaches. Rational approaches tended to perform the worst. Rooney & Murray (1996) compared the effectiveness of social influences, generic social skills and resistance skills approaches. They found that all three types were equally effective but the social influence programme was more effective when it addressed all drug use as opposed to just tobacco. Tobler's (1986) comprehensive review of prevention programmes found that 'peer programmes' (a term used to describe refusal skills and social/life skills approaches) were the most effective of all

approaches examined. In a follow-up study, using different criteria for categorising approaches, Tobler & Stratton (1997) and Tobler et al. (2000) found that interactive social influence programmes were more effective than every kind of non-interactive programmes. However, comprehensive 'interactive life skills' programmes (which include social influences elements) and 'multi-site' programmes were more effective than social influences programmes.

What is interesting is that these effects also endure for protracted periods of time. Botvin et al. (1995a) followed up thousands of young people six years after they had completed the Life Skills Training programme. Those young people who had completed the Life Skills group were less likely to experience frequent drunkenness than those in the control group even after this extended time period, whilst Schinke et al.'s (2000) long term follow-up of Native American children found that they were 7 per cent less likely to be weekly drinkers than a control group at a 3.5-year follow-up. Whilst these effects are promising, it is important to note that some studies have shown a boomerang effect with increased smoking rates in some groups post education sessions (Murray et al., 1988). However, the Life Skills model has demonstrated consistently positive outcomes for young people on a number of measures, including reducing the numbers of young people initiating use, delaying the onset of use, reducing the amounts used by those who have initiated consumption as well as prevention of further escalation in use, particularly in relation to tobacco use. Table 5.1 describes the outcomes of the Life Skills Approach on these various gradients of use.

Coggans et al. (2003) conducted an analysis of what made social influences approaches like Life Skills Training so effective. The social influence model assumes that there are six key protection factors to prevent drug use:

1. Assertiveness
2. Self-image
3. Social efficacy (social skills)
4. Social anxiety
5. Influence-ability
6. Locus of control.

These six mediators are strengthened through programme elements such as teaching resistance skills, general social skills (addressing self-esteem and assertiveness) and self-management skills

Table 5.1: Summary of prevention outcomes on a range of measures

Study	Substance	Sample size	Outcomes
Preventing initiation			
Botvin, Eng & Williams, 1980	Tobacco	281	Reduced initiation into smoking to 4 per cent compared to the control group of 16 per cent.
Botvin & Eng, 1982	Tobacco	426	Reduced initiation into smoking to 8 per cent compared to control group of 19 per cent.
Preventing escalation in frequency of use			
Botvin et al., 1984b	Alcohol/ Marijuana	1,311	Significant reductions in alcohol consumed per drinking occasion. Reduced monthly marijuana use by 71 per cent and weekly use by 83 per cent.
Botvin & Eng, 1982	Tobacco	426	Reduced weekly smoking by 56 per cent.
Botvin et al., 1983	Tobacco	902	Significant reductions in smoking maintained at 12 and 18 months post treatment.
Preventing heavy or problem use			
Botvin et al., 1984b	Alcohol	239	73 per cent reported lower rates of drunkenness.
Preventing escalation to heavy, multiple and illicit drug use			
Botvin et al., 1990; 1995a	Tobacco	6,000	Reduced cigarette use with long term reductions in other gateway drugs (marijuana and alcohol) and lower use of other illicit drugs at long term follow up than the control group.
Botvin et al., 2000	Gateway drugs	454	Long term reduced use of 13 different drugs compared to the control group. Particularly low levels of heroin and hallucinogenic drugs in the active intervention group, suggesting delay in initiation influenced subsequent gateway progression.

(skills to deal with peer and media influences). Coggans' research found that although the programmes were successful, very few of these mediators related to the programmes' outcomes. For example, young people who had engaged in the programme showed few changes in life skills, self-esteem, locus of control and social efficacy. Results were inconsistent for assertiveness, social anxiety and influence-ability. The Life Skills Programme did consistently show effects on improving knowledge or attitudes and challenging normative expectations of substance use. As positive expectations are highly influential in initiating use, the power of the programme may lie in challenging these positive expectancies in particular, resulting in a delay in initiation. The highly interactive nature of the programme itself was also related to programme effectiveness, as was high implementation quality.

Social influence appears particularly important in prevention programmes. Hansen (1990)

recognised that social influence can be direct and active or indirect and passive. Direct pressure emanates from peers and can take the form of offers, ridicule or threats. Pressure can also be inactive through the young person's perception of the general group or social norms which can assign low or high value to drugs or alcohol. As we have seen, the belief in young people that high numbers of adolescents take drugs is strong predictor of their own drug use (Conrad et al., 1992). Donaldson et al. (1994) compared two different social influence strategies in an alcohol prevention trial to identify the role of perceived norms in consumption. In this study, students were either assigned to a Resistance Skills Training programme to increase their capacity to refuse drugs or to a Normative Education programme that attempted to modify the participants' expectancies regarding use. Both approaches were effective in improving the targeted domains. Resistance Skills improved young people's ability to resist use, whilst the Normative Education programme altered young people's estimates of the prevalence of use. However, only the Normative Education programme predicted subsequent drug use, whilst Resistance Skills training alone did not predict future use. This led Donaldson et al. (1994) to suggest that without the active ingredient of normative education, Resistance Skills programmes alone would not impact on drug use.

Research analysis has consistently demonstrated that Normative Education in particular is a key driver of drug education outcomes. This is because of where expectancies sit in the sequence of risk factors. As we saw in Chapter 3, positive expectancies are critical to the initiation of use. They are the catalyst that realises the potential of background risk factors and opens up the possibility of future consequences. As the cross-cultural studies in Chapter 1 demonstrated, these positive expectancies exert greater influence on young people than awareness of negative consequences. Prevention and education's historical preoccupation with negative consequences has invested considerable effort into strengthening the weakest predictors of use whilst leaving overt positive expectancies unaddressed. This has diminished its effectiveness. This is illustrative of a tension in prevention and education between the concerns of adults who worry about consequences of use and young people who seek positive experiences through use. Where these programmes have adjusted to the young people's world view they have demonstrated much greater impact.

College and university based programmes

A specific constellation of risk factors applies to students who attend Higher Education at a particularly vulnerable phase of their life course. Young people face the stress of leaving home, maintaining performance in highly demanding educational environments and must form new friendship groups. As alcohol plays such a critical role in social bonding, alcohol consumption often peaks at these times. High rates of drug and alcohol use have a negative effect on academic performance and subsequent achievement. High use correlates with higher dropout rates and reduced grades. It may interfere with the

successful transition from adolescence into adult life, particularly the achievement of professional occupational status. This may create the same failure to integrate into the pro-social networks, which offer protection from continued high use, that occurs at a younger age with early onset groups.

Student consumption

High student consumption occurs within a set of established social norms regarding college or university life. Norms represent the dominant attitudes, expectations and behaviours that determine group actions in that particular setting. As we have seen, these expectancies have an extremely influential role in decision-making regarding drug and alcohol use. This can be further augmented when these expectancies are framed within a context of social normality. There is a strong tendency for human beings to comply with group rules, as a form of acceptance (Newcombe, 1943; Newcombe & Wilson, 1966) or group conformity (Asch, 1951; 1952), or through social comparison processes (Festinger, 1954). The result is that students are the highest alcohol consuming population, and during the college years consumption exceeds even that of the high risk early onset groups at his same stage of their lives.

Studies exploring the formation of norms amongst students have examined different sources of influence. Parents' norms have very little impact on subsequent student drinking behaviour once young people leave home (Wechsler et al., 1995; Lo, 1995; Perkins, 1987). This reflects the research examined in Chapter 2, which demonstrated how parental influence decreases dramatically across adolescence as young people increasingly select their own life choices and subsequent social environments. Research has been able to track this waning influence as young people move through the educational system (Beck & Trieman, 1996). There is an exception in the case of alcoholic parents, whose consumption can have greater negative impact on young people's future use (Bradley et al., 1992; Karwacki & Bradley, 1996). However, this influence may still be multi-faceted in combining both social and biological risk factors (Sher, 1991).

As in general populations, peers exert significant influence on consumption in student populations. Lo's (1995) study of first year university students found that peer norms were the single biggest predictor of level of intoxication. Perkins (1985) found that perception of peers' drinking norms and membership of a fraternity was a stronger predictor of patterns of use than religious, gender or parental attitudes. Peer intensity, moving away from home, and being younger than other students at university also predicted consumption. Wechsler et al. (1995) found consumption directly related to heavy peer exposure. Having 5 or more close friends, socialising for 2 hours or more a day and living in a fraternity or sorority house predicted higher drinking rates after controlling for all other factors. Students involved in athletics or teams sports are also high consumers due to the comradeship that comes with these intensive peer activities (Leichliter et al., 1998).

At the same time, students over-estimate the amount of alcohol and drugs that are consumed. In one survey of 100 colleges and universities in the US, most students perceived that alcohol consumption was far higher at university than it had been at school (Perkins et al., 1999). This also appeared to be the case with drugs too (Perkins, 1994; Perkins et al., 1999). Prentice & Miller (1993) found a wide gulf been students' perceptions of alcohol use and the actual consumption rate at Ivy League universities. The presence of these widely accepted norms of high consumption increased consumption by discouraging more responsible drinking or drug using behaviour. For example, Prentice & Miller (1993) found that when students with conservative views regarding alcohol mistakenly believed that their personal attitudes were in contradiction to perceived norms, they felt increasingly alienated from both university and from peer groups. This reversed the ego-discomfort described in Chapter 2. In the same way that marginalised young adolescents, who feel they are different from their peers, experience difficulty in joining pro-social peer groups, so low substance consuming students experience ego-discomfort amongst high consuming peer groups.

Faculty/department interventions

Prevention and education programmes in higher education have focussed on faculty or department interventions to reduce consumption as a primary source of influence on young peeple. Faculties have deployed general prevention strategies that increase students' knowledge around drug and alcohol use. But these have been largely ineffective in reducing consumption (Duitsman & Cychosz, 1997; Robinson et al., 1993) for the same reasons already examined in rational models of prevention for school children. Knowledge simply does not change behaviour. As attendance on these programmes has largely been voluntary, it is also means that they have been unlikely to reach the highest risk students. One important area that has been under-researched is the relationship young people have with faculty staff. Faculty staff could have a strong influence on student drinking as faculty members represent new role models for young students. However this potential to reduce consumption has been under-utilised.

Guidance in the UK

In the UK, there has been no evaluation of programmes designed to address high student consumption. Instead, the *Drugs Guidance for Schools* has now been extended to Further Education Institutions (Drugscope, 2004). It recognises the specific risks that student life entails in terms of substance abuse and recommends good practice that all colleges of further education should follow. It advises that education should focus on developing students' awareness of drugs and alcohol. This should include exploring what they already know about drugs and their underlying attitudes and beliefs. Drug issues should be connected to wider life issues such as sex, relationships, emotional health and well-being. Harm minimisation is also recommended as relevant to this population in terms of raising students' awareness of risk, developing communication skills, handling relationships, coping and accessing sources of support.

The *Guidance* also points out that universities and colleges should have a wide range of policies in place to deal with drug- and alcohol-related incidents, including ensuring that the law surrounding drug and alcohol use, and its enforcement on the institutions premises, is made clear to students. For example, Section 8 of the Misuse of Drugs Act (Home Office, 1971) applies to college campuses in particular, whereby it is an offence to knowingly permit the supply and production of any drug on premises. Policies on drug-related incidents are equally important. Such incidents can range from a specific issue with a student to the incidence of supply, or may emerge vicariously in the form of supplying students outside of the institution, paraphernalia being discovered or disclosure of another student's use. Any policies should link with wider policy frameworks. Consultations should be taken with the police, local drug and alcohol services, health promotions units, parents and the youth service in order to ensure equity and good practice in policy development. There should be specific policies applicable in higher education establishments (Drugscope, 2004), specifically:

- Management of medical emergencies
- Involving and working with the police
- Taking temporary possession and disposal of suspected illegal drugs
- Confiscation and disposal of illegal drugs
- Disposal of drug paraphernalia
- Detection
- Circumstances where searches are considered appropriate
- Recording of a drug-related incident.

Further to this, the *Guidance* continues, higher education institutions should also consider high risk populations. These include young people who are looked after, and those with a history of truancy, special needs, mental health issues or homelessness, as well as offenders and carers. Students who appear to be under-achieving, have poor attendance or raise other staff concerns should also be screened. Additional one-to-one tutor support can be offered and where this is not possible, referrals can be made to learning mentors or welfare services wherever appropriate. Staff training may be required to deliver drug education and to assist those who may have a higher indicated risk. However, the same report also identified that there was considerable scope for development and identified critical obstacles to the effective deployment of effective prevention and education strategies in Higher Education establishments (Drugscope, 2004), specifically:

- Lack of statutory requirement for drugs education.
- Few trained or confident staff to deliver drug education.
- Limited curriculum and resources.
- Diverse educational needs and reluctance by students to engage in anything that appears like 'school' drugs education.
- Poor partnership work with relevant agencies (police, Connexions, local drug services).

- Difficulties in achieving balance between strict codes of practice and supportive ethos.
- Confusion over the legal status of drugs, particularly cannabis.
- Part-time status of some students.

Strategies in US

The US has developed wider strategies and responses to drug and alcohol use on campus which have been subjected to more rigorous evaluation. This has taken two broad approaches including enforcement of regulations and specific programmes to address individual consumption. In terms of regulating alcohol consumption, over 32 per cent of campuses in the US have banned alcoholic beverages on site or at university sponsored events (Anderson & Gadaleto, 1991). Others have restricted the hours where alcohol may be consumed, such as restricting alcohol use to weekends only. Where alcoholic drinks are available, soft drink alternatives must also be available and many universities now demand waiter service at these events. Waiter services for alcoholic drinks have been shown to reduce general consumption in comparison to self-service. Other universities have used the timetabling of university events to coincide with peak periods of drinking. Many discount student nights operate in town centres on Thursday nights to attract student trade on otherwise typically quiet nights. California State University programmed alternative recreational activities for Thursday evenings, and scheduled examinations and important classes for Friday mornings. This had a significant impact on midweek drinking rates and improved class attendance rates on Fridays (Wilson, 1990).

Universities in US studies have also established more pragmatic prevention strategies. One of the most famous strategies was the development of 'designated driver,' which involves one person electing not to drink in order to transport their peers safely. This programme has been highly successful and has migrated out of universities into mainstream life, where the phrase and the tactic are now widely used. However, the designated driver scheme has generated some controversy in allowing high levels of intoxication to occur in the 'undesignated' group. Likewise, controlled drinking programmes and access to information on drugs and alcohol has also been attempted. Many of these programmes have used the intellectual resources of their own institutions to develop approaches and responses to alcohol and drug use on campus. This might entail law students disseminating legal advice or psychology departments developing education programmes for students as part of academic projects. This taps into the intellectual resources of the institutions and offers students opportunities to apply their learning in practical settings.

A number of specific prevention strategies have been developed and tested with student populations. One of the most interesting approaches was conducted by Goldman et al. (1993). In this experiment, heavy drinking students were taken to a party and asked to identify which guests had drunk alcohol and which ones had not. The students in this sample did no better than random chance. The heavy drinkers were then randomly assigned to three intervention groups. The first group attended a controlled drinking programme; the second group was asked to evaluate media messages regarding alcohol consumption compared to their actual experience; and a third group was left as a control. At follow-up it was found that the controlled drinking group's consumption of alcohol had increased with their new confidence in managing intoxication. The control group's alcohol remained stable. The expectancy group made the most significant reductions to their alcohol consumption. Specifically this occurred in the heaviest drinking students.

This research highlights the central importance of expectations of consumption in student populations, which parallels findings in school populations. A number of specific prevention initiatives have been developed that have explored this issue further. They have focussed on challenging the normative expectations of peer use in student populations. This is particularly important due to the role consumption plays in social bonding at this time of life. As we have seen, students' perception of consumption within higher education settings is often inaccurate in that they assume a far higher rate of consumption than actually occurs. This over-estimate may increase students' use, as they drink at higher rates, supposing them to be normative for the group. This behaviour is susceptible to challenge through the provision of normative feedback. As campuses are self-contained social networks, the normative data on actual drinking levels has been transmitted to students in a variety of ways, including classes, college radio, television and newsprint. The approach has demonstrated surprisingly powerful effects. Research studies have found that it is able to reduce consumption by 20 per cent (see Marlatt et al., 1995; Haines, 1998; Jeffrey, 2000). At the same time, the feedback can help strengthen and legitimise more conservative attitudes to lower consumption.

Beyond normative education, structured programmes have also been developed for students to reduce alcohol consumption. For example, Graham et al. (2004) developed an Alcohol-related Harm Prevention Programme (AHP) for college students. This was a two-session model that aimed to reduce alcohol-related harm by addressing alcohol-related risk taking behaviour. The assumption of this approach differed from other models. Most prevention and education models have operated on the assumption that behaviour is driven solely by motivation and ability. Therefore they have tried to increase motivation to change consumption and to develop students' skills to achieve this aim. Instead, the AHP programme focussed on the students' ability to foresee risks and plan to reduce their or their friends' risk taking behaviour around alcohol use. 'Thus, the main focus of the AHP program was to increase student motivation and skills regarding these kinds of action: harm reduction planning and intervention.' (Graham, 2004: 72). The programme focussed on the identification and response to 7 key risk areas:

1. Increase perception of taking care of friend's well-being.
2. Increase perception of risk behaviours being unacceptable.
3. Increase skills relating to harm-prevention planning.
4. Increase intention to intervene in a risk situation.
5. Increase intention to make harm reduction plans with friends.
6. Decrease inaccurate normative assumptions regarding peer use.
7. Increase the perception of peer non-use of alcohol as normative.

A total number of 681 students were enrolled into the AHP programme and 444 students completed both sessions. Follow-up studies showed specific effects for each of the key issues addressed in the programme. One of the strongest effects related to the element of normative education, which has already been established in this book as an important mechanism in challenging consumption. Also, the programme had a strong effect on increasing the unacceptability of certain behaviours under the influence, such as drink driving. Taking care of others and attempting to intervene also increased through the programme. Planning for risk situations in advance was less useful. However, this novel programme did appear to be successful in addressing many risk factors that contribute to poor health and social consequences that can affect young people, without focusing on the elimination of alcohol consumption itself.

Family based prevention approaches

The innovations in addressing high consumption in student populations, described in the previous section, offer greater insight into the unique challenges that put young people at risk at this life stage. Family influence is in dramatic decline and leaving home places these young people beyond the immediate influence of parental monitoring. During early stages of the life course, families have the ability to exercise greater influence on younger adolescents, but have been neglected as a source of prevention or education. Dishion et al. (1988) noted that the children of parents who are capable of applying family management skills, monitoring, problem solving and providing positive reinforcement tend to have less significant problems. This includes reductions in anti-social behaviour, experimentation with drugs or alcohol; and the children are more socially and academically proficient. As such, researchers have hypothesised that strengthening the relationship between parents and children in higher risk families should reduce their drug and alcohol use. The ability to achieve this may differ between early and later adolescent risk groups. Early involvement in drug and alcohol use may be indicated by heavy parental use or lack of parental supervision; whereas later adolescent involvement in drug and alcohol use may be the result of peer involvement, where monitoring may be more critical. The opportunity for these interventions may also be taken up in different ways by different families. Highly conscientious parents are the most likely to self-present for these family programmes but tend to have better relationships with their children anyway (Cohen & Linton, 1995).

Hawkins, J.D. et al.'s (1986; 1987) research stressed the importance of family discipline and monitoring, particularly in dysfunctional families. They identified that inconsistent expectations, poor parental monitoring, severe punishments, extreme poverty and low academic achievement were all contributory factors leading to youth involvement in drug and alcohol use. They suggested that drug and alcohol use in young people could be reduced by improving family management skills, reducing conflict and assisting parents in poverty to overcome such harsh conditions of life. However, families in crises with high levels of disorganisation present a challenge in terms of engagement and retention. This led to their development of the Homebuilders Programmes, an intensive family prevention service that consisted of 21 specific training modules covering areas such as anger management and problem solving, as well as the development of specific strategies to engage challenging families.

Results for this approach have been very positive. Kosterman et al. (2001) randomly assigned 209 families to an intervention or a waiting-list control group. Comparing the adjusted post-test scores revealed that parents in the intervention condition reported significant improvements in the parenting behaviours targeted by the specific intervention sessions they received when compared to the control group. Effects were most pronounced amongst mothers. Importantly, outcomes for young people were also related to the number of sessions attended. In a second study, 424 families were randomly assigned to an intervention or a control group. Again, the programme significantly reduced the development of alcohol problems and improved parent norms regarding adolescent alcohol use over time (Park et al., 2000). The programme has also been delivered in accessible formats, including a parent training TV special and a TV series entitled 'Preparing for the Drug (Free) Years'. The programmes were designed to increase motivation, teach skills and encourage parents to implement these new approaches. The success of this programme may be because it increased protection factors for the most vulnerable youth.

Kumpfer & Turner (1990) developed a family prevention model based on the assumption that young people who suffered from low self-esteem would be drawn into anti-social peer groups and hence increase their risk of involvement in drug and alcohol use. A structured equation model was developed in order to examine the sequence between these different domains. They hypothesised that a favourable family life would boost a student's self-esteem. Increases in self-esteem would increase their attachment to the school. This would lead to positive peer relationships, which in turn would reduce the likelihood of drug or alcohol involvement. Based on this, Kumpfer & Turner (1990) developed three different types of family orientated prevention programmes. The first included parent training, the second involved developing the young person's social skills and the third option was based on family skills training. The approach did appear to reduce risk for involvement in tobacco and alcohol use, but only when all three programmes were delivered at the same time.

Mass media campaigns

Family is an important stability zone in early adolescence but as the young person matures other influences supersede it. The young person begins to perceive the world through other external influences such as the wider mass media. The mass media has become an important means for broadcasting health prevention messages including drug and alcohol use. Its ability to reach huge national audiences and target hard to reach groups in particular make it a particularly powerful vehicle for promoting both prevention and education messages. It is effective in raising awareness by placing drug and alcohol use on the local and national agenda (Caswell et al., 1989) even if it is not effective at influencing behaviour change (Bauman et al., 1991). Though some researchers have suggested that media is an effective forum for motivating and mobilising responses at a community level by increasing the take up of help lines or local support services.

Early campaigns

Early attempts to change public behaviour through mass media were largely unsuccessful (Flay & Sobel, 1983). Messages lacked credibility with the intended audience. Recent decades have seen considerable innovation in the delivery of health care messages, through the adoption of marketing strategies developed in advertising, including: improved targeting of messages through better audience segmentation; greater use of formative research to identify what targeted groups respond to; improved production values of advertisements, allowing them to compete with advertisements for alcohol and tobacco. This has increased the persuasiveness of messages to avoid or cut down on drug and alcohol use (Backer, 1990; Perloff, 1993). Alongside this, improvements in research methods have allowed for more refined assessment of the impact of mass media campaigns. There is growing evidence that health promotion messages can have impact on drug- and alcohol-related beliefs, assumptions and subsequent behaviours (Beck et al., 1990; Flora et al., 1989; Zastony et al., 1993).

Prevention and education messages are often delivered via television. This may be done as public service broadcasts where airtime can be bought or donated by television stations. Donated airtime may be less effective as the timing of these broadcasts is likely to be offered during off-peak programming, which limits the ability of the campaign to target specific segments of the intended audience. Measuring the impact of these adverts is also difficult. Evaluations have focussed on media relevant issues rather than behaviour relevant outcomes. For example, some studies of television media campaigns focussed on the whether viewers could recall the channel that broadcast it or whether the message felt relevant, rather than what changes it elicited. The aim of the prevention advert has not always been clear. Messages can prevent the initiation of use, raise awareness of risk or try to reduce use for those already engaged in this behaviour. Furthermore, it is not always possible to disentangle the effects of a mass media campaign from other variables. Mass media campaigns may run in parallel and be attached to classroom-based prevention and education programmes.

Flynn et al. (1992; 1995) attempted to disentangle these different contributions to overall outcomes. Their studies followed a four-year anti-smoking campaign that compared a mass-media combined with school prevention strategy with a mass media campaign on its own. The mass media campaign was delivered in the form of 4 six-month public service campaigns over the four year period and was made using both purchased and donated television and radio air-time. Significant reductions were found in the mass media group only and these gains increased annually. In another long-term study, the Partnership for a Drug Free America examined the impact of a well-designed campaign that received over $3 billion worth of air-time and print space (Black, 1991; Zastony et al., 1993). Follow-up studies found that the campaign was effective in reducing cannabis, amphetamine and cocaine use. Critics argued that this research had failed to account for a decline in use that was already occurring and that the follow-up methods were flawed. However, public service broadcasts with high saturation of anti-drug and anti-alcohol messages can achieve reductions in consumption and intention to use, and can challenge drug-related attitudes and positive beliefs about the benefits of use (Black, 1991; Block et al., 1996).

Campaigns based on adolescent understandings

One finding from mass media education and prevention campaigns is that approaches informed by a clear understanding of adolescent drug and alcohol use are much more effective. A number of campaigns have called upon a wide range of behavioural theories such as social learning, protection motivation theory and theory of reasoned actions to enhance their message. One striking campaign was the SENTAR approach (SENsation-TARgetting) developed by Palmgreen et al. (2001) which was one of the first theory-driven media-based approaches. They based their approach on targeting the temperament factor, 'sensation seeking', as a critical risk factor for cannabis involvement. This programme developed an advertising campaign through three phases. Phase one included targeting the audience. Sensation seekers were chosen, as research had shown such a high prevalence of use in this population. Phase two comprised of designing messages that would resonate with this specific target audience. Through focus groups, sensation seekers reported a preference for novel, rapid-fire messages that elicited visual and emotional responses. Phase three included the identification of programming that was attractive to the target audience. Initial field trials on a public service broadcast elicited a very positive response. Over 2,100 callers subsequently phoned a hotline for more information on exciting alternatives to drug and alcohol use. Interestingly, 73 per cent of callers scored highly on sensation seeking.

The SENTAR model was broadcast in two matched cities in a larger clinical trial. It broadcast an anti-cannabis message using purchased and donated time. In order to measure impact the research team used an interrupted time method. This meant that the delivery of the anti-cannabis message would be introduced at different times across the two cities. This allowed for cross-comparison of its possible effect. Follow-up research showed that they were able not only to reduce cannabis use in the two cities but also to reverse the trend of consumption in high sensation seeking youth. In one city heavy cannabis use amongst young people had risen from 16.6 per cent to 33 per cent prior to the campaign. This was reduced to 24 per cent on the implementation of the campaign and these changes were sustained over a 12 month period. At cessation of the campaign, the use of cannabis began to rise, but then fell again after a 'booster' campaign was introduced in one city. Interestingly, the campaign had the greatest effect on young people with high sensation seeking temperaments.

Combined campaigns

Slater et al. (2006) tested the impact of stand-alone media campaigns versus media campaigns combined with school-based interventions in a large scale study involving 4,216 students. Using randomised procedures, 16 communities were assigned to either media only or media and community prevention strategies. Two schools also included an in-school prevention programme and two did not. The researchers supposed that the key issue in media-based campaigns was to ensure that the intended audience had sufficient exposure to the message (Hornik, 2000) and that the message was suitable to the target group (Pechmann et al., 2003). Social marketing principles were used to develop alcohol, tobacco and drug prevention messages. This included primary and secondary research to understand young people's attitudes, values and behaviours regarding substance use. Focus groups with young people identified products and media channels attractive to the adolescent audience. This culminated in the development of the 'Be Under your Own Influence' campaign. The message selected for this research study was to emphasise non-use as an expression of identity and promoted the idea that non-use was consistent with wider adolescent aspirations (Slater & Kelly, 2002).

Besides the use of media, the experiment also used a community-based prevention approach that had been shown to be effective in reducing drug or alcohol use (Aguirre-Molina & Gorman, 1996; Perry et al., 2002). This community-based participation programme consisted of a half day readiness workshop that identified people interested in prevention who were then asked to snowball attendance to others who might be interested. They then worked with individuals to identify prevention strategies and plans that were relevant to people's readiness to engage. This included a half-day workshop on the use of community messages such as leaflets, posters, brochures and ideas for special events. The in-school programme was based on a substance programme called All Stars (Trade Mark). This programme challenged using norms, strengthened young people's commitment to not use drugs and alcohol and enhanced school bonding (Harrington et al., 2003). It involved 13 sessions in the first year and 7 booster sessions in the second year.

The results of the programme showed superior outcomes for the combined media and in-school options, particularly for cannabis. Whilst the initial effects were small they increased steadily across the study. The stand-alone media intervention's impact was low on tobacco, which may be because only a few messages targeted tobacco, whereas all messages made references to drugs. However, the impact of the media programme on substance use was high. 'A particularly encouraging dimension of this intervention is that it appeared to influence several substance outcomes, marijuana and alcohol use in particular. The focus on autonomy and aspiration ('Be Under Your Own Influence') was equally applicable to both substances. Such multi-substance approaches are particularly advantageous given the limited resources and time available in most school settings.' (Slater et al., 2006: 164).

Other approaches

A slightly different approach to mass media campaigns was piloted in Switzerland. Advertisements there promoted the idea that self-change in drinking behaviour was an effective means of stopping problem use. The advertisements hoped to challenge negative expectancies regarding people's ability to stop consumption and to increase their belief that they could change themselves. This had positive effects in terms of acceptance and recall in audiences and appeared to augment decision making in those contemplating or preparing to initiate changes in behaviour (see Klingemann et al., 2001).

Backer et al. (1992) researched what works in mass media advertising. This was part analytic review and part interview with 29 leading experts in mass media communication. For example, it was found that multiple media that incorporate a degree of entertainment and repeat a simple message are more powerful, and it is important that the campaigns are targeted exactly. Segmenting the audience by psychological profiles was more effective than targeting audiences by demographics. In general, it was also found that mass media campaigns operated more effectively when they promoted a positive message rather than warned of the dangers of current behaviours.

Other mass media approaches have been used besides television. Health warning labels are a form of mass media advertising. This strategy relies on warning labels on packaging, billboards, posters and alcoholic beverages to educate the public regarding the specific risks of consumption. Recall for such messages is high and some research has demonstrated that young people believe that these measures are important, though they are unlikely to have a substantial impact on preventing behaviour in isolation (Paglia et al., 1996). Some studies have identified that health warnings on cigarette packets are more powerful on light or moderate smokers. Photographs of health conditions appear to influence young people who report that these images put them off smoking (Hammond et al., 2007). Whilst some studies have found a benefit in the use of these images, others have not. Repeat exposure to the same image means that the impact may wear off over time.

Computers have become an essential feature of everyday life, particularly for young people born into a highly advanced cyber-society. As such, the potential for computer-based interventions has been explored in a variety of health promotion initiatives targeting young people. Computer-based learning has generally shown positive outcomes. It has been found to increase young people's performance, speed of learning and motivation (Burns & Bozeman, 1981; McCollister et al., 1986). Computer-assisted learning is particularly helpful in health promotion as it is relatively easy to develop interactive software for a wide variety of health concerns which can motivate self-directed learning. Feedback processes built into the software can allow for greater personalisation, meaning that they can be tailored to each young person's needs with great adaptability and be delivered in a more confidential setting.

Chambers & Sprecher's (1980) early analysis of the impact of computer-assisted learning found that it could: produce equivalent outcomes or better than traditional teaching approaches; reduce learning time; and improve students' attitudes to learning via computer technology. However, despite an explosion in access to computer technology, there has been slow progress in the development of drug and alcohol education programmes. Pioneering models that have tried to use computers to alter behaviour have been positive. Tombari et al. (1985) studied the effect of teaching behavioural management skills via interactive software to young people who were disruptive in class. The programme was very successful in reducing their disruptive behaviour. The BARN Project (Body Awareness Resource Network) was a computer-based health promotion programme for young people and their families. Longitudinal follow-up of 800 young people who had tried the programme demonstrated a number of successful outcomes in the reduction of unhealthy behaviours, particularly amongst high risk youth.

The internet has opened up new possibilities in terms of the delivery of drug education and prevention programmes to young people as it is a medium that they value. Research by PricewaterhouseCoopers (2000) found that young people log on to the internet for a number of reasons. The main ones include checking email (83 per cent), research (68 per cent) and chatrooms (40 per cent). The internet can provide multi-media such as film and music to enhance its messages as well interactivity in terms of questionnaires and personal feedback. Young people have shown a high preference for internet based information in comparison to traditional leaflets (Di Noia et al., 2003). There has been limited study of the impact of internet approaches. Newton et al. (2010) studied the impact of an internet-based alcohol and cannabis prevention programme on 746 young people aged 13. A total of 397 young people were assigned to the Internet option whilst 367 young people attended the usual health education classes. At 12-month follow-up, students in the internet group showed significant improvements in alcohol and cannabis knowledge, a reduction in weekly alcohol consumption and a reduction in frequency of drinking to excess. No differences between groups were found on alcohol expectancies, cannabis attitudes or alcohol- and cannabis-related harms. The course was found to be acceptable by teachers and students.

Diversionary programmes

Diversionary approaches that encourage young people to engage in pro-social activities in preference drug and alcohol use have been popular since the 1970s. Anti-drug and anti-alcohol messages are not necessarily explicit in these approaches but the team building activities are designed to increase responsibility, self-esteem and fulfilment in young people. Youth groups in general are considered a sub-group of this category of education and prevention work, and incorporate recreation, community volunteering projects, community awareness campaigns and drug education. Some research has found that these are an effective approach to drug and alcohol prevention. In one 'drug-free' youth club, 90 per cent of youth abstained from alcohol and 97 per cent abstained from smoking over a six year follow-up period (Nelson-Simley & Erickson, 1995). This group was self-selecting to enter into the programme, but a third of the participants were from high-risk groups. These programmes may be enhanced if the activities are time-tabled during high risk times.

Anderson et al. (2006) reviewed the impact of recreational mentoring on young people. Their programme attempted to address barriers, such as cost, distance and time, to recreational activities for young people with mental health problems by using mentors to support them into diversionary activities in their community. The results demonstrated very high satisfaction rates (90 per cent), however no long term follow-up of impact was conducted nor were there control groups. Jones & Offord (1989) examined the use of after-school programmes for high-risk youth who were offered opportunities to engage in sports, music and the arts. During this 32-month programme arrest rates for young people declined dramatically, but these effects were not sustained after the programme finished. Nichols

& Crow (2004) examined seven different diversionary programmes and crime reduction, but found it difficult to draw any conclusions due to poor data collection. Types of groups, lengths of programme and attendance rates varied dramatically between projects.

Attention has been given to the use of theatre and the arts as a diversionary activity. Walters (1997) reviewed a programme of collaboration between actors and young people to develop a play that was performed across a number of venues. Without clear evaluation of outcomes, this study reported that only 1 in 22 young people had offended at 12-month follow-up. Ezell & Levy (2003) evaluated the impact of an arts project with young incarcerated offenders. This study was aimed at increasing young people's ability to self-reflect and occupy their time meaningfully. Institutional records showed a decline in reported rule violation amongst the offenders during the 6-month follow-up.

Diversionary sports programmes have been used extensively in order to increase engagement with young people who are socially marginalised, though the long-term effectiveness has not been clearly established. Smith & Waddington's (2004) review of clinical studies of diversionary sports activities concluded that the design and rationale of these programme was inconsistent and that they lacked clinical data on outcomes of the changes in young people's behaviour. Where positive changes in behaviour have been found they have tended to be short lived. For example, Hartman & Depro (2006) examined the use of 'midnight basketball' in deprived estates in the US. The midnight basketball programme is a sports scheme that commences at 10pm onwards and is voluntary for young people to attend. Leagues and cups are organised in high crime areas to divert young people into more pro-social recreation. They found that property crime did fall in neighbourhoods that offered the scheme but there was no decline in violent crime. As such, timetabling of alternative activities appears to influence pre-meditated crimes rather than impulsive criminal behaviour.

A three-year evaluation of the UK's Positive Futures programme examined the impact of 37 community projects to engage at-risk young people in sport. These programmes achieved high engagement rates and increased rates of young people moving into training and education. The programme reported improved relationships between the young people and staff, but no other outcomes were reported. A Home Office (2002) review of the UK Summer Splash programme was only able to establish data from three of the six case studies. Again there was little insight gleaned from what might constitute effective practice in retaining young people other than difficulties in recruiting staff who were able to forge strong alliances with the young people. In reviewing diversionary activities amongst young offenders in Australia, Mason & Wilson (1988) likewise reported a need for high quality staff in the delivery of diversionary sports programmes. Taylor et al.'s (1999) review of probation services' diversionary activities found that any benefit was derived from those staff who were able to operate under unique pressures with young people, rather than from the activities themselves. Similar results have also been found in relation to outward bound courses that have also demonstrated disappointing outcomes (McGuire et al., 2002).

Criticism has been levelled at diversionary sporting activities. Sport is often supposed to change behaviour by increasing the self-esteem of young people through competing and winning. However, as Smith & Waddington (2004) observed, what effect does this have on the losers in such activities? It is also important to consider that many team sports and clubs are also associated with heavy drinking which is counter-productive to the aims of substance misuse treatment services. The central problem in the provision of many sporting diversionary activities, and many other youth orientated programmes, is that they assume these programmes work by increasing self-esteem levels in young people, which in turn prompts behavioural change. Raising self-esteem levels as a form of protection from substance misuse and other anti-social behaviours is a very popular concept in youth work. However, research has not found that increases in self-esteem lead to, or enhance, behavioural change to any degree.

Whilst there has been a lack of research in this area, the current evidence suggests that diversionary programmes are not effective in preventing or reducing drug or alcohol use in the long term (Norman et al., 1997). At best, diversionary programmes appear to engage young people but do not induce enduring behavioural change. At the same time, limited study and poor design has meant that the potential of these programmes has not been fully realised. Additional consideration should be given to the fact that the skills young people learn in diversionary activities may not generalise to other domains of their life. For example, the skills necessary to overcome an Outward Bound challenge are the same as overcoming any challenge in life: planning, communication, teamwork, overcoming self-doubt, perseverance, etc. However, young people will not make this connection due to the situational nature of their behaviour. Greater focus on helping young people recognise the relevance of these skills in wider situations may facilitate their more effective transfer. Second, these studies have focussed on diversionary activities as stand-alone projects. Diversionary activities may be more viable when incorporated into a multi-dimensional programme, where they could provide an opportunity to test skills in more challenging environments or be used as contingency rewards for attendance on prevention and education programmes. Finally, as peer groups can exert such a profound influence on behaviours, diversionary activities could also be used as a route into new social groups.

Social/recreational counselling is an approach that is designed to generate ideas for alternative recreation, facilitate entry into the new recreational groups and support individuals to maximise engagement in these new activities. Whilst it has been used extensively within the Community Reinforcement Approach (see Chapter 6), it has not been used with young people as a diversionary prevention strategy. But it could hold considerable promise.

Multilevel community approaches

So far, prevention and education programmes have been reviewed as discrete elements. However, these approaches have often been combined in large scale multilevel, multisite programmes, incorporating all sectors of community involvement such as schools, parents, workplaces, churches, government agencies and the media. Project Northland was a randomised trial to reduce alcohol use amongst young people in 24 districts of northeast Minnesota involving 2,351 students. Minnesota was selected for the trial because it exhibited high rates of alcohol use amongst young people. This was an important study as it tried to combine two distinct interventions that aimed to reduce the demand and supply of alcohol to minors.

Phase One of the programme was delivered in 1991–94 and targeted young people in 6–8th grades at school. The prevention programme focussed on school-based educational and prevention messages, parental involvement, peer leadership and community task forces. Each intervention was branded with the Project Northlands logo and was informed by adolescent developmental processes. An Interim Phase was delivered in 1994–96 and involved limited interventions, whilst Phase Two was delivered in 1996–98 and included five strategies: community organisation to reduce access to alcohol, parent education and involvement in community actions, youth action teams targeting alcohol-related problems, use of print media to advertise community events, and targeting of older adolescents who often purchased alcohol for their younger peers. An outline of interventions is outlined in Table 5.2.

It was hoped that this large scale intervention would have several effects, including changing: young people's and adults' communication regarding alcohol, the functional meaning of alcohol amongst young people, and young people's ability to resist peer influences to drink alcohol. In addition, it hoped to challenge normative assumptions about alcohol use and address the ease with which alcohol was available to young people. Follow-up measures were based on these anticipated outcomes of behavioural change and were evaluated using multiple assessment tools, including annual student surveys, the number of alcohol purchase attempts by young people from shops and parent surveys. Attitudinal changes were evaluated by the development of a scale that measured the tendency towards using alcohol in youth. At the outset of the programme, young people reported higher alcohol use in the intervention areas than in the control group. Retention rates across the trial period after the initial school programme were very high. For example almost 50 per cent of young people engaged in peer led activities out of school, over 273 peer educators were trained and implemented the programme across all schools and 2,700 young people saw a drug education play entitled 'It's My Party' that was performed 20 times.

At follow-up, young people living in the intervention areas showed statistically significant lower scores for alcohol. This included reduction in 'past month' and 'past week' consumption of alcohol (21.1 per cent) in contrast to the

Table 5.2:   Summary of interventions in Project Northlands.

Intervention	Description
6th and 7th Grade	
Slick Tracy Family Fun	• Activity books completed by children with their parents. • Small discussion groups with parents. • Evening fairs for parents with student posters on display. • *Northland Notes for Parents* guidance on the programme.
Community task force	• Established 13 task forces of community activists across the area. • Drew on teaching, legal, police, business and government officials. • The task forces led to establishing five alcohol-related ordinances and three political resolutions including responsible beverage services training to prevent illegal alcohol sales. • Gold card discounts for students who pledged to be alcohol free.
Amazing Alternatives!	• Initiated with an evening party for parents. • 8-week peer-led and teacher-led classroom curriculum using discussion groups, games, problem solving and role plays. Peer leaders elected by other class members. • Peer participation programme identifying alcohol-free alternatives (T.E.E.N.S.). • Amazing Alternatives booklet for parents. • Additional *Northland Notes for Parents*.
8th Grade	
PowerLines	• 8-session classroom curriculum that introduced students to power groups in the community. These are groups that influence adolescent alcohol use and availability. • Students conducted a town meeting in order to make suggestions as to how to limit alcohol availability. • Theatre production of 'It's My Party' performed by 8th Grade actors. • Additional *Northland Notes for Parents*. • Continuation of T.E.E.N.S.

non-intervention control group (29.1 per cent). Findings from Phase 1 demonstrated reductions in youth drinking, less peer influence to use alcohol and knowing fewer peers who used alcohol. The programme was effective in reducing at its end the drinking rates of those who were not using alcohol at the initiation of the programme when compared to the control group (Perry et al., 1996). Amongst tobacco and cannabis users, there was no statistical difference between the intervention and the control groups. However the comparison for cigarette use showed as 19 per cent lower in the intervention group by the end of the study, and this score was approaching statistical significance. Young people in the intervention group were also far less likely to report smoking cigarettes and drinking at the same time. This is an interesting finding in relation to Gateway Theory, reviewed in Chapter 3, that delay in the initiation in one drug can delay involvement in others in the sequence.

Amongst young people receiving the intervention only 14.3 per cent reported smoking tobacco and drinking compared to 19.6 per cent of young people in the control group. This difference was statistically significant resulting in a 27 per cent reduction in 'gateway' drug use. Phase 2 was deemed necessary in light of a decaying effect of these prevention outcomes over a two year period (Perry et al., 1998). Komro et al. (2001) examined in detail what mediators were effective in reducing alcohol use in young people in the Project Northland study. Mediators are the critical risk or protection factors that were changed by the programme and which influenced the final outcome (Baron & Kenny, 1986). Analysis of Project Northland data found that the success of the programme was accounted for by its influence on four key areas:

1. Reduce peer influence to drink alcohol
2. Change functional meaning of non-using activities
3. Decreased the risk of developing alcohol problems
4. Increased alcohol related communication between adolescents and parents.

Project Northland decreased peer influence to use alcohol which is one of the greatest risk factors for involvement in alcohol use in general. This was achieved through the use of peer-led classroom curriculum interventions, parent education, peer-planned social activities and community involvement. For non-users at baseline, decreasing social problems prior to onset was important. This is because those young people who are most vulnerable to alcohol and substance problems are those who experience greater social problems prior to initiation. Ways of increasing vulnerable youth's self-belief in refusing alcohol were important mediators of their outcomes, which suggests that resistance skills may be more effective prior to involvement in alcohol.

This finding is interesting as these two measures – decreasing social problems and increasing self-belief – were not found to be significant in other trials such as Life Skills Training (Botvin et al., 1992) or the Midwestern Prevention Programme (MacKinnon et al., 1991). The Midwestern Prevention Programme is another example of this multilevel prevention approach and offers an interesting comparison to Project Northland. Conducted in Kansas City (Pentz et al., 1989), it covered 42 schools, eight of which were randomly assigned to the intervention or a control group. This multisite approach delivered prevention messages across five domains, and included: a 10-session school-based resistance programme; 10 joint homework sessions with parents; mass media advertising; community organisation; and policy changes to restrict access and availability. Whilst there were no differences in drug use between the students at initiation of the study, research at one-year follow-up demonstrated significantly lower rates of tobacco, alcohol and cannabis use in the intervention group compared to the control group (Pentz et al., 1989). These remained stable with the exception of alcohol at a three-year follow-up, though some methodological issues have undermined the confidence in some of these findings (Johnson et al., 1990).

Analysis of positive outcomes in this study identified that friends' negative reactions to drug use accounted for 66 per cent of the programme's effect on drug use and 45 per cent of the programme's effect on cigarettes. There was no clear impact of other elements of the programme, including resistance skills, perceived peer norms

or the negative consequences of drug use (MacKinnon et al., 1991). This suggests that peer influence is stronger in reducing drug use than alcohol use, which may be reflective of the cultural acceptability of alcohol versus drugs. Whereas young people operate in a culture which holds broadly positive views of alcohol, acceptance of drug use is much more restricted to their peer world.

Targeted interventions

The effectiveness of prevention and education approaches appears to rely on their ability to identify and address the actual risk factors in young people's lives as opposed to the presumed risk factors in their lives. However, young people may vary in their risk profiles, particularly amongst vulnerable youth populations. In the UK, a major review of the evidence base for prevention with specific vulnerable groups has been conducted by the National Collaborating Centre of Drug Prevention (Edmonds et al., 2005). This attempted to identify critical findings from a range of sources to inform best practice for specific risk groups. These vulnerable groups are unlikely to be attending school, so prevention interventions would need to occur in wider community settings. What is striking about the review is that every risk group identified is characterised by a lack of research into effective approaches for these groups. Rather, the report describes the needs of each sub-population and provides generalised guidance on types of support that may be appropriate for each group. Interestingly, all the groups described are those sub-populations of young people whose lives are characterised by weak social relationships. Their relationships with others are already compromised through the effects of poverty (as described in Chapter 1) as well as through family disintegration, poor academic attachments, and their vulnerability to being exploited by others. This places certain groups at high risk of developing substance misuse problems, such as:

- Young offenders
- Cared for children
- Young homeless people
- Young people excluded from school
- Sexually exploited young people and sex workers

- Young people from Black and Minority Ethnic communities who experience racial discrimination
- Carers of drug users
- Children of drug users

This report, and others like it, tends to suggest *where* the most at risk are liable to be rather than *what* their specific risk profiles are. As we have seen, demographic profiles are not as helpful in informing interventions as psychological profiles. Within these broad social groups may reside young people with very diverse personality types. It would be important to ascertain what specific risk factors influence these young people's drug and alcohol trajectories and whether they can be mediated by common protective factors or not. This might identify considerable crossover in these populations. As reviewed in Chapter 3, the risk and protection factors for substance abuse resemble the same factors that influence the development of mental health problems and offending (Kessler, 1995; Ollendick & King, 1994). Little consideration is given, either in the report or more generally, to whether some of the incumbent problems experienced by these young people are sourced in underlying mental health or behavioural problems induced by their life circumstances, which might demand a different response. The use of mental health assessment and interventions has been neglected in the prevention and education field, but could be vital if the highest risk groups are to be deflected from use.

Risk and protection factors in mental health and substance abuse

Research has demonstrated that specific efforts to reduce the risk factors and increase protective factors can have an impact on reducing the incidence of both mental health and substance abuse problems. This must occur within the developmental context of young people's lives and must address the particular risk factors that precipitate both sets of problems. Such early interventions are important in preventing or delaying the cascade effect of risk factors which snowball from initial conditions. This demands higher levels of intervention than universal education to address these more sophisticated and inter-related problems. Research does suggest that interventions delivered at opportune

times can be effective in reducing the severity of externalised and internalised disorders, as well as in diminishing adjunct substance abuse. Hawkins et al. (1997) iterated that five key principles can be used as guidance to address to these specific issues:

1. Systematic reduction of risk factors
2. Systematic enhancement of protective factors
3. Addressing factors at developmentally appropriate levels
4. Early intervention
5. Addressing multiple risk factors with multiple strategies.

The timing of an early intervention should be determined by the age of onset of underlying problems that contribute to the risk of drug and alcohol abuse. Externalised disorders have a very early onset in infancy, whereas internalised disorders, with the exception of anxiety, are more likely to present in early adolescence. Therefore, targeted prevention and education interventions that address mental health need to account for these different periods in development. The earliest interventions deployed in childhood will need to include the family system as it exerts such a powerful influence over children at this time and is where so many risks are sourced. Emphasis shifts to become more focussed on young people as increased autonomy means their own personal decisions increase their risk at this point.

Early intervention with externalised and internalised children

A number of education and prevention programmes have been developed and evaluated to target high risk groups for both internalised and externalised disorders in families at different stages of young people's development including infancy, childhood and adolescence. Externalised disorders commonly appear as early disruptive behaviour in nursery or kindergartens. Considerable attention has been given to the alleviation of externalised behaviours through early intervention. This has tried to address multiple risk factors that contribute to the disorder, specifically examining parent training and family interventions. The 'Triple P Stepped Care' approach (Sanders, 1999) and behavioural family interventions have demonstrated effective outcomes (Miller & Prinz, 1990). However, it has been recognised that recruited families often encounter their own mental health, financial or family problems that impede treatment gains. Oppositional Defiance Disorder appears most amenable to treatment interventions. However, Tremblay et al. (1995) found that disruptive nursery children from disadvantaged economic backgrounds allocated to a dual-focussed programme of parenting training and child social skills training demonstrated superior attendance in regular class and showed significantly less delinquent behaviour between the ages of 10 and 15 than did the control group.

One of the most effective approaches has been early intervention with at-risk parents selected via neonatal and antenatal clinics. Pregnant mothers have been targeted for their high risk factor indices such as living in poverty, teenage motherhood, being a single parent, low birth weight or a history of substance misuse, all of which are risk factors for early onset externalised disorders. Olds et al. (1998) collected data over a 15-year period on 400 at-risk mothers who were randomly assigned to a well-child programme that offered routine or intensive home visits from nursing staff. In the intensive home visit group, mothers were visited until the child's second birthday and were provided with a wide range of support and parenting skills. The intensive visiting group demonstrated significant outcomes for the children. This intervention reduced offending, anti-social behaviour, substance misuse and number of sexual partners by 50 per cent in these children at age 15 (Olds et al., 1998). Other studies have shown similar gains and provide substantial evidence that intensive early intervention with at-risk parents can create lasting long term effects on children's subsequent life trajectories (see Cole et al., 1998). Bernazzini (2001) reviewed 7 control trials where parenting interventions had been delivered before children were 3 years of age. The majority of these studies (6) involved intensive home visitation but with additional components. Positive results were found in 3 studies but no effects on behaviour were identified in 4 of the studies at follow-up.

Attempts at early intervention with internalised children are less impressive and tend to occur later in a child's life when the pattern of fretful or anxious behaviour emerges. LaFreniere & Capuano (1997) implemented a 6-month intensive home visiting prevention programme for mothers and their pre-school children who had been identified as being 'anxious-withdrawn' in temperament. This programme consisted of parenting skills, improving the family social network and addressing stresses in the parent. Children showed some reduction in anxious-withdrawn behaviour and improved social engagement, but little difference was detected in parental anxiety levels. Other studies targeting specific internalised risk groups have shown poorer outcomes (Roth & Dadds, 1999).

Late childhood intervention

Late childhood presents a promising opportunity to implement intervention strategies to address internalised and externalised disorders. As a child's own cognitive functioning develops, it is possible to engage them, as well as their family, directly in treatment interventions. However, methodological problems have dogged evaluations, so their value is difficult to discern. Evaluation difficulties may be further compounded by programmes which ask for parental involvement, as parents who take an active interest in their children's development and well-being are more likely to be attracted to these programmes, but are the least likely to experience problems. Recruitment and retention of parents is a particular issue, especially for those parents with substance misuse problems themselves. For young people, fears of stigma or negative judgments from peers can be a powerful block to them attending mental health services. Retention rates with young people are much higher in universal programmes than in targeted programmes, which suggests that broader programmes might usefully be adapted for young people with this risk profile.

Interventions that have targeted internalised disorders in children have shown more promising results in reducing drug and alcohol use. This may be due to the later onset of these problems and which have therefore not had time to entrench. A number of studies have found that Cognitive-Behavioural Therapy that targets improved anxiety management and increased social competency has demonstrated good outcomes in reducing subsequent drug and alcohol involvement. Kendall (1994) found that 16–20 sessions of Cognitive-Behavioural Therapy can eliminate symptoms of anxiety in over 60 per cent of children. Barret et al. (1996) showed similarly impressive outcomes with a combination of Cognitive-Behavioural Therapy and family treatment in group formats. Treatment effects were sustained at a 6-year follow-up. Cobham et al. (1999) found that reducing parental anxiety could also improve outcomes for children.

Evidence is also supportive of interventions designed to address externalised behaviours in later childhood. These programmes attempt to intercept externalised disorders as they become established. Greenberg et al. (2001) identified ten 'early intervention' programmes that demonstrated effective reductions in externalised behaviours or their risk factors. Again, these programmes draw upon child-cognitive skills, parent training or both. Reductions in fighting, and in drug and alcohol use, and improvements in family relationships have also been achieved with this group through mentoring programmes, though they did not reduce offending behaviour (Tierney et al., 1995). An obstacle for group programmes with externalised children is that the concentration of externalised youth in a single group tends to exacerbate their acting out behaviours. Pairing externalised children with non-aggressive peers through social competence programmes tends to reduce this effect and preserve intervention gains (Prinz et al., 1994; Hudley & Graham, 1995).

More comprehensive programmes have been designed to address a broader range of risk factors, including social competence and self-control in children, parenting and teacher training for classroom management with disruptive children. These comprehensive programmes have been found to be highly effective. Reid et al.'s (1999) sample of 671 children found significant reductions in playground aggression, improved mother-child relationships and classroom conduct, with immediate effect in each domain. Kazdin & Wassell's (2000) multisite programme also achieved a wide range of treatment gains in symptom reduction, reduced family stress and improvements in social and family functioning. Similar findings have been found in other comprehensive multisite studies. Dadds & McAloon (2002) identified five principle measures essential to the efficacy of these programmes:

1. Early identification and intervention
2. Incorporation of family-based intervention
3. Comprehensive models encompassing the ecology of child development
4. Longitudinal approach incorporating risk and protective factors and windows of opportunity

5. Combination of selected (poor neighbourhood), indicated (identified at risk young people) and universal (classroom programme) strategies.

Studies into the treatment of externalised and internalised disorders in later adolescence are more likely to occur where drug and alcohol consumption is already established and so may be more akin to treatment than to programmes of prevention aimed at addressing substance risk. Some research has found that some programmes can have a beneficial prevention effect though. Combined Behavioural Family Interventions and mentoring (Tierney et al., 1995) as well as anger management (Lochman, 1992) have shown some positive outcomes for externalised youth. In older adolescents internalised symptoms of depression, suicide, anxiety, substance misuse and self-harm are often florid. The programmes reviewed previously will remain relevant to adolescents up to the age of 14–15. However, more specialised programmes for older adolescents have been developed with internalised disorders. They have been able to achieve significant reductions in depression through problem solving, cognitive restructuring and anxiety management (Lewinsohn et al., 1990; Clarke et al., 1995) but again, they are primarily treatment orientated. However, approaches for internalised disorders have rarely included substance misuse outcomes, limiting their direct applicability to substance misuse reduction work. Common problems in all of these programmes are poor recruitment and higher drop-out rates as adolescents get older.

Personality traits and expectancies

Recent developments in education and prevention have begun to focus on how motivation to use drugs and alcohol is connected to the temperament of the young person. The trait-motivational model suggests that individual personality traits are directly connected to young people's expectancies of use and give rise to different types of susceptibility to alcohol (Conrod et al., 2000a; Pihl & Petterson, 1995; Theakston et al., 2004). The personality traits which appear particularly important in this process are sensation seeking and anxiety sensitivity (Comeau et al., 2001; Stewart & Devine 2000). Sensation seeking describes a thrill seeking, low impulse control personality trait whilst anxiety sensitivity refers to an anxious personality style. Studies have found that young people who score highly on either of these two use alcohol in highly maladaptive ways. For example, Comeau et al.'s (2001) investigation into young people's motivation to use alcohol revealed that sensation-seeking youth drank to enhance mood states. In contrast, anxiety sensitive youth valued the sedation effects of alcohol as it made them feel less anxious about fitting in, or reduced the stress from problems they faced.

The trait-motivation model assumes that by addressing these personality factors they can influence the degree of risk taking behaviour with alcohol. An initial study by Conrod et al. (2000b) showed promising results. They assessed the personality types of young women who engaged in heavy drinking and classified them as sensation seeking or anxiety sensitive. They were then assigned to a coping skills programme. They found significant reductions in drinking when these young women were matched to interventions appropriate to their drinking motives. This pilot led to a larger study that utilised manualised workbooks, psycho-education on personality traits and Cognitive-Behavioural strategies that were conducted on 4,882 young people aged between14 and 17 in Canada. Young people were selected for the programme on the basis that they had drank alcohol at least once in the last four months and that they also registered a positive score in psychological assessment tools which measured Sensation Seeking, Anxiety Sensitivity or Hopelessness (Conrod & Woicik, 2002). A total of 111 Anxiety Sensitive youth, 146 Sensation Seeking youth and 40 Hopelessness youth were identified, and they voluntarily entered into the programme. These groups did not differ in social demographics other than that the high Sensation Seeking groups tended to be heavier drinkers at intake. Participants were randomly assigned to different interventions consisting of just two sessions. This was either an appropriately matched intervention, a personality targeted intervention or a control group.

Follow-up at four months showed that few of the groups achieved abstinence, though the Hopelessness group showed the strongest trend in that direction. However, the programme did have a powerful influence on reducing binge drinking rates. Whilst 59.5 per cent of the control group continued to engage in binge drinking only 41.6 per cent of the personality targeted group did. The biggest reductions occurred in the Sensation Seeking group. The Anxiety Sensitive group showed significant reductions in alcohol-related consequences compared to the control group. The authors concluded that 'thus, it seems that these personality specific interventions are effective in reducing the very drinking behaviours that are more problematic for each personality type, thus providing further support for the necessity for matching early interventions to specific personality risk factors for alcohol misuse.' (Stewart et al., 2005: 283).

It is striking that the personality traits of Sensation Seeking and Anxiety Sensitivity/ Hopelessness are reflective of the sub-trajectories that have been described for externalised and internalised youths. This emergent research is an important development on a number of levels. First, this model is rooted in the risk factors of young people's lives. Furthermore, it is a multi-risk factor model linking personality traits, motivations and expectancies in a clear pathway. It has also demonstrated the validity of the assumption that young people in divergent trajectories may require more appropriately matched interventions which target their specific risk profiles. Finally, the model has also shown positive results in these groups after relatively brief exposure to prevention messages. This might suggest that the efficiency of interventions can be enhanced by focusing on the relevant risk profile that influences use.

The outcomes of prevention and education programmes

This chapter's review of the historical evolution of prevention and education programmes over the last hundred years has offered insight into the core assumptions, approaches and development of education and prevention. It has demanded that we make a critical shift from a moral, adult view of consumption towards young people's perspectives of consumption. As prevention and education models have incorporated a greater amount of research derived from the study of young people, their effectiveness has improved. However, the nature of these outcomes for young people is complex. Research has begun to illustrate these complexities through more detailed analysis. It offers important insight into the continued development of prevention and education programmes, with new perspectives on issues which occur regardless of the theoretical

Table 5.3:   Summary of short-term programme outcomes for different substances

Substance	Number of programmes	Positive outcomes*	No effect	Negative outcomes	Unclear
Alcohol	63	25	30	7	1
Tobacco	52	25	13	2	12
Cannabis	30	9	6	1	14

*Including partially effective outcomes, e.g. effects for one gender only.
Lister-Sharp et al., 1999.

orientation of the particular programmes deployed. Therefore, the rest of this chapter will review these issues more closely in order to answer critical questions about education and prevention work's effectiveness.

Large scale reviews

In light of these historical developments, recent programmes have undergone more stringent research analysis. White & Pitts' (1998) large scale review of programmes attempting to reduce specific drugs found that between 27 per cent and 56 per cent of programmes demonstrated a positive effect on drug use. Foxcroft et al.'s (2004) review of published studies identified that 35 per cent of alcohol programmes reported a positive short term effect; 36 per cent had a positive medium-term effect; and 38 per cent had an effect on long term use. This included school and non-school based interventions. Comparing the reductions in different types of substance *within* programmes that target all use can reveal important differences in outcome. Several reviews of published studies have compared 'in programme differences' in this way. Lister-Sharp et al. (1999) examined the effectiveness of generic school-based health interventions for alcohol, tobacco and drug outcomes separately. Their study included programmes that targeted one substance and programmes targeting all drugs. Nearly 40 per cent of programmes reported a positive effect on reducing alcohol use in the short-term, just under 50 per cent had a positive effect on tobacco, and approximately 33 per cent were positive for cannabis. Lister-Sharp et al. (1999) concluded that education programmes are slightly more effective at reducing tobacco use than alcohol or cannabis. However, alcohol programmes were more likely to be ineffective and harmful (see Table 5. 3).

Rundall & Bruvold's (1988) review examined the size of the effects prevention and education

on specific substances. They examined programmes that reported tobacco outcomes (47 studies), alcohol outcomes (29 studies) and programmes targeting both alcohol and tobacco (11 studies). They also included 7 alcohol only and 23 tobacco only programmes for comparison. They found that the initial short term impact of these programmes was very similar for tobacco and alcohol. However, the longer-term impact on smoking reduction was three times higher than the reductions in alcohol use (0.34 versus 0.12). This review also found that alcohol programmes were more likely to have no effect or a harmful effect in that they could increase drinking post-intervention.

Tobler's (1986) large-scale study of 143 school-based programmes also compared studies that addressed single substances versus studies of generic programmes that target all substances. This review also found that programmes appeared to be most effective in reducing tobacco, then 'all drugs', then alcohol and finally 'soft' drugs respectively. Some models were more effective than others. Refusal Skills and Life Skills programmes were most effective in reducing tobacco use. Other types of programme could reduce tobacco use to lesser extent and were ineffective at influencing alcohol, soft and all drug use. The overall conclusion from this review suggested that drug education programmes (including both single substance and generic programmes) appear to be more effective at influencing tobacco than other drug use. A later review by Tobler & Stratton (1997) of 120 school-based programmes found that more interactive programmes were more effective in addressing drug use (excluding cannabis) whilst non-interactive programmes tended to reduce tobacco use. So, the research suggests that prevention and education programmes are most effective at reducing tobacco use, have a smaller effect on drug use and can demonstrate contradictory finds for alcohol use.

Negative outcomes

It is important to note that some studies found that prevention and education programmes can increase use. These negative effects nearly always involve increased alcohol use triggered by attendance on drug specific education programmes. Currently there is no agreement on why this occurs. Different suggestions have been put forward but largely without any evidence to support the theories. Alcohol use may increase because, in contrast to the dangers of other drugs, it may appear to be a more safe and familiar option. The effectiveness of drug education might divert potential drug users into alcohol use instead. Alternatively, a positive group response to anti-drug messages within a programme could have a paradoxical effect. As we saw in Chapter 2, peer groups often define themselves in opposition to each other. A positive response in the majority to drug prevention could cause a 'salience response' in a minority where some young people take a contradictory stance as a form of augmenting an 'outsider' identity. This raises a similar issue in that young people from different sub-trajectories may respond very differently to the same message. For example, overemphasising the risks of use may make the concept of use more thrilling for externalised individuals.

At present there is also no agreement about why prevention and education messages are less successful at reducing alcohol use as well. This may be due to alcohol's unique role in Western society. As we saw in Chapter 1, the long tradition of alcohol use in the West has meant that this substance is deeply entwined into the fabric of social norms. Alcohol's symbolic meaning is synonymous with celebrations, commiserations and life transitions in a way that tobacco and more exotic drugs are not. Positive messages regarding alcohol use are more ambiguous, subconscious and socially accepted than any other substance. This wider social meaning may require a different kind of evaluation. Whereas the aims of tobacco and drug misuse programmes are clearly aimed at abstinence, the goals of prevention and education concerning alcohol use may be better achieved through promoting moderation.

Tobacco and timing

The fact that the majority of studies find that tobacco was the substance most likely to be reduced by prevention programmes also offers another key consideration. As we saw in Chapter 3, the Gateway Hypothesis suggests that early initiation into smoking tobacco tends to predict subsequent early involvement in alcohol and then cannabis use. Tobacco use is the touchstone of substance involvement. Tobacco use may be particularly amenable to change as it is the first substance young people use in the chain of consumption. As such, first initiation into its use represents a bigger psychological commitment than the movement from one substance to another. This suggests that the programmes designed to reduce smoking in young adolescents may have a powerful effect on interrupting their subsequent movement through the gateway sequence. As we have seen, this delay in onset could decrease a young person's subsequent using career and, even if they experience later problems, improve their treatment responsiveness should intervention be required.

Reducing tobacco use requires timing anti-smoking interventions prior to initiation. The value of timed interventions remains to be proven. Large-scale reviews of programmes have found contradictory results. Four reviews of prevention programmes (Tobler, 1986; Tobler et al., 2000; Wilson et al., 2001; Bangert-Drowns, 1988) did not find a strong relationship between age and programme outcome. In contrast, Gottfredson & Wilson (2003) found that programmes that targeted middle/junior high school pupils were slightly more effective than those that targeted younger or older students. Rooney & Murray (1996) found programmes targeting a younger age group (grade 6 or younger) were more effective. Bruvold (1993) found that better outcomes were always associated with targeting a higher grade level (nine or higher).

The reason that age ranges are not definitive may be because 'age specific' interventions make the assumption that all young people face the same risks at the same ages. However, the trajectory research reviewed in Chapter 3 suggests that early onset youth will confront risk factors at age 10 that their peers will confront later in adolescence. As such, programmes that target all young people at the same age may be delivered out of sequence for high risk externalised youth who have already initiated use by the time of the programme delivery. Meanwhile the same intervention programme may be premature for the later onset normative groups who will experience risk later. The aims of education and prevention programmes might also need to vary with age in order to have credibility with the target population. Prevention programmes based on abstinence may be more effective at younger age ranges whilst education-based harm reduction may be more effective for older youths.

Delaying the initiation into smoking can have multiple beneficial consequences. As early initiation of smoking is strongly association with rapid progression through the full spectrum of Gateway substances, theoretically, delaying the onset of tobacco use should also effect the progression through this Gateway sequence. This theory was tested by Scheier et al. (2001) who conducted a series of analyses on prevention's effect on future transitions in substance use. This study followed a sample of 2,030 young people who had been in a randomised Life Skills programme for three years. These studies were particularly interested in the impact of assertiveness training within the Life Skill's model. The key measurements taken at baseline are:

- Assertive behaviour (e.g. returning defective goods)
- Assertiveness efficacy (e.g. perceived assertive mastery)
- Drug refusal skills (e.g. frequency of rejecting drug offers)
- Drug refusal efficacy (e.g. perceived mastery in refusing drug offers).

Analysing the sequence of substance involvement in this population found strong evidence for a Gateway sequence. In this sample, early cigarette use predicted alcohol involvement and, later, marijuana use. Young people who initiated early alcohol use were much more likely to be involved in multiple substances by the end of the study. In comparison, reviewing the impact of increasing assertiveness in young people showed that it appeared to disrupt this sequence. Regardless of a young person's pattern of use at the entry point into the programme, increasing assertiveness reduced further involvement in consumption and broke the Gateway sequence. This reduction in risk appeared to reduce alcohol intake first, and then subsequent drug use. For every 10 per cent increase in assertiveness there was a correspondent 30–50 per cent reduction in drug use. Therefore, a modest increase in generic and specific assertiveness led to reductions in smoking, that transmitted through to reduction in alcohol use and which in turn reduced drug use.

Up-stream outcomes

Whilst research has suggested that some drug and alcohol prevention programmes can be effective in delaying or reducing use, it is difficult to measure the overall impact of even the most effective programmes, because the impact at the point of delivery is small, and the majority of long-term gains only begin 'up-stream' from the point of delivery. For example, many aspects of prevention programmes delivered to 13-year-olds may be attempting to address their consumption years in advance of risks or problems occurring, as young people are unlikely to get involved in the hardest range of drugs until they are considerably older. So there is a significant lag between the point of the delivery of a prevention programme and its desired effect several years into the future. Follow-up that extends to these lengths of time is rare in clinical studies, which leaves a significant gap in understanding the long term potential of prevention and education programmes and how they should be developed.

However, advances in computing mean that these up-stream outcomes of prevention can be mathematically modelled to give a clearer indication of the effect over longer periods of time. Two fascinating mathematical modelling studies were conducted by the RAND policy research centre in the US. Caulkins et al. (1999) achieved some success with an examination of the long term implications of cocaine prevention programmes. Their computer modelling procedure was then further developed to include the wide range of substances targeted by prevention and education programmes (Caulkins et al., 2002). The mathematical model was based on the most robust outcomes studies of effective education and prevention programmes. Programmes were chosen only if they had produced an optimal range of outcomes and met a strict set of criteria for quality of the research, such as:

- They had been published in peer-reviewed journals.
- They were universal programmes.
- They used pre- and post-test results.
- They were composed of treatment groups and control groups.
- They included adequate sample sizes.
- They utilised long-term follow-up (minimum 2–3 years).

These strict criteria yielded a limited number of studies for inclusion. Most were social influence models such as Project ALERT, Life Skills, the Alcohol Misuse Prevention Study (AMPS) and Project TNT (Toward No Tobacco use). They also included the Iowa Strengthen Families approach which was a composite of school-based resistance skills training combined with family involvement. Multisite programmes such as Project Northlands and the Midwest Prevention Programme (MPP) also met the selection criteria.

A difficulty in assessing the impact of prevention and education programmes is that the majority of young people would not use drugs or alcohol regardless of any prevention programmes that they attended. But comparing differences in initiation into substance use between young people attending a prevention programme and those who do not does offer insight into its effectiveness with at risk youth. Caulkins et al. (2002) used this approach in evaluating their selected studies to identify differences between young people involved in active intervention treatment programmes and control groups. They

calculated these differences by comparing percentage scores. For example, if 25 per cent of the control group went on to initiate alcohol use compared to only 20 per cent of the intervention group, this would be a 20 per cent reduction in initiation (expressed as −20 per cent) in those at risk. Conversely, if 10 per cent of the control group initiated use and 15 per cent of the intervention group did, this would be a 50 per cent increase in use (expressed as a +50 per cent). The outcomes of these comparisons are presented in Table 5.4. These figures reflect broader findings, for example those already reviewed in this chapter, in that: the greatest reductions occur in regard to tobacco use; and only one study produced an increase in use above that of the control group, and this involved alcohol use, possible reasons for which have been discussed.

From the overall data, Caulkins et al could derive an average reduction in use achieved in these gold standard studies. Estimating the impact of prevention and education on cocaine use was more difficult as this was not included in

Table 5.4:   Comparison of outcomes for tobacco, alcohol and marijuana use in model prevention programmes

	Project ALERT (%)	Lifeskills (%)	MPP (%)	Project Northland (%)	Project TNT (%)	Iowa (%)	Enhanced AMPS (%)
Marijuana							
Life time prevalence	−4.9	−	−	−	−	−	−
Annual prevalence	−	−	−	−14.0	−	−	−
Monthly use	−5.8	−	−	−	−	−	−
Monthly prevalence	−20.3	−7.1	−26.0	−	−	−	−
Weekly use	−18.0	−33.3	−22.8	−	−	−	−
Tobacco							
Life time prevalence	−4.3	−	−	−19.2	−21.5	−	−
Monthly use	−0.7	−	−	−	−	−	−
Monthly prevalence	−2.0	−19.7	−31.5	−	−	−	−
Weekly use	−7.9	−18.5	−30.3	−	−64.3	−	−
Daily use (packs of cigarettes a day)	−1.6	−20.8	−	−	−	−	−
Alcohol							
Lifetime prevalence	−4.1	−	−	−	−	−26	−
Annual prevalence	−	−	−	−	−	−	−3.3
Monthly use	−5.4	−	−	−	−	−	−
Monthly Prevalence	−2.1	−1.7	−30.8	−19.2	−	−	−
Weekly use	+2.2	−8.6	−42.0	−29.1	−	−	−
Heavy drinking	−	−16.3	−	−	−	−24.4	−4.5

Negative scores show reduction in use in the intervention group compared to the control group. Positive scores show increased use in the intervention group.
Caulkins et al., 2002; RAND Drug Policy Research Centre. Reprinted with permission.

these selected studies. Young people are more likely to initiate alcohol, tobacco and cannabis at an age which is either close to or during the delivery of the prevention or education programmes. Cocaine initiation tends to be deferred to much later in adolescence. To estimate cocaine reductions they reviewed the relationship between heavy early onset cannabis use and subsequent cocaine use in large scale US household surveys (see Caulkins et al., 1999). As the Gateway Theory suggested, they were able to predict levels of cocaine involvement based on these figures. Without hard data as to what degree prevention programmes had on lifetime use of cocaine, they modelled their cocaine reductions on the anticipated reductions in use of marijuana. Using three different mathematical procedures they estimated: a modest 2.9 per cent reduction in cocaine use; an average 7.6 per cent reduction; and an optimistic 13.6 per cent reduction.

Cost-effectiveness

Based on these averages, Caulkins et al. (2002) developed four different computer modelling programmes to chart the long term effects of prevention. This took into account the delayed effects of prevention, the length of young people's using careers across the life course, prevalence, individual consumption patterns, the social and

health cost generated by different substance's use as well as the cost of delivering 'model' prevention. Taking all of these factors into account, they were able to establish the cost-effectiveness of prevention programmes across the life course of young people. Their best estimate was that for every $150 spent on 'model' prevention programmes, there were social savings of $840. This only includes alcohol, tobacco, marijuana and cocaine in the calculations. If we take the prevention programmes' effect on other drugs (heroin, amphetamines and other controlled drugs) as being similar to that of cocaine, then this figure rises to $1,000 saving per each participant on educational and prevention programmes.

The most significant gains were derived from reductions in tobacco and alcohol use due to the high health care cost that these substances incur. As a result, the authors also stated that prevention and education programmes should primarily be understood as a health issue rather than a criminal justice issue. They also stressed that the effectiveness of education and prevention was not sufficient to warrant reallocation of funding away from supply reduction or treatment options. However, they had earlier demonstrated that their highest estimate of the long term effects of prevention is comparable to the impact of policing, criminal justice interventions and treatment (See Graph 5.1).

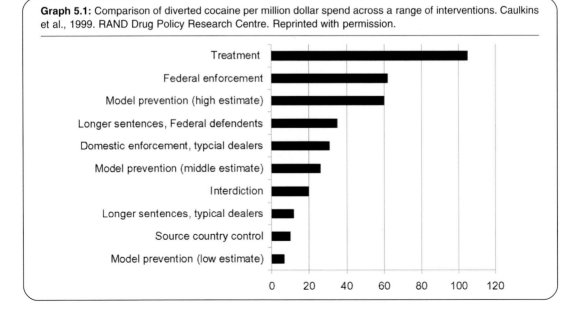

Graph 5.1: Comparison of diverted cocaine per million dollar spend across a range of interventions. Caulkins et al., 1999. RAND Drug Policy Research Centre. Reprinted with permission.

This research demonstrates the value of drug prevention and education as a worthwhile activity with significant social benefits. Whilst these programmes achieve modest gains at the time of delivery they lead to large outcomes across the life course. As we saw in Chapter 3, later initiation into drug and alcohol use is strongly associated with shorter using careers and diminished probability of developing chronic problems. Hser et al. (2007a) found only a six month difference in the age of initiation between opiate users who continued to use the drug across the life course and those who remitted in their twenties. Therefore even a small delay of 5 per cent in the age of initiation creates disproportionately large, positive outcomes over time as consumption becomes truncated.

Core elements of effective programmes

Education and prevention programmes have begun to demonstrate their worth in reduced usage across the life course. Within this, greater attention has also been given to understanding what specific elements are effective in its delivery. It has centred on the common factors that appear to be intrinsic to the effectiveness of any drug and alcohol education programme regardless of its orientation. They suggest that the style of delivery, types of deliverer, intensity and teaching style may all contribute to the outcomes of the programme.

Interactivity

A critical issue highlighted by research is the level of interactivity of the programme. First introduced to research studies by Tobler & Stratton (1997), this idea was further enhanced in subsequent studies (Tobler et al., 1999; Tobler et al., 2000). Tobler's definition recognised that 'how' a programme is delivered was a vital element that had been ignored. Interactive programmes encourage active participation by all students through discussion, word storming or skills practice. The interactive element occurs not simply between young people and the group leader but also amongst the young people themselves. Interactive components can be included in didactic prevention programmes, such as discussions, but these tend to be teacher-to-pupil rather than between peers.

Peer-led programmes significantly increase pupil-to-pupil interactions giving young people an even higher level of active participation. Tobler et al. (1997; 1999; 2000) consistently found that highly interactive programmes had greater effect in areas such as increasing knowledge, challenging attitudes and shaping behaviour. This was the case in universal school programmes as well as in family-focussed interventions (Kumpf & Alvarado, 2003). Non-interactive programmes are based on 'talk and chalk' presentations by teachers. They demonstrate far weaker effects, and any benefits are restricted to increasing knowledge only (Cuijpers, 2002a).

Interactivity is vital in education and prevention for two key reasons. First, people tend to learn more effectively when they are actively involved in their learning process. Second, interactivity is deeply linked to the social learning models that underpin recent developments in drug education, specifically those which focus on understanding, challenging and resisting peer influences. By its nature, this social learning approach lends itself to becoming part of peers' interaction in the educational process itself. For example, young people can learn to use negotiation skills when practising refusing offers and desisting from use whilst still maintaining their relationships with their using peers. Finally, through this learning through peer interactions, young people may also gain an understanding about the actual level of use amongst their peers which is more accurate than what they assume they use. This introduces a normative education element that is also integral to producing reduction in consumption.

The importance of interactivity is also supported by those programmes that do not produce good outcomes. In the US, the DARE programme is delivered by uniformed police and promotes resistance skills, but it also embraces wider concerns that have meant most research studies classify it separately from a social influences approach (Coggans et al., 2003; Tobler & Stratton, 1997; Tobler et al., 2000). It has been found to be ineffective, which appears to be related to its highly didactic format delivered by uniformed police officers (Ennett et al., 1994). It is important to stress that a programme's effectiveness is not solely governed by interactivity, but it does appear significant. For example, Tobler et al. (1999) examined 'placebo' interactive programmes. They were delivered using interactive methods but without any essential content. These interactive placebo programmes operated as well as non-interactive programmes such as DARE.

Who delivers

Besides interactivity, 'who' delivers the programme is also critical. Whilst it has in the past been difficult to establish robust research on the impact of peer-led programmes due to methodological challenges, more recent studies have found evidence in support of this approach. Cuijpers (2002b) found that peer-led programmes were more effective than adult-led programmes, but that the effects did not endure at 1- or 2-year follow-up. Similarly, Gottfredson & Wilson (2003) found that the benefits of peer-led interventions disappeared when sessions were co-led with a teacher. There has also been a suggestion that peer involvement tends to enhance programmes' effectiveness rather than create effective outcomes. In larger programmes, health professionals appear to be more effective delivery agents than peers, and peers appear to be more effective than teachers.

Gottfredson & Wilson (2003) also recognised that most prevention and education programmes were delivered by a range of individuals rather than through one person. Again, the limited available research suggests a contradictory pattern of findings. Whilst two large scale reviews suggest that peer delivery improves the effectiveness of programmes (Bangert-Drowns, 1988; Cuijpers, 2002b), others suggest that peer-led components only improve the effectiveness of alcohol and tobacco programmes, but not of drugs programmes (Lister-Sharp et al., 1999). Rooney & Murray (1996) found trained teachers and untrained peers are associated with greater effectiveness, and two studies suggested health professionals are the most effective facilitators for some programmes (Tobler & Stratton, 1997; Tobler et al., 2000).

These differences may be due to the level of interactivity that occurs in the programmes. Peer-led programmes have higher levels of interactivity in terms of peer-to-peer discussion, as opposed to peer-to-tutor, because they tend to be based on social influence models. As Tobler & Stratton (1997: 118) suggested 'without extra leaders to form small groups, the adolescents can only interact a few times and the essential part of the interactive programme is missing – that is,

active involvement, exchange and validation of ideas with their peers'. Peer-led programmes tend to offer greater interactivity by their nature compared to tutor-and teacher-delivered models. This gives young people a higher ratio of peer contact in these debates, which may be more powerful than tutor contact time.

Very little research has been conducted on whether in-house school training is better than delivery by invited external speakers. The range of external contributors can encompass anything from health professionals, people in recovery, grieving parents, religious agencies, drug and alcohol treatment providers and community drama groups, amongst others. White et al. (2004) reviewed studies examining the impact of 'external contributors' in schools' drug education programmes, but found the quality of research was too poor to draw any significant conclusions. They did examine what external contributors could contribute to school-based prevention, what external visitors actually delivered and whether external visitors are more effective at delivering certain elements of the programme. Based on the evidence available they concluded that peers, health professionals, guest experts and mentors could have a small benefit, but only as part of an intensive and highly structured package. They found little evidence to support the direct involvement of the police, except in a supplementary role to provide information on the law and on how legal consequences of arrest might affect young people's future lives.

But, external contributors may inspire a wide range of responses from young people. For example, Hammond et al. (2008) compared the satisfaction levels amongst young people who entered a DARE programme delivered by uniformed police in comparison to levels in response to other providers. They found that young people rated the police more highly than other professionals who were involved in the programme. However, young people with a history of delinquency rated the police contribution the lowest. This suggests that there may be a wide range of preferences amongst young people regarding who delivers a programme. Within this, peer-led programmes are the ones least likely to be rejected by the majority of young people.

Another important key issue resides in the fidelity of the programme delivery. This refers to how closely the programme is delivered to what is intended by the original authors. Evaluations of individual programmes (McBride et al., 2002; Phelps et al., 1994) found that training teachers and other facilitators in delivering drug education programmes increased their knowledge, confidence and skills. The closer their training mirrored the programme to be delivered, the less variability there was between individual teachers in how they interpreted written instructions (McBride et al., 2002). Coggans et al.'s (2003) review of Life Skills Training found that the quality of implementation was intrinsic to good outcomes for delivery by both teachers and peers alike. High fidelity may result from the deliverers being involved in a research study, as those delivering the programme are observed and monitored closely in such a context. In everyday settings though, the delivery of the drug and alcohol prevention may drift from the intended approach. Dusenbury et al. (2003) studied the fidelity with which teachers taught education programmes in daily practice compared to the material as stated in the guidance manuals. They showed that, whilst teachers presented the core messages of the programme very clearly, they tended to drift towards a didactic/knowledge-based approach, regardless of the stated programme content.

Intensity and credibility of delivery

Besides who delivers the programme, several reviews have examined the relationship between the intensity of the programmes and outcomes. In comparison to the amount of exposure that young people have to positive representations of drugs and alcohol from peers and from the media, exposure to prevention programmes is often minuscule. Again, it is hard to be definitive about the optimal length of a programme and its outcomes. This is because the most successful approaches like social influence programmes tend to be 10 or more sessions long. However, not all intensive programmes are effective. In comparison, 'rational' or 'affective' programmes remain ineffective regardless of the time invested in them, which suggests that the type of programme is more critical than the duration of the programme. Likewise, it is difficult to establish the value of 'booster sessions' that augment programme gains. These follow-up sessions can be delivered months or even years after the original programme. Whilst the most

effective programmes tend to have booster sessions in their overall design (Skara & Sussman, 2003), some research has not found them to be all that important in overall effect (Coggans et al., 2003). However, as Cujipers (2002a) observed, evaluating the initial programme outcomes and the outcomes of booster sessions separately has been under-researched, which compromises this general finding.

A more subjective quality to prevention and education programmes is their credibility. Credibility must exist within the programme design as well as in those delivering the programme, if young people are to engage in the learning process fully (Stead et al., 2001; MacKintosh et al., 2001; O'Connor et al., 1998; Anguelov et al., 1999). However, what might be credible for one social group is not for another. This requires that programmes are adaptable and can account for minority groups. In general, programmes are more credible when they relate to the reality of young people's lives rather than to adult assumptions about young people's lives. This may also account for emerging evidence which suggests that selected or indicated programmes are more effective than universal programmes for specific sub-groups (Gottfredson & Wilson, 2003). Selected or indicated programmes may offer a more precise focus on the risk factors of these specific groups. Universal programmes may be effective for normative youth, but externalised and internalised youth carry additional levels of complexity in their lives that a generic programme is unlikely to capture. Early intervention with programmes tailored to their needs is vital to address early risks before their life pattern becomes established and entrenched.

The need for credibility extends to minority cultural groups whose lives, cultural mores and wider life expectancies may differ significantly from the assumptions implicit in the majority culture. Culturally bespoke programmes have shown to be effective in reducing use in various ethnic groups (Hawkins et al., 2004). An example of culturally specific approaches to prevention and education was the Journey of the Circle project developed for the Pacific Coastal Canadian and Alaskan indigenous populations. In light of limited success in reducing high levels of alcohol use in these Native American populations, Marlatt et al. (quoted in Stewart et al., 2005) developed a prevention approach based on native traditions and customs. The central idea was not to simply revive these indigenous traditions but to find new contemporary meaning in them to make them relevant to urban youth.

The Journey of the Circle curriculum consisted of an 8-session Life Skills training programme that drew on the metaphor of a symbolic canoe journey taken each summer by Native American youths in the Pacific region. This embedded Life Skills into a symbolic representation of the journey of life, which is combined with the Medicine Wheel. This symbol has a resonance across many Native American tribes, but who can interpret it in different ways. Some tribes refer to it as the 'four directions' whilst others consider it akin to the 'circle of life'. In this study it was used as a reference point for self-reflection on balance, harmony and wholeness in life. Stories from Elders were also combined in the programme. 122 Native American youth attended the course and showed significant reductions in alcohol use, harmful consequences of drinking and all drug use except for tobacco.

There has been increasing interest in ethnic-specific interventions. They have achieved mixed results in terms of preventing drug and alcohol use. Some of the risk factors that may influence consumption in minority groups lie in the prejudices of the majority culture, expressed through racism or other forms of discrimination. Any form of discrimination precludes people from entering the pro-social structures of everyday life. Therefore drug and alcohol prevention work with minority cultures would need to address the barriers to social inclusion within the majority culture in order to be effective. However, most studies have focussed on the minority group's ability to preserve their own traditions and assimilate rather than the majority culture's ability to accommodate difference. For an extensive review of studies and critical challenges in the development of culturally specific approaches see Botvin et al. (1995b).

Summary

Prevention and education work with young people has undergone significant revision since its original inception. These revisions have seen prevention and education adopt a wide variety of guises, moving on from the initial moral, rational, self-esteem and values-based orientations. Whilst these programmes were well intended, they operated on adult assumptions regarding young people's drug and alcohol use. The lack of credibility of their approaches tainted the reputation of prevention and education work, and did much to undermine confidence in its value. Reducing the harm associated with use became a pragmatic if somewhat resigned response to these findings. However, renewed research interest was able to integrate research and theory into the development of social influence models. Social influence models not only began to identify critical risk factors for young people, but also began to address them through clear strategies that were subjected to rigorous evaluation and refinement. The consistent success of social influence models has seen a broadening of prevention and education work beyond the classroom. Recognising that risk factors reside in the wider context of a young person's life has seen prevention work annex the family, mass media and even entire communities into addressing drug and alcohol use. Further refinements have begun to recognise that the young people most vulnerable to problematic use share a number of divergent risk profiles. Progress has been made in the early identification of, and intervention with, young people with more complex needs. Intercepting the development and entrenchment of behavioural problems and significant mental illness may reduce the potential for additional complications later in their life course.

Not only has research strengthened the best prevention efforts, it has also begun to understand how outcomes are derived in these programmes. At the point of delivery, prevention and education work's gains appear small. However, these limited gains have increasing impact over the life course. This is because effective prevention and education can impede the snowball effect of risk factors. This can reduce heavy consumption, restrict progression into wider use of substances and significantly shorten the overall trajectory of use. Whilst gains are small at the point of delivery, they increase over time. The fact that these outcomes reside 'up-stream' from the point of their delivery has left many doubting the value of prevention and education work, even though they have shown significant results. Despite these findings, education and prevention as delivered in everyday practice remain dogged by their own historical assumptions regarding adult concerns about use. Dissemination of effective practice requires both a clearer theoretical understanding the clinical research, as has been summarised here, and the exorcism of these adult assumptions regarding young people's actual use. Otherwise, the central obstacle in improving these programmes will remain one of overcoming adults' preconceptions, and not the young people's.

CHAPTER 6

Does Treatment Work for Young People?

Introduction

'In four days the habit will be checked, in a week the desire to drink will be gone, in nine days it will be impossible to take alcohol into the system, and the manacles which bound the man for ten, twenty, or thirty years will be shattered and broken forever.' So claimed the advertisement for Dr Leslie E. Keeley's new wonder drug that was guaranteed to cure addictions of any kind including alcohol, opiates, cocaine and even tobacco. The Keeley Cure boasted a success rate of 95 per cent and even higher for morphine addiction. This miracle cure was based on the new wonder drug, the Double Chloride of Gold, that had amazing curative properties. 'It is the only antidote known to the world for the opium habit . . . By the magic of the Gold Remedy the opium habit is cast out easily and permanently.' The drug was developed by Dr Leslie Keeley, a physician who had become interested in alcoholism during his time serving in the American Civil War. But it was not until after the war when he settled in the small town of Dwight, Illinois, that he began to perfect his wonder drug, practicing on the local town 'bums'. In 1879 he opened the new Keeley Institute in partnership with a temperance minister, Frederick B. Hargreaves, and the Keeley Cure was born.

Thousands of people suffering from addictions, including physicians, politicians and celebrities, would flock to the Keeley Institute for the wondrous medication whose formulation was a fiercely guarded secret – except for the widely publicised element of gold. Patients received four injections a day drawn from red, white and blue liquids. This was accompanied by a tonic medication that was taken orally every two hours. Dr Keeley had first insisted that addictions were a genetic illness but changed his mind suggesting it was a disease caused by exposure to the toxins such as alcohol and other patent medications during childhood. The Double Chloride of Gold healed poisoned cells and returned them to their normal condition. Extensive advertising, promotions and publicity gimmicks turned the Keeley Cure into the brand leader in a highly competitive market place of cure-alls and snake oil. By 1893 it had become an international franchise with over 118 Keeley Institutes in the US, Great Britain, Finland, Denmark and Sweden, each paying a $50,000 buy-in fee, and all purchasing their medication through the founding centre in Dwight. By 1900, the Keeley Institute had turned over gross earnings of $2.7 million dollars.

Things began to unravel for Keeley towards the end of the century. Rival companies began attacking the cure by stating it was not a recognised medicine and could contain harmful contaminants. In 1891, four highly respected physicians claimed the cure was a fraud. A graduate of the Keeley Cure, J.F. Mines, publicly defended the cure but he subsequently relapsed and died in a media glare. Finally, an estranged early business partner, Frederick B. Hargreaves, testified at a court hearing launched by the Keeley Institute to stop a breakaway centre from continuing to ply the medication without a licence in 1907. In court, Hargreaves confessed that in the development of the cure, the only patient who received a dose of gold nearly died from it. Together, he and Keeley had spiked samples with gold in independent tests in order to confirm its presence but had used other secret ingredients in their daily treatment. The routine of daily injections that patients were given were placebos designed to keep them at the Keeley Institute for three to four weeks and the oral tonic was the only active medication that would suppress the desire for alcohol. Dr Lesley E. Keeley never faced public outcry though, as he had passed away with a heart attack in 1900.

There remains one unresolved issue in this fascinating episode in the history of addiction treatment. Despite the Double Chloride of Gold being a complete sham, the Keeley Cure worked for thousands of people who tried it. Such was the enthusiasm of ex-patients for Keeley that they set up their own Keeley League that supported 370 chapters across the US boasting 30,000 members. Even the critics of Keeley's research supported the efficacy of his treatment. The *Christian Advocate* journal polled 534 Keeley graduates and found that 51 per cent had remained alcohol free post treatment. Whilst this does not quite match the claims of Keeley, it is still an impressive success rate even by today's standards. So, how could a quack medicine prove so effective?

What Keeley had managed to do in the small town of Dwight was create a fraternity of recovery. There were no bars or chains in his centre, unlike in many rival sanatoriums. People were free to roam as they pleased in the company of others in recovery. He employed many former patients, including physicians, to work in his centres. Patients received lectures every morning, one-to-one support from former patients who would act as attendants in their early recovery, daily physical exercise and healthy food. Keeley pioneered alcohol and milk detoxification procedures and gradual reduction regimes for morphine. He standardised clinical practices by training all medical staff in every Institute and monitored their requests for the Double Chloride medication against the numbers of patients in their Institutes to ensure consistency of practice. Keeley's focus on medication bought into the belief systems of his patients. It may have been a gimmick but it was a powerful psychological device that sustained people through the early and difficult process of a carefully managed detoxification process. His oral tonic was an emetic, making those who drank alcohol violently ill, suggesting he had also discovered an early type of aversion therapy.

These were not the only changes he had inspired. Keeley educated patients to the notion of recovery. He reinforced changes that people made through recognition of their achievement and by use of positive role models within the treatment facilities itself. He emphasised relationship factors between the physicians, staff and patients through a sense of shared endeavour. And he enabled patients to create and enter into new social environments that supported the changes that they were making. The patients themselves were encouraged to help each other. New patients were greeted at the Dwight railway station by recovering patients who welcomed them warmly. These welcoming committees could be 2,000 strong, and appeared to reinforce their own recovery in contrast to those who stumbled dishevelled from the carriages. Ex-patients were encouraged to write weekly letters to new patients to detail their progress, again reinforcing the fraternity and optimism for change. The Keeley Institutes were warm, dignified and respectful. They opened their doors to men and women regardless of their age, ethnicity or religious beliefs. Furthermore, the whole town of Dwight welcomed this treatment population with open arms. It made the town wealthy, but its sympathetic townspeople were highly supportive of individuals who had been rejected and stigmatised in their own communities. Many former patients settled in Dwight, creating a unique district of recovery. Such was the scale and durability of the organisation he developed that the Keeley Cure, without injections of the Double Chloride of Gold, was still in operation until 1966.

Whilst Keeley had failed to create a magic bullet, many of the psychological and social interventions he developed remain critical in treatment outcomes today. The relationships and social environments that supported recovery then remain critical in treatment outcomes for adults now.

This chapter will seek to establish whether these and other treatment outcomes are possible for young people who experience substance misuse problems. The current research base, which will be reviewed in detail, offers an insight into the nature of young people's recovery that is particularly important for the orientation of their treatment services. However, the concept of measuring outcomes is difficult with young people, as there has been a tendency to use adult measures to define the nature of success. As young people's substance use problems differ radically from those of adults, a different approach to measuring treatment success is needed as well. So, various approaches to measuring outcomes will be examined and, based on state of the art research into what really drives treatment outcomes, this chapter will explain how treatment outcomes for adolescents can be both measured and optimised.

Careful review of the evidence is important, as young people's treatment responses are not uniform and follow divergent pathways. Treatment modalities that account for these differences are required. This chapter will review a range of modalities that are underpinned by a strong evidence base and are relevant to the different sub-trajectories of young people's use. To do this it will need to cover two areas. First, it will explore modalities that have been developed to address substance misuse directly. This will be followed by a review of wider treatment models that have been developed in order to address many of the incumbent problems associated with young people's use, including externalised and internalised behaviours.

Particular attention will be given to family involvement in the treatment processes, which is important as working with families offers the opportunity to influence a young person's immediate social environment beyond the treatment programme itself. Family can be involved in four different ways, namely its role in precipitating treatment entry, involvement in care planning, family therapy and becoming an active agent in treatment itself.

Finally, this chapter will review the importance of aftercare for young people. As young people are the least likely population to complete the optimal period of treatment, it will describe pioneering approaches to achieving the long term retention that is necessary to consolidate long term treatment outcomes.

Treatment outcomes with young people

Research on the effectiveness of specific treatment modalities for young people has been extremely limited. For example, whilst Miller et al. (1995) were able to call upon over 1,000 randomised control studies on adult alcohol treatment, Williams & Chang (2000) could only review 53 studies on young people. There has been a significant increase in clinical trials for young people conducted in the last few years. However, for the most part, the current range of interventions for young people are still modified from adult interventions to varying degrees, and the expanding research has generally not yet led to the establishment of specific youth interventions that are distinct from adult models. Whilst there has been some progress in integrating developmentally informed approaches into treatment modalities the availability of these programmes remains limited.

In particular, a weakness remains in our understanding of the relationship between adolescent development and treatment outcomes. For example, only a few studies include the age of young people in their analysis of treatment outcomes. They have not found any strong associations between age, treatment approach and outcome (Kelly et al., 2000), perhaps because these studies often use 'calendar age' which is a poor measure of a young people's emotional

maturity. As we have seen, most young people in treatment will have experienced some degree of developmental delay. Markers of life task achievement such as educational grade average have been found to show stronger links with treatment outcomes, but this is under researched (Brown et al., 2005b). Also, the vast majority of treatment programmes have focussed on older teens (15+), so there is a paucity of research on the outcomes for younger teens and pre-teens. This compromises the research base for early interventions. What robust research there is on the nature of substance misuse trajectories has largely been wholly ignored in treatment outcome research, with a few notable exceptions.

The establishment of a comprehensive research base is vital as young people present unique challenges to treatment services. They are experiencing accelerated transition from being embedded in family towards autonomous adulthood. The safety of parental influence falls into dramatic decline, whilst peer influences peak, giving rise to increased risk taking behaviours and experimentation on many levels besides drug and alcohol use (Spear, 2002). During this period they also demonstrate far higher levels of emotionality and life stresses than at any other point in the life course (Jorm, 1987) leading to increases in drug and alcohol consumption to alleviate life stress (Colder & Chassin, 1993). These pressures are not evenly spread throughout all populations of young people. Whilst young people are exposed to a multiplicity of risk factors, the risks cluster together and entrench into clearly demarcated trajectories of use that can deflect young people from their anticipated life course at key developmental stages. This excludes them from the pro-social structures where life tasks are rehearsed and accomplished, leading to rapid delay in their development. This has a profound impact on their treatment responsiveness. Long term exclusion does not simply impede the resources the young person has in managing the life course but also limits the resources they bring into the treatment. Not only can such exclusion result in their experiencing a breakdown in social functioning, but repeated exposure to substances can also lead to physical dependence too.

Large scale studies of effectiveness

Early studies into the effectiveness of treatment for young people reported less favourable outcomes than for adults. For example, the *Treatment Outcome Prospective Study* (TOPS) (Hubbard et al., 1985) demonstrated large reductions in drug use and criminality post-treatment. However 25 to 30 per cent of young people still reported daily use of cannabis and alcohol use. The *Services Research Outcomes Study* (SAMHSA, 1998) compared adolescent behaviours between the five years pre and post treatment, and found that alcohol use increased by 13 per cent and crack cocaine use doubled across this period.

The first dedicated large scale research study into young people's outcomes was the *Drug Abuse Treatment Outcome Study for Adolescents* (DATOS-A) (Hser et al., 2001). Conducted in Pittsburgh, Minneapolis, Chicago and Portland, it examined treatment outcomes of 1,167 young people in 23 community treatment settings, including 8 residential programmes. In this sample, 58.4 per cent of young people were involved in the criminal justice system whilst 63 per cent met the criteria for a concurrent mental health problem. The most common diagnoses were externalised disorders (57.3 per cent), such as conduct disorder, and there was a smaller internalised disorder group (15 per cent) with the most common disorder being depression. This multi-site research found that the principal outcomes of treatment were significant reductions in use across all treatment settings. They found that weekly cannabis use almost halved whilst crime and binge drinking was reduced by a third. But treatment had less impact on other illicit drug use, whilst cocaine use actually increased after treatment. This may have been a product of the Gateway Effect: as young people aged into early adulthood, they had greater disposable income and greater access to adult drug-using networks, so cocaine became more economically and socially available (see Table 6.1).

Besides reductions in use, DATOS-A also found positive lifestyle gains for young pole.

These young people reported greater school attendance, and they experienced improved grade averages and greater psychological adjustment, even though their drug and alcohol consumption was not eliminated entirely. DATOS-A also identified differences in treatment response by type of agency. The outcomes for outpatient drug programmes based on abstinence reported the worse outcomes. Where young people experienced no change in their use of stimulants or hallucinogens, and significantly increased their use of other illicit drugs besides cannabis. Although their criminal activity decreased post treatment, there was a slight increase in the number of arrests they experienced post-treatment. Abstinence orientated services also appeared unappealing to young people in this study as demonstrated by a poorer treatment retention rate. This was an important finding as the study also found that retention in treatment was the biggest factor in promoting treatment outcomes, regardless of the severity of the presenting problem or type of treatment. However, there was wide variance in how long young people were retained in treatment across all treatment services.

Factors linked to treatment outcomes

Abstinence as a goal in the treatment of young people presents a paradox. Other studies have shown that abstinence is significantly associated with better treatment outcomes. Abrantes et al. (2002) identified that young people who abstained from all drug and alcohol use demonstrated the highest rates of improvement in social functioning. Brown et al. (2001) also found that those who sustain abstinence for four years show the highest educational achievement and occupational status compared to their peers. But youth with intermittently heavy or chronic drinking continued to show the worst outcomes across a wide range of social domains. This

Table 6.1: Outcomes reported in DATOS-A

Substance and frequency	Pre-treatment score	Post-treatment score
Weekly cannabis use	80.4 per cent	43.8 per cent
Heavy drinking episodes	33.8 per cent	20.3 per cent
Cocaine use	16.5 per cent	19.2 per cent
Other illicit drug use	48.0 per cent	42.2 per cent
Criminal involvement	75.6 per cent	52.8 per cent

Hser et al., 2001.

suggests that whilst young people are more likely to accrue significant benefits from non-use, many find the idea of abstinence so unappealing that they do not complete the treatment course.

These more recent studies nevertheless demonstrate that treatment can be effective for young people. The major treatment gain appears to be reduction in consumption for the majority of young people, with only a minority achieving abstinence. Typically, these studies identified that at least 1 in 5 young people experienced no benefit from their treatment and that problematic use continued post-treatment. Reviewing the factors that influence the treatment course demonstrates some considerable variation (see Table 6.2). Several studies have identified that pre-treatment severity of use has an impact on treatment outcomes, but not all research supports this. Young people's pre-treatment motivation for change has been identified as an important predictor of treatment outcome.

A number of post-treatment factors have also been found to be important in sustaining long term change. Besides treatment drop out, a young person's environment appears to exert a major influence on long term gains. Young people who return to environments characterised by high consumption are unlikely to sustain treatment gains. For example, exposure to high levels of use in their family (parent or sibling) or amongst their peer group has been identified as a particularly powerful trigger to relapse in young people (Vik et al., 1992; Tomlinson et al., 2004). So research suggests that whilst pre-treatment risk factors predict problem severity, they do not necessarily predict recovery. As Latimer et al. (2000b) suggested, treatment outcomes may be influenced not just by the elimination of risk but also by increases in protection factors such as aftercare, pro-social groups and positive family supports.

In terms of post-treatment gains, most studies identified that treatment completion and aftercare support were the single biggest factors in producing optimum outcomes. Subsequent re-integration into pro-social networks was also vital. For example, entry into non-using peer groups and improved attendance in school has been found to be important in several studies. All of this is important in understanding the concept of recovery. Whilst there is much disagreement in the field regarding the nature of recovery, the clinical research on recovery is unequivocal. Recovery is the obverse of the nature of substance misuse problems (see Harris, 2007). As reviewed

in Chapter 4, drug and alcohol problems are characterised by breakdown in social functioning resulting in social exclusion and physical dependency. Every research study conducted on people who successfully recover from substance abuse problems is unanimous in identifying that recovery is the re-integration back into the social structures that define the life course and the abolition or control of dependence. Not only does the study of recovery support the same finding, it is true for all treatment pathways, regardless of whether recovery is attained with professional support (DeLeon, 1996; Moos, 2008) or through individuals' own efforts (Klingemann, 1992; Stall & Biernaki, 1986).

For example, studies have demonstrated that many young people naturally remit from problem drug and alcohol use without professional treatment. Brown et al., 1999 (see Wagner et al., 1999) interviewed young people who had experienced drug or alcohol problems but who had sustained at least one year of clean time without professional treatment. Examining which strategies were most helpful, these young people rated 'will power' as most important. This was followed by activities such as recreation, hobbies or voluntary work. School/work, friends and family received a middle range of endorsement. Attendance at 12 Step groups received the lowest approval with 82 per cent of young people giving it the lowest possible score. Interestingly, there was a pattern in the combination of strategies that young people adopted. Some young people reported a combination of 'family/friends/support groups' were of the greatest assistance. Whilst another group found that 'self-help/activities/school' were deeply connected. This suggests that, in order to achieve change, some young people invest in informal support networks whilst others invest in formal activities. Whilst these strategies differed, what is interesting is that both entailed the reintegration into pro-social networks, even if one was in the realms of a private network and the other in public networks.

Resolution of life tasks reduces consumption rates. Gotham et al. (2003) found that young people with alcohol disorders who married showed significant reductions in use, which replicates wider research such as that of Labouvie (1996), who suggested a process of 'maturing out' of use. This involved increasing an accomplishment in pro-social life tasks that crowded out use over time. An example is the

Table 6.2:   Factors associated with treatment outcomes for young people

Study	Pre-treatment factors	Post-treatment factors with positive impact	Post-treatment factors with negative impact
Brown (1993). Brown et al (1990).	Severity of substance use prior to treatment did not influence outcome.	Aftercare attendance. Staying in school. Improvement in grades at school.	Exposure to alcohol and drug use in social environment. Non-attendance in aftercare groups.
Latimer et al. (2000a).	Pre-treatment parental substance use. Pre-treatment sibling substance use. Pre-treatment deviant attitudes. Pre-treatment deviant behaviours. Pre-treatment levels of impulsivity.	Aftercare attendance. Increase in one or more protective factors.	
Latimer et al. (2000b).	Sibling substance use. Peer substance use. Pre-treatment levels of use. Gender. Alcohol use. Cannabis use.	Aftercare involvement. Treatment length.	
Winters et al. (2000).		Treatment completion.	
Cady et al. (1996). Friedman et al. (1994).	Pre-treatment levels of motivation for change predicted treatment outcome.		
Hawke et al. (2000).	History of sexual abuse increased problem severity and treatment drop out.		
Catalano et al. (1990).	Pre-treatment severity of use, legal problems, psychiatric problems, severity of use and school problems predicted treatment drop-out.		

establishment of a stable partner relationship which becomes a precursor to socialising with others in stable partner relationships. Employment is a precursor to socialising with work colleagues. Parenthood becomes associated with socialising with other parents. The achievement of life tasks and the entry into pro-social networks accounts for a huge decline in consumption as young people begin to take on new responsibilities within the context of new social norms.

Different young people, different outcomes

However, positive outcomes are not evenly spread through treated populations. The same studies also identified specific factors associated with poor outcomes that occurred in sub-populations of young people. Pre-treatment traits such as impulsive and deviant behaviour predicted poor outcomes. Parental drug and alcohol abuse was also linked to these findings. Whilst for other young people sexual abuse and mental health disorders appeared to influence them. Although not always examined within this framework, these factors are remarkably similar to the sub-trajectories of consumption amongst young people set out earlier in this book. These sub-trajectories not only influence young people's using careers but also their responsiveness to treatment. For example, in an interesting second study of DATOS-A data, Grella et al. (2001) re-examined the results of treatment on young people who also had significant behavioural or mental health problems. These youth were more likely to have the most severe range of problems,

meet the criteria for dependence, be poly-users and have the earliest age of onset at the outset of treatment. Their lives were also characterised by multiple problems in a wide range of social domains such as family, school and crime. These multiple-problem youth showed the worst treatment outcomes. Sub-trajectories of development and use have a direct impact on treatment outcomes.

Reviewing treatment outcomes in longer term follow-up studies reveals that young people from different sub-trajectories respond very differently to treatment. Most long term studies have been conducted primarily on problematic alcohol-using youth, but these young people are also likely to be poly-users at the same time. Chung et al.'s (2003) review of outcomes at three year follow-up showed very significantly varying treatment response rates amongst young people (see Graph 6.1). Young people with the highest number of alcohol symptoms prior to treatment entry appeared to improve one year after treatment. However they experienced a bounce back into heavy consumption within 3 years. Individuals with lower ranges of alcohol-related symptoms at intake all improved, but at different rates. The exception was those with a low severity score on alcohol symptoms prior to treatment who experienced little change in consumption over the three year period. Their more moderate range of problems remained moderate. Chung et al. found that this variation in treatment outcomes was not related to age, gender or mental health diagnosis, although positive treatment responders were less likely to be poly-users.

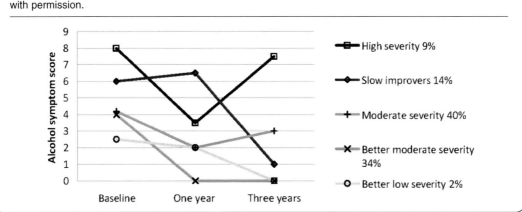

Graph 6.1: Treatment outcomes for young alcohol users at 3 year follow-up. Chung et al., 2003. Reprinted with permission.

Winters (see Chung et al., 2003) reported on five-year outcomes for a group of 179 young people who had been receiving 12 Step treatment with specific reference to the impact of internalising and externalising disorders on these outcomes. They were testing the hypothesis that early treatment interventions would predict better outcomes and that externalising youth were more likely to experience negative outcomes from treatment. They also included a control group of 66 non-treated problem-using young people for comparison. They identified that the recovery outcomes in young people were rarely characterised by abstinence, even though the young people were in a treatment modality that advocated it. Using measures of personality characteristics, they then separated their population into externalised youth (41 per cent of the sample), internalised youth (48 per cent of the sample) and other (11 per cent of the sample) and reviewed the treatment response rates.

'When outcome at five years was examined as a function of personality subtype, we found that externalisers reported significantly more abuse or dependence symptoms, greater alcohol use, greater marijuana and other drug use, and more negative consequences during the prior year.' (Chung et al., 2003: 257). This research also suggested that early treatment intervention improved outcomes for young people. In addition, aftercare appeared to be a much more important factor in the improvement of externalised youth than for any other sub-group. Those in treatment did produce a much better range of outcomes than the untreated group, in terms of higher rates of abstinence and lower lapse rates. This demonstrated the benefit of treatment over no-treatment for young people.

Abrantes et al. (2002) (c.f. Chung et al., 2003) reported on eight-year follow-up studies with particular reference to life functioning in 140 young people who had presented for treatment as problem drinkers. Their study included reference to the timing of important developmental markers such as leaving home, educational attainment, occupation status, etc. Again, they discovered a split in young people's treatment response. In this study 22 per cent achieved 'abstinence', 24 per cent became 'infrequent users,' 36 per cent 'got worse with time' post-treatment and 18 per cent became 'high frequent' users. In general, abstainers were more likely to be older, and to have been poly-users with a higher rate of withdrawal symptoms at intake. In comparison, the 'worse with time' group were more likely to hail from high-consuming families. They also experienced a 'bounce effect' in that they appeared to make similar treatment gains to those that the other treatment responsive sub-groups did at the 6-month point before experiencing dramatic escalation in use. Frequent users who experienced little gain from treatment and continued their high consumption tended to have more severe symptoms of alcohol dependence prior to treatment entry (see Graph 6.2).

In terms of life transitions, 67 per cent of the treatment group left home and moved into independent living during the course of the treatment study. Responses to leaving home varied, with 'infrequent users' declining in frequency of drinking whilst the 'worse with time' and 'frequent users' increased their drinking rate. Likewise, on other social functioning measures, 'abstainers' reported higher rates of family cohesion and achieved

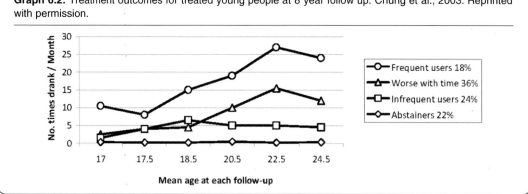

Graph 6.2: Treatment outcomes for treated young people at 8 year follow up. Chung et al., 2003. Reprinted with permission.

higher rates of educational attainment. 'Frequent drinkers' reported poor rates of interpersonal functioning and dramatically poorer relationships than the other groups, which is an important finding in that it suggests a strong link between young people's inability to form social attachments necessary to integrate into new social groups and continued high use. This study did not include psychological functioning or mental health diagnosis in its analysis.

Understanding how young people on different sub-trajectories respond to treatment is imperative for the advancement of effective interventions. Historically there has been a tendency to offer all young people the same treatment regardless of their pathway into drug and alcohol problems. But there are distinct differences in these sub-populations. Early onset externalised youth have poor impulse control, lack environmental supports and have long histories of poor academic achievement. Mid-onset internalised youth experience significant mental health problems that may relate to specific trauma in which the family may or may not be complicit. Late onset normative youth have few pre-existent personal or family problems and have higher levels of academic attainment. Planning treatment needs to respond to the fact that the age of onset of problematic use, and particularly the social complications that sever their pro-social attachments, will be indicative of young people's development delay. Those with long term exclusion will need more protracted support to catch up in life than those whose relationships are at threat of being broken. As the social functioning amongst normative youth is higher, these later onset youth have less severe symptoms and will experience the most benefit from treatment. The early onset externalised youth with high symptom severity will often show no treatment response or worsening of their condition. Without greater separation of these sub-groups in research and treatment, the positive responses of late onset normative users may mask the poorer treatment response rates of the early onset group. This can lead to a situation whereby apparently 'effective' services assist high functioning youth but leave unassisted the young people who are likely to experience the greatest personal and social harm. Not only does treatment need to support young people back into the integration of the pro-social networks of their life course, it must also recognise that the pathways to achieve this aim can vary across sub-populations of young people.

How can success be measured?

Young people on divergent consumption sub-trajectories may need very different treatment responses to account for their risk profiles. It is vital that different sub-trajectories' outcomes are monitored much more closely to establish whether there are optimal interventions for each group. As we have seen, taking an 'average' of treatment response in young people does not reveal the differences between these sub-groups. This is only revealed through tracking young people's outcomes within each sub-trajectory. However, addressing the issue of treatment effectiveness for young people is hampered by poor agreement on the best indicators of treatment success. Different research studies have used radically different measurements of treatment outcome and there is surprisingly little agreement in the field on the most important outcome measures. For example, Hays & Ellickson (1996) invited 10 experts on adolescent alcohol problems to rate 20 different measures of alcohol misuse that are based on frequency of consumption, high risk situations and negative consequences. Their scores were highly variable, especially with regard to those measures based on frequency of consumption, though most of the experts did agree that frequency of consumption should be graded by age, with higher consumption likely to be seen amongst older adolescents. A wide range of possible ways of measuring outcomes has been suggested, which are described in Table 6.3.

Treatment outcomes based on the diagnostic criteria, such as in *DSM (IV-TR)* would be the most effective measurement of treatment success. For example, if young people's problematic use is indicated by the presence of clear symptoms such as abnormal tolerance, role impairment, legal problems and withdrawal, outcome measures should detect changes to these key symptoms. They might include the elimination of high tolerance, role integration, absence of criminal involvement and the cessation of physical withdrawal. But the problem with *DSM (IV-TR)* is that its current classification of Abuse and Dependence are not well suited to young people (see Chapter 4) and so may not accurately assess either problematic use or its cessation.

Quantity, type and frequency of consumption are the most commonly used measures of treatment success but may provide misleading data about young people's response to treatment.

Table 6.3: Outcome measurements used in clinical studies

Outcome measure	Description
Frequency of consumption post-treatment	Classifying young people by the pattern of their consumption such as 'abstainers', 'relapsers', 'high users' etc.
DSM IV-TR post-treatment	Classifying young people according to whether they meet the DSM diagnostic criteria for abstinence, abuse or dependence.
Harm reduction post-treatment	Reporting on the range of reduction in frequency of hazardous use or reduced rates of consumption per drinking episode.
Specific high risk situations post-treatment	Reported reductions in specific high-risk behaviour such as the frequency of binge drinking.
Negative consequences post-treatment	Measurement of reported negative consequences of use such as quarrels at home, police involvement, etc.
Psychological indicators post-treatment	Reported reductions in indications of problem use such as cravings.
Reduction of health risk post-treatment	Reported reductions in behaviours such as unprotected sex, drink driving or concurrent drug use.

Based on Wagner, 2008.

Young people's desire for total abstinence from all substances varies enormously (Brown et al., 2000b). Adolescents appear more motivated to address the social consequences of their use than the substance use itself (Brown, 1999). Research suggests that young people are 10 times more likely to drop out of an abstinence-based alcohol programme than a controlled alcohol programme (Polich et al., 1981). Furthermore, research demonstrates that a significant proportion of youth continue to use drugs and alcohol *throughout the treatment course* itself. These 'continuing users' may differ from 'relapse users' in that their treatment goals were based on reductions in use and addressing wider social functioning rather than cessation (Chung & Maisto, 2006). In so doing, they might make significant improvement in social functioning, but it would not be captured by measuring their continued consumption.

Despite this reality, consumption rates are still heavily used as treatment outcomes in work with young people. The reason that measuring consumption rates is so pervasive as a treatment outcome is because it is so well established in measuring adult problem users' outcomes. Adults are much more likely to have advanced into heavy physical dependence characterised by physical withdrawal. Abstinence is often imperative for these adult treatment seekers because once they have achieved this high threshold of use, any return to drug and alcohol use can be catastrophic. For example, they may rapidly revert to pre-treatment use and re-experience the social breakdown associated with this level of consumption. Therefore consumption rates post-treatment can be a strong indicator of overall treatment outcome in adults. However, even in adult populations it is important to note that even those who go on to achieve successful recovery tend to have a 'jagged' pattern of consumption for at least two years before they attain stable abstinence (Vaillant, 1995).

In comparison, young people are unlikely to have arrived at physical dependence or any other imminent negative health consequences. Indeed, alcohol-consuming environments are likely to play an important part in young people's continuing development. They are where young people are likely to bond with peers and find future romantic partners. Because of this, many young people are reluctant to stop using substances altogether if there is no immediate necessity for them to do so. So, the measurement of consumption may again be reflective of what adults want for young people and not what young people wish to change. This means that young people who receive treatment could achieve important personal goals and stability, without it being reflected in the outcome measures that are used to assess their progress. So, if consumption rates are to be used, it may be more meaningful to compare reductions in use compared to normative levels of drug and alcohol use amongst non-problematic young people, rather than to abstinence.

The attainment of life tasks

An alternative measure may be the attainment of life tasks post-treatment. The breakdown in young people's social attachments and the failure to achieve important life task milestones are critical in substance misuse. Therefore, treatment must provide young people with the skills to achieve integration and maximise the opportunities it brings. For example, the twenties tends to be the decade of life of heaviest alcohol and drug consumption. Most people remit from heavy alcohol and drug use during this period when they gain access to employment, settle down with romantic partners, have children and nest-build. In this sequence, increased levels of social integration *precede* declines in consumption. So, just as risk factors chain together, it appears that protection factors do so as well during recovery. Research suggests that this reintegration occurs in a staged process. Improved school attendance will lead to greater educational achievement. Greater educational achievement opens up the possibility of quality employment, etc. Improvements in school performance occur in the first year post-treatment, whilst improvements in family relationships improve two years post treatment (Brown et al., 2001). As such, the attainment of key life tasks may offer a better indicator of treatment effectiveness than consumption rates. Research is yet to conclusively establish a concise framework for normative development. However, Brown (1993) identified a number of key life tasks strongly associated with reduction in alcohol use post-treatment (see Table 6.4).

Likewise, other proposed measures of effectiveness are difficult to normalise, such as reductions in negative consequences of use. Social consequences can vary according to culture, age, gender and social class. Normative patterns of use shift over time. Furthermore, establishing what causes the negative social consequences of problem use is equally difficult to establish in clinical studies. For example, a young person with externalised disorders may still act impulsively with negative consequences post treatment.

Table 6.4: Key social outcome indicators

Domain	Indicators
School	Attendance Academic performance Reduction in classroom disruption
Family	Cohesion Reduction in conflict
Social functioning	Reduction in interpersonal conflict Changes in peer social groups
Activities	Work Reduction in crime
Health	Physical Emotional

Based on Brown, 1993.

What really matters in treatment?

Rather than examining data from large-scale normative population studies, an easier way to benchmark outcomes is to measure the typical response rates of young people in treatment. This could identify the pattern of outcomes that is to be expected for young people. As young people display divergent patterns of response to treatment, these outcomes could be adjusted to track the outcomes of young people on different sub-trajectories of use. This average benchmark of treatment response would allow for more meaningful comparison with an individual client's score. A young person, a sub-trajectory or an entire agency's collective outcomes could then be compared to this benchmark in order to assess whether they are below, on track or above average in terms of achieving treatment outcomes. This approach would offer a means of ensuring that the services young people receive are helping them at an individual level, as well as offering accountability to agencies that are providing services funded by the taxpayer.

Randomised control trials and the evidence base

Working towards this goal requires a re-examination of what works in treatment and how best to achieve the optimal range of outcomes. Historically, low levels of accountability within the psychotherapy field sparked a debate regarding how best to assess the effectiveness of talking cures. These debates in the US and UK led to the formulation of an evidence-based practice agenda, which required that only those treatment modalities that had demonstrated their worth through systematic evaluation of their effectiveness should be used with clients. The evidence-based movement borrowed research practices that were established in medicine to test the effectiveness of different treatment modalities. The most important was the *randomised control trial*, where patients with similar health conditions are randomly assigned to different types of medication and their outcomes compared. The most effective medication is then promoted as evidence-based and disseminated within the field. Talking cures have adopted this approach where clients with a similar diagnosis are randomly assigned to gold standard treatments in clinical trials. In these trials practitioners use standardised manuals, videotape the sessions and receive expert supervision and training to ensure that they deliver the treatment exactly as intended. Outcomes are then compared between the different modalities in the trial to assess which intervention is superior for the treatment of that disorder. Furthermore, these studies also hope to identify what elements of the treatment approaches are most significant in producing positive outcomes. The models are then promoted in the field, but they must still be delivered according to the treatment manuals.

For example Project MATCH was a large-scale randomised control trial that assigned 1,726 adult problem drinkers to one of three therapies. Motivational Enhancement Therapy was a four-session brief intervention, based on Motivational interviewing. The Cognitive Behavioural Therapy option comprised of 12 sessions of structured relapse prevention group work. Whilst the Twelve Step Facilitation was a 12-session treatment model based on the Twelve Step treatment programme where these clients had to attend Alcoholics Anonymous meetings as well. This $36 million research study examined 64 different interactions that might predict outcomes within these models.

Whilst randomised control trials have been successful in medicine, there are difficulties in applying the methodology to talking cures. First, randomised control trials use 'single' diagnosis clients in their studies. If a potential research subject also has a co-occurring condition, such as bi-polar depression, they would be excluded from the trial. This excludes clients with greater complexity of need. In contrast, clients presenting in the community for treatment often have multiple problems and multiple diagnoses. Second, practitioners who deliver treatment in the randomised control trials are trained to deliver one specified treatment approach. In everyday practice this is not possible. Practitioners in the field have to manage clients who exhibit varying degrees of motivation and the practitioners are, as a result, required to deliver different types of intervention. Third, research subjects in these randomised control trials can be paid to attend additional days for assessment purposes. Financial incentives can improve a client's mood considerably. Again, the capacity to pay clients in community treatment is rare, but it can influence outcomes. Finally, randomised control trials pay special attention to engagement and retention strategies and promote them in order to preserve the attendance of their treatment group. This is important as statistical significance often depends on the size of the sample that completes treatment. But under the competing demands of everyday practice and outcome monitoring, the ability to incorporate special measures to improve retention can be lost. In light of these limitations, it has to be recognised that the ability to deliver treatment in an everyday setting in the same way as described in a randomised control trial is simply impossible.

Besides these problems in application, there is an even more profound problem with randomised control trials. When bona-fide structured treatment approaches are compared head-to-head at gold standard, the central finding of every randomised control trial is that no one treatment model has demonstrated that it is superior to any other. This is known as the 'dodo-bird effect' (Luborsky et al., 2002), in a reference to *Alice in Wonderland* where the Queen announces that everyone is a winner and that there are prizes for all. For example, Project MATCH found that the only variable that accurately predicted outcomes at treatment completion and at 10-year follow up was the working alliance between the therapist and the client, *regardless of treatment style*. This has been identified in numerous studies. Wampold (2001) conducted a large meta-analysis of randomised control trials. A meta-analysis is a statistical means of combining a large number of individual studies into one large-scale study. He found that treatment type only accounted for 1 per cent of

Table 6.5: Sources of outcome in treatment

Extra-therapeutic factors	Treatment factors
80–87 per cent of outcome	13–20 per cent of outcome
Readiness to change	Alliance effects (5–8 per cent)
Social functioning prior to the onset of problem	Model (1 per cent)
Social support	Placebo and allegiance (4 per cent)
Socio-economic status	Therapist effect (4–9 per cent)
Life events (or non-events)	

Adapted from International Centre for Clinical Excellence, 2011.

clinical outcomes. The majority of the treatment gains were driven by relationship factors and not the therapeutic model (see Table 6.5).

Lambert's (1992) studies of clinical outcome were more generous to method. Their research found that 15 per cent of outcomes were based on therapeutic approach, 15 per cent were a placebo response, whilst 40 per cent of outcome was attributed to extra-therapeutic factors, such as the client getting a job or entering a new relationship, etc. Within this, the final 30 per cent of outcomes were driven by the working relationship between the practitioner and the client. Hovarth & Symonds (1991) evaluated the impact of the relationship in a different way. They compared the outcomes of practitioners delivering the same treatment using a clinical manual. Despite them delivering exactly the same treatment intervention, the researchers found between 50–66 per cent variance in outcome. Based on research developed over a 60-year period, the most significant factor in driving clinical outcomes is the strength of the working alliance, regardless of therapeutic model (Bachelor & Hovarth, 1999).

In the limited number of randomised control trials conducted with young people the same problems persist. Despite differences in design and application of divergent treatment modalities, clinical trials tend to produce the same range of outcomes regardless of approach (see Waldron & Turner, 2008). Kazdin et al. (2006) examined the relationship in family therapy between practitioners and children aged between 6 and 14 who displayed oppositional, aggressive and anti-social behaviour. The biggest predictor of treatment outcomes was the young person's rating of the alliance with the practitioner. Furthermore, the alliance as rated by the parents

was also predictive of improvement in the child. This is supported by the conclusions of wider research into treatment, that the most effective practitioners are highly adaptive in their approach (Duncan et al., 2000). So, it is imperative that practitioners working with young people invest effort into the establishment and maintenance of positive working relationships with them, even in the event of the inevitable ruptures, tensions and conflicts that will arise (for a review, see Harris, 2006).

The working alliance

The research supporting the centrality of the working alliance in predicting outcomes requires further exploration to clarify key issues. First, it is important to recognise that outcomes in everyday practice can vary enormously from those in randomised control trials. What the 'dodo bird' effect demonstrates is that most structured treatment interventions can produce an *optimal* range of outcomes in an *optimal* treatment environment. But treatment in everyday practice settings can be sub-optimal. Second, whilst it is widely believed in the field that Cognitive Behavioural Therapy is superior to other forms of intervention this is not the case. This myth has developed because Cognitive Behavioural Therapy has been included in a greater number of randomised control studies, which means that a literature review on 'what works' will identify a large number of randomised control trials which have included a Cognitive Behavioural Therapy treatment option within them. However, *within* these studies, Cognitive Behavioural Therapy did not perform any better than other treatment approach.

Furthermore, no single study has ever been

able to identify a specific mechanism within any given treatment approach that is the catalyst for change. So whilst approaches like Neuro-Linguistic Programming (NLP) state that it takes the best elements of every model, this has never been validated in any research study ever undertaken. The continued finding of every study is that it is the common factors that are found in every treatment that drive outcomes rather than the specific elements of a given approach. Advances in research have identified that outcomes are derived from two key sources. One area is the *extra-therapeutic factors*, which are variables that are wholly independent of the treatment being delivered. The second source of outcomes are *treatment factors*, which are derived directly from the therapy being delivered. The contribution of each domain will be examined separately here.

Extra-therapeutic factors include the client's motivation for change, the client's level of social functioning prior to treatment, their social support, socio-economic status and the life events (or non-events) that occur during their treatment (Hubble et al., 2010). These extra-therapeutic factors are sometimes referred to as *social capital*. The social capital of an individual describes both their personal skills, resources and abilities *and* the opportunities, support networks and resources available to them in their environment. Both are important because all the skills in the world will not assist a client who has no opportunity. Likewise, opportunities are empty if individuals do not have the skills to take advantage of them. Wampold's (2001) large scale review of treatment outcomes suggested that that 80–87 per cent of outcomes were driven by extra-therapeutic factors in the client's life.

These findings have serious implications for the treatment of young people. Many extra-therapeutic factors embedded in young people's social environments can have a positive or negative impact on their treatment outcomes. Early onset externalised youth are liable to be exposed to a wide range of destabilising forces such as poverty, abuse and low expectancy of achievement. Parents with substance misuse problems or other complex problems are less able to provide them with support when preoccupied with their own life stresses. Continued parental use will expose young people to substance use post treatment, which is a critical factor in producing negative outcomes for any young people. Very early onset in use means that

externalised youth are also developmentally disadvantaged due to their protracted social exclusion.

Extra-therapeutic factors may vary more widely amongst internalised youth. This will depend on the circumstances contributing to their mental health status. Sexual, physical or emotional abuse in the home will remain a destructive influence. An entire family can be affected by traumatic life events, such as bereavement or bitter divorce, which can leave parents feeling guilty and bereft of emotional resources to support their children. In cases of abuse issues outside the family, parental belief in the young person's experience and supportive involvement in treatment can be enormously helpful in increasing the young person's environmental support.

Conversely, if the internalised disorders are rooted in temperament factors, such as a naturally fretful disposition, rolling back parent support may be necessary if the parents have become over protective. Protecting young people from their fears inadvertently sustains those fears, as young people do not develop the self-belief to overcome these triggers of anxiety. This needs to be a gradual process so as not to overwhelm the young person. Likewise, hypercritical or fretful parents may also transmit anxiety, though to a much lesser degree. Late onset normative users are much more likely to have attained greater educational achievement, have supportive families and have lives characterised by less complexity prior to the onset of problem use. Their social functioning is likely to be higher as they have remained socially intact for longer. This includes having maintained commitment to school, engaged in pro-social recreation and having experienced higher ranges of family cohesion. Their families are more likely to present to professional services for help.

This dramatic variance in environmental support and personal resources may account for the variance in outcomes for these different sub-trajectories of young people. Early onset youth outcomes are compromised by the limited recovery capital they possess prior to treatment. This limited capital also suggests that the reach of treatment needs to be wider, not necessarily focusing on a young person as an individual but within the context of the environment that exerts so much influence over them. Whilst not all extra-therapeutic factors can be made therapeutic, many of these wider factors can be embraced through treatment interventions that encompass family, school and even peer involvement.

Treatment effects account for the remaining 13–20 per cent of a young person's outcome. Treatment effectiveness is derived from several different sources. First, 'who' the practitioner is has a significant effect on outcome. This may include the personality style and credibility of the practitioner in the eyes of the young person. The practitioner's ability to foster positive expectations of change is also significant. This is referred to as a 'placebo effect', but the instigation of hope in the young person can have a powerful effect. Likewise, the greater the faith the practitioner has in their particular method of work will also enhance outcome. In contradiction to these personal qualities, therapeutic training, qualifications or clinical supervision have virtually no impact on improving a practitioner's outcomes (Baldwin et al., 2007).

The biggest single source of treatment outcome is the working alliance between the practitioner and the client. Research has consistently shown that the most effective therapists are those who are able to form effective alliances with a diverse range of clients (Brown, G.S. et al., 2005a; Luborsky et al., 1986). Norcross (2010) defines the alliance as the strength of the collaboration between the client and the practitioner. The centrality of alliance factors had been emphasised since the inception of talking cures with Freud. However, it was not until Bordin (1979) published his seminal research that the elements of the alliance began to be clarified. They identified three core components, though a fourth dimension has been added in terms of client preference (see Table 6.6). Research suggests that the establishment of these elements are not sequential, but that they inform each other. For example, a strong bond may increase the young person's engagement in the therapeutic tasks, and benefits derived from engaging in the therapeutic tasks may increase bond, etc.

The power of the alliance as the central factor in determining treatment outcome has been established in over 1,000 studies of treatment effectiveness (Orlinsky et al., 2004). For example, Norcross's (2011) large scale study of outcomes found that the alliance was 5–9 per cent more significant in influencing outcome than the therapeutic approach. Interestingly, Anker et al. (2010) found that therapeutic alliances that improve over time tend to produce better outcomes than those that started and remained positive.

The nature of treatment outcomes

Whilst advances in research have illuminated the dynamics of effective treatment, there has also been considerable progress in understanding the nature of treatment outcomes. Randomised control trials and meta-analysis studies have demonstrated that responses to treatment are highly predictable. Research demonstrates that early subjective improvement experienced by the client predicts long term outcome (see Howard et al., 1986). This is referred to as the 'rush-trickle effect' where the client experiences rapid gains early in the treatment process which then begin to slow as treatment progresses (see Graph 6.3). Young people with low functioning at the outset of treatment tend to make the greatest immediate treatment gains. However, as they then move towards normative levels of functioning a law of diminishing returns begins to impact and the rate of change slows down.

Table 6.6: Critical components of the therapeutic alliance

Component	Description
Bond	The practitioner's role in supporting this process, based on empathy, warmth, positive regard and a sincere desire to help.
Goals	The establishment of the goals or purpose of treatment, which offers some incentive to the young person to improve their life or reduce problems in it.
Tasks	The methods and approach used in treatment that the young person is expected to engage with in order to achieve their goal. These are the curriculum of treatment activities and vary from model to model. They can range from the experience of non-judgemental empathy in person-centred counselling to acquiring skills in cognitive behavioural models.
Preference	How well the young person's own views and preferences are accommodated in this process.

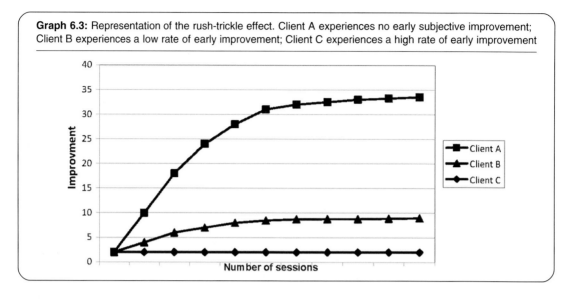

Graph 6.3: Representation of the rush-trickle effect. Client A experiences no early subjective improvement; Client B experiences a low rate of early improvement; Client C experiences a high rate of early improvement

For example, Brown et al. (1999) studied the treatment outcomes of clients of over 2,000 counsellors. They found that early subjective improvement was the biggest indicator of long term outcome. This was to the extent that clients who did not report any improvement by the third visit did not experience any gains at all. Clients with enduring mental illness were the exception as they reported that subjective improvement increased after 6 weeks of treatment. Clients who worsened by the third visit were twice as likely to drop out of treatment. This early subjective improvement was the only reliable predictor of long term outcome that occurred regardless of diagnosis, severity, family support and type of therapy. It might also explain why randomised control trials outcomes are similar. The rate of change Brown et al. observed was not determined by the particular counselling model but by the pace in which human beings can put change into place. So, the fact that treatment outcomes are similar between most counselling models suggests that they can promote a similar rate of change in people. This research also explains why this Baseline Assessment Reactivity (see Chapter 4) can make such a substantial contribution to overall outcome. As the majority of treatment gains occur so early in the treatment processes, a therapeutically designed assessment tool can maximise this early uplift. Conversely, a poorly designed assessment tool could have the potential for a catastrophic effect on long terms outcomes by diminishing this critical early response rate.

The rush-trickle effect in outcomes may also explain why young people within the different sub-trajectories appear to make similar progress in treatment, but also why these gains may deteriorate post treatment for the most high risk youth. Despite benefiting from treatment, these high risk young people remain exposed to drug and alcohol use in their family environments. Whilst they are in treatment the high level of support may insulate them from these environmental pressures. However, as the effect of this support decays post-treatment it may be too weak to address these threats. Hence aftercare becomes a more critical issue for high risk early onset users who will need continued support to navigate these pressures.

Whilst a number of outcome measurement tools have proliferated in recent years, many are often cumbersome, are not validated for young people or are simply not sufficiently practitioner-or service user-friendly. As we have seen, measurements of consumption rates, diagnosis or life task achievement are difficult to benchmark. In response to these demands, Duncan et al. (2000) have suggested an alternative to the evidence-based practice model. Rather than attempting to superimpose a randomised control trial on an everyday treatment settings, they have suggested that treatment outcomes focus on the two critical findings derived from over 60 years of research into the effectiveness of talking cures: that alliance factors are the single biggest driver of treatment outcome and that early subjective improvement predicts long term outcome. In order to measure this they have developed two simple outcome tools that are validated for adults, young people and children (available from www.scottmiller.com).

Using measurement tools to improve alliances

The *Outcome Rating Scale* developed by Duncan et al. is conducted at the start of each session and invites a young person to rate how well they feel they are progressing in four key social domains, including: 'individually' (in themselves); 'interpersonally' (in their close relationships); 'socially' (in wider relationships) and 'overall' (their general sense of wellbeing). The young person simply rates their progress on four unnumbered lines that are 10 centimetres long from poor to good. Measuring and combing these scores thus offers a range of 0–40. Charting these measures at the start of every session will reveal the subjective improvement that they are experiencing. Subjective improvement is a reliable measure as it runs in close accord with third party assessment of improvement. Young people who score 28 or above on this measure are like those young people who are not seeking professional help. In other words, they have achieved a normative level of social functioning. Where there is a poor early response, it can be identified quickly and the intervention adjusted for the specific young person. This increases the probability of a positive outcome.

It is possible to subscribe to a website where a young person can score their progress online and the software will analyse the data, predicting the young person's progress (see www.MyOutcomes.com). Furthermore, the website will analyse all clients' scores that are inputted from over 300,000 administrations and provide a global average response rate for this client group. This allows agencies to benchmark a young person's improvement against the global average of what is possible in terms of outcomes with this group. Benchmarking in this way allows practitioners and agencies to establish whether they are performing below, on or above the typical outcome range for these young people, which is vital to the development of effective services, as it sets a clear standard of treatment outcome. All too often, those purchasing treatment services on the behalf of the taxpayer may set wholly unrealistic targets for the agencies

that they commission. The outcomes that agencies do produce are meaningless, if there is no standard against which to evaluate them. In this way, the *Outcome Rating Scales* not only enhance treatment for young people but also allow agencies to demonstrate their worth to the public.

A second outcome tool, which can be utilised at the end of every session by a young person, is called the *Session Rating Scale*. Again, this is a simple tool with four unnumbered lines which are 10 centimetres long. It is used to invite the young person to rate the quality of the session, including: whether they felt 'respected' (bond); whether the session covered areas that were 'important' to them (goals); whether the practitioners approach was a 'good fit' (tasks); and how they felt the session went 'overall' (confidence in the practitioner). These scores can be measured and combined giving a range of 0–40. Where the young person rates the session 36 or less, they are invited to give feedback about what they felt was missing. The practitioner can respond to this feedback non-defensively and adjust their practice accordingly. This adjustment has the effect of boosting the client's future *Session Rating Scales* as the alliance becomes a better fit for the young person and then, as a result, improves the client outcomes. As research has continually re-iterated that alliance factors are critical in retaining young people in treatment, these tools can be especially important in their treatment.

The ability of these tools to detect poor initial response rates and poor alliances means that they do not simply measure outcomes but improve them. Through the use of these tools, with any model or method of practice, research shows that young people are far less likely to drop out of treatment and less likely to deteriorate during treatment and, critically, that the tools *double the number of clients achieving significant clinical outcomes*. This occurs without the practitioner adopting any specific model of practice other than adjusting their own intervention in light of client feedback. It ensures that the approach they use, whatever it is, is meaningful and relevant to each young person that they work with. The tools also offer other significant benefits to service development and should be considered the outcome tool of choice for children and young people.

These outcome ratings can also be linked to the sub-trajectory that young people belong to, which allows outcome evaluation to be conducted across the spectrum of presenting needs, so as to ensure that all young people are receiving effective treatment, not just the later onset normative users who are most treatment responsive, as we have seen earlier in this chapter can be the case. Patterns in outcome can provide agencies with vital feedback regarding the impact of their services and whose needs are, or are not, being met. This feedback can then be used to inform future service developments and increase the treatment gains for young people. This outcome-informed approach offers the ability to develop robust, clinically validated approaches in everyday settings without the limitation imposed by randomised control trials.

It is important to clarify a key issue regarding this research. The importance that it places on alliance factors does not mean that practitioners do not need models of practice. Research suggests that treatment approaches which lack focus and structure produce negative outcomes (Lambert & Bergin, 1994; Mohr, 1995). Practitioners need methods to identify goals with a young person and develop a curriculum of tasks that will help the young person to achieve them. Practitioners need to believe that the models that they use are helpful. It is the 'goodness of fit' between the practitioner's approach and the young person's own view of the world that is vital. Therefore it remains important that practitioners with young people have clearly defined treatment strategies that can then be adjusted according to the feedback of the young person.

Comprehensive treatment pathways

Treatment interventions for adolescent substance misuse will need to encompass a wide range of presenting needs. Based on the evidence reviewed in this book so far this requires treatment systems to address four critical aspects of young people's substance misuse problems:

1. Skills to change the established pattern of drug and alcohol use.
2. Life skills to address developmental delay.
3. Assessment and clinical management of physical withdrawal.
4. Specialist interventions to address sub-trajectory risk profiles.

1. Skills to change the established pattern of drug and alcohol use

Treatment will need to offer young people the skills needed to manage their substance use. This may involve resisting all use for some, as in the case of abstinence, or controlled use for others.

2. Life skills to address developmental delay

Treatment will need to address the developmental delay incurred by problematic use, by providing the life skills that the young person has missed. These life skills are essential. They are the means by which young people will integrate back into the pro-social structures of life. The extent of their need for help with life skills will also influence treatment prognosis. Early onset users will need greater support in the development of these skills, leading to longer treatment. Whilst young people who have received early interventions and normative users will have acquired greater life mastery, which makes brief intervention more appropriate.

3. Assessment and clinical management of physical withdrawal

A medical assessment is necessary to assess the need for a medically supervised detoxification to address physical dependence.

4. Specialist interventions to address sub-trajectory risk profiles

Finally, young people will require specialist interventions to address the behavioural problems or mental health issues that prompt use in ways that are specific to their sub-trajectories. These interventions must accommodate relational factors both in treatment and in the young person's family. For example, as externalised youth tend to be under-parented whilst internalised youth are over-parented, treatment must assist in changing the balance of these relationships.

These four aims need to be integrated into treatment systems for young people, starting with the comprehensive assessment that should identify physical dependence, breakdown in social attachments and the sub-trajectory profile of the young person. A treatment system should then offer clear pathways to support young people in these areas. In general terms there is a divide between the treatment of physical dependence and the treatment of social complications. Medical treatment for physical dependence is substance specific due to the unique actions of different drugs on the human brain. Treatment for social complications is not substance specific. This is because any substance can interfere with a young person's attachments leading to development delay, which means that psycho-social interventions that address social functioning are effective regardless of the substance used. Within this, treatment systems must account for the following divergent patterns of use.

Adapting treatment systems to young people

Externalised youth will need the most intensive support. Their early onset use will result in greater developmental delay requiring expansive life skills support, and their entrenched pattern of use will require deeper relapse prevention work. Their high impulse behaviour will also be indicated by poor impulse control, offending and risk-taking behaviour, demanding specialist interventions to address behavioural control. The more chaotic nature of their background will also require greater support for their families, whose lives tend to be characterised by complex needs of their own. The families may need support and stabilisation themselves before they can effectively support their children: parental management skills based on boundary setting, communication skills and improved parental monitoring.

Internalised youth will also require assessment of dependence and social functioning. Specialist support will also be needed to address or manage specific mental health issues. Their family roles may differ depending on the origins of their distress. Traumatised young people may benefit from family involvement in their treatment. Young people who experience generalised anxiety due to over-protective parenting will need their family to support them in achieving greater autonomy. Reductions in parental anxiety levels may also be critical.

Normative youth may benefit from brief interventions as their late onset of problematic use will mean they have already developed greater baseline social functioning. Besides relapse prevention work, they may need additional support to change their peer group and identify new support networks that promote more positive behaviours. Their parents are liable to be highly supportive. However, this support can inadvertently be misdirected towards an over-focus on minimising the negative impact of their offspring's consumption. This can have the opposite effect and actually sustain use as well as reduce motivation for change (Harris, P. 2011b). Therefore, psycho-education and adjusting the type and level of help that parents offer may assist these young people to sustain change.

All these treatment interventions need to be purposeful. As we have seen, recovery is not simply the absence of substances but the presence of a more fulfilling life. It is imperative to increase the protection factors which are located in the pro-social structures of the life course. Recovery is the re-integration back into these pro-social structures of life. Educational attainment, secure housing, family cohesion, pro-social networks, improved physical and emotional wellbeing, and no criminal involvement can all serve as positive markers of change, in addition to reduction of use. Once young people integrate into these pro-social networks of life, their sustained recovery will be greatly assisted by the backdraft of normative developmental processes. The comprehensive research base that has been presented here offers a clear framework in which to best organise treatment pathways for young people. Whilst there remains a paucity of truly developmentally informed models, this structure can house a variety of interventions designed to address the four critical components described at the start of this section. Figure 6.1 outlines this comprehensive treatment structure. The following sections will review the current evidence base concerning interventions to address critical areas within this framework, including detoxification/controlled use, substance-specific interventions and the evidence base for specialist interventions to address additional complexity in young people's lives.

Specific modalities: Pharmacotherapy

Pharmacological therapies for young people's substance misuse problems is an under-developed area and any conclusions about them are suggestive at best. Most research on adolescent withdrawal is based on retrospective self-report which has not been validated prospectively (Colby et al., 2000). A number of studies have been based on case studies or open

Figure 6.1: Scheme of treatment interventions for young people

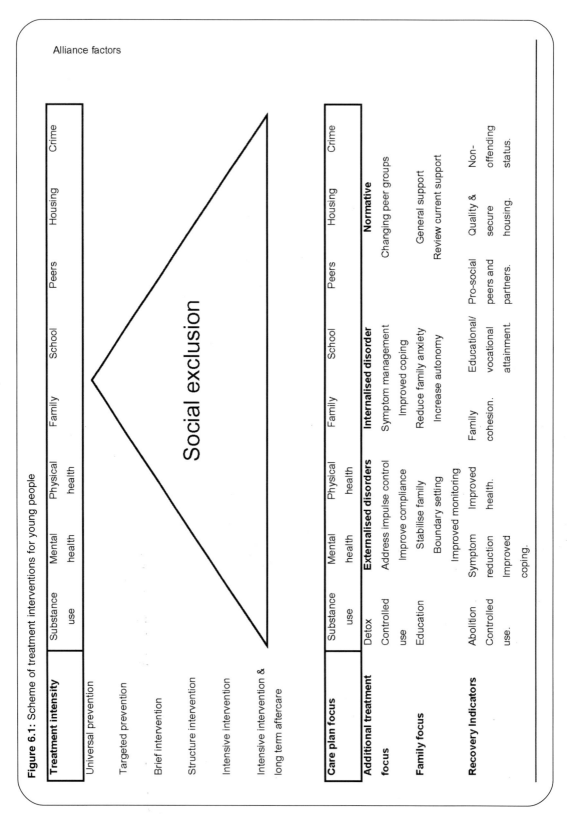

label trials, because ethical issues in prescribing placebo medications to young people mean that gold standard randomised control trials have not been applied. As withdrawal is rare in young people (Chung et al., 2000; Martin et al., 1995), they constitute a very small treatment population, making any research findings hard to substantiate, as there is an insufficient sample size for meaningful analysis. So, those studies that have been conducted are often inconclusive. Additional complications can also arise as the young people who are most likely to require medical management for dependence are liable to have concurrent mental health problems that will also need prescribed medications. The combination of prescribing can confound clear outcomes for any one medication.

As withdrawal states are rare in young people pharmacotherapy should only be used with them in exceptional circumstances, and only after a thorough medical assessment. Most of the existing medical based treatments for adolescents are similar to those used for adults but adjusted to account for age and size. In general, pharmacotherapy has been used to treat dependence in five different ways (see Table 6.7). As most medical authorities recommend detoxification for young people, this section will focus on detoxification and relapse prevention medications for specific substances.

As we have seen in Chapter 4, physical dependence occurs with depressant drugs (alcohol, benzodiazepines & opiates) where a strong relationship between tolerance and physical withdrawal requires medical attention.

The use of pharmacotherapy should only proceed where there is sufficient evidence of a withdrawal syndrome. The primary prescribing approach to detoxifying young people experiencing alcohol dependence is benzodiazepines (Lingford-Hughes & Nutt, 2003). Whilst no benzodiazepine has been shown to be more effective than any other, medical practitioners tend to use long acting medications such as Chlordiazepoxide or Diazepam. Shorter acting benzodiazepines can be used but tend to be reserved for patients with chronic liver damage. However, as the action of benzodiazepines is similar to alcohol there is always a danger of producing dependence on these medications. Alternative medications can be used with mild to moderate withdrawal symptoms such as Carbamazepine which can be prescribed in a 7-day reduction regime (Mayo-Smith, 1997; Holbrook et al., 1999). In a comparative trial, Carbamazepine appeared equally as effective as the more traditional Lorazepam detoxification (Malcom et al., 2002) though it can have side effects such as skin rashes and reducing white blood cell counts.

Besides detoxification, a number of medications have been developed to prevent relapse post-detoxification. Acamprosate is derived from an amino acid that is believed to act on NDMA receptors in the brain. These receptors become hyperactive as part of the withdrawal process leading to cravings to drink alcohol. Acamprosate operates by reducing this over-excitation and so reduces the cravings. This medication is prescribed for patients for one year after detoxification, and studies have shown that

Table 6.7: Pharmacological interventions for young people

Treatment	Function
Medical emergencies	Drugs administered to address overdose such as Naloxone to address overdose of opiates.
Substitute prescribing	Substitute medications can be prescribed to manage dependence on opiates such as Methadone or Buprenorphine.
Amelioration of withdrawal	Drugs administered to reduce the severity of withdrawal symptoms rather than substitute the primary drug of dependence such as such as Lofexidine for opiate detoxification.
Relapse prevention	Drugs can be prescribed to support relapse prevention in a number of different ways: • To block the action of drugs, such as Naltrexone for opiate use. • To reduce cravings such as Acamprosite for alcohol use. • To produce aversive side effects if taken in combination with primary drug of dependence such as Disulfirum which causes nausea if taken with alcohol.
Prescribing for mental health problems	A wide range of drugs can be prescribed to address either behavioural problems (e.g. Ritalin for Attention Deficit Disorder) or mental illness (e.g. anti-depressants).

it outperforms a placebo in reducing cravings (Slattery et al., 2003). A randomised control trial, with a small sample size of 26 young people aged 16–19, found that the Acamprosate group achieved greater cumulative days of abstinence in the 90 days post treatment compared to the placebo group (Niederhofer & Staffen, 2003a).

Disulfirum has been used with adults with severe alcohol problems, but its use with adolescents is rare (Bukstein, 1997). Disulfirum operates by blocking the production of the enzyme acetaldehyde dehydrogenase that metabolises alcohol in the liver. This leads to a build-up of the enzyme acetaldehyde when drinking, causing unpleasant physical reactions to alcohol such as flushing, nausea, headaches and tachycardia. This aversive response to alcohol breaks the expectation of positive effects of drinking such as euphoria and so becomes a deterrent to consumption. Disulfirum is prescribed for 3–6 months post detoxification (Edwards et al., 2003). Neiderhofer & Staffen (2003b) studied the impact of Disilfirum on a small sample of 26 adolescent problem drinkers. Those in the Disulfirum treatment group achieved much higher rates of abstinence across a 90-day trial than the control group (68.6 days versus 29.7 days). Issues regarding the safety of the drug and poor treatment compliance are major limitations to prescribing it to young people. As a result, some researchers have advised against its use for younger adolescents (Myers et al., 1994).

A further development in relapse prevention prescribing is the use of Naltrexone. Naltrexone is used extensively in the treatment of opiate problems, but as alcohol also triggers the release of natural opioid endorphins there is a crossover between these two forms of dependence. Naltraxone has a high affinity to opiate receptors in the brain and effectively 'caps' them rather than activates them. This means that alcohol (and opiates) are unable to bind to these receptor sites and thus cannot release endorphins. In alcohol patients, Naltrexone reduces the euphoria associated with alcohol consumption, diminishing its positive effects. Again, this can break the chain of expectancy between drinking alcohol and experiencing positive, rewarding responses. However, Naltrexone requires a high level of compliance in order to maintain its benefit. There can also be side effects in a small number of patients, such as liver problems, nausea and anxiety. Some studies have shown very positive results for Naltrexone in reducing

relapse rates and the number of drinking days in problem drinkers (Slattery et al., 2003). One small trial conducted by Neiderhofer et al. (2003) on 30 adolescent problem drinkers found that 20 participants in the Naltrexone group had sustained abstinence for the duration of the programme compared to only ten of the placebo group. Lifrak et al. (1997) also found positive results with the use of Naltrexone with alcohol dependent young people.

In terms of opiate use, the primary medication for the clinical management of withdrawal is Methadone, Buprenorphine or alpha-2 adrenergic agonists. Methadone is the most heavily researched medication in terms of detoxification. Methadone is an opioid, meaning it is produced synthetically in a laboratory rather than refined from the opium poppy as opiates are. It works on the same opiate receptors in the brain but is longer lasting than heroin. Whilst heroin stays active for 12 hours, methadone is active for 24 hours which means it can be prescribed daily. An equivalent dose of Methadone is prescribed to replace the heroin that a young person is consuming so as to prevent withdrawal. This can stabilise a young person so that they no longer have the urgent need to raise the funds to buy heroin. Methadone is considered most effective for young people when the dose is slowly reduced over a 3-month period. This gradual dose reduction reduces craving and withdrawal in a slowed-down detoxification process (Strang & Gossop, 1990).

Buprenorphine is a partial opiate agonist that has a high affinity with opiate receptors in the brain. As such, it not only binds to opiate receptors but also prevents other opiates such as heroin from binding as well. It has shown some promise in treatment for opiate dependence (Gowing et al., 2006). Its high affinity with opiate receptors means that it disengages from opiate receptors very gradually allowing for a more gentle withdrawal process. Alpha-2 adrenergic agonists are not opiate replacements but reduce the symptoms of withdrawal. Clonidine and Lofexidine are the principal medications used, though Lofexidine has fewer side effects. These drugs are used when individuals are detoxifying from low doses of opiates and essentially dampen the symptoms of withdrawal, making the process more comfortable for the patient.

An alternative to detoxification from opiates is the prescribing of substitute opiates as a maintenance regime. In these prescribing regimes, the patient is prescribed an equivalent dose of the replacement opiate and this is maintained for an indefinite period of time allowing the individual to stabilise and enter into structured support (Mattrick et al., 2003). Doses typically range between 60 and 100mg per day though may be lower for young people. Methadone maintenance has been shown to be effective in reducing harm associated with use, such as reducing blood borne viruses, drug related deaths and crime, and improving health. Buprenorphine has also been used as a maintenance medication though has been less researched. Doses of 8–16 mg have been found to be more effective in maintenance prescribing. Auriacombe et al. (2001) found Buprenorphine reduced mortality rates compared to Methadone. Research is extremely limited in terms of substitute prescribing for adolescents, but it has been shown to improve treatment retention rates in young people (Hopfer et al., 2002). Policy generally advises against maintenance prescribing for young people except in exceptional cases. Detoxification is the recommended approach due to young people's shorter using histories.

Naltrexone has been prescribed to assist recovery in opiate-using youth. Naltrexone has a very high affinity with opiate receptors. Once it binds with these receptors it caps them meaning that opiates cannot act on them, blocking all effects. However, Naltrexone must be taken daily and studies have found that young people have often failed to comply with the administration of the drug. Deas & Thomas (2001) found that the drug could be effective in reducing relapse rates if prescribed to highly motivated youth with supportive family environments.

Evidence on the efficacy of pharmacotherapy to block the effects of other drugs in young people is weak. Some case studies have found positive evidence for the use of Desipramine for cocaine-dependent youth (Kaminer, 1992). Nicotine patches have also been used as a replacement therapy for young people who smoke tobacco, but the clinical trials on their use with young people have shown poor results (Hurt et al., 2000; Smith et al., 1996). So, whilst there have been some positive suggestions regarding the effectiveness of prescribed medications, their overall efficacy is limited and most research suggests that prescribing must occur together with psycho-social interventions to be effective.

Specific modalities: Controlled drinking programmes

The main pharmacological interventions for young people are designed to reduce withdrawal. However, many young people do not require clinically managed detoxification. Furthermore, the majority of young people do not desire abstinence. As abstinence-based programmes are unpalatable for many young people, controlled drinking programmes can provide a more attractive and relevant option.

Controlled drinking programmes are a very controversial area of substance misuse treatment, particularly in the US whose treatment landscape is dominated by a Twelve Step philosophy that militates against such programmes. This view is derived from a number of sources. Many adult dependent drinkers attempt controlled use several times, and fail before they commit to abstinence. Such attempts at controlled drinking tend to be based on the individual taking a break from drinking before resuming. Time out of alcohol use, though, does not equip someone with the skills to drink moderately any more than dropping out of college for a year will help students to pass exams. Controlled drinking requires learning, applying and mastering new skills in a determined way. Also, whilst some individuals do relapse on controlled drinking programmes, it is also the case that many abstinent drinkers also relapse.

These controversies regarding controlled drinking programmes led to an intense research focus on their outcomes. These studies have revealed that controlled drinking is very effective for people with social complications arising from their alcohol use as opposed to physical dependence (See Sobell & Sobell, 1993). As the severity of physical dependence increases, the probability of achieving controlled use decreases sharply (see Miller & Munoz, 1982: Edwards et al., 2003). But as young people are unlikely to have physical dependency, it makes them strong candidates for such programmes. A number of factors other than dependence have also been identified that may influence an individual's ability to achieve controlled drinking, including psychological and social factors. For example, aggressive drinkers tend to have low impulse control, making them more sensitive to alcohol's effects. Individuals who operate in high drinking environments are more likely to succumb to the temptations of higher use. There may also be

Table 6.8:   Factors relevant to controlled drinking

Factors unfavourable to controlled use	Factors favourable to controlled use
• Severe dependence	• Mild or no signs of dependence
• Previous failures at controlled drinking	• Recent sustained normal drinking
• Strong desire in the drinker for abstinence	• Strong preference for normal drinking
• Commitment to AA	
• Poor self-control in other areas of life	• Evidence of self-control in other areas of life
• Mental illness or drug misuse	• No mental illness or concurrent drug abuse
• Severe organ damage from alcohol abuse	• Mild or no physical complications from drinking
• Heavy drinking family and social group	
• Heavy drinking in work settings	
• Social isolation	• Supportive family and friends
• Employment jeopardised by drinking problems	• Drinking does not affect work performance
• Violent when drinking	• Non-violent when drinking

Adapted from Edwards et al., 2003.

medical grounds that over-rule the individual's capacity to continue drinking, such as liver damage (see Table 6.8).

Whilst a number of different controlled drinking approaches have been developed, and researched deeply, the Behaviour Control Skills Training Programme (BCST) has shown particularly promising results with young people (Miller et al., 2001). It focuses on several aspects of controlled use, and begins with a systematic assessment process which reviews the individual's motivations for controlled drinking. This is combined with assessment tools that offer objective feedback on the severity of their alcohol problems and the probability of their achieving controlled use in light of this. This is based on extensive follow-up research on who is likely to achieve controlled use. Low order problem drinkers have a high probability of achieving controlled use, but as an individual moves closer to dependence their chances of achieving controlled use drop to zero. The assessment allows careful consideration in regards to entry on to the programme, and many candidates opt for abstinence at this stage. Those who do wish to progress in the programme are then asked to take two weeks out of drinking entirely in order to test resolve, identify difficult times and break established habits.

After this time-out period, drinking goals are established in two ways. One goal is based on a daily unit limit. This can be informed by the recommended daily unit limit but can be set higher in the interests of harm reduction. The daily unit limit can always be revised downwards in the future. A second drinking limit is set for 'special occasions' as people often want a different experience from drinking at these times. The special occasion drinking limit is based on the individual's Blood Alcohol Concentration (BAC) levels, which describes how much alcohol is in the blood stream at a given time. This is because levels of intoxication are not set by the number of units consumed. Rather they are set by how many units are consumed in what time. Drinking 2 units in two hours will result in low levels of alcohol concentration in the blood stream. Whereas drinking 2 units of alcohol in one minute will result in a higher rate of intoxication as the concentration level of alcohol peaks far more rapidly in the blood stream. The liver will also clear 1 unit of alcohol an hour, lowering the BAC further.

The BAC level is influenced by a number of other factors. Ethnicity, age, gender and body weight all influence BAC levels. Women are particularly prone to achieving higher BAC levels than men as they tend to be physically smaller, have smaller livers and more body fat. This means that they will achieve a far higher BAC level than male counterparts for the same number of units and time spent drinking. For example, a young woman who weighs 7 stone 2lbs and who drinks 9 units in three hours will achieve a BAC of 193 mg per cent. Her 10-stone boyfriend who drinks the same number of units in the same time period will achieve a BAC of 86mg per cent. The physiological effects from alcohol are derived from the level of the BAC. So whilst she will be profoundly impaired and close to blacking out at this range, her partner will only have impaired judgment (see Table 6.9).

Table 6.9: The blood alcohol concentration table.

BAC Level	Effect
20mg%	Subtle effects of alcohol become noticeable – usually after one drink.
40mg%	Feelings of relaxation, slowing of reaction times and fine motor skills which will impair driving.
55mg%	Positive effects of alcohol begin to diminish. Judgement, perception, learning, memory, coordination, sexual arousal, alertness and self-control begin to deteriorate. Memory impairment means you will tend to remember events preceding the 55mg% threshold but not after.
60mg%	Judgment is impaired. People are less able to make rational decisions and increase their risk-taking behaviour as they find it difficult to 'judge' their own judgment.
80mg%	Impairment in muscle coordination and driving skills. Drink drive limit.
100mg%	Clear deterioration in memory, reaction and movement.
120mg%	Vomiting occurs as the first defence against overdose.
150mg%	Balance is impaired and people find it difficult to walk in a straight line. Equivalent of half a pint of whisky in the blood stream.
200mg%	Experience of blackout at this level with people having no recall of events that occurred over this threshold. Can be a fatal dose for young people.
300mg%	People lose consciousness as a last defence against overdose.
450mg%	The average fatal dose of adults, breathing and heartbeat stop.

In setting a special occasion drinking limit, a young person is invited to identify what level of intoxication that they wish to achieve as their special occasion drinking goal, based on the BAC table. According to their gender and bodyweight, it is then easy to establish how many units they can consume in what time to achieve and remain at this level. There are now a number of very useful BAC calculators online (and available as free Apps on smart phones) that also factor in tolerance levels, making these calculations easy to do. The units can then be converted into beverage preference. This means that the young person can drink a lot of high-volume but low-alcohol beverages or a few low-volume high-alcohol beverages. As BAC levels increase, they affect decision-making, and so staying below their own pre-established threshold is more likely to result in success for each young person.

Once goals are established, the BCST programme provides young people with different sets of skills. The first is based on moderation skills that teach young people how to slow down their consumption, avoid heavy drinkers and identify high risk environments that prompt high use. They are asked to monitor each drinking occasion and record how much is being consumed and in what settings. This monitoring is important as it identifies when, where and why over-drinking occurs. It provides direction for further support in how to change the places, people, times and mood states in which they drink. More complex reasons may also underpin over-drinking, so the programme provides additional support to help manage stress, anxiety, social phobia, poor sleep and relaxation. Continued over-drinking will trigger a review, and treatment goals may be revised towards abstinence where the programme is not resulting in controlled use.

Behaviour Control Skills Training can be particularly effective for young people who must master intoxication management as a critical life skill. The programme has been modified and has shown very good outcomes with college-based youth in one-to-one and IT-based formats. It seems particularly helpful in pre-empting heavy drinking (see Miller et al., 2001). These are important findings, as controlled drinking appears to be a likely outcome for young people receiving treatment. For example Maisto et al. (2002) followed up 159 young problem drinkers who had presented for treatment. At 12-month follow-up, 17 per cent had remained abstinent, 60 per cent drank with at least one alcohol abuse symptom whilst 23 per cent drank with no alcohol related problems. Furthermore, improvements in social functioning were not very different between abstainers and non-problem drinkers. This suggests that controlled drinking skills may be a useful adjunct to treatment for problem using groups and may enhance treatment's positive outcomes.

Specific modalities: Motivational Interviewing

Brief interventions such as Motivational Interviewing (Miller & Rollnick, 1991) have been found to be effective with adolescent substance misusers in a number studies. This brief intervention was originally developed for adult problem drinkers, but the success of the model has meant it has been adopted in a wide range of clinical settings. Motivational Interviewing (MI) draws heavily on the Stages of Change research reviewed in Chapter 4. It recognises that motivation for change occurs in stages. In pre-contemplation a young person does not recognise any need for change. However, in light of increased consequences and external pressures they begin to re-evaluate their own behaviour. This re-evaluation is difficult. Substances can produce many positive consequences such as euphoria, relief, acceptance and excitement. At the same time, they can also generate problems including shame, conflict and a host of social and health complications. The co-existence of these contradictory emotions is referred to as ambivalence. In Motivational Interviewing, ambivalence is considered to be the central block in change because, whilst the pros and cons of use are evenly balanced, individuals will wait until the situation improves or worsens. This paralyses the change process and sustains use in the meantime.

Challenging an ambivalent client to change is counter-productive. When an ambivalent person is pressed towards change they tend to formulate an opinion in contradiction with a 'Yes, but . . .' response. This process is called reactance, and young people are particularly prone to taking this contradictory stance where they feel a sense of threat or a loss of personal freedom. In this way, Motivational Interviewing suggests that resistance to change is not necessarily caused by psychological denial but can be the product of a directing style of communication. So, it is essential that an MI practitioner does not present their opinions to their client, as this tends to cause reactance. Instead they adopt an *interviewing* style

where their role is to draw out the client's own reason for change.

It achieves this through utilising a distinct communication style called reflective listening, an advanced empathy technique that reflects back the deeper messages in the client's statement. Whilst paraphrasing is an element of this, reflective listening goes deeper. It will reflect back the implied meaning or emotional intent inherent in the client statements. Sometimes this is described as 'finishing the client's paragraph', in reflecting back what the client is not quite articulating. These reflections are selective in promoting 'change talk'. They gently direct the client to discuss the need for change, the benefits of change and their intention to change. This is often combined with a deep evaluation of the pros and cons of change in order to resolve mixed feelings towards it, which is seen as part of the process of committing to a change goal. It is imperative that conflict is avoided at all costs, and practitioners utilise a number of strategies to roll with any resistance to change.

A further consideration in Motivational Interviewing is the development of discrepancy within a young person. This is the discrepancy between, on the one hand, their stated goals and life aspirations, and their current behaviour on the other. As we have seen, the desire for internal consistency is a powerful drive in all human beings, and is especially important to young people who may be battling with identity formation. Motivational Interviewing's deep listening style reaches into the values of the individual in order to create a contrast between a young person's deeper beliefs and current behaviours. Where there is a profound contradiction between these elements of self it compels people to adjust. This can entail shifting someone's behaviour to be more harmonious with their aspirations. Alternatively people may shift their aspirations to account for the behaviour. When young people see a positive alternative to use which they believe they can attain, they strive for the former and amend behaviours accordingly. The approach has been manualised into a structured four-session model called Motivational Enhancement Therapy. It occurs within a framework of five key principles, sometimes referred to as the spirit of motivation (see Table 6.10).

Motivational Interviewing has shown very promising results with young people. Monti et al. (1999) studied the impact of Motivational

Table 6.10: Key principles of Motivational Interviewing

Principle	Description
Express empathy	Empathy – seeing the world through the client's eyes – is not a personal quality. Empathy is an active process whereby the practitioner must understand the deeper values, beliefs and wants of the client through reflective listening.
Avoid confrontation	Treatment outcomes are inversely proportional to the degree of confrontation experienced in treatment. High levels of confrontation lead to poor outcomes.
Roll with resistance	Resistance is part of the process of change. Resistance can be reduced by the communication style of the practitioner. Rolling with resistance with collaborative strategies is more helpful in overcoming these blocks to change than confronting it.
Develop discrepancy	Individuals desire internal consistency. Discrepancies between stated goals and current behaviour drive change as individuals feel compelled to close this gap. This is to the degree that where there is no internal discrepancy between the individual's aspirations and current behaviours, Motivational Interviewing is not possible.
Support self-efficacy	Self-efficacy describes the clients perception of their ability to perform a task to a given level. Clients with high self-efficacy persist in attaining tasks whilst those with low self-efficacy tend to give up. Motivational Interviewing helps the client to identify strategies that they believe will assist them to change. This is a democratic treatment process in supporting each individual client's belief in change.

Interviewing on 94 teens presenting at A&E department. These young people were randomly assigned to either Motivational Interviewing or Assessment & Information groups. At 6-month follow-up, the Motivational Interviewing group had a significantly reduced incidence of problem behaviours. They demonstrated a 32 per cent reduction in alcohol use and 50 per cent reduction in alcohol-related injuries compared to the young people in the Assessment & Information group. Motivational Interviewing not only appeared effective in reducing alcohol consumption in older teens but also produced significant reductions in their alcohol-related problems. This has been a consistent finding in a wide range of studies (Marlatt et al., 1998; Chick et al., 1985), and Motivational Interviewing appears to produce bigger reductions in consumption in young teens (Colby et al., 1999).

McCambridge & Strang (2004) studied the outcomes of Motivational Interviewing on 200 young people aged 16–20 who were using a wide range of substances. They were randomly assigned to either a single Motivational Interviewing session or a control group based on an Information Session. Comparison at follow-up showed a range of benefits for Motivational Interviewing. The control group increased smoking at three-month follow up by 12 per cent, whereas the Motivational Interviewing cohort reduced smoking tobacco by 21 per cent.

Furthermore, 25 per cent of the Motivational Interviewing group quit smoking compared to only 8 per cent in the control group. In terms of alcohol use, the control group increased units per week at follow-up by 12 per cent, whilst the Motivational Interviewing group decreased unit consumption by 39 per cent. In addition, 8 per cent of the Motivational Interviewing group quit drinking, whilst only 1 per cent of the control group did. The Motivational Interviewing cohort also reduced the frequency of cannabis smoking by 66 per cent (from 15.7 times a week to 5.4 times per week). In contrast the control group increased consumption by 27 per cent (from 13.3 times a week to 16.9). A further 16 per cent per cent of young people quit cannabis after receiving the Motivational Interviewing intervention compared to 5 per cent of the control group.

Brown (2001) adapted a brief intervention programme for young people called Project Options, which offered a wide range of choices and was heavily based on Motivational Interviewing. It was delivered in school settings where young people were offered a range of low intensity options to reduce or stop alcohol use. Brief interventions could be accessed through a variety of formats that included groups, individual sessions or a web-based intervention. The group programme was delivered across six sessions, the individual sessions were conducted in four sessions, whilst young people had unlimited access to the website. The interventions were developed in consultation with young people and focused on their concerns regarding alcohol use and preferred ways of managing problems. Extensive reviews were conducted to reduce barriers to accessing these interventions. The barrier that concerned young people the most was confidentiality. These interventions were designed to help young people evaluate their drinking, and receive feedback on their consumption and to reward their participation in the programme. The rewards were vouchers for clothing or food, which young people valued, but these were not available through the website-only option. It also combined many of the key findings from effective prevention programmes (based on Brown, 2001) that examined six key issues in alcohol use in a non-confrontational manner:

1. Prevalence and overestimations of normative consumption.
2. Expectancies regarding use.
3. Managing stress and urges without recourse to use.
4. Exploring the pros and cons of alcohol use.
5. Alternative rewarding activities to drinking.
6. Enhancing communication skills.

Project Options showed promising results at four-year follow up. Four schools were included in the initial programme with 6,000 students. Of these, a total number of 1,147 young people engaged in the programme. Those who engaged were younger and more likely to be African American or 'Multiple/Other' in ethnicity compared to the wider school population. A higher percentage of those teens who engaged in Project Options reported lifetime alcohol use (65 per cent vs. 60 per cent), however the school population reported more current drinking (during the previous 30 days). Boys were more likely to self-select the group format whilst ethnic minority youth were more likely to select the individual format. At follow-up, those that self-selected to enter the Project Options programmes exhibited high rates of reduced alcohol use and improvements in social functioning when compared to those that did not take up any option. Furthermore, the highest at-risk youth appeared to make the most substantial gains from the programme.

Project Options has shown the value of diversifying brief intervention options and adapting adult approaches for young people. It is important to recognise that brief interventions tend to operate on a 'mastery' approach. They identify previous strengths and resources that the individual has already acquired and helps re-direct those resources to addressing the current substance misuse issues. This means that they lend themselves to working with higher-functioning individuals who have developed personal resources. For example, many of the treatment population included in these studies were students who had achieved a high enough rate of life task accomplishment to have successfully progressed through the education system. As such, brief interventions can be effective stand-alone interventions for these individuals. Brief interventions may also be effective as an early intervention for those whose social attachments have not broken down yet. However, for young people who have profound experience of social exclusion, brief interventions may be less effective, as they will have greater skills deficits and less personal mastery to call upon. Here, Motivational Interviewing may be more effective as a primer for subsequent treatment. It may help these young people resolve to change their behaviour, but this would then need to be supported by additional treatment interventions. Individuals who receive an initial session of Motivational Interviewing tend to show higher compliance rates in subsequent treatment.

Specific modalities: Cognitive Behavioural and Behavioural approaches

The most common treatment delivered in community settings for young people with substance misuse problems is Cognitive Behavioural Therapy. Cognitive Behavioural Therapy is a generic name that covers a wide range of cognitive and behavioural approaches. A skills model based on social learning theory, it assumes that the human behaviours are primarily governed by individuals' self-efficacy belief. Self-efficacy belief is our expectation that we can perform a task to a given standard. As such, self-efficacy beliefs are highly specific. For example, a young person will have different self-efficacy beliefs regarding how good they are at mathematics, creative writing, a sport or dancing. However, self-efficacy belief is not the actual ability someone possesses, but their perception of it. In turn these beliefs regarding ability do affect their performance. For example, a young person who has negative self-efficacy beliefs regarding their ability to do mathematics will fear failure. They will invest less in trying to solve the problem and may give up easily. This failure then supports their negatives beliefs in their performance. Alternatively, a young person with high self-efficacy belief in their ability to do mathematics will invest more in trying to solve a problem and persist. As they do not fear failure, they focus on the task at hand. The successful resolution of the problem then increases their belief in their ability to resolve more challenging problems in the future. This is referred to as 'reciprocal determinism' and describes how belief, performance and response are inter-linked. If an individual's self-efficacy beliefs are very negative, they will avoid challenges completely. As a result they do not get an opportunity to evaluate their performance and correct it. This then sustains the negative expectations of performance.

Self-efficacy is derived from four key sources. The first of these, mastery, is the most powerful single source. It is only through performing a task that young people can assess their actual performance. Feedback and reflection can then refine the acquisition of the new skill. The second, comparison with others, can also shape self-belief. If a young person perceives someone who they believe is not very good at a task succeed, they will assume that they can achieve it too. Alternatively, if the young person perceives someone who they believe is proficient at a task fail, then it may reduce their own self-belief. The third, persuasion, trying to convince someone they have more ability than they actually have, is the least effective means of developing self-efficacy belief. Whilst praising achievement is helpful, simply trying to convince someone that they are good at something will not impact on

their self-efficacy belief at all. However, it is easy to play on their fears and undermine self-efficacy belief. The fourth source of self-efficacy is arousal. Individuals experience stress when they attempt a task as they focus on their anxiety. This reduces the performance considerably and generates more stress. As a result, stress management approaches always increase chances of positive treatment outcomes because it allows people to focus on the task achievement.

Cognitive Behavioural Therapy assumes that similar processes operate with substance use. Young people may lack self-efficacy belief in dealing with stress or difficult situations. They may therefore rely upon drugs or alcohol to cope with these demands as opposed to their own personal resources. This means that they do not develop self-efficacy belief in their own internal coping resources. This may also extend to other areas. They may not be confident in their ability to refuse drugs or alcohol, or to deal with urges, temptations or cravings to use. The Cognitive Behavioural Therapy approach operates by assessing a young person's triggers in high-risk situations and then teaches them a range of coping skills to help overcome the triggers without resorting to use. These skills can be 'global' in that they apply to all young people, like problem solving, or be specific in that they may apply to issues that are specific to particular young people, such as anger management (see Table 6.11). The practitioner's role in this is one of 'guided mastery'. It is closer to teaching than therapy in helping young people identify triggers, provide new strategies to deal with them and then provide feedback on their application of these skills in real-life settings. It is essential in Cognitive Behavioural Therapy that young people apply these skills in challenging situations. Without this level of personal mastery they will not foster their self-efficacy belief in managing triggers.

Table 6.11: Examples of coping strategies in Cognitive Behavioural Therapy.

Global coping strategies	Specific coping strategies
Dealing with urges and cravings	Assertiveness
Refusal skills	Anger management
Avoidance and escape	Dealing with intrusive memories
Problem solving	Anxiety management
Communication skills	Healthy relationships
Systematic relaxation	Dealing with grief

Kaminer et al. (1998) evaluated the outcomes of a number of Cognitive Behavioural Therapy programmes for adolescents based on the procedures developed for a treatment matching study. In this study, 32 dually diagnosed (i.e. substance misuse and mental health) young people aged 13–18 were randomly assigned to Cognitive Behavioural Therapy or a dynamic family group therapy for 12 weeks. The Cognitive Behavioural Therapy group made significant improvements more rapidly than the family group, but these advantages were not sustained at 12-month follow-up. In a larger study, Kaminer et al. (2002b) compared Cognitive Behavioural Therapy with psycho-education therapies. 88 dually diagnosed adolescents were randomly assigned to one of the two 8-week interventions. Older, male youths showed significant reductions in use in the Cognitive Behavioural interventions, with lower positive urinalysis test results. Self-reported drug use measures improved for both groups, but with a higher trend for the Cognitive Behavioural Therapy condition. Relapse rates were similar for both groups at 9-month follow-up.

Closely related to Cognitive Behavioural Therapy is Behavioural Therapy. Behavioural Therapy models also believe that behaviours like drug and alcohol use are learned. However it places greater emphasis on the environmental interactions in this learning through a process called operant conditioning. Operant conditioning suggests that when a given behaviour produces desirable consequences it will be repeated. Alternatively, if a given behaviour produces punishing consequences, it will reduce the behaviour that produced it. For example if you go to restaurant and the food is great, value for money and you get good service, you will visit that restaurant again. However, if the food is poor, expensive and the service terrible, you will stop going to that restaurant. Drug and alcohol use is conditioned by these same consequences. If using drugs or alcohol results in euphoria, excitement, acceptance and relief of stress, it will increase use. If the consequences are highly aversive, such as sickness, rejection and conflicts, then it will reduce use. As the beneficial effects of substance use are felt immediately and the negative consequences are delayed, drugs and alcohol are very powerful reinforcers for continued use. Behavioural models therefore assume that behaviours are shaped by the consequences they produce. In order to change drug and alcohol use, the consequence of consumption must become increasingly averse and the benefits of non-use must become increasingly attractive.

Behavioural therapies spend a great deal of time assessing the natural reinforcers in a young person's life, the desired activities in their wider life. Each young person is unique in the relationships, activities, behaviours and beliefs that they most value. Systematically identifying from this wide range of behaviours those that produce desirable consequences in every domain of the young person's life underpins the development of comprehensive care plans. This recovery-orientated plan maximises motivations in the young person to achieve the most highly desired outcomes. Behavioural Therapy models then offer a comprehensive programme of skills to help young people achieve those outcomes. The skills are not just linked to changing substance use, but may also encompass a wide range of life skills to facilitate access to better alternatives in things such as healthy relationships, social/recreational behaviour, communication skills and education/training, amongst others.

Contingencies

An adjunct to Behavioural Therapy is the use of contingencies to enhance treatment outcomes. Contingencies are rewards given to clients only when they successfully achieve stated goals such as providing clean urine samples or attending a set number of treatment appointments. Rewards can include vouchers, on-site retail items, social reinforcement, treatment privileges or access to highly prized recreational opportunities. The strength of the reward must be able to compete with the reinforcing effects of drugs or alcohol. Whilst contingency management strategies have demonstrated positive outcomes with adults they have been under-studied with adolescents. Some trials have been conducted but not in randomised conditions. Contingencies have been found useful with young people in cessation of smoking (Roll, 2005), cannabis use (Kamon, et al. 2005) and poly-drug use (Lott & Jenicus, 2009).

Public suspicion has limited the expansion of contingency management programmes. This suspicion may be due to the limits of language. The use of rewards to alter behaviour is often considered to be a form of bribery. However, bribes are the use of incentives to encourage anti-social behaviour, such as bribing a policeman to not charge you for breaking the law. Contingencies management on the other hand is explicitly designed to reward pro-social behaviour. People do not consider themselves bribed by wages and bonuses in the workforce, or to be bribed when they receive affection from their families. As we lack a word that denotes this positive bias, the use of contingencies is often seen as negative. The treatment field can also be suspicious of the use of incentives where change is often seen as its own reward. However, research demonstrates that successful changers use rewards heavily in their recovery, so they are a key mechanism in the change process (Prochaska et al., 1994).

The use of contingencies in treatment needs careful management. Petry (2000) recommended a set of procedures to optimise the use of rewards, including specifying the exact behavioural change that will be rewarded with incentives. The application of rewards should be simple, and be stated simply in a behavioural contract that states the period of time over which they will be applied. Behavioural approaches also require consistency. Applying rewards without meeting the stated requirement will not influence behaviour at all. It will also generate a sense of injustice in those who have maintained their contracts. But in contexts of low retention and treatment completion rates amongst young people, contingency management offers an additional strategy to enhance outcomes for young people.

Community reinforcement

The most fully developed Behavioural approach is the Community Reinforcement Approach (CRA) which was originally developed to treat long-term, highly excluded alcohol users. It is an intensive case management model that identifies positive reinforcers to change in wide range of social domains. This process is then combined with relapse prevention strategies and attention to a wide array of life skills. The success of the programme led to the development of the Adolescent-Community Reinforcement Approach (A-CRA) (Godley et al., 2009). This approach has proved equally effective with long-term socially excluded young people such as runaways and street homeless youth. For example, in one study (Slesnick et al., 2007) high-risk street homeless youth with high rates of mental illness were randomly assigned to either the A-CRA approach or treatment as usual. Youth assigned to the A-CRA approach significantly reduced substance use (37 per cent vs. 17 per cent reduction), reduced depression (40 per cent vs. 23 per cent) and increased social stability (58 per cent vs. 13 per cent). Both groups improved in many other domains such as substance use, internalising and externalising symptoms and coping. Azrin et al. (1994a; 1994b) conducted two trials comparing the CRA approach with generic supportive counselling for a mixed group of adults and 14 adolescents. This was followed up by a comparison study including 26 adolescents. Each modality was delivered once a week over a 12-month period. Follow-up results showed greater reductions in use and negative urine screens in the CRA groups.

One of the largest randomised control trials conducted on young people examined the effectiveness of both Cognitive Behavioural Therapy and A-CRA in the Cannabis Youth Treatment trial (Dennis et al., 2002). This was a large scale multi-comparison study conducted on 600 adolescents who were randomly assigned to one of five different interventions. They were then followed up at 3 and 12 months post treatment. Two Cognitive Behavioural Therapy group programmes were offered that initiated treatment with Motivational Enhancement sessions, followed by 3 or 10 CBT sessions. A third intervention included Motivational Enhancement and Cognitive Behavioural Therapy, plus a six-week family psycho-education add-on. In addition, a 12-week A-CRA and a 12-week family therapy intervention were also included. Dennis et al. (2004) reported significant reductions in use in all treatment interventions at 3- and 12-month follow-up, including reductions in problem behaviours. Cognitive Behavioural Therapy plus family support offered more rapid treatment gains than the brief Cognitive Behavioural Therapy intervention alone. The individual and group CBT produced better outcomes than family therapy. However, these advantages were not sustained at follow-up where outcomes equalised across all modalities. The biggest predictor of treatment gains was the initial level of subjective improvement. In general, it suggested that groups were an effective means of delivering treatment to young people with only smaller gains being made when CBT was delivered on a one-to-one basis.

Specific modalities: the Twelve Step Approach

A more traditional approach in the US has been the use of the Twelve Step Treatment programme. The Twelve Step programme was developed in the 1930s as a self-help movement to assist adult problem drinkers in the form of Alcoholics Anonymous. Lack of wider treatment services and an increasing social trend towards wider substance abuse led to the development of spin-off movements such as Narcotics Anonymous and Cocaine Anonymous which shared the same underlying aims and values as the original alcohol movement. The Twelve Step fellowship has since become a global movement whereby people with substance-related problems can attend meetings with others in recovery to find mutual support and encouragement based on the Twelve Step philosophy. This philosophy assumes that addictions are a disease and that total abstinence is the only route to recovery. Abstinence can be achieved through following the Twelve Steps, described in Figure 6.2.

The Twelve Steps are twelve therapeutic exercises that the person in recovery works through, either with a Twelve Step counsellor or through a sponsor. A sponsor is an individual who has progressed further in their own recovery and who offers a wide range of support to the new member working the programme. Usually the first steps are worked on in treatment centres followed by the later steps being conducted in the community. Proponents of the Twelve Steps believe that working this programme culminates in the achievement of a spiritual awakening that is transformative and supports sobriety for the rest of an individual's life. The effectiveness of the Twelve Step programme is difficult to evaluate for a number of reasons. First, as it is an anonymous self-help movement, it can be difficult to track over time the young people who have been involved. Second, the Twelve Step programme is often delivered by a range of services including professional inpatient treatment programmes, professional outpatient treatment programmes and community self-help groups. There can be a great deal of diversity in these meetings, depending on the age, composition and the values of the group members that attend. So, although the Twelve Step philosophy suggests a unified movement, in actual practice it is an extremely diverse organisation.

Although designed to address long term substance misuse problems in adults, the programme has been adapted to supporting young people (see Jaffe, 1990; 2000). Studies conducted on young people who attend the programme have shown promising results. The studies of Harris & Hoffman (1989) and Hsieh et al. (1998) followed 2,300 young people treated in

---

Figure 6.2: The Twelve Steps   Alcoholics Anonymous, 1952

1 We admitted that we are powerless over our addiction -that our lives had become unmanageable.

2 We came to believe that a power greater than ourselves could restore us to sanity.

3 We made a decision to turn our will and our lives over to the care of God as we understood God.

4 We made a searching and fearless moral inventory of ourselves.

5 We admitted to God, to ourselves, and to another human being the exact nature of our wrongs.

6 We were entirely ready to have God remove all these defects of character.

7 We humbly asked God to remove our shortcomings.

8 We made a list of all persons we had harmed, and became willing to make amends to them all.

9 We made direct amends to such people wherever possible, except when to do so would injure them or others.

10 We continued to take personal inventory and when we were wrong promptly admitted it.

11 We sought through prayer and meditation to improve our conscious contact with God as we understood God, praying only for knowledge of God's will for us and the power to carry that out.

12 Having had a spiritual awakening as the result of these steps, we tried to carry this message to other addicts, and to practice these principles in all our affairs.

24 different Twelve Step residential programmes and found an abstinence rate of 50 per cent at 12-month follow-up. Winters et al.'s (2000) systematic study compared the outcomes of 179 young people who received a Twelve Step treatment programme with 66 similar young people who could not access treatment. At one-year follow-up, 53 per cent of the Twelve Step group had achieved abstinence or a low rate of relapse compared to 28 per cent on the non-treated group. These benefits continued at 5-year follow-up, particularly for those young people who sustained Twelve Step engagement and attendance (Winters et al., 2007).

In an interesting series of studies, Kelly et al. examined the critical elements of the Twelve Steps that appeared to be particularly salient to young people. Kelly et al. (2000) found high rates of abstinence post-treatment for 99 young people who had received residential care. At 3-month follow-up 33 per cent had sustained abstinence, even after relatively short treatment episodes. This research suggested that attendance had increased young people's motivation for abstinence as a treatment goal. Furthermore, Kelly et al. (2002) found that the use of a sponsor *and* engaging in the Twelve Steps increased young people's motivation for abstinence to higher degree than just attendance at meetings. In terms of the benefits of inpatient Twelve Step treatment, Kelly et al. (2008) found that every group meeting that a young person attended equated to an additional two days clean time over an 8-year follow-up.

Whilst the limited research available does support the use of the Twelve Step programme for young people, many young people do not find the abstinence orientation appealing, as we have seen. This research may demonstrate that the programme may be most beneficial for those young people who find the approach meaningful rather than for the general population of young people as a whole, or for those who report more severe problem use. It is important to recognise that the community based Twelve Step programmes are unfacilitated groups with a wide age range of people in attendance. This may make it an inappropriate treatment setting for vulnerable young people. Kelly et al. (2005) found that the age composition of the group meetings was a critical factor in increasing adolescent's attendance.

Treatment matching interventions

The modalities reviewed so far pertain directly to substance misuse, including alcohol misuse. Whilst some have shown some promise in addressing wider mental health problems, they are not specifically developed to address these particular issues. Addressing mental health is vital to long term outcomes for young people. If their drug and alcohol use is influenced by mental illness, then drug and alcohol symptoms are liable to return after treatment that does not address mental health, which will undermine long-term drug and alcohol treatment gains. It is also important to recognise that what may be effective in addressing one mental health issue, for example poor impulse control, may differ from what might help another, such as depression. This suggests that matching treatment to the disorder may be helpful. Treatment matching is a process whereby an individual is 'matched' with a treatment approach that is most likely to offer the optimal treatment outcome for them. Interest has increased in treatment matching over the last 30 years, largely as a result of research advances and the proliferation of treatment models. This interest has focussed on a number of different ways that matching can be applied, including matching therapies to types of personality, matching intensity of treatment to functioning or identifying the key variables of therapies that different client groups respond to.

At present there has been mixed evidence to support the idea that matching clients to treatment modalities leads to improved outcomes (Magura et al., 2003; McKay et al., 1997; McLellan & McKay, 1998). For example, one of the central aims of Project MATCH, a $36 million randomised control trial for problem drinkers, was to attempt to identify what specific factors predicted treatment response to the three different therapies. This trial specifically tested 64 different variables, including the value of matching clients' personality to treatment type, but found no evidence to support this approach. All three treatment modalities produced a similar range of outcomes, regardless of the personality type of the clients involved. This inability to effectively match people into appropriate treatment has been attributed to a number of factors. Gastfreind et al. (2000) suggested that it was in part due to the multiple and complex problems that clients bring to treatment, making it difficult to determine which client characteristics should be matched with what treatment. Moyer et al. (2001) suggested that the research methodologies are not yet sufficiently advanced to analyse the data meaningfully.

It is important to note though that randomised control trials compare very similar treatment models which are appropriate to the disorder that this is being treated. For example, Project MATCH tested the efficacy of Motivational Enhancement Therapy, Cognitive Behaviour Therapy and Twelve Step Facilitation which are all specifically designed to address alcohol problems. But just because treatment matching at this level produced no differences does not mean that treatment matching should be ignored. No research has been done on comparing the outcomes of approaches which are not designed to treat the same disorder. For example, it is not known how a client with a Conduct Disorder would respond to a treatment approach designed to address an Anxiety Disorder. It is plausible that the client is unlikely to respond to, or even to continue to engage in, a programme that felt irrelevant to their presenting problem. Therefore the value of treatment matching may not lie so much in improving the success rate of outcomes of clients who do respond to the treatment, as they will always be capped by the pace at which the individual can implement change. But matching may assist in the *prevention of poorer outcomes* by ensuring that the treatment programme is relevant to the clients' lives.

Moreover, whilst matching the personality of clients to treatment has not shown any real advantage, there has been considerable progress in understanding the factors that influence an individual client's outcome and response to treatment. Greater severity of substance-related problems, the presence and severity of psychiatric problems, low social support and unemployment all have a strong influence on poor outcome response (McLellan & McKay, 1998). This is again indicative that it is the deficits in personal resources in the extra-therapeutic domain that have such a big impact on overall treatment outcome. Furthermore, there is a consistent research finding that addressing significant mental illness and substance misuse simultaneously is associated with improved outcomes (McLellan et al., 1993; 1997). For example, sequential treatment models, that address substance use and then mental illness (or vice versa) tend to produce worse outcomes than

integrated treatment that addresses both concurrently (Ridgely et al., 1986; 1987). This finding is important for the treatment of young people, as externalised and internalised mental health problems are such powerful and common pathways into young people's substance misuse problems. To this extent matching treatment approaches to the specific mental health disorder may improve outcomes for young people, especially amongst those with the poorest treatment response rate. At the very least, it may prevent the worsening of treatment response by increasing treatment's relevance to such young people's lives.

Treating substance misuse and mental health

There has been very little research on the effectiveness of treating both substance use and mental illness with young people. This is striking when considering that both disorders are so entwined in the sub-trajectories that lead young people into problem use. There have been large scale literature reviews and meta-analyses offering evidence that there is a treatment-matching effect in specific disorders in young people. The American Psychological Association (APA) developed the APA Division 12 Task Force Criteria for empirically supported treatment. These are strict criteria that are applied to published research in English. Based on outcomes and the quality of the research studies, these literature reviews categorise treatment evidence as 'well-established', 'probably efficacious', 'possibly efficacious' and 'experimental'. For the 'well-established' criteria to be met, the modality must be subject to evaluation from two independent research teams and must achieve clinically significant outcomes beyond medication, placebo or another treatment.

Based on these literature reviews we see a general trend in treatment outcomes amongst externalised and internalised disorders. In general, Behavioural models demonstrate more significant outcomes for externalised behavioural problems whereas Cognitive Behavioural Therapy shows greater efficacy with internalised disorders. Behavioural approaches with strong boundary setting and with focus on incentives to change may appeal more to externalised youth who need reigning in. Whilst the emphasis on improved coping skills and increased self-efficacy belief in Cognitive Behavioural Therapy would

Table 6.12: Overview of APA Task Force Reviews

Disorder	Well-established	Probably efficacious	Not supported
Attention Deficit Disorder	• Behavioural Parent Training • School based Behavioural Reinforcing • Summer Intensive (200–400 hours) day programmes focussed on Social Skills		• Non-behavioural models (Individual, Play, Cognitive) • Social Skills training in clinical settings
Conduct and Oppositional Defiance in adolescents	• CBT Group and Individual formats. (CBT models included MET and CRA) • Functional Family Therapy	• CBT (Rational Emotive Mental Health Program & Group Assertiveness training) • Multi-Systemic Therapy • Multi-Dimensional Foster Care • Family Behavioural Treatment • Functional Family Therapy	
Depression	• Coping with depression • Interpersonal therapy	• CBT • Interpersonal therapy	
Anxiety		• Coping Cat probably efficacious for separation anxiety, generalised anxiety and social phobia • CBT and Group CBT • Group CBT with parents • CBT for social anxiety • Social effectiveness training for social anxiety disorder • CBT for OCD	
PTSD	Trauma Focused CBT		

Based on Corcoran, 2011.

be more relevant to the internalised young people (see Table 6.12).

The Cochrane Collaboration is an international non-profit organisation that conducts systematic meta-analytic reviews on health and mental health treatment outcomes. Meta-analysis is a technique that combines treatment outcome results from numerous studies to produce a summary of empirical evidence. The Cochrane Collaboration meta-analysis concurs with the APA task force reviews. Reviewing published studies suggests Behavioural approaches are more effective in treating externalised disorders. Treating many of them also requires family involvement, for example as an adjunct to Behavioural approaches which look to influence behaviour by shaping environments that increase or decrease its occurrence. Cognitive Behavioural Therapy appears more helpful with internalised

disorders. Again, it is not always clearly stated whether these Cognitive Behavioural Therapy approaches are developmentally informed. The thinking processes of young people differ from those of adults due to meta-cognition in puberty. Adapting Cognitive Behavioural Therapy to account for these differences may improve its outcomes further (see Table 6.13).

In general, meta-analysis has demonstrated that treatment interventions produce moderate to mild outcomes for young people with both substance misuse and mental health disorders. It also recognises the substantial contribution that alliance factors contribute to these outcomes. But there appears to be bias favouring Behavioural approaches to help young people with externalised problems and to favouring Cognitive Behavioural approaches to assist young people with internalised disorders. It is important to

Table 6.13: Overview of Cochran Collaboration Findings

Disorder	Treatment
Externalised disorders	
Attention Deficit Disorder/Attention Deficit and Hyperactivity Disorder	• Parent Training • Behaviour Therapy
Oppositional Defiance/Conduct Disorder (Children)	• Behavioural Parent Training • Webster-Stratton Parent Training • Non-Behavioural Family Therapy • Social Skills • CBT demonstrated poor outcomes
Oppositional Defiance/Conduct Disorder (Adolescent)	• Family Behavioural Therapy • MST Family Therapy and CBT demonstrated poor outcomes • A-CRA/MET demonstrated promising outcomes
Externalised Disorders and Substance Abuse	• Individual Cognitive Problem Solving • Family Behavioural Treatment
Internalised disorders Anxiety Disorders	• CBT
Post-Traumatic Stress Disorder	• CBT had a modest effect • Parent Involved CBT
Depression	• Cognitive Behavioural Therapy • Social Skills had modest effect • Family Therapy • Interpersonal Therapy showed promising outcomes
Eating Disorders	• Maudsley Model of Family Therapy • CBT • MET showed promising outcomes

Based on Corcoran, 2011.

remember that this is not an exhaustive list of therapies open to young people. These are just the therapeutic models whose research base was sufficiently robust to evaluate. There could be other promising approaches which had not been evaluated sufficiently to be included in these large scale reviews.

Treatment for externalised disorders

The emergence of conduct disorders in early childhood increases the risk of substance involvement. In particular, the emergence of Oppositional Defiance Disorder in the later stage of early childhood appears to be a particularly strong predictor of future problem use (Sung et al., 2004). Other researchers have suggested that young people with a combination of ADHD (with its impulsive behaviour) and Conduct Disorder (which violates social norms) offers a substantially higher risk for drug and alcohol

involvement than one diagnosis alone (Molina et al., 2002). For example, Flory & Lynam (2003) consistently found that the ADHD diagnosis alone was highly predictive of tobacco use but not of other substances. Furthermore, substance use and externalising disorders appear to exacerbate each other (Hovens et al., 1994).

Early and chaotic involvement in alcohol and drug use may be an expression of an impulsive temperament (Kendler et al., 1993). As we have seen in Chapter 2, this impulsive temperament may have a genetic component. However, the emergence of impulsive temperament disorders is multi-faceted and shares in common many risk factors with the evolution of substance misuse disorders. These occur across multiple social domains of a young person's life including family, peers and school. For example, whilst most research suggests a genetic origin of externalised disorders, Rutter et al. (2006) found that environmental stresses predicted their form and severity. Externalised children in boundaried environments experience suppression of impulsivity. Externalised children in under-parented environments may entrench their impulsivity. This suggests that externalised disorders may be amenable to change through adjusting environmental supports, despite the genetic inheritability.

Young people with externalised disorders tend to show poorer outcomes in substance misuse treatment services, with high and early relapse rates (Brown et al., 1996; Clark & Scheid, 2001). Furthermore, 61 per cent of Conduct Disordered youth met the diagnosis for Anti-Social Personality Disorder at post-treatment follow-up and also exhibited higher levels of drug use than non-Conduct Disordered youth. Kaminer et al. (1992) found that Conduct Disordered youth had far higher drop-out rates in treatment than those with both Conduct Disorder *and* Depression. This pattern was also detected in the Complexity Index (Revised) reviewed in Chapter 3. As externalised youth age they appear to become more susceptible to internalised disorders such as depression. This may be the result of increased self-awareness in the young person who begins to recognise what impact their behaviour has had. This can result in exclusion, peer rejection and social impairment. This increased awareness may also increase their motivation to change. These older chaotic users with poly-drug use problems are also more likely to select abstinence as a treatment goal.

Several issues are pertinent to assessing young people with externalised disorder needs. It can be difficult to separate the symptoms of the externalised disorders from the effects of drugs and alcohol. For example, is shop lifting an impulsive act or is it driven by a compulsion to raise funds for drugs or alcohol? As externalised disorders precede drug and alcohol use, assessment should examine a young person's pre-use history. They are liable to exhibit a wide range of offending behaviour, exclusions from school and truancy prior to the age of 11. Externalised youth also appear to have a tendency to bias their descriptions of their consumption as less damaging than it is in reality. Rather than multiple assessment tools for each externalised disorder, it is preferable to use a single assessment tool, the Disruptive Behaviour Disorders Rating Scale (Pelham et al., 1992), which is based on the *DSM (IV-TR)* diagnostic criteria and which screens for all externalised disorders, and which suggests that externalised disorders may be amenable to change through adjusting these environmental supports.

In terms of treatment, a number of protocols have been developed for the treatment of adolescents with externalised disorders. In the UK, the National Institute of Clinical Excellence's (NICE, 2007) meta-analysis review of psycho-social treatment outcomes for children identified that clinically significant outcomes could be achieved with this treatment population through the use of parent training and education programmes. The outcomes included reduction in externalised symptoms in the child as well as well as reduction in parental depression (see Figure 6.3). These recommendations are also

---

Figure 6.3: Recommendations for treatment for Externalised disorders in children   NICE, 2007

- Group work parent-training programmes were optimal with one-to-one sessions only for parents with complex needs.

- Programmes should be informed by social learning theory.

- Programmes should include strategies to enhance parent-child relationships.

- Optimal treatment should be between 8 and 12 sessions lasting 1–2 hours.

- Enable parents to identify their own parenting objectives.

- Incorporate active learning processes such as role play and homework to generalise learning into the home situation.

- Be delivered by appropriately trained skilled facilitators who are supervised and have access to on-going professional development and who can foster positive working alliances with parents.

- Adhere to the programme manual and employ all necessary materials to ensure high treatment fidelity.

- Programmes should demonstrate effectiveness through randomised control trials or through suitable rigorous evaluation methods undertaken independently.

important in the treatment of older adolescents with behavioural problems.

The key finding for treatment research is that multi-modal and integrated treatment is most effective for externalised disorders. Where substance use is entrenched or chaotic in a young person, stabilisation of drug and alcohol use is preferable before commencing with treatment to address psycho-social problems. Medications to control impulse behaviours can be useful in the short term but should never be provided without comprehensive additional psycho-social support. Controversy exists on the use of prescribed medications for ADHD such as Methylphenidate which is a similar drug to cocaine. This medication binds more rapidly with dopamine transporter sites in the brain than cocaine does, although oral administration diminishes this rapid take-up effect (Kollins, 2007). Whilst no long term studies have been conducted on medications' role in prompting future levels of substance use, longitudinal research suggests that medications can be a protection factor insulating young people against future use (Wilens et al., 2003).

Whilst externalised youth may benefit from standard treatments for drug and alcohol use, certain modalities have been exposed to greater evaluation than others. Comprehensive Behavioural models produce the best outcomes, such as A-CRA, or the Behavioural/Family Therapy models that are reviewed in a subsequent section of this chapter. Cognitive Behavioural Therapy may be less useful because of the operation of the brain. Impulse behaviours are located in the limbic regions of the brain that control desires and emotions. These regions of the brain operate more quickly than the higher brain centres located in the pre-frontal cortex. This means that impulses can occur and be enacted before the brain can engage consciously with the thought processes which Cognitive Behavioural Therapy hopes to modify. In general, treatment prognosis is better for individuals who seek treatment early in their drug or alcohol using career, highlighting the importance of early interventions (McLellan et al., 1983).

Treatment for depression

Rates of depression increase across adolescence and there is a historical trend for depression to occur at increasingly low age ranges (Helzer &

Prybeck, 1988). As depression in youth is both chronic and episodic, the presence of depression in adolescence will increase the risk of depression in later life. Depression has been found to influence drug and alcohol treatment processes in a number of ways. Depressed youth show increased dropout rates, poorer treatment responses and earlier relapse (Curry et al., 2003). Depression has also increased the risk of suicide or attempted suicide. A large scale epidemiological study found that 75 per cent of young people with co-morbidity (drug/alcohol and mental health diagnoses) reported that depression preceded substance use (Reiger et al., 1990). Whilst this might suggest a self-medication theory of adolescent substance use, little empirical evidence supports this suggestion. There is no evidence, for example, that young people with certain disorders take specific drugs to manage specific symptoms. Rather, young people appear to take any substances that are available to them just to feel different. But there is considerable evidence that substance use increases the severity of depressive symptoms in young people (Tomlinson et al., 2005).

Grella et al. (2001) also found that young people with depression and substance-related disorders required much greater treatment time than youth with depression alone. Long term treatment may also be more effective than brief interventions. This has led to the suggestion that two phases of treatment are important for depressed youth who substance misuse. The first phase consists of an individually tailored treatment plan that addresses: substance use, psycho-education, the benefits of treatment, mental health and drug interactions, and consequences of non-engagement. The second phase should focus on relapse prevention in order to protect treatment gains. As such, optimal treatment for depressed youth may operate for 9–15 months.

In terms of psycho-social treatment, there have been numerous studies of young people that have included a large contingent of depressed youth, but the treatment response of the depressed sub-group is not always separated out in their analysis. It is important to establish whether treatment that focuses on depression and substance misuse is more effective than treating substance misuse treatment alone. Two studies have found that substance abuse treatment alone did not decrease symptoms of depression (Kaminer et al., 2002a; Riggs et al., 2005). This may be because of the issues in complex cases, described in Chapter 4, where treatment gains in one domain do not automatically generalise to other areas of life. Curry et al. (2003) developed a combined treatment programme that incorporated two substance misuse group sessions per week combined with one family therapy session per week in outpatient settings. This multi-modal approach has shown promising outcomes but conclusions are limited by a small sample population.

Some research has examined the outcomes of combined psycho-social treatment and medication. Riggs et al. (2005) studied the impact of Cognitive Behavioural Therapy, anti-depressants or a combination of both on 126 young people. Young people receiving the anti-depressant Fluoxetine demonstrated improved remission rates from depression over a placebo at and beyond 13 weeks. This reduction in depressive symptoms was strongly related to reduction in use of substances. Those young people who experienced no relief from depressive symptoms had little improvement in terms of substance use. Again, treatment outcomes also appeared to take longer in comparison to non-depressed youth, emphasising the importance of long term treatment. Cornelius et al.'s (2009) study of combined therapies found little difference between Fluoxetine and placebo groups, with both groups reporting improvement in depression and alcohol consumption. This may have been as a result of a smaller sample population or a more psycho-social intervention than was delivered in the Riggs et al. (2005) study.

Treatment for anxiety disorders

Anxiety disorders have been found to be the most common mental health problem in those young people presenting for substance use treatment, with specific phobias occurring in 5 per cent of community samples. The medium average age of onset is 15, which is an earlier onset than depression (medium age 19). Anxiety disorders can encompass a wide range of sub-groups including Social Phobia, Generalised Anxiety Disorder, Phobias, Obsessive Compulsive Disorder, Separation Anxiety and Panic Disorder. There is little clinical evidence to support the need for specific treatments for each sub-type of anxiety (Clark et al., 2008). This is because there

can be considerable overlap between Social Phobia, Separation Anxiety and Generalised Anxiety Disorder. Furthermore, anxiety is likely to co-occur with Depression though this is more likely to occur in females than in males (Clark et al., 1994).

Interactions between anxiety disorders and substance abuse may vary according to age. As we have seen in earlier chapters, children with anxiety disorders often delay the initiation of drug and alcohol use. However, once initiated, consumption increases dramatically. This suggests that young people with anxiety must cross a fear barrier of initiation, but that subsequent symptom relief may escalate their use rapidly. The nature of the anxiety disorder may also influence initiation. Social Anxiety has been found to be a strong determinant of problematic use (Buckner et al., 2008; Zimmermann et al., 2003). Goodwin et al. (2004) identified that the increased risk of anxiety disorders and substance use combined was not an independent variable, but linked to childhood experience, family/peer influences, prior use and co-morbid depression.

Treatment for anxiety disorders in young people has focussed on key areas. This has included psycho-education for children and parents, family therapy, individual psycho-social therapy and medications. There is some evidence that even after cessation of drug or alcohol use there is often continuation of anxiety symptoms young people. This disorder itself may also preclude certain forms of treatment. For example, Social Anxiety or Social Phobia may inhibit group participation. Conversely, Separation Anxiety may influence participation in therapy with or without parental involvement whereby young people may not agree to any form of therapy without parental involvement. This demands careful management in treatment. Whilst it is considered necessary to assist parents to create a stable environment for young people with substance misuse problems, anxiety disorders may require the parents to reduce their support gradually in order to foster greater autonomy and independence in the young person. Achieving this will require supporting parents to reduce their own anxiety at the same time. This shift from parental enmeshment to separation needs to be well timed in the treatment processes for both parties.

Limited studies have been conducted on treatment for anxiety in young people. Psychodynamic Therapy has proved more effective for pre-adolescent children than for adolescents (Target & Fonagy, 1994). Most studies conducted to date have centred on the use of Cognitive Behavioural Therapies. These studies have shown positive and enduring outcomes (Comptom et al., 2004; Kendall et al., 2004). This success may be located in Cognitive Behavioural Therapies' focus on increasing self-efficacy belief in managing anxiety-promoting situations. These programmes increase a young person's coping repertoire followed by gradual exposure to the anxiety-promoting trigger. This increases their confidence in managing the stressor in increasingly challenging circumstances. Cognitive restructuring can also help young people re-assess the negative thought patterns that can exacerbate their anxiety. If young people always fear the worst by catastrophising every situation it will arouse high levels of anxiety. Challenging these thinking patterns can reduce anxiety. Again, these thought re-structuring approaches need to take into account young people's unique thinking styles. For example, the invisible audience effect can generate deep anxiety in young people. Relaxation skills can relieve anxiety symptoms as well as help a young person to focus on immediate tasks rather than on their arousal. Combined psycho-social and medication therapies have received little clinical evaluation. Therefore the recommendations for prescribing to anxious youth with substance use disorders are similar for presenting to those without substance use problems.

Treatment for Post-Traumatic Stress Disorder

PTSD is the only mental illness that has an aetiology, whereby a young person must have been exposed to a life threatening or horrifying event. The symptoms include intrusive recall, avoidance, emotional numbing, an ability to experience joy and detachment. Whilst the occurrence of PTSD is 1 per cent (Copeland et al., 2007) in the general population, rates are far higher in clinical samples. Kilpatrick et al. (2003) found that 5 per cent of their treatment sample experienced PTSD. Abram et al. (2004) found an incidence rate of 11 per cent in youth justice samples. The incidence rate of problematic substance misuse is very high within populations diagnosed with the disorder. Kilpatrick et al. (2003) also found that 24 per cent of girls and 30

per cent of boys with PTSD had co-occurring substance misuse problems. The needs of the young people with PTSD were increasingly complex. They were four times more likely to have other, co-occurring mental health disorders in addition to their substance misuse. Furthermore, these concurrent mental illnesses tended to be twice as severe in PTSD disordered youth compared to their counterparts, and they were also more likely to have multiple substance use disorders. They also exhibited more chaotic lifestyle factors such as unprotected sex as well as self-harm (Lubman et al., 2007). Whilst Chapman & Ford (2008) found a very high incidence of suicide ideation in traumatised substance misusing young offenders.

Lopez et al. (2005) found that PTSD was the only anxiety disorder that predicted future substance abuse problems. The onset of PTSD preceded other mental health and substance misuse problems in approximately two thirds of sample populations (Epstein et al., 1998). Some research suggests that this disorder increases the odds ratio of substance use disorders by 3–14 times. However, older youth report that substance use precedes the onset of PTSD. This suggests that there may be two populations of PTSD youth. The first population is a young onset group who are traumatised prior to use and seek relief through consumption. In the later onset group, PTSD may result from the chaotic lifestyles of problematic drug and alcohol use that steer young people into high risk situations which are life threatening.

Psycho-social treatment studies of youth with PTSD are very limited with few treatment recommendations. Adult populations with PTSD have been found to show poorer treatment outcomes in response to drug- and alcohol-related interventions, though alcohol problems tended to improve before PTSD symptoms did (Najavits et al., 2006). Ouimette et al. (2003) found that in adults, concurrent treatment for PTSD reduced long term risk of relapse back into substance misuse problems, but only when long term aftercare was given to those leaving residential treatment. Adults often express a preference for combined substance use and PTSD treatment to be delivered concurrently (Read et al., 2004). No research has been done on concurrent PTSD and substance abuse in young people. One study did find that young people experiencing traumatic recall were more likely to end treatment prematurely, but no formal diagnoses of PTSD were made in this study (Jaycox et al., 2004).

Specific treatments for young people with PTSD without substance misuse problems have been evaluated. Seeking Safety was a programme designed for women who had experienced trauma that had been adapted for young women. This programme was 25 sessions long and included psycho-education, reviewing healthy relationships, cognitive restructuring and extensive case management. It reduced depression, self-harm and relief-seeking through substance use (Najavits et al., 2006). However, attendance rates were low (less than 50 per cent) and the treatment programme did not find benefit in the reduction of PTSD or substance abuse symptoms. Trauma Focussed Cognitive Behavioural Therapy has demonstrated positive results with children who have been sexually abused but there have been no trials with adolescents. The programme requires parental involvement and the avoidance of exposure to risk. This creates an issue in the treatment of PTSD, where continued exposure to risk within the family system (domestic violence, abuse etc.) will compromise treatment gains. This may be especially important as the maintenance of routine appears to particularly therapeutic for this group. Family involvement in treatment therefore becomes critical to long-term gains. Whilst the concurrence of PTSD and substance abuse problems requires more research, the multiplicity and severity of these problems may legislate against effective treatment in community settings, and it may be more appropriate for intensive inpatient settings.

Treatment for suicidal young people

Numerous studies have identified a prevalence of suicidal ideation in young people. Eaton et al. (2003) reported that 18.7 per cent of girls and 10.3 per cent of boys had contemplated suicide, whilst 13.4 per cent of girls and 9.2 per cent of boys had developed a suicide plan. Furthermore, 2.4 per cent of girls and 1.5 per cent of boys had attempted suicide. The peak in suicidal ideation tends to occur in early adolescence and is perhaps associated with cognitive shifts that may trigger a wide range of internalised disorders. Principle methods of suicide amongst youth are overdose or cutting, but few attempts result in death. Rates of suicidal ideation are higher in young people

with substance abuse. Between 18–36 per cent of clinical samples report a suicide attempt in the last twelve months (Kelly et al., 2001). Risk of successful suicide is also three times higher in substance abusing youth. Studies show that 28–33 per cent of young people who committed suicide are found to have had recent alcohol problems prior to their death (Houston et al., 2001). Poly-drug use and intravenous opiate use are the substances most associated with suicide.

The relationship between substance use and suicide is complex. At its simplest both substance use and suicide may each be a behavioural response to intolerable mood states. Both offer escape from emotional pain that an individual feels that cannot be reduced by other means. Furthermore, suicidality has been associated with multiple risk factors which are also concomitant with substance use. Mental illness, impulsivity, risk taking, family problems, poor educational achievement and poor coping are shared risk factors for both problems. Further to this, the rebound effects of drug and alcohol use on mood, disinhibiting behaviour or worsening life situations may conspire to increase a young person's sense of being overwhelmed. The availability of drugs also offers a clear means to commit suicide.

There have been no randomised control trials of treatment with suicidal substance using youth, but general studies of suicide offer some insight into effective treatment. Wood et al. (2001) studied the effect of group programmes for suicidal young people that were provided in addition to wider professional support. These young people also used drugs and alcohol heavily. Those attending the additional support group demonstrated reductions in self-harm and suicidal behaviour, but the study did not report outcomes on drug and alcohol use. Goldston (2004) found that a functional analysis of suicidal thoughts and behaviour was a powerful planning tool in both understanding and addressing suicidal thinking and action in young people. Functional analysis is a behaviour assessment tool that examines the critical factors that lead up to a suicide attempt. It involves reviewing the external factors, such as when, where and who else was involved, and the internal factors, including an assessment of the thoughts and feelings of the young person prior to the attempt. After examining the suicide attempt, it then reviews the short and long term consequences of the behaviour for the young person and others.

These triggers can then be addressed through the development of an individualised treatment plan that either eliminates them or highlights necessary coping skill to respond to them in other ways.

Kaminer et al. (2006) compared the outcomes of two different aftercare formats with suicidal young people. One aftercare service was delivered face-to-face and the other used telephone counselling after young people had completed a 9-week groupwork programme. Both interventions involved a combination of Cognitive Behavioural Therapy and Motivational Enhancement. Whilst suicidality was not addressed in these programmes, the face-to-face contact group showed significant reductions in suicidal behaviour. Esposito-Smythers and Goldston (2008) developed a comprehensive treatment package for substance using suicidal youth, including:

- case management,
- Cognitive Behavioural Therapy,
- Motivational Enhancement therapies,
- specialist counselling of parents and the young person delivered separately,
- medication.

The young people receiving this package were provided with 6 months of weekly interventions, a three-month bi-weekly aftercare and then a booster session every three months. Compared to an enhanced 'treatment as usual' group, this treatment group showed significant reduction in depressive symptoms, emergency room reports, hospitalisations, running away, arrests and suicidal behaviours. Brown, G.K. et al. (2005) reported the outcomes of a 10-week Cognitive intervention with adults and young people presenting to emergency rooms. Whilst it reduced suicide attempts by 50 per cent, there was no reported data of the impact on drug or alcohol consumption. Dialectal Behavioural Therapy, a Cognitive Behavioural Therapy style programme that incorporates Mindfulness, has been adapted for young people. It includes developing an understanding of boundaries versus personal freedom and the involvement of parents, but there have been no clinical trials on this adapted approach as yet.

Goldston et al. (2011) proposed a specific model for addressing suicidality in young people with substance abuse problems. In this approach, a young person is first encouraged to tell their story regarding the behaviour, and this can be combined with Motivational Interviewing approaches and involve parents. Based on functional analysis, a safety plan is developed specifically for the young person and a safety review is conducted with parents to remove any means for suicide from the home. Whilst suicidal behaviour is monitored in subsequent sessions, greater attention is also given to recreational counselling to increase the range of pleasurable activities in the young person's life.

The abandonment of pleasurable activities is a key feature of both substance abusing and depressed youth. Adhedonia (an inability to experience joy) may contribute to both conditions (Carey et al., 1986). This suggests that social/recreational counselling can have a positive impact on both conditions, but it has been under-researched. In addition, Speckens & Hawton (2005) developed problem-solving strategies for suicidal youth. They involve a problem solving formula that begins by generating possible solutions and evaluating the best strategies. An option is then selected, implemented and reviewed for continued refinement. This is a helpful approach as many suicidal individuals have been found to have poor coping and problem solving skills, resulting in them ruminating on suicide as the only perceived option for responding to problems. Increased problem solving and enhanced thinking skills are especially important for this population.

Family involvement in treatment

Historically, families have been under-utilised in the treatment of young people for substance misuse. This has occurred for a number of reasons. First, the lack of developmentally informed approaches has forced the adolescent substance misuse field to adopt or adapt adult models of practice. However, adults are free to make choices, which differs from young people who cannot escape their embeddedness in their social environment. In Western societies this freedom has created highly individualistic adult treatment models, whose assumptions have shaped young people's treatment models, which often focus on individual choices, perceptions and wants as opposed to the wider web of relationships that provide the context of an individual's life. This has meant that less attention has been given to approaches that involve these wider relationships, leaving a gap in knowledge. It is not that youth services do not recognise the importance of family in the lives of young people in comparison to adults, it is that they often do not know how to involve the family. There is no tradition, nor are there any precedents, to call upon in order to guide or shape practice. Even though family therapies have become more widely available, they have not become mainstream in many youth services and remain difficult to access in many areas.

There can also be a more insidious reason why family is excluded from the treatment processes. As we saw in Chapter 2, there is a powerful assumption in Western cultures that parental influence is the central driver of child and adolescent development, both when it goes well and when it doesn't. Whilst this infantile determinism (the ideas that parenting style can account for all problems in adolescence) is a fallacy, it remains an active cultural assumption, which may result in a prejudicial attitude in services towards families, some of whom can come to be seen as the real problem. For example, Campbell's (1992) analysis of counsellors' notes found that 90 per cent of counsellors' comments were negative in regard to their clients' families. Whilst Balaban & Melchionda (1979) found that workers frequently got into conflict with family members over their clients, forcing clients to drop out as the only way to ease the worker-family tensions. Sher (1991) also found that professional attitudes towards the parents of problem users tended to be negative, again with a strong assumption that the family were primarily responsible for the substance misuse problems of their children. Whilst this may sometimes be true for the early onset externalised group, it may often have no bearing on other sub-populations' use. Negative attitudes towards parents will not encourage parents' engagement with support services to change the life situation of their offspring, or indeed of themselves.

In contrast to this, many concerned families want to help their loved ones deal with pressing substance-related issues, but simply do not know how. Parents often attempt dramatic and well-intended strategies to assist their loved one that can unintentionally be counter-productive and increase use. Whilst many practitioners would accept that families can have a negative influence over young substance users, the field has been far more reluctant to accept the positive influence they can have on reducing use. Yet parents are extremely well placed to exert a great deal of influence over the lives of young people.

Family life events, relationships and dynamics in the home are the backdrop to a young person's life and, as such, parents constitute a substantial proportion of the extra-therapeutic forces that are beyond the immediate reach of formal treatment. The next sections of this chapter will review how families can influence drug and alcohol use and can contribute to the change process in profound ways. This can occur on several levels. First, families can play an active role in facilitating unmotivated young people to enter into treatment. Second, they can contribute to a deeper assessment of a young person's drug and alcohol use, and offer a wider perspective on consumption than a young person might do without them. Third, the following sections of this chapter will review models of practice that involve the family in treatment processes in a variety of roles, including family therapy, becoming part of a treatment team or through the care planning processes. Each area will be examined separately to evaluate the relative contribution that each role provides.

Family involvement: motivating young people for treatment

Problematic drug or alcohol use has a profound affect not just on the user but on those around them as well. Paolino & McCrady (1977) suggested that for every problem alcohol user, five other people are adversely affected. At the same time, research demonstrates that in any given year, 90–95 per cent of problem alcohol users do not seek help (Kessler et al., 1994; Price et al., 1991; Reiger et al., 1993; Sobell et al., 1996). This leaves a huge population of family members isolated and struggling to manage the unbearable burden of a loved one's escalating addiction. Velleman et al. (1993) identified that families experience a wide range of short- and long-term consequences. In the short term, family members affected by others' problem use are more likely to experience social isolation, fatigue, anxiety, guilt, fear and may even become suicidal. In the long term they were likely to experience physical health problems, depression and anxiety attacks as well as an increased drug and alcohol intake of their own.

Research has demonstrated that the greater the pressure that families experience from a young person's use, the more motivated they become to address it. However, historically, the treatment field's response to this need has been poor. The overt focus of treatment in clinical practice on individualism has assumed that authentic motivation for change must emanate solely from the individual. Therefore, when parents have made contact with services they are often rebuffed by agencies who suggest that there is nothing that can be done until the young person asks for help. This means that the opportunity for an effective early intervention into that young person's use is missed. Their problematic use escalates and becomes entrenched whilst the family become increasingly exhausted. Reviewing research on the factors that lead to all young people's treatment entry, it is clear that internally driven motivation for change is weak. The vast majority of clients who present for services do so because of family pressure (for an extensive review of these mechanisms, see Harris, 2011a; Harris, 2011b.) Rather than impotent bystanders, families are often the central driving force in treatment entry. In recent years there have been important treatment advances which have capitalised on this reality and which have demonstrated considerable effectiveness in facilitating early treatment entry in unmotivated problem users.

An early pioneering approach was developed by the Johnson Institute and is known as 'the intervention' (Johnson, 1998), which was originally designed for use with adults, but has since been extensively used with young people. The intervention consisted of a secret meeting between significant members of a problem user's family who devise a surprise ambush. Members of this group compose letters to describe how the user's drug and alcohol use has hurt them by drawing on concrete examples. The intervention is then conducted on the victim (sic) and all members read their letters. The young person must then agree to attend a pre-arranged appointment with a treatment provider or face ultimatums. Whilst the Johnson Institute reports very high success rates on its approach, subsequent research has questioned its findings. This observed that the success rates reported on were based only on those families who are actually willing to conduct the intervention. But many families are unwilling to do so and drop out of the process. Drop-out rates can be enormous with 75–100 per cent of families withdrawing (Landau et al., 2004).

Variations on the intervention have been developed that attempt to reduce the more humiliating aspects of the original public tribunal approach. The programme called A Relational Sequence for Engagement (ARISE) utilises a slower paced and staggered approach. It comprises of three stages of increasingly directive interventions. Stage One comprises an informal intervention without professional assistance. Concerned others contacting the service are invited to attend a joint appointment accompanied by other concerned individuals as well as the young person, so there is no secrecy involved. If the young person does not attend this first session then Stage Two is introduced. Working with the group of concerned others, the practitioner helps them collectively assess useful strategies that may motivate the problem user into treatment. The problem user is then contacted directly by telephone at this meeting. If this fails, a gentler intervention in the Johnston mould is then implemented at Stage Three. Stanton (1997) found that ARISE enabled 55 per cent of unmotivated drug users and 70 per cent of unmotivated problem drinkers to enter treatment. One study included a cohort of 13 young people out of 84 treatment subjects and resulted in 83 per cent subsequently entering treatment. This was achieved in 1–6 sessions. These models have shown a great utility in instigating rapid treatment entry with minimum intervention. Landau et al. (2004) were able to instigate 50 per cent of their sample into treatment within one week, 76 per cent by the second week and 84 per cent by the third week. The average intervention length was only 88 minutes of clinician time.

Some models of early intervention have specifically targeted young people. For example, the Intensive Parent and Youth Intervention (Donahue et al., 1998) aims to increase attendance of youth offenders and parents in treatment within 2–7 days. It includes standardised telephone induction, extolling the advantages of engagement, combined with positive feedback from workers about the programme and how it can alleviate punitive court sanctions. It has also been combined with telephone reminders two days prior to the appointment. In one clinical trial of this intervention, involving 39 dually diagnosed youth, up to 89 per cent attended their first treatment after a 2-hour parental intervention, whilst Szapocznik et al.'s (1988) Strategic Structural Systems Engagement model developed a six-step staged approach to facilitate treatment entry with young people, based on a family ecology model of intervention. In their sample, 108 parents were able to facilitate 91 per cent of their substance-misusing offspring into treatment within 1–3 hours. However, not all youth-based approaches are as successful. The Co-operative Counselling approach developed in the UK by Yates (1988) consisted of a rapid access outreach programme that was instigated in response to a family member contacting an agency regarding a young person's alcohol use. As part of this process, the problem-using young person was invited to an advice session that included information, counselling and educational materials. In their sample of 30 young people, only 21 per cent took up the treatment option.

Young people who enter into treatment via this pathway demonstrate good treatment outcomes. In an interesting study, Waldron et al. (2008) evaluated the efficacy of Cognitive Behavioural Therapy for 30 young people who initially refused to enter treatment but subsequently did as a result of a parental intervention. They were heavy drug and alcohol users and completed 8.1 the of the 12 therapy sessions. Despite this they showed significant reductions in cannabis consumption at 6-month follow-up.

Concerned others

There is a long standing research finding, though, that treatment entry subsequent to interventions involving parents does not translate into improvements in the parents' own lives (see Barber & Crisp, 1995). This is an important finding, as family members should not merely be seen as a resource but as human beings with needs in their own right. Programmes which initiate treatment entry and improve their concerned others' lives have been developed, but they tend to involve longer treatment. The most influential early model was Community Reinforcement Training (CRT). This was an offshoot of the CRA programme (see Chapter 4) and entailed: developing the concerned others' skills to intervene in their loved one's use by offering competing rewards to compromise use; and allowing natural consequences of use to impact upon the user. In the very first study, Sission & Azrin (1986) randomly assigned 12 concerned others to either the prototype Community Reinforcement Training or a traditional treatment approach based on the Twelve Steps. The Community Reinforcement Training assisted six out of seven resistant problem drinkers to enter into treatment after an

average of 7.2 sessions (58.2 days). They also found that these individuals had halved their drinking during this period. None of the drinkers in the traditional treatment group of the study took up treatment.

Early promising results stimulated further development, which resulted in the development of the Community Reinforcement and Family Therapy (CRAFT) (Smith & Meyers, 2004). This behavioural programme has three core aims. The first aim is to enable the concerned others to assist their unmotivated loved ones into treatment without conflict. The second aim of CRAFT is reduce the stress and suffering of the concerned others themselves. This includes diminishing conflict, domestic violence and stress. The third aim is to improve the concerned others' own lives after years of self-neglect whilst supporting their problematically using loved ones. In one study, 130 concerned others of problem drinkers were randomly assigned to CRAFT, Al Anon or the Johnson Intervention (Miller et al., 1999). Each programme was based on 12 hours of treatment with a manual-based approach. CRAFT significantly out-performed the other approaches in securing treatment entry for the problem loved one. This was achieved within 47 days of the first appointment, with the concerned others having completed 4.7 sessions on average. The CRAFT groups also showed considerable improvement in stress reduction and improvements in quality of life.

In a second non-controlled CRAFT study, 62 concerned others of problem drug users were recruited into the treatment programme (Meyers et al., 1999). In this trial, 74 per cent of problem users were engaged in treatment. This was achieved within 4.8 sessions over 48 days on average. All the concerned others demonstrated significant reductions in anger, anxiety, depression and other problems. Other studies based on CRAFT have been conducted with similar results. Kirby et al.'s (1999) multi-site study of CRT found that 64 per cent of the concerned others of problem drug users were able to motivate their loved ones into treatment compared to 17 per cent in the Al Anon treatment group of the study. A more recent study (Meyers et al., 2002) compared CRAFT with CRAFT plus CRA aftercare and with an Al-Narc facilitation programme based on Al Anon principles but for drug users. This research found that the CRAFT conditions successfully engaged 67 per cent of problem users and the Al-Narc engaged only 29 per cent. The study included measurements of the concerned others' functioning prior to and after treatment. Significant reductions were found in the levels of depression, stress and anger.

Comparative results have also been found with the Parents and Carers Training (PACT) developed in South Wales, UK (See Harris, 2011a). This model was developed on behavioural principles but uses a stepped care approach. It begins with a comprehensive assessment which may detect current motivation in a loved one leading to a rapid treatment response. Where existing motivation is not present in the problem user, the approach offers family members the skills to facilitate treatment entry. It does this by reducing positive aspects of use through using rewards to compete with use and by reducing conflicts. At the same time it looks to increase the negative consequences of use by reducing the 'helping behaviours' employed by family members that diminish the negative consequences of use. The programme also offers support to concerned others in improving their own lives, reducing their stress and offering strategies to help concerned others support a loved one who is in treatment. These elements of the programme are delivered in a menu format, where the family members can chose one or all of these four different elements.

The PACT programme has not been evaluated with a randomised control trial as it adopts a different treatment methodology. In light of the limitations of the randomised control trial application to everyday practice reviewed earlier, it has adopted an *outcome informed approach*. This approach does not attempt to re-create the findings of a randomised control trial, but instead monitors the treatment response of each client who engages with a service. Using the Outcome Rating Scales and Session Rating Scales discussed earlier in this chapter, family members provide on-going feedback on their progress in treatment as well as rating the helpfulness of each session. This feedback is routinely assessed and patterns in family members' feedback lead to refinement of the programme. As a result, every concerned other that has engaged in the programme has contributed to its development through this continual process. As such, the programme has demonstrated very robust results in everyday clinical settings with unfiltered client groups.

One data sample was collected on treatment completers in the programme and demonstrated favourable results for the PACT programme compared to a general counselling option (Harris, 2011c). During the sample period 28 clients were engaged in the PACT programme whilst 25 clients were in general counselling. In collecting outcome data it is important to recognise that the individual scores on outcome measuring tools are not the whole picture. For example, how does a family member who moved from 12 points to 28 points compare to a family member who moved from 19 points to 35 points at the end of treatment? Outcome research requires an understanding of the significance of the change experienced rather than just of the numbers. The significance of change is identified through a Reliability Change Indication (RCI), which can identify the kind of change that occurred. This is important because when people seek treatment there can only be four possible outcomes. The Reliability Change Indication calculates what outcome the individual has experienced by comparing their initial intake score to the final treatment completion score:

1. **Deteriorates:** The client has worsened during their treatment.
2. **No change:** The client experiences no change during their treatment – some clients may show some slight improvement but this is natural remission and is not influenced by the treatment.
3. **Reliable change:** The client has improved as a result of the treatment that they have received.
4. **Clinically significant change:** The client has experienced the highest level of change and their social functioning is akin to those that do not require professional help.

The Reliability Change Indication demonstrated a far higher treatment response rate for PACT clients compared to those in general counselling. Not only did PACT clients fare better in treatment, they were also less likely to deteriorate or experience no change than those in counselling (See Graph 6.4). In the PACT cohort, 85.7 per cent of concerned others achieved clinically significant levels of change – the highest possible rate of change in treatment. In comparison, 56 per cent of clients in counselling achieved the same range. The same team delivered both interventions so, even accounting for the alliance factors, the PACT programme showed superior outcomes.

Seventy per cent of concerned others in the PACT programme selected motivating their loved ones to enter treatment as their goal. Of these, 68 per cent were successful in motivating

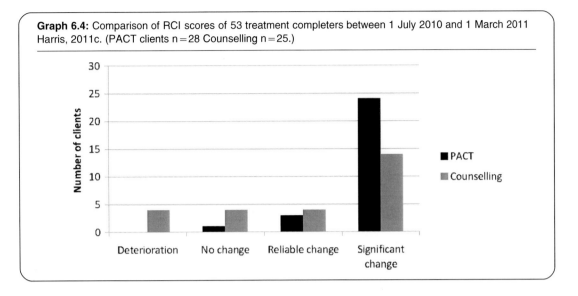

Graph 6.4: Comparison of RCI scores of 53 treatment completers between 1 July 2010 and 1 March 2011 Harris, 2011c. (PACT clients n = 28 Counselling n = 25.)

the unmotivated user into treatment. There was no difference in treatment entry whether the problem using family member was a young person or adult. In comparison, only 21 per cent of problem users subsequently entered treatment in the general counselling group of the study. Dropout rates for both interventions were very low with only 3.1 per cent of the PACT group and 5.5 per cent of the counselling group failing to complete their treatment. As such, the PACT programme has demonstrated very effective outcomes in everyday clinical settings for both young people and their families, and numerous small sample studies done in situ are being brought together to develop a bigger research base.

Family involvement: family therapy

The parents of young people should be actively involved and supported in a young person's treatment. Parental involvement can improve treatment outcomes. For example, Dakof et al. (2001) found that parents who recognised that their young people had problems, demanded they desist and supported academic achievement increased their engagement rates in treatment considerably. Clarke et al. (2005) found that young people with high parental supervision fared better in treatment than those with low parental supervision. Besides facilitating and strengthening treatment attendance, parents can become part of the treatment process through

family therapy. This is particularly important for those young people whose risk factors extend beyond their own choices and peer groups and are embedded in the family structure itself.

Family therapy is a broad name for a wide range of treatment modalities that focuses on two or more people who are related by birth, marriage or adoption. The function of the therapy is to help families to clarify communication, rules, hierarchies and boundaries as well as to resolve conflict and enhance emotional cohesion. It is important to note that some family therapy approaches, such as systemic models, have developed from clinical experience and not through research (Bry, 1988). This means that many of studies on systemic family therapy have not incorporated the methodological standards of evaluation into their studies that are necessary to reliably substantiate their outcomes. However, as the family remains a significant mechanism for socialisation, family therapy would seem apposite as an intervention for young people experiencing drug and alcohol problems. There are two broad schools of family therapy which offer different theoretical perspectives on approaching substance use/misuse issues. These are referred to as Systemic and Behavioural models, and will be reviewed separately.

Systemic family therapy

Systemic family therapy emerged in the 1940s and 1950s in light of growing dissatisfaction with psychodynamic therapy approaches with children, which had not accounted for the impact of family on children's lives. Instead, Systemic family therapy drew upon a range of sources such as anthropology and sociology which had begun to explore the social context in which people lived their lives. From this perspective a family is understood as a social unit with its own governing rules, characteristics and norms. Through these rules each individual influences a family and, in turn, the family influences the individual. As such, a collective family system rather than specific individuals is the driving force in problems. However, families are prone to focussing on an individual as the source of family distress even though they are not the problem. Instead, in Systemic family therapy, an 'identified patient' who is experiencing difficulties is seen as an expression of the dysfunctional family relationships. For example, where tension increases between two family members, as in the case of marital conflict, a third family member may be co-opted into the situation in order release unresolved tensions in a less emotionally charged manner. They become the focus of others' concern as a means of avoiding conflict in a process described as triangulation. In this way, the 'identified patient' is not necessarily the cause of family discord but is an expression of conflicts within the family system as a whole; and this pattern of relating can become stable, creating a dysfunctional pattern within the family system.

As such, Systematic therapies are more concerned with readjusting the relationships that perpetuate problems rather than identifying causes of the presenting problem. They attempt to interrupt this status quo through examining the family roles, allegiances and boundaries that determine family interactions. This can be achieved through the use of devices such as genograms which analyse not only family ancestry but also roles that are inherited from grandparents and even beyond. In this way, systematic therapies are trans-generational and often require a whole family to engage in the treatment process in order to reorganise their family system into a new set of more functional ways of relating (Carr, 2000).

Behavioural family therapy

Behavioural family therapy takes a different view and draws on the work of behavioural psychologists such as Skinner (2002). Skinner believed that psychology should be a scientific discipline and base itself on observation and empirical data and, importantly, be able to predict future behaviours. As such, it has adopted a more rigorous methodological approach than systemic therapy. Behaviourism is interested in the way behaviours are learnt through a process of *operant conditioning*, which was reviewed earlier in this chapter. Operant conditioning assumes that behaviour is either reinforced or punished by the consequences it generates. For example, if people drink alcohol and derive pleasure from it, they will repeat the behaviour that produced these consequences, i.e. drink more. Alternatively, a behaviour that produces punishing consequences such being violently sick after drinking too much vodka will reduce the frequency of this behaviour.

Behavioural approaches are less interested in the family system but focus on how behaviours are supported or negated in the here and now. Families can shape the consequences of behaviour without realising, by inadvertently rewarding negative behaviours. For example, if a young drug user incessantly pesters their parent for money for drugs it increases the stress levels of the parent. In order to alleviate this stress, the parent may succumb and give them money because a consequence of doing so stops the unpleasant pressure. However, the young person has now learned that incessant pestering brings about a desired outcome, i.e. money for drugs, which will increase the frequency of this behaviour in the future. Conversely, parents may inadvertently reduce the negative consequences of drug and alcohol use. In light of the stresses and pressure that stem from use the parents may step in and help the young person persist with their problems. This might entail making excuses for them, keeping their use a secret from others, paying their fines or giving them attention when in crises. In this way, the punishing consequences of drug and alcohol are reduced. This may sustain continued use as all the punishing consequences are abated.

Behavioural family therapy teaches parents key skills to shape a young person's behaviour in a positive direction. This involves identifying rewards for pro-social behaviour and how to consistently implement sanctions for negative behaviours. Whereas Systemic therapies explore family roles and patterns, Behaviour therapies teach skills to shape behaviours in more pro-social ways. This includes communication to reduce conflict, boundary setting, problem-solving and developing the parents' conscious awareness of behavioural interactions. For example, when an anticipated reward is withheld from a young person they will automatically enact an 'extinction burst' of behaviour. This is an intensification of the behaviour that occurs prior to it extinguishing. Many parents interpret this increased difficulty as a signal that their approach is not working and give in to this increased pressure. However, the extinction burst is a sign that the behaviour is changing. Once parents understand this process they are more likely to remain consistent and not succumb to the pressure. Behaviour therapies do not require all the family members to attend sessions. Those present can still acquire the skills that influence the problem user's consumption patterns regardless.

Comparative assessment of family therapies

Systemic and Behavioural schools of family therapy have shown positive results with some variation. Whilst both family models produce positive outcomes, Behavioural approaches tend to achieve them over a much shorter time period. Long-term follow-up studies have also supported Behavioural family therapies' ability to create sustained long term outcomes (Waldron et al., 2001). Interestingly, Multi-systemic Therapy (Henggeler et al., 1991; 1996) a Systemic approach that has drawn most heavily on research studies on risk factors and adolescent development, has tended to show poorer treatment responses. For a comparison of outcomes between family interventions specifically developed for substance misusing youth, see Table 6.14.

Family therapy has demonstrated important findings in relation to improving engagement rates with young people. Whilst practitioners often have low expectations of engagement rates with the families of problem using youth, family therapies have consistently demonstrated enhanced retention rates in comparisons with individual therapies. For example, Donohue et al. (1998) found that they could engage 89 per cent of families in family based treatment services compared to 60 per cent of parent alone programmes. Liddle & Darkof (2002) found 95 per cent engagement rates for intensive Multi-Dimensional Family Therapy in comparison to 59 per cent retention in residential treatment. This was a particularly salient finding

as this study was conducted on young substance misusers who were diagnosed with mental health problems as well.

Treatment completion rates also appear to be significantly higher. Henggeler et al.'s (1991; 1996) studies of offenders found that 98 per cent of young offenders assigned to Multi-Systemic Family Therapy completed the full course of treatment. Whilst Liddle & Darkof (2002) found that 88 per cent of young people completed their Multi-Dimensional Family Therapy compared to 24 per cent of youth in residential treatment. Whilst treatment completions are significantly higher in family therapy models compared to 'treatment as usual,' direct comparison of family therapy versus state of the art manualised individual or group therapies has shown more modest completion rates. Liddle et al. (2004) found Multi-Dimensional Family Therapy accounted for 95 per cent retention rates compared 88 per cent of participants in manualised individual therapy.

Family trajectories

The increased retention rates of family therapies may be age related. Younger adolescents for example appear to make more significant gains from family therapies than older adolescents (Waldron et al., 2001), which may be driven by the maturational process. As we saw in Chapter 2, families have a high degree of influence over children that wanes across adolescence as young people achieve increased autonomy. This means that when family influence is high, family therapy is more potent in shaping a young person's behaviour. Once the young person emotionally separates from them at 14 years old and moves into peer groups, this influence is considerably compromised. Hence family therapy effectiveness declines as a young person matures.

It is important to recognise that family therapy models are mostly theoretically driven, informed by the core assumptions of their model and not necessarily by empirical data on adolescent development. This is an important observation for two reasons. First, the orientation of family therapy models may be important when considering the nature of a presenting adolescent substance misuse disorder. As we have seen in the review of one-to-one structured interventions for youth earlier in this chapter, Behavioural models show favourable outcomes for

able 6.14: A comparison of family therapy approaches involving young substance misusers and their outcomes

odel	Studies	Treatment length	Outcomes
ulti-Systemic Therapy (MST) regards substance misuse problems as multidetermined, so operates by addressing the individual, family, peer, school and social network of the young person. The intervention is delivered in the young person's own environment where possible.	Henggeler et al., 1999	60 Treatment hours	Offending youth reduced consumption but gains decayed at 6 months follow up.
	Henggeler et al., 2002	60 Treatment hours	Four year follow-up found no reductions in offending, drug use or mental health problems, though aggressive crime reduced.
rief Strategic Family Therapy (BSFT) was assigned for Hispanic Youth and draws on a wide nge of structured interventions.	Santistenban et al., 2003	4–20 weeks of treatment	Randomly assigned 126 participants to group therapy or the BSFT. BSFT reduced conduct disorders, delinquency and drug use. No differences were found in alcohol use between the two treatment groups. The BSFT group also showed improved family functioning. No long term follow up.
ulti-Dimensional Family Therapy (MDFT) is an tervention designed for multi-problem youth. It perates by focusing on multiple ecologies of a young erson's development and the circumstances that romote continued substance use.	Liddle, 2001	12–16 sessions	182 cannabis or alcohol abusing young people were randomly assigned to either MDFT, Multifamily Education Group or Adolescent Group Therapy. MDFT model showed the greatest improvement on drug use, grade average and family functioning even at one year follow-up.
	Liddle et al., 2001	2–16 sessions	224 inner city youth with high co-morbidity were assigned to MDFT or individual CBT. Both groups showed improvement in reducing substance misuse, internalised and externalised symptoms at treatment completion. Gains were only maintained at the 12 month follow-up in the MDFT group.
ehavioural Family System Treatment or unctional Family Therapy (FFT) is a multisystemic pproach that links cognitive and behavioural aspects f treatment to the formation of family conflict. Initially eveloped for young offenders and runaways, recent udies have found it can be very effective when linked ith other treatment interventions.	Waldron et al., 2001	8–15 sessions	114 adolescents were randomly assigned to FFT, CBT, a combination of FFT and CBT or Psycho-education Therapy. Followed up at 4 and 7 months, the FFT and combined therapy showed significant reductions in use. All interventions were effective but the rate of change and stability of outcomes differed between modalities.
ehavioural Family Treatment (BFT) is based on the neoretical foundations of behavioural therapy uggesting that behaviours are learned and reinforced y the environments in which they occur. It operates y using behavioural contracting and other	Azrin et al., 2001	15 sessions	Compared BFT to standard cognitive problem solving amongst adolescents with a dual diagnosis who were followed up at six months. Both interventions were equally effective at reducing depression and conduct symptoms, substance use and improving lifestyle.

externalised disorders whilst Cognitive Behavioural Treatment shows a bias in the direction of internalised disorders. The same appears to be true for family therapy. The parents of externalised young people will need to improve boundary setting, communication and monitoring as well as deal with disruptive behaviours. Behavioural family models' focus on behaviour management appears to be more effective in setting these limits on behaviour. Systemic models may be more helpful to support internalised disorders, for example where more than one family member experiences depression or anxiety, or where a child's anxiety is increased by a parent's depressions, and so on.

However, both schools remain locked into their own assumptions, which may limit these models' ability to address the wider risk factors that shape each sub-trajectory. As Liddle's (2004) review of family therapy models noted: 'As advances in the basic science of adolescent substance abuse continue, these findings will continue to raise important implications for therapy development and treatment science . . . One example is the work in co-morbidity and the specification of adolescent substance use typologies . . . For example, the issue of subgroups/typologies is subsumed under the broader issue of heterogeneity of substance abusers, which many researchers now see as the rule not the exception. How to best capture this heterogeneity is a future challenge.' (Liddle, 2004: 84).

Family therapies share the same problem as individual treatment modalities for young people. Scant attention has been given to the differing treatment responses of the families of externalised, internalised or normative youth. However, this issue may be far broader in family therapy. It is vital to recognise that family therapy may not simply be attempting to tackle different sub-trajectories of use in young people but is working with different sub-types of family. The families of externalised youth are liable to have levels of complexity of their own. Families of internalised youth may be overprotective and share the same trauma as their offspring. Whilst normative families may be confused by their offspring's problems, and this lack of understanding can be inverted on to themselves in the form of guilt and shame. Greater understanding of these family trajectories is needed to inform family therapy beyond the historical assumptions that shaped its initial development.

Family involvement: Family Conferencing and Network Therapy

The inclusion of families in the treatment of young people has broadened beyond the idea of family therapy. Innovative new approaches have begun to develop in which family members work alongside the treatment process not as 'clients' who need personal assistance in their family relationships or parenting style, but as members of the treatment team. These new roles for parents have expanded the range of possible roles that they might play in the treatment. In particular they hope to strengthen the treatment engagement and outcomes of young people. Two notable developments in this area are Family Case Conferencing and Network Therapies.

Family Case Conferencing

Family Case Conferencing is a participatory approach to case management that was first developed in New Zealand to support Maori families to address the disproportionate numbers of their children being removed into care. The process has since been adopted in over 20 countries and appears to demonstrate high degrees of family and professional satisfaction (Lupton & Nixon, 1999). It has also been piloted in a wide range of young people's support services. Nixon et al.'s (2005) international review of the application of Family Case Conferencing found that 60 per cent of conferences focused on child protection, 58 per cent on criminal justice, 32 per cent for domestic violence and 29 per cent on mental health. Whilst the Family Case Conference model has been adapted to suit these various support settings, the approach is always based on four key principles:

1. **Referral**: agency and family agree that a Family Case Conference would be helpful and a co-ordinator is appointed.
2. **Preparation**: the coordinator identifies the family network and meets with participants to outline the purpose of the conference and invite their engagement.
3. **Meeting**: the family and all involved professionals meet to discuss the situation and explain the possible treatment options to the family. Afterwards the family meet in private to discuss the optimal plan. This is sometimes done with a lead worker to act as advocate for the beliefs and rights of the young person. The plan is agreed and implemented.

4. **Review**: the plan is reviewed and amended if necessary.

In line with the United Nations Rights of the Child, the Family Case Conference offers the opportunity for the child or young person to voice their concerns in the development of a care plan. Whilst they have no formal rights within the family conferencing settings, the appointment of a youth worker to provide advocacy for them can assuage these weaknesses in the model. As a result, children and young people report positive experiences of the approach (Marsh & Crow, 1998).

Despite the increased popularity of the model there have been few empirical studies conducted regarding its efficacy. Only one long term follow-up study has been conducted. Sundell & Vinnerljung (2004) followed 97 children involved in 66 Family Case Conferences between November 1996 and October 1997 in Sweden. They also included a comparison group of 142 children from a random sample of 104 traditional child protection investigations by the Child Protection Services. All children were tracked for 3 years for future maltreatment events. Effects were modelled using multiple regressions that controlled for the child's age, gender, family background and type and severity of problems. After controlling for these initial differences, Family Case Conference children experienced more difficulties than the control group. They had higher rates of re-referral to Child Protection Services compared to the group that had been processed in traditional investigations. They were more often re-referred due to abuse, were more often re-referred by the extended family, and were longer in out-of-home placements, but they tended over time to get less intrusive support from the Child Protection Services. Furthermore, Family Case Conferences did not reduce re-referrals for neglect, or the number of days of received services, or increase case closure after three years.

These results suggested that the impact of the Family Case Conferencing was scant in that it only accounted for 0–7 per cent statistical variance in effectiveness. Whilst the model has been widely adopted and shows promise, it appears to require greater refinement in its delivery, but could offer a potential strategy to engage young people in substance abuse services. It might be an option for resistant families that have shown a poor response to previous treatment attempts or are in minority ethnic groups who place greater priority on family involvement.

Network Therapies

A further development of the inclusion of families in the treatment process itself is the rise of Network Therapies, pioneered in the US by Galanter (1990). Social Behavioural Network Therapy developed and expanded these ideas in the UK into a comprehensive substance specific treatment programme (Copello et al., 2009). In this model practitioners work jointly with the problem drinker to identify individuals in their social network who would be willing to support them implement changes to their drinking. These networks can include friends, family, neighbours and work colleagues who are considered to have needs in their own right. The whole network then attends the treatment sessions together. The practitioner can take a very directive role by setting the agenda for sessions and providing advice and feedback as well as offering practical support. Delivered over eight sessions, treatment takes place in the home at times convenient for the network and follows a set structure:

- Identify potential network members in the client's support network.
- Engage network members with the treatment process.
- Agree on a drinking goal which may be moderation or abstinence.
- Review current interactions regarding responses to problematic use.
- Develop relapse management strategies.
- Identify strategies to sustain long term gains.

Network Therapies have shown positive outcomes. A feasibility study of Network Support Therapy (Ellis, 1998) found that the approach led to improved relationships between the problem users and the social network members. Network members felt more supported and were more confident in dealing with relapse. The network relationships also endured post treatment and offered a more rapid response to relapse. The effectiveness of Social Behavioural Network Therapy was explored in a large randomised control trial conducted in the Alcohol Treatment Trial in the UK. This multi-centre study compared Social Behavioural Network Therapy with Motivational Enhancement Therapy. Both models were equally effective in reducing alcohol consumption by 48 per cent at three months and by 45 per cent at 12-month follow-up (UKATT Research Team, 2005). Alcohol-related problems also reduced to the same degree in both groups, falling by 44 per cent at three months and 50 per cent at 12 months. Whilst the Social Behavioural Network Therapy did not demonstrate superior outcomes to other forms of therapy, it offers a very different alternative to traditional treatment models with its inclusion of network members. It may be a particularly attractive option to families of young people, as they often want to assist the young people in their families but are not always certain how this might best be achieved.

Aftercare

Despite the benefits of active treatment, effective aftercare is critical to ensure that treatment gains are sustained. This is important, as young people appear more susceptible to relapse than adults for a number of reasons. Young people's self-efficacy belief in change is lower than adults'. Adults may have attempted change several times and drawn valuable insights and learning from each of these experiences. Conversely, if it is the first change attempt that a young person has made, they have little prior experience to call upon. Also, the accelerated rate of developmental change and life task accomplishment during adolescence may also increase the pressure on them to adapt rather than sustain behaviours. Moreover, as no developmentally informed treatment approaches are currently available, the unique drivers of their consumption may not always be adequately addressed in their primary treatment, leaving them vulnerable to forces unaccounted for in their treatment planning. Finally, even a highly individualistic treatment for a young person will not necessarily eliminate the risk factors or increase the protection factors in their social environments that feature so highly in our understanding of young people's post treatment response rates.

Research has also demonstrated key differences in young people's relapse patterns compared to adults'. Alcohol use is the most likely substance to trigger relapse in young people even if it was not their primary drug of choice prior to treatment (Brown et al., 2000b). This demands that special attention is given to controlled drinking as a core component of treatment. Adolescent thought processes may also make

them prone to reacting powerfully to even minor setbacks, which they may interpret as being catastrophic. This may make young people liable to give up their attempts to change as a result.

Research also shows that young people are liable to relapse for different reasons than adults. Long term follow-up studies of individuals of all ages leaving treatment have consistently identified 8 key determinants of relapse in all treated populations (Marlatt & Gordon, 1980). These determinants can be categorised into two sub-groups: *intrapersonal* stresses that occur within the individual and *interpersonal* events that occur between people (see Figure 6.4).

Each individual will vary in their susceptibility to relapse in each of these areas, which creates a unique risk profile for each person. However, there are age-related patterns in these determinants.

Long-term adult users are more likely to relapse due to unpleasant mood states and conflict. This is because their expectations of use are already strongly associated with the removal of negative mood states. However, unpleasant mood states or conflict are rarely reported as reasons by young people who relapse (Brown et al., 1989). Instead, young people are more likely to relapse for positive emotional states and social pressure. This is reflective of their positive expectations that substances enhance such mood states, and is more likely to occur in a peer setting, making it a powerful trigger to relapse.

Many relapse prevention programmes do not take sufficient account of these differences, but they may be important, as we see different motivations for use in different sub-trajectories of young people. Externalised youth may be more vulnerable to relapse because of urges, whereas internalised youth may be more likely to relapse in unpleasant moods. For normative youth, social pressure and pleasant times with others may be more significant. Assessment tools have been developed, such as The Inventory of Drug/Alcohol Taking Situations (Annis et al., 1996), that can identify the unique risk profiles of individuals. Based on this assessment it is then possible to select coping skills and interventions that will address each particular profile. For example, a young person scoring highly on relapsing in response to unpleasant mood states may benefit from support with depression. Alternatively, a young person who scores highly on areas such as social pressure may benefit from help with assertiveness and refusal skills.

Figure 6.4: The 8 key determinants of relapse   Marlatt & Gordon, 1980

Intrapersonal :

1. **Unpleasant emotional states:** people may use substances to deal with difficult emotional states. These include negative feelings such as frustration/anger due to hassles of daily life or feelings of loneliness, boredom, worry or depression.

2. **Physical discomfort:** substances are used to ease physical pain. This includes physical states which relate to prior drug use such as physical withdrawal or cravings. It also relates to non-drug using physical discomfort such as illness, fatigue or injury.

3. **Pleasant emotions:** substances are used to enhance positive emotions such as feeling joy, being in control or happiness.

4. **Testing personal control:** this is the user's desire to test their willpower by using substances 'just the once' to see if they can manage it now.

5. **Urges:** These are desires to re-create the old using experience. Whilst cravings are physical and can result from withdrawal, urges are psychological temptations to use.

Interpersonal:

6. **Conflict:** substance use is resumed after arguments or disagreements with other people. These encounters leave people in negative emotional states such as being frustrated, angry or guilty. At other times people might feel anxious or apprehensive, or worry about the implications of the conflict.

7. **Social pressure:** substance use can resume because of direct social pressure such as being offered the drug. Or it can be indirect through observing others use and wishing to participate.

8. **Pleasant times:** substances can be taken to enhance pleasant occasions such as a party, holiday, sex or celebrations like birthdays. Although this enhances a positive mood, substance use occurs in context of social interactions.

However, there have been no clinical trials of this structured relapse prevention with young people to establish its merit.

Besides relapse prevention, aftercare should also focus on improvements in social functioning. Young people need to re-enter pro-social networks after protracted periods of social exclusion. As a result of their developmental delay they will experience new difficulties and pressures in these environments. Shifting family relationships, educational attainment, moving into new peer groups and the initiation of new romantic partners, all bring new challenges. Setbacks in these areas can be interpreted by young people as signifying their innate inability to manage these life tasks as opposed to having to catch up in the curriculum of life. From this perspective, aftercare should be considered the critical transition point from professional support into the informal social environment that can support the changes that a young person has made.

Indeed, research has also begun to illuminate critical features of effective aftercare and assess what contributes to outcomes following treatment, and how. It was once believed that people who remained committed to treatment plans for extended periods of time were able to do so simply because they were more motivated. But, this is not the case. The impact of external aftercare provision is at least as important as internal motivation. For example, Vannicelli's (1978) research demonstrated that sustained attendance within programmes promoted sobriety. Walker et al. (1983) took this further, in finding that problematic alcohol users who attended a 9-month aftercare programme were three times more likely to sustain abstinence compared to non-attenders in the same aftercare. In this study, aftercare attendance was a better predictor of eventual outcomes than 10 other variables within the prior treatment, which had been thought to have been the factors most closely associated with achieving optimal outcomes. Ito & Donavan (1990) also found that attendance in aftercare predicted the nature of eventual outcomes amongst problem drinkers to a greater degree than clients' social profiles, their ages of onset of drinking and their coping repertoire. It has also been found that dropping out of post treatment plans tends to occur prior to relapse rather than after it.

Research consistently shows that the longer that someone is engaged in aftercare then the better their eventual outcomes become. This is a particularly important issue for young people, because they show high drop-out rates from post treatment plans. Hser et al.'s (2001) DATOS-A study found that only 28 per cent of dually diagnosed (substance misuse and mental health) youth completed the optimal 90 days of treatment and post treatment plans. They acknowledged that increasing engagement rates with aftercare was one of the most difficult challenges for those providing treatment to young people. However, as engagement rates differed dramatically across agencies, they also suggested that treatment engagement rates could be improved dramatically, if services employed proactive strategies to improve them.

Most studies on aftercare have been conducted on adult populations. But, as studies of treatment engagement show that it appears predictive of both adult and young people's outcomes, aftercare parallels can be drawn for young people. Studies have shown that outcomes in adult aftercare are not related to the *intensity* of aftercare but its *duration*. The reason for this may be explained by the 'rush-trickle effect' described earlier. The majority of gains occur early in the treatment process and then begin to diminish as the clients move towards normative social functioning. More intensive treatment will not improve the rate of change once this law of diminishing returns begins. In fact it may be counter-productive. As the client continues to put high effort into change but no longer experiences the same subjective improvement they assume

that they are failing and can drop out of their treatment feeling demoralised. This has been known as the 'failure zone' of treatment and was first recognised in the 1950s. However, what they are in fact experiencing is the typical rate in which change unfolds. At its simplest, more treatment at this stage will not equate with more change. Continued support, even if it is less frequent, is more helpful in dealing with these new challenges than intensive support. One of the extensive studies on this aftercare effect was conducted by Moos et al. (1999). Their study found that 34 per cent of clients who did not enter into aftercare remained abstinent at 12-month follow-up compared to 65 per cent of clients who attended at least two aftercare sessions a month for 7 months (see Graph 6.5). Treatment gains were highest for those who attended a combination of formal treatment and self-help groups such as AA or NA. These positive outcomes were sustained at two- and eight-year follow-up (Moos & Moos, 2003).

These research findings strongly suggest that maintaining engagement in aftercare for seven months is important for establishing long term gains. For externalised young people, who often show a deterioration in outcomes at the 12-month mark, their aftercare should be longer, and they may benefit from booster sessions. But even though this is such an important finding, there has been very little research conducted on the management of aftercare either for adults or young people. Most studies of 'treatment retention' with young people (how long they sustain a commitment to a post-treatment plan) have focussed on the importance of alliance

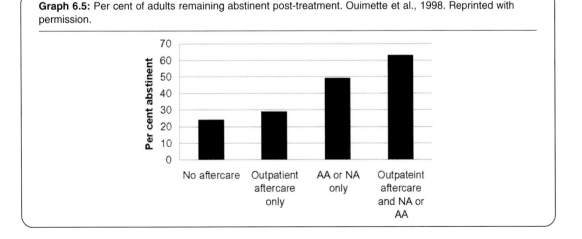

Graph 6.5: Per cent of adults remaining abstinent post-treatment. Ouimette et al., 1998. Reprinted with permission.

factors increasing a service's engagement rates. However, more recent studies have evaluated the impact of a wider range of strategies thought to be important in increasing long term engagement.

Lash et al. (1996; 2001; 2004; 2005; 2006) devised an interesting series of experiments to test the value of three key strategies to improve services' long term retention rates, including the use of behavioural contracting, prompts and rewards reinforcements. Those undergoing aftercare treatment in the various experiments were adults, primarily male (95–100 per cent) and Caucasian (42–62 per cent) and most had received residential treatment prior to aftercare (86–100 per cent), whilst a smaller cohort (0–14 per cent) had been outpatients. All clients then attended a Cognitive Behavioural relapse prevention programme in addition to Twelve Step self-help groups. The Contract, Prompt and Reinforce procedures were developed as an adjunct to this aftercare treatment, and in ways that allowed the specific behavioural principles that were applied in the clinical trials to be applied subsequently in any aftercare setting.

The experiment was conducted over four trials that were designed to test the value of the procedures incrementally by adding Contracting, Prompt and Reinforcement components one at a time. Each strategy would be retained only if it increased retention rates. So the first experiment tested whether simple exposure to an aftercare group without any additional techniques increased attendance. The second phase then tested whether clients who signed a behavioural contract demonstrated better retention rates in aftercare than those who did not. If the behavioural contract group showed better retention rates, it would become the standard condition for the next trial. The next trial would then compare a behavioural contract group with those who not only signed a behavioural contract but were also prompted to attend their sessions. If those who had signed the behavioural contract and received prompts led to higher retention rates, this would be the next standard approach. In the final study, both groups would sign a behavioural contract and receive prompts, but only one cohort would also be reinforced in their attendance with the use of rewards.

Within this sequence, exposing individuals to a video extolling the virtues of aftercare compared to introducing other individuals to an aftercare group showed little difference in subsequent aftercare treatment entry. Asking clients to sign a

behavioural contract to attend an agreed number of sessions increased aftercare treatment initiation, but only when this procedure was conducted by a member of staff and not by a volunteer. Prompts to attend groups, combined with feedback on progress did increase retention rates, but only for three months. The addition of social reinforcement and symbols of achievement (certificates, engraved medals) at landmark moments in the aftercare treatment process did increase the number of clients who attended for the optimal length of time of seven months. The awarding of these small tokens of achievement was conducted in the group. The individual in receipt of these tokens made a statement regarding how the aftercare treatment assisted them and received social reinforcement in the form of praise from other group members and staff. This was a highly cost effective contingency, but appeared particularly powerful.

The differences in overall aftercare treatment retention were stark. In the initial video/group introduction condition only 32 per cent attended a first aftercare session. In contrast, those receiving Contract/Prompt/Reinforcement achieved a 100 per cent attendance at the first session. Whilst only 18 per cent of the video/group introduction group completed three months of attendance, 71 per cent of the Contract/Prompt/Reinforcement approach did. Furthermore, whilst no clients in the original group achieved attendance at the 7-month point, 50 per cent of the Contract/Prompt/ Reinforcement approach did so. At this point aftercare treatment attendance and gains stabilised suggesting that it is the optimal aftercare length. Not only was their attendance rate higher but, at 6-month follow-up, 76 per cent of the reinforced group were still abstinent of all drugs and alcohol, compared to 40 per cent of the control group. These gains occurred even though the majority of clients in the last group of the experiment were dually diagnosed with substance misuse and mental health problems, and had the most complex needs at intake. Normally, these groups tend to exhibit the poorest retention rates in aftercare treatment.

This promising approach offers a powerful addition to the development of services for young people. Moreover, the technology is currently available to conduct many of these procedures by text over a mobile telephone. The addition of these procedures allows for aftercare treatment processes to be strengthened through a medium that is highly prized by young people, which could enhance the retention and engagement rates in a very cost effective manner. The author is currently trialling the use of the principles with mobile telephone technology in the UK to see if these proactive retention strategies can improve engagement rates and subsequent outcomes in young people who are so vulnerable to dropping out of treatment.

Summary

Whilst considerable progress has been made in the last twenty years, treatment for young people remains underdeveloped. Young people tend to show poorer outcomes than adults. Whilst those that do achieve abstinence tend to show the highest improvements in social functioning, the majority of young people are not motivated to attain this goal. Instead they are more motivated to reduce social problems generated by their use rather than to reduce consumption itself. This desire for controlled use may stem from the fact that they are unlikely to be experiencing physical dependence or severe health consequences at this stage of their using history. Furthermore, a preference for controlled use may be indicative of their developmental pathway where alcohol will continue to feature in their social forums. The use of adult measures of treatment outcomes therefore offers a poor fit in terms of measuring the treatment gains that young people achieve.

In general, treatment interventions appear to be effective when stratified. Brief interventions can be highly effective for high functioning youth, but longer term therapies are required for highly excluded youth who are more likely to have incumbent complex needs, both within themselves and in their immediate environment. Enhancing those factors shared in common by many treatments and known as the working alliance, is essential to maximise treatment gains. Whilst a number of substance use treatment models have been developed for young people, most are not specifically developmentally informed, which may diminish their effectiveness and may reduce their relevance to young people's lives. Greater understanding is needed to address the unique needs of different sub-trajectories of young people, who display divergent patterns of response to treatment. This is the weakest area of the evidence base, where little attention has been given to the co-occurrence of behavioural

problems or mental illness in young people who are experiencing substance use problems. Research on the existing evidence base does suggest that Behavioural approaches are more effective with young people with externalised disorders and Cognitive Behavioural Therapy models are more effective with internalised disorders. However, as the research base is so limited, this is not to say that other models will not show equally optimal outcomes but await rigorous evaluation.

These differences are carried through into family therapies. Scant attention has been given here to interactions between parental style and a young person's temperament due to the limited scale of the research and evidence base. It is important to recognise that the families of young drug and alcohol users are liable to share similar profiles that are indicative of their offspring. Externalised youth tend to hail from chaotic families who are battling with their own wide range of social problems. Internalised families may have been traumatised by similar events as their offspring. Normative families will often be much more stable but less aware of drugs and the problems that they and alcohol can elicit. Whilst family therapies show high retention rates, especially for young adolescents, there remains a paucity of research on family therapies' impact on different sub-trajectories of young people. This may limit the therapies' range considerably. Within this, the role of family has become greatly extended in recent years, during which the importance that family can have in the lives of young people has been recognised. New models that can precipitate treatment entry – Family Case Conferencing and Network Therapies – have opened new points of inclusion for those families that want to help and support their offspring.

Finally, it has here only been possible to pay scant attention to treatment retention and aftercare, again because of the limited scale of the research and evidence base. Whilst research has continually highlighted the importance of aftercare, particularly for the highest risk groups, there has been little attention given to how various aftercare strategies can maximise long term outcomes for young people. It is essential that young people are not simply supported in overcoming their drug and alcohol consumption, but are also given the means to re-enter the social structures that comprise their life course. Treatment studies have continually demonstrated that long terms gains are not simply shaped by the elimination of risk factors, but by the increasing of protection factors. Essentially these protection factors lie in the accomplishment of a more fulfilling life, which embraces the opportunities and currents that shape all our lives. Only then, with the provision of increased protection factors, will young people who have had difficulties with alcohol and substance use be able to transit into an adult life where their full potential will ultimately be realised.

Epilogue

This book set out to identify the specific differences between young people's problematic substance use and that of adults. These differences are located in a complex, multi-disciplinary set of interactive forces. These processes are located in the biology and personality of the young person that interact with their immediate family and peer environments as well as with more distant cultural norms. Adolescent development, and the development and rise of substance misuse issues, are the product of this dynamic interplay.

Incident rate

We can see that the majority of young people do not use drugs or alcohol, but that the incident rate increases dramatically with age. Whilst consumption is decreasing slightly in Western societies, use is increasing in the minority that do use substances. Patterns of use in young people are a mirror of established social norms within a society which promotes powerful expectancies of use. Not only does this give rise to distinctive patterns of consumption but it also determines the type, intensity and frequency of problems associated with use. Furthermore, this occurs within the context of the young person's particular social and historical environment. Young people adopt drug use not necessarily to experience the specific pharmacological properties of a given substance but because of what the drug symbolises. Use is connected with wider associations for young people, involving identity, lifestyle and social bonding.

Developmental processes

Substance misuse has a more profound effect on developmental processes in youth as adolescence is a period of such rapid transition. Brain development and rapid transition towards adult life give rise to new ways of understanding the self and the world, and bring with them novel life experiences that require mastery. Young people's thought processes and reactions to life differ greatly from adults'. Substance use has a direct impact in critical developmental processes such

as cognitive development, life task achievement, identity formation and shifts in relationships. If use erodes the social attachments of the young person, it leads to profound development delay, curtailing the young person's preparedness for increasingly sophisticated demands within the life course. This marks the age of initiation as particularly important, as early initiation impedes this developmental process more profoundly. Within this, young people's use is determined by a constellation of risk factors emanating from both themselves and the environments they occupy. These risk factors cluster together forming distinct pathways into problematic use. High risk youth are exposed to a greater range of risk at a younger age, leading to early involvement. These 'externalised' youth experience a wide range of behavioural problems and experience the most profound developmental delay. In contrast, 'internalised' youth experience a greater frequency of mental illness, particularly at the time of puberty, whilst 'normative' use occurs later in adolescence as peer influence peaks, and both tend to have much higher levels of social functioning. Their different sequence of drug and alcohol involvement reflects patterns of deeper entrenchment in their social attachments and more restricted access to substances. The key Gateway substance is tobacco, followed by alcohol and cannabis. These substances are cheap and easily available. Technological advances in the form of the internet are likely to have a profound effect on these patterns of involvement in the future though.

Assessment

The nature of young people's problematic use does not reflect the diagnostic criteria developed for adults. Existing diagnostic criteria are designed to assess long term exposure to drugs or alcohol and largely centre on concepts of substance Abuse and substance Dependence. Whilst young people are more liable to experience Abuse, as defined through increased rates of social complications, the inherent weaknesses of these diagnostic criteria have limited their utility. Moreover, young people are far less likely than adults to experience physical withdrawal, rendering the Dependence criteria unsuitable. As such, young people are more likely to present as diagnostic imposters or orphans. However, research has identified the sequence of onset of these symptoms and this may provide improved direction in assessment processes. They can build on the evidence that those assessment processes which are tailored to capturing the nature and sequence of young people's use provide objective feedback and can increase their belief that change can make a significant contribution to their clinical outcomes.

Prevention

In terms of prevention, many of the historical models failed to produce any significant outcomes because they were largely reflective of adult concerns regarding drug and alcohol use, and not young people's. Advances in prevention have been able to identify the key risk factors that influence young people's use and have begun to demonstrate significant outcomes. However, these outcomes operate in more complex ways than previously imagined. As patterns of drug and alcohol use are predicted by the age of onset of use, even small delays in initiation or consumption can have profound consequences up-stream from the point of delivery of education and/or prevention measures. At their best, education and prevention shorten a young person's using career, reduce their liability to experiencing problematic use and prevent young people travelling through the spectrum of use to higher end substances. Prevention has proven particularly effective for 'externalised' high risk groups when they have been targeted by psychological profiles as opposed to demographic ones. Such profiles appear to reflect the distinctions between externalised, internalised and normative youth who express profoundly different motivations for use, influenced by their temperament.

Treatment

In terms of treatment, young people have historically demonstrated a poorer outcomes profile than adults. Again, treatment responsiveness appears to be influenced by a young person's sub-trajectory. Externalised youth progress during treatment but can experience a collapse of outcome post-treatment, due to the continuation of risk factors in their environments. Internalised and normative youth display better long term outcomes which may also be influenced by their higher range of social functioning at treatment outset. These extra-therapeutic factors contribute to the majority of treatment outcomes. In terms of treatment provision, factors which are common to all interventions, such as the working alliance between the young person and the practitioner, are the single largest source of type of treatment outcomes. Therefore, pro-active strategies should be employed to maximise this relational element of treatment, which can have a major up-lift on treatment outcomes. Whilst there is limited research on optimal treatment modalities with young people, there is a promising emergent evidence base. However, truly developmentally informed approaches are yet to be fully realised. Treatment systems need to incorporate four key elements:

- Clinically managing physical dependence if present.
- Equipping young people with the skills to stop or control their use.
- Providing specialist support to address complex issues in their risk profile, such as behaviour problems or mental illness.
- Offering a broad range of life skills to address developmental delay.

Recovery and aftercare

The recovery process is characterised by reintegration into the pro-social structures that constitute the individual young person's life course. This requires not simply the elimination of risk factors but the promotion of protective factors to sustain these gains as well. As the family constitutes a substantial element of this social structure, its involvement needs to be promoted in the treatment of young people. Family involvement can occur at a number of points including promoting treatment entry, family therapy and adjunct support such as case conferences and network therapies. However, family interventions have not yet accounted for the diversity of family profiles that are reflective of young people's various sub-trajectories. Finally, whilst aftercare has been a much neglected area of study, research consistently agrees that it is essential if positive outcomes are to endure for the most vulnerable young people. The duration of aftercare appears intrinsically important for sustained long-term outcomes. Research has begun to support innovative proactive strategies that can enhance retention rates.

New understanding and old ideas

Prevention and treatment interventions for young drug and alcohol users are at an exciting juncture in their development. Advances in research, particularly in understanding developmental processes and longitudinal studies, have discovered compelling and robust evidence describing the natural history of young people's use as it occurs. Whilst previous generations in the field could only rely upon speculative theories of human nature and problem use, we now possess an empirically validated foundation of knowledge to inform future development. The progress of any discipline requires two things.

First is the advance of new understanding and theories that take better account of the facts. Second is the elimination of older theories that have not stood up against the test of evidence. Whilst the fields of psychology and psychotherapy are very good at the former, they tend to poor at the latter. The field remains haunted by ideological models which have not been substantiated by subsequent research but which, like a ghost net, continue to capture the imagination of practitioners. Philosophically, if anything goes then everything stays. The possibility of truly developmentally informed approaches to young people requires not simply the incorporation of research but also the letting go of established modes of practice. Young people will not benefit from our loyalty to certain models. They will benefit from an openness to our own and their future possibilities.

References

Abram, K.M. et al. (2004) Posttraumatic Stress Disorder and Trauma in Youth in Juvenile Detention. *Archives of General Psychiatry*. 61, 403–10.

Abrantes, A. et al. (2002) *Long-Term Trajectories of Alcohol Involvement Following Addictions Treatment in Adolescence*. Symposium presented at The Research Society on Alcoholism, California.

ACMD Report (1998) *Drug Misuse and The Environment*. HMSO.

Aguirre-Molina, M. and Gorman, D.M. (1996) Community-Based Approaches for the Prevention of Alcohol, Tobacco and Other Drug Used. *Public Health*. 17, 337–58.

Alcoholics Anonymous (1952) *The Twelve Steps and Twelve Traditions*. Alcoholics Anonymous World Services.

Allen, J.P. et al. (1997) A Review of Research on The Alcohol Use Disorders Identification Test (AUDIT) *Alcoholism: Clinical and Experimental Research*. 21: 4, 613–9.

Allport, G.W. and Odbert, H.S. (1936) Trait Names: A Psycho-Lexical Study. *Psychological Monographs*. 47: 1, 211.

American Academy of Pediatrics (2002) Make Time to Screen for Substance Abuse During Office Visits (Committee on Substance Abuse). *AAP News*. 21: 14, 34.

Amonini, C. and Donovan, R.J. (2006) The Relationship Between Youth's Moral and Legal Perceptions of Alcohol, Tobacco and Marijuana and Use of the Substances. *Health Education Research: Theory and Practice*. 2: 2, 276–86.

Anderson, B. et al. (2007) *Alcohol and Drug Use Among European 17–18 Year Old Students: Data From The ESAPD Project*. The Swedish Council for Information on Alcohol and Other Drugs.

Anderson, D.S. and Gadaleto, A.F. (1991) *The College Alcohol Survey*. George Mason University.

Anderson, T. et al. (2006) The Recreation Mentoring Program: A Community Engagement Initiative for Children. *Journal of The Canadian Academy Child and Adolescent Psychiatry*.15: 2, 59–63.

Anderson, T.L. (1993) Types of Identity Change in Drug Using and Recovery Careers. *Sociological Focus*. 26: 2, 133–45.

Anderson, T.L. (1994) Drug Abuse and Identity: Linking The Micro and Macro Factors. *Sociology Quarterly*. 35: 1, 159–74.

Anderson, T.L. and Mott, J.A. (1998) Drug Related Identity Change: Theoretical Development and Empirical Assessment. *Journal of Drug Issues*. 28: 2, 299–328.

Anguelov, A., Petkova, E. and Lazarov, P. (1999) Promoting Health Educational Programmes for The Prevention of Tobacco, Alcohol and Drug Abuse in The School Environment. *Drugs: Education, Prevention and Policy*. 6: 3, 333–5.

Anker, M.G. et al. (2010) The Alliance in Couple Therapy: Partner Influence, Early Change, and Alliance Patterns in a Naturalistic Sample. *Journal of Consulting and Clinical Psychology*. 78: 5, 635–45.

Annis, M., Herrie, M.A. and Watkin-Merek, L. (1996) *Structured Relapse Prevention*. Addiction Research Foundation.

Antony, J.C., Warner, L. and Kessler, R.C. (1994) Comparative Epidemiology of Dependence on Tobacco, Alcohol, Controlled Substances and Inhalants: Basic Findings for The National Co-Morbidity Survey. *Experimental and Clinical Psychopharmacology*. 2, 244–68.

APA (2000) *Diagnostic and Statistical Manual of Mental Disorders DSM-IV-TR*. 4th edn. American Psychiatric Publishing.

APA (In Press) Diagnostic and Statistical Manual of Mental Disorders DSM-V. 5th edn. American Psychiatric Publishing.

Armstrong, T.D. and Costello, E.J. (2002) Community Studies on Adolescent Substance Use, Abuse, or Dependence and Psychiatric Co-Morbidity. *Journal of Consulting and Clinical Psychology*. 70, 1224–39.

Arnett, J.J. (1999) Adolescent Storm and Stress, Reconsidered. *American Psychologist*. 54, 317–26.

Asch, S.E. (1951) *Social Psychology*. Prentice Hall.

Asch, S.E. (1952) Effects of Group Pressure on The Modification and Distortion of Judgement. In Guetzkow, H. (Ed.) *Groups, Learning and Men: Research in Human Relations*. Carnegie Press.

Ashtari, M. et al. (2009) Diffusion Abnormalities

in Adolescents and Young Adults With a History of Heavy Cannabis Use. *Journal of Psychiatric Research*. 43: 3, 189–204.

Auriacombe, M., Franques, P. and Tignol, J. (2001) Deaths Attributable to Methadone Versus Buprenorphine in France. *JAMA*. 285, 45.

Austin, E.W., Chen, M.J. and Grube, J.W. (2006) How Does Alcohol Advertising Influence Underage Drinking? *Journal of Adolescent Health*. 38: 4, 376–84.

Azrin, N.H., et al. (1994a) Youth Drug Abuse Treatment: A Controlled Outcome Study. *Journal of Child and Adolescent Substance Abuse*. 3, 1–16.

Azrin, N.H., et al. (2001) A Controlled Evaluation and Description of Individual Cognitive Problem-solving and Family Behaviour Therapies in Dually Diagnosed Conduct Disordered Substance Dependant Youth. *Journal of Child and Adolescent Substance Abuse*, 11: 1, 1–43.

Azrin, N.H., McMahon, P. and Donohue, B. (1994b) Behaviour Therapy for Drug Abuse: A Controlled Outcome Study. *Behaviour Research and Therapy*. 32, 857–66.

Bachelor, A. and Hovarth, A. (1999) The Therapeutic Relationship. In Duncan, B.L. et al. (Eds.) *The Heart and Soul of Change: Delivering What Works in Therapy*. American Psychological Association.

Bachman, J.G. and Schulenberg, J. (1993) How Part-Time Work Intensity Relates to Drug Use, Problem Behaviour, Time Use, and Satisfaction Among High School Seniors: Are These Consequences or Merely Correlates? *Developmental Psychology*. 29, 220–35.

Bachman, J.G. et al. (1997) *Smoking, Drinking, and Drug Use in Young Adulthood: The Impacts of New Freedoms and New Responsibilities*. Lawrence Erlbaum Associates.

Bachman, J.G. et al. (2008) *The Education-Drug Use Connection: How Successes and Failures in Schools Relate to Adolescent Smoking, Drinking, Drug Use and Delinquency*. Lawrence Erlbaum Associates.

Backer, T.E. (1990) Comparative Synthesis of Mass Media Health Behaviour Campaigns. *Knowledge: Creation, Diffusion, Utilization*. 11: 3, 315–29.

Backer, T.E. Rogers, E.M. and Sopory, P. (1992) *Designing Health Communication Campaigns: What Works?* Sage.

Baker, K. (2008) *Assessment, Planning Interventions and Supervision – Key Elements of Effective Practice*. London: YJB.

Balaban, B.J. and Melchionda, R. (1979) Outreach Redefined: The Impact on Staff Attitudes of a Family Education Project. *International Journal of Addiction*. 14: 6, 833–46.

Baldwin, S.A., Wampold, B.E. and Imel, Z.E. (2007) Untangling the Alliance-Outcome Correlation: Exploring the Relative Importance of Therapist and Patient Variability in the Alliance. *Journal of Consulting and Clinical Psychology*. 75: 6, 842–52.

Ball, S., Bowe, R. and Gerwitz, S. (1996) School Choice, Social Class and Distinction: The Realisation of Social Advantage in Education. *Journal of Education Policy*. 11, 89–113.

Baltes, P.B., Reese, H.W. and Lipsitt, L.P. (1980) Life Span Development Psychology. *Annual Review of Psychology*, 31, 65–110.

Bandura, A. (1977a) *Social Learning Theory*. Prentice-Hall.

Bandura, A. (1977b) Self-Efficacy: Toward a Unifying Theory of Behavioural Change. *Psychology Review*. 84: 2, 191–215.

Bandura, A. (1986) *Social Foundations of Thought and Action: A Social Cognitive*. Prentice Hall.

Bangert-Drowns, R.L. (1988) The Effects of School-Based Substance Abuse Prevention: A Meta Analysis. *Journal of Drug Education*. 18: 3, 243–64.

Barbeau, E., Krieger, N. and Soobader, M.J. (2004) Working Class Matters: Socioeconomic Disadvantage, Race/Ethnicity, Gender, and Smoking in NHIS 2000. Eratum. *American Journal of Public Health*. 94, 1295.

Barber, J.G. and Crisp, B.R. (1995) The Pressures to Change Approach to Working With the Partners of Heavy Drinkers. *Addiction*. 90, 269–76.

Barbor, T.F. et al. (1989) *AUDIT: The Alcohol Use Disorders Identification Test: Guidelines for Use in Primary Care*. WHO publication No. 89.4. WHO.

Barnow, S. et al. (2004) Do Alcohol Expectancies and Peer Delinquency/Substance Use Mediate The Relationship Between Impulsivity and Drinking Behaviour in Adolescence? *Alcohol and Alcoholism*. 39: 3, 213–9.

Baron, R.M. and Kenny, D.A. (1986) The Moderator-Mediator Distinction in Social Psychology Research: Conceptual, Strategic, and Statistical Considerations. *Journal of Personality and Social Psychology*. 51, 1173–82.

Barret, P.M., Dadds, M.R. and Rapee, R.M. (1996) Family Treatment of Childhood Anxiety: A Controlled Trial. *Journal of Consulting and Clinical Psychology*. 64, 333–42.

Bates, M.E. and Labouvie, E.W. (1997) Adolescent Risk Factors and The Prediction of Persistent Alcohol and Drug Use Into Adult Life. *Alcoholism: Clinical and Experimental Research.* 21, 944–50.

Bauman, K.E. et al. (1991) The Influence of Three Mass Media Campaigns on Variables Related to Adolescent Cigarette Smoking: Results of a Field Experiment. *American Journal of Public Health.* 81, 597–604.

Baumeister, R.F. (1994) The Crystallization of Discontent in The Process of Major Life Change. In Heatherton, T.F. and Weinberg, J.L. (Eds.) *Can Personality Change?* American Psychological Association.

Baumeister, R.F. et al. (2003) Does High Self-Esteem Cause Better Performance and Interpersonal Success or Healthier Lifestyles? *Psychological Science in The Public Interest.* 4, 1–44.

Baumrind, D. (1971) Current Patterns of Parental Authority. *Developmental Psychology.* 4: 1.2, 1–103.

Baumrind, D. and Moselle, K.A. (1985) A Developmental Perspective on Adolescent Drug Abuse. *Advances in Alcohol and Substance Abuse.* 4, 41–67

Beck, E.J. et al. (1990) Update on HIV-Testing at a London Sexually Transmitted Disease Clinic: Long Term Impact of The AIDS Media Campaign. *Genitourinary Medicine.* 66, 142–7.

Beck, K.H. and Trieman, K.A. (1996) The Relationship of Social Context of Drinking, Perceived Social Norms, and Parental Influence to Various Drinking Patterns of Adolescents. *Addictive Behaviour.* 21, 633–44.

Becker, J. and Roe, S. (2005) *Drug Use Among Vulnerable Groups of Young People: Findings From The 2003 Crime and Justice Survey.* Home Office.

Behrens, D.A. et al. (1999) A Dynamic Model of Drug Initiation: Implications for Treatment and Drug Control. *Mathematical Biosciences.* 159, 1–20.

Behrens, D.A. et al. (2000) Optimal Control of Drug Epidemics: Prevent and Treat – But Not at The Same Time. *Management Science.* 46: 3, 333–47.

Behrens, D.A. et al. (2002) Why Present-Orientated Societies Undergo Cycles of Drug Epidemics. *Journal of Economic Dynamics and Control.* 26: 6, 919–36.

Bell, M. et al. (2010) *Northern Ireland Registry of Deliberate Self-Harm Western Area, Two Year Report. January 1st 2007–31 December 2008.* National Suicide Research Foundation.

Bernazzini, O. (2001) Early Parent Training to Prevent Disruptive Behavior Problems and Delinquency in Children. *The Annals of The American Academy of Political and Social Science.* 578, 90–103.

Berry, E.H. et al. (2001) Multi-Ethnic Comparisons of Risk and Protective Factors for Adolescent Pregnancy. *Journal of Child and Adolescent Social Work.* 17, 79–96.

Best, J. et al. (1988) Preventing Cigarette Smoking Among School Children. *Annual Review of Public Health.* 15, 161–201.

Birmaher, B. et al. (2006) Clinical Course of Children and Adolescents With Bipolar Spectrum Disorders. *Archives of General Psychiatry.* 63: 2, 175–83.

Black, G.S. (1991) Changing Attitudes Towards Drug Use: Effects of Advertising. In Donohew, L. et al. (Eds.) *Persuasive Communication and Drug Abuse Prevention.* Lawrence Erlbuam.

Blitzer, R.D., Gil, O. and Lundau, E.M. (1990) Long Term Potentiation in Rat Hippocampus is Inhibited by Low Concentrations of Ethanol. *Brain Research.* 537: 1–2, 203–8.

Block, L.G., Morwitz, V.G. and Sen, S.K. (1996) *Does Anti-Drug Advertising Work?* Proceedings of The Marketing and Public Policy Conference, Washington DC.

Blum, R.H. (1976) *Drug Education: Results and Recommendations.* Lexington Books.

Blum, R.H. and Blum, E.M. (1969) A Cultural Case Study. In Blum, R.H. et al. (Eds.) *Drugs I: Drugs and Society.* Jossey-Bass.

BMRB (British Market Research Bureau) (2007) *Scottish Schools Adolescent Lifestyle and Substance Use Survey (SALSUA) National Report: Smoking, Drinking and Drug Use Among 13–15 Year Olds in Scotland in 2006.* BMRB Social Research.

Bordin, E.S. (1979) The Generalizability of The Psychoanalytic Concept of The Working Alliance. *Psychotherapy: Theory, Research and Practice.* 16: 3, 252–60.

Borkenau, P. et al. (2001) Genetic and Environmental Influences on Observed Personality: Evidence From The German Observational Study of Adult Twins. *Journal of Personality and Social Psychology.* 80, 655–68.

Botvin, G.J. and Eng, A. (1982) The Efficacy of a Multi-Component Approach to The Prevention of Cigarette Smoking. *Journal of Preventative Medicine.* 11, 199–211.

Botvin, G.J. and Tortu, S. (1998) Peer Relationships, Social Competence and Substance Abuse Prevention: Implications for

The Family. In Coombs, R.H. (Ed.) *The Family Context of Adolescent Drug Use*. Hawthorn Press.

Botvin, G.J., Eng, A. and Williams, C.L. (1980) Preventing The Onset of Cigarette Smoking Through Life Skills Training. *Preventative Medicine*. 9, 135–43.

Botvin, G.J. et al. (1984b) Prevention of Alcohol Misuse Through The Development of Personal and Social Competence: A Pilot Study. *Journal of Studies on Alcohol*. 45, 550–2.

Botvin, G.J. et al. (1989a) A Psychosocial Approach to Smoking Prevention for Urban Black Youth. *Public Health Reports*. 104, 573–82.

Botvin, G.J. et al. (1989b) A Skills Training Approach to Smoking Prevention Amongst Hispanic Youth. *Journal of Behavioural Medicine*. 12, 279–96.

Botvin, G.J. et al. (1990) Preventing Adolescent Drug Abuse Through a Multimodal Cognitive-Behavioural Approach: Results of a 3-Year Study. *Journal of Consulting and Clinical Psychology*. 58: 4, 437–46.

Botvin, G.J. et al. (1992) Smoking Prevention Among Urban Minority Youth: Assessing the Effects on Outcome and Mediating Variables. *Health Psychology*. 11, 290–9.

Botvin, G.J. et al. (1995a) Long Term Follow-Up Results of a Randomised Drug Abuse Prevention Trial in a White Middle Class Population. *Journal of The American Medical Association*. 273, 1106–12.

Botvin, G.J. et al. (1995b) Effectiveness of Culturally Focused and Generic Skills Training Approaches to Alcohol and Drug Abuse Prevention Among Minority Adolescents: Two-Year Follow-Up Results. *Psychology of Addictive Behaviours*. 9, 183–94.

Botvin, G.J. et al. (1997) School-Based Drug Abuse Prevention With Inner-City Minority Youth. *Journal of Child and Adolescent Substance Abuse*. 6: 1, 5–19.

Botvin, G.J. et al. (2000) Preventing Illicit Drug Use in Adolescents: Long-Term Follow-Up Data From a Randomized Control Trial of a School Population. *Addictive Behaviors*. 25: 5, 769–74.

Botvin, G.J. et al. (2001) Drug Abuse Prevention Among Minority Adolescents: Posttest and One-Year Follow-Up of a School-Based Preventive Intervention. *Prevention Science*. 2: 1, 1–13.

Botvin, G.J., Renick, N. and Baker, E. (1983) The Effects of Scheduling Format and Booster Sessions on a Broad Spectrum Psychosocial

Approach to Smoking Prevention. *Journal of Behavioural Medicine*. 6, 359–79.

Botvin, G.J., Schinke, S. and Orlandi, M.A. (Eds.) (1995) *Drug Abuse Prevention With Multiethnic Youth*. Sage.

Botwin, M.D. and Buss, D.M. (1989) Structure of Act-Report Data: Is The Five-Factor Model of Personality Recaptured? *Journal of Personality and Social Psychology*. 56, 988–1000.

Boucharde, T.J. and McGue, M. (1990) Genetic and Rearing Environmental Influences on Adult Personality: an Analysis of Adopted Twins Reared Apart. *Journal of Personality*. 58, 263–92.

Bourdieu, P. (1977) Cultural Reproduction and Social Reproduction. In Karabeland, J. and Halsey, A. (Eds.) *Power and Ideology in Education*. Oxford University Press.

Bowlby, M. (1961) *Child Care and The Growth of Love*. Penguin.

Boys, A. and Marsden, J. (2003) Perceived Functions Predict Intensity of Use and Problems in Young Polysubstance Users. *Addiction*. 98, 951–63.

Boys, A. et al. (1999) What Influences Young People's Use of Drugs? A Qualitative Study of Decision Making. *Drugs: Education Prevention and Policy*. 6, 374–87.

Boys, A. et al. (2003) Psychiatric Morbidity and Substance Use in Young People Aged 13–15: Result of a Child and Adolescent Survey of Mental Health. *British Journal of Psychiatry*. 182, 509–17.

Boys, A., Marsden, J. and Strang. J. (2001) Understanding Reasons for Drug Use Amongst Young People: A Functional Perspective. *Health Education Research Theory and Practice*. 16, 457–69.

Bradley, J.R., Carman, R.S. and Petree, A. (1992) Personal and Social Drinking Motives, Family Drinking History, and Problems Associated With Drinking in Two University Sample. *Journal of Drug Education*. 22, 195–202.

Breakwell, G. and Fife-Shaw, C. (1992) Sexual Activities and Preferences in a United Kingdom Sample of 16–20 Year Olds. *Archives of Sexual Behaviour*. 21, 271–93.

Bronfenbrenner, U. (1979) *The Ecology of Human Development: Experiments by Nature and Design*. Harvard University Press.

Brook, J.S., Cohen, P. and Brook, D.W. (1998) Longitudinal Study of Co-Occurring Psychiatric Disorders and Substance Use. *Journal of The American Academy of Child and Adolescent Psychiatry*. 37, 322–30.

Brooks-Gunn, J and Paikoff, R. (1997) "Sex is a Gamble, Kissing is a Game": Adolescents' Sexuality and Health Promotion. In Millstein, S.G. et al. (Eds.) *Promoting The Health of Adolescents: New Directions for The Twenty-First Century*. O.U.P.

Brown, G.K. et al. (2005) Cognitive Therapy for The Prevention of Suicide Attempts: A Randomised Controlled Trial. *Journal of The American Medical Association*. 294, 563–70.

Brown, G.S. et al. (2005) Identifying Highly Effective Psychotherapists in a Managed Care Environment. *Journal of Managed Care*. 11: 8, 513–20.

Brown, J., Dries, S. and Nace, D.K. (1999) What Really Makes A Difference in Psychotherapy Outcome? Why Does Managed Care Want to Know? In Hubble, M.A., Duncan, B.L. and Miller, S.D. (Eds.) *The Heart and Soul of Change: What Works in Therapy?* American Psychological Association.

Brown, P. and Scase, R. (1994) *Higher Education and Corporate Realities*. UCI Press.

Brown, S.A. (1993) Recovery Patterns in Adolescent Substance Abuse. In Baer, J.S. and Marlatt, G.A. (Eds.) *Addictive Behaviour Across The Life Span: Prevention, Treatment, and Policy Issues*. Sage Publications.

Brown, S.A. (1999) Treatment of Adolescent Alcohol Problems: Research Review and Appraisal. *NIDA Extramural Scientific Advisory Board*.

Brown, S.A. (2001) Facilitating Change for Adolescent Alcohol Problems: A Multiple Options Approach. In Wagner, E.F. and H.B. Waldron, H.B. (Eds.) Innovations in Adolescent Substance Abuse Interventions. Pergamon/Elseveir.

Brown, S.A. et al. (1980) Expectations of Reinforcement From Alcohol: Their Domain and Relation to Drinking Patterns. *Journal of Clinical and Consulting Psychology*. 48, 419–26.

Brown, S.A. et al. (1996) Conduct Disorder Among Adolescent Alcohol and Drug Users. *Journal of Studies on Alcohol*. 57, 314–24.

Brown, S.A. et al. (2000a) Neurocognitive Functioning of Adolescence: Effects of Protracted Alcohol Use. *Alcoholism: Clinical and Experimental Research*. 24: 2, 164–71.

Brown, S.A. et al. (2000b) The Role of Alcohol in Adolescent Relapse and Outcome. *Journal of Psychoactive Drugs*. 32, 107–15.

Brown, S.A. et al. (2001) Four Year Outcomes From Adolescent Alcohol and Drug Treatment. *Journal of Studies on Alcohol*. 62, 381–8.

Brown, S.A. et al. (2005a) Facilitating Youth Self-Change Through School Based Interventions. *Addictive Behaviour*. 30: 9, 1797–810.

Brown, S.A. et al. (2005b) Treatment of Adolescent Alcohol Related Problems. In Galante, M. (Ed.) *Recent Developments in Alcoholism*. Kluwer Academic/Plenum.

Brown, S.A., Mott, M.A. and Myers, M.G. (1990) Adolescent Alcohol and Drug Treatment Outcome. In Watson, R.R. (Ed.) *Drug and Alcohol Abuse Prevention*. Humana Press.

Brown, S.W., Vik, P.W. and Creamer, V.A. (1989) Characteristics of Relapse Following Adolescent Substance Abuse Treatment. *Addictive Behaviours*. 14: 3, 291–300.

Bruvold, W.H. (1993) A Meta-Analysis of Adolescent Smoking Prevention Programs. *American Journal of Public Health*. 83, 872–80.

Bry, B.H. (1988) Family-Based Approaches to Reducing Adolescent Substance Abuse: Theories, Techniques and Findings. *NIDA Research Monograph*. 77, 39–68.

Bry, B.H., Mckeon, R. and Pandina, R.J. (1982) Extent of Drug Use as a Function of Number of Risk Factors. *Journal of Abnormal Psychology*. 91, 273–9.

Buckner, J.D. et al. (2008) Specificity of Social Anxiety Disorder as a Risk Factor for Alcohol and Cannabis Dependence. *Psychiatry Research*. 42, 230–9.

Bui, K.V.T., Ellickson, P.L. and Bell, R.M. (2000) Cross-Lagged Relationship Among Adolescent Problem Drug Use, Delinquent Behaviour and Emotional Distress. *Journal of Drug Issues*. 30, 283–304.

Bukstein, O. (1997) Practice Parameters for the Assessment and Treatment of Children and Adolescents With Substance Use Disorders. *Journal of The American Academy of Child and Adolescent Psychiatry*, 36, 140s-56s.

Burke, J.D., Loeber, R. and Birmaher, B. (2002) Oppositional Defiance Disorder and Conduct Disorder: A Review of the Past Ten Years. *Journal of The American Academy of Child and Adolescent Psychiatry*, 41, 1293.

Burns, P.K. and Bozeman, W.C. (1981) Computer Assisted Instruction and Mathematic Achievement: Is There a Relationship? *Educational Technology*. 21, 29–32.

Cady, M.E. et al. (1996) Motivation to Change as a Predictor of Treatment Outcome for Adolescent Substance Abusers. *Journal of Child and Adolescent Substance Abuse*. 5, 73–91.

Campbell, T.W. (1992) Therapeutic Relationships and Iatrogenic Outcomes: The Blame-And-Change Manoeuvre in Psychotherapy. *Psychotherapy.* 29: 3, 474–80.

Carey, M.P. et al. (1986) Relationship of Activity to Depression in Adolescents: Development of Adolescent Activity Checklist. *Journal of Consulting Clinical Psychology.* 54, 320–2.

Carney, R.E. (1971) An *Evaluation of The Effect of a Values Orientated Drug Abuse Education Program Using The Risk Taking Attitude Questionnaire.* Coronado Unified School District.

Carney, R.E. (1972) An *Evaluation of The Tempe, Arizona 1970–1971 Drug Abuse Prevention Education Program Using The RTAQ and B-VI: Final Report.* Tempe School District.

Carr, A. (2000) Evidenced-Based Practice in Family Therapy and Systemic Consultation: Child Focussed Problems. *Journal of Family Therapy.* 22, 29–60.

Casswell, S. et al. (1989) Changes in Public Support for Alcohol Policies Following a Community-Based Campaign. *British Journal of Addictions.* 84, 515–22.

Casswell, S., Pledger, M. and Pratap, S. (2002) Trajectories of Drinking 18–26: Identification and Prediction. *Addiction.* 97, 1427–37.

Castro, F.G. et al. (1987) A Multivariate Model of The Determinants of Cigarette Smoking Among Adolescents. *Journal of Health and Social Behaviour.* 28, 273–89.

Catalano, R.F. et al. (1990) Evaluation of The Effectiveness of Adolescent Drug Abuse Treatment, Assessment of Risks for Relapse, and Promising Approaches for Relapse Prevention. *International Journal of Addictions.* 25, 1085–140.

Catalano, R.F. et al. (1998) Comprehensive Community and School Based Interventions to Prevent Antisocial Behavior. In Loeber, R. and Farrington, D.P. (Eds.) *Serious and Violent Juvenile Offenders: Risk Factors and Successful Interventions.* Sage Publications.

Cattell, R.B. (1943) The Description of Personality: Basic Traits Resolved Into Clusters. *Journal of Abnormal and Social Psychology.* 38, 476–507.

Cattell, R.B. (1947) Confirmation and Clarification of Primary Personality Factors. *Psychometrika.* 12, 197–220.

Caulkins, J.P. et al. (1999) An *Ounce of Prevention, A Pound of Uncertainty: The Cost Effectiveness of School Based Drug Prevention Programs.* RAND Drug Policy Research Centre.

Caulkins, J.P. et al. (2002) *School Based Prevention: What Kind of Drug Use Does it Prevent?* RAND Drug Policy Research Centre.

Chambers, J.A. and Sprecher, J.A. (1980) Computer-Assisted Instruction: Current Trends and Critical Issues. *Communications of The ACM.* 23, 332–42.

Chan, Y.F., Dennis, M.L. and Funk, R.R. (2008) Prevalence and Comorbidity of Major Internalizing and Externalizing Disorders Among Adolescents and Adults Presenting to Substance Abuse Treatment. *Journal of Substance Abuse Treatment.* 34, 14–24.

Chapman, J.F. and Ford, J.D. (2008) Relationship Between Suicide Risk, Traumatic Experiences, and Substance Use Amongst Juvenile Detainees Screened With MAYSI-2 and Suicide Ideation Questionnaire. *Archives of Suicide Research.* 12, 50–61.

Chassin, L., et al. (1996) The Relation of Parent Alcoholism to Adolescent Substance Use: A Longitudinal Follow-Up Study. *Journal of Abnormal Psychology.* 105, 70–80.

Chassin, L., Pitts, S.C. and Prost, J. (2002) Binge Drinking Trajectories From Adolescence to Emerging Adulthood in a High Risk Sample: Predictors and Substance Abuse Outcomes. *Journal of Consulting and Clinical Psychology.* 70, 67–78.

Chau, N.E. et al. (2008) Social Inequalities and Correlates of Psychotropic Drug Use Among Young Adults: A Population Based Questionnaire Study. *International Journal for Equity in Health.* 7: 1, 3.

Chick, J. (1980) Alcohol Dependence: Methodological Issues in its Treatment: Reliability of The Criteria. *British Journal of Addictions.* 75, 175–86.

Chick, J., Lloyd, G. and Crombie, E. (1985) Counselling Problem Drinkers in Medical Wards: A Controlled Study. *British Medical Journal.* 290, 965–7.

Chief Medical Officers' Report (2009) *Draft Guidance on The Consumption of Alcohol by Children and Young People.* Chief Medical Officers of England, Wales and Ireland.

Chilcoat, H. and Breslau, N. (1999) Pathways From ADHD to Early Drug Use. *Journal of The American Academy of Child and Adolescent Psychiatry.* 38: 11, 1347–54.

Chou, S.P. and Pickering, R.P. (1992) Early Onset of Drinking as a Risk Factor for Lifetime Alcohol Problems. *British Journal of Addiction.* 87, 1199–204.

Christiansen, B.A. et al. (1989) Using Alcohol

Expectancies to Predict Adolescent Drinking Behaviour After One Year. *Journal of Consulting and Clinical Psychology*. 57, 93–99.

Chung, T. and Maisto, S.A. (2006) Review and Reconsideration of Relapse as A Change Point in Clinical Course in Treated Adolescents. *Clinical Psychology Review*. 26, 149–61.

Chung, T. and Martin, C.S. (2001) Classification and Course of Alcohol Problems Among Adolescents in Addiction Treatment Programs. *Alcoholism: Clinical and Experimental Research*. 26, 485–92.

Chung, T. and Martin, C.S. (2005) Classification and Short Term Course of Cannabis, Hallucinogen, Cocaine, and Opioid Disorders in Treatment Adolescents. *Journal of Consulting and Clinical Psychology*. 73, 995–1004.

Chung, T. et al. (2000) Screening Adolescents for Problem Drinking in a Hospital Setting. *Journal of Studies on Alcohol*. 61, 579–87.

Chung, T. et al. (2002) Prevalence of DSM-IV Alcohol Diagnosis and Symptoms in Adolescent and Community and Clinical Samples. *Journal of American Academy of Child and Adolescent Psychiatry*. 41, 546–54.

Chung, T. et al. (2003) Course of Alcohol Problems in Treated Adolescents. *Alcoholism: Clinical and Experimental Research*. 27: 2, 253–61.

Clark, D.B. and Scheid, J. (2001) Comorbid Disorder in Adolescents With Substance Abuse Disorders. In Hubbard, J.R. (Ed.) *Substance Abuse in The Mentally and Physically Disabled*. Marcel Dekker.

Clark, D.B. et al. (1994) Anxiety Disorders in Adolescents: Characteristics, Prevalence and Comorbidities. *Clinical Psychology Review*. 14, 113–37.

Clark, D.B. et al. (1997) Gender and Comorbid Psychopathology in Adolescents With Alcohol Dependence. *Journal of The American Academy of Child and Adolescent Psychiatry*. 36: 9, 1195–203.

Clark, D.B., Thatcher, D.L. and Cornelius, J.R. (2008) Anxiety Disorders and Adolescent Substance Use Disorders. In Kaminer, Y. and Bukstein, O.I. (Eds.) *Adolescent Substance Abuse: Psychiatry, Comorbidity and High-Risk Behaviours*. Routledge.

Clarke, D.B., Thatcher, D.L. and Maisto, S.A. (2005) Supervisory Neglect and Adolescent Alcohol Use Disorders: Effects AUD Onset and Treatment Outcome. *Addictive Behaviours*. 30: 9, 1737–50.

Clarke, G.N. et al. (1995) Targeted Prevention of Unipolar Depressive Disorder in an At-Risk

Sample of High School Adolescents: A Randomised Trial of a Group Cognitive Intervention. *Journal of The American Academy of Child Adolescent Psychiatry*. 34, 312–21.

Clayton, R.R. (1992) Transitions in Drug Use: Risk and Protective Factors. In Glantz, M.D. and Pickins, R. (Eds.) *Vulnerability to Drug Abuse*. American Psychological Association.

Clearly, P.D. et al. (1988) Adolescent Smoking: Research and Health Policy. *Milbank Quarterly*. 66: 1, 137–71.

Clifford, P.R. et al. (2000) Alcohol Treatment Research Follow Up Interviews and Drinking Behaviour. *Journal of Studies on Alcohol*. 61: 5, 736–43.

Clifford, P.R., Maisto, S.A. and Davies, C.M. (2007) Alcohol Treatment Research Assessment Exposure Subject Reactivity Effects, Part I: Alcohol Use and Related Consequences. *Journal of Studies on Alcohol and Drugs*. 68, 519–28.

Cobham, V.E., Dadds, M.R. and Spence, S.H. (1999) The Role of Parental Anxiety in The Treatment of Childhood Anxiety. *Journal of Consulting and Clinical Psychology*. 66, 893–905.

Coggans, N., Cheyne, B. and Mckellar, S. (2003) *The Life Skills Training Drug Education Programme: A Review of Research*. Scottish Executive Drug Misuse Research Programme, Effective Interventions Unit.

Cohen, D.A. and Linton, K.L. (1995) Parent Participation in Adolescent Drug Abuse Prevention Programme. *Journal of Drug Education*. 25, 159–69.

Cohen, H. (1981) The Hashish Culture, A Death Announcement. *Tijdschr Alcohol Drugs*. 7, 3–8.

Cohen, P. et al. (1993) An Epidemiological Study of Disorders in Late Childhood and Adolescence: Age and Gender-Specific Prevalence. *Journal of Child Psychology and Psychiatry*. 34, 851–66.

Colby, S.M. et al. (1999) Effects of a Brief Motivational Interview on Alcohol Use and Consequences: Predictors of Response to Intervention Among 13–17-Year-Olds. In Longabaugh, R. and Monti, P. (Chairs) *Brief Motivational Interventions in The Emergency Department for Adolescents and Adults*. Symposium at The Annual Meeting of The Research Society on Alcoholism.

Colby, S.M. et al. (2000) Are Adolescent Smokers Dependent on Nicotine? A Review of The Evidence. *Journal of Drug and Alcohol Dependence*. 59, S83–S95.

Colder, C.R. and Chassin, L. (1993) The Stress and

Negative Affect Model of Adolescent Alcohol Use and the Moderating Effects of Behavioural Under Control. *Journal of Studies on Alcohol*. 54: 3, 326–33.

Colder, C.R. et al. (2002) A Finite Mixture Model of Growth Trajectories of Adolescent Alcohol Use: Predictors and Consequences. *Journal of Consulting and Clinical Psychology*. 70, 976–85.

Cole, D.A. et al. (1998) A Longitudinal Look at The Relation Between Depression and Anxiety in Children and Adolescents. *Journal of Consulting and Clinical Psychology*. 66, 451–60.

Comeau, N., Stewart, S.H. and Loba, P. (2001) The Relations of Trait Anxiety, Anxiety Sensitivity, and Sensation Seeking to Adolescents' Motivation for Alcohol, Cigarettes, and Marijuana Use. *Addictive Behaviours*. 26, 803–35.

Comptom, S.N. et al. (2004) Cognitive-Behavioural Psychotherapy for Anxiety and Depressive Disorders in Children and Adolescents: an Evidence Based Medicine Review. *Journal of The American Academy of Child and Adolescent Psychiatry*. 43, 930–59.

Connors, G.J., Donovan, D.M. and DiClemente, C.C. (2001) *Substance Abuse Treatment and The Stages of Change: Selecting and Planning Interventions*. Guildford Press.

Conrad, K.M., Flay, B.R. and Hill, D. (1992) Why Children Start Smoking Cigarettes: Predictors of Onset. *British Journal of Addiction*. 87, 1711–24.

Conrod, P.J. and Woicik, P. (2002) Validation of a Four-Factor Model of Personality Risk for Substance Abuse and Examination of a Brief Instrument for Assessing Personality Risk. Presented at The Annual Symposium of The Society for The Study of Addiction, November 2001. *Addictive Biology*. 7, 2329–46.

Conrod, P.J. et al. (2000a) Validation of a System of Classifying Female Substance Abusers Based on Personality and Motivational Risk Factors for Substance Abuse. *Psychology of Addictive Behaviour*. 14, 243–56.

Conrod, P.J. et al. (2000b) Efficacy of Brief Coping Skills Interventions That Match Different Personality Profiles of Female Substance Abusers. *Psychology of Addictive Behaviour*. 14: 3, 231–42.

Copeland, W.E. et al. (2007) Traumatic Events and Posttraumatic Stress in Childhood. *Archives of General Psychiatry*. 64, 577–84.

Copello, A. et al. (2009) *Social Behaviour and Network Therapy for Alcohol Problems*. Routledge.

Corcoran, J. (2011) *Mental Health Treatment for Children and Adolescents*. Oxford University Press.

Cornelius, J.R. et al. (2009) Fluoxetine in Adolescent With Major Depression and Alcohol Use Disorder: an Open-Label Trial. *Addictive Behaviour*. 26, 735–9.

Cottino, A. (1995) Italy. In Heath, D.B. (Ed.) *International Handbook on Alcohol and Culture*. Greenwood.

Cottler, L.B. (1993) Comparing The DSM-IIIR and ICD10 Substance Abuse Disorders. *Addictions*. 88, 689–96.

Cottler, L.B. et al. (1997) Concordance of DSM-IV Alcohol and Drug Use Disorder Criteria and Diagnosis as Measured by AUDADIS-ADR, CIDI and SCAN. *Drug and Alcohol Dependence*. 47, 195–205.

Cottler, L.B., Phelps, D.L. and Compton, W.M. (1995) Narrowing of The Drinking Repertoire Criterion: Should it Have Been Dropped From ICD10? *Journal of Studies on Alcohol*. 56, 173–6.

Coulthard, M. et al. (2002) *Tobacco, Alcohol and Drug Use and Mental Health*. HMSO.

Crockett, L. et al. (1996) Timing of First Sexual Intercourse: The Role of Social Control, Social Learning and Problem Behaviour. *Journal of Youth and Adolescence*. 25, 89–112.

Crum, R. et al. (2008) Depressed Mood in Childhood and Subsequent Alcohol Use Through Adolescence and Young Adulthood. *Archive of General Psychiatry*. 65: 6, 702–12.

CSAT (1999) *Screening and Assessing Adolescents for Substance Use Disorders*. Treatment Improvement Protocol, Series 31.

Cuijpers, P. (2002a) Effective Ingredients of School Based Drug Prevention Programs: A Systematic Review. *Addictive Behaviours*. 27, 1009–23.

Cuijpers, P. (2002b) Peer-Led and Adult-Led School Drug Prevention: A Meta-Analytic Comparison. *Journal of Drug Education*. 32, 107–19.

Cunningham, H. (2006) *The Invention of Childhood*. BBC Books.

Curry, J.E. et al. (2003) Cognitive-Behavioural Interventions for Depressed Substance Abusing Adolescents: Development and Pilot Testing. *Journal of The American Academy of Child and Adolescent Psychiatry*. 42, 656–65.

D'Unger, A.V. et al. (1998) How Many Latent Class of Delinquent / Criminal Careers? Results From Mixed Poisson Regression Analysis. *American Journal of Sociology*. 103, 1593–630.

Dadds, M.R. (1996) Conduct Disorder. In Ammerman, R.T. and Hersen, M. (Eds.) *Handbook of Prevention and Treatment With Children and Adolescents.* John Wiley.

Dadds, M.R. and McAloon, J. (2002) Prevention. In Essua, C.A. (Ed.) *Substance Abuse and Dependence in Adolescence: Epidemiology, Risk Factors and Treatment.* Brunner-Routlege.

Dakof, G.A., Tejeda, M. and Liddle, H.A. (2001) Predictors of Engagement in Adolescent Drug Abuse Treatment. *Journal of The American Academy of Child and Adolescent Psychiatry.* 40: 3, 274–81.

Dawson, D.A. (2000) The Link Between Family History and Early Onset Alcoholism: Earlier Initiation of Drinking or More Rapid Development of Dependence? *Journal of Studies on Alcohol.* 61, 636–46.

De Bellis, M.D. et al. (2005) Prefrontal Cortex, Thalamus, and Cerebellar Volumes in Adolescents and Young Adults With Adolescent Onset Alcohol Use Disorders and Comorbid Mental Disorders. *Alcohol: Clinical Experimental Research.* 29, 1590–600.

Deardorff, J. et al. (2005) Early Puberty and Adolescent Pregnancy: The Influence of Alcohol Use. *Pediatrics.* 116, 1451–6.

Deas, D. and Thomas, S.E. (2001) An Overview of Controlled Studies of Adolescent Substance Abuse Treatment. *American Journal on Addictions.* 10, 178–89.

Deas, D. et al. (2000) Adolescents Are Not Adults: Development Considerations in Alcohol Users. *Alcoholism: Clinical and Experimental Research.* 24, 232–7.

DeLeon, G. (1996) Integrative Recovery: A Stage Paradigm. *Substance Abuse.* 175, 1–63.

DeMause, De, L. (1976) *The History of Childhood.* Souvenir Press.

Dennis, M.L. et al. (2002) The Cannabis Youth Treatment (CYT) Experiment: Rationale, Study Design and Analysis Plans. *Addiction.* 97, Supplement 1, 58–69.

Dennis, M.L. et al. (2004) Main Findings of The Cannabis Youth Treatment (CYT) Randomised Field Experiment. *Journal of Substance Abuse Treatment.* 28, Supplement 1, S51–S62.

DeWit, D.J. et al. (1995) The Construction of Risk and Protective Factors for Adolescent Alcohol and Other Drug Users. *The Journal of Drug Issues.* 25, 837–63.

Di Noia, J. et al. (2003) The Relative Efficacy of Pamphlets, CD-ROM, and The Internet for Disseminating Adolescent Drug Abuse Prevention Programs: an Exploratory Study. *Preventive Medicine.* 37: 6, 646–53.

Difranza, J.R., Richards, J.W. and Paulman, P.M. (1991) RJR Nabiscos' Cartoon Camel Promotes Cigarettes to Children. *Journal of The American Medical Association.* 226, 3149–53.

Dillon, D. et al. (2006) *Risk, Protective Factors and Resilience to Drug Use: Identifying Resilient Young People and Learning From Their Experiences.* Home Office Report.

Dishion, T.J., Reid, J.B. and Patterson, G.R. (1988) Empirical Guidelines for a Family Intervention for Adolescent Drug Use. *Journal of Chemical Dependency Treatment.* 1, 189–224.

Donahue, B. et al. (1998) Improving Initial Session Attendance of Substance Abusing and Conduct Disordered Adolescents: A Control Study. *Journal of Child and Adolescent Substance Abuse.* 8, 1–13.

Donaldson, S.I., Graham, J.W. and Hansen, W.B. (1994) Testing The Generalizability of Intervening Mechanism Theories: Understanding The Effects of Adolescent Drug Use Prevention Interventions. *Journal of Behavioral Medicine.* 17: 2, 195–216.

Donnellan, M.B. et al. (2005) Low Self-Esteem Is Related to Aggression, Antisocial Behaviour and Delinquency. *Psychological Science.* 16, 364–8.

Donovan, C. and Spence, S. (2000) Prevention of Childhood Anxiety Disorders. *Clinical Psychology Review.* 20, 509–31.

Dorn, N. and Murji, K. (1992) *Drug Prevention: A Review of The English Language Literature.* ISDD Research Monograph 5, London.

Douglas, M. (1987) A Distinctive Anthropological Perspective. In Douglas, M. (Ed.) *Constructive Drinking: Perspectives on Drink From Anthropology.* Cambridge University Press.

Douvan, E. and Adelson, J. (1966) *The Adolescent Experience.* John Wiley.

Drew, D., Gray, J. and Sime, N. (1992) *Against The Odds: The Education and Labour Market Experiences of Young Black People.* Employment Department.

Drugscope (2004) *Drugs: Guidance for Further Education Institutions.* Drugscope.

Drury, J. et al. (1998) Exploring Teenagers' Accounts of Bad Communication: A New Basis for Intervention. *Journal of Adolescence.* 21, 177–96.

Dryfoos, J.G. (1990) *Adolescents at Risk.* Oxford University Press.

Duffy, M. et al. (2008) *Cannabis Supply and Young*

People: It's a Social Thing. Joseph Rowntree Foundation.

Duitsman, D.M. and Cychosz, C.M. (1997) The Efficacy of University Drug Education Course on Factors That Influence Alcohol Use. *Journal of Drug Education.* 27, 223–9.

Duncan, B.L., Miller, S.D. and Sparks, J. (2000) *The Heroic Client.* John Wiley.

Dunn, M. and Goldman, M. (1998) Age and Drinking-Related Differences in The Memory Organization of Alcohol Expectancies in 3rd, 6th, 9th, and 12th Grade Children. *Journal of Consulting and Clinical Psychology.* 66, 579–85.

Dunphy, D. (1972) Peer Group Socialisation. In Hunt, F. (Ed.) *Socialisation in Australia.* Angus and Roberstson.

Dusenbury, L. et al. (2003) A Review of Research on The Fidelity of Implementation: Implications for Drug Abuse Prevention in School Settings. *Health Education Research: Theory and Practice.* 18: 2, 237–56.

Eaton, D.K. et al. (2003) Youth at Risk Surveillance – United States 2007. *MMWR Surveillance Summary.* 57–131.

Edmonds, K. et al. (2005) *Drug Prevention Among Vulnerable Young People.* National Collaboration Centre for Young People.

Edwards, G. and Goss, M.M. (1976) Alcohol Dependance: Provisional Description of a Clinical Syndrome. *British Medical Journal,* 1, 1058–61.

Edwards, G., Marshall, E.J. and Cook, C.C. (2003) *The Treatment of Drinking Problems.* Cambridge University Press.

Eisenstadt, S. (1956) *From Generation to Generation.* Collier-Macmillan.

Elkind, D. (1967) Egocentrism in Adolescence. *Child Development.* 38, 1025–34.

Ellickson, P.L. and Bell, R.M. (1990a) Drug Prevention in Junior High: A Multi-Site Longitudinal Test. *Science.* 247, 1299–305.

Ellickson, P.L. and Bell, R.M. (1990b) *Prospects for Preventing Drug Use Among Young Adolescents.* The RAND Corporation.

Ellickson, P.L. and Morton, S.C. (1999) Identifying Adolescents at Risk for Hard Drug Use: Racial/Ethnic Variations. *Journal of Adolescent Health.* 25, 382–95.

Ellickson, P.L. and Robyn, A. (1987) Goal: Effective Drug Prevention Programs. *California School Boards.* 45: 4, 24–7.

Ellis, J.A. (1998) *Quasi Experimental Trial of Network Support Therapy for Alcohol Problems.* University of Birmingham: Unpublished Clin PsyD Thesis.

Ennett, S.T. et al. (1994) How Effective is Drug Abuse Resistance Education? A Meta-Analysis of Project DARE Outcome Evaluations. *American Journal of Public Health.* 84: 9, 1394–401.

Enright, R., Shukla, D. and Lapsley, D. (1980) Adolescent Egocentrism, Sociocentrism and Self-Consciousness. *Journal of Youth and Adolescence.* 9, 101–16.

Epstein, E.E. et al. (2005) Is Alcohol Assessment Therapeutic? Pretreatment Change in Drinking Among Alcohol-Dependent Women. *Journal of Studies on Alcohol.* 66, 369–78.

Epstein, J.N. et al. (1998) PTSD as a Mediator Between Childhood Rape and Alcohol Abuse in Adult Women. *Child Abuse and Neglect.* 22, 223–34.

Erikson, E.H. (1968) *Identity: Youth and Crises.* W.W. Norton.

Erikson, E.H. (1995) *The Childhood and Society.* Vintage.

Esposito-Smythers, C. and Goldston, D.B. (2008) Challenges and Opportunities in the Treatment of Adolescents With SUD and Suicidal Behaviour. *Substance Use.* 29, 5–17.

Essua, C.A. (2000) *Angst Und Depression Bei Jugendlichen.* Habilitationschrift, University of Bremen.

Eysenck, H.J. (1952) *The Scientific Study of Personality.* Routledge and Kegan Paul.

Ezell, M. and Levy, M. (2003) An Evaluation of an Arts Program for Incarcerated Juvenile Offenders. *Journal of Correctional Education.* 54: 3, 108–14.

Farrell, A.D. and Danish, S.J. (1993) Peer Drug Associations and Emotional Restraint: Causes and Consequences of Adolescent Drug Use? *Journal of Consulting and Clinical Psychology.* 61, 327–34.

Farrell, M. et al. (1997) *Nicotine, Alcohol and Other Drug Dependence and The Association With Deprivation.* C.F. ACMD (1998) Drug Misuse and The Environment. HMSO.

Federal Trade Commission (1997) *Tar, Nicotine and Carbon Monoxide of The Smoke of 1252 Varieties of Domestic Cigarette for The Last Year.* Www.Ftc.Gov.

Feingold, A. and Rounsaville, B. (1995) Construct Validity of The Dependence Syndrome as Measured by DSM-IV for Different Psycho-Active Substances. *Addiction.* 90, 1661–9.

Ferdinand, R.F., Blum, M. and Verhurst, F.C. (2001) Psychopathology in Adolescence

Predicts Future Substance Use in Young Adulthood. *Addiction*. 96, 861–70.

Fernandez, E., Garcia, M. and Schiaffano, A. (2001) Smoking Initiation and Cessation by Gender and Educational Level in Catalonia, Spain. *Prevention Medicine*. 32, 218–23.

Ferri, E., Bynner, J. and Wadsworth, M. (2003) Changing Lives. In Ferri, E., Bynner, J. and Wadsworth, M. (Eds.) *Changing Britain, Changing Lives*. Institute of Education.

Festinger, L. (1954) A Theory of Social Comparison Processes. *Human Relationship*. 7, 117–140.

Festinger, L. (1957) *A Theory of Cognitive Dissonance*. Harper and Row.

Filmore, K.M. (1975) Relationships Between Specific Drinking Problems in Adulthood and Middle Age. *Journal of Studies on Alcohol*. 36, 882–907.

Filmore, K.M. (1987) Women's Drinking Across the Life Course as Compared to Men's. *British Journal of Addictions*. 82, 801–11.

Filmore, K.M. and Midanik. L. (1984) Chronicity of Drinking Problems Among Men: A Longitudinal Study. *International Journal of Alcohol*. 45, 228–36.

Filmore, K.M. et al. (1988) *Spontaneous Remission From Alcohol Problems: A Critical Review*. Paper Commissioned and Supported by The Institute of Medicine.

Fishbein, M. and Ajzen, I. (1975) *Belief, Attitude, Intention and Behavior: an Introduction to Theory and Research*. Addison-Wesley.

Fiske, D.W. (1949) Consistency of The Factorial Structures of Personality Ratings From Different Sources. *Journal of Abnormal and Social Psychology*. 44, 329–44.

Flay, B.R. (1985) Psychosocial Approaches to Smoking Prevention: A Review of Findings. *Health Psychology*. 4: 5, 449–88.

Flay, B.R. and Sobel, J.L. (1983) The Role of Mass Media in Preventing Adolescent Substance Abuse. In Glynn, T.J. et al. (Eds.) *Preventing Adolescent Drug Abuse: Intervention Strategies*. NIDA.

Flay, B.R. et al. (1985) Are Social-Psychological Smoking Prevention Programs Effective? The Waterloo Study. *Journal of Behavioral Medicine*. 8: 1, 37–59.

Flora, J.A., Maibach, E.W. and Maccoby, N. (1989) The Role of Media Across Four Levels of Health Promotion Intervention. *Annual Review of Public Health*. 10, 1881–2001.

Flory, K. and Lynam, D.R. (2003) The Relationship Between ADHD and Substance Abuse: What Role Does Medication Play? *Clinical Child and Family Psychology Review*. 6, 1–16.

Flory, K. et al. (2004) Early Adolescent Through Young Adult Alcohol and Marijuana Use Trajectories: Early Predictors, Young Adult Outcomes and Predictive Utility. *Development and Psychopathology*. 16, 193–213.

Flynn, B.S. et al. (1992) Prevention of Cigarette Smoking Through Mass Media Intervention and School Programs. *American Journal of Public Health*. 82: 6, 827–34.

Flynn, B.S. et al. (1995) Cigarette Smoking Prevention Effects of Mass Media and School Interventions Targeted to Gender and Age Groups. *Journal of Health Education*. 26, 45–51.

Fogelman, K. (1976) *Britain's 16 Year Olds*. National Children Bureau.

Fossey, E. (1994) *Growing Up With Alcohol*. Tavistock/Routlege.

Foxcroft, D.R. et al. (2004) *Primary Prevention for Alcohol Misuse in Young People (Cochrane Review) The Cochrane Library, 1*. John Wiley.

Freud, A. (1958) Adolescence. *Psychoanalytic Study of The Child*. 13, 255–78.

Friedman, A., Granick, S. and Kreisher, C. (1994) Motivation for Adolescent Drug Abusers for Help and Treatment. *Journal of Child and Adolescent Substance Abuse*. 3, 69–88.

Frisher, M. et al. (2007) *Predictive Factors for Illicit Drug Use Among Young People: A Literature Review*. Home Office Report.

Furedi, F. (2001) *Paranoid Parenting: Why Ignoring The Experts May Be Best for Your Child*. Allen Lane.

Furnham, A. et al. (1997) A Content Analysis of Alcohol Portrayal and Drinking in British Soap Operas. *Health Education Research: Theory and Practice*. 12: 4, 519–29.

Gabhainn, S.N. and Francois, Y. (2000) Substance Use. In WHO-EURO. *Health Behaviour in School Children*. WHO-EURO. 97–114.

Galanter, M. (1990) *Network Therapy for Alcohol and Drug Abuse*. Guildford Press.

Gamela, J.F. (1995) Spain. In Heath, D.B. (Ed.) *International Handbook on Alcohol and Culture*. Greenwood.

Gardner, M. and Steinberg, L. (2005) Peer Influence on Risk Taking, Risk Preference, and Risky Decision Making in Adolescence and Adulthood: an Experimental Study. *Developmental Psychology*. 41: 4, 625–35.

Gastfreind, D.R., Lu, S. and Sharon, E. (2000)

Placement Matching: Challenges and Technical Progress. *Substance Use and Misuse*. 35, 2191–213.

Gecas, V. and Seff, M. (1990) Families and Adolescents: A Review of The 1980s. *Journal of Marriage and The Family*. 52, 941–58.

Geckova, A.M. et al. (2003) Influence of Risk Behaviour and Socio-Economic Status on Health of Slovak Adolescents. Croatian Medical Journal. 44: 1, 41–9.

Genesee, F. (1989) Early Bilingual Development: One Language or Two? *Journal of Child Language*. 16, 161–79.

Giancola, P.R. and Parker, A.M. (2001) A Six Year Prospective Study of Pathways Towards Drug Use in Adolescent Boys With and Without a Family History of a Substance Use Disorder. *Journal of Studies on Alcohol*. 62, 166–78.

Giedd, J.N. et al. (1999) Brain Development During Childhood and Adolescence: A Longitudinal MRI Study. *Nature Neuroscience*. 2, 861–3.

Gil, A.G., Wagner, E.F. and Tubman, J.G. (2004) Associations Between Early-Adolescent Substance Use and Subsequent Young-Adult Substance Use Disorders and Psychiatric Disorders Among a Multi-Ethnic Male Sample in Florida. *American Journal of Public Health*. 94: 9, 1603–9.

Giovino, G. et al. (1995) Epidemiology of Tobacco Use and Dependence. *Epidemiological Reviews*. 17, 48–65.

Glassner, B. and Berg, B. (1980) How Jews Avoid Alcohol Problems. *American Sociological Review*. 45, 647–64.

Godley, S.H. et al. (2009) Adolescent Community Reinforcement Approach. In Springer, D.W. and Rubin, A. (Eds.) *Substance Abuse Treatment for Youth and Adults: Clinician's Guide to Evidence-Based Practice*. John Wiley.

Goldman, M.S., Brown, S.A. and Christiansen, B.A. (1987a) Expectancy Theory: Thinking About Drinking. In Blane, H.T. and Leonard, K.E. (Eds.) *Psychological Theories of Drinking and Alcoholism*. Guildford Press.

Goldman, M.S., Christiansen, B.A. and Brown, S.A. (1987b) *Alcohol Expectancy Questionnaire: Adolescent Form*. Psychological Assessment Resources.

Goldman, M.S., Del Boca, F.K. and Darkes, J. (1999) Alcohol Expectancy Theory: The Application of Neuroscience. In Blane, H.T. and Leonard, K.E. (Eds.) *Psychological Theories of Drinking and Alcoholism*. Guildford Press.

Goldman, M.S. et al. (1993) Alcoholism and Memory: Broadening The Scope of Alcohol-Expectancy Research. *Psychological Bulletin*. 110, 137–46.

Goldston, D.B. (2004) Conceptual Issues in Understanding The Relationship Between Suicidal Behaviour and Substance Use During Adolescence. *Drug and Alcohol Dependence*. 76, (Supplement 17) S79–91.

Goldston, D.B. et al. (2011) Assessment and Treatment of Suicidal Behaviour. In Kaminer, Y. and Winters, K.C. (Eds.) *Clinical Manual of Adolescent Substance Abuse Treatment*. APA.

Golub, A. and Johnson, B.D. (2002) The Misuse of The 'Gateway Theory' in US Policy on Drug Abuse Control: A Secondary Analysis of The Muddle Deduction. *International Journal of Drug Policy*. 13, 5–19.

Gooden, W.E. (1989) Development of Black Men in Early Adulthood. In Jones, R.L. (Ed.) *Black Adult Development and Aging*. Cobb and Henry.

Goodnow, J. and Collins, A. (1990) *Development According to Parents*. Lawrence Erlbaum.

Goodstadt, M. (1986) School-Based Drug Education in North America: What Is Wrong? What Can Be Done? *Journal of School Health*. 56: 7, 278–81.

Goodwin, R.D., Fergusson, D.M. and Horwood, L.J. (2004) Association Between Anxiety Disorders and Substance Abuse Disorders Among Young Persons: Results of a 21 Year Longitudinal Study. *Journal of Psychiatric Research*. 38, 295–304.

Gordon, R. (1987) an Operational Classification of Disease Prevention. In Steinberg, J.A. and Silverman, M.M. (Eds.) *Preventing Mental Disorders*. Department of Health and Human Science.

Gotham, H.J., Sher, K.J. and Wood, P.K. (2003) Alcohol Involvement and Developmental Task Completion in Young Adulthood. *Journal of Studies on Alcohol*. 64, 32–42.

Gottfredson, D.C. and Wilson, D.B. (2003) Characteristics of Effective School Based Substance Abuse Prevention. *Prevention Science*. 4, 27–38.

Goulden, C. and Sondhi, A. (2001) at *The Margins: Drug Use by Vulnerable People in 1998/1999 Youth Lifestyles Survey*. Home Office Research, Development and Statistics Directorate Research Study, 228.

Gowen, L.K. et al. (2004) A Comparison of The Sexual Behaviours and Attitudes of Adolescent Girls With Older vs Similar-Aged Boyfriends. *Journal of Youth and Adolescence*. 33: 2, 167–75.

Gowing, L., Ali, R. and White, J. (2006) Buprenorphine for The Management of Opiate Withdrawal. *Cochrane Database of Systematic Reviews* 2009, Issue 3. Art. No.: CD002025. DOI: 10.1002/14651858.CD002025.pvb4.

Graham, D.L. and Diaz-Granados, J.L. (2006) Periadolescent Exposure to Ethanol and Diazepam Alters The Aversive Properties of Ethanol in Adult Mice. *Pharmacology, Biochemistry and Behavior*. 84: 3, 406–14.

Graham, J.W. et al. (2004) Prevention Alcohol-Related Harm in College Students: Alcohol-Related Harm Prevention Programme Effects on Hypothesized Mediating Variable. *Health Education Research*. 19: 1, 71–84.

Grant, B.F. and Dawson, D.A. (1997) Age at Onset of Alcohol Use and its Association With The DSM-IV Alcohol Abuse and Dependence: Results From The National Longitudinal Alcohol Epidemiologic Survey. *Journal of Substance Abuse*. 9, 103–10.

Grant, B.F. et al. (1992) DSM-IIIR and Proposed DSM-IV Alcohol Use Disorders, United States 1988. A Methodological Comparison. *Alcoholism: Clinical and Experimental Research*. 16, 215–21.

Grant, B.F. et al. (2004) Prevalence and Co-Occurrence of Substance Use and Independent Mood and Anxiety Disorders: Results From The National Epidemiologic Survey on Alcohol and Related Conditions. *Archives of General Psychiatry*. 61, 807–16.

Grant, B.F. et al. (2005) The Epidemiology of Social Anxiety Disorder in The United States: Results From The National Epidemiologic Survey on Alcohol and Related Conditions. *The Journal of Clinical Psychology*. 66: 11, 1351–61.

Grant, B.F., Stinson, F.S. and Harford, T.C. (2001) Age of Onset of Alcohol Use and DSM IV Alcohol Abuse and Dependence: A 12 Year Follow-Up. *Journal of Substance Abuse*. 13, 493–504.

Grant, J.D. et al. (2006) Adolescent Alcohol Use Is a Risk Factor for Adult Alcohol and Drug Dependence: Evidence From a Twin Design. *Psychological Medicine*. 36, 109–18.

Gray, D., Amos, A. and Currie, C. (1997) Decoding The Image-Consumption, Young People, Magazines and Smoking: an Exploration of Theoretical and Methodological Issues. *Health Education Research: Theory and Practice*. 12: 4, 505–17.

Green, B., Young, R. and Kavanagh, D. (2005) Cannabis Use and Misuse Prevalence Amongst Young People With Psychosis. *British Journal of Psychiatry*. 187, 306–13.

Greenberg, M.R. et al. (2001) *The Prevention of Mental Disorder in School Age Children: A Review of The Effectiveness of Prevention Programmes*. College of Health and Human Development, Pennsylvania State University.

Grella, C.E. et al. (2001) Drug Treatment Outcomes for Adolescents With Comorbid Mental and Substance Use Disorders. *Journal of Nervous and Mental Disorders*. 189, 384–92.

Greydanus, D.E. and Shrek, D. (2009) Deliberate Self-harm and Suicide in Adolescents. *Keio Journal of Medicine*, 58: 3, 144–51.

Grotevant, H. and Cooper, C. (1986) Individuation in Family Relationships: A Perspective on Individual Differences in The Development of Identity and Role-Taking Skills in Adolescence. *Human Development*. 29, 82–100.

Gruber, E. et al. (1996) Early Drinking Onset and Its Association With Alcohol Use and Problem Behaviour in Late Adolescence. *Preventative Medicine*. 25: 3, 293–300.

Gruer, L. et al. (1997) Extreme Variations in The Distribution of Serious Drug Misuse-Related Morbidity in Greater Glasgow. Personal Communication. C.F. ACMD Report (1998) *Drug Misuse and The Environment*. HMSO.

Gusfield, J.R. (1987) Passage to Play: Rituals of Drinking Time in American Society. In Douglas, M. (Ed.) *Constructive Drinking: Perspectives on Drink From Anthropology*. Cambridge University Press.

Hadju, D. (1988) Commercials on Cassette. *Video Review*. December, 33–5.

Haggerty, R., et al. (Eds.) (1994) *Stress, Risk and Resilience in Children and Adolescents: Processes, Mechanisms and Interventions*. Cambridge University Press.

Haines, M.P. (1998) Social Norms in a Wellness Model for Health Promotion in Higher Education. *Wellness Management*. 14, 1–10.

Hall, G.S. (1916) *Adolescence*. (Vols 1–2) Appleton.

Hammond, A. et al. (2008) Do Adolescents Perceive Police Officers as Credible Instructors of Substance Abuse Prevention Programmes? *Health Education Research*. 23: 4, 682–96.

Hammond, D. et al. (2007) Communicating Risk to Smokers: The Impact of Health Warnings on Cigarette Packs. *American Journal of Preventive Medicine*. 32: 3, 202–9.

Hancock, D.R. (2002) Influencing Graduate Students' Classroom Achievement, Homework

Habits and Motivation to Learn With Verbal Praise. *Educational Research.* 1, 83–95.

Hansen, W.B. (1990) Theory and Implementation of The Social Influence Model of Primary Prevention. In Rey, K. Faegre, C. and Lowery, P. (Eds.) *Prevention Research Findings: 1988, OSAP Prevention Monograph Number 3.* OSAP, Rockville, Md.

Hansen, W.B. (1992) School-Based Substance Abuse Prevention: A Review of The State of The Art in Curriculum. *Health Education Research.* 7: 3, 403–30.

Hansen, W.B. et al. (1988) Affective and Social Influences Approaches to The Prevention of Multiple Substance Abuse Among Seventh Grade Students: Results From Project SMART. *Prevention Medicine.* 17: 2, 135–52.

Harrell, A. and Wirtz, P.M. (1989) Screening for Adolescent Problem Drinking: Validation of a Multidimensional Instrument for Case Identification. *Psychological Assessment.* 1, 61–3.

Harrington, N.G. et al. (2003) Persuasive Strategies for Effective Anti-Drug Messages. *Communication Monographs.* 70: 1, 16–38.

Harris, J. et al. (2009) Smoking. In Fuller, E. (Ed.) *Smoking, Drinking and Drug Use Among Young People in England in 2008.* NHS Information Centre for Health and Social Care.

Harris, J.R. (1999) *The Nurture Assumption.* Bloomsbury.

Harris, P. (2006) Where It All Begins: Growing Up and The Helping Relationship. In Harbin, F. and Murphy, M. (Eds.) *Secret Lives: Growing With Substance: Working With Children and Young People Affected by Familial Substance Misuse.* Russell House Publishing.

Harris, P. (2007) *Empathy for The Devil: How to Help People Overcome Drugs and Alcohol Problems.* Russell House Publishing.

Harris, P. (2011a) *The Concerned Other: How to Change Problematic Drug and Alcohol Users Through Their Family Members: A Complete Manual.* Russell House Publishing.

Harris, P. (2011b) *The Concerned Other: New Theory and The Evidence Base for Changing Problematic Drug and Alcohol Users Through Their Family Members.* Russell House Publishing.

Harris, P. (2011c) *A Review of DAFS Outcomes: Outcomes for Concerned Others in a Range of Treatment Options.* Presentation to The Reach-Out Conference, Bristol, March 2011.

Harris, P. (2011d) *Complexity Index.* (Revised) Unpublished.

Harrison, P., Fulkerson, J.A. and Beebe, T.J. (1998)

DSM-IV Substance Abuse Disorder Criteria for Adolescents: Critical Examination Based on a Statewide School Survey. *American Journal of Psychiatry.* 155, 486–92.

Harrison, P.A. and Hoffmann, N. (1989) *CATOR Report: Adolescent Treatment Completers One Year Later.* CATOR.

Harter, S. (1988) The Construction and Conservation of The Self: James and Cooley Revisited. In Lapsley, D. and Power, F. (Eds.) *Self, Ego and Identity.* Springer Verlag.

Harter, S. (1990) Self and Identity Development. In Feldman, S. and Elder, G. (Eds.) At *The Threshold: The Developing Adolescent.* Harvard University Press.

Hartmann, D. and Depro, B. (2006) Rethinking Sports-Based Community Crime Prevention: A Preliminary Analysis of The Relationship Between Midnight Basketball and Urban Crime Rates. *Journal of Sports and Social Issues.* 30: 9, 180–96.

Hasin, D. et al. (1997) Nosological Comparison of Alcohol and Drug Diagnosis: A Multisite, Multi-Instrument International Study. *Drug and Alcohol Dependence.* 47, 217–26.

Hasin, D. et al. (2000) Withdrawal and Tolerance: Prognostic Significance in DSM IV Alcohol Dependence. *Journal of Studies on Alcohol.* 61, 431–8.

Havinghurst, R. (1952) *Developmental Tasks and Education.* Mckay.

Hawke, J.M., Jainchill, N. and De Leon, G. (2000) The Prevalence of Sexual Abuse and Its Impact on The Onset of Drug Use Among Adolescents in Therapeutic Community Drug Treatment. *Journal of Child and Adolescent Substance Abuse.* 9, 35–49.

Hawkins, E., Cummins, L.H. and Marlatt, G.A. (2004) Preventing Substance Abuse in American Indian and Alaska Native Youth: Promising Strategies for Healthier Communities. *Psychological Bulletin.* 130, 304–23.

Hawkins, E. et al. (1987) *Childhood Predictors and The Prevention of Adolescent Substance Abuse.* National Institute of Drug Abuse Monographs. 56, 75–126. U.S. Government Printing Office.

Hawkins, J.D. et al. (1986) Childhood Predictors of Adolescent Substance Abuse: Toward an Empirically Grounded Theory. *Journal of Children in Contemporary Society.* 8, 11–48.

Hawkins, J.D., Catalano R.F. and Miller, J.Y. (1992) Risk and Protective Factors for Alcohol and Other Drug Problems in Adolescence and

Early Adulthood: Implications for Substance Abuse Prevention. *Psychological Bulletin.* 112: 1, 64–105.

Hawkins, J.D. et al. (1987) Delinquents and Drugs: What The Evidence Suggests About Prevention and Treatment Programming. In Brown, B.S. and Mills, A.R. (Eds.) *Youth at High Risk for Substance Abuse.* NIDA.

Hawkins, J.D. et al. (1997) Substance Use and Abuse. In Ammerman, R.T. and Hersen, M. (Eds.) *Handbook of Prevention and Treatment With Children and Adolescents.* John Wiley.

Hawkins, J.D. et al. (2002) Substance Use Norm and Transitions in Substance Use: Implications for The Gateway Hypothesis. In Kandel, D.B. (Ed.) *Stages and Pathways of Drug Involvement: Examining The Gateway Hypothesis.* Cambridge University Press.

Hay, G., Gannon, M. and Casey, J. (2011) *National and Regional Estimates of The Prevalence of Opiate And/Or Crack Cocaine Use 2009/10: A Summary of Key Findings.* The Centre for Drug Misuse Research, University of Glasgow, NTA, Department of Health.

Hays, R.D. and Ellickson, P.L. (1996) What is Adolescent Alcohol Misuse in The United States According to The Experts? *Alcohol and Alcoholism.* 31: 3, 297–303.

Health Study for England (1998) *Cardiovascular Disease. Vol. 1.* HMSO.

Heath, D.B. (1998) Cultural Variations Among Drinking Patterns. In Grant, M. and Litvak, J. (Eds.) *Drinking Patterns and Their Consequences.* Taylor and Francis.

Heather, N., Rollnick, S. and Winton, M. (1983) A Comparison of Objective and Subjective Measures of Alcohol Dependence as Predictors of Relapse Following Treatment. *British Journal of Clinical Psychiatry.* 22, 11–7.

Helzer, J.E. and Prybeck, T.R. (1988) The Co-Occurrence of Alcoholism With Other Psychiatric Disorders in The General Population and Its Impact on Treatment. *Journal of Studies on Alcohol.* 49, 219–24.

Henderlong, J. and Lepper, M.R. (2002) The Effects of Praise on Children's Intrinsic Motivation: A Review and Synthesis. *Psychological Bulletin.* 5, 774–95.

Henderson, N.D. (1982) Human Behavioural Genetics. *Annual Review of Psychology.* 33, 403–40.

Hendry, L. et al. (1993) *Young People's Leisure and Lifestyles.* Routledge.

Henggeler, S.W. et al. (1991) Effects of Multisystemic Therapy on Drug Use and Abuse in Serious Juvenile Offenders: A Progress Report From Two Outcome Studies. *Family Dynamics of Addiction Quarterly.* 1, 40–51.

Henggeler, S.W. et al. (1996) Eliminating (Almost) Treatment Dropout of Substance Abusing or Dependent Delinquents Through Home Based Multi-Systemic Therapy. *American Journal of Psychiatry.* 153, 437–28.

Henggeler, S.W., Clingempeel, W.G. and Brondino, M.J. (2002) Four Year Follow-up of Multi-systemic Therapy with Substance-abusing and Substance-dependant Juvenile Offenders. *Journal of the American Academy of Child and Adolescent Psychiatry,* 41, 868–74.

Henggeler, S.W., Pickeral, S.G. and Brondino, M.J. (1999) Multi-systemic Treatment of Substance-abusing and Dependant Delinquents: Outcomes, Treatment Fidelity and Transportability. *Mental Health Services Research,* 1: 171–84.

Hibell, B. et al. (2001) *The 1999 ESPAD Report: Alcohol and Other Drug Use Among Students in European Countries.* Swedish Council for Information on Alcohol and Other Drugs.

Hibell, B. et al. (2004) *The 2003 ESPAD Report: Alcohol and Other Drug Use Among Students in 30 European Countries.* Swedish Council for Information on Alcohol and Other Drugs.

Higgins, P.S. (1988) *The Prevention of Drug Abuse Among Teenagers: A Literature Review.* Amherst H. Wilder Foundation.

Hill, F.E. and Bugen, L.A. (1979) A Survey of Drinking Patterns Amongst College Students. *Journal of College Student Personnel.* 20, 236–43.

Hill, K.G. et al. (2000) Early Adult Outcomes of Adolescent Binge Drinking: Person and Variable Centred Analysis of Binge Drinking Trajectories. *Alcoholism: Clinical and Experimental Research.* 24, 892–901.

Hingson, R. et al. (2003) Age of First Intoxication, Heavy Drinking, Driving After Drinking and Risk of Unintentional Injury Among U.S. College Students. *Journal of Studies of Alcohol.* 64, 23–31.

Hingson, R.W. et al. (2006) Age at Drinking Onset and Alcohol Dependence: Age at Onset, Duration, and Severity. *Archives of Pediatrics and Adolescent Medicine.* 160, 736–46.

Hoare, J. (2009) *Drug Misuse Declared: Findings From The 2008/9 British Crime Survey England and Wales.* Statistical Bulletin. Home Office.

Holbrook, A.M. et al. (1999) Meta-Analysis of Benzodiazepine Use in The Treatment of Acute

Withdrawal. *Canadian Medical Association Journal.* 160, 649–55.

Home Office (1971) *Misuse of Drugs Act (1971).* HMSO.

Home Office (2002) *Summer Splash Schemes 2000: Findings From Six Case Studies.* HMSO.

Hopfer, C.J. et al. (2002) Adolescent Heroin Use: A Review of Descriptive and Treatment Literature. *Journal of Substance Abuse Treatment.* 23, 231–7.

Hornik, R.C. (2000) Exposure Theory and Evidence About All the Ways it Matters. *Social Marketing Quarterly.* 8: 3, 30–7.

Houston, K., Hawton, K. and Shepperd, R. (2001) Suicide in People Aged 15–24: A Psychological Autopsy Study. *Journal of Affective Disorders.* 63, 159–70.

Hovarth, A.O. and Symonds, B.D. (1991) Relation Between Working Alliance and Outcome in Psychotherapy: A Meta-Analysis. *Journal of Consulting and Clinical Psychology.* 38: 2, 139–49.

Hovens, J.G., Cantwell, D.P. and Kiriakos, R. (1994) Psychiatric Co-Morbidity in Hospitalised Adolescent Substance Abusers. *Journal of American Academy of Child and Adolescent Psychiatry.* 33, 476–83.

Hover, S. and Gaffney, L.R. (1991) Relationship Between Social Skills and Adolescent Drinking. *Alcohol and Alcoholism.* 26, 207–14.

Howard, K.I. et al. (1986) The Dose-Effect Relationship in Psychotherapy. *American Psychologist.* 41: 2, 159–64.

Hser, Y.I., Chou, C.P. and Anglin, M.D (2007a) Trajectories of Heroin Addiction: Growth Mixture Modelling Results Based on A 33-Year Follow-Up Study. *Evaluation Review.* 31: 6, 548–63.

Hser, Y.I. et al. (2001) an Evaluation of Drug Treatments for Adolescents in 4 US Cities. *Archives of General Psychiatry.* 58, 679–85.

Hser, Y.I., Longshore, D. and Anglin, M.D. (2007b) The Life Course Perspective on Drug Use: A Conceptual Framework for Understanding Drug Use Trajectories. *Evaluation Review.* 32: 6, 515–47.

Hsieh, S., Hoffman, N.G. and Hollister, D.C. (1998) The Relationship Between Pre-, During-, Post-Treatment Factors, and Adolescent Substance Abuse Behaviours. *Addictive Behaviours.* 23: 4, 477–88.

Hubbard, R.L. et al. (1985) Characteristics, Behaviour, and Outcomes for Youth in The TOPS. In Freidman, A.A. and Beschner, G. (Eds.) *Treatment Services for Adolescent Substance Abusers.* National Institute on Drug Abuse.

Hubble, M.A., Duncan, B.L. and Miller, S.D. (2010) *The Heart and Soul of Change: Delivering What Works in Therapy.* American Psychological Association.

Hudley, C. and Graham, S. (1995) School-Based Intervention to Reduce Peer Directed Aggression Among African American Boys. *Child Development.* 64, 124–38.

Huisman, M., Kunst, A.E. and Mackenbach, J.P. (2005) Educational Inequalities in Smoking Among Men and Women Aged 16 Years and Older in 11 European Countries. *Tobacco Control.* 14, 106–13.

Humphrey, J.A. and Friedman, J. (1986) The Onset of Drinking and Intoxication Amongst University Students. *Journal of Studies on Alcohol.* 47, 455–8.

Hunt, S. (2005) *The Life Course: A Sociological Introduction.* Palgrave Macmillan.

Hurt, R.D. et al. (2000) Nicotine Patch Therapy in 101 Adolescent Smokers. *Adolescent Medicine.* 154, 31–7.

Hussong, A., Bauer, D. and Chassin, L. (2008) Telescoped Trajectories From Alcohol Initiation to Disorder in Children of Alcoholic Parents. *Journal of Abnormal Psychology.* 117: 1, 63–78.

Hutchings, J. and Levesley, T. (2008) *Education, Training and Employment: Key Elements of Effective Practice.* YJB, London.

Instel, T.R. (1992) Oxytocin: A Neuropeptide for Affiliation: Evidence From Behaviour, Receptor, Autoradiographic, and Comparative Studies. *Pyschoneuroendocrinology.* 17: 1, 3–35.

International Centre for Clinical Excellence (2011) *Manual 1: What Works in Therapy.* ICCE.

Ito, J.R. and Donavan, D.M. (1990) Predicting Drinking Outcome: Demography, Chronicity, Coping and Aftercare. *Addictive Behaviours.* 15, 553–9.

Jaffe, S.L. (1990) *Step Workbook for Adolescent Chemical Dependency Recovery: A Guide to The First Five Steps.* American Psychiatric Press.

Jaffe, S.L. (2000) *Adolescent Substance Abuse Intervention Workbook: Working a First Step.* American Psychiatric Press.

Jahnke, H. and Blanchard-Fields, F. (1993) A Test of Two Models of Adolescent Egocentrism. *Journal of Youth and Adolescence.* 22, 313–26.

Jahoda, G. and Cramond, J. (1972) *Children and Alcohol.* HMSO.

Jaycox, L.H. et al. (2004) Trauma Exposure and Retention in Adolescent Substance Abuse Treatment. *Journal of Trauma Stress.* 17, 113–21.

Jeffrey, L.R. (2000) *The New Jersey Higher Education*

Consortium Social Norms Project: Decreasing Binge Drinking in New Jersey Colleges and Universities by Correcting Student Misconceptions of College Drinking Norms. Centre for Alcohol Studies.

Jellinek, E.M. (1960) *The Disease Concept of Alcoholism*. Hillhouse Press.

Jessor, R., Donovan, J.E. and Costa, F.M. (1991) *Beyond Adolescence: Problem Behaviour and Young Adult Development*. Cambridge University Press.

Johnson, C.A. et al. (1990) Relative Effectiveness of Comprehensive Community Programming for Drug Abuse Prevention With High to Low Risk Adolescents. *Journal of Consulting and Clinical Psychology*. 58, 447–57.

Johnson, R.A. and Gerstein, D.R. (1999) Initiation of Use of Alcohol, Cigarettes, Marijuana, Cocaine, and Other Substances in US Birth Cohorts Since 1919. *American Journal of Public Health*. 88: 1, 27–33.

Johnson, V.E. (1998) *Intervention: A Step-By-Step Guide for Families and Friends of Chemically Dependent Persons*. Hazelden.

Johnston, L.D., O'Malley, P.M. and Bachman, J.G (1998) *National Survey Results on Drug Use From The Monitoring The Future Study, 1975–97*. National Institute on Drug Abuse.

Johnston, L.D., O'Malley, P.M. and Bachman, J.G. (1991) *Drug Use Amongst American High School Seniors, College Students and Young Adults, 1975–1990*. National Institute of Drug Abuse.

Jones, A. (2002) Wage and Non-Wage Compensation Among Young Alcoholic and Heavy Drinking Women: A Preliminary Analysis. *Journal of Family Economic Issues*. 23, 3–25.

Jones, G. and Wallace, C. (1992) *Youth, Family and Citizenship*. Open University Press.

Jones, M.B. and Offord, D.R. (1989) Reduction of Antisocial Behaviour in Poor Children by Nonschool Skill Development. *Journal of Child Psychology and Psychiatry*, 30: 5, 737–50.

Jorm, A.F. (1987) Sex and Age Differences in Depression: A Quantative Synthesis of Published Research. *Australian and New Zealand Journal of Psychiatry*. 21, 46–53.

Kahn, R.L. and Antonucci, T.C. (1980) Convoys Over The Life Course: Attachment, Roles and Social Support. In Baltes, P.B. and Brim, O.G. (Eds.) *Life-Span Development and Behaviour*. Academic Press.

Kaminer, Y. and Bukstein, O. (2008) *Adolescent Substance Abuse: Psychiatric Comorbidity and High-Risk Behaviours*. Routledge.

Kaminer, Y., Burleson, J.A. and Burke, R.H. (2008) Efficacy of Outpatient Aftercare for Adolescents With Alcohol Use Disorders: A Randomised Controlled Study. *Journal of American Academy of Child and Adolescent Psychiatry*, 47, 1405–12.

Kaminer, Y., Burleson, J.A. and Goldberger, R. (2002a) Cognitive Behavioural Coping Skills and Psychoeducation for Adolescent Substance Abuse. *Journal Nervous and Mental Disorders*. 190, 737–45

Kaminer, Y., Burleson, J.A. and Goldberger, R. (2002b) Psychotherapies for Adolescent Substance Abusers: Short- and Long-Term Outcomes. *Journal of Nervous and Mental Disease*. 190, 737–45.

Kaminer, Y. et al. (1992) Comparison Between Treatment Completers and Noncompleters Among Dually Diagnosed Substance Abusing Adolescents. *Journal of The American Academy of Child and Adolescent Psychiatry*. 31, 1046–9.

Kaminer, Y. et al. (1998) Measuring Treatment Process in Cognitive Behavioural and Interactional Group Therapies for Adolescent Substance Abusers. *Journal of Nervous and Mental Diseases*. 186, 407–13.

Kaminer, Y. et al. (2006) Suicidal Ideation Among Adolescents With Alcohol Use Disorders During Treatment and Aftercare. *American Journal of Addictions*. 15, Supplement, S43–S49.

Kaminer, Y.A. (1992) Desipramine Facilitation of Cocaine Abstinence in an Adolescent. *Journal of American Academy of Child and Adolescent Psychiatry*. 31, 312–7.

Kamon, J.L., Budney, A.J. and Stranger, C.S. (2005) A Contingency Management Intervention for Adolescent Marijuana Abuse and Conduct Problems. *Journal of The American Academy of Child and Adolescent Psychiatry*. 44, 513–21.

Kandel, D.B. (1975) Stages in Adolescent Involvement in Drug Use. *Science*. 190, 912–4.

Kandel, D.B. (1995) Ethnic Differences in Drug Use: Patterns and Paradoxes. In Botvin, G. et al. (Eds.) *Drug Abuse Prevention With Multiethnic Youth*. Sage

Kandel, D.B. (2002) Examining The Gateway Hypothesis: Stages and Pathways of Drug Involvement. In Kandel, D.B. (Ed.) *Stages and Pathways of Drug Involvement: Examining The Gateway Hypothesis*. Cambridge University Press.

Kandel, D.B. and Yamaguchi, K. (1993) From Beer to Crack: Development Patterns of Drug

Involvement. *American Journal of Public Health.* 83, 851–5.

Kandel, D.B. and Yamaguchi, K. (2002) Stages of Drug Involvement in The US Population. In Kandel, D.B. (Ed.) *Stages and Pathways of Drug Involvement: Examining The Gateway Hypothesis.* Cambridge University Press.

Kandel, D.B. et al. (1999) Psychiatric Co-Morbidity Among Adolescents With Substance Use Disorders: Findings From The MECA Study. *Journal of The American Academy of Child and Adolescent Psychiatry.* 38, 693–9.

Kane, P. and Garber, J. (2004) The Relations Among Depression in Fathers, Children's Psychopathology, and Father Child Conflict: A Meta-Analysis. *Clinical Psychology Review.* 24: 3, 339–60.

Kaplan, H.B. et al. (1986) Escalation of Marijuana Use: Application of a General Theory of Deviant Behaviour. *Journal of Health and Social Behaviour.* 27, 44–61.

Karwacki, S.B. and Bradley, J.R. (1996) Coping, Drinking Motives, Goal Attainment Expectancies and Family Models in Relation to Alcohol Use Among College Students. *Journal of Drug Education.* 26, 243–55.

Kazdin, A.E. and Wassell, G. (2000) Therapeutic Changes in Children, Parents and Families Resulting From Treatment of Children With Conduct Problems. *Journal of The American Academy of Child and Adolescent Psychiatry.* 39, 414–20.

Kazdin, A.E., Whitley, M. and Marciano, P.L. (2006) Child-Therapist and Parent-Therapist Alliance and Therapeutic Change in the Treatment of Children Referred for Oppositional, Aggressive and Anti-Social Behaviour. *Journal of Child Psychology and Psychiatry.* 47,5: 436–45.

Kegan, R. (1982) *The Evolving Self: Problems and Process in Human Development.* Harvard University Press.

Kelly, J.F. et al. (2008) Social Recovery Model: an 8-Year Investigation of Youth Treatment Outcome in Relation to 12-Step Group Involvement. *Alcoholism: Clinical and Experimental Research.* 32, 1468–78.

Kelly, J.F., Myers, M.G. and Brown, S.A. (2000) A Multivariate Process Model of Adolescent 12-Step Attendance and Substance Use Outcome Following Inpatient Treatment. *Psychology of Addictive Behaviours,* 14: 4, 376–89.

Kelly, J.F., Myers, M.G. and Brown, S.A. (2002) Do Adolescents Affiliate With 12-Step Groups?

A Multivariate Process Model of Effects. *Journal of Studies on Alcohol.* 63, 293–304.

Kelly, J.F., Myers, M.G. and Brown, S.A. (2005) The Effect of Age Composition of 12-Step Groups on Adolescent 12-Step Participation and Substance Use Outcome. *Journal of Child and Adolescent Substance Abuse.* 15, 63–72.

Kelly, T. et al. (2001) Alcohol Use Disorders and Risk Factor Interactions for Adolescent Suicidal Ideation and Attempts. *Suicide and Life Threatening Behaviour.* 31, 181–93.

Kendall, P.C. (1994) Treating Anxiety Disorders in Children: Results of a Randomised Clinical Trial. *Journal of Consulting and Clinical Psychology.* 62, 100–10.

Kendall, P.C. et al. (2004) Child Anxiety Treatment: Outcomes in Adolescence and Impact on Substance Use and Depression at 7.4-Year Follow-Up. *Journal of Consulting and Clinical Psychology.* 72, 276–87.

Kendler, K.S. et al. (1993) The Structure of Genetic and Environmental Risk Factors for Common Psychiatric and Substance Use Disorders in Men and Women. *Archives of General Psychiatry.* 60, 929–37.

Kessler, R.C. (1995) Epidemiology of Psychiatric Comorbidity. In Tsuang, M.T. and Tohen, M. (Eds.) *Textbook of Psychiatric Comorbidity.* Wiley-Liss.

Kessler, R.C. et al. (1994) Lifetime and Twelve Month Prevalence of DSM-III-R Psychiatric Disorders in The United States: Results From The National Co-Morbidity Survey. *Archives of General Psychiatry.* 51, 8–19.

Kessler, R.C. et al. (1995) Post-Traumatic Stress Disorder in The National Comorbidity Survey. *Archives of General Psychiatry.* 52, 1048–60.

Kilpatrik D.G. et al. (2003) Violence and The Risk of PTSD, Major Depression, Substance Abuse/Dependence and Comorbidity: Results From The National Survey of Adolescents. *Journal of Consulting and Clinical Psychology.* 71, 692–700.

Kinder, B., Pape. N. and Walfish, S. (1980) Drug and Alcohol Education Programs: A Review of Outcome Studies. *International Journal of Addiction.* 15: 7, 1035–54.

King, K.M. and Chassin, L. (2007) A Prospective Study of The Effects of Age of Initiation of Alcohol and Drug Use on Young Adult Substance Dependence. *Journal of Studies on Alcohol and Drugs.* 68, 1–10.

Kirby, K.C. et al. (1999) Community Reinforcement Training for Family and

Significant Others of Drug Abusers: A Unilateral Intervention to Increase Treatment Entry of Drug Users. *Drug and Alcohol Dependence*. 56, 85–96.

Klingemann, H. and Gmel, G. (2001) *Mapping The Social Consequence of Alcohol Consumption*. Kluwer Academic Publishers.

Klingemann, H. et al. (Eds.) (2001) *Promoting Self-Change From Problem Substance Use: Practical Implications for Policy, Prevention and Treatment*. Kluwer Academic Publishers.

Klingemann, H.K.H. (1992) Coping and Maintenance Strategies of Spontaneous Remitters From Problem Use of Alcohol and Heroin in Switzerland. *The International Journal of Addictions*. 27: 12, 1359–88.

Klonsky, E.D. (2011) Non-Suicidal Self-Injury in United States Adults: Prevalence, Socio-Demographics, Topography and Functions. *Psychological Medicines*. 41, 1981–6.

Knight, J.R. (1999) *The CRAFFT Questions: A Brief Screening Test for Adolescent Substance Abuse*. Children's Hospital Boston.

Knight, J.R. et al. (2002) Validity of The CRAFFT Substance Abuse Screening Test Among Adolescent Clinic Patients. *Archives of Pediatric Adolescent Medicine*. 6, 607–14.

Knight, J.R. et al. (2003) Validity of Brief Alcohol Screening Tests Amongst Adolescents: A Comparison of The AUDIT, POSIT, CAGE and CRAFFT. *Alcoholism: Clinical and Experimental Research*. 27, 67–73.

Kollins, S.H. (2007) Abuse Liability of Medications Used to Treat ADHD. *American Journal of Addiction*.16, Supplement 1, S35–S42.

Komro, K.A. et al. (2001) How Did Project Northland Reduce Alcohol Use Among Young Adolescents? Analysis of Mediating Variables. *Health Education Research: Theory and Practice*. 16: 1, 59–70.

Kooiker, S. and Christiansen, T. (1995) Inequalities in Health; The Interaction of Circumstances and Health Related Behaviour. *Social Health and Illness*. 17, 495–524.

Kosterman, R. et al. (2001) Preparing for The Drug Free Years: Session-Specific Effects of a Universal Parent-Training Intervention With Rural Families. *Journal of Drug Education*. 31: 1, 47–68.

Kracke, B. and Noacke, P. (1998) Continuity and Change in Family Interactions Across Adolescence. In Hofer, M. et al. (Eds.) *Verbal Interactions and Development in Families With Adolescents*. Ablex Publishing.

Kroger, J. (Ed.) (1993) *Discussion on Ego Identity*. Lawrence Erlbaum.

Kroger, J. (1996) *Identity in Adolescence: The Balance Between Self and Other*. Routledge.

Krug, I. et al. (2008) Present and Lifetime Comorbidity of Tobacco, Alcohol and Drug Use in Eating Disorders: A European Multicentre Study. *Drug and Alcohol Dependence*. 97, 169–79.

Kumpfer, K.L. and Alvardo, R. (2003) Family Strengthening Approaches to The Prevention of Youth Problem Behaviours. *American Psychologist*. 58, 457–65.

Kumpfer, K.L. and Baxley, G.B. (1997) *Drug Abuse Prevention: What Works?* National Institute of Drug Abuse.

Kumpfer, K.L. and Turner, C.W. (1990) The Social Ecology Model of Adolescent Substance Abuse: Implication for Prevention. *International Journal of Addictions*. 25: 4A, 435–63.

Kuperman, S. et al. (2001) Developmental Sequence From Disruptive Behavior, Diagnosis to Adolescent Alcohol Dependence. *American Journal of Psychiatry*. 158, 2022–6.

Kurdek, L. and Fine, M. (1994) Family Acceptance and Family Control as Predictors of Adjustment in Young Adolescents: Linear, Curvilinear, or Interactive Effects? *Child Development*. 65, 483–99.

Kypri, K. et al. (2006) Assessment May Conceal Therapeutic Benefit: Findings of a Randomised Control Trial for Hazardous Drinking. *Addiction*. 102: 1, 62–70.

Labouvie, E. (1996) Maturing Out of Substance Use: Selection and Self-Correction. *Journal of Drug Issues*. 26: 2, 457–76.

LaFreniere, P.J. and Capuano, F. (1997) Preventative Intervention as a Means of Clarifying Direction of Effects on Socialization: The Case of Anxious-Withdrawn Preschoolers. *Development and Psychopathology*. 9, 551–64.

Lambert, M.J. (1992) Implications of Outcome Research for Psychotherapy Integration. In Norcross, J.C. and Goldfrieds, M.R. (Eds.) *Handbook of Psychotherapy Integration*. Basic Books.

Lambert, M.J. and Bergin, A.E. (1994) The Effectiveness of Psychotherapy. In Bergin, A.E. and Garfield, S.L. (Eds.) *Handbook of Psychotherapy and Behaviour Change*. Wiley.

Landau, J. et al. (2004) Outcomes With ARISE Approach to Engaging Reluctant Drug- and Alcohol-Dependent Individuals in Treatment. *The American Journal of Drug and Alcohol Abuse*. 30: 4, 711–48.

Langenbucher, J.W. and Martin, C.S. (1996) Alcohol Abuse: Adding Content to Category. *Alcoholism: Clinical and Experimental Research.* 20, 270–5.

Larsen, R.J. and Buss, D.M. (2005) *Personality Psychology: Domains of Knowledge About Human Nature.* McGraw-Hill International.

Lasch, C. (1979) *The Culture of Narcissism.* W.W. Norton.

Lash, S.J. and Dillard, W. (1996) Encouraging Participation in Aftercare Group Therapy Among Substance-Dependent Men. *Psychological Reports.* 79, 585–6.

Lash, S.J., Burden, J.L. and Fearer, S.A. (2006) Contracting, Prompting and Reinforcing Substance Abuse Treatment Aftercare Adherence. In Bennett, L.A. (Ed.) *New Topics in Substance Abuse Treatment.* Nova Science Publishers.

Lash, S.J. et al. (2001) Social Reinforcement of Substance Abuse Aftercare Group Therapy Attendance. *Journal of Substance Abuse Treatment.* 20, 3–8.

Lash, S.J. et al. (2004) The Impact of Social Reinforcement of Substance Abuse Treatment Aftercare Participation on Outcome. *Addictive Behaviours.* 29, 337–42.

Lash, S.J. et al. (2005) Improving Substance Abuse Treatment Aftercare Adherence and Outcome. (Project IIR 99-282-2) for Co-Morbid Adolescent Drug Users. *Drug and Alcohol Dependence.* 66, S2–S202, S103.

Latimer, W.W. et al. (2000a) Adolescent Substance Abuse Treatment Outcome: The Role of Substance Abuse Problem Severity, Psychosocial and Treatment Factors. *Journal of Consulting and Clinical Psychology.* 68, 684–96.

Latimer, W.W. et al. (2000b) Demographic, Individual, and Interpersonal Predictors of Adolescent Alcohol and Marijuana Use Following Treatment. *Psychology of Addictive Behaviours.* 14, 162–73.

Lee, C.S., Winters, K.C. and Wall, M.W. (2010) Trajectories of Substance Use Disorders in Youth: Identifying and Predicting Group Membership. *Journal of Child and Adolescent Psychiatry.* 19, 135–57.

Leichliter, J.S. et al. (1998) Alcohol Use and Related Consequences Among Students With Varying Levels of Involvement in College Athletics. *Journal of American College Health.* 46, 257–62.

Leigh, B.C. and Stacy, A.W. (1993) Alcohol Outcome Expectancies: Scale Construction and Predicative Utility in Higher Order Confirmation Models. *Psychological Assessment.* 5, 216–29.

Lemert, E.M. (1964) Forms and Pathology of Drinking in Three Polynesian Societies. In Mac Marshall (Ed.) *Beliefs, Behaviours and Alcoholic Beverages: A Cross Cultural Survey.* University of Michigan Press.

Lerner, R.M., Ostrom, C.W. and Freel, M.A. (1997) Preventing Health Compromising Behaviours Among Youth and Promoting Their Positive Development: A Development Contextual Perspective. In Schulenberg, J. Maggs, J.L. and Hurrelman, K. (Eds.) *Health Risks and Development Transitions During Adolescence.* Cambridge University Press.

Levin, H.S. et al. (1991) Developmental Changes in Performance on Tests of Purported Frontal Lobe Functioning. *Developmental Neuropsychology.* 7: 3, 377–95.

Levinson, D. (1978) *The Seasons of a Man's Life.* A.A. Knopf.

Lewinsohn, P.M. et al. (1990) Cognitive-Behavioural Treatment for Depressed Adolescents. *Behaviour Therapy,* 21, 385–401.

Lewinsohn, P.M. et al. (1993) Adolescent Psychopathology: Prevalence and Incidence of Depression and Other DSM-III-R Disorders in High School Students. *Journal of Abnormal Psychology.* 102, 133–44.

Lewinsohn, P.M., Rohde, P. and Seeley, J.R. (1996) Alcohol Consumption in High School Adolescents: Frequency of Use and Dimensional Structure of Associated Problems. *Addiction.* 91, 375–90.

Liddle, H.A. (2004) Family-based Therapies for Adolescent Alcohiol and Drug Use: Research Contributions and Future Research Needs. *Addiction,* 99, 76–92.

Liddle, H.A. and Darkof, G.A. (2002) A Randomised Control Trial of Intensive Outpatient, Family Based Therapy vs. Residential Drug Treatment. *Drug and Alcohol Dependence.* 66: 385, S2–S202. S103.

Liddle, H.A. et al. (2001) A Multi-dimensional Therapy for Adolescent Drug Abuse: Results of a Randomised Trial. *American Journal of Drug and Alcohol Abuse,* 27: 4, 651–88.

Liddle, H.A. et al. (2004) Early Intervention for Adolescent Substance Abuse: Pretreatment and Posttreatment Outcomes of a Randomised Control Trial Comparing Multidimensional Family Therapy and Peer Group Treatment. *Journal of Psychoactive Drugs.* 36, 49–63.

Liddle, H.A. et al. (2008) Treating Adolescent Drug Abuse: A Randomised Control Trial Comparing Multi-dimensional Family Therapy and Cognitive Behaviour Therapy. *Addiction*, 103: 10, 1660–70.

Lifrak, P.D. et al. (1997) Naltraxone for Alcoholic Adolescents. *American Journal of Psychiatry*. 154, 439–41.

Lingford-Hughs, A.R. and Nutt, D. (2003) Neurobiology of Addiction and Implications for Treatment. *British Journal of Psychiatry*. 182, 97–100.

Linkovich-Kyle, T.L and Dunn, M.E. (2001) Consumption Related Difference in The Organisation and Activation of Marijuana Expectancies in Memory. *Experimental and Clinical Psychopharmacology*. 9: 3, 334–42.

Lipsey, M.W. and Wilson, D.B. (1998) Effective Interventions for Serious Juvenile Offenders: A Synthesis of Research. In Loeberandd, R. and Farringinton, P. (Eds.) *Serious Violent Juvenile Offenders: Risk Factors and Successful Interventions*. Sage.

Lister-Sharp, D. et al. (1999) Health Promoting Schools and Health Promotion in Schools: Two Systematic Reviews. *Health Technology Assessment*. 3, 22.

Lo, C.C. (1995) Gender Differences in Collegiate Alcohol Abuse. *Journal of Drug Issues*. 25, 817–36.

Lochman, J.E. (1992) Cognitive Behavioural Intervention With Aggressive Boys: Three Year Follow-Up and Preventative Efforts. *Journal of Consulting and Clinical Psychology*. 60, 426–32.

Loeber, R. et al. (1998) The Development of Male Offending: Key Findings From The First Decade of Pittsburgh Youth Study. *Studies on Crime and Crime Prevention*. 7: 2, 141–71.

Lolli, G. et al. (1958) *Alcohol in Italian Culture*. Free Press.

Lopez, B., Turner, R.J. and Saavedra, L.M. (2005) Anxiety and Risk for Substance Dependence Among Late Adolescents / Young Adults. *Journal of Anxiety Disorders*. 19, 275–94.

Lott, D.C. and Jenicus, S. (2009) Effectiveness of Very Low-Cost Contingency Management in a Community Adolescent Treatment Program. *Drug and Alcohol Dependence*. 102, 162–5.

Lubman, D.I. et al. (2007) The Impact of Co-Occurring Mood and Anxiety Disorders Among Substance-Abusing Youth. *Journal of Affective Disorders*. 103, 105–12.

Luborsky, L. et al. (1986) Do Therapists Vary Much in Their Success? Findings From Four Outcome Studies. *American Journal of Orthopsychiatry*. 56: 4, 501–12.

Luborsky, L., Rosenthal, R. and Diguer, L. (2002) The Dodo Bird Verdict is Alive and Well – Mostly. *Clinical Psychology Science and Practice*. 9, 3–12.

Lupton, C. and Nixon, P. (1999) *Empowering Practice? A Critical Appraisal for The FGC Approach*. Policy Press.

Lyon, A., Dalton, S. and Hoy, A. (2006) 'Hardcore Drinking': Portrayals of Alcohol Consumption in Young Men's and Young Women's Magazines. *Journal of Health Psychology*. 11: 2, 223–32.

Lyskey, M. and Hall. W. (2000) The Effects of Adolescent Cannabis Use on Educational Attainment: A Review. *Addiction*. 95: 11, 1621–30.

MacAndrew, C. and Edgerton, R.B. (1969) *Drunken Comportment: A Social Explanation*. Aldine.

Maccoby, E.E. and Martin, JA. (1983) Socialization in The Context of The Family: Parent-Child Interaction. In Mussen, P. and Hetherington, E.M. (Eds.) *Handbook of Child Psychology, Volume IV: Socialization, Personality, and Social Development*. 4th edn. Wiley.

MacDonald, S. (1994) Whisky, Women and The Scottish Drinking Problem. A View From The Highlands. In Mcdonald, M. (Ed.) *Gender, Drink and Drugs*. Berg.

Mackesey-Amiti, M.E., Fendrich, M. and Goldstein, P.J. (1997) Sequence of Drug Use Among Serious Users: Typical vs Atypical Progression. *Drug and Alcohol Dependence*. 45, 185–96.

MacKinnon, D.P. et al. (1991) Mediating Mechanisms in a School-Based Drug Prevention Program: First Year Effects of The Midwestern Prevention Project. *Health Psychology*. 10, 164–72.

MacKintosh, A.M. et al. (2001) *NE Choices: The Results of A Multi-Component Drug Prevention Programme for Adolescents*. DPAS Paper 14. London: Home Office.

Maddahian, E., Newcomb, M.D. and Bentler, P.M. (1988a) Adolescent's Drug Use and Intention to Use Drugs: Concurrent and Longitudinal Analysis of Four Ethnic Groups. *Addictive Behaviours*. 13, 191–5.

Maddahian, E., Newcomb, M.D. and Bentler, P.M. (1988b) Risk Factors for Substance Abuse: Ethnic Differences Among Adolescents. *Journal of Substance Abuse*. 1, 11–23.

Magura, S. et al. (2003) Predicative Validity of The ASAM Patient Placement Criteria for Naturalistically Matched vs Mismatched Alcohol Patients. *American Journal of Addiction.* 12, 386–97.

Maisto, S.A. et al. (2002) Nonproblem Drinking Outcomes in Adolescents Treated for Alcohol Use Disorder. *Experimental and Clinical Pharmacology.* 10: 3, 324–31.

Malcom, R., Myrick, H. and Roberts, J. (2002) The Effects of Carbamazepine and Lorazepam on Single Versus Multiple Previous Alcohol Withdrawals in an Outpatient Randomised Control Trial. *Journal of General Internal Medicine.* 17, 349–55.

Malinowski, B. (1922) *Argonauts of The Western Pacific.* Routledge.

Mandelbaum, D.G. (1965) Alcohol and Culture. *Current Anthropology.* 6: 3, 281–93.

Marcia, J. (1966) Development and Validation of Ego-Identity Status. *Journal of Personality and Social Psychology.* 3, 551–8.

Marcia, J. (1993) The Relational Roots of Identity. In Kroger, J. (Ed.) *Discussion in Ego Identity.* Lawrence Erlbaum.

Marlatt, G.A. and Gordon, J.R. (1980) Determinants of Relapse: Implications for The Maintenance of Behavioural Change. In Davidson, P. and Davidson, S.M. (Eds.) *Behavioural Medicine: Changing Health Lifestyles.* Pergamon.

Marlatt, G.A., Baer, J.S. and Larimer, M. (1995) Preventing Alcohol Abuse in College Students: A Harm Reduction Approach. In Boyd, G.M. et al. (Eds.) *Alcohol Problem Among Adolescents: Current Directions in Prevention Research.* Lawrence Erlbaum.

Marlatt, G.A. et al. (1998) Screening and Brief Intervention for High-Risk College Student Drinkers: Results From a Two Year Follow-Up Assessment. *Journal of Consulting and Clinical Psychology.* 66: 4, 604–15.

Marsh, P. and Crow, G. (1998) *Family Group Conferences in Child Welfare.* Blackwell.

Marshall, M. (1979) *Weekend Warriors: Alcohol in a Micronesian Culture.* Mayfield.

Martin, C.S. (1999) *Contrasting Alternative Diagnostic Criteria for Adolescent Alcohol Use Disorders.* Paper Presented to The Annual Meeting of The Research Society on Alcoholism, Santa Barbara.

Martin, C.S. and Chung. T. (2008) How Should We Revise Diagnostic Criteria for Substance Use Disorders in The DSM-V? *Journal of Abnormal Psychology.* 117: 3, 561–75.

Martin, C.S. and Winters, K.C. (1998) Diagnosis and Assessment of Alcohol Use Disorders Among Adolescents. *Alcohol Health and Research World.* 22, 95–105.

Martin, C.S. et al. (1995) Patterns of DSM IV Alcohol Abuse and Dependence Symptoms in Adolescent Drinkers. *Journal of Studies on Alcohol.* 56, 672–80.

Martin, C.S. et al. (1996) Staging The Onset of DSM IV Alcohol Abuse and Dependence Symptoms in Adolescent Drinkers. *Journal of Studies on Alcohol.* 56, 672–80.

Maruna, S. and Roy, K. (2007) Amputation or Reconstruction? Notes on The Concept of 'Knifing Off' and Desistance From Crime. *Journal of Contemporary Criminal Justice.* 23: 1, 104–24.

Mason, G. and Wilson, P. (1988) *Sport, Recreation and Juvenile Crime: an Assessment of The Impact of Sport and Recreation Upon Aboriginal and Non-Aboriginal Youth Offenders.* Australian Institute of Criminology.

Mathews, S., Brasnett, L. and Smith, J. (2006) *Underage Drinking: Findings From The 2004 Offenders, Crime and Justice Survey.* Home Office.

Mattrick, R.P. et al. (2003) *Methadone Maintenance Therapy Versus No Opioid Replacement for Opioid Dependence.* Cochrane Database Systematic Review: CD002207.

Mayer, J. and Filstead, W.J. (1979) The Adolescent Alcohol Involvement Scale: an Instrument for Measuring Adolescent Use and Misuse of Alcohol. *Journal of Studies on Alcohol.* 40, 291–300.

Mayo-Smith, M. (1997) Pharmacological Management of Alcohol Withdrawal. *JAMA,* 278, 144–51.

McBride, N. (2003) A Systematic Review of School Drug Education. *Health Education Research.* 18: 6, 729–42.

McBride, N. et al. (2000) Harm Minimization in School Drug Education: Final Results of The School Health and Alcohol Harm Reduction Project (SHAHRP). *Addiction.* 99,3: 278–91.

McBride, N. et al. (2004) Harm Minimization in School Drug Education: Final Results of The School Health and Alcohol Harm Reduction Project (SHAHRP). *Addiction.* 99: 3, 278–91.

McBride, N., Farrington, F. and Midford, R. (2002) Implementing a School Drug Education Programme: Reflections on Fidelity. *International Journal of Health Promotion and Education.* 40: 2, 40–50.

McCambridge, J. and Strang, J. (2004) The

Efficacy of Single Session Motivational Interviewing in Reducing Drug Consumption and Perceptions of Drug Related Risk and Harm Among Young People: Results From A Multi-Site Cluster Randomized Trial. *Addiction.* 99, 39–52.

McCambridge, J. and Strang, J. (2005) Deterioration Over Time in Effect of Motivational Interviewing in Reducing Drug Consumption and Related Risk in Young People. *Addiction.* 100, 470–8.

McClelland, D.C. et al. (1972) *The Drinking Man.* Free Press.

McCollister, T.S. et al. (1986) Effects of Computer Assisted Instruction and Teacher Assisted Instruction on Arithmetic Task Achievement Scores of Kindergarten Children. *Journal of Educational Research.* 80: 2, 121–5.

McCrae, R.R. and Costa, P.T. (1990) *Personality in Adulthood.* Guildford Press.

McGrath, Y. et al. (2006) *Drug Use Prevention Among Young People: A Review of Reviews.* The National Institute of Clinical Excellence.

McGue, M. (1999) Behavioural Genetics Models of Alcoholism and Drinking. In Leonnard, K.E. and Blane, H.T. (Eds.) *Psychological Theories of Drinking and Alcoholism.* Guildford Press.

McGuire, J., Kinderman P. and Hughes C. (2002) *Offending Behaviour Programmes.* YJB.

McGuire, W. (1964) Inducing Resistance to Persuasion: Some Contemporary Approaches. *Advances in Experimental and Social Psychology.* 1, 191–229.

McKay, J.R. et al. (1997) An Initial Evaluation of Psychosocial Dimensions of The American Society of Addiction Medicine Criteria for Inpatient Versus Outpatient Substance Abuse Rehabilitation. *Journal of Consulting and Clinical Psychology.* 58, 2329–52.

McLellan, A.T. and McKay, J.R. (1998) The Treatment of Addictions: What Can Research Offer Practice? In Lamb, S. et al. (Eds.) *Bridging The Gap Between Practice and Research: Forging Partnerships With Community Based Drug and Alcohol Treatment.* National Academy Press.

McLellan, A.T. et al. (1983) Increased Effectiveness of Substance Abuse Treatment: A Prospective Study of Patient Treatment Matching. *Journal of Nervous and Mental Disorders.* 171, 597–605.

McLellan, A.T. et al. (1993) The Effects of Psychosocial Services in Substance Misuse Treatment. *JAMA.* 269, 1953–9.

McLellan, A.T. et al. (1997) Problem-Service

'Matching' in Addictions Treatment: A Prospective Study in Four Programmes. *Archives of General Psychiatry.* 54, 730–5.

McLeod, B.D., Wood, J.J. and Weisz, J.R. (2007) Examining The Association Between Parenting and Childhood Anxiety: A Meta-Analysis. *Clinical Psychological Review.* 27: 2, 155–72.

Mead, M. (1928) *Coming of Age in Samoa.* Morrow.

Meehan, J.P., Webb, M.G. and Unwin, A.R. (1985) The Severity of Alcohol Dependence Questionnaire (SADQ) in a Sample of Irish Drinkers. *British Journal of Addictions.* 80, 57–63.

Melrose, M. et al. (2007) *The Impact of Heavy Cannabis Use on Young People: Vulnerability and Youth Transition.* Joseph Rowentree Foundation.

Meyers, R.J. et al. (1999) Community Reinforcement and Family Training (CRAFT): Engaging Unmotivated Drug Users in Treatment. *Journal of Substance Abuse.* 10, 291–308.

Meyers, R.J. et al. (2002) A Randomised Control Trial of Two Methods for Engaging Treatment-Refusing Drug Users Through Concerned Significant Others. *Journal of Consulting and Clinical Psychology.* 70, 1182–85.

Midford, R. et al. (2002) Principles That Underpin Effective School-Based Drug Education. *Journal of Drug Education.* 32: 4, 363–86.

Miller, B. and Bingham, C. (1989) Family Configuration in Relation to Sexual Behaviour of Female Adolescents. *Journal of Marriage and Family.* 51, 499–506.

Miller, E.T. et al. (2001) Alcohol Skills Training for College Students. In Monti, P.M. Colby, S.M. and O'Leary, T.A. (Eds.) *Adolescent Alcohol and Substance Abuse: Reaching Teens Thorough Brief Interventions.* Guildford Press.

Miller, G. (1985) *The Substance Abuse Subtle Screening Inventory-Adolescent Version.* SASSI Institute.

Miller, G.E. and Prinz, R.J. (1990) Enhancement of Social Learning Family Interventions for Childhood Conduct Disorder. *Psychological Bulletin.* 108, 291–307.

Miller, R. (2012) *Needs Analysis in The Three Counties of Dyfed.* (Unpublished).

Miller, W.R. and Munoz, R.F. (1982) *How to Control Your Drinking.* University of New Mexico Press.

Miller, W.R. and Rollnick, S. (1991) *Motivational Interviewing: Preparing People to Change Addictive Behaviour.* The Guilford Press.

Miller, W.R. et al. (2001) Community

Reinforcement and Traditional Approaches: Findings of a Controlled Trial. In Meyers, R.J. and Miller, W.R. (Eds.) *A Community Reinforcement Approach to Addiction Treatment.* Cambridge University Press.

Miller, W.R. et al. (1995) What Works? A Methodological Analysis of The Alcohol Outcome Treatment Literature. In Hester, H.A. and Miller, R.W. (Eds) *Handbook of Alcoholism Treatment Approaches.* Allyn and Bacon.

Miller, W.R. et al. (2003) What Works? A Methodological Analysis of The Alcohol Outcome Treatment Literature. In Hester, H.A. and Miller, W.R. (Eds.) *Handbook of Alcoholism Treatment Approaches.* Allyn and Bacon.

Miller, W.R., Meyers, R.J. and Tonigan, J.S. (1999) Engaging The Unmotivated in Treatment for Alcohol Problems: Comparisons of Three Strategies for Intervention Through Family Members. *Journal of Consulting and Clinical Psychology.* 67, 688–97.

Mita, T.H., Dermer, M. and Knight, J. (1977) Reversed Facial Images and The Mere-Exposure Hypothesis. *Journal of Personality and Social Psychology.* 35: 8, 597–601.

Moffit, T.E. (1997) Adolescence-Limited and Life Course Persistent Offending: A Complimentary Pair of Developmental Theories. In Thornbury, T.P. (Ed.) *Developmental Theories of Crime and Delinquency.* Transaction.

Mohr, D.C. (1995) Negative Outcome in Psychotherapy: A Critical Review. *Clinical Psychology: Science and Practice.* 2: 1, 1–27.

Molina, B.S., Bukstein, O.G. and Lynch, K.G. (2002) ADHD and Conduct Disorder Symptomology in Adolescents With Alcohol Use Disorder. *Psychology of Addictive Behaviour.* 16, 161–4.

Montgomery, S.M. et al. (1998) Substance Abuse: Unemployment, Cigarette Smoking, Alcohol Consumption and Body Weight in Young British Men. *European Journal of Public Health.* 8, 21–7.

Monti, P.M. et al. (1999) Brief Intervention for Harm Reduction With Alcohol-Positive Older Adolescents in Hospital Emergency Department. *Journal of Consulting and Clinical Psychology.* 67, 989–94.

Monti, P.M. et al. (2005) Adolescence: Booze, Brains, and Behaviour. *Alcoholism: Clinical and Experimental Research.* 29, 207–20.

Moore, K.A. et al. (1995) *Adolescent Sex, Contraception and Child Bearing: A Review of Recent Research.* Child Trends.

Moos, R.H. (1977) *Evaluating Educational Environments.* Jossey-Bass.

Moos, R.H. (1986) *Coping With Life Crises: an Integrated Approach.* Plenum.

Moos, R.H. (2008) Addictive Disorders in Context: Principles and Puzzles of Effective Treatment and Recovery. In Marlatt, G.A. and Witkiewitz, K. (Eds.) *Addictive Behaviors: New Readings on Etiology, Prevention and Treatment.* American Psychological Association.

Moos, R.H. and Moos, B.S. (2003) Long Term Influence of Duration and Intensity of Treatment on Previously Untreated Individuals With Alcohol Use Disorders. *Addition.* 98, 325–37.

Moos, R.H. et al. (1999) A Comparative Evaluation of Substance Abuse Treatment: I. Treatment Orientation, Amount of Care, and 1 Year Outcomes. *Alcoholism: Clinical and Experimental Research.* 23, 529–36.

Morral, A.R., McCaffrey, D.F. and Paddock, S.M. (2002) Reassessing The Marijuana Gateway Effect. *Addiction.* 97, 1493–505.

Moyer, A.A. et al. (2001) Can Methodological Features Account for Patient-Treatment Matching Findings in The Alcohol Field? *Journal of Studies on Alcohol.* 62, 62–73.

Munsch, J. and Kinchen K. (1995) Adolescent Sociometeric Status and Social Support. *Journal of Early Adolescence.* 15, 181–202.

Muntaner, C. et al. (2004) Socioeconomic Position and Major Mental Disorders. *Epidemiologic Reviews.* 26, 53–62.

Murji, K. (1999) White Lines: Culture, 'Race' and Drugs. In South, N. (Ed.) *Drugs: Cultures, Control and Everyday Life.* Sage.

Murphy, E.F. (1922) *The Black Candle.* Thomas Allen.

Murray, D.M. et al. (1988) Four- and Five-Year Follow up Results From Four Seventh-Grade Smoking Prevention Strategies. *Journal of Behavioural Medicine.* 11, 395–405.

Musto, D.F. (1987) *The American Disease: Origins of Narcotic Control.* Oxford University Press.

Muthen, B.O. and Muthen, L.K. (2000) The Development of Heavy Drinking and Alcohol Related Problems From Ages 18 to 37 in a US National Sample. *Journal of Studies on Alcohol.* 61, 290–300.

Myers, W.C., Donahue, J.E. and Goldstein, M.R. (1994) Disulfirum for Alcohol Use Disorders in Adolescents. *Journal of American Academy of Child and Adolescent Psychiatry.* 33, 484–9.

Nagin, D.S., Farrington, D.P. and Moffit, T.E.

(1995) Life Course Trajectories of Different Types of Offenders. *Crminology*. 33, 111–39.

Najavits, L.M., Gallop, R.J. and Weiss, R.D. (2006) Seeking Safety Therapy for Adolescent Girls With PTSD and Substance Use Disorder: A Randomised Control Trial. *Journal of Behavioural Health Service Research*. 33, 453–63.

National Centre of Social Research (2007) *Smoking, Drinking and Drug Use Among Young People in England 2006*. The Information Centre. National Centre of Social Research.

Neale, J. (2006) Social Exclusion, Drugs and Policy. In Hughes, R., Lart, R. and Higate, P. (Eds.) *Drugs: Policy and Politics*. Open University Press.

Nelson-Simley, K. and Erickson, L. (1995) The Nebraska 'Network of Drug Free Youth' Program. *Journal of School Health*. 65, 49–53.

Neugarten, B. (1965) *Norms, Age Constraints and Adult Socialisation*. Foreman.

Neve, R.J., Diedriks, J.P. and Knibbe, R.A. (1993) Development of Drinking Behaviour in The Netherlands From 1958 Until 1989 With Respect to Age and Gender. *Tijdschr Alcohol Drugs*. 19: 2, 91–106.

Newcomb, M.D. (1995) Drug Use Etiology Among Ethnic Minority Adolescents: Risk and Protective Factors. In Botvin, G.J., Schinke, S. and Orlandi, M.A. (Eds.) *Drug Abuse Prevention With Multi-Ethnic Youth*. Sage Publications.

Newcomb, M.D. and Bentler, P.M. (1986) Substance Use and Ethnicity: Differential Impact of Peer and Adult Models. *Journal of Psychology*. 120, 83–95.

Newcomb, M.D. and Bentler, P.M. (1987) Impact on Adolescent Drug Use and Social Support on Problem Young Adults: A Longitudinal Study. *Journal of Abnormal Psychology*. 97, 64–75.

Newcomb, M.D. and Felix-Ortiz, M. (1992) Multiple Protective and Risk Factors Drug Use Amongst Adolescents: Cross Sectional and Prospective Findings. *Journal of Personality and Social Psychology*. 63, 280–96.

Newcomb, M.D. et al. (1987) Substance Abuse and Psychosocial Risk Factors Among Teenagers: Associations With Sex, Age, Ethnicity, and Type of School. *American Journal of Drug and Alcohol Abuse*. 13, 413–33

Newcombe, T.M (1943) *Personality and Social Change: Attitude Formation in a Student Community*. Dryden Press.

Newcombe, T.M. and Wilson, E.K. (1966) *College Peer Groups: Problems and Prospects for Research*. Aldine.

Newlin, D.B. and Thomson, J.B. (1999) Chronic Tolerance and Sensitization to Alcohol in Sons of Alcoholics: Replication and Reanalysis. *Experimental and Clinical Psychopharmacology*. 7, 234–45.

Newman, B. and Newman, P. (1995) *Development Through Life: A Psychosocial Approach*. Brooks/Cole.

Newton, N.C. et al. (2010) Internet-Based Prevention for Alcohol and Cannabis Use: Final Results of the Climate Schools Course. *Addiction*. 105, 4: 749–59.

NICE (2007) *Parent-Training / Education Programmes in The Management of Children With Conduct Disorders*. Technology Appraisal Guidance, 102. NICE.

Nichols, G. and Crow, I. (2004) Measuring The Impact of Crime Reduction Interventions Involving Sporting Activities for Young People. *Howard Journal of Criminal Justice*. 43: 3, 267–83.

Niederhofer, H. and Staffen, W. (2003a) Acamprosate and Its Efficacy in Treating Alcohol Dependent Adolescents. *European Child and Adolescent Psychiatry*. 12, 144–8.

Niederhofer, H. and Staffen, W. (2003b) Comparison of Disulfirum and Placebo in Treatment of Alcohol Dependence in Adolescents. *Drug and Alcohol Review*. 22, 295–7.

Niederhofer, H., Staffen, W. and Mair, A. (2003) Comparison of Naltrexone and Placebo on Treatment of Alcohol Dependence of Adolescents. *Alcohol Treatment Quarterly*. 21, 87–95.

Nigg, J. and Huang-Pollock, C. (2003) *An Early Onset Model of The Role of Executive Functions and Intelligence in Conduct / Delinquency. Causes of Conduct Disorder and Juvenile Delinquency*, Guildford Press.

NISRA (Northern Ireland Statistics and Research Agency) (2008) *Young Persons Behaviour and Attitude Survey 2007*. Central Survey Unit, NISRA.

Nixon, P., Burford, G. and Quinn, A. (With Edelbaum, J.) (2005) *A Survey of International Practice, Policy and Research on Family Group Conferencing and Related Practices*. American Humane Association.

Norcross, J.C. (2010) The Therapeutic Relationship. In Duncan, B.L. et al. (Eds.) *The Heart and Soul of Change: Delivering What Works in Therapy*. 2nd edn. American Psychological Association.

Norcross, J.C. (Ed.) (2011) *Psychotherapy*

Relationships That Work: Evidence Based Responsiveness. Oxford.

Norman, E. et al. (1997) Prevention Programmes Reviewed: What Works? In Norman, E. (Ed.) *Drug-Free Youth Work: A Compendium for Prevention Specialists.* Garland Publishing.

Norman, W.T. (1963) Toward an Adequate Taxonomy of Personality Attributes: Replicated Factor Structure in Peer Nomination Personality Ratings. *Journal of Abnormal Psychology.* 66, 574–83.

Norström, T. (2002) *Alcohol in Postwar Europe: Consumption, Drinking Patterns, Consequences and Policy Responses in 15 European Countries.* National Institute of Public Health.

NTA Report (2010) *Drug Treatment in 2009–2010.* Department of Health.

O'Connor, L., Best, D. and Best, R. (1998) What 'Works' in Drugs Education? In O'Connor, L. et al. (Eds.) *Drugs: Partnerships for Policy, Prevention and Education: A Practical Approach for Working Together.* Cassell.

O'Malley, P.M., Johnston, L.D. and Bachman, J.G. (1998) Alcohol Use Amongst Adolescents. *Alcohol Health and Research World.* 22, 85–93.

Oesterle, S. et al. (2004) Adolescent Heavy Episodic Drinking Trajectories and Health in Young Adulthood. *Journal of Studies on Alcohol.* 65, 204–12.

Oetting, E.R. and Beauvais, F. (1986) Peer Cluster Theory: Drugs and The Adolescent. *Journal of Counselling and Development.* 65, 17–22.

Offer, D., Ostrov, E., Howard, K. and Dolin, S. (1992) *The Offer Self-Image Questionnaire for Adolescents-Revised.* Western Psychological Services.

Office for National Statistics (2008) *Results From The 2006 General Household Survey.* ONS.

Olds, D. et al. (1998) Long Term Effects of Home Nurse Visitation on Children's Criminal and Antisocial Behaviour: 15 Year Follow Up of A Randomised Control Trial. *Journal of The American Medical Association.* 280: 14, 1238–44.

Ollendick, T.H. and King, N.J. (1994) Diagnosis, Assessment, Treatment of Internalising Problems in Children: The Role of Longitudinal Data. *Journal of Consulting and Clinical Psychology.* 62, 918–27.

Orlinsky, D.E., Ronnestad, M.H. and Willurzki, U. (2004) Fifty Years of Psychotherapy Process-Outcome Research: Continuity and Change. In Lambert, M.J. (Ed.) *Bergin and Garfield's Handbook of Psychotherapy and Behaviour Change.* Wiley.

Ouimette, P.C. and Brown P.J. (2003) *Trauma and Substance Misuse.* American Psychiatric Association.

Ouimette, P.C., Moos, R.H. and Finney, J.W. (1998) Influence of Outpatient Treatment and 12 Step Group Involvement on 1-Year Substance Abuse Treatment Outcomes. *Journal of Studies on Alcohol.* 59, 513–22.

Ouimette, P.C., Moos, R.H. and Finney, J.W. (2003) Substance Use Disorder-Posttraumatic Stress Disorder Comorbidity. A Survey of Treatments and Proposed Practice Guidelines. *Journal of Consulting & Clinical Psychology.* 71: 2, 410–14.

Ozechowski, T.J. and Liddle, H.A. (2000) Family-Based Therapy for Adolescent Drug Abuse: Knowns and Unknowns. *Clinical Child and Family Psychology Review.* 3, 269–98.

Paglia, A. et al. (1996) Beliefs and Attitudes. In Stephens, S. and Morin, M. (Eds.) *Youth Smoking Survey, 1994: Technical Report.* Minister of Supply and Services Canada.

Palmgreen, P. et al. (2001) Television Campaigns and Adolescent Marijuana Use: Tests of Sensation Seeking Targeting. *American Journal of Public Health.* 91, 292–6.

Paolino, T.J. and Mccrady, B.S. (1977) *The Alcoholic Marriage: Alternative Perspectives.* Grune and Statton.

Pape, H. and Hammer, T. (1996) How Does Young People's Alcohol Consumption Change During The Transition to Early Adulthood? A Longitudinal Study of Changes at Aggregates and Individual Level. *Addiction.* 91: 9, 1345–57.

Park, J. et al. (2000) Effects of The 'Preparing for The Drug Free Years' Curriculum on Growth in Alcohol Use and Risk for Alcohol Use in Early Adolescence. *Prevention Science.* 1: 3, 125–38.

Parker, H., Bakx, K. and Newcombe, R. (1988) *Living With Heroin: The Impact of a Drugs 'Epidemic' on an English Community.* Open University Press.

Parkes, C.M. (1991) *Bereavement Studies of Grief in Adult Life.* Penguin.

Paus, T. et al. (1999) Structural Maturation of Neural Pathways in Children and Adolescents: in Vivo Study. *Science.* 283: 5409, 1908–11.

Pechmann, C. and Shih, C.F. (1999) Smoking Scenes in Movies and Antismoking Advertisements Before Movies Effects on Youth. *Journal of Marketing.* 63, 1–13.

Pechmann, C. et al. (2003) What to Convey in Antismoking Advertisements for Adolescents: The Use of Protection Motivational Theory to

Identify Effective Message Themes. *Journal of Marketing.* 67: 2, 1–18.

Pederson, N.L. (1993) Genetic and Environmental Change in Personality. In Bouchard, T.J. and Proping, P. (Eds.) *Twins as Tools of Behaviour Genetics.* Wiley.

Pelham, W.E. et al. (1992) Teacher Ratings of DSM-III-R Symptoms of Disruptive Disorders. *Journal of The American Academy of Child and Adolescent Psychiatry.* 31, 210–8.

Pentz, M.A. et al. (1989) A Multicommunity Trial for Primary Prevention of Adolescent Drug Abuse. *Journal of The American Medical Association.* 261, 3259–66.

Perkins, H.W. (1985) Religious Traditions, Parents, and Peers as Determinants of Alcohol and Drug Use Among College Students. *Review of Religious Research.* 27, 15–31.

Perkins, H.W. (1987) Parental Religion and Alcohol Use Problems as Intergenerational Predictors of Problem Drinking Among College Students. *Journal of The Scientific Studies on Religion.* 26: 3, 340–57.

Perkins, H.W. (1994) The Contextual Effect of Secular Norms on Religiosity as a Moderator of Student Alcohol and Other Drug Use. In Lynn, M. and Moberg, D. (Eds.) *Research in The Social Scientific Study of Religion.* JAI Press.

Perkins, H.W. et al. (1999) Misperceptions of The Norms of The Frequency of Alcohol and Other Drug Use on College Samples. *Journal of American College Health.* 47, 253–8.

Perloff, R.M. (1993) *The Dynamics of Persuasion.* Lawrence Erlbaum.

Perry, C.L. et al. (1996) Project Northland: Outcomes of A Communitywide Alcohol Use Prevention Program During Early Adolescence. *American Journal of Public Health.* 86, 956–65.

Perry, C.L. et al. (1998) *Project Northland – Phase II: Community Action to Reduce Adolescent Alcohol Use.* Paper Presented at The Fourth Symposium on Community Action Research and The Prevention of Alcohol and Other Drug Problems: Russell, New Zealand.

Perry, C.L. et al. (2002) Project Northlands: Long Term Outcomes of Community Action to Reduce Adolescent Alcohol Use. *Health Education Research.* 17, 117–32.

Petchers, M. and Singer, M. (1990) Clinical Applicability of A Substance Abuse Screening Instrument. *Journal of Adolescent Chemical Dependency.* 1, 47–56.

Petersen, A.C. and Leffert, N. (1995) What is Special About Adolescence? In Rutter, M. (Ed.) *Psychosocial Disturbances in Young People: Challenges of Prevention.* Cambridge University Press.

Petraitis, J., Flay, B.R. and Miller, Q.T. (1995) Reviewing Theories of Adolescent Substance Abuse: Organising Pieces in The Puzzle. *Psychological Bulletin.* 117, 67–86.

Petry, N.M. (2000) A Comprehensive Guide to The Application of Contingency Management Procures in Clinical Settings. *Drug and Alcohol Dependence.* 58, 9–25.

Phelps, F.A. et al. (1994) Sex Education: The Effect of A Peer Programme on Pupils (Aged 13–14 Years) and Their Peer Leaders. *Health Education Journal.* 53, 127–39.

Phinney, J. and Goosens, L. (Eds.) (1996) Identity Development in Context. *Journal of Adolescence.* 19, 401–500.

Piaget, J. (2001) *The Language and Thought of The Child.* 3rd edn. Routledge.

Pihl, R.O. and Petterson, J.B. (1995) Alcoholism: The Role of Different Motivational Systems. *Journal of Psychiatry and Neuroscience.* 20, 372–96.

Pikanen, T., Lyyra, A.L. and Pulkkinnen, L. (2005) Age of Onset of Drinking and The Use of Alcohol in Adulthood: A Follow-Up Study From Age 8–42 for Females and Males. *Addiction.* 100, 652–61.

Pittman, D.J. and White, H.R. (Eds.) (1991) *Society, Culture and Drinking Patterns Re-Examined.* Rutgers Centre of Alcohol Studies.

Plomb, H.N., Kirschner, W. and Van Der Hek, H. (1996) Explanation of National Variations in Alcohol and Cannabis Consumption: A Comparative Study in a Dutch and Adjoining German Region. *European Journal of Public Health.* 6: 2, 118–25.

Plomin, R. and Spinath, F.M. (2004) Intelligence: Genetics, Genes and Genomics. *Journal of Personality and Social Psychology.* 86, 112–29.

Polich, J.M., Armor, D.J. and Braiker, H.B. (1981) *The Course of Alcoholism: Four Years After Treatment.* Wiley.

Pollay, R. et al. (1996) The Last Straw? Cigarette Advertising and Realised Market Shares Among Youths and Adults, 1979–93. *American Marketing Association Journal of Marketing.* 60, 1–16.

Pollock, N.K. and Martin, C.S (1999) Diagnostic Orphans: Adolescents With Alcohol Symptoms Who Do Not Qualify for DSM IV Abuse or Dependence Diagnosis. *American Journal of Psychiatry.* 156, 897–901.

Pope, H.G. et al. (2003) Early Onset Cannabis Use and Cognitive Deficits: What Is The Nature of The Association? *Drug and Alcohol Dependence.* 69, 303–10.

Poulin, C. et al. (2005) Gender Differences in The Association Between Substance Use and Elevated Depressive Symptoms in a General Adolescent Population. *Addiction.* 100, 525–35.

Prentice, D.A. and Miller, D.T. (1993) Pluralistic Ignorance and Alcohol Use on Campus: Some Consequences of Misperceiving The Social Norms. *Journal of Personality and Social Psychology.* 243–56.

Prescott, C.A. and Kendler, C.S. (1999) Age of First Drink and Risk of Alcoholism: A Noncausal Association. *Alcoholism: Clinical and Experimental Research.* 23, 101–7.

Price, R.K., Cottier, L.B. and Robins, L.N (1991) Patterns of Drug Abuse Treatment Utilization in a General Population. In Harris, L. (Ed.) *Problems of Drug Dependence, 1990.* National Institute of Drug Abuse Research Monograph No. 15. US Government Printing Office.

PricewaterhouseCoopers (2000) *Teen Purchasing Power Weak in Online Shopping Arena.* www.Pwcglobal.com

Primack, B.A. et al. (2008) Content Analysis of Tobacco, Alcohol and Other Drugs in Popular Music. *Archives of Pediatrics and Adolescent Medicine.* 162: 2, 169–75.

Prinz, R.J., Blechman, E.A. and Dumas, J.E. (1994) an Evaluation of Peer Coping – Skills Training for Childhood Aggression. *Journal of Clinical Child Psychology.* 23, 193–203.

Prochaska, J.O. and DiClemente, C.C. (1992) Transtheoretical Approach. In Norcross, J.C. and Goldfried, M.R. (Eds.) *Handbook of Psychotherapy Integration.* Basic Books.

Prochaska, J.O., Norcross, J.C. and DiClemente, C.C. (1994) *Changing for Good.* William Morrow & Co.

Pull, C.B. et al. (1997) Concordance Between ICD-10 Alcohol and Drug Use Disorder Criteria and Diagnosis as Measured by The AUDADIS-ADR, CIDI, and SCAN: Results of A Cross-National Study. *Drug and Alcohol Dependence.* 47, 207–16.

Rahdert, E. (Ed.) (1991) *The Adolescent Assessment/Referral System Manual.* DHHS Pub. No. (ADM) 91–1735. National Institute on Drug Abuse.

Rankin, H., Stockwell, T. and Hodgson, R. (1982) Cues for Drinking and Degrees of Alcohol Dependence. *British Journal of Addiction.* 77, 287–96.

Rasmussen, S.A. and Tsuang, M.T. (1986) Clinical Characteristics and Family History in DSM-III Obsessive-Compulsive Disorder. *American Journal of Psychiatry.* 143, 317–22.

Read, J.P., Brown, P.J. and Kahler, C.W. (2004) Substance Use and Posttraumatic Stress Disorders: Symptom Interplay and Effects on Outcome. *Addictive Behaviors.* 29, 1665–72.

Redmond, W. (1999) Effects of Sales Promotion on Smoking Amongst US Ninth Graders. *Preventative Medicine.* 98, 243–50.

Reese, H.W. and Smyer, M.A. (1983) The Dimensionalization of Life Events. In Callahan, E.J. and Mccluskey, K.A. (Eds.) *Life-Span Developmental Psychology: Nonnormative Life Events.* Academic Press.

Rehm, J. (2001) Concepts, Dimensions and Measures of Alcohol-Related Social Consequences – A Basic Framework for Alcohol Realted Benefits and Harm. In Klingmann, H. and Gmel, G. (Eds.) *Mapping The Social Consequence of Alcohol Consumption.* Kluwer Academic Publishers.

Reid, J.B. et al. (1999) Description and Immediate Impacts of A Preventative Intervention for Conduct Problems. *American Journal of Community Psychology.* 27, 483–517.

Reiger, D.A. et al. (1990) Comorbidity of Mental Disorders With Alcohol and Other Drug Abuse: Results From The Epidemiologic Catchment Area (ECA) Study. *JAMA.* 264, 2511–8.

Reiger, D.A. et al. (1993) The De Facto US Mental and Addictive Disorders Service System. *Archives of General Psychiatry.* 50, 84–94.

Reinherz, H.Z. et al. (1993) Prevalence of Psychiatric Disorders in a Community Population of Older Adolescents. *Journal of The American Academy of Child and Adolescent Psychiatry.* 32, 369–77.

Rey, J.M. et al. (2002) Mental Health of Teenagers Who Use Cannabis; Results of an Australian Survey. *British Journal of Psychiatry.* 180, 216–21.

Ridgeley, M.S., Goldman, H.H. and Talbot, J.A. (1986) *Chronically Mentally Ill Young Adults With Substance Abuse Problems: A Review of The Literature and Creation of A Research Agenda.* Mental Health Policy Studies.

Ridgely, M.S., Osher, F.C. and Talbot, J.A. (1987) *Chronically Mentally Ill Young Adults With Substance Abuse Problems: Treatment and Training Issues.* Mental Health Policy Studies.

Riggs, P.D. et al. (2005) A Randomised Control Trial of Fluoxetine and Cognitive Behavioural

Therapy in Adolescents With Major Depression, Behavioural Problems and Substance Use Disorders. *Archive of Paediatric Adolescent Medications.* 161, 1026–34.

Roberts, P. and Newton, P.M. (1987) Levinsonian Studies of Women's Adult Development. *Psychology and Aging.* 2, 154–63.

Robins, L.N. and Przybeck, T.R. (1985) Age of Onset of Drug Use as a Factor in Drug and Other Disorders. In Jones, C.L. and Battjes, R.J. (Eds.) *Aetiology of Drug Abuse.* NIDA.

Robinson, S.E. et al. (1993) Influence of Substance Abuse Education on Undergraduates' Knowledge, Attitudes and Behaviours. *Journal of Alcohol and Drug Educations.* 39: 1, 123–30.

Roehrich, L. and Goldman, M. (1995) Implicit Priming of Alcohol Expectancy Memory Processes and Subsequent Drinking Behaviour. *Experimental Clinical Psychopharmacology.* 3, 402–10.

Roll, J.M. (2005) Assessing The Feasibility of Using Contingency Management to Modify Cigarette Smoking in Adolescents. *Journal of Applied Behavioural Analysis.* 38, 463–7.

Room, R. (1983) Alcohol and Crime: Behavioural Aspects. In Kadish, S.H. (Ed.) *Encyclopaedia of Crime and Justice: Volume 1.* The Free Press.

Room, R. (2003) *Use of Alcohol and Drugs: Patterns, Pleasures, Problems.* International Conference on Public Health, Bergen, Norway, 15th-17th of June. Ministry of Health.

Room, R. (2007) Taking Account of Cultural and Societal Influences on Substance Use Diagnosis and Criteria. *Focus.* 5: 2, 199–207.

Rooney, B.L. and Murray, D.M. (1996) A Meta-Analysis of Smoking Programs After Adjusting for Error in The Units of Analysis. *Health Education Quarterly.* 23: 1, 48–64.

Root, T.L. et al. (2010) Substance Use Disorders in Women With Anorexia Nervosa. *International Journal of Eating Disorders.* 43: 1, 14–21.

Rosenberg, M.F. and Anthony, J.C. (2001) Early Clinical Manifestations of Cannabis Dependence in a Community Sample. *Drug and Alcohol Dependence.* 64, 123–31.

Roth, J. and Dadds, M.R. (1999) *Reach for Resilience: Evaluation of a Universal Program for The Prevention of Internalizing Problems in Young Children.* Griffith Early Intervention Project, School of Applied Psychology, Griffith University.

Ruffin, J.E. (1989) Stages of Adult Development in Black Professional Women. In Jones, R.L. (Ed.) *Black Adult Development and Aging.* Cobb and Henry.

Rundall, T.G. and Bruvold, W.H. (1988) A Meta-Analysis of School-Based Smoking and Alcohol-Use Prevention Programs. *Health Education Quarterly.* 15: 3, 317–34.

Russell, M., Cooper, M.L. and Frone, M.R. (1990) The Influence of Sociodemographic Characteristics on Familial Problems: Data From A Community Sample. *Alcoholism: Clinical and Experimental Research.* 14, 221–6.

Rutter, M., Moffitt, T.E. and Caspi, A. (2006) Gene-Environment Interplay and Psychopathology: Multiple Varieties But Real Effects. *Journal of Child Psychology and Psychiatry.* 3–4, 226–61.

Ryan, B.E. and Mosher, J.F. (1991) *Progress Report: Alcohol Promotion on Campus.* The Martin Institute.

Sadava; S.W. and Pak, A.W. (1994) Problem Drinking and Close Relationships During The Third Decade of Life. *Psychology of Addictive Behaviour.* 8, 251–8.

SAMHSA (Substance Abuse and Mental Health Services Administration) (1998) *Services Research Outcome Study.* Office of Applied Studies.

Sanders, M.R. (1999) Triple P-Positive Parenting Program: Towards an Empirically Validated Multilevel Parenting and Family Support Strategy for The Prevention of Behaviour and Emotional Problems in Children. *Clinical Child and Family Psychological Review.* 2: 2, 71–90.

Sanju, G. and Hamday, M. (2005) 'Gateway Hypothesis' – A Preliminary Evaluation of Variables Predicting Non-Conformity. *Addictive Disorders and Their Treatment.* 4, 39–40.

Santisteban, D.A. et al. (2003) Efficiency of Brief Strategic Family Therapy in Modifying Hispanic Adolescent Behavior Problems and Substance Abuse. *Journal of Family Psychology,* 17, 121–31.

Saunders, J.B. et al. (1993) Development of The Alcohol Use Disorder Test (AUDIT): WHO Collaborative Project on Early Detection of Persons With Harmful Alcohol Consumption. II. *Addiction.* 88, 791–804.

Schaps, E. et al. (1981) A Review of 127 Drug Abuse Prevention Evaluations. *Journal of Drug Issues.* 11, 17–43.

Schaps, E. et al. (1986) Evaluation of Seven School-Based Prevention Projects: A Final Report on The Napa Project. *International Journal of The Addictions.* 21, 1081–112.

Scheier, L.M., Botvin, G.J. and Griffin, K. (2001) Preventive Interventions, Effects on

Developmental Progression in Drug Use: Structural Equation Model Analysis Using Longitudinal Data. *Preventative Science.* 2, 89–100.

Scheier, L.M., Newcomb, M.D., and Skager, R. (1994) Risk, Protection, and Vulnerability to Adolescent Drug Use: Latent-Variable Models of Three Age Groups. *Journal of Drug Education.* 24, 49–82.

Schinke, S.P., Tepavac, L. and Cole, K.C. (2000) Prevention Substance Use Among Native American Youth: Three Year Results. *Addictive Behaviour.* 25, 387–97.

Schlegal, A. and Barry, H. (1991) *Adolescence: an Anthropological Inquiry.* The Free Press.

Schlossberg, N.K. (1995) *Counselling Adults in Transition: Linking Practice With Theory.* Springer.

Schroeder, D.S., Laflin, M.T. and Weis, D.L. (1993) Is There a Relationship Between Self-Esteem and Drug Use? Methodological and Statistical Limitations of The Research. *The Journal of Drug Issues.* 23: 4, 645–65.

Schuckit, M.A. et al. (1997) Periods of Abstinence Following The Onset of Alcohol Dependence in 1853 Men and Women. *Journal of Studies on Alcohol.* 58, 581–9.

Schuckit, M.A. et al. (1998) Clinical Relevance of The Distinction Between Alcohol Dependence With and Without A Physiological Component. *American Journal of Psychiatry.* 41, 1043–9.

Schulenberg, J. et al. (1996a) Adolescent Risk Factors for Binge Drinking During The Transition to Young Adulthood: Variable and Pattern Centred Approaches to Change. *Developmental Psychology.* 32, 659–79.

Schulenberg, J. et al. (1997) Negotiating Development Transitions During Adolescence and Young Adulthood: Health Risks and Opportunities. In Schulenberg, J.L., Maggs, J. and Hurrelman, K. (Eds.) *Health Risks and Development Transitions During Adolescence.* Cambridge University Press.

Schulenberg, J. et al. (2004) *How Social Role Transitions From Adolescence to Adulthood Relate to Trajectories of Wellbeing and Substance Use.* Monitoring The Future Occasional Paper, 56.

Schulenberg, J. et al. (2005) Trajectories of Marijuana Use During The Transition to Adulthood: The Big Picture Based on National Panel Data. *Journal of Drug Issues.* 35: 2, 255–79.

Schwartz, R.H. and Wirtz, P.W. (1990) Potential Substance Abuse: Detection Among Adolescent Patients Using The Drug and Alcohol Problem (DAP) Quick Screen, A 30 Item Questionnaire. *Clinical Pediatrics.* 29, 38–43.

Shapiro, H. (2003) *Shooting Stars: Drugs, Hollywood and The Movies.* Serpent's Tail.

Shedler, J. and Block, J. (1990) Adolescent Drug Use and Psychological Health: A Longitudinal Study. *American Psychologist.* 45: 5, 612–30.

Sher, K.J. (1991) *Children of Alcoholics: A Critical Appraisal of Theory and Research.* University of Chicago Press.

Sherif, M. et al. (1961) *Intergroup Cooperation and Competition: The Robbers Cave Experiment.* University Book Exchange.

SHEU (2001) www.SHEU.org.uk

Shucksmith, J. and Hendry, L. (1998) *Health Issues and Adolescents: Growing Up and Speaking Out.* Routledge.

Shucksmith, J., Hendry, L.B. and Glendinnning, A. (1995) Models of Parenting: Implications for Adolescent Well-Being Within Different Types of Family Context. Journal of Adolescence. 18, 253–70.

Silbereisen, R.K. and Kracke, B. (1997) Self-Report Maturational Timing and Adaption in Adolescence. In Schulenberg, J., Maggs, J.L. and Hurrelman, K. (Eds.) *Health Risks and Development Transitions During Adolescence.* Cambridge University Press.

Silva, P.A. and Stanton, W.R. (1996) *From Child to Adult: The Dunedin Multidisciplinary Study.* Oxford University Press

Simmons, R. and Blythe, D. (1987) *Moving Into Adolescence: The Impact of Pubertal Change and School Context.* Aldine De Gruyter.

Sisson, R.W. and Azrin, N. (1986) Family-Member Involvement to Initiate and Promote Treatment of Problem Drinkers. *Journal of Behavior Therapy and Experimental Psychiatry.* 17, 15–21.

Skara, S. and Sussman, S. (2003) A Review of 25 Long Term Adolescent Tobacco and Other Drug Use Prevention Programme Evaluations. *Preventative Medicine.* 37, 451–74.

Skinner, B.F. (2002) *Beyond Freedom and Dignity.* Hachette Publishing.

Slater, M.D. and Kelly, K.J. (2002) Testing Alternative Explanations for Exposure Effects in Media Campaigns: The Case of a Community Based in School Media Drug Prevention Project. *Communication Research.* 29, 367–89.

Slater, M.D. et al. (2006) Combining In-School and Community-Based Media Uptake Among Younger Adolescents. *Health Education Research: Theory and Practice.* 21: 1, 157–67.

Slattery, J. et al. (2003) *Prevention of Relapse in Alcohol Dependence.* Health Technology Assessment Report 3. Health Technology Board for Scotland.

Slesnick, N. et al. (2007) Treatment Outcome for Street-Living, Homeless Youth. *Addictive Behaviors.* 32: 2, 1237–51.

Slotkin, T.A. (2002) Nicotine and The Adolescent Brain: Insights From an Animal Model. *Neurotoxicology and Teratology.* 24, 369–84.

Smetana, J. (1988) Adolescents' and Parents' Conceptions of Parental Authority. *Child Development.* 59, 321–35.

Smetana, J. (1989) Adolescents' and Parents' Reasoning About Actually Family Conflicts. *Child Development.* 60, 1052–67.

Smith, A. and Waddington, I. (2004) Using Sport in The Community Schemes to Tackle Crime and Drug Use Among Young People: Some Policy Issues and Problems. *European Physical Education Review.* 10: 3, 279–98.

Smith, J.E. and Meyers, R.J. (2004) *Motivating Substance Abusers to Enter Treatment: Working With Family Members.* Guildford Press.

Smith, R.F. (2003) Animal Models of Periadolescent Substance Abuse. *Neurotoxicology and Teratology.* 25, 291–301.

Smith, T.A. et al. (1996) Nicotine Patch Therapy in Adolescent Smokers. *Paediatrics.* 98, 659–67.

Smucker-Barnwell, S. and Earlywine, M. (2006) Simultaneous Alcohol and Cannabis Expectancies Predict Simultaneous Use. *Substance Abuse Treatment, Prevention and Policy.* 1: 29, 1–9.

Sobell, L.C., Cunningham, J.A. and Sobell, M.B. (1996) Recovery From Alcohol Problems With and Without Treatment: Prevalence in Two Population Surveys. *American Journal of Public Heath.* 86, 966–72.

Sobell, M.B. and Sobell, L.C. (1993) *Problem Drinkers: Guided Self-Change Treatment.* Guildford Press.

Spear, L.P. (2000) The Adolescent Brain and Age-Related Behavioural Manifestation. *Neuroscience and Biobehavioural Reviews.* 24: 4, 417–63.

Spear, L.P. (2002) The Adolescent Brain and The College Drinker: Biological Bias of Propensity to Use and Misuse Alcohol. *Journal of Studies on Alcohol. Special Issue: College Drinking, What Is it, and What to Do About It: Review of The State of The Science.* Supplement 14, 71–81.

Speckens, A.E. and Hawton, K. (2005) Social Problem-Solving With Adolescents With Suicidal Behaviour: A Systematic Review. *Suicide and Life Threatening Behaviour.* 35, 365–87.

Spock, B. (2011) *Baby and Child Care.* 9th edn. Gallery Press.

Stacey, J. (1996) *In The Name of Family: Rethinking Family Values in The Postmodern Age.* Beacon Press.

Stall, R. and Biernacki, P. (1986) Spontaneous Remission From Problematic Use of Substances: An Inductive Model Derived From a Comparative Analysis of The Alcohol, Opiate, Tobacco, and Food/Obesity Literatures. *The International Journal of the Addictions.* 21: 1, 1–23.

Stanton, M.D. (1997) The Role of Significant Others in The Engagement and Retention of Drug-Dependent Individuals. In Onken, S., Blaine, J.D. and Boren, J.J. (Eds.) *Beyond The Therapeutic Alliance: Keeping Drug Dependent Individuals in Treatment.* NIH 97-4142, 157–80. National Institute on Drug Abuse.

Stattin, H. and Kerr, M. (2003) What Parents Know, How They Know It, and Several Forms of Adolescent Adjustment: Further Support for A Reinterpretation of Monitoring. *Developmental Psychology.* 36, 366–80.

Staulcup, H., Kenward, K. and Frigo, D. (1979) A Review of Federal Primary Alcoholism Prevention Projects. *Journal of Studies in Alcohol.* 40: 11, 943–68.

Stead, M. et al. (2001) Preventing Adolescent Drug Use: The Development, Design and Implementation of The First Year of NE Choices. *Drugs: Education, Prevention and Policy.* 8: 2, 151–75.

Stein, K., Goldman, M.S. and Del Boca, F.K. (2000) The Influence of Alcohol Expectancy Priming and Mood Manipulation on Subsequent Alcohol Consumption. *Journal of Abnormal Psychology.* 109: 1, 106–15.

Steinberg, L. (2001) We Know Some Things: Parent-Adolescent Relationships in Retrospect and Prospect. *Journal of Research on Adolescence.* 11, 1–19.

Steinberg, L. and Silverberg, S. (1986) The Vicissitudes of Autonomy in Early Adolescence. *Child Development.* 57, 841–51.

Steinberg, L., Dorrnbusch, S.M. and Brown, B.B. (1992) Ethnic Differences in Adolescent Achievement: an Ecological Perspective. *American Psychologist.* 47, 723–9.

Steinberg, L. et al. (1991) Authoritative Parenting and Adolescent Adjustment Across Various

Ecological Niches. *Journal of Research on Adolescence.* 1, 19–36.

Stewart, S.H. and Devine, H. (2000) Relations Between Personality and Drinking Motives in Young Adults. *Personality and Individual Difference.* 29, 495–511.

Stewart, S.H. et al. (2005) New Developments in Prevention and Early Intervention for Alcohol Abuse in Youths. *Alcoholism: Clinical and Experimental Research.* 29: 2, 278–86.

Stockwell, T. et al. (1979) The Development of a Questionnaire to Measure Alcohol Dependence. *British Journal of Addiction.* 74, 145–55.

Stockwell, T., Murphy, D. and Hodgson, R. (1983) The Severity of Alcohol Dependence Questionnaire: Its Use, Reliability and Validity. *British Journal of Addiction.* 78, 145–55.

Strang, J. and Gossop, M. (1990) Comparison of Linear Versus Inverse Exponential Methadone Reduction Curves in The Detoxification of Opiate Addicts. *Addictive Behaviour.* 15, 541–7.

Stronski, S.M. et al. (2000) Protective Correlates of Stages in Adolescent Substance Use: A Swiss Study. *Journal of Adolescent Health.* 26, 420–7.

Stuart, J. (1974) Teaching Facts About Drugs: Pushing or Preventing? *Journal of Educational Psychology.* 66, 189–201.

Sullivan, T.N. and Farrell, A.D. (1999) Identification and Impact of Risk and Protective Factors for Drug Use Among Urban African American Adolescents. *Journal of Clinical Child Psychology.* 29, 122–36.

Sundell, K. and Vinnerljung, B. (2004) Outcomes of Family Group Conferencing in Sweden: A 3-Year Follow-Up. *Child Abuse and Neglect.* 28: 3, 267–87.

Sung, M. et al. (2004) Effects of Age at First Substance Use and Psychiatric Comorbidity in The Development of Substance Use Disorders. *Drug and Alcohol Dependence.* 75, 287–99.

Sutherland, I. (2004) *Adolescent Substance Misuse: Why One Young Person May Be More at Risk Than Another, and What You Can Do to Help.* Russell House Publishing.

Szapocznik, J. et al. (1988) Engaging Adolescent Drug Abusers and Their Families in Treatment: A Strategic Structural-Systems Approach. *Journal of Consulting and Clinical Psychology.* 56, 552–7.

Target, M. and Fonagy, P. (1994) The Efficacy of Psychoanalysis for Children: Prediction of Outcome in A Developmental Context. *Journal of The American Academy of Child and Adolescent Psychiatry.* 33, 1134–44.

Tarter, R.E. et al. (1992) Validation of The Adolescent Drug Use Screening Inventory: Preliminary Findings. *Psychology of Addictive Behaviors.* 6, 322–6.

Taylor, P. et al. (1999) *Demanding Physical Activity Programmes for Young Offenders Under Probation Supervision.* University of Sheffield.

Temple, M.T. and Filmore, K.M. (1985) The Variability of Drinking Patterns Among Young Men, Aged 16–31: A Longitudinal Study. *The International Journal of the Addictions.* 20, 1595–620.

Theakston, J.A. et al. (2004) Big-Five Personality Domains Predict Drinking Motives. *Personality and Individual Difference.* 37, 971–84.

Thomas, D.W. (1990) *Substance Abuse Screening Protocol for The Juvenile Courts.* National Centre for Juvenile Justice.

Thundal, K.I., Granbom, S. and Allebeck, P. (1999) Women's Alcohol Dependence and Abuse: The Relation to Social Network and Leisure Time. *Scandinavian Journal of Public Health.* 27, 30–7.

Tierney, J.P., Grossman, J.B. and Resch, N.L. (1995) *Making a Difference: The Impact Study of Big Brother/Sister.* Public/Private Ventures, Philadelphia.

Tobler, N.S. (1986) Meta-Analysis of 143 Adolescent Drug Prevention Programs: Quantitative Outcome Results of Program Participants Compared to a Control or Comparison Group. *Journal of Drug Issues.* 16: 4, 537–67.

Tobler, N.S. and Stratton, H. (1997) Effectiveness of School-Based Drug Prevention Programmes: A Meta-Analysis of The Research. *Journal of Primary Prevention.* 18: 1, 71–128.

Tobler, N.S. et al. (1999) Effectiveness of School-Based Drug Prevention Programs for Marijuana Use. *School Psychology International.* 20: 1, 105–37.

Tobler, N.S. et al. (2000) School-Based Adolescent Drug Prevention Programs: 1998 Meta-Analysis. *Journal of Primary Prevention.* 20: 4, 275–336.

Tombari, M.L., Fitzpatrick, S.J. and Childress, W. (1985) Using Computers as Contingency Managers in Self-Monitoring Interventions: A Case Study. *Computers in Human Behaviour.* 1, 75–82.

Tomlinson, K.L., Brown, S.A. and Abrantes, A. (2004) Psychiatric Comorbidity and Substance Use Treatment Outcomes of Adolescents. *Psychology of Addictive Behaviors.* 18, 160–9.

Tomlinson, K.L. et al. (2005) An Examination of Self-Medication and Rebound Effects: Psychiatric Symptomology Before and After Alcohol or Drug Relapse. *Addictive Behaviour.* 31, 461–74.

Townsend, J.L., Roderick, P. and Cooper, J. (1994) Cigarette Smoking by Socio-Economic Group, Sex and Age: Effects of Price, Income, and Health Publicity. *British Medical Journal.* 309, 923–6.

Tremblay, R.E. et al. (1995) A Bimodal Preventative Intervention for Disruptive Kindergarten Boys: Its Impact Through Mid-Adolescence. *Journal of Consulting and Clinical Psychology.* 63, 560–8.

Tucker, J.S., Orlando, M. and Ellickson, P.L. (2003) Patterns and Correlates of Binge Drinking Trajectories From Early Adolescence to Young Adulthood. *Health Psychology.* 22, 79–87.

Turkheimer, E. et al. (2003) Socioeconomic Status Modifies Heritability of IQ in Young Children. *Psychological Science.* 14, 623–8.

Twenge, J.M. (2000) The Age of Anxiety? The Birth Cohort Change in Anxiety and Neuroticism, 1952–1993. *Journal of Personality and Social Psychology.* 79: 6, 1007–21.

Tyrer, P. and Casey, P. (Eds.) (1998) *Social Functioning in Psychiatry: The Hidden Axis of Classification Exposed.* Wrightson Biomedical Publishing.

Udry, J. and Billy, J. (1987) Initiation of Coitus in Early Adolescence. *American Sociological Review.* 52, 841–55.

UKATT Research Team (2005) Effectiveness of Treatment for Alcohol Problems: Findings of The Randomised United Kingdom Alcohol Treatment Trial (UKATT). *British Medical Journal.* 331, 544–58.

Ustun, B. et al. (1997) WHO Study on The Reliability and Validity of The Alcohol and Drug Use Disorder Instruments: Overview of Methods and Results. *Drug and Alcohol Dependence.* 47, 161–9.

Vaillant, G.E (1995) *The Natural History of Alcoholism – Revisited.* Harvard.

Vaillant, G.E. (1977) *Adaptions to Life: How The Brightest and Best Come of Age.* Little Brown.

Vannicelli, M. (1978) Impact of Aftercare in The Treatment of Alcoholics. *Journal of Studies on Alcohol.* 39, 1875–86.

Vega, W.A. et al. (1993) Risk Factors for Early Adolescent Drug Abuse in Four Ethnic Racial Groups. *American Journal of Public Health,* 83, 185–9.

Vega, W.A. et al. (2002) Prevalence and Age of Onset for Drug Use in Seven International Studies: Results for an International Consortium of Psychiatric Epidemiology. *Drugs and Alcohol Dependence.* 68, 285–97.

Velleman, R. et al. (1993) The Families of Problem Drug Users: The Accounts of Fifty Close Relatives. *Addiction.* 88, 1275–83.

Velting, O.N., Setzer, N.J. and Albano, A.M. (2004) Update on and Advances in Assessment and Cognitive-Behavioural Treatment of Anxiety Disorders in Children and Adolescents. *Professional Psychology: Research and Practice.* 35: 1, 42–54.

Verhulst, F.C. et al. (1997) The Prevalence of DSM-III-R Diagnosis in a National Sample of Dutch Adolescents. *Archives of General Psychiatry.* 54: 4, 329–36.

Viera, D.L., Ribeiro, M. and Laranjeira, R. (2007) Evidence of Association Between Early Alcohol Use and Risk of Later Problems. *Review Brasil Psiquitra.* 29: 3, 222–7.

Vik, P.W., Grizzle, K.L. and Brown, S.A. (1992) Social Resource Characteristics and Adolescent Substance Abuse Relapse. *Journal of Adolescent Chemical Dependency.* 2, 59–74.

Wagner, E.F. (2008) Developmentally Informed Research on The Effectiveness of Clinical Trials: A Primer for Assessing How Developmental Issues May Influence Treatment Responses Among Adolescents With Alcohol Use Problems. *Pediatrics.* 121, Suppl 4, S337–47.

Wagner, E.F. et al. (1999) Innovations in Adolescent Substance Abuse Intervention. *Alcoholism: Clinical and Experimental Research.* 23: 2, 236–49.

Wagner, E.F., Lloyd, D.A. and Gill, A.G. (2002) Racial/Ethnic and Gender Differences in The Incidence and Onset of The DSM IV Alcohol Use Disorder Symptoms Among Adolescents. *Journal of Studies on Alcohol.* 63, 609–19.

Wakefield, M. et al. (2003) Role of The Media in Influencing Trajectories of Youth Smoking. *Addiction.* 98, Supl 1, 79–103.

Waldron, H.B. and Turner, C.W. (2008) Evidence-Based Psychosocial Treatments for Adolescent Substance Abuse. *Journal of Clinical Child and Adolescent Psychology.* 37, 238–61.

Waldron, H.B. et al. (2001) Treatment Outcomes for Adolescent Substance Abuse at 4- and 7-Month Assessments. *Journal of Consulting and Clinical Psychology.* 69, 802–13.

Waldron, H.B. et al. (2008) Engaging Resistant Adolescents in Drug Treatment. *Journal of Substance Abuse Treatment,* 32: 2, 133–42.

Walker, R.D. et al. (1983) Length of Stay, Neuropsychological Performance, and Aftercare: Influences on Alcohol Treatment Outcome. *Journal of Clinical and Consulting Psychology.* 51, 900–11.

Wallace, J.M. and Bachman, J.G. (1993) Validity of Self-Reports in Student Based Studies on Minority Populations: Issues and Concerns. In De Le Rosa, M.R. and Adrados, J.L. (Eds.) *Drug Abuse Among Minority Youth: Advances in Research Methodology.* National Institute of Drug Abuse.

Walters, R. (1997) Big Art: The Theatrical Side of Youth Crime Prevention. *Youth Studies Australia.* 16: 4, 22–6.

Wampold, B.E. (2001) *The Great Psychotherapy Debate: Models, Methods, and Findings.* Lawrence Erlbaum.

Wanless, D. (2003) *Securing Good Health for The Whole Population: Population Health Trends.* HMSO.

Warren, S. et al. (1997) Child and Adolescent Anxiety Disorder and Early Attachment. *Journal of The American Academy of Child and Adolescent Psychiatry.* 36: 5, 637–44.

Watson, J.B. (1928) *Psychological Care of The Infant.* Norton.

Weber, M.D. et al. (1989) Evidence of Two Paths of Alcohol Use Onset in Adolescents. *Addictive Behaviour.* 14, 399–408.

Wechsler, H. et al. (1995) Correlates of College Student Binge Drinking. *American Journal of Public Health.* 85, 921–6.

Weinberg, N.Z. et al. (1998) Adolescent Abuse: A Review of The Past 10 Years. *Journal of The American Academy of Child and Adolescent Psychiatry.* 37, 252–61.

Weisheit, R. (1983) The Social Context of Alcohol and Drug Education: Implications for Program Evaluations. *Journal of Alcohol and Drug Education.* 29: 1, 72–81.

Weiss, G. and Trokenberg-Hechtman, L. (1993) *Hyperactive Children Grown Up: ADHD in Children, Adolescents, and Adults.* Guildford Press.

West, D.J. (1982) *Delinquency: Its Roots Careers and Prospects.* Harvard University Press.

White, A.M. and Swartzwelder, H.S. (2004) Hippocampal Function During Adolescence: A Unique Target of Ethanol Effects. *Annals of The New York Academy of Science.* 1021, 206–20.

White, D. and Pitts, M. (1998) Educating Young People About Drugs: A Systematic Review. *Addiction.* 93: 10, 1475–87.

White, D., Buckley, E. and Hassan, J. (2004) *Literature Review on The Role of External Contributors in School Drug, Alcohol and Tobacco Education.* Centre for Health Psychology Staffordshire University. DfES.

White, H.R. and Labouvie, E.W. (1989) Toward The Assessment of Adolescent Problem Drinking. *Journal of Studies on Alcohol.* 50, 30–7.

White, H.R., Johnson, V. and Buyske, S. (2000) Parental Modelling Behaviour Effects on Offspring, Alcohol and Cigarette Use: A Growth Curve Analysis. *Journal of Substance Abuse.* 12, 287–310.

White, V.M., Hayman, J. and Hill, D.J. (2008) *Can Population-Based Tobacco-Control Policies Change Smoking Behaviour of Adolescents From Socio-Economic Groups? Findings From Australia: 1987–2005 Cancer Causes and Control.* Published Online.

Wichstrom, L. (1998) Alcohol Intoxication and School Dropout. *Drug and Alcohol Review.* 17, 413–21.

Wiederman, M.W. and Pryor, T. (1996) Substance Use and Impulsive Behaviours Among Adolescents With Eating Disorders. *Addictive Behaviours.* 21: 2, 269–72.

Wilens, T.E. et al. (2003) Does Stimulant Therapy of ADHD Beget Later Substance Abuse? A Meta-Analytic Review of The Literature. *Paediatrics.* 111, 179–85.

Williams, R.J. and Chang, S.Y. (2000) A Comprehensive and Comparative Review of Adolescent Substance Abuse Treatment Outcome. *Clinical Psychology: Science and Practice.* 7: 2, 138–66.

Wilson, D.B., Gottfredson, D.C. and Najaka, S.S. (2001) School-Based Prevention of Problem Behaviours: A Meta-Analysis. *Journal of Quantitative Criminology.* 17, 247–72.

Wilson, R. (1990) *Better Times at Chicago State: Prevention File.* University of California at San Diego.

Winters, K.C. (1992) Development of an Alcohol and Other Drug Abuse Screening Scale: Personal Experience Screening Questionnaire. *Addictive Behaviours.* 17, 479–90.

Winters, K.C. et al. (2000) The Effectiveness of The Minnesota Model Approach in The Treatment of Adolescent Drug Abusers. *Addiction.* 95, 601–12.

Winters, K.C. et al. (2007) Long-Term Outcome of Substance Dependent Youth Following 12 Step Treatment. *Journal of Substance Treatment.* 33, 61–9.

Wolfson, A.R. and Carskadon, M.A. (1998) Sleep Schedules and Daytime Functioning in Adolescents. *Child Development.* 69: 4, 875–87.

Wong, M.M. et al. (2006) Behavioural Control and Resiliency in The Onset of Alcohol and Illicit Drug Use: A Prospective Study From Preschool to Adolescence. *Child Development.* 77, 1016–33.

Wood, A. et al. (2001) Randomised Trial of Group Therapy for Repeated Deliberate Self-Harm in Adolescents. *Journal of The American Academy of Child and Adolescent Psychiatry.* 40, 1246–53.

Woodward, L.J. and Fergusson, M. (2001) Life Course Outcomes of Young People With Anxiety Disorders in Adolescence. *Journal of the American Academy of Child and Adolescent Psychiatry.* 40: 9, 1086–93.

Wu, P. et al. (2006) Childhood Depressive Symptoms and Early Onset of Alcohol Use. *Paediatrics.* 118, 1907–15.

Wymbs, B.T. et al. (2008) Rate and Predictors of Divorce Among Parents of Youth With ADHD. *Journal of Consulting and Clinical Psychology.* 76: 5, 735–44.

Yager, J. et al. (2002) Practice Guideline for The Treatment of Patients With Eating Disorders. In American Psychiatric Association (2002) *Practice Guidelines for The Treatment of Psychiatric Disorders: Compendium 2002.* American Psychiatric Association.

Yates, F.E. (1988) The Evaluation of a 'Co-Operative Counselling' Alcohol Service Which Uses Family and Affected Others to Reach and Influence Problem Drinkers. *British Journal of Addiction.* 83, 1309–19.

Young, R. et al. (2006) The Role of Alcohol Expectancy and Refusal Self-Efficacy Beliefs in University Student Drinking. *Alcohol and Alcoholism.* 41: 1, 70–5.

Zabin, L.S. (1990) Adolescent Pregnancy and Early Sexual Onset. In Lahey, B.B. and Kazdin, A.E. (Eds.) *Clinical Child Psychology.* Plenum Press.

Zabin, L.S., Kantner, J.F. and Zelnik, M. (1979) The Risk of Adolescent Pregnancy in The First Months of Intercourse. *Family Planning Perspective.* 11, 215–22.

Zajonc, R.B. (1968) Attitudinal Effects of Mere Exposure. *Journal of Personality and Social Psychology.* 9: Suppl 2, Part 2.

Zastony, T.R. et al. (1993) Sociodemographic and Attitudinal Correlates of Alcohol and Other Drug Use Among Children and Adolescents: Analysis of A Large-Scale Attitude Tracking Study. *Journal of Psychoactive Drugs.* 25: 3, 223–37.

Zimmermann, P. et al. (2003) Primary Anxiety Disorders and The Development of Subsequent Alcohol Use Disorders: A 4 Year Community Study of Adolescents and Young Adults. *Psychology and Medicine.* 33, 1211–22.

Zucker, R.A. (2006) Alcohol Use and Alcohol Use Disorders: A Developmental-Biopsychosocial Systems Formulation Covering The Life Course. In Cicchetti, D. and Cohen, D.J. (Eds.) *Developmental Psychopathology: Vol 3. Risk, Disorder, and Adaption.* Wiley.

Zucker, R.A. (2008) Anticipating Problem Alcohol Use Developmentally From Childhood Into Middle Adulthood: What Have We Learned? *Addiction.* 103: Suppl S100–8.

Zucker, R.A. et al. (1994) Pathways to Alcohol Problems and Alcoholism: A Developmental Account of The Evidence for Multiple Alcoholisms and for Contextual Contributions to Risk. In Zucker, R.A., Howard, R.J. and Boyd, G.M. (Eds.) *The Development of Alcohol Problems: Exploring The Biopsychosocial Matrix of Risk.* NIAAA Research Monograph No. 26, NIH Publication No. 94–3495, 255–90.

Other books from Russell House Publishing

The concerned other
How to change problematic drug and alcohol users through their family members: a complete manual
By Phil Harris

'Introduces, then describes and then provides an intervention-based programme to help family and friends (the concerned others) bring about change in people close to them who are experiencing problems with drugs and/or alcohol . . . a welcome addition to the toolkit for working with those affected.' *BJSW*

'Focuses on what the concerned other can do and provides a very specific tool to do it, providing an overt challenge that awakens us brusquely to the great potential for change that exists within a highly crucial relationship.' *Child Abuse Review*

'Offers practical help, support and a framework to be used . . . comprehensive . . . well explained and detailed . . . well researched . . . highly adaptable . . . a useful tool in many settings.' *Addiction Today*

The 68 pages of copiable material to be found in this 304-page manual (a complete worksheet-based programme) are also available as a FREE PDF to customers who subsequently register their purchase with RHP, using the form in the manual.

978-1-905541-48-5

The concerned other
New theory and the evidence base for changing problematic drug and alcohol users through their family members
By Phil Harris

Setting out ideas that have been demonstrated to work in a context of 'payment by results', academic and practitioner Phil Harris sees the concerned other as the person most able to effect change in the user's life, whilst also taking good care of themselves. Here, he presents the thoroughly researched and carefully argued theoretical underpinning of his work with substance users and their families. Containing the text of Part One of the above manual, this book is essential reading for academics, researchers, students, policy-makers.

978-1-905541-66-9

Empathy for the devil
How to help people overcome drugs and alcohol problems
By Phil Harris

Examining the core skills necessary for effecting change in problematic substance users, this important book explores practical ways of establishing or improving your practice. It steps beyond clinical, theoretical and moral undertones to the reality of working with substance misuse. Where society, the media and our imaginations are full of the modern day social demons of drug users, it provides positive and reflective support for both experienced and novice workers – or those affected by others' use. It suggests ways ahead to workers stuck in seemingly perennial impasses, as they strive with their colleagues to address multi-faceted and entrenched problems.

Increasingly, social policy now demands evidence-based practice, putting ever greater pressure on professionals from all disciplines to grasp the core ideas and skills drawn from research findings. But this research is often too arid and abstract to overlay upon the life of the individual sat before us, and can make the lay person feel even more under skilled. This book bridges this chasm, **bringing together a wide range of proven skills in supporting people through change in an open and accessible way**. It:
- invites you to re-consider your own experiences so as to illuminate the key ideas, skills and techniques in addiction work
- lucidly explains the latest findings in effective practice
- illustrates them with case examples
- provides optional **self-reflective exercises and activities to aid learning and training**.

Empathy for the Devil will give anyone working with people whose lives are affected by drugs or alcohol new ideas and perspectives to address old and intractable problems.

'Discusses the complexity of drug and alcohol problems with more references to cultural and social aspects than previous work that I have read in this area . . . The focus is explicitly and empathically on helping clients to establish and achieve their own goals to overcome their addiction. However Harris does not treat people as living in a vacuum, but as living within and being part of an extremely influential cultural context. I particularly enjoyed Harris's astute reflections upon the therapeutic relationship, something not always talked about, and found the chapter on solution-focused therapy so inspiring that I wanted to rush out and try it . . . I thoroughly enjoyed this book, it is a great read.' *The Psychologist*

'Book of the month . . . his bibliography makes for extensive further reading.' *Drugscope Members Briefing*

978-1-903855-54-6

Drug Induced
Addiction and treatment in perspective
By Phil Harris

'It would be difficult for anyone involved in working with addiction whether as a practitioner, or manager, or policy maker to come away from reading this informative and interesting book without some spur to reflecting on and changing their own thinking and practice.' *VISTA*

'Should be essential reading ... his critique of peer pressure, the importance of relationships throughout adolescence and why some young people are more prone to drug dependency than others are brilliant ... **an excellent book** ... Much to my own surprise I thoroughly enjoyed *Drug Induced* and found myself repeating to colleagues much of what I read. I found it to be a refreshing, courageous book that radically challenges many of our widely held beliefs about addiction and treatment: it is just up to you now to read it.' *Youth & Policy*

'This **thought-provoking** book challenges many aspects of the theoretical base and clinical practices prevalent in the addictions field today ... The disease concept, motivational interviewing, stages of change and dual diagnosis are all examined in a way which will, hopefully, **encourage alcohol and drug workers to re-evaluate their 'sacred cows'**. The authors' clinical experience shines through what I largely experienced as a social-science perspective with a developmental and environmental focus.' *Addiction Today*

'He supports his arguments with a comprehensive array of references from both friend and foe of his stance ... it hangs together well ...' *Journal of Mental Health*

978-1-903855-53-9 2005

Secret lives: growing with substance
Working with children and young people affected by familial substance misuse
Edited by Fiona Harbin & Michael Murphy

Including the chapter *Where it all begins: growing up and the helping relationship* by *Phil Harris*

Secret Lives offers new and challenging insights into the task of working with children and young people who are affected by substance misuse. This includes the needs of children brought up in substance misusing households, and young people who are beginning to misuse substances themselves.

'The authors aim to help practitioners and managers in the identification, assessment, treatment and support of the children and siblings of substance misusers. Buy this book as a reference and investment.' *Addiction Today*

'All the contributions are interesting, and informed my knowledge of what services should be available to assist children ... the book succeeds in allowing the views of children and young people caught in this sad situation poignantly to come through.' *Seen & Heard*

'Founded on current research ... informed, accessible and relevant.' *Rostrum*

'Most books of this genre discuss either how to assess the issue or how to work with it: this book does both ... I recommend this book.' *Community Care*

'Impressive ... for anyone working with children, young people, parents and families.' *Community Safety Journal*

978-1-903855-66-9